# Texas Vistas

Selections from the *Southwestern Historical Quarterly*

Third Edition



Texas State Historical Association

Austin

Printed in the United States of America.

*Library of Congress Cataloging-in-Publication Data*

Texas vistas : selections from the Southwestern historical quarterly / edited by Ralph A. Wooster, Robert Calvert, Adrian Anderson.—3rd ed.
p. cm.
Includes index.
ISBN 0-87611-219-X (alk. paper)
1. Texas-History. I. Wooster, Ralph A. II. Calvert, Robert A. III. Anderson, Adrian N. IV. Southwestern historical quarterly. V. Texas State Historical Association.

F386.5.T49 2006
976.4—dc22 2006020914

10 9 8 7 6 5 4 3 2 1

Published by the Texas State Historical Association in cooperation with the Center for Studies in Texas History at the University of Texas at Austin.

The paper used in this book meets the minimum requirements of the American National Standard for Permanence of Paper for Printed Library Materials, Z39.48-1984.

*Front cover:* Gonzales County Courthouse. *Photograph copyright Richard Payne, used by permission.*

# Contents

**Reconstruction and After**

# Preface

For more than one hundred years some of the finest articles on the history of Texas have appeared in the *Southwestern Historical Quarterly* published by the Texas State Historical Association. In 1980 the Association published in paperback form *Texas Vistas*, a collection of articles from the *Quarterly*. In selecting articles the compilers attempted to provide a sampling of Texas history from early Spanish exploration through the twentieth century. Minor revisions to the original edition appeared in 1987.

Since the publication of the earlier editions two decades ago many articles have appeared in the *Southwestern Historical Quarterly* that better reflect the rich diversity of Texas history, especially in the areas of gender and ethnic studies. The editors of the newest edition have brought together eighteen essays (twelve of which were published in the past two decades) that reflect the best of scholarship in Texas history.

The collection has been designed primarily as a collateral reading book for college and university students of Texas history, but it is believed the work will appeal to all readers interested in the history of Texas. In making selections the compilers tried to include examples of political, social, economic, and military history. Each essay is accompanied by brief introductory remarks prepared by the compilers. The essays include the footnotes and other documentation as they appeared when first published in the *Quarterly*.

We wish to dedicate this work to the late Robert A. Calvert of Texas A&M University, who was one of the original compilers of *Texas Vistas*.

Ralph A. Wooster
Adrian Anderson

# In Search of Cabeza De Vaca's Route across Texas: An Historiographical Survey

Donald E. Chipman*

*Modern Texas history began in November 1525 when Spanish survivors of the Narváez Florida expedition attempting to reach settlements in Mexico landed on the coast west of Galveston Island. After several years among native Americans on the Texas coast, four survivors of the party, including Cabeza de Vaca and an African named Estevanico, began a long overland journey to reach Spanish settlements in Mexico.*

*As Donald E. Chipman, professor of history at the University of North Texas, points out in this essay, historians, anthropologists, geographers, and novelists have long debated the route that de Vaca and his party traveled across Texas. While all scholarly accounts agree that the Spanish castaways journeyed westward from the coast before eventually reaching the northern Spanish outpost at Culiacán in western Mexico, they disagree as to the route taken through Texas and northern Mexico. In this article Chipman describes the various arguments over the path de Vaca and his party followed. Chipman concludes that, while the exact route cannot be determined precisely, a major portion of their travel took them through northern Mexico.*

*For more on Spanish exploration in Texas see Chipman's longer study,* Spanish Texas, 1519–1821 *(Austin: University of Texas Press, 1992) and Fanny Bandelier (trans.),* The Narrative of Alvar Núñez Cabeza de Vaca *(Barre, Mass.: Imprint Society, 1972).*

*Donald E. Chipman, "In Search of Cabeza de Vaca's Route across Texas: An Historiographical Survey," *Southwestern Historical Quarterly*, 91 (Oct., 1987), 127–148. Donald E. Chipman wishes to thank Professor William M. Holmes for his assistance in preparing the figure 1 map.

Modern Texas history begins in November, 1528, when two makeshift barges bearing several dozen Spaniards landed west of Galveston Island. Nearly eight years later, four survivors, destined to become famous as the Four Ragged Castaways, arrived at Culiacán, a Spanish outpost near the Pacific coast of Mexico. If the overland route the four men traveled in traversing Texas can be determined with a high degree of certainty, the accounts written later by three of them will provide the earliest information on landforms, flora, and fauna in what was to become the Lone Star State. Historians, however, are in substantial disagreement over the path followed by the Four Ragged Castaways across Texas. The purpose of this paper is to survey previous writing and to suggest the route interpretation that is most probably correct.

A brief outline of the circumstances that brought Spaniards to the Texas coast at that early date is essential to understanding events that transpired after the landing. The men were members of an expedition that had left Spain the previous year under the command of Pánfilo de Narváez. Narváez, a minor participant in the conquest of Mexico, had lost an eye and command of his army to Fernando Cortés, and in the early 1520s had returned to Spain seeking redress from the king. His efforts were finally rewarded with a royal patent to establish a colony in "Florida," a term applied to the Gulf coast stretching from the province of Pánuco in Mexico to the Florida peninsula. Don Pánfilo set sail from the mouth of the Guadalquivir River in Spain in June, 1527.[1]

Narváez spent the fall and winter months in Cuba, where his expedition suffered losses as a result of desertions and a hurricane, and in April of 1528 he sailed with five ships and 400 men to the west coast of Florida, landing near Tampa Bay. There he decided to separate 300 men from the support ships and reconnoiter the land, despite protests from the expedition's treasurer, Alvar Núñez Cabeza de Vaca, who thought it foolish to leave the vessels. Narváez mistakenly believed that he was only a few leagues from the Pánuco River, when the actual distance was more than 1,500 miles via the coast. By mid-June of 1528, Narváez's overland expedition, in search of riches and an ideal location for a colony, had marched up the interior coast to northwestern Florida, where it

---

[1]Henry R. Wagner, *The Rise of Fernando Cortés* (Los Angeles: Cortés Society, 1944), 266–285; Michael C. Meyer and William L. Sherman, *The Course of Mexican History* (2nd ed.; New York: Oxford University Press, 1983), 117–120. Pánuco was an ill-defined province lying inland from the Mexican port of Tampico. Its northern boundary was the Río Soto la Marina, known in colonial times as the Río de las Palmas. See Donald E. Chipman, *Nuño de Guzmán and the Province of Pánuco in New Spain,* 1518–1533 (Glendale, Calif.: Arthur H. Clark Co., 1967), 39–73; William H. Prescott, *History of the Conquest of Mexico, and History of the Conquest of Peru* (New York: Modern Library, n.d.), 627–628; Fanny Bandelier (trans. and ed.), *The Journey of Alvar Núñez Cabeza de Vaca and His Companions from Florida to the Pacific, 1528–1536* (1904; reprint, New York: Allerton Book Co., 1922), 1 (quotation). The first name of Cortés is often rendered as Hernán or Hernando, but he preferred Fernando. Wagner, *The Rise of Fernando Cortés,* vi.

remained for approximately three months. Faced with hostile natives and food shortages, Narváez elected to build improvised barges and to exit Florida by sea. His command, which had dwindled to less than 250 men, packed themselves into five craft and set out for Pánuco on September 22. The first month at sea went fairly well. Hugging the coast, the small flotilla approached the mouth of the Mississippi River. On the thirty-first day, according to Cabeza de Vaca, troubles began. A storm caught the barges and tossed them like driftwood. Several days after passing the mouth of the great river, Narváez released his command with the advice that "each must do as he thought best to save himself." His own efforts, however, were insufficient: later his poorly anchored boat was blown into deep water off the Texas coast and presumably sunk. On November 6, 1528, the barge bearing Cabeza de Vaca and an undetermined number of other men landed near the western extremity of Galveston Island. A second boat containing Andrés Dorantes de Carranza, his African-born slave Estevanico, Alonso Castillo Maldonado, and perhaps forty-five others had apparently landed nearby on the previous day, making them the first non-Indians in Texas.[2]

There have been and are difficulties in projecting the path of the four survivors from the Galveston area to Culiacán—problems that will never be resolved to everyone's satisfaction, for no one can prove beyond a doubt the route taken on any part of the journey. It is the Texas portion of the odyssey, however, that has received by far the most attention. James A. Michener, for example, in his epic novel *Texas,* mapped the route of Cabeza de Vaca and his three companions from the Galveston area to El Paso, with virtually every mile of it in the Lone Star State.[3] For purposes of fiction, Michener chose a nearly all-Texas route interpretation, one that is in agreement with an abundance of writing on the subject. But was the first leg of the overland trek, that from Galveston Bay to the environs of El Paso, wholly within the present borders of Texas, or did parts of it traverse northern Mexico? A totally trans-Texas route for the first segment of the overland march defies both logic and documentation. It defies logic in that the overall goal of the Narváez expedition from the time it left Florida was to reach Pánuco, not to explore the interior. It defies

---

[2] Cyclone Covey (trans.), *Cabeza de Vaca's Adventures in the Unknown Interior of America* (1961; reprint, Albuquerque: University of New Mexico Press, 1984), 7, 27–52, 53 (quotation), 54–59. Narváez's boat was blown into the Gulf off Matagorda Bay, not at the Mississippi Delta as claimed by Frederick W. Hodge. Frederick W. Hodge (ed.), "The Narrative of Alvar Núñez Cabeza de Vaca," in *Spanish Explorers in the Southern United States, 1528–1543* (New York: Charles Scribner's Sons, 1907), 62. See Gonzalo Fernández de Oviedo [y Valdés], *Historia general y natural de las Indias* (5 vols.; Madrid: Real Academia Española, 1959), IV, 297. The Spanish use of "Espíritu Santo" to designate both the Mississippi River and Matagorda Bay has apparently led to this confusion.

[3] James A. Michener, *Texas* (New York: Random House, 1985), 12. See fig. 1.

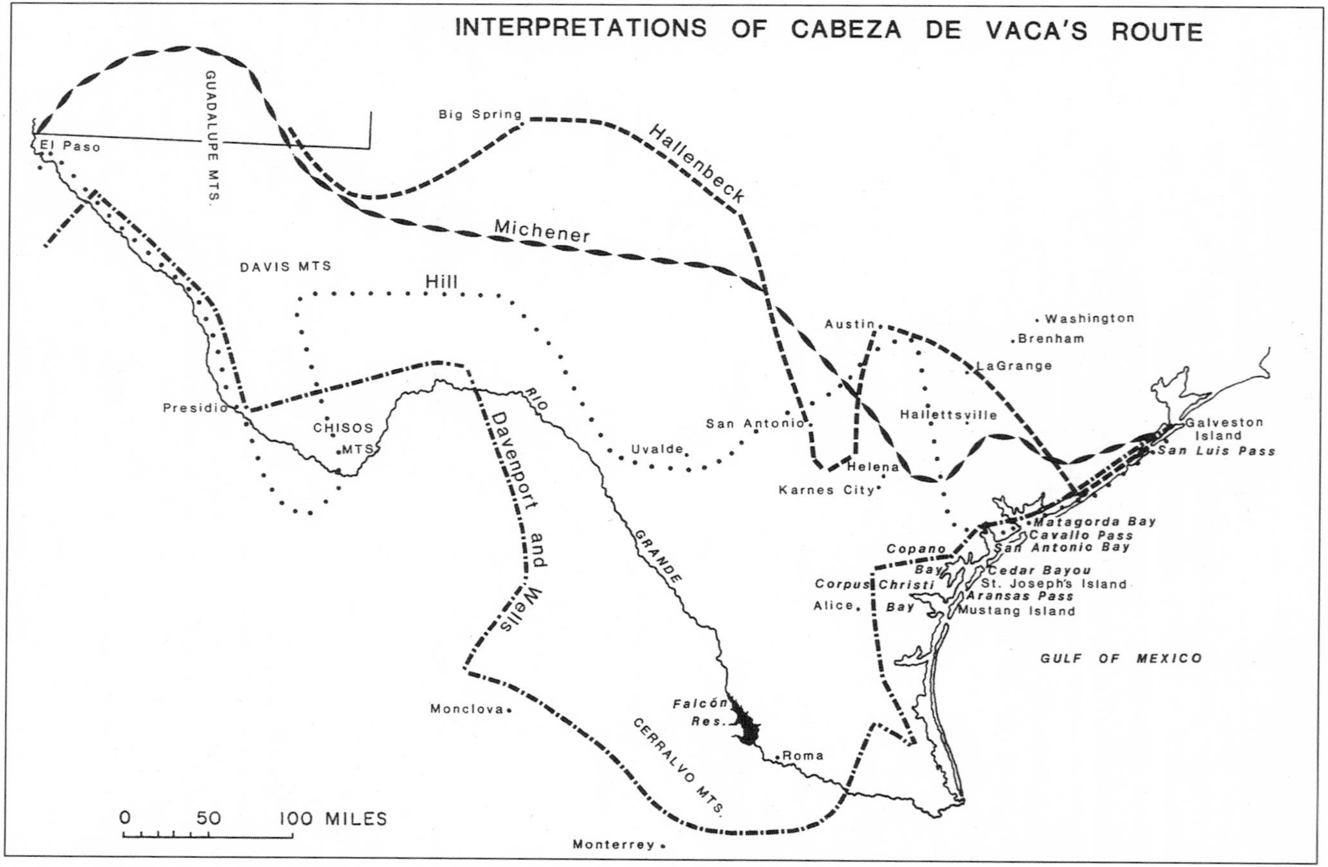


Four interpretations of Cabeza de Vaca's route across Texas and Mexico.

documentation in that it is frequently at variance with evidence in the two original accounts on which all route interpretations must ultimately rest.

Los Naufragios [Shipwrecks], as the work is generally known, was composed by Cabeza de Vaca, probably within two or three years after his trek ended in 1536, and published in 1542 at Zamora, Spain. A subsequent edition, with slight alterations, was printed at Valladolid, Spain, in 1555. A second document, commonly referred to as the Joint Report, or the Oviedo account, was drawn up in 1536 by Cabeza de Vaca, Dorantes, and Castillo in Mexico City for the Audiencia of Santo Domingo. It is presumed, since the original has never been found, that the version in Gonzalo Fernández de Oviedo's *Historia general y natural de las Indias* is an amended account.[4] A common failing among early students of the journey was to ignore the Oviedo account, or to disregard parts of both narratives and to send Cabeza de Vaca "where the route interpreter wanted him to go, not where . . . [he] plainly indicates that he went."[5]

The two narratives, both of which were written from memory rather than field notes, deserve attention for several reasons. First, they are primary documents on the Indians of South Texas, for Cabeza de Vaca lived with natives of the region and survived to write about them. No other Spaniard was able to do this. He was also the only Spaniard to record the names of Indians in the area and to locate them relative to each other. His accounts of the Mariames and Avavares, with whom he lived for about eighteen months and eight months, respectively, make them the best described Indians of southern Texas. In the words of T. N. Campbell and T. J. Campbell, "his cultural information

[4] *La relacion que dio Aluar nuñez Cabeça de vaca de lo acaescido enlas Jndias enla armada donde yua por gouernador Páphilo de narbaez, desde el año de veynte y siete hasta el año d'treynta y seys que boluio a Seuilla con tres de su compañia* (Zamora: Impresso por Augustin de paz y Juan Picardo, a costa de Juan pedro musetti mercader de libros, vezino de Medina del campo, 1542); *La relacion y comentarios del gouernador Aluar nuñez cabeça de vaca, de lo acaescido en las dos jornadas que hizo a las Indias, con priuilegio* . . . (Valladolid: Francisco Fernandez de Cordoua, 1555). A complete copy of the original 1542 edition is housed in the New York City Public Library; the Barker Texas History Center at the University of Texas at Austin has a copy of the 1555 edition. The account may also be found in Fernández de Oviedo [y Valdés], *Historia general,* IV, 287–318. For translations of Naufragios, see Bandelier (trans. and ed.), *Journey,* and Hodge (ed.), "Narrative of Alvar Núñez Cabeza de Vaca," 3–126. For the best translation of the Joint Report, see Basil C. Hedrick and Carroll L. Riley, *The Journey of the Vaca Party: The Account of the Narváez Expedition, 1528–1536, as Related by Gonzalo Fernández de Oviedo y Valdés* (Carbondale, Ill.: Southern Illinois University, 1974). A brief, fragmentary document published in *Colección de documentos inéditos, relativos al descubrimiento, conquista y organización de las antiguas posesiones españolas en América y Oceanía sacados de los Archivos del Reino, y muy especialmente del de Indias* (1864–1884; reprint, 42 vols., Vaduz: Kraus Reprint, 1964–1966), XIV, 265–279, contains no information that is useful to route interpretation.

[5] T. N. Campbell and T. J. Campbell, *Historic Indian Groups of the Choke Canyon Reservoir and Surrounding Area, Southern Texas* (San Antonio: Center for Archaeological Research, University of Texas at San Antonio, 1981), 4.

quantitatively exceeds that of all his successors combined."[6] Second, Cabeza de Vaca, Dorantes, Castillo, and Estevanico were the first non-Indians to set foot on the soil of the Lone Star State and the first to cross the North American continent. As noted above, if it can be determined *where* they went and *what* they saw, their experiences can also supply valuable data on early Texas landforms, flora, and fauna. There are, for example, gross landscape features described in the narratives that ought to be identifiable. The initial landing was on an island off the Texas coast whose dimensions and location relative to another island and four successive streams were given; inlets *(ancones)* along the coast toward Pánuco were described; a river of nuts and extensive stands of prickly pear cactus were mentioned; a large stream comparable in width to the Guadalquivir River had to be crossed; and mountains near the coast that ran from the direction of the "North Sea" were observed soon after the river was forded.[7] In reconstructing the most likely route on the basis of these narratives, one should be sensitive to the compatibility of biotic, ethnographic, and physiographic information. Not surprisingly, some writers have done a better job than others in correlating all the data.

First impressions in the United States of the Cabeza de Vaca journey came from translations of his narrative by Buckingham Smith (1851 and 1871), from a brief route interpretation by Hubert H. Bancroft (1884), and from the writings of Adolph Bandelier on the Spanish Southwest (1890). All three authors were generally vague in their assertions. Smith placed the initial landfall east of the Mississippi River in the environs of Mobile Bay.[8] Bancroft did not give much credence to the narrative, regarding it as "fragmentary, disconnected, contradictory, and often unintelligible." But he positioned the first landing somewhere on the eastern coast of Texas, and he believed the overland passage started between Galveston and the San Antonio River, then continued "north-westward through Texas."[9] Bandelier also regarded the narrative as confused and "unsatisfactory in precision and detail," not, however, because of intent to deceive, but because of adverse conditions that affected the writing. He believed the

---

[6]Ibid., 64, 65 (quotation).

[7]In Spanish nomenclature, "North Sea" referred to the Atlantic Ocean and embraced the Gulf of Mexico. Robert S. Weddle, *Spanish Sea: The Gulf of Mexico in North American Discovery,* 1500–1685 (College Station, Tex.: Texas A&M University Press, 1985), 201–202.

[8]Buckingham Smith (trans.), *Relation of Núñez Cabeza de Vaca, by Alvar Núñez Cabeza de Vaca* (Ann Arbor: University Microfilms, 1966), 64, n. 2. See also Buckingham Smith (trans.), *The Narrative of Alvar Núñez Cabeza de Vaca* (Washington, D.C.: [George W. Riggs], 1851); Buckingham Smith (trans.), *Relation of Alvar Núñez Cabeza de Vaca* ([Albany: J. Munsell for H. C. Murphy], 1871).

[9]Hubert Howe Bancroft, *History of the North Mexican States and Texas* (2 vols.; San Francisco: History Co., 1884–1889), I, 63 (1st quotation), 64 (2nd quotation). Bancroft's total attention to the Cabeza de Vaca route occupied only eleven pages of his two-volume work. For a map depicting the trans-Texas route, see ibid., 67.

barges were grounded west of the Mississippi River on the coast of Louisiana. The castaways then wandered toward Texas and encountered the land of prickly pear cactus immediately west of the Sabine River. Bandelier identified four rivers crossed along an east to west route through Texas as the Trinity, Brazos, Colorado, and Río Grande; and he believed that the four pedestrians left the state at the junction of the Río Conchos and Río Grande.[10]

Interest in the Cabeza de Vaca route was also reflected in the earliest issues of the *Quarterly* of the Texas State Historical Association. Beginning with volume 1 and continuing through volume 22, five route interpretations with a cumulative total of 319 pages of text were devoted to the topic.[11] Later, in his presidential address to the Association, Thomas F. Harwood would remark that "no one subject [in Texas history] has inspired so many different local authors. . . ."[12] After 1919 no other interpretative article on the Cabeza de Vaca journey appeared in the *Southwestern Historical Quarterly,* but this did not mean that controversy had ended.

A substantial contribution to the Cabeza de Vaca route interpretation appeared in the *Quarterly* in 1898. Two undergraduates at the University of Texas, Miss Brownie Ponton and Bates McFarland, challenged the conclusions of "three eminent historians." Ponton and McFarland gave credence to the Cabeza de Vaca narrative and believed that they could pinpoint the initial landing on the Texas coast. Cabeza de Vaca named the island where the barges first landed "Malhado" (Isle of Misfortune). Near Malhado and toward Pánuco were four successive streams, the second of which flowed directly into the Gulf of Mexico without entering a bay. Ponton and McFarland believed Malhado to have been Galveston Island and the waterways, Oyster Creek, the Brazos River, the San Bernard River, and Caney Creek. Their identification of the streams is

---

[10]A. F. Bandelier, *Hemenway Southwestern Archaeological Expedition: Contributions to the History of the Southwestern Portion of the United States* (Cambridge, Mass.: John Wilson & Son, 1890), 31, 49, 50 (quotation), 51–54. For a map depicting the trans-Texas route, see the frontispiece of the volume.

[11]Brownie Ponton and Bates H. M'Farland, "Alvar Núñez Cabeza de Vaca: A Preliminary Report on His Wanderings in Texas," *Quarterly of the Texas State Historical Association,* I (Jan., 1898), 166–186; O. W. Williams, Route of Cabeza de Vaca in Texas," ibid., III (July, 1899), 54–64; Bethel Coopwood, "The Route of Cabeza de Vaca," ibid. (Oct., 1899), 108–140, (Jan., 1900), 177–208, (Apr., 1900), 229–264, IV (July, 1900), 1–32; James Newton Baskett, "A Study of the Route of Cabeza de Vaca," ibid., X (Jan., 1907), 246–279, (Apr., 1907), 308–340; Harbert Davenport and Joseph K. Wells, "The First Europeans in Texas, 1528–1536," *Southwestern Historical Quarterly* (hereafter cited as *SHQ),* XXII (Oct., 1918), 111–142, (Jan., 1919), 205–259.

[12]T. F. Harwood, "Review of the Work of the Texas State Historical Association," *SHQ,* XXXI (July, 1927), 10. A translation by Harbert Davenport that appeared in the *Southwestern Historical Quarterly* does not offer a different route interpretation. See Harbert Davenport (ed.), "The Expedition of Pánfilo de Narváez by Gonzalo Fernández Oviedo y Valdez," ibid., XXVII (Oct., 1923), 120–139, (Jan., 1924), 217–241, (Apr., 1924), 276–304, XXVIII (July, 1924), 56–74, (Oct., 1924), 122–163. Bernardo Calero and Joseph K. Wells assisted Davenport with the translation.

beyond dispute. At no other place between the Río Grande and the Mississippi River is there even one river that flows directly into the Gulf.[13]

After identifying the four waterways that were first crossed by the castaways, Ponton and McFarland admitted to problems in tracing the onward journey. They projected a trans-Texas route and believed the first mountains mentioned in the narratives to have been the southern limit of the Edwards Plateau on the San Antonio River, but they were unable to reconcile Cabeza de Vaca's statement that information from Indians placed the mountains within fifteen leagues of the coast.[14]

Oscar W. Williams offered a brief route refinement in volume 3 of the *Quarterly*. His article appeared without footnotes and was based primarily on personal knowledge of topography in southern Texas. Williams sought to establish the northern limits of prickly pear cactus stands and the southern boundaries of the buffalo range. The fruit of the cactus (tuna) was an important, seasonal staple in the diet of Coahuiltecan tribes; and it appears from the narratives that Cabeza de Vaca rarely encountered bison, for he mentioned seeing them only three times. Williams, like Ponton and McFarland, supported a trans-Texas passage, in this case based on floral and faunal evidence in the narrative.[15]

In the same volume of the *Quarterly* there appeared a lengthy, four-part article by Bethel Coopwood. For the most part, Coopwood's treatise on the journey of the castaways rambled badly, but in several instances he made significant contributions. Coopwood raised questions about Galveston Island's being Cabeza de Vaca's Isle of Misfortune, for it is too wide and too long to fit the dimensions stated in the narrative; he deduced that trees along the river of nuts were pecan, not walnut as claimed by earlier writers; he was the first to suggest that the large river crossed by Cabeza de Vaca and his companions was the lower Río Grande; he believed the first mountains encountered by the travelers to have been the Pamoranes of Nuevo León; and he established that the southern limits of the buffalo range extended into northern Coahuila. Once the castaways forded the Río Grande, Coopwood projected the possibility of two totally trans-Mexico routes. His preferred southern path has been labeled a "bizarre scheme," for it traversed virtually impassable mountains and denied that the men passed through Culiacán.[16]

---

[13]Hodge (ed.), "Narrative of Alvar Núñez Cabeza de Vaca," 50 (2nd quotation); Ponton and M'Farland, "Alvar Núñez Cabeza de Vaca," 175–177, 178 (1st quotation). Technically, as Ponton and McFarland acknowledged, Bandelier was an archaeologist rather than a historian. Ibid., 179. See also Davenport and Wells, "First Europeans" (Oct., 1918), 119.

[14]Ponton and M'Farland, "Alvar Núñez Cabeza de Vaca," 182.

[15]Williams, "Route of Cabeza de Vaca in Texas," 54–64.

[16]Coopwood, "Route of Cabeza de Vaca" (Oct., 1899), 117, 120–121, 134–135, (Jan., 1900), 178–179, (Apr., 1900), 232–233. For a map depicting Coopwood's route interpretation, see ibid. (Jan., 1900), 192–193 (between pages). See also Baskett, "Study of the Route of Cabeza de Vaca" (Apr., 1907), 329 (quotation).

The flurry of publication on the Cabeza de Vaca route that had marked the first four volumes of the *Quarterly* then subsided for seven years. In 1907 James N. Baskett somewhat apologetically "ventured to submit yet another study of the journey." Baskett recognized the importance of the shorter Joint Report as a complement to the Cabeza de Vaca narrative, arguing, as Oviedo had, that "the testimony of three, fresh from the scenes, is better than that of one, recorded some years later. . . ." Like Ponton and McFarland, he believed that Galveston Island must have been the Spaniards' Malhado.[17]

After the initial landfall, two parties of Spaniards made their way along the Texas coast from the Galveston area toward Matagorda and Corpus Christi bays. Twelve or thirteen, including Dorantes, Castillo, and Estevanico, made the trek in the spring of 1529, followed by Cabeza de Vaca along a slightly more inland path in the winter of 1532–1533. Baskett, in tracing the first part of the overland journey, made an important contribution to route interpretation. From the Oviedo account he was able to differentiate Spanish terminology for bays, swamps, and inlets. The latter were then identified in sequence as Pass Cavallo, Cedar Bayou, and Aransas Pass. He also recognized the Guadalupe as the river of nuts where Cabeza de Vaca rejoined his companions, and he attempted an analysis of the complete route from the Texas coast to Culiacán. In dealing with the Texas journey beyond the Guadalupe River, Baskett lost focus. To his credit, he tried to correlate ethnographic information, but he was hampered by the dearth of reliable data on Texas Indians. He identified the Guadalquivir-like river as the Frío, and the mountains as the dissected Cambrian escarpment near Uvalde, Texas, dismissing Cabeza de Vaca's remark that these mountains were fifteen leagues from the sea. In other instances when he could not reconcile the Texas landscape with the narratives, he hedged with statements such as: "I am inclined to believe that Cabeza [de Vaca] has erred here. . . ."[18]

Following the appearance of Baskett's article, a hiatus of eleven years ensued before the *Southwestern Historical Quarterly* published a landmark, two-part study of the Cabeza de Vaca route by Harbert Davenport and Joseph K. Wells. "The First Europeans in Texas, 1528–1536" represented a synthesis of earlier works in the *Quarterly* and a careful correlation of Naufragios and the Joint Report; it was based on greater knowledge of the topography along the border of Texas and Mexico; and it incorporated the work of Herbert E. Bolton and his associates on Texas Indians. Davenport and Wells reconfirmed the first four streams crossed by the castaways and provided logical explanations for changes that had occurred in drainage channels over four centuries. They were the first to conjecture, correctly in this author's opinion, that Cabeza de Vaca's Malhado was a combination of

[17]Baskett, "Study of the Route of Cabeza de Vaca" (Jan., 1907), 246 (quotations), 249, 250, 264.

[18]Ibid., 258–259, 265–272, 278 (quotation).

present San Luis Island and Oyster Bay peninsula in the Brazosport area. Silting from the discharge of rivers and the impact of hurricanes, they argued, had turned what had been an elongated island in Cabeza de Vaca's time into a peninsula. Once San Luis Island proper and Oyster Bay peninsula are connected, then the island described by Cabeza de Vaca as lying behind Malhado (toward Florida) becomes Galveston Island, and the reconstructed island is "just where Mal-Hado *[sic]* ought to be" relative to the four rivers.[19]

Davenport and Wells agreed with Baskett's identification of the inlets. They were also able to identify Mustang Island and Corpus Christi Bay from the narratives and to confirm Baskett's deduction that the Guadalupe was the river of nuts. From the Guadalupe River to the Land of Tunas the four men had traveled toward Pánuco for a distance of thirty or forty leagues, a journey that the Indians annually took along the coast near the end of May. The coastal route was favored by the Indians because they were able to drive deer into the sea and hold them there until they drowned. Significantly, after Cabeza de Vaca was reunited with Dorantes, Castillo, and Estevanico, the men planned their escape from the Land of Tunas at the end of summer, when the prickly pear cactus was playing out.[20]

Location of the tuna region on the Texas coastal plain was therefore an important consideration. Davenport and Wells were aware that a great freeze in February, 1899, coupled with "root rot," had thinned the prickly pear cactus stands just south of the Nueces River. Prior to 1899 a thick Land of Tunas was located in the Texas counties of Kleberg, Jim Wells, Duval, Live Oak, and in a part of Nueces. South of this first region of tunas was a great sand plain not conducive to the growth of cactus. But beyond the sand plain a second stand of prickly pear cactus, even more abundant than the first, characterized vegetation along the lower Río Grande in Hidalgo, Starr, and Cameron counties.[21]

As Davenport and Wells emphasized, to read the narratives is to be impressed with the castaways' determination to go forward toward Pánuco. It was to reach Pánuco that the Spaniards had built boats on the Florida coast, and toward that goal the survivors had moved down the Texas coast after landing near Galveston Island. From the Land of Tunas, since the castaways were still intent on reaching Mexico, they must have crossed the Río Grande, the

---

[19]Davenport and Wells, "First Europeans" (Oct., 1918), 112–113, 119–122, 123 (quotation). This land form in the Brazosport area, now named Follets Island (actually a peninsula), was also known as Velasco Peninsula. See W. L. Fisher et al., *Environmental Geologic Atlas of the Texas Coastal Zone—Galveston-Houston Area* (Austin: Bureau of Economic Geology, University of Texas at Austin, 1972), Map II—Physical Properties Map; and Walter Prescott Webb, H. Bailey Carroll, and Eldon Stephen Branda (eds.), *The Handbook of Texas* (3 vols.; Austin: Texas State Historical Association, 1952, 1976), II, 558. The correspondence of Follets Island and Velasco Peninsula is confirmed by their southwestward relationship to San Luis Pass. See fig. 1.

[20]Davenport and Wells, "First Europeans" (Oct., 1918), 133, 141–142, (Jan., 1919), 205–208.

[21]Ibid. (Jan., 1919), 208, 209 (quotation), 210.

first river "in the direction of Mexico . . . which conceivably could be compared to the Guadalquivir at Sevilla." And there is the matter of mountains, first observed soon after the castaways crossed a wide river. Indians informed the four men that these mountains were within fifteen leagues of the ocean. As mentioned earlier, Coopwood identified them as the Pamoranes, an outlying spur of the Cerralvo mountains in the Sierra Madre Oriental range.[22]

The ethnographic information presented by Davenport and Wells is better than in previous route interpretations, thanks primarily to the work of Bolton on Texas Indians, but it is not convincing. In many instances, the Indian groups specifically named by Cabeza de Vaca were linked by the authors to later Indians of the coastal region on the basis of similar orthography and pure guesswork. The most notable contributions by the two men were to make plausible correlations with Texas land forms through a careful reading of Naufragios and the Oviedo account, and to stress the continued desire of the castaways to travel south toward the Christian community in Pánuco.[23] Subsequent interpretations of the Cabeza de Vaca journey would have benefited from a careful consideration of Davenport and Wells. Instead, writers over the next several decades followed a pattern already established in earlier volumes of the *Quarterly*. They traced a coastal route from Malhado to the Guadalupe River and then projected a westward journey across Texas, often without regard to topography or to the succession of facts stated in the narratives.

That trend received impetus in the 1930s from Robert T. Hill, a distinguished geologist, and Carlos E. Castañeda, an emerging Texas historian. Hill's work was triggered by publication in 1933 of *The Odyssey of Cabeza de Vaca,* by Morris Bishop. Bishop, a professor of romance languages at Cornell University, had been much impressed by Cabeza de Vaca's travels on two continents, and he had written a breezy narrative spiced with imaginary dialogue. The Cornell professor made no attempt to advance a new route interpretation but instead accepted the conclusions of Davenport and Wells, set forth some fourteen years earlier.[24] The realization that a significant portion of Cabeza de Vaca's travels had been removed from Texas to Mexico proved intolerable for Hill.

Hill's talents and accomplishments in the field of Texas and Mexican geology and physiography were unexcelled. He had worked out the complex geology of the Austin area, giving name to the Balcones Escarpment in 1887, and had authored an impressive string of scientific publications. In 1931 Hill began a series of articles for the Dallas *Morning News,* commenting in Sunday editions

[22]Ibid., 223–224, 233–234 (quotation).

[23]Ibid., 222.

[24]Morris Bishop, *The Odyssey of Cabeza de Vaca* (New York: Century Co., 1933); *The Book Review Digest* . . . (New York: H. W. Wilson Co., 1934), 86–87. In the early 1540s Cabeza de Vaca walked from the Brazilian coast to Asunción (Paraguay).

on such a variety of topics as East Texas oil fields, archaeological sites, and 3.2 alcoholic beverages. In 1933 and 1934 the noted geologist wrote twenty-two lengthy articles on the route of Cabeza de Vaca.[25] At that time Hill was the retiring chairman of the Cordilleran section of the Geological Society of America and was the elected president of the Texas Geographic Society.[26] When he undertook the Cabeza de Vaca route interpretation he did so with the zeal of a true Texas nationalist.

For some years Hill had been convinced that all previous route interpretations by historians had been wrong. Why? Because "I personally was familiar with the geographic and geologic features of the countries through which the party traveled and the historians were not so." In his opening article, Hill likened the heresy of moving Cabeza de Vaca out of Texas to landing the Pilgrims in Canada or to placing John Smith and Pocahontas in Ohio. To accept the trans-Mexico route, he railed, was to take away "Cabeza's Texas citizenship," and he chastised the citizens of his adopted state for allowing themselves to "sit complacently by and see the very beginnings of our history taken from us, the scene of its story wrongly transferred across the Río Grande into a foreign country, Mexico. . . ." With great passion, Hill announced his goal in the forthcoming articles: "If there was but one thing left to do in this life for me, it would be to endeavor to relocate the scene of Cabeza's route upon the Texas map where it justly belongs, and from where it was most unjustly and wrongfully removed." The record, he vowed, must be set straight, and Cabeza de Vaca must be restored among the "pantheon of heroes." That Hill succeeded in his mission is beyond dispute; that he could tell a difficult story in nearly two dozen segments over ten months "so plain that even a child who runs may read it" was another matter.[27]

Hill's articles were occasionally learned discourses on the geology of a particular region with little mention of Cabeza de Vaca and his companions, and they reflect a man who did not suffer indecision in advocating a trans-Texas route. Malhado, the coastal rivers, and the river of nuts, as accepted by Davenport and Wells, gave Hill no cause for concern. From the Guadalupe River, however, he projected a more northern route than had other writers. The factors that had determined the path of the castaways, Hill insisted, were physiographical, sources of water being the primary one, although he paid some attention to flora and fauna. He placed the Land of Tunas on the Washington prairies near the town sites of Washington, Brenham, Hallettsville,

[25]Webb, Carroll, and Branda (eds.), *Handbook of Texas,* I, 813–814; Nancy Alexander, *Father of Texas Geology: Robert T. Hill* (Dallas: SMU Press, 1976); Dallas *Morning News,* July 2, 9, 16, 23, 30, Aug. 20, 27, Sept. 10, 17, 24, Oct. 8, 15, 22, 29, Nov. 5, 19, 1933; Feb. 18, Mar. 4, 11, May 27, June 10, Dec. 30, 1934.

[26]Dallas *Morning News,* July 2, 1933.

[27]Ibid. (2nd–6th quotations), Dec. 30, 1934 (1st quotation).

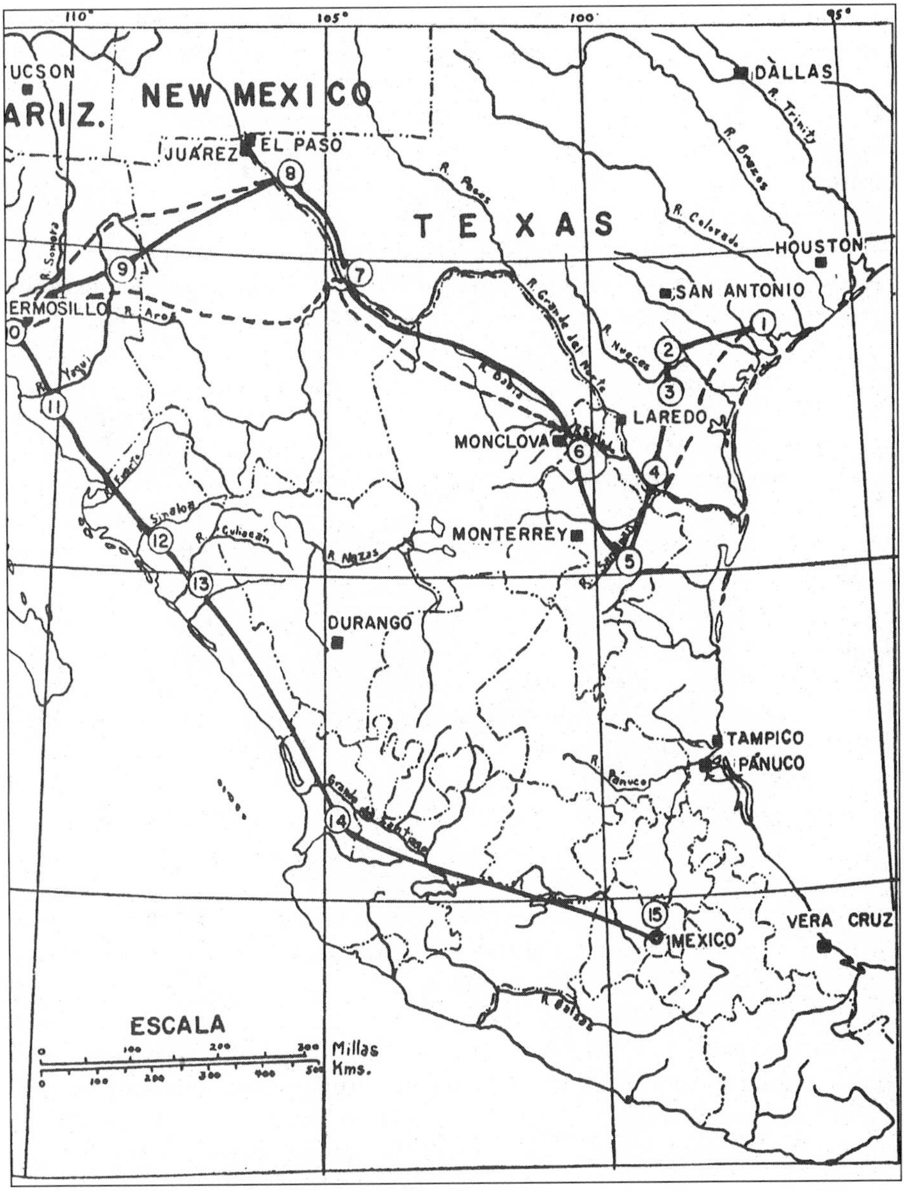


Alex D. Krieger's interpretation of Cabeza de Vaca's most probable route from the Guadalupe River to Mexico City. Krieger's alternate route interpretation is shown with broken lines. From Krieger, "The Travels of Alvar Núñez Cabeza de Vaca in Texas and Mexico, 1534–1536," in *Homenaje a Pablo Martínez del Río. . . . Courtesy Benson Latin American Collection, University of Texas, Austin.*

La Grange, Karnes City, and Helena. The large river like the Guadalquivir may have been the Colorado near Austin or the Guadalupe north of New Braunfels, and the first mountains were the Balcones Escarpment.[28] In projecting a route close to Austin, Hill could not resist chiding the "learned professors" at the University of Texas who daily viewed a portion of Cabeza de Vaca's journey, yet insisted that it lay in "distant Mexico."[29] From Austin or San Marcos, according to Hill, the path led to San Antonio, then westward to the mouth of Devils River, where it turned northward. Hill placed the first crossing of the Río Grande just west of the Chisos Mountains, followed by a quick recrossing of the river from the south at Presidio, Texas. Thus a tiny portion of the route identified by Hill did cross Mexican soil.[30] Several months after his concluding article on Cabeza de Vaca, Hill offered a self-serving assessment of his own work. The lengthy title for his valedictory, probably chosen by the newspaper itself, was "Cabeza de Vaca Comes Back to Texas. This Time to Stay. His Texas Route as Set Forth in The News is Approved and Vindicated." The source of Hill's elation was correspondence from an unnamed but "able professor of Latin American history at the University of Texas." Professor X had informed the famous geologist that his route interpretation had been accepted by the department of history and was being taught in its classes. That news, confessed Hill, "so filled my old heart with joy and excitement that it sent me to bed for twenty-four hours."[31]

Hill's route interpretation was plausible, especially if one chose to ignore portions of the narratives and to concentrate on geographic and geologic determinants. The unspecified professor at the University of Texas was undoubtedly Charles W. Hackett, a Bolton-trained scholar. Hackett later directed the M.A. thesis (1939) of Albert C. Williams, entitled "The Route of Cabeza de Vaca in Texas: A Study in Historiography." Williams accepted Hill's route interpretation, regarding it as "fundamentally unitary in nature, being based upon the geological evidences primarily." But the young student was somewhat troubled, admitting "that the route given by Davenport and Wells most nearly avoids contradiction of the literal wording of the *Relation*. . . ."[32]

Another scholar at the University of Texas, soon to attain the rank of associate professor in the department of history, was Carlos E. Castañeda. In the first volume

---

[28]Ibid., Aug. 27, Sept. 10, 24, Oct. 15, Nov. 19, 1933.

[29]Ibid., Oct. 15, 1933.

[30]Ibid., Nov. 19, 1933, Feb. 18, Mar. 4, 1934. For a map of Hill's trans-Texas route, see ibid., June 10, 1934, and fig. 1.

[31]Ibid., Dec. 30, 1934.

[32]John Francis Bannon, *Herbert Eugene Bolton: The Historian and the Man,* 1870–1953 (Tucson: University of Arizona Press, 1978), 284; Albert Calvin Williams, "The Route of Cabeza de Vaca in Texas: A Study in Historiography" (M.A. thesis, University of Texas, 1939), 86 (quotations), 87. Some authors prefer to use the title *Relación,* rather than Naufragios, when citing the account by Cabeza de Vaca.

(1936) of his massive work, *Our Catholic Heritage in Texas,* Castañeda acknowledged the Davenport and Wells analysis as "the most detailed and scholarly." Like Hill, he accepted their route interpretation as far as the Guadalupe River. For the remainder of the trek to El Paso, however, Castañeda essentially followed the journey as outlined a few years earlier in the Dallas *Morning News.*[33] The fact that two scholars at the University of Texas had accepted the conclusions of Robert T. Hill was of great importance to the historiography of the Cabeza de Vaca odyssey. Hill's articles have never been very accessible to scholars or the reading public, but Hackett and Castañeda have had a tremendous impact on the teaching and writing of Texas history. Through their lectures and publications, the blatant Texas nationalism of Hill influenced history textbooks read by thousands of Texas school children.[34] And there was worse to come.

In 1940 Cleve Hallenbeck, a nonacademic historian, published the first book-length study of the Cabeza de Vaca route. His work consisted of three parts. Part 1 narrated the journey from Florida to Culiacán and Mexico City; Part 2 presented a new route interpretation across Texas; and Part 3 assessed the routes "traced by others." Hallenbeck claimed firsthand knowledge of Texas topography and biota, and he argued that the castaways followed established Indian trails across Texas. His trans-Texas route was based on astonishing conjecture—suppositions that no one else had dared to make. In the introduction, for example, he speculated that the four "could have" erected piles of stone marking their path, making it possible to trace the route after four centuries; inscriptions "could have" been carved on soft sandstone and limestone cliffs in West Texas; a walking staff "arbitrarily scaled into uniform graduations, easily could have been prepared," in order to determine latitude by the length of the shadow cast at noon; and animal skins, "one to the man, would have permitted them" to map their route across the North American continent. Never mind that skins were so lacking that Cabeza de Vaca at times described his wretched condition with such words as "I wended my way naked as the day I was born."[35]

---

[33]Carlos E. Castañeda, *Our Catholic Heritage in Texas,* 1519–1936 (7 vols.; Austin: Von Boeckmann-Jones Co., 1936–1958), I, 55, n. 33 (quotation), 59–80. Castañeda became an associate professor in 1939. Webb, Carroll, and Branda (eds.), *Handbook of Texas,* III, 150.

[34]For example, see Adrian N. Anderson and Ralph A. Wooster, *Texas and Texans* (rev. ed.; Austin: Steck-Vaughn Co., 1978), 58; Allan O. Kownslar, *The Texans: Their Land and History* (New York: American Heritage Publishing Co., 1972), 66; Jim B. Pearson, Ben H. Procter, and William B. Conroy, *Texas: The Land and Its People* (Dallas: Hendrick-Long Publishing Co., 1972), 57; James V. Reese and Lorrin Kennamer, *Texas, Land of Contrast: Its History and Geography* (Austin: W. S. Benson & Co., 1978), 92–93.

[35]Cleve Hallenbeck, *Alvar Núñez Cabeza de Vaca: The Journey and Route of the First European to Cross the Continent of North America,* 1534–1536 (Glendale, Calif.: Arthur H. Clark Co., 1940), [5] (1st quotation), 26 (2nd, 3rd, and 5th quotations), 27 (4th quotation), 105–113; Covey, *Adventures,* 86 (6th quotation).

In projecting his trans-Texas route, Hallenbeck insisted that Galveston Island was Cabeza de Vaca's Malhado, the river of nuts was the Colorado, and the Land of Tunas lay immediately south of San Antonio. After fleeing the Mariames, the castaways traveled north by northwest from San Antonio to Big Spring, Texas. The wide river the four men waded was the Concho; the first mountains were the Davis and Guadalupe of West Texas; Cabeza de Vaca's statement that the first mountains he saw were near the coast and ran from the direction of the North Sea was attributed to imperfect communication with the Indians and consequent misunderstanding.[36]

In short, the first book on the subject contradicted many of the initial landmarks of the journey that had been accepted for over twenty years. As one critic of Hallenbeck has remarked, his work was "an incredible series of errors in geography, travel time and distance, Indian customs, distribution of native plants and animals, etc. . . ." Regrettably, the Hallenbeck route interpretation has gained wide circulation and acceptance, even among academic historians.[37]

Since 1940 three scholars, all anthropologists, have undertaken a careful reexamination of the Cabeza de Vaca journey. The pioneer in this endeavor was Alex D. Krieger, ably supported by the careful research of T. N. Campbell and T. J. Campbell. All have failed to attract the attention they deserve. Krieger's doctoral dissertation, submitted in Spanish to the faculty of the Universidad Nacional Autónoma de México (1955), has never been published. A précis in English of the dissertation (1961) was published in Mexico, but it is not well known in the United States. The Campbells' cooperative work (1981) suffers from a title, *Historic Indian Groups of the Choke Canyon Reservoir and Surrounding Area, Southern Texas,* which contains not a clue that it relates to Cabeza de Vaca.[38]

Any detailed analysis of the Cabeza de Vaca journey requires a book-length monograph, for the route interpreter must carefully coordinate the texts of

---

[36]Hallenbeck, *Alvar Núñez Cabeza de Vaca,* 119–127, 136–140, 147–171, 175–177. See also fig. 1. Hallenbeck stated that he was "not certain" of Cabeza de Vaca's meaning for "North sea" (p. 174). (For this body of water, see note 7.)

[37]Alex D. Krieger, "The Travels of Alvar Núñez Cabeza de Vaca in Texas and Mexico, 1534–1536," in *Homenaje a Pablo Martínez del Río en el vigésimoquinto aniversario de la primera edición de "Los orígenes americanos"* (Mexico City: Instituto Nacional de Antropología e Historia, 1961), 465 (quotation). Hallenbeck heavily influenced Covey's route interpretation in *Cabeza de Vaca's Adventures,* first published by Collier Books in 1961 and reprinted by the University of New Mexico Press in 1983 and 1984. See Covey (trans.), *Adventures,* 7–8, and the map in the first edition on pages 18–19. See also John Francis Bannon's introduction in Fanny Bandelier (trans.), *The Narrative of Alvar Núñez Cabeza de Vaca* (Barre, Mass.: Imprint Society, 1972), xi–xxxi.

[38]Alex D. Krieger, "Un nuevo estudio de la ruta seguida por Cabeza de Vaca a través de Norte America" (Ph.D. diss., Universidad Nacional Autónoma de México, 1955); Krieger, "Travels," 459–474; Campbell and Campbell, *Choke Canyon.*

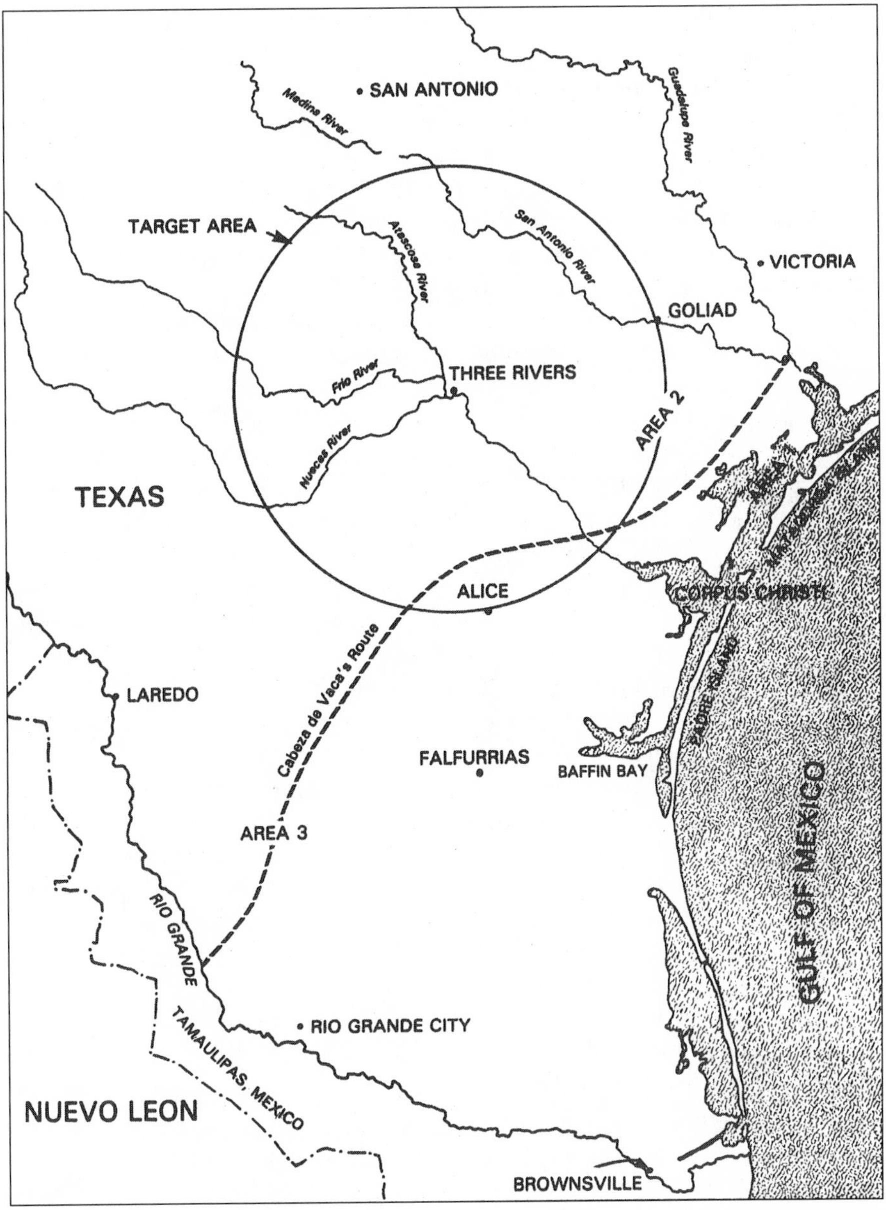


T. N. and T. J. Campbell's interpretation of Cabeza de Vaca's probable route from the Guadalupe River to the lower Rio Grande and the locale of named Indian groups. From Campbell and Campbell, *Historic Indian Groups. . . . Courtesy T. N. Campbell.*

Naufragios and the Joint Report with all available data—physiography, time and distance of travel, ethnographic information, biota, geographic knowledge, geographic *perceptions* of the castaways, and the overall objective of the trek, which, to repeat, was to reach Pánuco on the Gulf coast of Mexico. The problem with too many route interpretations has been the lack of objectivity, or a somewhat myopic concentration on only one or two indices. Fueled by Texas nationalism, for example, writers have sought to prove that Cabeza de Vaca waded a specific river, crossed this or that arroyo, saw a particular mountain, or trod the site of a modern town; or they have concentrated on geology or Indian trails, which, coupled with a loose reading of the documents, makes it possible to project an almost limitless number of routes across Texas and Mexico.[39]

Alex D. Krieger's route interpretation meets the criteria of thoroughness and objectivity. His approach was systematic, breaking the journey into ten chronological segments. It is well to remember, as Krieger emphasized, that the castaways did not wander in the wilderness for eight years. In reality, they were only on the march during the last twenty-two months of their odyssey (September, 1534–July, 1536), and only in the last thirteen months were they "continuously" on the move. Krieger calculated actual days of progress at 230–238 over a distance of 2,480–2,640 miles.[40] Second, Krieger studied the *entire* route from the Texas coast to Culiacán and Mexico City, making full use of Naufragios and the Joint Report. Third, he carefully analyzed previous route interpretations, coordinated topography, ethnology, and biota, and illustrated every mile of the journey with twelve maps. His route interpretation for the portion of the overland trek that lay near the Texas-Mexico border is essentially a refinement—an important refinement, to be sure—of that advanced by Davenport and Wells in 1919. Because of firsthand knowledge of border topography, Krieger was able to dovetail convincingly the Mexican part of the overland trek with the Texas route. His placement, however, of the Land of Tunas in Texas has been challenged by the Campbells.

It seems certain that the castaways crossed the lower Río Grande into Mexico, where they soon encountered the Sierra de Cerralvo in northern Nuevo León. Cabeza de Vaca described the peaks with the words *sierras,* while the Joint Report rendered them *cordillera,* but in either case, "mountains." It can be argued that Cabeza de Vaca knew the difference between hills or escarpments and peaks. He was familiar with mountains along the coast of his native land in southern Spain, which rise to 6,000 feet, and his narrative was composed *after* he had seen the Sierra Madre Occidental of western Mexico, one of the most formidable mountain ranges on the North American continent.

[39]Krieger, "Nuevo estudio," 9.

[40]Ibid., 229 (quotation). Even after the castaways were in transit, they were delayed, sometimes for days, by circumstances such as swollen streams. Covey, *Adventures,* 122.

Further, as Krieger noted, the Sierra de Cerralvo runs roughly north-south, precisely as described by Cabeza de Vaca, and at the southern end these mountains are "almost exactly" forty-five miles, or fifteen leagues, from the coast.[41]

Once Cabeza de Vaca and his companions encountered the mountains, they decided to turn inland rather than head eastward toward the Gulf coast. That decision, which contradicted their original intent to travel toward Pánuco, was probably based on several considerations. Friendly Indians reminded them that the shoreline groups were "very bad," while those in the interior were better disposed and possessed more food.[42] Krieger also argued logically that the four men believed the Pacific Ocean could be reached at about 105° west longitude, and that it was no further away than Mexico City. Here, perceptions of geography must be kept in mind. When the Narváez expedition set out in 1528, its leaders knew of Pacific coast settlements in Mexico as far north as the state of Jalisco, where the coast lay at roughly 105° west longitude. But they had no way of knowing that the coast of Mexico above Cabo Corrientes plunges northwestward at a nearly 135° angle toward the Gulf of California. In reality, at the latitude where the four men turned westward, the Pacific coast was actually situated at approximately 110° west longitude. Finally, as Cabeza de Vaca admitted, by traveling inland they also had an opportunity to discover new lands and collect important information.[43]

The path of the castaways across northern Mexico is convincingly analyzed by Krieger, but is beyond the defined limits of this paper. In their travels the four men again struck the Río Grande, this time near its confluence with the Río Conchos in eastern Chihuahua. Almost every route interpreter has placed contact by the travelers with Indians who lived in fixed houses at La Junta de los Ríos, near Presidio, Texas. Krieger believed the castaways ascended the Río Grande on the east, or Texas, bank for some seventeen days, recrossed the river about seventy-five miles downriver from El Paso, and then turned westward toward the Pacific coast.[44]

---

[41] *La relación y comentarios del gouernador Aluar nuñez cabeça de vaca,* capítulo XXVIII; Hedrick and Riley, *Journey,* 136; Campbell and Campbell, *Choke Canyon,* 8–9; Krieger, "Travels," 467 (2nd quotation). Krieger placed the Río Grande crossing near Roma, Texas. Ibid., 459–474.

[42] Quoted in Krieger, "Travels," 467. This reminder was hardly necessary, given what the castaways knew about the fate of their colleagues.

[43] Ibid., 462–464. Land expeditions by Nuño de Guzmán and sea explorations by Fernando Cortés increased geographic knowledge of the Pacific coast above Cabo Corrientes in the early 1530s.

[44] Ibid., 467–470. In 1582 the expedition of Antonio de Espejo contacted Indians at La Junta de los Ríos who remembered the appearance there of three Christians and a black man forty-seven years earlier. Herbert Eugene Bolton (ed.), *Spanish Exploration in the Southwest, 1542–1706* (1908; reprint, New York: Barnes & Noble, 1959), 173.

The later work of T. N. and T. J. Campbell at the University of Texas may be properly called a refinement of the Krieger interpretation for a portion of the Texas route. Their contribution was essentially new in that they went through all the relevant primary Spanish documents with a fine-tooth comb and sorted out all information about each *named* Indian group. The synthesized Indian data were used, along with terrain and biotic data, as criteria for their route evaluation. Once this was accomplished, it became apparent to the Campbells that those who advocate a totally trans-Texas route must move the Texas Indians contacted by Cabeza de Vaca to parts of the state "where they obviously never lived."[45]

As the Campbells cautioned, it will never be known *precisely* where Cabeza de Vaca encountered each Indian group in South Texas. But, of the twenty-three Texas groups named by Cabeza de Vaca, "all of them can be linked with the outer part of the Texas coastal plain, extending from the vicinity of Galveston Island to the vicinity of Falcon Lake, an overland distance of some 300 miles." Six of these groups lived east of the lower Guadalupe River: the Capoques, Chorruco, Doguenes, Han, Mendica, and Quevenes. The remaining seventeen were situated between the lower Guadalupe River and the Río Grande. Four of this number, the Guaycones, Quitoles, Camoles, and Fig People, were shoreline Indians located between the Guadalupe River and San Antonio Bay. Eleven groups occupied the inland region between the lower Guadalupe and lower Nueces. The northern groups of them regularly moved southwestward in the summer to the prickly pear region. Arranged roughly in order of their locations along a northeast-southwest axis they were the Mariames, Yguazes, Atayos, Acubadaos, Avavares, Anegados, Cutalchuches, Maliacones, Susolas, Comos, and Coayos. The remaining two groups mentioned by Cabeza de Vaca, the Arbadaos and Cuchendados, appear to have lived west of the sand plain of Brooks and Kenedy counties.[46]

Aside from their substantial contribution in supplying ethnographic data for route interpretation, the Campbells also provided a logical and defensible location for the Land of Tunas. As implied earlier, it is here that they differ with the route interpretation of Krieger. Krieger positioned the tuna area south of the Atascosa River, some thirty to forty miles due south of San Antonio. But he was troubled by the Oviedo account, which suggests a more coastal location. Indeed, Krieger acknowledged the possibility of an "alternate" route for this portion of the journey. The Campbells offered convincing evidence that Krieger's "alternate" route should be his "preferred" route. They placed the prickly pear area near the Nueces River, west and northwest of Corpus Christi Bay. Cabeza de Vaca and his companions intended to escape toward Pánuco

---

[45]T. N. Campbell to D. E. C., Apr. 16, 1985.

[46]Campbell and Campbell, *Choke Canyon*, 9 (quotation), 10–32, 37–40.

when their captors, the Mariames, were at the tuna collecting grounds. If the prickly pear area were not south of the lower Guadalupe, they would have attempted escape from the river of nuts. Second, the Oviedo account made reference to a communal deer hunt en route to the Land of Tunas. Deer were drowned by driving them into the waters of a coastal bay as the Indians skirted its shorelines. The Campbells believed this body of water to have been Copano Bay. Third, escape plans of the four were laid for the end of the prickly pear season (September), when the Mariames would be returning north to their winter range. As this occurred, the castaways would flee south in the opposite direction. Finally, like Davenport and Wells before them, the Campbells pointed to the fact that prickly pear cactus grew in super abundance near the lower Nueces River until 1899, when a severe freeze reduced its stands. They placed the tuna gathering area in the general vicinity of Alice, Texas, in Jim Wells County.[47]

Once the Land of Tunas is located in Jim Wells County, the route projected by the Campbells for the men's escape from the Mariames and for their later departure from the Avavares is supported nicely by the documentation. Their path toward the Río Grande was probably southwestward, thereby avoiding both the barren sand plain and hostile coastal Indians. Like Krieger, the Campbells postulated a Río Grande crossing in the area of Falcon Lake.[48]

This essay is intended to provide historical perspective on interpretations of Cabeza de Vaca's route in Texas. It will not "solve" the problem of determining precisely where three Spaniards and an African traveled on an odyssey that began in Texas and ended in Mexico City some 450 years ago. But a careful reading of the literature on the subject, especially the work of Davenport and Wells, Krieger, and the Campbells, suggests that those who persist in advocating a totally trans-Texas route for the first leg of the overland journey should reassess the soundness of scholarship on which it rests. Historical accuracy is important in itself; moreover, a more precise route interpretation contributes to a better understanding of early Texas ethnography, geography, and biology. And, in any case, the possibility that a sizable portion of the Four Ragged Castaways' route lay across northern Mexico hardly denies their importance to the history of Texas. They were, after all, the first non-Indian pioneers of Texas, and lived continuously for nearly seven years in the area that would become the Lone Star State.

---

[47]Krieger, "Travels," 466 (author's quotation marks). See fig. 2. Campbell and Campbell, *Choke Canyon*, 4–6, 7 (quotations); Davenport and Wells, "First Europeans" (Jan., 1919), 209–210.

[48]Campbell and Campbell, *Choke Canyon*, 8. See fig. 3.

# Tios and Tantes: Familial and Political Relationships of Natchitoches and the Spanish Colonial Frontier

Patricia R. Lemée*

*In this essay Patricia R. Lemée, an independent researcher and visiting professor at the University of Texas at Austin, describes the relationship between residents of the French outpost in Natchitoches, Louisiana, and the Spanish and Native Americans in East Texas. She pays particular attention to the role played by a French colonial trader, Louis Juchereau de St. Denis (1674–1744), and his family in maintaining a continuing influence with Native Americans in Louisiana and Texas.*

*A native of Canada, St. Denis first came to Louisiana in 1699 with an expedition commanded by Pierre Le Moyne, Sieur d'Iberville. Sent to Spanish Texas by the French governor of Louisiana in response to a request from Father Francisco Hidalgo of the Spanish mission San Juan Bautista to help with missionary activity in Texas, St. Denis quickly established himself as a major figure in activities along the borders of French Louisiana and Spanish Texas. After St. Denis's death in 1744 his sons and other descendants continued to play an important role in trade and Indian affairs along the Louisiana-Texas border for many years.*

*Readers interested in learning more about the influence of St. Denis and his family should see Patricia R. Lemée, "Ambivalent Successes and Success in Failures: St. Denis, Aguayo, and Juan Rodriquez," in François Lagarde (ed.),* The French in Texas: History, Migration, Culture *(Austin: University of Texas Press, 2003); Donald Chipman,* Spanish Texas, 1519–1822; *Ross Phares,* Cavalier in the Wilderness: The Story of the Explorer and Trader Louis Juchereau de St. Denis *(Baton Rouge: Louisiana State University Press, 1952); and Robert S. Weddle,* The French Thorn: Rival Explorers in the Spanish Sea, 1682–1762 *(College Station: Texas A&M University Press, 1991).*

* Patricia R. Lemée, "Tios and Tantes: Familial and Political Relationships of Natchitoches and the Spanish Colonial Frontier," *Southwestern Historical Quarterly*, 101 (Jan., 1998), 343–358.

The Mexican town of Guerrero, Coahuila, is near the Rio Grande in the drought-ridden, semi-arid desert that characterizes northeastern Mexico and southwestern Texas.[1] Situated about thirty-five miles downriver from present-day Piedras Negras, Coahuila, and its sister city of Eagle Pass, Texas, Guerrero retains much of its historical character. The contemporary town is the home to impressive ruins, including the Misión de San Bernardo and a still-functioning irrigation system designed nearly three hundred years ago. Historians of the Spanish colonial borderlands have termed this Rio Grande settlement "the gateway to Spanish Texas."[2]

The name of the first mission at the Guerrero site, San Juan Bautista, became the generic name for the settlement that included Presidio de Rio Grande and missions San Francisco de Solano and San Bernardo. Through this frontier outpost passed some of the most important colonial expeditions from northeast Mexico across the Rio Grande into the Province of Texas, which is why it is called a gateway. The term "gateway," however, by no means should be considered exclusive. While San Juan Bautista served as the gateway from the south, another similarly named colonial settlement on the northeast side of the region also served as an entry point—the French post Saint-Jean-Baptiste des Natchitoches on the Red River at present-day Natchitoches, Louisiana.[3]

A study of the people—Spanish, French, and Indian—who moved between the two fringe settlements reveals relationships that produced a remarkable interaction across the land that became the state of Texas. The links forged between these groups, sometimes cemented by kinship, had both economic and political implications that endured through much of the eighteenth century. During that time, French traders from Natchitoches influenced or controlled commercial

---

[1]Guerrero, Coahuila, is not to be confused with Guerrero Viejo or Nuevo Guerrero, Tamaulipas. Originally named Revilla, the Tamaulipas town was renamed on November 12, 1827, to honor the Mexican military hero Vicente Guerrero. Construction of Falcón Dam on the Rio Grande and the subsequent flooding of that river to create Falcón Lake precipitated the relocation of various towns in Tamaulipas, including Guerrero, which was renamed Nuevo Guerrero. The former townsite became known as Guerrero Viejo. Mario L. Sánchez (ed.), *A Shared Experience: The History, Architecture and Historical Designations of the Lower Rio Grande Heritage Corridor*, 2nd ed. (Austin: Los Caminos del Rio Heritage Project and the Texas Historical Commission, 1994), 201.

[2]Robert S. Weddle, *San Juan Bautista, Gateway to Spanish Texas* (1968; reprint, Austin: University of Texas Press, 1991).

[3]Jean Baptiste Le Moyne, Sieur de Bienville, brother of Pierre Le Moyne, Sieur d'Iberville, was among the Natchez Indians in June 1716 when he learned that a Spanish entrada commanded by Domingo Ramón was approaching the French colony. Upon reaching the Red River later that month, Ramón found a French garrison which, under Bienville's command, had fortified the outpost only ten days prior. The exact date in June that Post Saint-Jean-Baptiste des Natchitoches was established is uncertain. Possibly it was June 24, the Feast Day of Saint-Jean-Baptiste, patron saint of Canada. Dunbar Rowland and Albert Godfrey Sanders (eds.), *Mississippi Provincial Archives 1701–1729 French Dominion* (3 vols.; Jackson: Press of the Mississippi Department of Archives and History, 1929), III, 515 (cited hereafter as *MPA*).

activity along the Red River. Significantly, traces of the same French influence eventually spread across much of Texas through trade and Indian relations. These French actions often were associated with frontier trade cartels that were predominantly familial in nature. Established by Frenchmen, the cartels grew through alliances and kinship to include Indian and Spanish members.

One of the most influential French colonial traders was Louis Juchereau de St. Denis. His interaction with Frenchmen, Spaniards, and Indians in Louisiana, the Spanish province of Texas, and the interior of Mexico illustrates how the complex relationships of one such frontier cartel formed. The cartel St. Denis established strongly influenced the political and military setting throughout the Province of Texas during much of the eighteenth century.

St. Denis arrived on the Louisiana Gulf Coast in 1700 with his nephew-in-law Pierre Le Moyne, Sieur d'Iberville, a French Canadian who had established the Louisiana colony the previous year.[4] St. Denis himself was a third generation French Canadian, said to have been educated formally at Le Collège Royale in Paris.[5]

By 1701, St. Denis had explored a considerable distance up the Red River. He developed amiable relations with some indigenous groups and engaged in trade with the Caddoan confederacies, possibly including the Hasinai in East Texas.[6] When the Natchitoches Indians' corn crop failed the next year, they

---

[4]In 1696 Pierre Le Moyne married Marie Pollet, the daughter of Louis Juchereau de St. Denis's older sister, Marie Anne, and François Pollet de la Combe Pocatière, a French army captain. Marie Anne's second husband was François Madeleine Fortune Ruette d'Auteuil, Procureur General of the Sovereign Council of Nouvelle France or present-day Canada. Genealogical information from author's personal files.

[5]St. Denis's ancestors, Jean Juchereau, Sieur de St. Maur, and Robert Giffard, Sieur de Beauport, were among the early colonists of New France. In 1687, the lieutenant governor of New France recommended the Sieur de St. Maur to Louis XIV and requested a patent of nobility for him to reward his faithful services to the crown. Juchereau did not live to receive the patent. He died in 1672 at Beauport on the concession of his son, Nicholas Juchereau de St. Denis. Eighteen years later, it was Jean Juchereau's seventy-year-old son who came to the attention of Louis XIV. In 1680, when Quebec was threatened with seige by an English fleet, Nicholas Juchereau successfully led his three hundred militiamen for three days against the English landing party at Beauport. In recognition for his heroism, Nicholas Juchereau de St. Denis and his legitimate descendants were granted a patent of nobility from Louis XIV in February, 1692. Nicholas Juchereau de St. Denis and his wife, Marie Thérese Giffard, had twelve children—among them, Louis Juchereau de St. Denis. Abbé Cyprien Tanguay, *Dictionnaire Généalogique des Familles Canadiennes Depuis la Fondation de la Colonie Jusqu'a Nos Jours* (2 vols., Baltimore: Genalogical Publishing Company, 1967), I, 328.

[6]John R. Swanton, "Source Material on the History and Ethnology of the Caddo Indians," Bureau of American Ethnology Bulletin 132 (Washington, D.C.: U.S. Government Printing Office, 1942), 51. The Caddos in Texas, Oklahoma, Louisiana and Arkansas comprised three known confederacies—the Hasinai, the Kadohadacho, and the Natchitoches. As trading partners, these confederacies gave the French access to the Wichita, Kichai, Taovayas, Waco, Yscani, and Tawakoni, collectively known as the Norteños or "Nations of the North," of the Canadian, Arkansas, and upper Red Rivers, as well as their Comanche allies.

moved south from their village on the Red River to the banks of Lake Pontchartrain near St. Denis's property along Bayou Saint Jean in present-day New Orleans.[7] The Natchitoches remained there until St. Denis departed for New Spain in September 1713, then ascended the Red River with him.[8] As the Indians re-established themselves at the site of their abandoned village, St. Denis gave them seeds to plant and promised that Frenchmen would reside among them permanently.[9] In return, the Natchitoches constructed two buildings for St. Denis—one to store French provisions and the other to lodge the Frenchmen St. Denis had instructed to remain there until he returned from New Spain.

In general, the earliest French colonists in Louisiana seem to have been those who expected easy fortunes from the New World's mineral wealth or the poor and idle who intended to subsist on the crown's benevolance.[10] Discouragement and disappointment were constant companions of the first colonists, as fortunes were not quickly made, the crown supplied the colony infrequently, and provisions were received only sporadically. Early attempts at agriculture, better described as gardening rather than farming, were unsuccessful. Although soils were well-suited for planting, the colonists lacked the appropriate tools, skills, and desire for the task.[11]

Throughout the first two decades of the colony's often-destitute existence, the nearby Indians contributed to its subsistence needs by trading food for European goods and the protection of the French.[12] St. Denis appears to have valued and long remembered the natives' contributions to the colony.

The French historian Marcel Giraud suggests it was St. Denis's personal relationship with the local Indian groups that made him a logical candidate to lead a French trading venture to New Spain. Giraud writes, "The command was conferred upon St. Denis because of his enterprising spirit and his knowledge

[7]Richebourg G. McWilliams, *Fleur de Lys and Calumet: Being the Penicaut Narrative of French Adventure in Louisiana* (Baton Rouge: Louisiana State University Press, 1953), 100. The Natchitoches were a tribe within the confederacy of the same name. Their ancestral home was along the Red River near present-day Natchitoches, Louisiana.

[8]Marcel Giraud, *A History of French Louisiana*, trans. Joseph C. Lambert (3 vols.; Baton Rouge: Louisiana State University Press, 1974), I, 366. Originally published as *Histoire de la Louisiana française* (5 vols., Paris: Presses Universitairs de France, 1953), three of the five volumes have been translated and published to date.

[9]McWilliams, *Fleur de Lys and Calumet*, 149.

[10]Amos Stoddard, *Sketches, Historical and Descriptive, of Louisiana* (Philadelphia: Mathew Carey, 1812), 25.

[11]Rowland and Sanders, *MPA*, II, 72, 82.

[12]Stoddard, *Sketches of Louisiana*, 11, 36; Giraud, *History of French Louisiana*, I, 100; Fred Kniffen, Hiram Gregory and George Stockes, *The Historical Indian Tribes of Louisiana* (Baton Rouge: Louisiana State University Press, 1976), 71.

of the people of the Red River, with whom he had maintained a commerce in skins, maize, fruits and melons from his residence at Biloxi."[13] Plans for the French expedition were initiated in Mobile in 1713 when Governor Cadillac received a Fray Francisco Hidalgo letter written two years earlier from New Spain.[14] Hidalgo's missive, reportedly written in Latin, inquired about the Tejas Indians he had served at the Spanish missions in East Texas from 1690 to 1693.[15]

Recently unsuccessful at establishing French trade with New Spain via the Gulf route from Louisiana to Veracruz, Governor Cadillac issued St. Denis a passport stating his official purpose for visiting New Spain: to contact Hidalgo in response to the Franciscan's inquiry. While the passport made reference to no other purpose, longstanding French interest in New Spain's mineral riches seemed to assure that St. Denis would make every attempt to explore the region's mining activities.[16] Cadillac and St. Denis's primary interest, however, was trade. Their interest in the Spanish mines lay in the mines' potential to produce wealth that could be used to purchase French goods.

Antoine de la Mothe, Sieur de Cadillac, suffered as little success on the lower Mississippi as he had previously as commander of Fort Pontchartrain at Detroit. The record of his administration at the northern post has been described as "incoherent, inefficient, self-interested, and marred by his difficulties with religious orders."[17] A French official sent to investigate the numerous charges lodged against Cadillac in 1708 reported that he was hated equally by the French and Indians. "The tyranny that he maintains over them both is sufficient to warrant it," the investigating officer wrote.[18] Recalled to France in 1710 following accusations of financial misappropriations, Cadillac was instrumental in convincing Antoine Crozat, Marquis de Chatel, to invest in North

[13]Giraud, *History of French Louisiana*, I, 366.

[14]Gerardo Mora, "Relacion hecha por Don Luis de San Dionis y Don Medar Jalot del viaje que ejecutaron desde la Movila hasta el Presidio de Diego Ramón," Archivo General de la Nacion, Provincias Internas, Vol. 181, 11 (Center for American History, University of Texas at Austin; cited hereafter as CAH); Rowland and Sanders, *MPA*, III, 176.

[15]Rowland and Sanders, *MPA*, II, 182.

[16]Cadillac to Pontchartrain, Feb. 20, 1716, Archives Nationales, Paris, Archives des Colonies, C13A, 3: 417–454; Charmion Clair Shelby, "St. Denis's Second Expedition to the Rio Grande," *Southwestern Historical Quarterly*, 27 (Jan., 1924), 193.

[17]Giraud, *History of French Louisiana*, I, 251. The self-styled Cadillac was born Antoine Laumet on March 5, 1658, in Saint Nicolas de la Grace, Montauban, France. After Laumet's older brother squandered their father's estate, Laumet changed his name and joined the French army in 1677.

[18]W. J. Eccles, *The Canadian Frontier, 1534–1760*, (Albuquerque: University of New Mexico Press, 1992), 136; Sr. d'Aigremont au Ministre, Que., Nov. 14, 1708, Paris Archives Nationales Colonies, C11A, 3:26–777.

America.[19] A grateful French crown not only forgave Cadillac of his sins, but appointed him governor of the Louisiana colony, and Crozat made Cadillac an agent of his Company of Louisiana, the sole purpose of which was to establish regular commerce with New Spain and New Mexico.[20]

Cadillac received his appointment as Louisiana governor in 1710 from minister Jérôme Phélypeaux, Comte de Pontchartrain, and arrived in the colony in early summer 1713 to find it struggling for survival. Provisional authorities were at loggerheads, inadequate provisions had reduced the population to poverty, and, as a result, the garrison had taken to the woods to live and hunt among the Indians for survival.[21] Cadillac's relatively short tenure was plagued with controversy and ended in disgrace. By 1715 the lengthy list of his enemies included the colony's financier, Antoine Crozat. The governor complained that Crozat had not given him "supreme authority" in the colony's trade.[22] Less than a year later, in December 1716, Crozat's investment in his Company of Louisiana showed a deficit of 1,250,000 livres and he petitioned the king to be released from his obligations. The petition was granted and soon thereafter the Council of the Navy, while recognizing Cadillac's occasional contributions to the colony, concluded that he no longer should govern Louisiana. Almost exactly three years after he assumed command on the lower Mississippi, the governor's career there ended. For a second time, Cadillac was recalled to France.[23]

Cadillac's successor at Fort Pontchartrain was François Dauphine de la Forest, a native of France who had come to Canada in 1675 as a lieutenant of René-Robert Cavelier, Sieur de la Salle. La Forest and the historically better known of La Salle's lieutenants, Henri de Tonti, formed a trading company that was partially financed on one occasion with a loan of 7,000 livres from two of St. Denis's siblings, Charles and Charlotte Françoise Juchereau de St. Denis, who reportedly made substantial loans to several traders.[24] Charles Juchereau de

---

[19]Charles J. Balesi, *The Time of the French in the Heart of North America, 1673–1818,* (Chicago: Alliance Française, 1992), 140. At the time of his death in 1728, Crozat reportedly was the wealthiest man in France. Crozat acquired his wealth in maritime commerce and in offices of finance. Attracted by promises of mineral riches, Crozat speculated in the Louisiana colony with an initial capital of six hundred thousand to seven hundred thousand livres. Future events proved that his decision to reserve the option to abandon or pursue his interests in the colony depending on results was a wise one. Information from author's personal files.

[20]Roland and Sanders, *MPA*, II, 89; Duclos to Pontchartrain, Ministry of the Colonies, Paris, Archives Nationales Colonies, C13, 3: 113–122.

[21]Roland and Sanders, *MPA*, II, 80, 166–169, 178.

[22]Giraud, *History of French Louisiana*, II, 74.

[23]McWilliams, *Fleur de Lys and Calumet*, 203, 204.

[24]John Fortier and Donald Chaput, "A Historical Reexamination of Juchereau's Illinois Tannery," *Journal of the Illinois State Historical Society*, 62 (Winter, 1969), 386.

St. Denis, a military officer-turned-royal judge-turned-trader from Montreal, established a tannery on the Ouabache River in 1703. His father-in-law, interestingly, personally had advanced large sums of cash to La Salle, including 46,000 livres in 1678–1679.[25] Charlotte Françoise, a wealthy widow, married La Forest in 1702.[26] La Forest and Tonti controlled or directly influenced trade and politics throughout the Illinois Territory during the last decades of the seventeenth century. Their trading company ultimately was so negatively impacted by the French crown's commercial policy changes that it was forced to dissolve.[27]

For Louis Juchereau de St. Denis, about to embark on his first journey to New Spain, it was his contract with Crozat's company that imposed strictures. The agreement forced him to sign a note for the trade goods and supplies issued to him and required him to repay in specie. Cadillac's report to Crozat in his letter dated October 26, 1713, included a vague comment that the enterprise was "executed at the cost and expense of the party, the Company entering into it only to the extent of one hundred pistoles."[28]

Jean-Baptiste du Bois du Clos, Sieur de Montigny, detailed a different perspective on the 1713 French trading expedition to New Spain in a memoir to his superior, Pontchartrain. Duclos, *commissaire ordonnateur* of the colony, accused Cadillac of violating the company's agreement with the explorers.[29] According to Duclos, "one of the conditions of their agreement already has been broken which stipulated that the Company should advance to each of the explorers one hundred piastres in goods at one hundred per cent more than the price in France according to the bill, and when it was seen that they were involved in the enterprise so that they could no longer withdraw from it, no bills were found and they have been obliged to take the said goods on the basis that the Company wished with only an increase of twenty piastres in goods for

---

[25]Norman W. Caldwell, "Charles Juchereau de St. Denys: A French Pioneer in the Mississippi Valley," *Mississippi Valley Historical Review*, 28 (June, 1941), 564. Charles Juchereau de St. Denis married fourteen year old Denise-Thérése Migeon de Bransac in 1692. Her father was the wealthy Jean Baptiste Migeon de Bransac, lieutenant general of Montreal. Information from author's personal files.

[26]Charlotte Françoise Juchereau de St. Denis was widowed by François Viennay-Pachot, a wealthy merchant from Grenoble, France, with whom she had sixteen children. Caldwell, "Charles Juchereau de St. Denys," 570.

[27]Clarence Walworth Alvord, *The Illinois Country, 1673–1818* (Springfield: Illinois Centennial Commission, 1920), 100–102.

[28]Giraud, *History of French Louisiana*, I, 366; Rowland and Sanders, *MPA*, I, 131.

[29]Duclos letter to Pontchartrain, *MPA*, II, 79–143. The *ordonnateur* in French Louisiana was responsible for directing the colony's accounts. Giraud explains in *History of French Louisiana*, I, 252, that the *commissaire ordonnateur* in a French port was a naval commissioner. Although Duclos had been selected from the *commissaires ordonnateurs* of the French ports, in Louisiana he was a general administrative officer in charge of the colony's finances.

men."[30] Duclos writes that Cadillac's actions so greatly discouraged the explorers that they were persuaded they never would realize a profit from their efforts—even if they were successful in establishing trade with the Spaniards—and that each explorer had left Mobile determined to leave the colony upon returning from the journey to New Spain.

Before departing France, Cadillac and Duclos had clashed when Duclos violated the company's commercial policy by bringing to Louisiana a cargo of trade goods that the twenty-nine-year-old *commissaire* persuaded Pontchartrain he needed to establish himself in Louisiana—items Duclos indeed did later trade. By the time they arrived in Louisiana aboard the *Baron de la Fauche*, the two men were as antagonistic as were the colonial officials before them. Whether unable or unwilling to prepare the traditional joint administrative report for authorities in France, the men submitted individual reports to their respective superiors in October 1713. Not surprisingly, the reports are incompatible and, as a result, they pose more questions than answers for the modern historian.[31]

St. Denis knew before he left Mobile that arriving with trade goods at the Spanish presidio of San Juan Bautista would violate the King of Spain's order prohibiting the entry of foreign traders or their merchandise into New Spain.[32] Therefore, it was not a surprise to St. Denis when he reached his destination that Diego Ramón, the presidial commandant, detained him and his companions and sent word of the visitors to the Spanish viceroy. Ramón also wrote to Hidalgo and listed the Frenchmen who were detained at San Juan Bautista: St. Denis; the two Talon brothers, Pierre and Robert, who had survived the massacre of La Salle's abortive colony on the Texas coast; and a fourth Frenchman described only as St. Denis's companion. Neither this man (Medard Jallot) nor "the captain," Ramón said, spoke Spanish. Hidalgo was informed that with this group there were four Tejas (Haisinai) Indians, including Bernardino; Francisco, who spoke Spanish; a Capitan Bosalon; and another who had visited Hidalgo in the past.[33]

---

[30]Duclos letter to Pontchartrain, *MPA*, II, 89–90.

[31]Carl A. Brasseaux, "The Cadillac-Duclos Affair: Private Enterprise versus Mercantilism in Colonial Mobile," *The Alabama Review*, 37 (Oct., 1984), 257–271. Determining the accuracy of Duclos's allegations that Cadillac had deceived members of the expedition to New Spain is beyond the scope of this article.

[32]Rowland and Sanders, *MPA*, II, 89–90.

[33]Capitan Diego Ramón to Fray Francisco Hidalgo at Queretaro, 1714, Film II, Frame 1396 (microfilm; Old Spanish Missions Research Library, Our Lady of the Lake University, San Antonio). Ramón's letter contradicted the assertions of one André Pénicaut, who claimed to have been in New Spain with St. Denis when he wrote what he claimed was a first-person account of the expedition. McWilliams, *Fleur de Lys and Calumet*, 144–157.

Not until March 1715 did the viceroy respond to Ramón's letter. St. Denis, meanwhile, passed the time at Presidio de San Juan Bautista in confinement that appropriately can be described as informal—so informal that he was able to court Ramón's step-granddaughter, Manuela Sánchez Navarro. Manuela was related to Ramón because he had married her paternal grandmother, Feliciana Camacho y Botello, the widow of Diego Sánchez Navarro. Manuela, who was baptized April 26, 1697 at Santiago Apostólica in Monclova, Coahuila, was the daughter of Diego Sánchez Navarro y Camacho and Mariana Gómez Mascorró y Garza.[34]

It is hard to believe that a man of Ramón's experience and stature could be persuaded solely on the basis of St. Denis's personal charm. Diego Ramón was a veteran frontiersman whose long political and military service to the Spanish crown was instrumental in the pacification of Coahuila. Ramón had fought the Toboso Indians in 1687 with Alonso de León, the newly appointed governor of Coahuila.[35] When De León died in 1691, Ramón succeeded him as interim governor. Ramón was named captain of the flying company at the Presidio de San Juan Bautista in 1701 and led a punitive expedition against Indians north of the Rio Grande in 1707.[36] Ramón reportedly sought out and returned from Rancheria Grande apostates who fled the Rio Grande missions in 1714.[37] One must ask why Ramón would risk becoming involved with an individual whose actions violated Spanish law and whose standing with the viceroy remained questionable at best. What inspired the strong bonds that quickly developed between these two men?

---

[34]Parroquia de Monclova, Iglesia de Santiago Apostolica, Libro de Bautismos, V 1A, Principia 1666, Termina 1750 (Archivo Diosia de Saltillo, Cathedral Santiago del Saltillo, Saltillo, Coahuila, México); Patricia R. Lemée, "Manuela Sánchez Navarro," *The Natchitoches Genealogist,* 20 (Oct., 1995), 17–21.

[35]Weddle, *San Juan Bautista,* 13.

[36]Testimonio del Decreto de Fundacion del Presidio de San Juan Bautista, Archivo General de la Nacion, Historia, vol. 20, 72–75; Diego Ramón to Fray Francisco Hidalgo, July 22, 1714, K, Legajo 19, No. 19, Herbert E. Bolton Transcripts, Colegio de Santa Cruz de Queretaro, Various Sources: 2Q235, vol. 745, 16–17, (CAH).

[37]Diligas. que hiso el Colegio año de 1729 para la mudanze de las Missiones de Texas, Archivo del Colegio de la Santa Cruz, K. Legajo 19, No. 10, BANC MSS C-B 840, Herbert Eugene Bolton Papers (Bancroft Library, University of California, Berkeley); Herbert Eugene Bolton, *Texas In The Middle Eighteenth Century, Studies in Spanish Colonial History and Administration* (Austin: University of Texas Press, 1970), 143; Robert S. Weddle, "Rancheria Grande," in Ron Tyler, et al. (eds.), *The New Handbook of Texas,* (6 vols.; Austin: Texas State Historical Association, 1996), VI, 429. The phrase *rancheria grande* was used by some eighteenth-century Spaniards to describe an unusually large temporary settlement or encampment of diverse Indian groups. Historians disagree whether the Rancheria Grande Diego Ramón encountered south of the Nueces River in Texas in 1707 was the same Rancheria Grande the Domingo Ramón expedition of 1716 recorded in Central Texas.

Did Ramón and St. Denis have Old World family ties? That possibility is suggested by the presence of the French fleur de lis on the Ramón branding iron. One is tempted to consider that the two men might have met before St. Denis arrived at San Juan Bautista. One might speculate also that Hidalgo had known of some prior relationship between the two when he wrote to the French in 1711. On the other hand, St. Denis's arrival on the doorstep of Diego Ramón may have been strictly fortuitous.

At the same time, a motivation for St. Denis's relationship with Manuela is far from clear. Was it precipitated by love, passion or entrepreneurship? Or was it perhaps a convenient tool for St. Denis's self-preservation when he was dealing with the viceroy in Mexico City? In any event, it served him well. The viceroy named St. Denis the conductor of supplies for an expedition to establish missions in East Texas as a buffer against French intrusion, which became the first permanent Spanish settlements in the province.[38]

This 1716 entrada, commanded by Diego Ramón's son Domingo and guided by St. Denis, left Presidio de San Juan Bautista in April, reportedly soon after St. Denis's marriage to Manuela. St. Denis returned to the Rio Grande the following year with Domingo's brother Diego, who had accompanied the 1716 expedition.[39]

St. Denis returned to New Spain in 1717 with a story that the goods he had brought with him were merely what was necessary to establish his business there in order to support himself and his young family. Spanish authorities probably would have accepted the claim if St. Denis had come alone. However, other Frenchmen had accompanied him, including François Guyon Desprez

---

[38]Charmion Clair Shelby, "St. Denis's Declaration Concerning Texas in 1717," *Southwestern Historical Quarterly*, 26 (Jan., 1923), 166–167.

[39] In 1721–1722 under Domingo's direction and on orders from the Marqués de Aguayo, Misión Nuestra Señora del Espíritu Santo de Zuñiga and a presidio, Nuestra Señora de Loreto, were founded at La Bahía del Espíritu Santo, built on the former site of the French Fort St. Louis that La Salle had established near Garcitas Creek. Ramón commanded there until his death in 1723 when he was succeeded by his son, Diego Ramón III, not to be confused with Diego Ramón II, Domingo's brother. Diego Ramón III, grandson of the San Juan Bautista commandant, married the daughter of another commandant, Nicolás Flores de Valdez, of San Antonio de Bejar. Relieved of his command at La Bahia, Ramón later was appointed by his cousin Toribio Urrutia, another Flores y Valdez son-in-law, to be lieutenant at the San Xavier missions on the present San Gabriel River. This command was shorter-lived than the first. Later, when the San Xavier missions were abandoned, Ramón was instrumental in relocating Misión San Francisco de San Xavier to its second and third temporary sites on the rivers San Marcos and Guadalupe, respectively. Information from author's personal files.

d'Herbanne.[40] To the surprise of the French, which well may have been feigned, Commandant Ramón confiscated their merchandise. Shortly afterward, St. Denis traveled to Mexico City to protest Ramón's action.

St. Denis was imprisoned in Mexico City while Governor Martín de Alarcón investigated the matter in Coahuila. Alarcón concluded that Ramón had confiscated only a portion of the merchandise and, further, that the balance had been conveyed to José de Urrutia, Protector of the Indians in Nuevo León and Ramón's son-in-law.[41]

Although not conclusive, there was sufficient evidence of Ramón's participation in illicit French trade that in January 1719 a royal cédula ordered that St. Denis and his wife be deported to Guatemala and Ramón be removed from his command at San Juan Bautista. Before the order could be executed, however, St. Denis escaped from New Spain and returned to Louisiana, where Manuela and their children joined him. Not long afterward, Diego Ramón died, on April 9 or 10, 1719, at Presidio de San Juan Bautista.[42]

---

[40]Records for the Church of Saint Francis and the post Saint-Jean-Baptiste at Natchitoches (microfilm; CGHRC); Gerald E. Poyo and Gilberto M. Hinojosa (eds.), *Tejano Origins in Eighteenth-Century San Antonio* (Austin: University of Texas Press for the University of Texas Institute of Texan Cultures at San Antonio, 1991), 101; Cyprien Tanguay, *Dictionnaire Généalogique des Familles Canadiennes* (7 vols.; Quebec, 1871), I, 295; Role de la Garrison laissée au fort Maurepas, Aout 25, 1699, Archives Nationales, Paris, Archives des Colonies, Series C13A, 1: 209, (microfilm copy; Colonial Records Collection, Center for Louisiana Studies, University of Southwestern Louisiana, Lafayette). D'Herbanne was one of the original colonists of the Louisiana colony. His paternal grandfather, Jean Guyon *dit* Deprez, helped colonize Canada, arriving there with St. Denis's ancestors, Jean Juchereau and Robert Giffard. The French term *dit* translates as "called." Some individuals were better known by their *dits* than by their surnames. Among the upper classes it was not uncommon to use one's seignerie or nobility title in conjunction with or in preference to one's surname, i.e. St. Denis, d'Iberville. In 1736, the son of d'Herbanne and his wife, a former Chitimacha slave, married the daughter of José Gonzales, commandant at the Spanish presidio Nuestra Señora del Pilar de Los Adaes. The couple eventually moved to San Antonio where their son Manuel Berbán (the Spanish spelling of the French surname) married Teresa de Armas, widow of Francisco Xavier Péres and daughter of Canary Islander Ignacio Lorenzo de Armas. In 1796 Manuel entered the cabildo in San Antonio serving as a councilman and, in 1801, as attorney. The Berbán surname survives to the present time in San Antonio while Louisiana descendants use the French spelling Derbanne.

[41]The record is unclear how or from whom Urrutia received the merchandise. Joseph de Urrutia married Diego Ramón's daughter Antonia in Monclova, Coahuila, on January 6, 1697. Their sponsors were Gregorio Salinas Varona and his wife Francisca de Castro. In 1731, Urrutia became commandant of the Spanish presidio at San Antonio de Bejar. When Urrutia died there in 1740, he was succeeded by his son Toribio. Information from author's personal files.

[42]Lemée, "Manuela Sánchez Navarro," 17–21. The author is in possession of copies of two documents, both privately held in México: the first, Diego Ramón's *testamento*, or will, written at Presidio de San Juan Bautista and dated April 9, 1719, and the second, dated April 28, 1719, written by Martín de Alarcon, Governor of the Province of Texas and Coahuila, to "El Rey Nuestro Señor." Alarcon writes, "pro cuanto el dia 10 del corriente mes, fallecio Diego Ramón."

St. Denis, persona non grata in New Spain, still was well regarded in Louisiana. He assumed command there of the upper part of Rivière aux Cannes by 1721. Nine months later his command was extended to include the region of the Natchitoches and the Nassonites, a move calculated to bolster St. Denis's influence with the Indians in case the French needed their help against the Spaniards. That same year, a Spanish force commanded by the Marqués de Aguayo reoccupied the abandoned missions in East Texas and established a presidio only seven leagues west of the French at Natchitoches.

With Presidio Nuestra Señora del Pilar de Los Adaes established, a lucrative trade between the Spaniards there and St. Denis at the Natchitoches post began soon after Aguayo departed the region to return to Coahuila. St. Denis's account with the Company of the Indies indicated that between 1723 and 1726 he drew goods valued at more than 3,500 livres from the king's storehouse in Natchitoches.[43] What percentage of those goods was sold to Spaniards is uncertain.

During the next twenty years, St. Denis's family grew and his business prospered. His sons-in-law were given positions of authority in the family business. When d'Herbanne, keeper of the royal storehouse at Natchitoches, died in 1730, it was Pierre Duplessis, St. Denis's son-in-law, who filled the vacancy. In 1733, St. Denis's daughter Marie Rose married Jacques de la Chaise *fils*, whose father was *commissaire ordonnateur* at New Orleans.[44] The couple's son, Louis Antoine, later became the first alcalde in New Orleans under the Spanish dominion of Louisiana.

When St. Denis died in 1744, his family lost its patriarch, the post lost its commander, the Indians lost their trusted ally, and the trade cartel lost its leader. St. Denis was so influential that his death prompted Justo Boneo y Morales, the Spanish governor of Texas, to write the viceroy that "St. Denis is dead. Now we can breathe easier."[45] It is an interesting postscript to St. Denis's life that, the year before his death, St. Denis had petitioned the French crown for permission to resign his command and move to New Spain with his wife and minor children. Although St. Denis's resignation was accepted, he was encouraged to remain in the colony. Also, St. Denis was promised that his children would be placed as advantageously as possible in the service of the French crown.[46]

---

[43]Melrose Scrapbook, 70, 72 (CGHRC).

[44]Records for the Church of Saint Francis and Post Saint-Jean-Baptiste at Natchitoches (microfilm; CGHRC); Elizabeth S. Mills, *Natchitoches 1729–1803: Abstracts of the Catholic Church Registers of the French and Spanish Post of St. Jean Baptiste des Natchitoches in Louisiana,* (New Orleans: Polyanthos, 1977), 18.

[45]Bolton, *Texas in the Middle Eighteenth Century*, 41; (Cebrian y Augustin, Pedro) El Conde de Fuenclara, México, to Justo Boneo y Morales, Nuestra Señora del Pilar de Los Adaes, Aug. 8, 1744, The Papers of Mirabeau Buonaparte Lamar, 2827 (Texas State Library, Austin).

[46]Minister of Marine to Governor Vaudreuil and Minister of Marine to St. Denis, Archives Nationales, Paris, Archives de Colonies, Series B (Ordres du Roi), V 78, Folio 448, Colonial Records Collection (microfilm; Center for Louisiana Studies, University of Southwestern Louisiana, Lafayette).

St. Denis's request startled French provisional authorities who were preoccupied with the English threat on the colony's eastern boundary. When faced with the expressed desire of this particular Frenchman to leave the colony, the crown finally may have comprehended the magnitude of the man's influence, not only with the Indians along the Red River and throughout East and Central Texas, but also his relationship with the Spaniards. Inducements subsequently offered to St. Denis hint strongly that the crown realized that the Indians were loyal to St. Denis personally; that the Spaniards feared St. Denis personally; and that, in any eventuality, measures must be taken to ensure the continuing stability of the region. Subsequent events demonstrate the wisdom of those measures.

French trading activities among East Texas Indian villages, meanwhile, provoked a response by Spanish Governor Jacinto de Barrios y Jáuregui. In 1752 Barrios moved to oust the French traders. The governor sent Manuel Antonio de Soto y Bermúdez, his second-in-command, to investigate French trade in the area.[47] After De Soto's life was threatened by the chief of the Nadotes, who fiercely opposed any change in area trade relations, he retreated to safety at Los Adaes. Soon thereafter Louis de St. Denis *fils* responded to a request to meet with five hundred Indian warriors who were hostile to the Spaniards and who shared the Nadote chief's concerns.

Like his late father, the younger St. Denis was a trader. More important to the Spaniards, whose annihilation the warriors plotted, was his personal influence with the Indians—influence that sufficed to dissuade the Indians from their plans for attacking the Spaniards. Barrios, upon learning from a Spanish priest what had transpired between St. Denis and the Indians, acknowledged that indeed it was St. Denis alone who had saved the lives of all Spaniards in East Texas. Barrios realized that the Spaniards could not breathe as easily as Boneo y Morales had believed in 1744 when the elder St. Denis died.[48]

In 1767, area Indian tribes, again angered by Spanish efforts to interrupt their trade relations with the French, assembled to prepare an attack against the Spaniards at Los Adaes. Fray Ygnacio Laba, a Zacatecan friar assigned to

---

[47]Charles Wilson Hackett (ed.), *Pichardo's Treatise on the Limits of Louisiana and Texas* (4 vols.; Austin: University of Texas press, 1946), IV, 54; Elizabeth A. H. John, *Storms Brewed in Other Men's Worlds* (Lincoln: University of Nebraska Press, 1981), 344. Less than two years later, on June 2, 1754, Manuel Antonio de Soto y Bermúdez married Marie De Neiges Juchereau de St. Denis, daughter of the deceased French commandant. Records for the Church of Saint Francis and Post Saint-Jean-Baptiste at Natchitoches (microfilm: CGHRC).

[48]Hackett (ed.), *Pichardo's Treatise on the Limits of Louisiana and Texas*, IV, 57, 61; Timothy K. Perttula and Kathleen K. Gilmore, *Archaeological Survey Along Mill Race Creek and Tributaries, Wood County, Texas* (Denton: Institute of Applied Sciences, University of North Texas, 1987–1988), 91–94.

San Miguel, the Los Adaes mission, personally witnessed the younger St. Denis calm the Indians and dissuade them from the attack.[49]

Five years later, in 1772, Athanase de Mézières, lieutenant governor of the Natchitoches post in Spanish Louisiana, learned of two threats to Spanish interests in the Province of Texas: first, the Panis-mahas were moving south from the Missouri River region and, second, the Taovayas and other area Indian tribes were trading with the English.[50] Horses were bartered for guns and other European goods. In a move designed to stop their trade with the English, De Mézières appealed to the Taovayas to move father south to the Brazos River, and he petitioned Spanish authorities for a new presidio on the Brazos to protect them.[51]

When the proposal reached the hands of the Spanish governor, Barón de Ripperdá, he conferred with Fray Pedro Ramírez, president of the Zacatecan missions of Texas. Ramírez, who reportedly knew Louis de St. Denis only by reputation, urged that the Frenchman be appointed commandant of the proposed presidio. Describing him as the person most suitable for the charge, the friar stated that St. Denis "is loved by the surrounding nations, who after the loss of his father, danced before him in preference to the commandant of the post."[52] Ramírez stressed St. Denis's standing with the Indians, his knowledge of both their languages and Castillian, and his facility for dealing with the natives in the most appropriate manner.

The presidio never was established, and Louis de St. Denis died on February 7, 1778, at Natchitoches. Still very much alive, however, was the long-

[49]John, *Storms Brewed in Other Men's Worlds,* 379.

[50]In the preface to Herbert Eugene Bolton (ed.), *Athanase De Mézières and the Louisiana-Texas Frontier, 1768–1780,* (2 vols; Cleveland, The Arthur H. Clark Company, 1914; New York: Kraus Reprint Co., 1970), I, 13. De Mézières is described as "the foremost Indian agent and diplomat of the Louisiana-Texas frontier . . . comparable in this respect with Saint Denis." Athanase Christophe Fortunat de Mézières was born in Paris in 1721, the only son of Louis Christophe Claude de Mézières and Marie Josephe Ménard de Mauguet. De Mézières' widowed mother married the Marquis de la Haye de Rious. The Rev. Dr. J. Edgar Bruns, Historian of the Archdiocese of New Orleans, says that De Mézières' half-sister, Charlotte Béraud de la Haye de Riou, married, in secret, Louis Philippe Duc d'Orléans, first Prince of the Blood, in 1773. Bruns did not explain the reason for secrecy. Athanase de Mézières married first Marie Petronille Juchereau de St. Denis, daughter of the late commandant. The widower De Mézières later married Pélagie Fazende. After Louisiana was ceded to Spain in 1763, De Mézières served as Lieutenant Governor of the Natchitoches post and its district, and was commissioned as a captain of the militia. Later appointed governor of the Spanish province of Texas, De Mézières died in San Antonio in 1779 before assuming office. He is buried in that city at San Fernando Cathedral. J. Edgar Bruns, "Athanase Christophe Fortunate De Mézières (1721–1779), An Extraordinary Man and His Extraordinary Relatives in France and Louisiana," *The Louisiana Genealogical Register,* 32 (Mar., 1985), 4.

[51]Bolton (ed.), *Athanase de Mézières and the Louisiana-Texas Frontier,* I, 97.

[52]Ibid., I, 324–325.

standing bond between the St. Denis family and numerous Indian groups, both in Louisiana and in Texas. Evidence of the family's continuing influence over the natives is recorded in the diary of François Grappe, *dit* Touline.[53] A non-commissioned officer in the Natchitoches militia, Grappe accompanied Gil Ybarbo's Spanish trading expedition to the Kichai Indians in 1783.

One band of the Kichai, seeking protection from the invading Osages, had moved their village from Spanish Texas to be near their Caddo allies in Spanish Louisiana. There the Kichai traded with two French partners who were members of the St. Denis cartel—Louis Charles de Blanc, grandson of the late commander Louis Juchereau de St. Denis, and Paul Boüet Laffitte.[54] Ostensibly to reestablish trade relations between the Kichai and the Spaniards at Nacogdoches, Gil Ybarbo organized an expedition to the Kichai village at its new location. He also may have sought to enhance the profits of his illicit trade with Etienne Vaugine, then the commander of the fort at Natchitoches. On Vaugine's orders, Grappe accompanied Ybarbo.

Having reached their destination late in the evening of September 19, the Spaniards departed the next afternoon after a heated exchange between Ybarbo and the medal chief of the Kichai. Ybarbo touted himself as the great chief. The Kichai chief angrily retorted that his tribe recognized all chiefs; but the chief of the Kichai was the elder Louis Juchereau de St. Denis. St. Denis had died and left a descendant whom they subsequently recognized as their chief, and they similarly would regard St. Denis's descendants as long as there were some. Ybarbo, not descended from St. Denis, returned to Nacogdoches empty-handed, and trade between the Kichai and the St. Denis family continued.[55]

---

[53]Journal of François Grappe, Sept. 24, 1783, Natchitoches, Archivo General de Indias, Seville, Papeles Procedentes de Cuba, Legajo 196, Folio 586, Roll 35, The Historic New Orleans Collection (microfilmed copy; CGHRC); David La Vere and Katia Campbell, "An Expedition to the Kichai: The Journal of François Grappe, September 24, 1783," *Southwestern Historical Quarterly*, 98, (July, 1994), 58–78.

[54]Paul Boüet Laffitte's first wife was Marie Madeleine Grappe. She and her brother François Grappe *dit* Touline were baptised in Natchitoches. They were born at the French post Saint Louis near present-day Texarkana where their father, Alexis Grappe, a trader and a non-commissioned officer, was in charge. Louis Marguerite Guedon, their mother, was half Chitimacha Indian and half French. After Madeleine's death in 1781, Laffitte married Eulalie Marie Anne de Soto, daughter of the Spaniard Manuel Antonio de Soto y Bermúdez and his half-French, half-Spanish wife, Marie de Neiges Juchereau de St. Denis. Eulalie Marie Anne de Soto was a first cousin of Louis Charles de Blanc de Neuville, a commander of Saint-Jean-Baptiste at Natchitoches and, later, of the Attakapas Post at present-day St. Martinville, Louisiana. The birth and marriage records for these individuals are found in the Records for the Church of Saint Francis and Post Saint-Jean-Baptiste at Natchitoches (microfilm: CGHRC).

[55]Journal of Francis Grappe, Sept. 24, 1783, Natchitoches, Archivo General de Indias, Seville, Papeles Procedentes de Cuba, Legajo 196, Folio 586, Roll 35, The Historical New Orleans Collection (microfilmed copy; CGHRC); La Vere and Campbell, "An Expedition to the Kichai: The Journal of François Grappe," 58–78.

A document in the Natchitoches archives dated January 6, 1785, is proof of the continuing conflict between Vaugine and the St. Denis family over Indian trade, and the continuing influence of the St. Denis trading family with area Indian groups. Following a fistfight between the two men, Laffitte filed suit against Vaugine. Soon thereafter Vaugine resigned his command at the Natchitoches post and Laffitte resumed his trading activities; he sold sixty horses, twenty-nine mares and colts and two stallions in 1786 for $3,287. The next year Laffitte purchased a tract of land from the Yatasi Chief Antoine for five hundred pounds of Limbourge cloth, a white cover, one shirt, two pounds of gun powder, two twists of tobacco, and ten pounds of salt.[56]

The French crown's regard for St. Denis's unique relationship with the Indians is suggested by the fact that it kept its promises to him, promises that were reaffirmed to St. Denis's widow: their sons were made chevaliers of the Military Order of Saint Louis, and two of their daughters, Marie Petronille and Marie des Douleurs, married men who later commanded the Natchitoches fort and were themselves awarded the Cross of the Military Order of Saint Louis—César de Blanc de Neuville and Athanase de Mézières, respectively.[57] Louis de Blanc, St. Denis's grandson and César's son, also commanded at Natchitoches.

And so it was from the post at Natchitoches in French Louisiana that Louis Juchereau de St. Denis and Manuela Sánchez Navarro and at least three generations of their descendants, in unique relationship with the Indians and by means of the cartel St. Denis had established with Diego Ramón, influenced trade and trade relations on the Red River and across much of the Spanish province of Texas throughout most of the eighteenth century.

---

[56]Paul Boüet Laffitte v. Etienne de Vaugine, Jan. 6, 1785, Document 1782, Vol. 18, Office of the Clerk of Court, Natchitoches Parish, Natchitoches, La.; Aubra Lane Lee, "Fusils, Paint, and Pelts: An Examination of Natchitoches Based Indian Trade in the Spanish Period, 1766–1791," (M.A. thesis, Northwestern State University, 1990). This document provides detailed information about area Indian trade competition between Vaugine and Laffitte.

[57]Vaudreuil to Maurepas, December 29, 1744, Vaudreuil Papers (Huntington Library and Art Gallery, San Marino, Calif.). Pierre de Rigaud, Marquis de Vaudreuil, was royal governor of the French province of Louisiana from 1743 through 1753. The text of his letter to St. Denis's widow indicates that she had reminded Vaudreuil of the crown's promises to her late husband concerning advancement of their children in the service and, possibly, her intention to leave the French colony in the event those promises were not kept. Vaudreuil assured Manuela Sánchez Navarro of the crown's faithfulness to its word, and wrote to her of the anticipated advancement of Louis, her older son, from the next promotion list. De Blanc de Neuville succeeded Louis Juchereau de St. Denis as commander at Saint-Jean-Baptiste.

# The Partnership of Stephen F. Austin and Joseph H. Hawkins

Gregg Cantrell*

*The role played by Stephen F. Austin in the Anglo American colonization of Texas is well known. Less known is the valuable financial assistance given to Austin by New Orleans lawyer Joseph H. Hawkins. Between 1820 and the time of his death in 1823 Hawkins invested more than $7,000 in Austin's Texas colonization plan. Without this financial assistance and support from Hawkins, Austin's colonization efforts would have been much more difficult.*

*In this article, Gregg Cantrell, award-winning biographer of Stephen F. Austin, examines the relationship between Austin and Hawkins. He notes that Texas historians have disagreed as to the importance of Hawkins in the Texas venture. In the first major biography of Austin, historian Eugene C. Barker downplayed Hawkins's role. A later scholar, Malcolm D. McLean, argued that the financial assistance by Hawkins was vital to the success of Austin's colonization scheme. As readers will note in this article Cantrell takes the middle ground, concluding that Hawkins provided extremely valuable but "not necessarily indispensable" assistance to Austin in the colonization efforts.*

*For more on the Austin-Hawkins relationship see Cantrell's* **Stephen F. Austin: Empresario of Texas** *(New Haven: Yale University Press, 1999) as well as Eugene C. Barker,* **The Life of Stephen F. Austin, Founder of Texas, 1793–1836: A Chapter in the Westward Movement of the Anglo-American People** *(Nashville and Dallas, 1926; reprint; Austin: University of Texas Press, 1969) and Malcolm D. McLean (comp. and ed.),* **Papers Concerning Robertson's Colony in Texas** *(19 vols.; 3 vols.; Fort Worth: Texas Christian University Press, 1974–1976; 16 vols.; Arlington: University of Texas at Arlington Press, 1977–1993), especially volume II.*

---

*Gregg Cantrell, "The Partnership of Stephen F. Austin and Joseph H. Hawkins," *Southwestern Historical Quarterly*, 99 (July, 1995), 1–24. Grants from Sam Houston State University and the National Endowment for the Humanities helped make this article possible. The author wishes to thank James E. Crisp, Sally Hawkins, Joseph W. McKnight, and Thomas Primrose for their helpful comments.

Students of early Texas history may be vaguely familiar with the name of Joseph H. Hawkins. A prominent New Orleans attorney, Hawkins in 1820 met the penniless Stephen F. Austin, who had recently moved from Arkansas Territory in search of a fresh start after having failed in a variety of business ventures. Hawkins took a keen interest in the young man and became his friend and mentor. Several months later, when Austin's father, Moses, obtained permission from the Spanish authorities in Mexico to introduce American settlers into Texas, Hawkins offered to invest in the enterprise. Moses accepted the offer, in which Hawkins agreed to provide financial support in return for half of whatever lands and profits Austin might realize from Texas colonization. When Stephen Austin inherited the project following his father's death, he and Hawkins formalized the agreement. The result was a partnership which successfully inaugurated the Anglo American colonization of Texas.

Beyond this broad outline, the story of the Austin-Hawkins partnership has been poorly understood and rarely told. Most of what has been written on the topic has been based upon an incomplete command of the historical sources or has been colored by either a pro- or anti-Austin bias. The following account of the Austin-Hawkins relationship will resolve much of this confusion and shed light on an important aspect of the American colonization of Texas. It will also provide fresh insight into the character of the often-enigmatic Stephen F. Austin.

When Austin moved to New Orleans in the fall of 1820, it was the action of a man in near-desperate financial straits. For a decade he had become increasingly involved in the management of his father's failing lead mining business at Potosi, Missouri. Instead of being able to rescue the Austin family from financial disaster, Stephen Austin himself had fallen deeply in debt along with his father.[1] In 1818–1819 he had plunged into high-risk land speculation in Arkansas, which had only worsened his debt burden.[2] A stint as a territorial

---

[1]Moses Austin's financial difficulties are ably chronicled in David B. Gracy II, *Moses Austin: His Life* (San Antonio: Trinity University Press, 1987), chaps. 9–11. Stephen F. Austin's biographer is almost totally silent on the nature and magnitude of Stephen F. Austin's financial problems; see Eugene C. Barker, *The Life of Stephen F. Austin, Founder of Texas, 1793–1836: A Chapter in the Westward Movement of the Anglo-American People* (1925; reprint, Austin: University of Texas Press, 1980), 22. Presenting all the evidence of Stephen F. Austin's indebtedness would require a separate article, but for two major examples (among many) of his Missouri debts, see Statement of Account, Dec. 22, 1818, in Eugene C. Barker (ed.), *The Austin Papers,* Annual Reports of the American Historical Association for the Years 1919 and 1922 (2 vols.; Washington, D.C.: Government Printing Office, 1924, 1928), I, pt. 1, p. 334 (cited hereafter as *Austin Papers*); and Robert D. Dawson to Stephen F. Austin, June 16, 1827, ibid., pt. 2, pp. 1658–1659. Years later, Austin paid off another of his large Missouri debts, in the amount of $5,767 to Anthony Butler; see entry dated Apr. 16, 1833, Austin Account Book (Center for American History, University of Texas at Austin; cited hereafter as CAH).

[2]Through a complex speculation involving the purchase of New Madrid Land Certificates, Austin and a partner tried unsuccessfully to establish title to the site upon which Little Rock,

judge in the summer of 1820 proved short-lived when the court to which he was appointed was almost immediately abolished by the Arkansas legislature.[3] Reflecting on his troubles in April 1820, Austin lamented that "My opinion of mankind has, unfortunately perhaps, been as bad as it could be for some years, but the longer I live the worse it grows. . . . I shall remain here [in Arkansas] this summer, and after that it is uncertain where I shall go. . . . I believe I am nearly indifferent what becomes of me, or whether I live or die, unless I am to be of use to my Family by living, and then I should be as anxious to live as any one." This pessimism, coupled with a strong sense of familial duty, would become one of the hallmarks of Austin's personality in the coming tumultous years.[4]

As Austin's father made preparations for a trip to Texas to investigate colonization opportunities, Stephen abandoned Arkansas for New Orleans. As the commercial and financial center of the Deep South, New Orleans seemed to offer the best opportunity for a well-educated, well-connected, ambitious young man to get back on his feet. "I came here," he wrote his mother in January 1821, "with a hope of getting employ; I offered to hire myself out as clerk, as an overseer, or anything else, but business is too dull here to get into business. There are hundreds of young men who are glad to work for their board." He also pointedly told his mother that "I know nothing as to my father's objects or prospects," suggesting that he would probably be happy to remain as disconnected as possible from his father's visionary schemes.[5]

Despite the grim report about business opportunities, Austin actually had reason for optimism. Shortly after coming to New Orleans, he had made the acquaintance of Joseph Hawkins. Born about 1786 in Powhatan County, Virginia, Hawkins had studied law and moved to Lexington, Kentucky, as a young man. He married George Anne Nicholas, daughter of Col. George Nicholas, one of Kentucky's most influential early statesmen. His abilities,

---

Arkansas would soon be built. See Memoranda Concerning Land Speculations, Jan. 30, Feb. 25, 1819, *Austin Papers,* I, pt. 1, p. 337; Stephen F. Austin to William M. O'Hara, Apr. 5, 7, 1819, ibid., 341–343; Promissory Note from Stephen F. Austin to William M. O'Hara, Mar. 5, 1819, in Chester Ashley Papers (Special Collections and Archives, University of Arkansas at Little Rock).

[3]Stephen F. Austin's Commission as Judge, *Austin Papers,* I, pt. 1, pp. 365–366; *Arkansas Gazette* (Arkansas Post), July 15, Oct. 28, 1820. Austin did briefly preside at court; see E[lias] A. E[lliott] to James Bryan, July 28, 1820, *Austin Papers,* Series II (CAH); Skipper Steely, *Forty Seven Years* (Paris, Tex.: Northeast Texas Historical Preservation Association in cooperation with Wright Press, 1988), 155.

[4]Stephen F. Austin to James Bryan, Apr. 30, 1820, *Austin Papers,* I, pt. 1, pp. 358, 359 (quotation).

[5]Stephen F. Austin to His Mother, Jan. 20, 1821, *Austin Papers,* I, pt. 1, p. 373.

along with the Nicholas connection, helped Hawkins win election to the Kentucky House of Representatives in 1810. Not yet thirty years old, he served two terms as speaker of the Kentucky house (1812–1813 and 1813–1814) and saw military service as an officer in the Kentucky militia in the War of 1812. When Henry Clay was sent to Europe to negotiate the end of the war, Hawkins was chosen to fill Clay's seat in congress, which Hawkins held for a year. In March 1815 he returned to Kentucky to pursue his private business and legal interests. Some time prior to 1820 he moved to New Orleans.[6]

The descendants and heirs of Hawkins and Austin believed that the two men had known each other when Austin was a student at Transylvania University in Lexington in 1808–1810, but apparently they had never met before Austin came to New Orleans in 1820.[7] However, Austin was a friend of Hawkins's brother Littleberry in Kentucky, and that connection, along with Joseph Hawkins's political prominence during those years, would certainly have made Austin know Hawkins by reputation. In addition, Moses Austin had long

[6]Information on the life of Joseph Hawkins is extremely scarce. William B. Victor, *Life and Events* (Cincinnati: Applegate & Co., 1859) gives more information than any other source, but it contains inaccuracies and was produced for partisan purposes (it was apparently an outgrowth of Victor's Memorial to the Legislature, which will be discussed at length later in this article). In answer to a query from the present writer, the staff at the Kentucky Historical Society prepared a biographical sketch of Hawkins, from which most of the information in the preceding paragraph is taken. This sketch will be cited hereafter as Kentucky Historical Society, "Joseph H. Hawkins," and copies can be obtained from me or from the Kentucky Historical Society in Frankfort. I am indebted to Dr. Thomas Appleton and his staff for making this information available to me.

[7]In 1859 William B. Victor, a son-in-law of Hawkins, wrote that Stephen F. Austin had actually lived in the Hawkins household while a student in Lexington, and that Moses Austin had also become personally acquainted with Hawkins at that time. This story was embroidered upon in a 1925 newspaper article, which stated that Hawkins had become "strongly attached" to both Moses and Stephen in Lexington. See Victor, *Life and Events,* 128; clipping from Austin *American Statesman* Sunday Magazine, Nov. 1, 1925 (quotation), in S. F. Austin Scrapbook (CAH). Austin's nephew, Guy Bryan, repeated a slightly different version of this story, describing Hawkins as Austin's "old friend and classmate." See Guy Bryan, "Sketches of Moses and Stephen F. Austin," in Dudley G. Wooten (ed.), *A Comprehensive History of Texas, 1685 to 1897* (2 vols.; Dallas: William G. Scarff, 1898), I, 445. The two men obviously were not classmates at Transylvania, since Hawkins was married, a practicing lawyer, and a member of the Kentucky legislature when Austin was a teenaged student there. Bryan probably had Joseph Hawkins confused with Hawkins's younger brother Littleberry, who does seem to have attended Transylvania with Austin. The most definitive evidence that the men were not personally acquainted before Austin's move to New Orleans comes from Austin himself. Neither Stephen F. Austin nor Hawkins ever alluded to a prior acquaintance, and in his January 20, 1821, letter to his mother, Austin writes that after arriving in New Orleans, "it was my good fortune to get acquainted with Joseph H. Hawkins . . . a man who two months ago was a stranger to me. . . ." *Austin Papers,* I, pt. 1, pp. 373–374.

been acquainted with another Hawkins relative, Maj. John T. Hawkins (probably an uncle or cousin), in Missouri.[8]

The exact circumstances of their meeting are not known, but the struggling young Austin had only been in New Orleans a short time when Hawkins befriended him and came to his rescue. Hawkins not only gave Austin "employ in an office," but he took him into his own household and advanced him enough money for Austin to purchase some groceries to send to his destitute mother and sister in Missouri. Austin told his mother of the generous arrangement that Hawkins had made with him: "if I will remain with him he will board me, permit me the use of his books, and money for clothes, give me all the instruction in his power until I am well fitted to commence the practice of law in this country—for my board and the use of his books he will charge nothing, and for the money he advances he will wait until I make enough by my profession to repay him. . . ." So moved was Austin by these acts of kindness that it "almost made me change my opinion of the human race." Though worried that his Missouri creditors would "prosecute," Austin nonetheless believed that "If I am left alone a few years I may get up and pay all off; it will take me 18 months to become acquainted with civil law which is in force in this country and learn the French language—that once done I then shall have the means of fortune within my reach. I am determined to accept of Hawkins offer." In the meantime, probably through Hawkins's influence, he also got a part-time job helping to edit a New Orleans newspaper, the *Louisiana Advertiser.*[9]

Austin had found a benefactor, and he was grateful. But while Hawkins's generosity was freely given, it rested upon a shaky foundation. He had left Kentucky a few years earlier under financial duress, a victim of the same unstable economic conditions that had ruined Moses and Stephen Austin and many others on the American frontier during and after the War of 1812. In 1815 Hawkins and his brother Littleberry had been "compelled to Dispose of their property" in a manner that apparently netted little return.[10] Austin himself acknowledged in January 1821 that while "Mr. Hawkins is a lawyer of the [highest]

[8]Duff Chadwell to Moses Austin, Sept. 11, 1807, *Austin Papers,* I, pt. 1, p. 136; Joseph H. Hawkins to Stephen F. Austin, Feb. 8, 1822, ibid., 478; Stephen F. Austin to J. E. B. Austin, May 10, 1823, ibid., 639; Littleberry Hawkins to Stephen F. Austin, Oct. 7, 1824, ibid., 921. Both Littleberry Hawkins and Maj. John T. Hawkins eventually emigrated to Austin's colony.

[9]Stephen F. Austin to His Mother, Jan. 20, 1821, *Austin Papers,* I, pt. 1, pp. 373 (1st quotation), 374 (2nd–5th quotations). The only surviving issues of the *Advertiser* dating from the approximate time that Austin was working on the paper are the months of October–December 1820, housed at the Library of Congress. These make no mention of Austin. His association with the paper may not have begun until January, when he wrote the above letter to his mother, or there may simply have been no reason to print the name of a part-time editor in the paper. In any case, nothing more is known of Austin's journalistic career, and he never mentioned it in his surviving correspondence.

[10]Lexington *Kentucky Gazette,* Oct. 30, 1815; Kentucky Historical Society, "Joseph H. Hawkins."

standing in this place—he is not rich. . . ."[11] Hawkins's generosity would contribute significantly to his own financial undoing in the coming years, an undoing that figures prominently in the subsequent story of the Austin-Hawkins partnership.

To the probable surprise of just about everyone but himself, Moses Austin succeeded in his mission to Texas. Returning to Missouri after securing permission to establish his colony, the ailing Moses did two things. First, he wrote to his son's friend Hawkins, and proposed that Hawkins take a "joint interest" in the colonization scheme. Next, he wrote to Stephen, urging him to "Discharge your Doubts, as to the Enterprise. . . . raise your Spirits times are changing a new chance presents itself nothing is now wanting but Concert and firmness."[12]

Nearly everybody concerned with the project was more excited about it than Stephen. A letter from his brother-in-law, James Bryan, did more to convince him than did his father's urgings, but the enthusiasm of Joseph Hawkins may have been the decisive factor in Austin's decision to participate actively in his father's scheme. "[Believing] the enterprise laudable, and perhaps promising some reward to those who would toil in its prosecution," Hawkins wrote, "I agreed to meet the proposition of [Moses Austin], and take a joint interest in the grant and settlement. . . ." Now an active partner in the decision-making, Hawkins explained that he and Stephen "both concluded it was best for him [Stephen] to set out immediately and meet the Spanish officers waiting at Nachitoches, to conduct him to the grant. . . ." Hawkins advanced Stephen "all the funds he desired for the expedition and have promised to furnish more as he requires them. . . ." With Stephen on his way to Texas by land, the plan had been for Moses to come on to New Orleans, presumably to sign a written contract with Hawkins and to bring emigrants by sea, but Moses died in Missouri on June 10. Hawkins learned of Moses's death on June 27, two weeks before Stephen got the news in Natchitoches.[13]

The next four months were a whirl of activity for both men. Austin proceeded to Texas, where he met with the governor and received provisional confirmation as the heir to his father's concession. He spent several weeks exploring the grant, and by November 10 he was back in New Orleans. Hawkins, in the

---

[11]Stephen F. Austin to His Mother, Jan. 20, 1821, *Austin Papers,* I, pt. 1, p. 374.

[12]Joseph H. Hawkins to Mrs. Maria Austin, June 27, 1821, *Austin Papers,* I, pt. 1, p. 398 (1st quotation); Moses Austin to Stephen F. Austin, May 22, 1821, ibid., p. 393 (2nd quotation). It is possible that Moses Austin and Joseph Hawkins had met some time in past years, but more likely Stephen had simply told Moses of Hawkins's interest in the Texas plan.

[13]Joseph H. Hawkins to Mrs. Maria Austin, June 27, 1821, *Austin Papers,* I, pt. 1, pp. 397 (1st and 2nd quotations), 398 (3rd and 4th quotations). Hawkins learned of Moses Austin's death on the day he wrote this letter. Ten days earlier Stephen had left to meet the Spanish officials in Natchitoches. Stephen was there on July 13 when an express letter from Hawkins informed him of his father's death. See Stephen F. Austin to Maria Austin, July 13, 1821, ibid., 401.

meantime, had been busy arranging for the onset of immigration. He had seen to it that announcements of Austin's grant were published in western newspapers,[14] and consequently word of the enterprise was spreading. As soon as Austin arrived, he and Hawkins located and arranged for the purchase of a small schooner, the *Lively,* and began preparing it to carry the first settlers to Texas.[15] "Just then Stephen Austin and Joe Hawkins were crying up Texas—beautiful country[,] land for nothing etc.," recalled one of the settlers who had shortly thereafter sailed from New Orleans for Texas.[16]

One of Austin's tasks upon his return to New Orleans was to formalize his arrangement with Hawkins. On November 14, 1821, the two men signed a legal contract setting in writing the informal agreement that Hawkins and Moses Austin had made previous to Moses's death. The new written contract specified that Stephen F. Austin, as heir and agent of his father, was now bound by these same provisions. In the contract Austin acknowledged to have received $4,000 from Hawkins. In return, Austin promised:

> that after meeting the necessary expenses of surveying the said Hawkins shall be entitled to and receive one equal half part of the monies, effects, property and profits arising from the sale of lands, lotts, or from any other sources growing out of the grant of lands before referred to, or the settlement thereof, And all lands lotts and other property so derived shall be from time to time divided between said parties hereto in equal moities.
>
> And it is furthermore covenanted and agreed by and between the parties hereto that a joint and equal copartne[r]y is established between said S. F. Austin and said Hawkins in all matters and concerns touching the lands to be granted to them or

---

[14]Stephen F. Austin to [Joseph H. Hawkins], July 20, 1821, *Austin Papers,* I, pt. 1, pp. 402–404. This letter soliciting emigrants appeared first in the *Louisiana Advertiser* (New Orleans) on September 3, 1821, and later in the *Arkansas Gazette* (Little Rock) of October 6. It probably appeared in other major western newspapers at about the same time.

[15]Stephen F. Austin to [Edmund H.] Martin, Sept. 14, 1832, *Austin Papers,* II, 859–865; [W. S.] Lewis, "The Adventures of the 'Lively' Immigrants," *Quarterly of the Texas State Historical Association,* III (July, 1899), 11–12; Lester G. Bugbee, "What Became of the Lively?," *Quarterly of the Texas State Historical Association,* III (Oct., 1899), 141–148. The circumstances surrounding the purchase and outfitting of the *Lively* are as confusing as the subsequent fate of the ship. There is no doubt that Hawkins played a large role in making all the arrangements concerning the *Lively.* However, the only detailed account of those arrangements comes from Austin himself, many years after the fact. Austin stated that the *Lively* was purchased for $600, of which he furnished $400 and Hawkins only $200. Hawkins paid an unknown amount for "her outfit." See Stephen F. Austin to [Edmund H.] Martin, Sept. 14, 1832, *Austin Papers,* II, 860, 861 (quotation). However, the men shared in the costs of a portion of the supplies that went out on the ship. See Price List: Supplies of Schooner Lively, Oct. 29, 1821, ibid., I, pt. 1, pp. 422–423 (Hawkins paid $50 and Austin $40 on this account).

[16]Angelina Eberly to Mary Austin Holley, "Notes Made by Mrs. Holley in Interviews with Prominent Texans of the Early Days" (recopied by George W. Hill), p. 8, Mary Austin Holley Papers (CAH).

> either of them, or touching the emoluments or profits claimable from said Grant of lands or to the sale or settlement thereof, and all other purposes and objects in which they may embark in said province of Texas.
>
> The said Austin furthermore covenants and agrees to cause as many individual grants of lands to be made to said Hawkins and himself and to such persons as they shall name as can be obtained from the proper and legal authority in said province of Texas, and in all lands, granted to said Austin and Hawkins either party is at liberty to consider himself a joint owner should he elect to do so.
>
> In embarking in objects requiring addition disburcements of monies or monied responsibilities it must be done by joint and mutual consent.[17]

Austin departed for Texas ten days later, never to see Hawkins again. The *Lively*, with about twenty settlers, sailed soon thereafter (about November 27) for the mouth of the Colorado. The ship landed its passengers at the Brazos by mistake, and Austin spent many days trying unsuccessfully to locate them.[18] Other settlers soon began arriving in Texas by land, but Austin was not able to spend much time getting them settled. Mexico had won its independence from Spain, and in April 1822 he was forced to travel to Mexico City to get his grant confirmed by the new government. To his great frustration, the errand took a full year.

Meanwhile, fearing for the *Lively*, Hawkins in about February 1822 secured another vessel, a sloop called the *Only Son*, to sail to Texas to search for the lost schooner, or to carry another load of emigrants to the colony, or both. Returning to New Orleans after achieving its mission, the *Only Son* then made two more voyages to Texas between June and September, apparently carrying a considerable number of settlers each time. At the same time the *Only Son* was making either its second or third voyage, a third ship, a sloop named the *Good Intent*, also sailed for Texas. According to one of these settlers' recollections thirty years later, Hawkins had not only chartered all these ships for their multiple voyages but had paid for the passage and supplies of many of the poorer emigrants and was personally involved in the hands-on preparation of the vessels for departure. The extent of Hawkins's financial involvement in all of these voyages cannot be stated with certainty, but in the case of the *Only Son*, it appears that he had actually purchased the vessel. In a May 1822 letter he mentioned his "interest in the *Only Son*" and stated that he "was compelled to sell

---

[17] Agreement Between Austin and Joseph H. Hawkins, Nov. 14, 1821, *Austin Papers*, I, pt. 1, pp. 428–429.

[18] For unclear reasons, the *Lively* did not return to New Orleans for several months. When it did return, some time in the spring of 1822, it once again took on passengers and supplies (probably again financed by Hawkins, although there is no documentation for that supposition), and sailed for Texas. On this voyage the schooner was wrecked on Galveston Island, although the passengers were saved. See Bugbee, "What Became of the Lively?"

one half—the vessell, and may be forced to sell the other." And in 1823 Austin's brother also referred to "the sloop Only Son . . . owned by J. H. Hawkins."[19]

Letters written by Hawkins to Austin in early 1822 provide a glimpse into how deeply Hawkins had invested his energy and his hopes—along with his money—into the Texas colonization effort. Though an able lawyer, Hawkins

---

[19] Joseph H. Hawkins to Stephen F. Austin, May 31, 1822, Austin Papers, I, pt. 1, p. 521 (1st and 2nd quotations); J. E. B. Austin to Stephen F. Austin, May 25, 1823, ibid., 649 (3rd quotation). The true circumstances of the voyages of the Only Son and the Good Intent are exceedingly difficult to state with exactitude. This much is certain: The *Only Son* made three round-trip voyages from New Orleans to Texas in 1822, arriving back in New Orleans on May 7, July 11, and September 18, respectively. The *Good Intent* made one round trip, arriving back in New Orleans on August 5; see Milton P. Rieder Jr. and Norma Gaudent Rieder (eds.), *New Orleans Ship Lists* (2 vols.; Metairie, La.: Privately Published Typescript, 1968), II, 33, 38, 39, 42. These records are transcriptions of the "Passenger Lists of Vessels Arriving at New Orleans, 1820–1902," in the National Archives, and were verified by the author.

Apart from above-cited evidence of Hawkins's ownership of the *Only Son,* the documentation that Joseph Hawkins played the major role in the chartering, outfitting, and financing of both ships comes from only one source, the recollections of settler Angelina Peyton Eberly, many years after the fact. Eberly's accounts come to us from three different sources: notes made by Mary Austin Holley in an undated interview (ca. early 1840s) with Eberly; information collected from Eberly by Mirabeau B. Lamar (also ca. 1840s); and an affidavit given by Eberly in 1855, which was solicited from her by William Victor, a son-in-law of Joseph Hawkins who was seeking compensation from the State of Texas for Hawkins's services in promoting Texas colonization. The three accounts contradict one another in some respects: the Holley and Lamar interviews have Eberly sailing on the *Good Intent,* while Eberly's 1855 affidavit has her sailing on the *Only Son;* the number of passengers on her voyage also differs in the various accounts; and in the Lamar account Joseph Hawkins himself sails to Texas on the *Only Son,* returning to New Orleans in the fall (which certainly did not happen). Only in the 1855 affidavit does Eberly discuss the active role of Hawkins in underwriting the voyages, although in the interview with Holley she does mention that both Austin and Hawkins were "crying up Texas" in New Orleans in 1821. See Eberly to Holley in Holley, "Notes Made by Mrs. Holley in Interviews with Prominent Texans of the Early Days," p. 8; M. B. Lamar, "Difficulties with Karankawa Indians" [Information Derived from Mrs. Eberly], in C. A. Gulick Jr. et al. (eds.), *Papers of Mirabeau Buonaparte Lamar* (6 vols.; Austin: Texas State Library, 1921–1927), IV, 255–257; Affidavit of Mrs. Angelina B. Eberly, June 26, 1855, in Wm. B. Victor, *Memorial to the Legislature of Texas* (Cincinnati: Wrightson and Co., 1859), 10–13.

While the entire document containing the 1855 affidavit must be interpreted cautiously due to its potential for bias (as will be explained later in this article), Eberly's affidavit on the whole is probably correct in ascribing an active role to Hawkins, after one makes allowance for the passage of more than thirty years and the possible prodding of Eberly by William Victor to make her enhance Hawkins's contributions. It should be realized, however, that Hawkins was already hopelessly in debt by the time of the *Only Son's* first voyage, and he simply may not have had the means to do all that Eberly credits him with in the outfitting of the two ships. See Joseph H. Hawkins to Stephen F. Austin, Feb. 6, 1822, *Austin Papers,* I, pt. 1, pp. 476–478. In this same letter (p. 476) Hawkins also mentions a fourth vessel: "Of the $7,000 advanced for the Providence I have not one cent return. . . ." It is unclear whether the *Providence was* a ship carrying emigrants to Texas, or if it was one of Hawkins's side-ventures. It is not mentioned in New Orleans shipping records and no other references to it have been found.

Oil portraits of Col. Joseph H. Hawkins and George Anne Nicholas Hawkins, attributed to Matthew Harris Jouett. Jouett lived in Lexington, Kentucky, at the same time that Stephen F. Austin attended Transylvania University there. *Courtesy Kentucky Museum, Western Kentucky University, Bowling Green, Kentucky.*

was never an astute businessman. He apparently spent his last dime on Austin's venture and by the beginning of 1822 was deeply in debt. "I am bent down almost to the very ground," Hawkins wrote to Austin in February.

> . . . In fact my dear Sir I turn my mind towards you as the wrecked mariner does towards the glimerings of the light house which promises a Haven of safety— Were it not for you my path would now be cheerless if not hopeless.
>
> If I could obtain through your efforts the means to pay my debts I would join you immediately and spend my life in plowing the soil—and teaching our children the ways of virtue.[20]

Austin, petitioning the government in Mexico City and subsisting in part on funds provided by Hawkins, could do nothing to relieve his friend.

It is difficult to say whether Hawkins's leveraged investment in Austin's venture was the principal cause of this wretched financial state, or whether Hawkins, already deeply in debt from other business reverses, had gambled on Austin as a last-gasp tactic to save himself from otherwise-certain ruin. One suspects the latter. Hawkins had left Kentucky several years earlier in poor financial shape, and undoubtedly he had made other bad investments since then. Two of these investments were associated with Texas but apparently not with Austin. In one of them, Hawkins had invested heavily with his brother

[20] Joseph H. Hawkins to Stephen F. Austin, Feb. 6, 1822, *Austin Papers,* I, pt. 1, pp. 476 (quotation), 477–478.

Littleberry in a scheme to sell horses, mules, and other trade goods in Texas. In the other, as Austin later related it, Hawkins had lost "a vast sum in the negro speculation of which John Botts had the management. . . ." The details of these enterprises are not fully known, but clearly they were unsuccessful and greatly compounded Hawkins's debt burden.[21]

As Hawkins's creditors pressed him ever harder, he placed even greater hopes on Austin's success. "The glimmerings of hope sometimes break in upon me, and the visions are almost golden," he wrote to Austin in May 1822. "I do [not] mean the sordid acquisition of wealth—but release from debt in other words freedom—To die a slave would be insupportable—To leave as the only legacy to my children *hungry creditors* would be to have lived in vain and die miserable." Hawkins, apparently in ill health by this time and realizing that he might not live to see the fulfillment of his and Austin's dreams, told Austin that he had persuaded his wife "to look to and rely on you as the firmest pillar in our *building*. . . ."[22] Austin sincerely reciprocated these warm feelings, telling his own brother in June 1823 that "Joseph H. Hawkins is my *adopted brother*, a better or truer friend never existed."[23]

Hawkins anxiously monitored the progress of Austin's negotiations with the Mexican government. He also kept in touch with Austin's mother in Missouri. In spite of his own hardship, he again offered to send Maria Austin some groceries. But he also reminded her of the amounts he had invested in the venture, which he now calculated at over $7,000. "It is time therefor[e] for us to have some return," he stated candidly.[24]

On October 1, 1823, shortly after Austin had returned to Texas from Mexico, Joseph Hawkins died in Madisonville, Louisiana.[25] Austin seems to have taken the loss of his friend and partner hard. "My good friend J. H. Hawkins is dead," he wrote to one of his closest friends among the colonists. "I have met with some things to vex me and fear my best friends will sometimes think my temper a little unruly—but they must bear with me and in the end they will find that my heart is right."[26]

---

[21]Stephen F. Austin to [Edmund H.] Martin, Sept. 14, 1832, *Austin Papers*, II, 861 (quotation). In the the fall of 1824 John Botts briefly discussed his failed slave-trading expedition. See J. Botts to Stephen F. Austin, Sept. 14, 1824, *Austin Papers*, I, pt. 1, pp. 895–896. A few weeks later Littleberry Hawkins gave Austin a much more lengthy but quite convoluted account of his failed attempt to sell livestock and merchandise in Texas. See Littleberry Hawkins to Stephen F. Austin, Oct. 7, 1824, ibid., 917–923.

[22]Joseph H. Hawkins to Stephen F. Austin, May 31, 1822, *Austin Papers*, I, pt. 1, p. 521.

[23]Stephen F. Austin to J. E. B. Austin, June 13, 1823, *Austin Papers*, I, pt. 1, p. 672.

[24]Joseph H. Hawkins to Mrs. Maria Austin, Mar. 29, 1823, *Austin Papers*, I, pt. 1, p. 628 (quotation). See also Nathaniel Cox to Stephen F. Austin, June 3, 1824, ibid., 807–808.

[25]New Orleans *Louisiana Gazette*, Oct. 3, 1823; Victor, *Life and Events*, 149.

[26]Stephen F. Austin to Josiah H. Bell, Jan. 8, 1824, *Austin Papers*, I, pt. 1, p. 722.

Hawkins's widow was left to administer the estate, but feeling herself incapable of the task she appointed Nathaniel Cox to act in her behalf. Cox, a New Orleans businessman who was close to Austin as well as to Hawkins, soon wrote to Austin informing him of the status of the estate and of Hawkins's family. The story was a grim one. There were not enough assets in the estate to pay legal fees, much less satisfy the many creditors. It was agreed that if Austin were to settle his debt now with the Hawkins estate, all of the proceeds would go into the hands of the creditors, leaving nothing for the widow and five young children. It was clear by this point that the only significant asset Austin would eventually realize from his Texas project would be land, although he had not yet received title to any of his lands from the Mexican government. Austin and Cox simultaneously proposed to one another that for the time being all the titles be put in Austin's name. Later, after all the affairs of the Hawkins estate had been settled, Austin would then divide the lands as proposed in the original contract, thus securing a legacy for the Hawkins heirs. This maneuver would no doubt leave many of Hawkins's creditors out in the cold, but Austin and Cox were determined to see to the interests of the family. Destitute and grieving, the widowed George Anne Hawkins agreed to this arrangement and, borrowing money for the journey, moved with her children to Kentucky to live with relatives.[27] About four months after learning of Hawkins's death, Austin wrote a long letter of condolence to George Anne Hawkins. The delay in writing seems inexcusable given the closeness of the Austin-Hawkins relationship and the debt that Austin owed his late friend. In partial explanation, if not defense, of Austin's actions, it must be remembered that the demands on Austin's time were absolutely enormous during this period.

The colony had almost foundered during his year's absence in Mexico, and now he was working around the clock to perform the countless tasks associated with establishing a viable colony. He had not yet received Cox's letter with the proposal about settling the estate, so he did not know the wishes of the family regarding the land titles, nor did he even know who was in charge of administering the estate, although he assumed it would be Cox. He also did not know where in Kentucky George Anne Hawkins had settled. Under these circumstances it must have been easy for him to procrastinate in the painful chore of writing to his friend's widow. When he did force himself to sit down and write to her in care of Nathaniel Cox, Austin wrote a touching letter that seems entirely sincere: "I scarcely know in what language to express how much I sympathise with you and for the great loss you have sustained in the death of your

[27]Nathaniel Cox to Stephen F. Austin, Mar. 20, 1824, *Austin Papers,* I, pt. 1, pp. 754–755. Also see Cox to Stephen F. Austin, June 3, 1824, ibid., 807–808; and Cox to Stephen F. Austin, Aug. 8, 1824, ibid., 872–873.

kind and affectionate husband—I have so long esteemed Mr. Hawkins as a brother, as a bosom friend that indeed I feel too much in need of consolation myself for his loss to be able to offer it to others." He went on to pen a heartfelt, poignant eulogy on his late friend, and to offer whatever aid he could to the family. If Mrs. Hawkins wished to settle in Texas with her family, Austin would make the same accommodations for her that he was then planning for his own mother and sister when they arrived from Missouri. But Austin discouraged such a move (as he had done for two years with his own female relatives), citing the hardships and dangers of the frontier. Without going into the details of the plan that he and Cox were developing to save the lands for the heirs, he assured Mrs. Hawkins that she and her children "will in the end be greatly benefited" by his "labors in these wild deserts."[28]

Over the following months Cox and Austin corresponded several times about setting Hawkins's affairs. Austin was taken aback when Cox, having pored over Hawkins's ill-kept books, concluded that the amount Hawkins had expended in Texas totalled over $30,000. It is crucial to examine this figure carefully, because it obviously greatly exceeds the other three figures that have thus far been put forward as Hawkins's contribution to Texas colonization. The first of those figures, it will be recalled, was the $4,000 that Austin acknowledged having received from Hawkins in the original 1821 partnership contract. In July 1822, Hawkins estimated that he had now spent $6,000 on Austin's venture, and in March 1823, only five months before his death, he updated the estimate to $7,000. Surely Hawkins himself is the most reliable source for how much he had invested. From a legal standpoint, however, the payment of the original $4,000 alone entitled Hawkins to half of Austin's profits. Nowhere was it ever specified that the contribution of additional amounts by Hawkins to the enterprise would in any way entitle him to anything more than that.[29] Even if

---

[28]Stephen F. Austin to Mrs. Joseph H. Hawkins, Apr. 20, 1824, *Austin Papers,* I, pt. 1, pp. 773 (1st quotation), 774, 775 (2nd and 3rd quotations). In his *Papers Concerning Robertson's Colony,* Malcolm D. McLean makes much of the four-month gap between Austin's learning of Hawkins's death and his writing of the letter of condolence. This delay, according to McLean, stands as evidence of Austin's ingratitude toward the Hawkinses. Professor McLean reminds his readers of this episode in a later volume of his work, when he charges that Austin betrayed the Hawkins heirs in the final settlement of the contract—a charge that will be refuted later in this article. See Malcolm D. McLean (comp. and ed.), *Papers Concerning Robertson's Colony in Texas* (16 vols.; Arlington: University of Texas at Arlington Press, 1974–1992), II, 45–46.

[29]The only thing that the 1821 contract said about the expenditure of funds above and beyond $4,000 was this clause: "In embarking in objects requiring additional disburcements of monies or monied responsibilities it must be done by joint and mutual consent." This may have happened, but it in no way alters Austin's obligation to share equally with Hawkins in the profits of the colony. Agreement Between Austin and Joseph H. Hawkins, Nov. 14, 1821, *Austin Papers,* I, pt. 1, p. 429 (quotation). For the $6,000 and $7,000 estimates, see Joseph H. Hawkins to Stephen F. Austin, July 23, 1822, ibid., 532; and Hawkins to Mrs. Maria Austin, Mar. 29, 1823, ibid., 628.

we accept for the moment Cox's later claim that the amount expended was actually $30,000, the figure is irrelevant; Austin still owed him half the profits to be derived from the colony.

Legalities notwithstanding, the $30,000 figure still should be analyzed. For the figure to have been truly accurate, Hawkins would have had to spend $23,000 in the five months after he himself had estimated his outlays at $7,000—expenditures that would have been virtually impossible given his desperate financial plight in the last five months of his life. However, Cox, who came up with the $30,000 figure after his own post-mortem examination of Hawkins's papers, readily admitted that "this includes the purchas[e] of Vessells, Cargoes, and disbursements to officers and seamen—Loans to individuals traveling to and from the grant, who are unknown to me, and lost to his Heirs Except as a charge to the grant—payments made to you and on your draft—and the dreadfull Item of Usurious Interest to money Brokers for loans at diff$^{t}$. times." There was no way for Cox or anyone else but Hawkins really to know which of these expenditures were previously agreed-upon colonization expenses, which were unilateral expenditures by Hawkins, and which were side ventures (such as the aforementioned enterprises of Littleberry Hawkins and John Botts) entirely unconnected with Austin. The most important fact is this: In mentioning the legally irrelevant $30,000 figure, Cox himself did not suggest that it bound Austin to any obligation other than the fulfillment of the terms of the original contract. Indeed, in this same letter Cox expressly told Austin, "I fully approve the resolution you have adopted with regard to the Texas property. . . . [T] he only plan wh. can avail Mrs. Hawkins and her children is the one you have adopted—and the time may come when it may make them independent."[30]

In a later letter, disturbed that Austin might have interpreted his mentioning of the $30,000 amount as meaning that Austin owed more than what the original contract called for, Cox even more explicitly reassured Austin that "I did not even for a moment suppose he had any other claim on you than what you have mentioned to wit One half of the Grant. . . ." He also informed Austin that Mrs. Hawkins had indeed declined the offer of settling in Texas; her relatives in Kentucky "wont listen to any thing of the kind." And significantly (in light of developments yet to come), Cox gave Austin one other assurance which came directly from George Anne Hawkins: "On the subject of a division of the Grant, she has instructed me to say that she cannot find any person to act as agent in whom she has the same confidence as yourself, and that she leaves the division entirely to you."[31]

---

[30]Nathaniel Cox to Stephen F. Austin, June 3, 1824, *Austin Papers,* I, pt. 1, p. 808. These sentiments are repeated in Cox's letter of August 6, 1824, ibid., 871–872.

[31]Nathaniel Cox to Stephen F. Austin, Nov. 16, 1824, *Austin Papers,* I, pt. 1, pp. 941 (1st quotation), 942 (2nd quotation).

As compensation for his labor as empresario, Austin was to receive 22½ leagues designated as "premium land"—almost exactly 100,000 acres—from the Mexican government. Originally Austin had believed that he would be able to charge a small per-acre fee to the colonists, each of whom normally was granted about 4,600 acres. The Mexican authorities had soon overruled this plan, allowing Austin to charge only for the expenses of surveying the land and processing the official paperwork for the titles. Given the heavy expenses of conducting the colony's business, these fees rarely were enough to cover Austin's costs. Furthermore, as long as the government was essentially giving land away, converting land into cash was a near-impossibility. Austin thus spoke truly when he told the Hawkinses and Cox that the premium lands constituted the only profits to be realized from the colonizing venture. In a 50-50 division, the Hawkins heirs would be entitled to 11¼ leagues, or nearly 50,000 acres.[32]

Later that year (1824) Austin again wrote to George Anne Hawkins and urged her to send an agent to Texas to handle the division of the lands. Apparently fearing that her late husband's creditors would get wind of the transaction and end up with the land, she replied that "I do not think it would be advisable in the present state of things to do so. . ." Instead she expressed her "reliance on the goodness of your heart" and was "perfectly willing to resian [resign] the welfare of my Fatherless Children to you. . . ." "write often," she urged her husband's old friend.[33]

Three years later, in 1827, she wanted to send a legal representative to Texas to proceed with the division of the lands, but she feared she would "not be able to engage a suitable one for some time."[34] As chance would have it, Austin was not able to perfect the titles to his 22½ leagues of premium land until the following year, so any division before then would have rested upon a shaky legal basis. But in March 1829 Austin notified Nathaniel Cox that he was ready to divide the land. George Anne Hawkins had trusted Austin to make a fair division, but the empresario told Cox he preferred "laying the plats all before you, as the agent and friend of the heirs and I also wish to consult with you as to the best mode of Making the Estate of some value to the heirs." Under Mexican law, title to the land could not be vested in a non-resident alien, so Austin offered to "take charge of the property and sell parts of it, or lease and

[32]Austin himself gave the most succinct explanation of the complex history of the land and fee system in Stephen F. Austin to [Edmund H.] Martin, Sept. 14, 1832, *Austin Papers,* II, 859–863, 864 (quotation), 865. See also Barker, *The Life of Stephen F. Austin,* 37, 89–90, 97–106.

[33]G. A. [Mrs. Joseph H.] Hawkins to Stephen F. Austin, Oct. 9, 1824, *Austin Papers,* I, pt. 1, p. 923.

[34]Mrs. J. H. Hawkins to Stephen F. Austin, Aug. 4, 1827, *Austin Papers,* I, pt. 2, p. 1674.

settle other parts," or to "cheerfully and faithfully" do anything else she desired, "but this should be done under the authority of special instructions to that effect—from the legal agent of the Estate after the division is made and Hawkins part designated."[35]

The wheels continued to turn slowly—much too slowly, as far as Austin was concerned. The bulk of his 100,000 acres of premium land lay along the lower Brazos River in modern-day Brazoria County. It was in Austin's interest to have the division of the lands made, because the value of his own property depended in part on the overall economic development of the area. That economic development was stunted as long as large tracts of land adjoining his remained unoccupied and unimproved. The sooner titles could be made to the Hawkins heirs for their share and the land be cultivated, leased, or sold, the better it would be for Austin.[36]

George Anne Hawkins finally appointed her brother, R. C. Nicholas, to go to Texas and arrange for the division of the lands. But Nicholas did not come at once, and George Anne died soon after. Over the next three years three more men were named to represent the family in the matter of the lands, but nothing of consequence happened.[37] In the meantime, the Hawkins children—four boys and a girl—were growing up. In 1831 Austin received one of the sons, Edmund St. John Hawkins, as a colonist, securing him a grant of land and helping him get settled in Texas.[38] Finally, in the fall of 1832, the heirs of Joseph Hawkins and their legal representatives were ready to receive their long-awaited legacy.

Austin spent parts of September, October, and November in Brazoria, studying the deeds and surveys and running the lines that would divide the premium lands into equal parts for himself and the heirs of Hawkins. In a letter to his sister Emily he remarked that he had given up at least a fourth of what he was entitled to, but he did so just to get the matter settled.[39] On November 8, 1832, Austin and the heirs signed a legal agreement specifying exactly which lands the heirs were to receive. Accordingly, several weeks later, in January

---

[35]Stephen F. Austin to Nathaniel Cox, Mar. 10, 1829, *Austin Papers,* II, 181.

[36]Austin was so anxious to settle the Hawkins business that he returned to Texas after attending the 1832 session of the state legislature in Saltillo rather than traveling to Mexico City as he had earlier planned. See Stephen F. Austin to Samuel M. Williams, Apr. 12, 1832, *Austin Papers,* II, 764.

[37]R. C. Nicholas to Stephen F. Austin, Oct. 11, 1829, *Austin Papers,* II, 263–264; Richard Hawes to Stephen F. Austin, Aug. 29, 1831, ibid., 691–692; Stephen F. Austin to [Edmund H.] Martin, Sept. 14, 1832, ibid., 859–865. Martin eventually acted as the agent for three of the heirs, and William H. Wharton represented two others.

[38]Entries dated Nov. 17, 1831, Austin Account Book.

[39]Stephen F. Austin to James F. Perry, Sept 27, 1832, *Austin Papers,* II, 867; Stephen F. Austin to Emily M. Perry, Nov. 5, 1832, ibid., 884.

1833, the deeds for approximately 42,000 acres of land were transferred into Edmund St. John Hawkins's name (acting as agent for his brothers and sister, since they were not resident in Texas). Prior to the agreement Austin had sold portions of the land amounting to about 9,000 acres to eight individuals, and Austin agreed to pay the heirs half of the proceeds of those sales. After the costs of surveying the lands were deducted as per the original contract, the Hawkinses received about $2,000 in cash in addition to the 42,000 acres of land.[40]

Thus, after weighing upon Austin's mind for more than a decade, his obligation to Joseph Hawkins was finally discharged. But while the 1832 agreement explicitly stated that it was "final and conclusive between the parties aforesaid of all partnership concern of every kind whatever which heretofore existed between Stephen F. Austin and the late Joseph H. Hawkins," the intrinsic fairness of the settlement is still in question. Did Austin take advantage of his superior knowledge of the lands to saddle the youthful heirs with an inferior half? Fortunately, the agreement itself, along with a remarkable map from the archives of the General Land Office, answers that question convincingly.

Instead of taking the 100,000 acres of land (minus the fraction that had been sold previously) and lopping off the poorest or least accessible half of it for the Hawkinses, Austin took each individual tract—seventeen of them in all—and split them exactly down the middle. All but four of these tracts were located in or around the town of Brazoria, and several of them adjoined the plantation known as Peach Point, where the Austin-Bryan-Perry family made their home. As a result, the Hawkins heirs received about 32,000 acres of their land in the very heart of the most productive (and valuable) part of Austin's colony, and the rest lay in nearby areas almost as choice. After running the division lines, Austin had surveyor Thomas H. Borden draw a map of the Brazoria-Peach Point area, showing in precise detail the division of the lands. This map strikingly reveals the fairness of the division. Tracts lying on the Brazos River are

[40]Austin-Hawkins Agreement, Nov. 8, 1832, Deed Book A, pp. 86–89 (Brazoria County Clerk's Office, Angleton, Texas). This document presented the terms of the settlement between Austin and the Hawkins heirs; the deed records showing the actual transfer of the various parcels of land are in Transcribed Spanish Records, 1823–1836, pp. 46–55, in the Brazoria County Clerk's Office. William H. Wharton acted as legal representative for two of the heirs, and given his animosity toward Austin it is safe to assume that he zealously represented the interests of his clients. One of the tracts that had been sold was a 3,000-acre tract on Chocolate Bayou that Austin had sold to his brother-in-law James Perry for $500. However, Austin agreed to value the land at $3,000 for purposes of determining the monetary settlement on it—further evidence of his willingness to meet the heirs more than halfway in order to get the business settled. For the subsequent cash payments to Edmund St. John Hawkins, see Accounts dated Feb. 20, 1833, in the unpublished Austin Papers, Series III, 1831–1834 (CAH).

divided so that Austin and the Hawkinses each received equal amounts of river frontage. Tracts nearer the town of Brazoria and town lots within the town are laid off in a checkerboard fashion, with Austin and the Hawkinses receiving alternating shares.[41] Five young people in their teens and twenties, four of whom had never set foot on Texas soil, were now among the largest landowners in Texas. In 1837, court-appointed Brazoria County appraisers appraised the Hawkins land at more than $129,000.[42]

During the discussions that led to the division of the lands, Edmund St. John Hawkins, the only one of the heirs actually in Texas, had expressed some reservations about Austin's handling of the settlement. As Austin told the family's longtime friend and lawyer, Nathaniel Cox, "After the many years of labor and hardships and perplexities I have undergone in this country by which I have secured a handsome fortune for the heirs, I was not prepared to receive censure from any of them, because I thought I did not merit it." But Austin was pleased to learn that the "incorrect impressions" Edmund had received "from some persons who are unfriendly to me . . . are removed now and that he is very well satisfied." Cox, who knew more about the Austin-Hawkins relationship than anyone besides Austin himself, approved of Austin's conduct, an approval which Austin found "very gratifying."[43]

The partnership between Stephen F. Austin and Joseph H. Hawkins is important for two reasons. First, there is the matter of evaluating the material contribution that Hawkins made to the founding of Austin's first colony, and thus to Anglo American Texas. Second, there is the question of what the Hawkins affair tells us about Austin's character. These two issues in fact become interrelated when one considers whether or not Austin gave proper credit to Hawkins for his role in building Texas.

Historians have handled these questions in curious ways. Austin's biographer, Eugene C. Barker, downplays Hawkins's role. In doing so, Barker relies almost exclusively on Austin's own statements, particularly an 1832 letter to the family's legal agent, Edmund H. Martin. In this letter Austin had sought to

---

[41]Thomas H. Borden, "Sketch of Surveys on Peach Point," Dec. 1832, in Austin Colony Maps, Folder Y7 (Archives and Records Dvision, Texas General Land Office, Austin). I am grateful to Galen Greaser of the GLO Archives for calling this map to my attention.

[42]Inventory and Appraisment of the Estate of E[dmund] St. John Hawkins, June 13, 1837, Probate Records, Brazoria County Clerk's Office, Angleton, Texas. The total amount of land as of that date was 42,941 acres, valued at $3 per acre, plus town lots in Brazoria valued at $1,000. John A. Wharton was one of the appraisers. The titles to all the Hawkins land were still in Edmund's name, probably because he was holding them in trust for his siblings who were not of majority age.

[43]Stephen F. Austin to Nathaniel Cox, Apr. 2, 1833, *Austin Papers,* II, 941.

satisfy Martin that nothing beyond half the premium lands was owed to the heirs, and that even that was a generous settlement given the relative contributions of Hawkins and himself. Austin only acknowledged Hawkins's outfitting of the *Lively* and his partial underwriting of Austin's expenses for the 1822 Mexico City trip. Hawkins "could not have been much aid in sending out emigrants, for he died before there was much emigration," Austin explained. While this was true enough if one compares the pre-1823 to the post-1823 levels of emigration, it no doubt understates the part that Hawkins played in "sending out" the crucial earliest emigrants—perhaps as many as six shiploads of them. Austin simply failed to mention that Hawkins apparently outfitted the *Lively* not once but twice, and that he probably had a significant financial (and certainly a managerial) role in sending the *Only Son* on its three voyages and the *Good Intent* on its one. He denied that the amount expended by Hawkins ever approached even the $4,000 mentioned in the 1821 contract. "The truth is," Austin stated emphatically, "that I could have done all that I have done, had I never known Hawkins, nor received one cent, nor aid, from any quarter beyond my own resources."[44]

This was at best disingenuous on Austin's part, and also on the part of Barker, who tacitly accepts Austin's contention.[45] In fairness to Austin, it must be pointed out that he may not have been aware of all that Hawkins had done in sending emigrants, for he had been occupied with business in Mexico City during the time of these voyages. Still, as difficult as it was for Austin to get his first colony established and confirmed by the Mexican government, it would have been much harder if not for the support of Hawkins. That support came not just in the form of outfitting ships, bankrolling emigrants, and contributing money for Austin's 1821–1822 travel expenses, but also in the six months that Austin lived under the Hawkins roof and ate at the Hawkins table. It came in the form of the part-time work that Hawkins helped Austin secure when he first came to New Orleans. It came in the form of the legal instruction that Austin received in Hawkins's law office—experience that would be invaluable in helping him draft a workable legal code for his colony.[46] And it came in the form of

---

[44]Stephen F. Austin to [Edmund H.] Martin, Sept. 14, 1832, *Austin Papers*, II, 859–860, 861 (1st and 2nd quotations), 862–865.

[45]Barker, *The Life of Stephen F. Austin*, 249–252.

[46]Although it was not a part of the November 1821 Austin-Hawkins contract, Austin earlier had informally promised to repay Hawkins the small sums of money that Hawkins had advanced him for clothes, groceries, and other sundry living expenses while Austin was rooming with Hawkins and studying law in early 1821. The reimbursement was not expected to be made until after Austin was fully trained in the law and making a living from his practice—which of course never happened. See Stephen F. Austin to His Mother, Jan. 20, 1821, *Austin Papers*, vol. I, pt. 1,

the encouragement that Hawkins rendered to a moody and often depressed young man down on his luck.

Austin possessed many sterling qualities, but among his shortcomings was a tendency to view his life as a struggle of Stephen F. Austin alone against a hostile world, a point of view that became more pronounced as the years went by. This aspect of Austin's character manifested itself not so much in overt egotism, but rather in a propensity to overlook the contributions of others and magnify his own achievements. Austin should have given Hawkins more credit; his biographer Barker should have viewed Austin's self-serving statements with a more critical eye.

In his massive multi-volume work *Papers Concerning Robertson's Colony in Texas,* Malcolm D. McLean takes a very different attitude than Barker toward Austin's treatment of the Hawkins partnership. In his first volume, McLean includes a section entitled "Joseph H. Hawkins, Unrewarded Benefactor of Moses and Stephen F. Austin," and states outright that "Hawkins was never repaid for the money he had advanced to the Austins." McLean returns to this theme several times in subsequent volumes, using it to portray the empresario as ungrateful and unfaithful to the man "who financed Austin."[47] Such an interpretation, based upon a highly selective and incomplete reading of the sources, leaves the false impression that Hawkins was the sole and utterly indis-

---

p. 374. On Austin's legal training and its role in helping him draft the legal code for his colony, see Joseph W. McKnight, "Stephen Austin's Legalistic Concerns," *Southwestern Historical Quarterly,* LXXXIX (Jan., 1986), 239–268.

[47]McLean (comp. and ed.), *Papers Concerning Robertson's Colony,* I, liv-lv (1st and 2nd quotations); II, 62 (3rd quotation), 314. McLean also makes much of the "startling" (II, 46) fact that some of the money that Hawkins advanced Austin may have come from a mortgage executed between Hawkins and Gen. James Wilkinson. The "sources" (plural in McLean's footnote on II, 179) that McLean cites for this information are actually a single source—a letter from Nathaniel Cox, dated February 24, 1824. This letter does not survive in the original, but it is partially reprinted in the 1859 William Victor *Memorial* discussed elsewhere in this article. In this letter, Cox is quoted as saying, "The house and lot [of Joseph Hawkins] are mortgaged to Gen. Wilkinson, for the four thousand dollars obtained from him to advance Austin." See Victor, *Memorial to the Legislature,* 21 (p. 3 of the appendix identifies the recipient of this letter as Lewis Sanders, a kinsman of Hawkins). However, in the voluminous Austin correspondence neither Hawkins nor Cox nor anyone else ever mentions James Wilkinson as one of Hawkins's sources of financing. Nor did a search of notarial records in New Orleans turn up such a mortgage. But there are several references to "the dreadfull Item of Usurious Interest to money Brokers [plural—not just Wilkinson or any single individual] for loans at diff. times" incurred by Hawkins (see Cox to Stephen F. Austin, June 3, 1824, in *Austin Papers,* I, pt. 1, p. 808), and certainly one of these brokers may have been James Wilkinson. It is a far cry, however, from this poorly documented, third-hand evidence that James Wilkinson may have furnished some of the money that Hawkins furnished Austin to Malcolm McLean's sweeping generalization "that Wilkinson financed Hawkins, and that Hawkins financed Austin." See McLean (comp. and ed.), *Papers Concerning Robertson's Colony,* II, 46, 62, 179 (quotation).

pensable source of Austin's financing—clearly an exaggeration, even when we acknowledge the importance of Hawkins's aid. More egregiously, it ignores the genuine concern that Austin showed the Hawkins heirs and completely overlooks the large 1833 land transfer.

At this point, in order to evaluate fully and fairly Professor McLean's charge that Austin maliciously betrayed the Hawkins heirs, it is necessary to take a closer look at McLean's principal source for the accusation. This fascinating and little-known document itself constitutes an important part of the larger Austin-Hawkins story.

In 1859 a Kentuckian named William Victor published a lengthy *Memorial to the Legislature of Texas*. Victor was the second husband of Mary Jane Hawkins, who was the last surviving child of Joseph Hawkins. Victor's petition asked the Texas Legislature to render a "tribute of voluntary justice to the memory of Joseph H. Hawkins" by appropriating $100,000, half in land and half in money, for his wife. Victor argued that the lands the heirs received from Austin in 1833 were merely the share due them as a result of Hawkins's initial $4,000 investment in Austin's colony; the additional $25,000 Hawkins had allegedly invested had given the heirs the right to an equal share of all subsequent premium lands Austin had been granted as a result of his later empresario contracts. With interest, this $25,000 obligation now totalled over $100,000.[48]

It is true that the 1821 contract had specified that Austin and Hawkins would share in "all lands" that Austin might get from the Spanish government, and that Austin was obligated "to cause as many individual grants of lands to be made to said Hawkins and himself" as possible.[49] But it is difficult to proceed from this contractual language to the conclusion (reached by Victor and cited by McLean) that the Hawkins heirs were due the value of half of all premium lands granted to Austin for his subsequent empresario contracts and that, additionally, Austin somehow also owed the heirs for the money Hawkins had contributed to the venture.

Two prominent legal scholars consulted for the writing of this article agree that the November 1821 contract between Austin and Hawkins applied only to the premium lands Austin received for the first colony. Moses (and subsequently Stephen) Austin only promised Hawkins in 1821 to obtain as much land as possible from the Spanish government; upon achieving independence, Mexico honored the Austins' Spanish contract by granting Stephen 100,000 acres (22½ leagues), half of which Austin ultimately signed over to the Hawkins heirs as per the 1821 agreement. By the time Austin signed his second

---

[48]Victor, *Memorial to the Legislature,* 3 (quotation), 29–35.

[49]Agreement Between Austin and Joseph H. Hawkins, Nov. 14, 1821, *Austin Papers,* I, pt. 1, pp. 428 (1st quotation), 429 (2nd quotation).

empresario contract, it was the spring of 1825, Hawkins had been dead for more than a year, and the new empresario contract was a totally separate agreement between Stephen Austin and the state government of Texas y Coahuila. Legal historian Joesph W. McKnight of the Southern Methodist University School of Law explains that "the terms of the partnership were those agreed between Moses Austin and Hawkins, and that Hawkins's interest was limited to lands acquired under the agreement with the Spanish government as ratified by the Mexican government." Therefore the contract could not, as McLean argues, have been "open-ended in that it covered all lands to be acquired by Austin in Texas in the future, without any time limitation. . . ." In short, Austin did fulfill all the legal requirements of the 1821 contract.[50]

It should be recalled that the Hawkins heirs, in writing, recognized the settlement at the time as being "final and conclusive."[51] Even William Victor in his 1859 *Memorial* denied "any intention or wish to impeach the honor or injure the fame of Col. Austin" and openly acknowledged that Austin fulfilled his legal requirements stemming from the first colony. The inescapable conclusion is that Victor's *Memorial* was a rather pitiful attempt to extract "a generosity from the state of Texas" (to quote Professor McKnight again), an attempt based on absolutely no legal grounds (as even Victor admitted) and on a thoroughly flawed interpretation of Austin's moral obligation to the Hawkins heirs.[52] Victor may even have come to realize it himself, for there is no record that he ever actually presented the *Memorial* to the legislature. It may also be significant that Victor claimed to have drawn up the *Memorial* without the knowledge of his wife Mary Jane, the only living child of Joseph Hawkins. Mary Jane Hawkins had gradually sold off her massive tracts of Texas lands over the years before she married Victor, realizing hefty cash profits from the sales.[53] Yet Professor McLean cites the William Victor *Memorial* as proof that "Hawkins was never repaid for the money he had advanced to the Austins."[54] The 1821 contract, as

---

[50]Joseph M. McKnight to Gregg Cantrell, Dec. 16, 1994 (1st quotation) (letter in possession of the author); McLean (comp. and ed.), *Papers Concerning Robertson's Colony,* II, 46 (2nd quotation). Professor Hans Baade of the University of Texas School of Law concurs in Professor McKnight's opinion, stating that holding Austin liable to share with Hawkins half of all land grants that he might obtain from Mexico during the rest of his life would have constituted something akin to "slavery" and could never have been legally upheld. Hans Baade to Gregg Cantrell, July 1994 (interview).

[51]Austin-Hawkins Agreement, Nov. 8, 1832.

[52]Victor, *Memorial to the Legislature,* 31 (1st quotation); Joseph W. McKnight to Gregg Cantrell, Dec. 16, 1994 (2nd quotation).

[53]Victor, *Memorial to the Legislature,* 3–4. Between June 1840 and November 1847, Mary Jane Hawkins Davis (her first husband's last name was Davis) sold nineteen individual tracts of land

this article has shown, never required the repayment of cash but rather the division of Austin's premium lands. Thus McLean bases much of his criticism of Austin upon this moot point of owed money, all the while completely ignoring the ample evidence in the Austin Papers and other sources cited herein showing that Austin settled the debt with the heirs by dividing the premium lands of the first colony, which secured the surviving heirs a handsome fortune in their lifetimes.

Both Barker and McLean, then, have transmitted to future generations flawed understandings of the Austin-Hawkins partnership. Hawkins, as we have seen, deserves more credit than Barker will allow him, but less than McLean suggests. Conversely, Barker has exaggerated the single-handedness of Austin's very real accomplishments, while McLean is far too zealous in denying Austin the credit due him. The truth lies in the middle ground: Stephen Austin inaugurated the Anglo American colonization of Texas with a tremendously important, though not necessarily indispensable, assist from Joseph Hawkins.

Similar errors have been made in using the Hawkins episode as a basis for evaluating the empresario's character. As we have seen, Barker tended to accept Austin's estimation of his own virtue and selflessness. McLean, in his eagerness to present a revisionist view of Austin, seizes on every piece of negative evidence connected with the Austin-Hawkins affair and ignores many counterbalancing documents in order to vilify and discredit the man he clearly views as undeserving of the title "Father of Texas." But neither Barker nor McLean, nor any other scholar to date, has properly recognized the one indisputable fact connected with this case: Whether or not he publicly expressed proper gratitude to his

---

totalling more than 21,000 acres, not including various town lots and some sales in which the amount of land sold was not clearly stated. Land in the lower Brazos River in this period generally sold for between two and three dollars per acre. The most conservative estimate, therefore, places her cash income from these sales at $42,000, a considerable sum for the time; see Direct Index to Deeds, A-D (Brazoria County Clerk's Office, Angleton, Texas). In one transaction, for example, she sold a 4,263-acre tract for $9,948.68, which comes to $2.33 per acre. See Deed Book D, pp. 492–493. The only male Hawkins heir who survived beyond 1837, Joseph Thomas Hawkins, actually moved to Brazoria County and lived there until his death in 1850. He, too, sold considerable amounts of land in the 1840s and realized handsome returns. See Direct Index to Deeds, E-K. He died in 1850 and left all his property to an uncle in Kentucky. See Last Will and Testament of Joseph T. Hawkins, Will Records, Book E,515 (Brazoria County Clerk's Office, Angleton, Texas).

[54]McLean (comp. and ed.), *Papers Concerning Robertson's Colony,* I, lv.

one-time partner and friend, when it came to actions Austin proved he was a man of his word. His settlement with the Hawkins heirs was honorable and scrupulously fair. As a result of the agreement made in New Orleans in 1821, Edmund, Norbourne, George, Thomas, and Mary Jane Hawkins ultimately received a rich legacy of 42,000 acres of fertile land and $2,000 in cash, and young Stephen Austin was given a much-needed hand in launching the enterprise that forever changed Texas history.[55]

---

[55]These are the names given as the heirs of Hawkins in the 1832 land settlement, and it seems safe to assume that they were the four sons and daughter of Joseph Hawkins alive in 1832. There are, however, confusing discrepancies among the various sources that give the names of the Hawkins children. The 1823 "Inventory of the Estate of Joseph H. Hawkins" in the New Orleans Public Library lists five heirs: Mary, Norbourne, John, Joseph, and Thomas. Another 1823 New Orleans Court of Probates record, the "family meeting of the heirs and friends of the late Joseph Hawkins" (MF VCH 20, roll 105) (New Orleans Public Library), lists six children: George, Edmund St. John, Mary Jane, Norbourne, Joseph, and Thomas. William Victor's 1859 *Memorial*, 32, mentions only four children: Mary Jane, Norbourne, Edmund, and George. Mary Jane and Norbourne are the only two names that appear in all sources. Edmund St. John Hawkins is almost certainly the person listed as Edmund in one source and John in another. Land and probate records for the Hawkins heirs in Brazoria County definitively identify Joseph Thomas Hawkins as the brother of Norbourne, Edmund St. John, George, and Mary Jane. Why "Joseph" and "Thomas" are listed as separate people in the New Orleans probate records remains a mystery.

Norbourne Hawkins (there is considerable disagreement about his middle name or names) came to Texas as a teenager, enlisted in the revolutionary army, and died in the Goliad massacre. Edmund St. John Hawkins, the first to come to Texas (and the one whom Austin had welcomed as a colonist before the land distribution), died soon thereafter. George Nicholas Hawkins, the eldest son (see Littleberry Hawkins to Austin, Aug. 6, 1826, *Austin Papers*, I, pt. 2, p. 1399), likewise came to Texas and soon died. The estates of Norbourne, Edmund, and George were all probated in close succession in Brazoria County in 1837. Oddly, William Victor fails to mention the fourth son, Joseph Thomas Hawkins, by name, and only alludes to him in passing (see p. 32). There may, however, be an explanation. Joseph Thomas Hawkins was the only male heir to survive beyond 1837, and he ultimately inherited half of his brothers' land and lived until 1850 as a planter in Brazoria County (with his then-absent sister, Mary Jane, inheriting the other half of the family land). Victor may have conveniently omitted any specific discussion of this most important Hawkins heir because members of the state legislature might have connected the late, land-wealthy Joseph Thomas Hawkins of Brazoria County with the supposedly mistreated heirs of Joseph H. Hawkins, giving the lie to Victor's tale of injustice. Also, the fact that Joseph Thomas Hawkins willed all his lands to his uncle in Kentucky instead of to his sister, Mary Jane Hawkins Victor, may have miffed William Victor so much that he purposely omitted his late brother-in-law from the *Memorial*. See Inventories of the Estates of Edmund St. John, Norbourne, George, and Joseph T. Hawkins, Probate Records (Brazoria County Clerk's Office, Angleton, Texas), and the various land records cited previously in this article. None of these Hawkinses should be confused with the Maj. John T. Hawkins (a more distant kinsman of Joseph Hawkins and himself later a settler in Austin's colony) mentioned earlier in this article.

# Tory Sentiment in Anglo-Texas Public Opinion, 1832–1836

MARGARET SWETT HENSON*

*The Texas Revolution and struggle for independence from Mexico has attracted much attention from historians. Numerous books and articles describe the gallant stand of William B. Travis, Jim Bowie, David Crockett, and others at the Alamo. Several biographers chronicle the life of the hero of San Jacinto, Sam Houston. Other accounts relate the story of James W. Fannin Jr., Sidney Sherman, Mirabeau B. Lamar, and Stephen F. Austin. Until recently, however, little has been written about those Texans who did not support the independence movement.*

*The late Margaret S. Henson, a history professor at the University of Houston, Clear Lake, wrote a succinct account of those Texans who opposed the Revolution. In this article she pointed out that these Texas "tories" tended to be longtime residents in Texas with a vested interest in land or power, while the rebels were younger, brasher newcomers who had less land or power. She also noted that some of those who originally opposed separation from Mexico, such as David G. Burnet, Thomas Jefferson Chambers, and Thomas McKinney, eventually came to support the Revolution for a variety of reasons. Others, especially a group of conservative cattle ranchers along the lower Trinity River, never supported independence. In their case, "preservation of economic gains in land and livestock gained under Mexican rule," she writes, "apparently outweighed appeals to defend political rights."*

*For more on divisions within Texas during the Revolution see Paul D. Lack,* The Texas Revolutionary Experience: A Political and Social History, 1835–1836 *(College Station: Texas A&M University Press, 1992), and Andres Tijernia,* Tejanos and Texas under the Mexican Flag, 1821–1836 *(College Station: Texas A&M University Press, 1994).*

*Margaret Swett Henson, "Tory Sentiment in Anglo-Texan Public Opinion, 1832–1836," *Southwestern Historical Quarterly*, 90 (July, 1986), 1–34.

Public support in Texas for the acts of violence against the centralist administration of Mexico was not unanimous, but this fact has received little attention from historians. Texas public opinion during this period in general has drawn few scholars. William C. Binkley mentioned public opinion as one factor that led the Anglo-Texans toward revolution, but he did not develop it as a separate topic. Eugene C. Barker, in his biography of Stephen F. Austin, referred to public attitudes and the empresario's efforts to shape them. Barker also focused on public opinion during the spring and summer of 1835 in a 1911 essay that sought to explain the commencement of separationist sentiment, but the article was limited to that brief period.[1] Most histories have concentrated instead on the more exciting military and political events. The present essay, while mentioning those events, will explore tory sentiment that arose in 1832 and 1835–1836 in Anglo-Texan neighborhoods.

Nineteenth-century writers, often closely associated with participants of the Texas Revolution, mentioned the similarities between the Texas and American revolutions and usually lauded the successful patriots. They noted that both movements had committees of correspondence, preliminary battles, and subsequent declarations of independence, but they did not usually mention tory dissidents.[2] A few contemporaries labeled the 1832 dissenters tories, a word associated with both English history and the American Revolution, but the negative connotation caused most historians to avoid it. The two sides of the issue in 1835 were characterized at the time by the terms peace party, on the one hand, and war party, or occasionally tories, on the other. Tory was an especially popular term for those dissenters living east of the San Jacinto River, who clung to their loyalist position until after the battle of San Jacinto in April, 1836.

---

[1]William C. Binkley, *The Texas Revolution* (Baton Rouge, 1952), 47, 57, 120; Eugene C. Barker, *The Life of Stephen F. Austin, Founder of Texas, 1793–1836: A Chapter in the Westward Movement of the Anglo-American People* (2nd ed.; Austin, 1949), 337–339, 345, 353, 358, 376, 411–413, 425–426; Eugene C. Barker, "Public Opinion in Texas Preceding the Revolution," American Historical Association, *Annual Report*, 1911 (Washington, D.C., 1913), 219–228.

[2]See Henry Stuart Foote, *Texas and the Texans* . . . (2 vols.; Philadelphia, 1841), II, 93–96, for comparisons of the revolutions. David B. Edward, *The History of Texas* . . . (Cincinnati, 1836), 249, mentions both "Whigs" and "Tories" in his description of the events of 1832, but he was a Scot and sympathetic toward Mexico. Ibid., ix, xi–xii.

Modern historians who have referred to the tories include Frank X. Tolbert, *The Day of San Jacinto* (New York, 1959), 65, 100, 199, 246; Andrew Forest Muir, "Tories in Texas, 1836," *Texas Military History*, IV (Summer, 1984), 81–94, who concludes that there were none on the San Jacinto River; Clyde Allen True, "John A. Williams: Champions of Mexico in the Early Days of the Texas Revolution," *Southwestern Historical Quarterly*, XLVII (Oct., 1943), 107–119 (the *Quarterly* is cited hereafter as *SHQ*); and Kent Gardien, "Kokernot and His Tory," *Texana*, VIII, No. 3 (1970), 269–294, who says there was at least one tory in 1836.

Dictionaries agree that a tory is a conservative in any party: in English history tories were those who supported the Crown against the progressive Whig party, and during the American Revolution tories were loyalists who sustained the claims of the king. The term, therefore, can apply to those Texans who opposed the attacks against Anahuac and Velasco in 1832 and the efforts of the peace party in 1835–1836. The word tory in this essay is interchangeable with conservative, loyalist, and peace party.

Dissent appeared inevitable in Texas, given the contentious nature of Anglo-Americans. As sons and grandsons of the American Revolution, with inherited notions of their rights as free men, Anglo-Texans protested when acts of the Mexican government violated their perceptions of liberty and justice. But these new Mexican citizens could not agree on proposed remedies or on who was to lead them. Individualism and independent action, more than a united planned remonstrance, characterized the reactions of the Anglo-Texans.

Erroneously assuming that republics were alike, most immigrants from the United States failed to understand that the Mexican Constitution of 1824 lacked a bill of rights providing such traditional American guarantees as trial by jury, the right to assemble, and freedom of speech. For their part, the Mexicans wanted immigrant frontiersmen to develop agriculture on their northeastern border and to defend the area from hostile Indians because the new republic was without the means to do so. Founded by idealists who lacked a tradition of self-government, the Mexican Republic soon floundered amid constant turmoil as ambitious men of opposing political philosophies struggled for dominance. The leaders of Mexico divided between the federalists, who favored a liberal republic vaguely like that of the United States, but with a weak central government and strong, independent states, and centralists, who wanted a strong national government and weak states. Stephen F. Austin guided his colonies along a neutral course and away from taking sides in the political arguments. He and many others personally favored the federalist philosophy but felt that Mexico was ill prepared for self-government. Many Anglos blamed the resulting coups and countercoups on presumed racial and cultural inferiority. They did, however, resist efforts of the successful centralist faction in 1830 to rid Mexico of republicanism and to establish a country more in keeping with Spanish heritage, which had almost always been monarchical.[3]

---

[3]Margaret Swett Henson, "Hispanic Texas, 1519–1836," Donald W. Whisenhunt (ed.), *Texas: A Sesquicentennial Celebration* (Austin, 1984), 49–50; Barker, *Life of Stephen F. Austin,* 76. See David J. Weber, *The Mexican Frontier, 1821–1846: The American Southwest under Mexico* (Albuquerque, 1982) for an overview of events in Mexico and Texas, especially pages 20, 22, 24, 31, 162–170.

The Anglo-Texans first acted in opposition to Mexico in 1832, when they expelled military garrisons placed in Texas by the centralist administration two years earlier. Troops had been sent to Texas in 1830 to enforce new laws restricting further immigration from the United States and to aid in the collection of the national tariff. Both measures angered most Anglo-Texans, many of whom were expecting relatives in the U.S. to immigrate also, and who mistakenly assumed that the temporary exemption from customs duties granted to the colonists would continue forever. This atmosphere of distrust was intensified by the actions of the Anahuac commandant, Colonel Juan Davis Bradburn. Bradburn's orders denying titles to settlers, interfering with elected local officials, and imprisoning civilians, although entirely legal under Mexican law, appeared arbitrary and authoritarian to the colonists, who were ignorant about the power traditionally exercised by the Mexican military. The fact that Bradburn was a former countryman and well known to some of the Anglo-Texans made his actions appear even more insulting, and he soon became a special target for their displeasure.[4]

The crisis came at Anahuac in June, 1832, when about 150 armed men marched from the Brazos River and Harrisburg, without the approval of the local authorities, to attack Bradburn because he would not release his civilian prisoners, including William B. Travis. After initial skirmishes, the Anglo-Texans realized that they needed cannon and sent a party to the Brazos to bring several small field pieces stored there. Other volunteers camped north of Anahuac on Turtle Bayou, where they drafted an explanation of their recent attack against the garrison. The insurgents aligned themselves with the federalist movement led by Antonio López de Santa Anna, whose troops had recently won victories in the civil war that had kept Mexico in turmoil for two years. The Texan rebels announced that they were opposing centralism at Anahuac as *santanistas.*[5]

Conservatives in San Felipe, traditionally the center of political power in Anglo-American Texas, deplored the attack at Anahuac and in letters to the civil and military authorities at San Antonio disavowed the rebels. San Antonio was the seat of government for Texas, although it was subservient to Saltillo, the state capital for Coahuila y Texas. The San Felipe *ayuntamiento* (town council) asked the political *jefe* (chief) at San Antonio to come to San Felipe to help cool emotions during the emergency. On June 25 he addressed a public meeting at San Felipe warning the insurgents not "to assume to themselves the rights of the majority." The residents passed resolutions condemning the rebels by a sixty-six

---

[4]Margaret Swett Henson, *Juan Davis Bradburn: A Reappraisal of the Mexican Commander at Anahuac* (College Station, Tex., 1982), 49–96.

[5]Ibid., 96–105.

to one tally, but it was too late. The action at Anahuac against the centralist outpost was compounded even as the jefe spoke, for Anglo-Texans were moving into position to attack Velasco, the fort at the mouth of the Brazos. Colonel Domingo de Ugartechea resisted as long as he could but capitulated on June 29.[6]

The use of the word tory appeared in a letter written on July 4, 1832, perhaps inspired by that significant date. Others may have used the prejudicial term earlier, but William H. Wharton of Brazoria, a supporter of the insurgents, is the first known to have recorded it. Wharton wrote, "I have received several letters . . . breathing all the same toryish spirit and shewing that we have as much opposition to expect from our own country men as from the Mexicans."[7]

Rumors about the events at Anahuac reached Colonel José Antonio Mexía, the victorious federalist commander, near Matamoros, and he invited Colonel José María Guerra, his centralist counterpart, and Stephen F. Austin, who happened to be visiting the area, to accompany him to Texas. If the rebels intended to sever Texas from the Mexican union, the combined troops of Mexía and Guerra would quash the movement. Five vessels bearing four hundred troops arrived at the mouth of the Brazos River on July 16, and the Brazoria alcalde, John Austin, who had participated in both attacks, presented the Turtle Bayou Resolutions to Mexía as evidence that the Texans were fighting for the federalist cause. The attacks against Anahuac and Velasco were portrayed as actions against centralist commanders, not against Mexico. Mexía accepted the disingenuous explanation and the residents of Brazoria held a dinner and ball in honor of the visitors. The empresario sent a courier to San Felipe to explain to his lieutenant, Samuel May Williams, and others of conservative bent that he, Austin, had embraced the federalist position and urged the ayuntamiento to endorse Santa Anna. Local rowdies in Brazoria showed their contempt for the San Felipe tories by hanging in effigy the advocates of the status quo: Samuel May Williams, Thomas Jefferson Chambers, and Ira R. Lewis.[8]

Austin's sudden change from his long-held position of absolute neutrality to outright endorsement of *santanismo* took the San Felipe conservatives by surprise. The empresario advised Williams to ignore the hanging; after all, he said,

---

[6]Citizens' Meeting, June 25, 1832, Charles Adams Gulick, Jr., et al. (eds.), *The Papers of Mirabeau Buonaparte Lamar* (6 vols.; Austin, 1968), I, 120–121; Ramon Musquiz to the People, June 25, 1832, ibid., 121, 122 (quotation); San Felipe Ayuntamiento to the Citizens, June 26, 1832, ibid., 123–124; Report of Ugartechea, July 1, 1832, ibid., 132–136; John Austin to Samuel May Williams, June 19, 1832, Samuel May Williams Papers (Rosenberg Library, Galveston); William Chambers, *Sketch of the Life of Gen. T. J. Chambers* (Galveston, 1853), 15–17.

[7]William Brown, Asa Mitchell, and William H. Wharton to Committee, July 4, 1832, Gulick et al. (eds.), *Papers of Mirabeau Buonaparte Lamar,* I, 139–140.

[8]Margaret Swett Henson, *Samuel May Williams, Early Texas Entrepreneur* (College Station, Tex., 1976), 39–41.

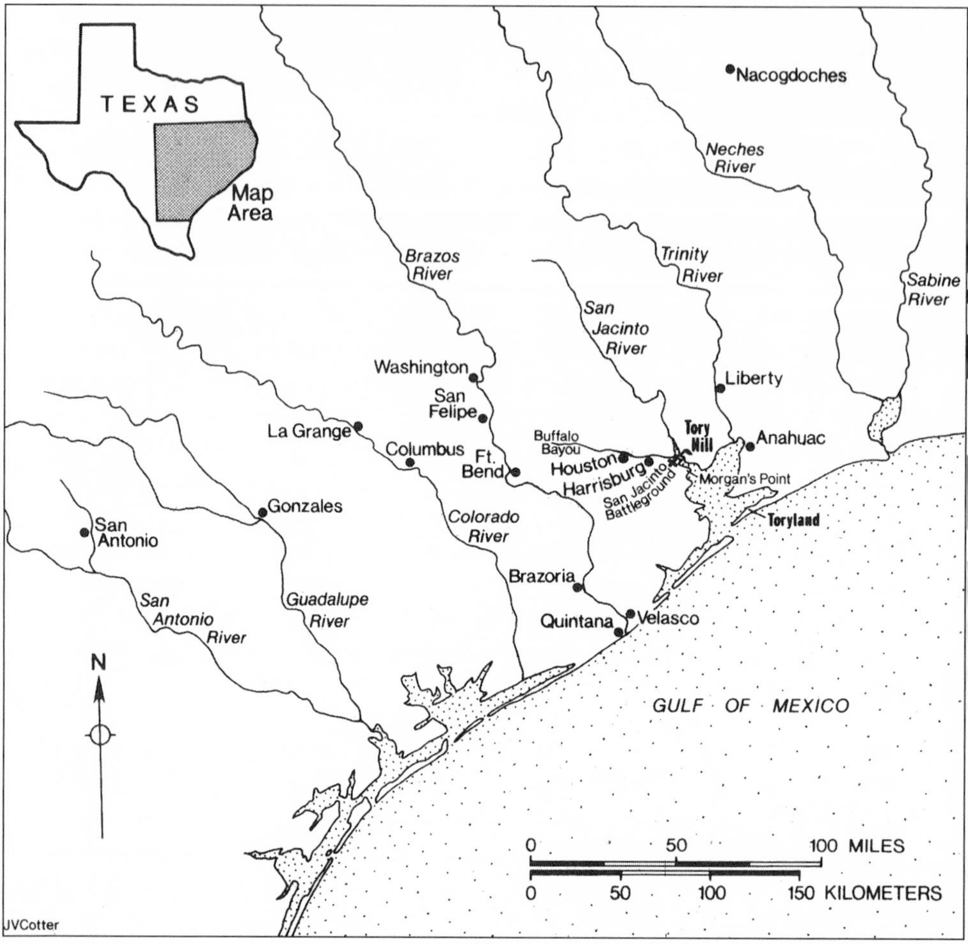


it had happened to some of the best men in the United States. Williams should explain to his critics that he had only been doing his best but "may have been mistaken as to the means." Williams's reaction to Austin's suggestions is not recorded, but Chambers published a pamphlet explaining that he was a "victim" of public opinion. It was not fair being labeled an "enemy" when he had merely had "an honest difference of opinion." Never a friend of the empresario, Chambers called him a "hypocrite" who pursued a double course.[9]

[9]Ibid., 41, 42 (1st quotation); Stephen F. Austin to S. M. Williams, July 19, 1832, Williams Papers; Chambers, *Life of Gen. T. J. Chambers*, 11,15 (2nd–4th quotations), 16 (5th quotation).

In San Felipe the returning troops, once called rebels, assembled as the Santa Anna Volunteer Company and on July 25 welcomed Austin and the vanquished commander from Velasco. Colonel Ugartechea had refused to join the *santanista* movement and was shepherding his men in a retreat to San Antonio and ultimately the Rio Grande. Elaborate ceremonies punctuated with cannon fire marked the occasion and a dinner followed; no one recorded whether or not the former tories attended.[10]

While the loyalists on the Brazos River suffered verbal and visual abuse, those around Anahuac endured physical blows. When the volunteers had first reached Anahuac, twenty-nine of the fifty-one residents of that area refused to join the attack against Bradburn. William B. Scates, the town's carpenter, recalled the event thirty-nine years later and castigated the "tories, by which name I like to call them even until now [1871] for I know the trouble they gave us." Colonel José de las Piedras, the commandant at Nacogdoches, responding to the emergency, reached Anahuac on July 1 with about a hundred troops, but fearful that he was outnumbered by Anglo-Texans, he acquiesced to the insurgents' demands. Piedras allowed Bradburn to resign his command, and, after naming a replacement and releasing the prisoners to the civil government, he left for Nacogdoches on July 8, rightly suspecting that a revolt might take place there also. The troops at Anahuac mutinied against the few remaining centralist officers and joined the *santanistas,* which forced Bradburn to flee to New Orleans. Scates and others rounded up the despised loyalists and rewarded them with "a full suit of tar and feathers, whilst others were stripped and taken into the Bay and scoured with corn cobs to scrub their Bradburn sins off. . . ."[11]

What divided Anglo-Texans into two factions in 1832? It is no easier to explain and categorize people then than now, but in general, tories were longtime residents in Texas with a vested interest in land or power, while the rebels tended to be younger, brash newcomers who either did not qualify for large land grants or found that all of the best land was already claimed and thus had to buy land from the pioneer settlers. Place of origin also provides a pattern. Most of the firebrands came from frontier settlements in the lower South. They possessed strong feelings about personal liberty and American constitutional rights as understood by frontiersmen. The Brazos conservatives were just as concerned about liberty and justice, but their reactions appear to be more judicious, due partly, perhaps, to their places of origin, which tended to be older, established areas, coupled with the caution associated with property holders.

---

[10]Mary Austin Holley, *Texas: Observations, Historical, Geographical, and Descriptive . . .* (Baltimore, 1833), 141–143.

[11]Henson, *Bradburn,* 109–112, 140–141; W. B. Scates, "Early History of Anahuac," James M. Day (comp.), *The Texas Almanac, 1857–1873: A Compendium of Texas History* (Waco, Tex., 1967), 681 (1st quotation), 688 (2nd quotation).

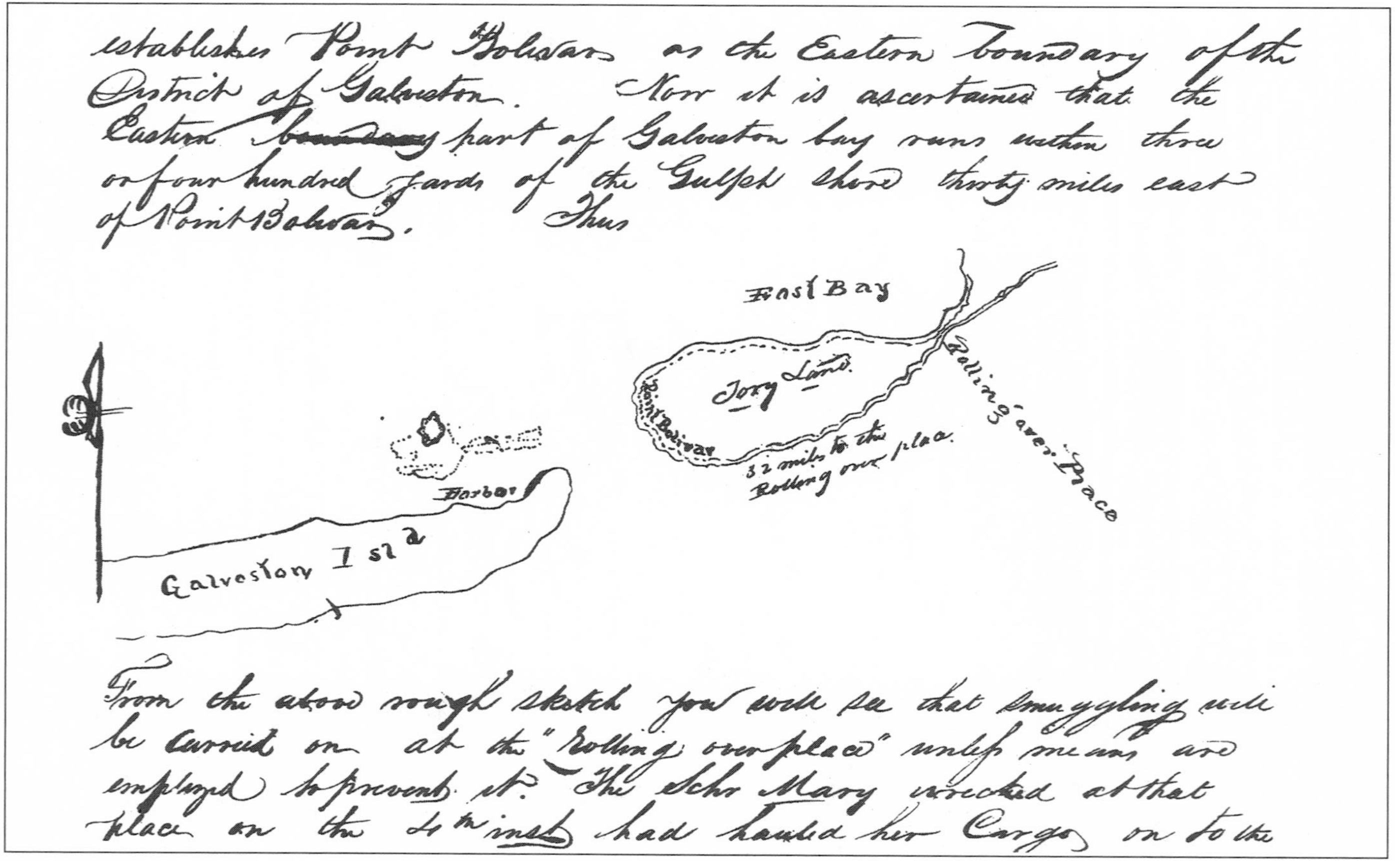
establishes Point Bolivar as the Eastern boundary of the District of Galveston. Now it is ascertained that the Eastern ~~boundary~~ part of Galveston bay runs within three or four hundred yards of the Gulfph shore thirty miles east of Point Bolivar. Thus



From the above rough sketch you will see that smuggling will be carried on at the "Rolling over place" unless means are employed to prevent it. The Schr Mary wrecked at that place on the 2nd inst had hauled her Cargo on to the

A sketch by Gail Borden of Bolivar Peninsula, labeled Tory Land, in a letter dated September 15, 1837. Courtesy Rosenberg Library,

An in-depth quantitative study might prove or disprove this assumption, something this writer will not attempt. A casual review of vital statistics available in *The Handbook of Texas* and the respective land grants made to eleven of the leaders involved in the 1832 crisis supports the thesis. Stephen F. Austin, Samuel May Williams, Thomas Jefferson Chambers, Ira R. Lewis, and Horatio Chriesman represent the conservative element. Their ages range from thirty to forty years, and all except Lewis had been in Texas or Mexico for at least eight years. Austin owned over forty-five leagues (one league is 4,428 acres); Williams, eleven; Lewis, one; and Chambers, none. Chambers had been appointed surveyor general in 1829, and with the support of influential men in the state and national capitals expected greater appointments, which in fact came in 1834, all accompanied by large land grants. All but one were born in Virginia and had moved west; Williams was a native of Rhode Island and a cosmopolitan by experience. Chambers had received legal training in Mexico City; Lewis, an American law education; while the others were entrepreneurs with some mercantile and surveying experience.[12]

On the other hand, rebels William B. Travis, Patrick C. Jack, William H. Jack, and Robert M. Williamson were natives of Georgia and had been in Texas less than four years; all were lawyers educated in the southern states, and the maximum amount of land granted to any was one league. William H. Wharton was a native of Virginia but matured in Tennessee; he had legal training, and when he came to Texas in 1827, he married the only daughter of wealthy Jared E. Groce. The young couple lived in Tennessee for a few years; when they returned, they built a large home on land owned by her father near the mouth of the Brazos. Wharton received no headright and thus felt no obligation to Mexico. The man in this group with the most to lose by rebellion was John Austin, a distant cousin of the empresario and a native of Connecticut. He had filibustered with James Long in 1820 to help the Mexican republicans expel Spain from Mexico. Austin received two leagues and a *labor* of land, partially in recognition of his contributions toward Mexico's independence and also because he intended to develop commerce. While his colleagues ranged in age from twenty-two to twenty-six, John Austin was a mature thirty-one.[13]

While the tories in San Felipe had interests in land and position and supported the empresario's traditional policy of neutrality in the ongoing civil war, the conservatives on the lower Trinity, in the area that became Chambers

[12]Walter Prescott Webb, H. Bailey Carroll, and Eldon Stephen Branda (eds.), *The Handbook of Texas* (3 vols.; Austin, 1952, 1976), I, 81, 326, 344, 915, II, 52; Virginia H. Taylor, *The Spanish Archives of the General Land Office of Texas* (Austin, 1955), 155, 169, 170, 207, 255.

[13]Webb, Carroll, and Branda (eds.), *Handbook of Texas,* I, 80, 899, II, 91, 889–890; Taylor, *Spanish Archives,* 200, 248, 254, 255. Wharton is not listed because he had no headright.

County, tended to differ slightly. A few, like John A. Williams, who was a long-time resident and who exercised a moderate amount of political power as alcalde, resembled the San Felipe conservatives. The others, however, were largely apolitical. Many had roots in southern and western Louisiana, where their fathers had settled as early as the 1780s, coming from Natchez and the Carolinas. Some may have been related to former British loyalists or, at least, to those who had favored neither side during the American Revolution. When Louisiana became a part of the United States in 1803, some of these families began moving west to the Calcasieu River, the border of the Neutral Ground, which stretched west to the Sabine River.[14] The sanctuary had been created in 1806 in an attempt to prevent bloodshed between the forces of the United States and Spain, but it became a haven for those engaged in illicit trade in Spanish Texas. Seemingly, these men felt no particular loyalty to the United States and had little interest in politics.

These families supported themselves by hunting, trading, and cattle raising. By 1822 they had begun moving to the Trinity River, where they squatted on homesteads until 1831, when a Mexican land commissioner finally issued titles. Heads of families received one league of grazing land upon payment of modest fees to the surveyor, the commissioner, and for writing the deed, just as in Austin's colony. Living outside of Austin's jurisdiction, they looked to Nacogdoches for departmental guidance. In 1831, however, the federalist state-appointed land commissioner organized an ayuntamiento at Liberty in defiance of the centralist administration, which expected Bradburn to maintain sole governance of the area at Anahuac. In general, Bradburn was supported by those residents who did business with the fort, such as James Taylor White, who supplied cattle; Dr. Nicholas D. Labadie, the pharmacist and surgeon; and merchants who had flocked to the military town in 1831.[15]

James Taylor White was representative of former Louisianians in the lower Trinity neighborhood, such as Elisha H. R. Wallis, James McFadden, Joseph Dunman, Solomon Barrow, Benjamin Winfree, Silas Smith, and John M. Smith, in that he took no active role in politics, preferring instead to attend to his ranch. He was, however, loyal to Mexico, although, like Winfree, Wallis, and the Smiths, he had not received a land grant in 1831. Nevertheless, he appreciated

---

[14]Webb, Carroll, and Branda (eds.), *Handbook of Texas,* II, 913 (for J. A. Williams); Margaret Swett Henson, "History of Chambers County," manuscript of book in progress, based in part on genealogical files of pioneer families in Chambers County at Wallisville Heritage Park. Those living on the Calcasieu River before 1819 are listed in *American States Papers . . . ,* Class VIII: *The Public Lands* (8 vols.; Washington, D.C., 1790–1837), IV, 72–73; Gifford White, *James Taylor White of Virginia* (Austin, 1982), 3, 5, 18–21, 66, 71, 81, 86.

[15]Mary McMillan Osburn, "The Atascosita Census of 1826," *Texana,* I (Fall, 1963), 305–321; Henson, *Bradburn,* 55–56, 58–67.

the economic opportunities for ranching and cattle trading present in Mexican Texas, and also the benign neglect of the government relative to illegal cattle drives from the Trinity River to Louisiana.[16]

Labadie, merchant James Morgan, and a few others, however, broke with Bradburn in June, 1832, and joined the insurgents. In part, their renunciation stemmed from personal pique. Labadie was unable to collect his fees from the administration and blamed the colonel. Likewise, Morgan resented Bradburn's policy of harboring fugitive slaves from Louisiana. Slaveholders feared that such an example might endanger their bondsmen if the blacks discovered that Mexico allowed no slavery. While Austin's colony had been granted an exemption that permitted residents to hold black indentured servants, slavery, in theory, was prohibited in areas outside of his jurisdiction. Neither Labadie nor Morgan was eligible for a headright, and both sympathized with Travis and the others who had been arrested. They even joined in an unsuccessful plan to effect the prisoners' escape.[17]

In sum, toryism in 1832 depended on length of time in Texas, plus the desire to preserve economic, political, and social gains acquired with citizenship in Mexico. Near Anahuac, passive loyalty to Mexico and the nearby garrison was challenged by a few who violently objected to Bradburn's policies. The short time span in which the crisis developed, from May to June, allowed little time for introspective discussions about oaths of loyalty to Mexico, an issue that arose during the events of 1835–1836.

After the successful expulsion of centralist troops from Texas in 1832, Anglo-Texans held a convention in San Felipe, October 1–6, 1832, to consider how best to capitalize on their alignment with Santa Anna's forces. At least ten members of the convention had participated in the recent rebellion, but the more cautious element dominated the session. Stephen F. Austin was chosen over William Wharton as presiding officer by a vote of thirty-one to fifteen. The election marked the beginning of factions supporting and opposing the empresario, with the latter group headed by Wharton. The Whartonites deplored Austin's proclivity for appeasing the Mexican authorities and preferred instead to demand rights similar to those in the United States. Some threatened to

---

[16]Henson, "Chambers County"; original land-grant map of Chambers County (General Land Office, Austin). For comments on marketing cattle in Louisiana see *A Visit to Texas in 1831 . . .* (3rd ed.; Houston, 1975), 61, 76–80.

[17]Day Book of Dr. Nicholas D. Labadie, Feb., 1834, trying to collect his fees at Matamoros (San Jacinto Museum of History, Deer Park, Texas; cited hereafter as SJMH); Henson, *Bradburn,* 94–95; J. Lindsay to R. M. Williamson, May 18, 1832, Gulick et al. (eds.), *Papers of Mirabeau Buonaparte Lamar,* I, 90; Monroe Edwards to Robert M. Williamson, May 24, 1832, ibid., 91–92; Nicholas D. Labadie, "Narrative of the Anahuac; or, Opening Campaign of the Texas Revolution," Day (comp.), *Texas Almanac,* 130–131.

break ties with Mexico and ask for union with the United States if reform was not forthcoming.[18]

The convention asked for three major reforms: repeal of the ban on immigration from the United States, extension of the exemption from the tariff, and separate statehood for Texas. Since 1824, when the national government had joined Texas and Coahuila as a single state because of their low population, Texans, both native-born and Anglo, had chafed at the inconvenience of conducting business in Saltillo, the capital, more than 700 miles from the Brazos. Moreover, the state legislature was heavily weighted in representation from Coahuila, a ranching area that had little understanding of, or sympathy for, Anglo-Texan culture or agricultural needs. All Texans agreed that separate statehood could solve many of the current problems.[19]

While no native-born Texans had attended the convention, many in San Antonio agreed in principle with the demands. The convention, however, was an illegal gathering under Mexican law and the jefe condemned the proceedings, which should have been preceded by sending remonstrances through proper channels in order that the jefe could instigate the meeting. On December 19, 1832, the ayuntamiento at San Antonio issued the proper remonstrance and made plans to hold a meeting there in the spring.[20]

The members of the Wharton faction were impatient, and while the empresario was in San Antonio completing plans for a cautious program of reform, they called for a second meeting to be held at San Felipe in April, 1833. Adopting techniques of the American Revolution, the Anglo-Texans had already formed a central standing committee of vigilance and correspondence at San Felipe to funnel information to the various local committees organized the previous year. While Stephen F. Austin was named to the central committee, most members were more radical than the empresario and were able to counter his conservative course. When the central committee urged calling a second convention, only alcalde John A. Williams of Liberty, once a Bradburn supporter, refused to do so. The toryish alcalde denounced the Liberty delegation to the 1832 convention (which had included Patrick Jack and William Hardin, Travis supporters) as having "exercised a power that was never delegated to them" by endorsing the petitions adopted at the convention. He added that

---

[18]Barker, *Life of Stephen F. Austin*, 348–351, 386; H. P. N. Gammel (comp.), *The Laws of Texas, 1822–1897*... (10 vols.; Austin, 1898), I, 475; S. F. Austin to James F. Perry, Aug. 25, 1834, Eugene C. Barker (ed.), *The Austin Papers* (3 vols.; Vols. I, II, Washington, D.C., 1924–1928; Vol. III, Austin, 1927), II, 1,076.

[19]Barker, *Life of Stephen F. Austin*, 349–350; S. F. Austin to S. M. Williams, Dec. 6, 1832, Williams Papers (also in Barker [ed.], *Austin Papers*, II, 898).

[20]Barker, *Life of Stephen F. Austin*, 351–357; S. F. Austin to S. M. Williams, Dec. 6, 1832, Williams Papers (also in Barker [ed.], *Austin Papers*, II, 898).

"not five men" in his neighborhood favored the second call, which was not needed.[21]

The convention that met in San Felipe in April, 1833, elected Wharton president over the empresario, indicating a more radical membership. The delegates readopted the 1832 proposals and went one step further by drafting a state constitution to be submitted to the national government for approval. The document included many of the familiar privileges guaranteed by the United States Bill of Rights: trial by jury, habeas corpus, the right to bail, freedom of the press, and so forth. While Austin and two other men were named to take the documents to Mexico City, the latter two did not make the trip. The responsibility thus fell upon the empresario, although many believed that his commitment was not sincere and others feared that he was not aggressive enough to secure separate statehood.[22]

After several months in Mexico City with little success, Stephen F. Austin wrote a compromising letter to the San Antonio ayuntamiento urging that it take unilateral steps to organize a separate state government for Texas. Unable to suppress such a treasonable letter, the council forwarded it to state authorities, which ultimately led to Austin's arrest at Saltillo in January, 1834. He was returned to prison in the national capital, where he remained until the end of the year. Paroled but unable to leave Mexico City, Austin remained away from Texas until September, 1835. The Texans, once so confident that Santa Anna's victories and 1833 election to the presidency were in their favor, at last learned that the general was not necessarily their friend.[23]

Nevertheless, many of the requested reforms were approved in 1834, including the repeal of the restriction against immigration from the United States and the postponement of tariff collection until 1835. Texas, however, remained wedded to Coahuila, and while Austin was incarcerated, the Texans remained quiet in order not to put him in jeopardy.[24]

A schism in the governance of Coahuila in 1834, when centralist and federalist factions organized rival capitals, created an opportunity for reopening the question of separate statehood for Texas. Upon the recommendation of

---

[21]Circular, Call for a Convention, Nov. 20, 1832 (written even before Austin left, but apparently without his knowledge), Barker (ed.), *Austin Papers,* II, 891–893; John A. Williams to S. F. Austin, Dec. 18, 1832, ibid., 904–905, 906 (quotations); D. W. Anthony to S. F. Austin, Dec. 26, [1832] (saying Central Committee acted), ibid., 910–911; S. F. Austin to S. M. Williams, Jan. 12, 1834 (happened during his absence), Williams Papers (also in Barker [ed.], *Austin Papers,* II, 1,025); Barker, *Life of Stephen F. Austin,* 350–351 (for Central Committee); *Biographical Directory of the Texan Conventions and Congresses,* 1832–1845 (Austin, [1942]), 15–16.

[22]Barker, *Life of Stephen F. Austin,* 359–363; Edward, *History of Texas,* 196–205; S. F. Austin to J. F. Perry, Apr. 22, 1833, Barker (ed.), *Austin Papers,* II, 960; John P. Coles to Anthony Butler, July 15, 1833, ibid., 988; S. F. Austin to J. F. Perry, Aug. 25, 1834, ibid., 1,078.

[23]Barker, *Life of Stephen F. Austin,* 372–388.

[24]Ibid., 374, 381; Binkley, *Texas Revolution,* 18–19.

Thomas Jefferson Chambers, recently named superior judge for Texas, and the Texas legislators, a public gathering in San Antonio, sanctioned by the jefe, called for a meeting of Texans to be held in San Antonio to discuss the situation and what steps to take. Even before receiving the official announcement, Henry Smith, a Whartonite and the recently appointed political chief for the new department of the Brazos, a man extremely prejudiced against native Mexicans, issued his own call for action. The central committee at San Felipe, however, fearing for Austin's safety in Mexico City, opposed Smith and stressed the recent reforms as an indication of improving conditions. Ironically, the committee included six men who had attacked Anahuac and Velasco two years earlier: Wylie Martin, Robert Peebles, William Pettus, William B. Travis, William H. Jack, and Francis W. Johnson. These temporary defenders of the status quo managed to defeat the call for a convention with the aid of James F. Perry, the empresario's brother-in-law, and Thomas F. McKinney, a merchant and partner of Samuel May Williams. McKinney denounced Smith and the Whartonites as "Demagogues and scoundrels" and prayed that "the vengeance of heaven [,] earth and hell fall upon them. . . ."[25]

The calm imposed by the conservative San Felipe committee disintegrated in January, 1835, when, after a hiatus of almost three years, customs collectors returned to Texas. No troops were sent to the Brazos River, but forty soldiers reinforced the deputy collector at Anahuac.

Andrew Briscoe, a new merchant at Anahuac, objected to the tariff because he believed it was not uniformly collected at all Texas ports, and he organized protest meetings. In May the captain of a government schooner seized a vessel from New Orleans at Anahuac on the pretext of smuggling; he confiscated the cargo and arrested passengers without passports. The sudden enforcement of maritime laws long ignored drew protests from a Harrisburg resident, who said he was ready to retaliate and warned that "we are determined not to stand It." From San Felipe, Travis agreed that such "piracies & robberies. . . . will not be borne. Nothing has ever . . . arroused *[sic]* the indignation & resentment of the whole people."[26] The hot-headed defenders of Anglo-American rights had found an issue around which to rally.

---

[25]Barker, *Life of Stephen F. Austin,* 400–402; Henson, *Samuel May Williams,* 63; Thomas F. McKinney to J. F. Perry, Nov. 4, 1834, Barker (ed.), *Austin Papers,* III, 16 (quotations); J. F. Perry to S. F. Austin, Dec. 7, 1834, ibid., 33–35. The *Handbook of Texas* account of the schism in the article "Coahuila and Texas" is not altogether reliable. Webb, Carroll, and Branda (eds.), *Handbook of Texas,* I, 365.

[26]Andrew Briscoe to John K. Allen, Apr. 14, 1835, Andrew Briscoe Collection (SJMH); Anahuac resolutions, May 4, 1835, John H. Jenkins (ed.), *The Papers of the Texas Revolution,* 1835–1836 (10 vols.; Austin, 1973), I, 90–91; Anahuac petition, May 5, 1835, ibid., 92–93; Juan Calvi to Antonio Tenorio, May 7, 1835, ibid., 101; Robert Wilson to William B. Travis, May 13, 1835, ibid., 107, 108 (1st quotation); Travis to David G. Burnet, May 21, 1835, ibid., 12 (2nd quotation), 122.

The same captain captured McKinney's new ship at the mouth of the Brazos and treated the cargo and passengers in the same manner. While many residents complained about official behavior, the toryish spirit prevailed. Mrs. Mary Austin Holley, the empresario's cousin, was visiting on the Brazos and followed Austin's traditional philosophy. McKinney was at fault, she assumed, for bringing passengers without passports and bringing goods to the Brazos without the proper papers from the Mexican consul in New Orleans. "The Texas people are ungrateful to Mexico to whom they owe so much. Not satisfied with very lenient laws, they evade all law."[27]

Excitement over the tariff momentarily took a back seat when news arrived from the state capital that the legislature had made huge grants of unlocated land in Texas to various men, including Sam Williams and Frank Johnson, former alcalde of San Felipe and commander of the attack against Anahuac in 1832. Land speculating was held in low repute among those who recalled the outrages perpetrated in Kentucky, Tennessee, and Mississippi. When the participants in the "Monclova speculations" arrived in San Felipe and warned their neighbors that President Santa Anna was leading an army north into Zacatecas and perhaps Coahuila to punish dissidents, nobody believed them. Anglo-Texans who preferred the status quo said that the speculators cried "wolf, wolf . . . war, to arms, to arms!" only to protect their "Mammouth *[sic]* Speculations . . . They talk of nothing but declaring ourselves Independent, of granting letters of marque . . . and all such nonsense. . . ." This critical reaction notwithstanding, the information that the speculators brought was correct. Zacatecas, Coahuila's southern neighbor, fell to Santa Anna, punished because it had refused to comply with his order reducing the state militia to an ineffective force. Instead of invading Coahuila, the president sent his brother-in-law, commandant general of the northeastern states Martín Perfecto de Cós, to Saltillo. Coahuila y Texas had not reduced its militias either, and, furthermore, it had granted large tracts of vacant land to Williams and others as a means of raising men and funds to oppose Santa Anna. In panic, the governor, legislators, and speculators fled toward Texas in May, 1835.[28]

A military courier en route to Anahuac in June with messages promising reinforcements was intercepted in San Felipe. The fire-eaters of 1832

[27]Ammon Underwood, "Journal of Ammon Underwood, 1834–1838," ed. James K. Greer, *SHQ*, XXXII (Oct., 1928), 134; *Mary Austin Holley: The Texas Diary, 1835–1838*, ed. J. P. Bryan (Austin, 1965), 23; Tenorio to Domingo de Ugartechea, June 25, 1835, Jenkins (ed.), *Papers*, I, 167–168.

[28]Henson, *Samuel May Williams*, 65–76; John G. McNeel to J. F. Perry, [ca. June 22 (probably June 24), 1835], Jenkins (ed.), *Papers*, I, 160; James Kerr to Thomas J. Chambers, July 5, 1835 (2nd and 3rd quotations), Bexar Archives (microfilm, Eugene C. Barker Texas History Center, University of Texas, Austin).

immediately demanded action to prevent additional troops from reaching San Antonio and Anahuac, and also to rescue the governor, who was a prisoner in Monterrey. Public opinion, however, was not in favor of precipitate action. Nevertheless, Travis led about twenty-five volunteers to Anahuac, where they captured the small garrison on June 29, 1835.[29]

The public denounced Travis's unauthorized act, and the conservatives tried to repair the damage by treating the captives with great courtesy. Surprised at the response to his actions, Travis published a notice asking the public to suspend judgment until he had an opportunity to present his case, which he finally did in September. Tension eased when there was no immediate military reprisal from San Antonio, but rumors that reinforcements were on the way kept the Anglo-Texans uneasy. Alcalde John A. Williams, criticized as a tory since 1832, wrote from the Trinity that he was "sickened to the soul . . . Oh Sanity! Oh Ignorance! What have ye done. . . ."[30]

The peace party, favoring conciliation, wrote letters to the authorities trying to heal the breach. The majority, however, not knowing what to believe, withheld judgment and support from both sides. "The truth is," wrote Travis from San Felipe, "the people are much divided here. The peace-party . . . I believe, are the strongest, and make much the most noise. Unless we [the war party] could be united, had we not better be quiet, and settle down for a while?"[31]

The war party received unexpected support in July and August when Ugartechea, acting on orders from Cós, ordered the arrest of F. W. Johnson, R. M. Williamson, W. B. Travis, S. M. Williams, Mosely Baker, and Lorenzo de Zavala. Local officials made excuses for not arresting the proscribed men, saying that they were unable to locate them. The centralists wanted the six for political reasons. The Anglo-Texans had either participated in the land speculations, tampered with government dispatches, or attacked Anahuac, but Santa Anna particularly wanted to punish Zavala, who had deserted the administration and was critical of the president. An ardent federalist, Zavala had resigned

---

[29]Barker, *Life of Stephen F. Austin,* 407–408; Williamson address, June 22, 1835, Gulick et al. (eds.), *Papers of Mirabeau Buonaparte Lamar,* I, 212; J. G. McNeel to J. F. Perry [ca. June 22 (probably June 24), 1835], Jenkins (ed.), *Papers,* I, 160; Travis to Henry Smith, July 6, 1835, ibid., 209–210; San Felipe pledge, June 22, 1835, ibid., 161–162; account of capture of Anahuac, [June, 1835?], ibid., 294–296.

[30]Frank W. Johnson, *A History of Texas and Texans,* ed. Eugene C. Barker (5 vols.; Chicago, 1914), I, 209–210; Travis's card, July 18, 1835, Jenkins (ed.), *Papers,* I, 253; Travis to Public, Sept. 1, 1835, ibid., 385; James B. Miller to Ugartechea, July 16, 1835, ibid., 245; John A. Williams circular, July 3, 1835, ibid., 186–187 (quotation).

[31]William H. Jack et al. to Miller, July 3, 1835, Jenkins (ed.), *Papers,* I, 180–182; Miller to Jack et al., July 3, 1835, ibid., 182; Miller to Ugartechea, July 16, 1835, ibid., 247; Travis to Bowie, July 30, 1835, ibid., 289 (quotations), 290.

his post as the Mexican minister to France to return and oppose Santa Anna's new centralizing policies. The military demand that they arrest citizens offended the Anglo-Texans, of course, and, when coupled with renewed rumors that Cós was bringing more troops to Texas, prompted many to forsake the peace party. Local committees of correspondence endorsed a call for a consultation of representatives to discuss the recent developments. Travis wrote that the "tories and cowards" were working to suppress such a gathering, but he believed that they were losing influence and were "almost as bad off as they were in 1832. 'Heaven's hangman will lash the rascals round the world.'"[32]

Stephen F. Austin arrived home on September 1, 1835, and surprised the peace party by endorsing the call for a consultation. From San Felipe, the empresario reported that "there is the most perfect union in this part of the country." In a circular he warned the people that conciliatory measures with the military at San Antonio were hopeless and urged unity. "War is our only resource. There is no other remedy but to defend our rights, ourselves, and our country. . . ." A war-party member in Columbia put it even more strongly: "an honest difference of opinion can no longer exist. . . . he who . . . recommends a supine course, is a *traitor*. . . ."[33]

Before the Consultation could take place, a confrontation at Gonzales on October 2, 1835, plunged Texas into armed resistance. Volunteers, including the empresario and many delegates to the proposed conference, rushed to the Guadalupe River to help the citizens of Gonzales successfully defend their right to keep an old cannon previously loaned to them by the government for defense against the Indians.

The Consultation had a quorum on November 3. Four days later it voted to remain in the Mexican nation as a separate state, rather than declare independence, by a margin of two to one, a tally that indicated the conservatives were in charge. While still loyal to Mexico, the delegates vowed to oppose Santa Anna's troops as long as they remained on Texas soil and to unite with others (meaning the old federalists) in defense of the Mexican Constitution of 1824.

---

[32]Binkley, *Texas Revolution,* 52–67. For sequence of arrests, see Ugartechea to political chief, July 31, 1835 (Zavala), Jenkins (ed.), *Papers,* I, 293; Martín Perfecto de Cós to Ayuntamiento of Columbia, Aug. 1, 1835 (Travis), ibid., 296; Ugartechea to political chief, Aug. 4, 1835 (for six), ibid., 309; Cós to Ugartechea, Aug. 20, 1835, ibid., 359. For resistance to carrying out order, see Martin to Ugartechea, Aug. 5, 16, 25, 1835, ibid., 311, 348, 370; Travis to John W. Moore, Aug. 31, 1835, ibid., 382 (quotations).

See Raymond Estep, "Zavala and the Texas Revolution," *SHQ,* LVII (Jan., 1954), 322–335, for details about Zavala.

[33]S. F. Austin to public, Sept. 8, 1835, Jenkins (ed.), *Papers,* I, 423–427; S. F. Austin to J. F. Perry, Sept. 14, 1835, ibid., 444 (1st quotation), 445; circular from committee of Austin, Sept. 18, 1835, ibid., 455, 456 (2nd quotation); Branch T. Archer to people . . . of Columbia, [ca. Sept. 20, 1835], ibid., 467 (3rd quotation), 468–469.

In other words, they endorsed resumption of the civil war between federalism and centralism. The members adopted measures for supplying the volunteer army camped at Gonzales and for recruiting men and funds in the United States, issued letters of marque, and created a provisional state government for Texas. They selected a general council composed of one member from each municipality, most of whom favored cooperation with the federalists, and, somewhat illogically, chose Henry Smith, a war-party member favoring independence, for governor.[34] The subsequent bickering between the governor and council hindered the pursuit of their common goal of defeating Santa Anna and also alienated many Texans from the provisional government.

Public opinion remained divided between the war and peace party strategies during the winter months of 1835 and 1836. One of the new recruits from Georgia wrote to his father describing the situation in Texas: "the wild malignant demon of party spirit has appeared here in its most virulent form." He described the two parties: one (the peace party) favored reestablishing the Constitution of 1824, with Texas as a separate state with its own laws; and the other (the war party) wanted secession and independence. The secessionists, the largest faction, were divided into three groups: the first wanted annexation to the United States; the second wanted to sell Texas to the United States and become a territory, thus avoiding the high expenses of statehood until there was a larger population; and the third favored a separate and independent nation.[35]

The peace party gradually lost influence between November, 1835, and February, 1836, when its opponents began calling it the Mexican party or the Mexican tory party. McKinney, for example, was appalled at the number of articles favoring independence that appeared in the Brazoria newspaper, the only publication in Texas. Preferring cooperation with the Mexican federalists, he wrote an article in opposition to the war party. Although the editor agreed to run it, John Wharton, who controlled the paper, suppressed publication. McKinney complained to Stephen F. Austin on December 17, 1835, "I am truly surprised that public opinion should be thus forestalled" by "a wild unthinking faction."[36]

Stephen F. Austin deplored some unprincipled men in the war party who supported the movement for independence solely for personal aggrandizement. Theirs was a devious plot, he said, to injure old settlers by demanding independence. Nationhood would require a large expensive standing army, the

---

[34]Declaration of the People of Texas, Nov. 7, 1835, ibid., II, 346–348; John Henry Brown, *Life and Times of Henry Smith, the First American Governor of Texas* (Dallas, 1897), 79.

[35]John Sowers Brooks to father, Jan. 20, 1836, Jenkins (ed.), *Papers,* IV, 82, 83 (quotation), 84–85.

[36]McKinney to S. F. Austin, Dec. 17, 1835, ibid., III, 228, 229 (quotations).

cost of which would fall on the pioneer men of property. Austin had been selected by the council to accompany William H. Wharton and Branch T. Archer, both ardent advocates of independence, on a mission to the United States to raise money for Texas's struggle. A week in the company of these two in January, 1836, changed Austin's mind, particularly after he heard that Mexican federalists might join Santa Anna to quash any revolt in Texas. Writing to his cousin, Henry Austin, and General Sam Houston from New Orleans in January, 1836, the empresario said that he now believed independence was the only course. McKinney, still bound to the federalists by ties of friendship, was furious upon receiving word of Austin's reversal. He scribbled a message to the empresario saying, "you can not be any thing else but an injury to your country. . . . I do not intend to say you are dishonest . . . but you are from your nature useless in any thing like a public capacity. . . ." McKinney, still clinging to a conservative approach, wrongly predicted that Texans would not accept the new course.[37]

Thomas Jefferson Chambers was quicker to sense the change in public opinion. On January 1, 1836, he asked for and received a commission from the general council as a major general to raise a division of volunteers in the United States. He had been, he said, opposed to "hostile measures" until after the attack on Gonzales, but had been unable to join the fray until the present. According to his memoirs, he had been organizing courts in San Antonio and San Felipe and trying to preserve his sinecure.[38]

The lower Trinity neighborhood again earned the reputation as the center of toryism in 1835–1836. As early as August 15, 1835, a public meeting at Nacogdoches censured John A. Williams for "maligning" his fellow citizens in a private letter to the general government. In October, the Liberty delegates to the Consultation urged the permanent council to arrest him, a step they hoped would cool the ardor of other tories. Williams, they said, had organized a band of fifty-eight tories in September to oppose the raising of volunteers, who were to meet on the Colorado River to prevent the reinforcing of San Antonio; moreover, he had a boat that Santa Anna could use once the president reached Galveston Bay. The council, however, declined to act. Saying it lacked authority, it forwarded the request to Stephen F. Austin as commander-in-chief of the volunteers; he refused to accept jurisdiction and characteristically urged caution. On October 28, the council published the names of three men who were aiding the enemy and damaging the Texan cause: Thomas Jefferson Chambers,

[37]S. F. Austin to F. W. Johnson et al., Dec. 22, 1835, ibid., III, 282–283; S. F. Austin to Henry Austin, Jan. 7, 1836, ibid., 429–430; S. F. Austin to Sam Houston, Jan. 7, 1836, ibid., 432–433; T. F. McKinney to S. F. Austin, Feb. 22, 1836, ibid., IV, 405, 406 (quotation).

[38]Chambers memorial to General Council, Jan. 1, 1836, ibid., Ill, 399 (quotation), 400; Council to Chambers, Jan. 7, 1836, ibid., 451–452; Chambers, *Life of Gen. T.J. Chambers,* 38–39.

John A. Williams, and Don Carlos Barrett. Chambers, as has been mentioned, and Barrett managed to salvage their reputations, but Williams finally fled to Louisiana, where he was living in 1837. The following year he sold his headright on the Trinity, and in 1840 he died near Beaumont.[39]

David G. Burnet practiced law in Liberty and for awhile had close ties with the local tories. His change from tory to patriot illustrates pragmatic adaptation. Before settling on the San Jacinto in 1831, Burnet, a native of New Jersey, had aided Spanish republicans in Venezuela and studied law in Ohio. The generous grants to empresarios offered by Coahuila y Texas attracted him to Saltillo in 1827, where he received a contract encompassing an area west of Nacogdoches above the old Spanish road. Unable to attract investment capital to develop his grant, he contacted two other unsuccessful empresarios whose grants adjoined his on the south, Lorenzo de Zavala and Joseph Vehlein, a resident of Mexico City. The trio sold their interests in the large area stretching from Galveston Bay to the Sabine River and northwest to Nacogdoches to a group of New York and Boston investors in October, 1830, a step illegal under Mexican law. Using the proceeds, Burnet married, bought steam mill machinery, and immigrated to the San Jacinto River, where he bought land from Nathaniel Lynch for his mill and home.[40]

Without a headright or an empresario grant, Burnet remained loyal to Mexico and was slow to oppose centralism. He took no part in the events at Anahuac in 1832, but represented Liberty in the 1833 convention. His neighbors believed him to be an educated man with influence in both the United States and Mexico. In 1834 the state named him chief justice for the Department of the Brazos, which aligned him with others having a vested interest in preserving the status quo. But in August, 1835, when he discovered that Santa Anna was centralizing the government by reducing state power and intended to use the army to enforce his changes, Burnet drafted a cautious resolution critical of the president for a meeting at Lynchburg. Strongly opposed to military rule, Burnet argued that citizens had a right to reject the new system in favor of the former republic, and he expected that old-time republicans would not allow despotism to win. Moderate in tone, the San Jacinto

---

[39]Nacogdoches resolutions, [Aug. 15, 1835], Jenkins (ed.), *Papers,* I, 345 (quotation); Richard R. Royall to S. F. Austin, Oct. 16, 1835, ibid., II, 140–141; Royall to S. F. Austin, Oct. 19, 1835, ibid., 286; S. F. Austin to Council (confidential), Oct. 24, 1835, ibid., 207–208; Resolution of Permanent Council, Oct. 28, 1835, ibid., 252; Royall to Chambers, Oct. 31, 1835, ibid., 281. Contrary to the statement in Webb, Carroll, and Branda (eds.), *Handbook of Texas,* II, 913, Williams did not disappear from Texas history. See citations to deed records in Liberty and Jefferson counties in Miriam Partlow, *Liberty, Liberty County and the Atascosito District* (Austin, 1974), 94.

[40]Dorothy Louise Fields, "David Gouverneur Burnet," *SHQ,* XLIX (Oct., 1945), 215–220; Virginia Henderson, "Minor Empresario Contracts for the Colonization of Texas," *SHQ,* XXXI (Apr., 1928), 302–305.

Resolutions also endorsed the call for the Consultation and named Burnet and one other to represent Lynchburg at the meeting. Burnet took copies to the political chief on the Brazos and to the editor of the newspaper at Brazoria. The resolutions were not published, and later Burnet offered two explanations: one, the paper was already full, and two, the editor demanded prepayment. During the vicious 1841 presidential campaign, however, Sam Houston accused Burnet of pocketing the document when he learned that Santa Anna was considering him as a candidate for political chief under the new regime. Some residents of Lynchburg, Houston said, had suggested hanging Burnet for treason, but cooler heads had saved him. The unfavorable indictment is not unfounded, judging by subsequent actions of his neighbors, and particularly the lack of pro-Burnet votes in elections between 1836 and 1841.[41]

Burnet later claimed illness prevented him from attending the Consultation, but it appears that neither Liberty nor Harrisburg municipalities elected him as representative, overriding the early Lynchburg endorsement. His conservative philosophy was more popular on the Trinity River than on the San Jacinto, but when he told prospective constituents at Liberty that he would not be bound by any instructions they might want to impose, they did not endorse him. Burnet attended the organizational meeting of the Liberty committee of safety on October 6, which named Joseph Bryan to represent the town on the permanent council at San Felipe. By the end of the month and after the confrontation at Gonzales, Burnet and the other members of the Liberty committee urged "worthy and patriotic citizens" to relinquish the "sanctity of their oath of allegiance" to Mexico because the constitution that they had sworn to uphold was destroyed. Oath-takers in the nineteenth century took their vows seriously and felt that any violation of their swearing loyalty reflected upon their personal honor. Zavala had argued the point in a written address to the Lynchburg meeting in August, noting that he had helped form the constitution but now felt no disgrace in opposing the centralist faction. Burnet wrote, "If Santa Ana *[sic]* and his myrmidons be the government you desire, then avow yourselves the degraded minions of . . . despotism." The committee continued its appeal by saying that "those who are not for us are against us." Evidently the

---

[41]Fields, "Burnet," 221; Truth [Sam Houston] to Burnet, Aug. 18, 1841, *The Houstonian,* Aug. 18, 1841, in Amelia W. Williams and Eugene C. Barker (eds.), *The Writings of Sam Houston,* 1813–1863 (8 vols.; Austin, 1970), I, 382, 383; San Jacinto resolutions, Aug. 8, 1835, Jenkins (ed.), *Papers,* I, 317–321; Burnet to Martin, Aug. 14, 1835, ibid., 336. Burnet refused to return to his home because of the enmity of Lynch and William Scott. Andrew M. Clopper to Nicholas Clopper, Dec. 18, 1836, Edward N. Clopper, *An American Family* (Cincinnati, 1950), 270 (also in "The Clopper Correspondence, 1834–1838," *Quarterly of the Texas State Historical Association,* XIII [Oct., 1909], 139). Houston defeated Burnet at Lynchburg by 115 to 17, and at nearby Cedar Bayou by 29 to 1. Harris County voter records, 1841, Election Returns, Secretary of State Records (Archives Division, Texas State Library, Austin).

immediate vicinity of Liberty (but not necessarily the rest of the municipality) heeded the warning, because on November 9 the committee confidently announced that everyone was in agreement. But like conservatives on the Brazos, the members advised against a "premature declaration of independence" that might alienate friends in the United States.[42]

The general council called for a convention to meet on March 1, passing it over the governor's veto. Voting for candidates committed to one course or the other was lively, but when the delegates assembled at Washington-on-the-Brazos the peace party was in the minority, and they accepted the inevitable. On March 2 the delegates, including federalist Zavala, unanimously adopted and signed the Declaration of Independence.[43]

In spite of his moderation, Burnet was not chosen a delegate to the convention. Nevertheless, he attended the session. Carrying a petition for clemency for two clients (tory John M. Smith and his son, who had killed Smith's son-in-law) and also armed with a remonstrance against independence written by himself and signed by a number of lower Trinity tories, he hurried to Washington-on-the-Brazos in March. Arriving after the approval of the Declaration of Independence, Burnet buried the document, which argued that Texas had too few people and too few resources to maintain itself as an independent nation. Like Poland, it said, Texas could expect no sympathy from other nations.[44] The closing paragraph summed up tory sentiment in what would become Chambers County, and predicted tory action in April, 1836:

> Fellow-citizens . . . especially members of the Convention—the select of the land—we leave the subject with you. We have discharged a solemn duty, and if Texas is doomed to destruction, our hands are clean.[45]

Burnet, the document suppressed, began campaigning for the ad interim presidency.

---

[42]Burnet to William Hardin, Sept. 24, 1835, Hardin Papers (Sam Houston Regional Library and Research Center, Liberty); Liberty Meeting, Oct. 6, 1835, Jenkins (ed.), *Papers,* II, 59–60; Tanner et al to Bryan, Oct. 24, 1835, ibid., 212 (1st quotation), 213 (2nd–4th quotations); Lorenzo de Zavala to colonists, [ca. Aug. 7, 1835], ibid., I, 313–315; Liberty Committee to Archer, Nov. 9, 1835, ibid., II, 366, 367 (5th quotation). Fields, "Burnet," 222, says that Burnet was ill, but the citation does not prove the fact. Burnet to Houston, Nov. 26, 1835, merely says he regrets not being there. Ibid., I, 511.

[43]William Fairfax Gray, *From Virginia to Texas, 1835: Diary of Col. Wm. F. Gray . . .* (1909; reprint, Houston, 1965), 89–91; T. H. Borden to voters, Jan. 19, 1836, Jenkins (ed.), *Papers,* IV, 70–71; Journals of the Convention . . . , Mar. 2, 1836, ibid., IX, 303.

[44]For details of the John M. Smith case see Partlow, *Liberty,* 117–122; Truth [Houston] to Burnet, Aug. 18, 1841, Williams and Barker (eds.), *Writings of Sam Houston,* II, 285–286; copy of document (from Burnet's papers) in *Life and Times of David G. Burnet, First President of the Republic of Texas* (Galveston, 1871), 9–12, and in Day (comp.), *Texas Almanac,* 721–724.

[45]Day (comp.), *Texas Almanac,* 723.

Most former advocates of the peace party on the Brazos River changed their course after learning about the Declaration of Independence and the March 6 defeat at the Alamo. McKinney, for example, abandoned his opposition to independence and devoted his energy and capital to supplying the Texas army, although he may have retained private doubts about the wisdom of this course. While most of the families from the Brazos fled eastward before Santa Anna's army in March and April in what was called the Runaway Scrape, one family at Fort Bend, named Johnson, was rumored to be joining the Mexicans, and General Houston ordered an investigation and arrest. General José de Urrea had sent agents ahead as he swept along the coast from Victoria to Columbia to assure Texans that loyalist property would be respected, and he claimed that "many English, American, and German" colonists greeted him at Brazoria. Texan accounts, however, indicated that most residents fled, and Urrea's claim seems an exaggeration.[46]

While tories on the Brazos River had time to change direction and salvage their reputations during the Runaway Scrape, those east of the San Jacinto River were branded as tories after April 21. When Santa Anna occupied James Morgan's house near present-day LaPorte on April 17, he sent word around the neighborhood by one of Morgan's slaves that persons not in arms and their property were safe. Morgan was in command at Galveston Island, aided by a number of local men. All of the families on both sides of the San Jacinto had been evacuated, except for those of Dr. Harvey Whiting and Benjamin Page on Goose Creek. Page was elderly, and Whiting claimed that family responsibilities and poverty prevented him from leaving. Two single men remained near Morgan's place on the west bank; James Routh was in poor health but vacated his cabin for Colonel Juan Almonte, while Fabricus Reynolds sought favor with Santa Anna by taking him a tub of fresh butter. Always suspicious, the president made Reynolds eat the gift, suspecting that it had been poisoned.[47]

Upon learning that loyalists would be respected, Whiting and Page crossed the San Jacinto in Whiting's broad-beamed boat to visit Santa Anna on April 18 or 19. The pair had a friendly interview with the president, witnessed by two Texans captured by the Mexicans, printer Isaac D. Boyce and courier Andrew M. Clopper. Burnet's enemies believed that Whiting and Burnet had

[46]Henson, *Samuel May Williams,* 81; José Urrea, *Diary of the Military Operations . . .*, in Carlos E. Castañeda (trans.), *The Mexican Side of the Texas Revolution . . .* (Dallas, 1928), 241 (quotation), 242; Warren D. C. Hall to Rusk, Mar. 30, 1836, Jenkins (ed.), *Papers,* V, 242; J. M. Allen to Houston, Mar. 31, 1836, ibid., 245; Houston to Wylie Martin, Apr. 2, 1836, ibid., 294; Collinsworth to Convention, [Mar. 16, 1836], ibid., 88–89.

[47]Harvey Whiting to James Morgan, May 3, 1836, James Morgan Papers (Rosenberg Library, Galveston) (also in Jenkins [ed.], *Papers,* VI, 157); *Board of Land Commissioners, Harrisburg District,* 1838, Class 1 ([Anahuac], 1980), 63–64; Robert P. Boyce, Memoir (Houston Metropolitan Research Center Archives, Houston Public Library; cited hereafter as HMRC).

exchanged powers of attorney before Burnet left home and thus could protect each other's property, no matter which side was victorious. Whiting said later that the Mexicans confiscated his boat in order to transport their army across the San Jacinto River because all the boats had been removed from Lynch's ferry. Returning home in a skiff provided by Almonte, Whiting and Page took a message to the tories on the Trinity to meet Santa Anna at Lynch's place at noon on April 20 to guide him toward the Sabine River. Whiting always denied this accusation of his neighbors, but he was the only one who could have summoned the horsemen who appeared at the ferry from the east on April 20.[48]

Sam Houston's army had occupied the west bank at the ferry landing earlier that morning and saw Whiting's vessel approaching, loaded with supplies seized from Morgan's warehouse. When the Texans fired, the Mexican soldiers jumped overboard, leaving Boyce, the printer, who called for assistance. Thus supplies originally destined for the Texas army were recovered. The twenty tories on the east bank noted the adverse turn of affairs, wheeled around, and rode off the rise, which ever since has been known as Tory Hill. The Texans, believing the horsemen to be fresh recruits, were astonished to see them ride eastward. Although no proof exists, the group must have included some of the Barrows, the Winfrees, and various members of the other families labeled tory since 1832.[49]

According to Lieutenant David L. Kokernot, a search of Santa Anna's baggage after the battle revealed a list of maybe 150 Trinity loyalists, probably supplied by John A. Williams, but the incriminating evidence has disappeared. If Williams was indeed responsible for the list, the figure was perhaps closer to 58, the number of tories Williams had been accused of organizing in September, 1835.[50]

Few if any tories answered the militia call on March 6. Some pleaded illness; others hired substitutes. On March 21, William Hardin, the new alcalde for Liberty, writing from Beaumont, endeavored to arouse the tories to duty:

---

[48]Whiting to Morgan, May 3, 1836, Morgan Papers; Testimony of A. M. Clopper and Isaac D. Boyce in *Board of Land Commissioners, Harrisburg,* 15, 65; Truth [Houston] to Burnet, Aug. 18, 1841, Williams and Barker (eds.), *Writings of Sam Houston,* II, 284.

[49]N. D. Labadie, "San Jacinto Campaign," Day (comp.), *Texas Almanac,* 157; I. D. Boyce Testimony, *Board of Land Commissioners, Harrisburg,* 65. Kokernot says there were twenty to thirty tories. Gardien, "Kokernot and His Tory," 276. The question of who appeared on Tory Hill is still a sensitive issue in the neighborhood. Some descendants of Solomon Barrow say oral tradition has it that he was there, but others claim he was not. Mrs. Loraine Silva and Mrs. Villamae Williams to M. S. H., interviews. Kent Gardien told the author that his first inquiries about tories in Chambers County met with hostility, although later informants proved hospitable and helpful.

[50]D. L. Kokernot's reminiscences, Gonzales *Inquirer,* 1878, in Gardien, "Kokernot and His Tory," 269–272; Z. N. Morrell, *Flowers and Fruit in the Wilderness. . .* (St. Louis, 1872), 203; Rusk to Morgan, Mar. 29, 1836, Jenkins (ed.), *Papers,* V, 236; Morgan to Rusk, Apr. 8, 1836, ibid., 384–385; Whiting to Morgan, May 3, 1836, ibid., VI, 156–158; Burnet to Morgan, May 16, 1836, ibid., 308–309.

"we must lay all business aside until the enemy is driven from our borders." It was better, he said, to let business suffer than to sacrifice property to the enemy. The only business in the area was cattle raising, but ranchers had already decided to move their herds east if either army approached. Taylor White conducted an annual roundup in March or April and left his ranch with 500 head of cattle before April 18. The herd, reduced to 330 by accident and theft, was seen by one of the fugitives from Texas well east of Calcasieu (Lake Charles, Louisiana) on April 27. Prices were higher in Opelousas and New Orleans than in Texas; two years earlier, yearlings had sold in New Orleans for twelve dollars or more, while the Texas price was about five dollars. There was no point, therefore, in risking seizure by one army or the other, when the owners would receive only vouchers that might or might not be redeemable later.[51]

Tories east of the San Jacinto River became the target for revenge by some of their neighbors. Lieutenant David L. Kokernot, armed with an order purportedly signed by General Houston but not in his hand, seized 300 head of livestock east of the San Jacinto River. The order, dated April 30, specified rounding up all the horses and cattle east of the river except those belonging to "honest citizens." Kokernot noted that for his trouble he got "a hell of a cursing." In June, apparently after orders to take the animals back, Burnet warned Kokernot that as long as he was unable to return the livestock to the Liberty neighborhood, he must advertise them so that each man could recover his property.[52]

In May an over-zealous English officer serving in the Texas army seized James Taylor White, Martin and Reuben Dunman (White's nephews), Amos Barbour and his son, A. J. Winfree, and James McGaffey as tories, probably for refusing to give up their cattle, and delivered the men to James Morgan on Galveston Island. As soon as President Burnet learned about the arrests, he instructed the secretary of war to release them.[53]

---

[51]Hardin to McGaffee and others, Mar. 21, 1836, Hardin Papers; Gray, *Diary,* 165, 171; David Woodman, Jr., *Guide to Texas Emigrants* (1835; reprint, Waco, Tex., 1974), 63 (for prices). Meredith Duncan to Burnet, May 1, 1836, said he was ill. Jenkins (ed.), *Papers,* VI, 140–141. Reuben Barrow hired Patrick Green as a substitute for three months in exchange for eight gentle cows. Contract, June 21, 1836, Morgan Papers. Whiting sent his future son-in-law, Gilbert Brooks, to Galveston Island in April, 1836. Whiting to Morgan, Apr. 8, 1836, ibid.

[52]There are two orders: Houston to David L. Kokernot, Apr. 29, 1836 (signature not in hand of Houston), Hardin Papers; Houston to Kokernot, Apr. 30, 1836, Gardien, "Kokernot and His Tory," 272 (see page 287, note 13, for provenance of document [also in Jenkins (ed.), *Papers,* VI, 129 (2nd quotation), citing Gardien as source]; Burnet to Kokernot, June 9, 1836, Jenkins (ed.), *Papers,* VII, 88. The presence of loyalist boatmen living on Bolivar Peninsula inspired its nickname of Tory Land. Gail Borden's map labeling Bolivar Peninsula "Toryland," Customs House Record Book for Port of Galveston (1837–1844), 24 (Rosenberg Library, Galveston).

[53]E. H. Stanley to Morgan, May 15, 1836, Jenkins (ed.), *Papers,* VI, 299; Burnet to Morgan, May 16, 1836, ibid., 308–309.

Some of those reluctant to become involved produced creditable excuses. Meredith Duncan, whose father was a good friend of Burnet, wrote the president on May 1 that "a great enmity" existed against him in the army because he was too ill to answer draft calls coming from Lynchburg and Liberty. Because he lived between the two places, both had called him to military duty. He said that he had offered twenty dollars per month to anyone who would serve in his place but could find nobody. Duncan was willing to do anything for Texas and, if need be, would send all of his cattle, except for a few milk cows. He had advised his brother to join the army (he enlisted for three months in July), and he asked Burnet to use his influence to aid both his brother and himself. Duncan hoped that he would not be "soon caught in a like scrape again."[54]

Whiting wrote to James Morgan on May 3 in a similar vein. "The almost Meraculous *[sic]* turn of events which [had] recently taken place" had prompted many charges against Whiting, inspired by desire to "revenge an old grudge." He explained his actions between April 15 and 19, as well as the seizing of his boat, but now, he complained, the "most exaggerate *[sic]* tales are told" that he had turned tory. The doctor expected Kokernot to punish him because the lieutenant believed Whiting had plundered his house. Whiting had endeavored to cancel ill will by furnishing goods and caring for some of the sick soldiers, but, he complained, he had received neither money nor receipts for his contributions.[55]

Dr. Labadie remarked that after April 22 a number of new faces appeared at the battleground, when some tories belatedly decided to join the fray. Military records, recreated after a fire consumed them in 1855, show that some former tories joined the army for their three months' duty on May 7 and another group on July 7. Emotions about service before and after April 21, 1836, continued to cause friction as late as the 1870s, when the veterans began holding reunions and pensions became available. At least two Chambers County women who applied for widows' pensions offered no proof of their husband's service, only substantiation from kinsmen; nevertheless, in spite of adverse and contradictory testimony, the county court approved the claims.[56]

---

[54]Meredith Duncan to Burnet, May 1, 1836, ibid., VI, 140 (1st quotation), 141 (2nd quotation).

[55]Whiting to Morgan, May 3, 1836 (quotations), Morgan Papers (also in Jenkins [ed.], *Papers,* VI, 156–158); Whiting to Morgan, July 19, 1836, Morgan Papers. Whiting's claims for 1836–1837 include shoes, boots, and beef. Audited Accounts, Republic Payments for Service (Archives Division, Texas State Library, Austin).

[56]Labadie, "San Jacinto," 166; Thomas Lloyd Miller, *Bounty and Donation Land Grants of Texas, 1835–1888* (Austin, 1967), 92 (Reuben Barrow), 113 (William Bloodgood), 238 (W. B. Duncan), 696 (A. B. J. Winfree); petition of Elizabeth Barrow, widow of Solomon, February session, Chambers County Court (courthouse records do not exist), Audited Military Claims, Pensions to Veterans (Archives Division, Texas State Library, Austin); Gardien, "Kokernot and His Tory," 293 (for Mary Winfree, widow of Jacob F.). An undated fragment of a clipping from the Houston *Age* offers tantalizing evidence. Robert P. Boyce scrapbook (HMRC). No extant copies of this paper have been located.

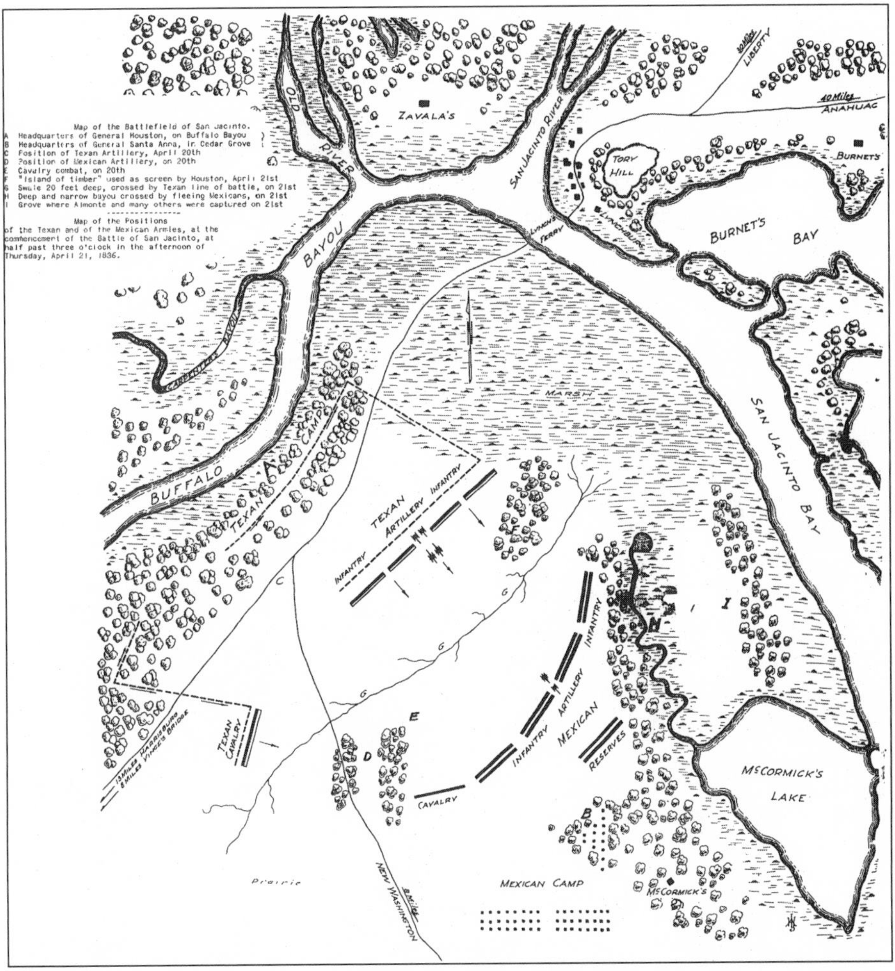


Map of the San Jacinto battlefield featuring Tory Hill, from Andrew Jackson Houston's *Texas Independence* (1938). *Courtesy Eugene C. Barker Texas History Center, University of Texas, Austin.*

As in 1832, the tories in 1835 and 1836 refrained from joining their more radical contemporaries because of perceived self-interest. Loyalty to Mexico was a strong factor, and the rebels struggled to convince the old-timers that their oaths to uphold the 1824 constitution were no longer binding because of Santa Anna's dictatorial course. While conservatives along the Brazos River reacted pragmatically, and perhaps resignedly, to the Declaration of Independence and the threat of the advancing Mexican army, tories east of the San Jacinto felt less immediate pressure and resisted joining the insurgents. While men like Thomas F. McKinney, Thomas Jefferson Chambers, and David G. Burnet could forsake their previous loyalties and change with the tide of public opinion, the cautious ranchers along the lower Trinity River could not. Historians can only sift what few historical facts remain and draw conclusions about the feelings and motives of these tories. Preservation of economic gains in land and livestock garnered under Mexican rule apparently outweighed appeals to defend political rights.

## Appendix 1

The following well-known men favored the peace party between June, 1835, and February, 1836. Some were willing to oppose Santa Anna, but most preferred to aid the federalist party and to remain within the Mexican Republic.

Stephen F. Austin
Don Carlos Barrett
David G. Burnet
Thomas Jefferson Chambers
James Kerr
Thomas F. McKinney
Pleasant D. and Sterling McNeel (brothers)
James F. Perry (Austin's brother-in-law)
James W. Robinson
Samuel May Williams
Lorenzo de Zavala

## Appendix 2

William B. Scates, a carpenter in Anahuac, recalled that twenty-nine of fifty-one residents in the area refused to join the attack against Juan Davis Bradburn in June, 1832. The following men lived in the vicinity and may have been tories, judging from their later activities and family tradition. Some can be documented as such. (W. B. Scates, "Early History of Anahuac," James M. Day [comp.], *The Texas Almanac, 1857–1873: A Compendium of Texas History* [Waco, Tex., 1967], 681–691.)

1. Samuel Barber
2. Ben Barrow
3. Reuben Barrow
4. Solomon Barrow
5. James Campbell

6. Moses Alfred Carroll (ward of John M. Smith, soon to be his son-in-law)
7. Martin Dunman (nephew of James Taylor White)
8. Reuben Dunman (nephew of James Taylor White)
9. Meredith Duncan
10. William Duncan[a]
11. Burrell Franks
12. Benedict or Clement Haden[b]
13. Joseph Lawrence
14. James McFadden
15. Andrew Roach
16. John M. Smith[c]
17. Silas Smith[d]
18. William M. Smith (son of John M. Smith)
19. Charles N. Tilton
20. Elisha H. R. Wallis
21. Charles C. P. Welch
22. James Taylor White[d]
23. John A. Williams[e]
24. A. J. Winfree
25. Jacob F. Winfree[f]
26. Robert Wiseman

---

SOURCES:

[a] Walter Prescott Webb, H. Bailey Carroll, and Eldon Stephen Branda (eds.), *The Handbook of Texas* (3 vols.; Austin, 1952, 1976), I, 525.

[b] The brothers Benedict and Clement Haden are listed in Nicholas D. Labadie's Account Book for 1833–1840 (San Jacinto Museum of History, Deer Park, Texas). Francis W. Johnson refers to a Haden as a "creature of Jno. M. Smith." Francis W. Johnson, "Further Account by Col. F. W. Johnson of the First Breaking Out of Hostilities," James M. Day (comp.), *The Texas Almanac, 1857–1873: A Compendium of Texas History* (Waco, Tex., 1967), 138. See also W. B. Scates, "Early History of Anahuac," ibid., 686–687.

[c] Johnson, "Further Account," 138; Peter J. Menard to Richard R. Royall, Oct. 19, 1835, John H. Jenkins (ed.), *The Papers of the Texas Revolution, 1835–1836* (10 vols.; Austin, 1973), II, 285.

[d] N. D. Labadie, "Narrative of the Anahuac; or, Opening Campaign of the Texas Revolution," Day (comp.), *Texas Almanac*, 129.

[e] Johnson, "Further Account," 139.

[f] Kent Gardien, "Kokernot and His Tory," *Texana*, VIII, No. 3 (1970), 280–281.

## Appendix 3

The following men lived east of the San Jacinto River in 1836 and were accused or suspected of being tories. The loyalty of some was questioned simply because they did not want to give up cattle to the Texas army and herded their animals instead to Louisiana. The Barbers, Barrows, Dunmans, Whites, Winfrees, and Wallis were related to each other by either blood or marriage (signified by an asterisk).

*Amos Barber (son of Samuel Barber)[a]
*Samuel Barber[b]
*Benjamin Barrow[b]
*Reuben Barrow[b]
*Solomon Barrow[b]
Meredith Duncan[c]
*Martin Dunman (cousin of Reuben Dunman)[a]
*Reuben Dunman[a]
Burrell Franks, or his sons[d]
Joseph Lawrence[e]
James McGaffie[a]
Benjamin Page[f]
John M. Smith[g]
Silas Smith[h]
William M. Smith (son of John M. Smith)[g]
*Elisha H. R. Wallis[b]
*James Taylor White[a]
*John White (son of James Taylor White)[i]
Harvey Whiting[f]
John A. Williams[g]
*A. J. Winfree[a]
*Jacob F. Winfree[j]

SOURCES:

[a] E. F. Stanley to James Morgan, May 15, 1836, John H. Jenkins (ed.), *The Papers of the Texas Revolution,* 1835–1836 (10 vols.; Austin, 1973), VI, 299.

[b] John Middleton (descendant of Elisha H. R. Wallis) to M. S. H., 1983, interview; Barrow folder (Wallisville Heritage Park). Family tradition has it that Wallis joined the Texas army in May or June, 1836, but no record of his service has been found.

[c] Meredith Duncan to David G. Burnet, May 1, 1836, Jenkins (ed.), *Papers,* VI, 140–141.

[d] Thomas J. Rusk to Morgan, ibid., V, 236.

[e] L. Lawrence to Morgan, June 7, 1836, James Morgan Papers (Rosenberg Library, Galveston).

[f] Harvey Whiting to Morgan, May 3, 1836, Jenkins (ed.), *Papers,* VI, 156–158.

[g] Peter J. Menard to Richard R. Royall, Oct. 19, 1835, ibid., II, 285.

[h] No service record can be found.

[i] Burnet to Morgan, May 16, 1835, Jenkins (ed.), *Papers,* VI, 308–309.

[j] Kent Gardien, "Kokernot and His Tory," *Texana,* VIII, No. 3 (1970), 269–294.

# "Tryels and Trubbles": Women in Early Nineteenth-Century Texas

Fane Downs*

*The role played by women in Texas history has received more attention from scholars in the past three decades. In this article, Fane Downs, formerly chair of the history department at McMurry College and president of the West Texas Historical Association, describes the difficulties women in early Texas faced. She points to the contributions of women in the areas of immigration and home-building, education, religion, and the Texas Revolution. She notes that pioneer Texas women faced problems and overcame difficulties similar to those of other frontier women. "Their migrations to Texas," she concludes, "were marked by both grief and joy, and their settlement by hardships and happiness. They coped with danger, illness, loss, and isolation, and privations; yet they found strength and stamina in themselves, their families, and friends."*

*Readers interested in learning more about women in early Texas should also see Margaret Henson,* **Anglo American Women in Texas, 1820–1850** *(Boston: American Press, 1980); Jo Ella Powell Exley,* **Texas Tears and Texas Sunshine: Voices of Frontier Women** *(College Station: Texas A&M University Press, 1985); Ann Patton Malone,* **Women on the Texas Frontier: A Cross-Cultural Perspective** *(El Paso: Texas Western Press, 1983); and Paula Mitchell Marks,* **Hand to the Spindle: Texas Women and Home Textile Production, 1822–1880** *(College Station: Texas A&M University Press, 1998).*

Recent scholarship in regional history has established women's presence as integral in the fabric of historical experience of Texas and the West. Similarly, recent scholarship in women's history has revealed the richness and variety of women's experiences on the frontier. Using these two approaches

* Fane Downs, "'Tryels and Trubbles': Women in Early Nineteenth-Century Texas," *Southwestern Historical Quarterly*, 90 (July, 1986), 35–56.

historians are rewriting and reinterpreting the history of the West.[1] In a large number of books and articles historians have corrected the traditional male bias in western history, which asserted either that women were "invisible, few in number, and not important in the process of taming a wilderness," or, on the other hand, that they were the saintly sentimental heroines of male imagination. Attacks on these two sets of misconceptions have effectively discredited any view which would stereotype western women or ignore them.[2]

Texas women's history has likewise come under closer examination by historians of women and of more traditional topics. In common with women's history in the larger context, Texas women's history has moved from the historiographical stage of "oh look! oh look!" which catalogued women and affirmed their presence,[3] to works of synthesis and interpretation, which are attempting to describe the larger issues in women's history, to be inclusive of all

---

[1]The most useful historiographical essay in this regard is Joan Jensen and Darlis Miller, "The Gentle Tamers Revisited: New Approaches to the History of Women in the American West," *Pacific Historical Review,* II (May, 1980), 173–213.

[2]Ibid., 173–175, 176 (quotation), 177–182; Beverly Stoltje, "A Helpmeet for Man Indeed: The Image of Frontier Woman," *Journal of American Folklore,* LXXXVIII (Jan./Mar., 1975), 25–41; Ronald W. Hogeland, "'The Female Appendage': Feminine Life-Styles in America, 1820–1860," *Civil War History,* XVII (June, 1971), 101–114; Paula Treckel, "An Historiographical Essay: Women on the American Frontier," *The Old Northwest,* I (Dec. 1975), 391–403; Sandra Myres, *Westering Women and the Frontier Experience, 1800–1915* (Albuquerque, 1982), 1–11; Glenda Riley, "Images of the Frontierswoman: Iowa as a Case Study," *Western Historical Quarterly,* VIII (Apr., 1977), 198–202.

Perhaps the definitive signal that women in the West cannot be ignored nor their experiences devalued is the appearance of Sandra Myres's *Westering Women,* a volume in the authoritative Histories of the American Frontier series, edited by the late Ray A. Billington. Other works useful in filling in the women's record are Joanna Stratton, *Pioneer Women: Voices from the Kansas Frontier* (New York, 1981); Julie Roy Jeffrey, *Frontier Women: The Trans-Mississippi West, 1840–1880* (New York, 1979); John Mack Faragher, *Women and Men on the Overland Trail* (New Haven, 1979); Jerena East Giffin, "'Add a Pinch and a Lump': Missouri Women in the 1820's," *Missouri Historical Review,* LXV (July, 1971), 478–504; T. A. Larson, "Women's Role in the American West," *Montana: The Magazine of Western History,* XXIV (Summer, 1974), 3–10.

[3]Early works describing notable Texas women include Mrs. M. [Adele B.] Looscan, "The Women of Pioneer Days in Texas—Domestic and Social Life in the Period of the Colonies, the Revolution, and the Republic," Dudley G. Wooten (ed.), *A Comprehensive History of Texas, 1685–1897* (2 vols.; Dallas, 1898), I, pt. 1, pp. 649–668; Aurelia Hadley Mohl, "Women of the Texas Republic and Revolution," typescript, Aurelia Hadley Mohl Papers (Eugene C. Barker Texas History Center, University of Texas, Austin; hereafter cited as BTHC); Evelyn Carrington (ed.), *Women of Early Texas* (Austin, 1975); Annie Doom Pickerell, *Pioneer Women in Texas* (Austin, 1970). Recent collections of short biographies have appeared, which are more useful than the earlier ones because of their more rigorous scholarship and restraint. These include Ann Fears Crawford and Crystal Sasse Ragsdale, *Women in Texas: Their Lives, Their Experiences, Their Accomplishments* (Burnet, Tex., 1982); James M. Day et al., *Women of Texas* (Waco, Tex., 1972); Mary Beth Rogers, Sherry A. Smith, and Janelle D. Scott, *We Can Fly: Stories of Katherine Stinson and Other Gutsy Texas Women*

women in Texas, and to explore the experiences of women as groups in addition to individual women.[4]

A comprehensive study of women of the 1820–1845 period should include Indian, Hispanic, and Anglo women of all ages, in all classes, in rural areas and towns, who were single, married, or widowed, who worked at home or away from home. Such a study would need to encompass material on immigration, homebuilding, family life, community life and leadership, church roles, education, health and medical practices, legal status, homemaking tasks, work other than homemaking, and so forth. This article will attempt to treat but a few of these topics: immigration and homebuilding, education, religion, and the Texas Revolution.

Women moved to Texas with their families, with larger groups, and alone. Their reactions to immigration ranged from eager expectation at beginning anew, through sober resignation at the necessity of accompanying husbands, to abject grief at leaving friends and families. Many women were of pioneering stock and possessed the necessary skills to make the transition to the Texas frontier rather easily; others, less schooled in pioneer life, experienced difficulties in establishing their new homes.

In the fall of 1823, eighteen-year-old Mary Crownover Rabb left Jonesboro, Arkansas, with her husband and a large group of Rabb kinfolks, to start a new life in Texas. Mary's memoirs do not reveal that she dreaded the trip to Texas, regretted the move, or that she was ill-equipped to cope with the pioneer life. Mary Rabb described little of their journey to Texas. Details of the trip are scanty "untell we got to Colerrado[.] we come to it where LaGrange now is, but

---

(Austin, 1983). A useful collection that includes women of folklore as well as history is Francis Edward Abernethy, *Legendary Ladies of Texas,* Publications of the Texas Folklore Society XLIII (Dallas, 1981). There are, of course, a number of biographies and published writings of individuals: for example, Rebecca Smith Lee, *Mary Austin Holley: A Biography* (Austin, 1962), and C. A. Clausen (ed.), *The Lady with the Pen: Elise Waerenskjold in Texas* (Northfield, Minn., 1961).

[4]A watershed in Texas women's studies was "Texas Women: A Celebration of History," an exhibit created by the Texas Women's History Project and now permanently housed at Texas Woman's University. The catalogue of that exhibit, *Texas Women: A Celebration of History* (Austin, 1981), is a useful introduction to the broader topics of women's history. The *Texas Women's History Project Bibliography,* edited by Ruthe Winegarten (Austin, 1980), which grew out of exhibit research, indicates that Texas women's history is maturing with its own scholarly aids. Two pioneering studies are Ann Patton Malone, *Women on the Texas Frontier: A Cross-Cultural Perspective,* Southwestern Studies No. 70 (El Paso, Tex., 1983), and Jane Dysart, "Mexican Women in San Antonio, 1830–1860: The Assimilation Process," *Western Historical Quarterly,* VII (Oct., 1976), 365–375. Also useful is Margaret Henson, *Anglo American Women in Texas,* 1820–1850 (Boston, 1982). Chapters in two college texts are broad attempts to define and describe part of the Texas women's experience: Necah Furman, "Texas Women versus Texas Myth," Ben Proctor and Archie P. McDonald (eds.), *The Texas Heritage* (St. Louis, 1980), 167–184; and Fane Downs, "Texas Women at Work," Donald W. Whisenhunt (ed.), *Texas: A Sesquicentennial Celebration* (Austin, 1984), 309–325.

thare was no house thare then nore nothing but a wilderness not eaven a tree cut down to marke that plais[.]" The river was running swiftly but "thare was no dainger." On her horse, Tormenter, she arrived safely across the river, where she joined her mother-in-law and others. They proceeded to Indian Hill, where a small house built by Rabb's father and brothers was located. "[W]e got thare a bout the 15 of december 1823 thare we got to ouer gerneys end safe[.]"[5]

While Mary Rabb's support group moved to Texas with her, some women came alone or with children. It was not uncommon for widows with children to move to Texas. Stephen F. Austin's "Register of Families" shows twenty widows, most with children. In 1835 Abigail Fokes, a widow with six children, moved to Texas from Florida and located a headright on the San Gabriel River. Mary Peevyhouse Smith likewise moved to Texas as a widow with her children in 1833.[6]

Whether they came alone or with their families, their departures were often difficult. Mary Maverick, who came to Texas with her husband and family in 1837, remembered,

> With heavy hearts we said goodbye to Mother, and my brothers, and sister. Mother ran after us for one more embrace. She held me in her arms and wept aloud, and said, "Oh, Mary, I will never see you again on Earth." I felt heartbroken and often recalled that thrilling cry; and I have never beheld my dear Mother again.[7]

Similarly, Millie Gray, wife of William Fairfax Gray, experienced grief at departing from her friends and family in Fredericksburg, Virginia, in 1838. She recorded that in the days before leaving, she visited friends, which was "a melancholy pleasure." The night before they left, many family members and friends gathered, and "it was a heart rending scene when the hour came for us to go down to the Boat—too painfull for any attempt at description."[8] Even after her arrival in Houston, Millie had difficulty conquering her sadness,

> although every thing looks better than I had expected, my heart feels oppressed [etc.] and it requires an effort to wear the apearance of cheerfulness—I could (if I

---

[5]Mary Crownover Rabb, *Travels and Adventures in Texas, Being the Reminiscences of Mary Crownover Rabb* (Waco, Tex., 1962), iii, 1–2 (quotations); Mary Rabb Family Papers (BTHC); Walter Prescott Webb, H. Bailey Carroll, and Eldon Stephen Branda (eds.), *The Handbook of Texas* (3 vols.; Austin, 1952, 1976), III, 768. For a literary analysis of Mary Rabb's memoirs, see Bessie Malvina Pearce, "Texas through Women's Eyes" (Ph.D. diss., University of Texas, Austin, 1965), 7–14.

[6]"Register of Families," Gifford White, 1830 Census of Texas (Austin, 1983), 1–42; Mary Fokes Locklin, "Experiences of Abigail McLennan Fokes and Family as Told by her Daughter," typescript, 2 (BTHC); Mohl, "Women of the Texas Republic and Revolution," 9–10. Mohl records experiences of other women who moved to Texas after their husbands died.

[7]Rena Maverick Green, *Memoirs of Mary A. Maverick,* arranged by Mary A. Maverick and George Madison Maverick (San Antonio, 1921), 12.

[8]Millie Richards Gray, *The Diary of Millie Gray, 1832–1840* (Houston, 1967), 121.

> were a weeping character) sit down & fairly weep—and if asked for what, I could not tell—merely because all is strange [etc.] and I fear to look forward— . . .[9]

Not all departures were this gloomy: Angelina Peyton (later Eberly) noted that

> Just then [in 1822] Stephen Austin & Joe Hawkins were crying up Texas— beautiful country, land for nothing &c. —Texas fever rose then, as it has often since, there we must go. —there, without much reflection we did go. I was full of it, went to buy whatever was necessary for housekeeping—dishes & — &c[10]

In sharp contrast to the experiences of free women immigrants to Texas, black slave women moved to Texas involuntarily and often experienced brutal conditions of travel. Silvia King recalled that she was taken from Africa to New Orleans, where she was sold.

> We were all chained, and they stripped all our clothes off, and the folks who were going to buy us came around and felt us all over. . . . [T]hey chained us together and marched us up near LaGrange in Texas. . . . That was an awful time, because we were all chained up, and what one did all had to do. If one drank out of the stream, we all drank; when one got tired or sick, the rest had to drag and carry him.[11]

William Fairfax Gray observed slaves who had recently been imported to Texas from the West Indies and Cuba in 1836.[12]

Mary Rabb's first house, like that of many immigrants, was crude and small, although it was better than some of the temporary shelters she lived in later. Since the original house built by her father-in-law was so small, her husband and a friend "bilt a hous in a weeak." This log house had an "aerthing floor," a chimney, and a sturdy door so "the Indians could not get in." After Indians stole some of their livestock, John Rabb decided to leave Indian Hill for a location on the Brazos. While John was gone, Mary spent ten fearful days and nights alone with her "little Babe." She allayed her fears by using the spinning wheel Andrew Rabb had made for her. "Now lonely as I was after riseing early in the morning and attending to makeing meal for the day I kept my new spinning wheel whisling all day and a good part of the night for while the wheel was rowering it would keep me from hearing the Indians walking around hunting michieaf [.]" Mary coped with frequent moves and other vicissitudes of pioneer life, with her spinning wheel serving almost as a talisman to diminish fear and anxiety.[13]

---

[9]Ibid., 52.

[10]Mary Austin Holley, "Notes Made by Mrs. Holley in Interviews with Prominent Texans of Early Days," 8, Mary Austin Holley Papers (BTHC).

[11]Ronnie C. Tyler and Lawrence R. Murphy (eds.), *The Slave Narratives of Texas* (Austin, 1974), 3.

[12]William Fairfax Gray, *From Virginia to Texas, 1835: Diary of Col. Wm. F. Gray* (Houston, 1965), 147, 158.

[13]Rabb, *Travels,* 2 (1st–3rd quotations), 3–4 (4th and 5th quotations).

Mary's descriptions of small, rude dwellings and camps are not unique. Many pioneer women lived in equally primitive shelter—sometimes because of lack of materials, at other times for lack of pioneering skills. The latter circumstance caused Texas's first German family considerable discomfort and inconvenience. Caroline Ernst von Hinueber recalled that their first house "was a miserable little hut, covered with straw and having six sides, which were made out of moss." Because the roof was not water-proof, they often held an umbrella over the bed when it rained at night. "Of course, we suffered a great deal in the winter. My father had tried to build a chimney and fireplace out of logs and clay, but we were afraid to light a fire because of the extreme combustibility of our dwelling. So we had to shiver." They did not know how to make shoes or clothing and, therefore, had to do without. "No one can imagine what a degree of want there was of the merest necessities of life, and it is difficult for me now to understand how we managed to live and get along under the circumstances. Yet we did so in some way."[14]

Whether widowed or unmarried, single women were in an awkward position. Lydia Ann McHenry, a single woman, immigrated to Texas in 1833 with her sister and brother-in-law, Maria and John Wesley Kenney. She lived with the Kenneys most of her life; her experiences reveal some of the peculiar problems faced by single women in nineteenth-century Texas. Lydia's status as "maiden aunt" living with her sister's family caused her considerable difficulty. She inherited property and slaves from her parents but was never free from financial worries.[15] She felt her dependence on her sister in Texas and brothers in Kentucky keenly. Out of patience with her brother's advice, she wrote in exasperation,

> For Gods sake do not you & Martin any longer treat me as an idiot who requires a guardian, but what little I have, let it be my own & not partnership property. . . . You know I am not avaricious! that I care for nothing more than the supply of moderate wants, . . . but I ought to be independent.[16]

She objected to her brother's "reproachful & lordly" attitude as if she were "some refractory child, & it was his business to bring me into subjection."[17]

Lydia McHenry's immigration to Texas was not entirely felicitous, and her attempts to establish independence were generally unsuccessful. Moreover, her hardships were similar to those of other single and married women of limited means whose early years in Texas were marked by great effort to create stable

[14]Caroline von Hinueber, "Life of German Pioneers in Early Texas," *Quarterly of the Texas State Historical Association,* II (Jan., 1899), 229 (this journal is hereafter cited as *QTSHA).*

[15]Lydia Ann McHenry to John Hardin McHenry, Feb. 12, July 4, 1835, July 17, 1836, George R. Neilsen (ed.), "Lydia Ann McHenry and Revolutionary Texas," *Southwestern Historical Quarterly,* LXXIV (Jan., 1971), 394–395 (the *Quarterly* is cited hereafter as *SHQ).*

[16]Ibid., 401–402.

[17]Ibid., 401.

homes for themselves and their families. These experiences were those of women on all frontiers; the Texas frontier was not unique in this regard.

Texas women's experiences with schooling and religion were likewise common to those on other frontiers. Educational opportunities for girls and teaching positions for women were limited in Texas. Thinly populated and poor, Texas was not an environment in which education enjoyed high priority. The government of Coahuila y Texas made a number of laws calling on ayuntamientos to establish schools; however, paucity of municipal funds militated against success. Efforts at schooling were made in Bexar, Nacogdoches, Goliad, and Victoria in the 1820s and 1830s, but none was particularly successful.[18]

Frances Trask opened the first boarding school for girls in Cole's Settlement (later Independence) in late 1834. She sold it to Henry F. Gillette in 1839; Gillette donated the school to Baylor University in 1845. Trask continued to teach off and on until 1860, when she left Texas.[19]

Texas newspapers carried a number of notices for boarding and day schools and academies. Samuel Peniston of San Felipe advertised the opening of a school for "youth of either sex," with instruction in English education in its "several branches." Some school notices specified that the schools were principally for girls; Mrs. F. A. Andrews proposed to open a school in Houston "principally for young ladies; yet a few boys under the age of 12 will be received until further notice." The Reverend and Mrs. Caleb S. Ives advertised an academy in Matagorda in 1840. Mrs. Ives had been educated in the "best schools for young ladies in New England" and had taught in a female seminary in Hartford, so presumably she was well-prepared for Texas girls.[20]

Scattered evidence suggests that in many communities schools and teachers were available for Texas girls, although support for the education for girls was not profound. During the period of the Texas Republic, several civic leaders urged the establishment of a system of education. At least one emphasized the importance of education for girls. "The early education of the daughter ought to be more thorough, deep and clear, sounder, more extensive, and better than the education of the son, because the daughter early in life becomes a wife and mother, retires from the world to her own peculiar empire—her home." The daughter "must learn early in life or never learn." The writer called for girls to learn to cook, wash, iron, nurture the children. Significantly this

---

[18]Fane Downs, "The History of Mexicans in Texas, 1820–1845" (Ph.D. diss., Texas Tech University, 1970), 134–165.

[19]Webb, Carroll, and Branda (eds.), *Handbook of Texas,* I, 543, 876, II, 774; Frances Trask file, Texas Women: A Celebration of History Exhibit Archives (Library, Texas Woman's University). The exhibition archives are cited hereafter as Texas Women Exhibit Archives.

[20]*Texas Gazette* (San Felipe), Oct. 30, 1830 (1st and 2nd quotations); *Telegraph and Texas Register* (Houston), Nov. 11, 1837 (3rd quotation); *San Luis Advocate,* Sept. 14, 1840 (4th quotation).

author saw education as a means of reinforcing the domestic role of women, not of giving them any citizenship training.[21]

There appear to have been more men teachers than women, though teaching was an acceptable occupation for women—particularly single women and widows. Lydia McHenry, for example, opened a boarding school at the David Ayres home in Washington County in the fall of 1835. The Ayres children and others attended, among them Charles Travis, son of William Barret Travis. Lydia apparently intended to expand her school; she placed notices in the *Telegraph and Texas Register* for the opening of a boarding school for girls. The "scholars" would be boarded in the Ayres home, "where the best care will be taken of their health and morals." The curriculum would include orthography, reading, writing, and arithmetic. The Texas Revolution and the Runaway Scrape interrupted these plans. Lydia, however, did continue to teach. After the Runaway Scrape several of the children she had taught at the Ayres's accompanied her and the Kenneys home "to attend to their books with me & as we are confined at home, Maria agreed to board them, so that unintentionally we have our hands full of business." Her young nephew recalled years later that there were some twenty children at the school. He remembered the experience very fondly: the "brave and cheery little company" studied reading and other subjects. The school was not financially successful and closed after some months.[22]

The two cornerstones of civilized society were schools and churches. Women were perhaps even more active in the establishment and nurture of churches than schools. Lydia McHenry and Mary Rabb were two among many who actively supported the church. Mary Rabb wrote, "how many tryels and trubbles have we past threw to gather here in texas and no oppertunity of going to church yet god was mindfull of us and blesst us and gave us his sparit and made us feel that we was his [.]" She herself played a significant role in helping establish the Methodist Church in Texas; after her husband joined the church in the 1830s they were both active supporters and benefactors of the church. Mary held a life membership in the Foreign Missionary Society of the church, and John donated land for its work. She hosted itinerant Methodist preachers; moreover, it is likely that Methodists preached in her home before the organization of the church. So long as Texas was a part of Mexico, Protestants were not supposed to conduct services; it is clear, however, that a number of them did.[23]

---

[21] *The Red-Lander* (San Augustine), Oct. 7, 1841.

[22] Mrs. A. J. Lee, "Some Recollections of Two Texas Pioneer Women," *Texas Methodist Historical Quarterly,* I (Jan., 1910), 209 (this journal is hereafter cited as *TMHQ); Telegraph and Texas Register* (San Felipe), Nov. 14 (1st and 2nd quotations), 21, 1835. L. A. McHenry to J. H. McHenry, Nov. 21, 1836, Neilson (ed.), "Lydia Ann McHenry," 408 (3rd quotation); M. M. Kenney, "Recollections of Early Schools," *QTSHA,* I (Apr., 1898), 286 (4th quotation).

[23] Rabb, *Travels,* 14 (quotation); Pickrell, *Pioneer Women,* 92; Walter Vernon et al., *The Methodist Excitement in Texas: A History* (Dallas, 1984), 30.

Lydia Ann McHenry was even more ardent and active in her support of the Methodist Church. Her brother-in-law John Wesley Kenney was a Methodist minister, and Lydia and her sister Maria assisted him in his part-time ministry. In the fall of 1834, Kenney, Henry Stephenson, and others, including some Presbyterians, conducted a camp meeting on Caney Creek; the Methodists present organized a church. A second camp meeting near the site of the first was held in the fall of 1835; since Kenney was again one of the preachers, it is likely that his wife and sister-in-law were present and active in the proceedings. Even though Stephen F. Austin had warned as early as 1829 that "it will not do to have the Methodist excitement raised in this country," the Methodists regularly conducted worship services, prayer meetings, and Sunday schools in Texas homes.[24]

Lydia and Maria were only two among many active churchwomen; David Ayres, an active Methodist layman, recalled that after the Revolution he started a prayer meeting in his home. In a "back room a few pious females met with my family." He conducted a Sunday school with the assistance of his wife and daughter; moreover, they had a large class of blacks to whom they read the Bible.[25]

Women did not take a public role in the Texas Methodist church; the most recent history of Texas Methodism asserts, however, that "a striking fact in this whole story is the extent to which women played a significant role in the planting and nurturing of the Methodist faith."[26] In those early years, of course, most church meetings were held in homes, which gave the women a particular responsibility.

Women were similarly active in other denominations. Presbyterianism came to Texas with Mary McKinzie (Mrs. Josiah) Bell in 1821. As zealous as she was, Mary Bell could do little to advance Presbyterianism until Texas Independence. Tradition holds that she conducted a funeral service for a friend when no minister was available. Her home was "the Mecca for Presbyterian preachers" and "a welcome home to every stranger." Another significant Presbyterian woman was Belinda McNair (Mrs. Peter Hunter) Fullinwider, who, with her husband, taught a Sunday school in San Felipe in 1834. Fullinwider, and probably his wife, participated in the Caney Creek camp meetings of 1834 and 1835.[27]

---

[24]Lee, "Some Recollections," 209; Vernon et al., *Methodist Excitement,* 30 (quotation).

[25]"Reminiscences of David Ayers," *TMHQ,* I (July, 1909), 42 (quotation), 43. Ayres's name was frequently spelled Ayers, though he apparently spelled it Ayres.

[26]Vernon et al., *Methodist Excitement,* 33.

[27]William Stuart Red, *A History of the Presbyterian Church in Texas* ([Austin], 1936), 3, 359–361, 362 (quotations); Webb, Carroll, and Branda (eds.), *Handbook of Texas,* I, 655.

Some women felt keenly the lack of church services and the support of a congregation. Dilue Rose Harris recalled that her mother grieved for lack of Protestant services. In April, 1834, Mrs. Rose persuaded a minister to preach a sermon because she had been in Texas for a year and had not heard one. After the Revolution the Rose family moved near Houston and were grateful that they could attend church regularly in that town.[28]

Perhaps the most poignant story of coping without a minister concerned a couple who were old and ill. Since they thought themselves near death, they wanted to take communion. No minister was available; therefore, they "determined through faith, to take other elements, trusting their acceptability." They prayerfully administered communion to each other, which consisted of "nice corn bread and strong coffee."[29]

Although the Catholic religion was the only one sanctioned in Mexican Texas, Hispanic Texans were nearly as unchurched as the Anglo and European immigrants. The lack of priests and resources hampered the work of the church. Women contributed from their resources to repair parish churches in Nacogdoches and San Antonio. Doña Patricia de la Garza de León, wife of the empresario Martín de León, supported the parish church of Victoria generously. After her return to Victoria following the Revolution, she continued to support the church.[30]

Religion for slave women served the same purpose as for free women: it provided a source of comfort and strength, both spiritual and emotional. Worship services frequently occurred in houses—in the slave quarters—and consisted of preaching, singing, and praying. "Right fine meetings, too." Often the slaves' religious expression was more emotional than that of whites. One slave recalled, "I saw some powerful figurations of the spirit in those days." A few slave men were allowed to preach, but often the slaves attended the "white folks' church."[31] The blacks also held prayer meetings in the woods.

> Us niggers used to have a praying ground in the hollow and sometimes we came out of the field between 11 and 12 at night, . . . and we wanted to ask the good Lord to have mercy. . . . Some got so joyous they started to holler loud, and we had to stop up their mouths. I saw niggers get so full of the Lord and so happy they dropped unconscious.[32]

---

[28]Dilue Rose Harris, "Reminiscences of Dilue Harris," *QTSHA,* IV (Oct., 1900), 102, (Jan., 1901), 188, VII (Jan., 1904), 215.

[29]Julia Lee Sinks, "Chronicles of Fayette," manuscript, 33, Julia Lee Sinks Papers (BTHC).

[30]Downs, "History of Mexicans in Texas," 90–133; Doña Patricia de la Garza de León file, Texas Women Exhibit Archives.

[31]Tyler and Murphy (eds.), *Slave Narratives of Texas,* 81 (1st and 2nd quotations), 83 (3rd quotation).

[32]Ibid., 82.

Another slave recalled,

> Marse Tom didn't mind us singing in our cabins at night, but we'd better not let him catch us praying. Seems like us niggers just got to pray. Half their life was spent in praying. . . . They circled themselves on the floor in the cabin and prayed. They go moaning low and gentle. "Some day, some day, this yoke is going to be lifted off of our shoulders."[33]

Religion was significant in the lives of Texas women because they lacked other opportunities to associate with one another and to make effective contributions beyond their families. Participation in religious services and teaching Sunday school gave women a sense of worth and status unavailable in any other area of life. Largely excluded from public life, women could fill their needs for service to others and for female companionship through the churches. They were instrumental in establishing and nurturing churches in all parts of Texas.

Virtually all women, slave or free, who lived in Texas in the 1835–1836 period were affected by the Revolution. Unlike the American Revolution, however, the Texas Revolution had little long-term impact on women's lives and work. Because the war was short and small-scale, women did not experience significant change in their roles or responsibilities. The principal effect of the war for Texas women was grief at loss and temporary (though traumatic) dislocation. Many women contributed to the war effort in various ways, and even more of them were caught up in what may be the most commonly shared experience of early Texas women—the Runaway Scrape.

Women's contributions to the war effort varied. Women of means often provided money and livestock for the cause. Patricia de León was generous in supporting the Texas effort, a fact which did not lessen the postwar hostility toward her and her family.[34] Jane McManus proposed to borrow money against her land in Texas in order to contribute to the war cause.

> [E]very Texan will be called on to yield his utmost assistance to the cause of freedom and justice as a female I cannot bear arms for my adopted country— but if the interest I possess in her soil, will be a guarantee for any money, I will with joy contribute my mite to purchase arms for her brave defenders— . . . I firmly believe these threats of evil are but the precursors to redoubled prosperity.[35]

The *Telegraph and Texas Register,* generating enthusiasm for the war, announced that "even the ladies, bless their souls, volunteer their services in

---

[33] Ibid., 83.

[34] Janelle D. Scott, "Patricia de la Garza de León: Pioneer Woman from Mexico," typescript, 9, Patricia de León file.

[35] Jane M. McManus to Joseph D. Powers [?], New York, Oct. 29, 1835, Jane McManus Storms Cazneau Papers (BTHC).

moulding and patching bullets, making cartridges, &c. and if necessary, would even enter the ranks, and fight manfully for the rights of the country."[36]

When their husbands, sons, or fathers left to join Texan forces, women had to supervise farm work or do it themselves. In addition, there were instances of women making cartridges and providing clothing and livestock for the army. One woman proposed that Texas women sew clothing for the soldiers; indeed, she anticipated the women could provide clothing for 1,000 men. She appealed to the patriotic sentiments of her sisters: "While our husbands, brothers, fathers, and sons vanquish an invading tyrant, let us be busy in preparing them comfortable raiment." Clinching her argument, she suggested that since the women of Kentucky had supported the American Revolution in this way, could Texas women do less? Another suggested in the *Telegraph and Texas Register* that women sew bags so that each man could have two to fill with sand for instant defensive breastworks.[37]

Sometimes women contributed their goods to the war effort involuntarily. Angelina Peyton, innkeeper of San Felipe, had some difficulty in getting compensation for oxen "pressed into service"; it seems she had not submitted her claim to the government in the proper form! The Widow McElroy suffered losses of several head of cattle and a wagon. Because she and her family were in great distress, President David G. Burnet ordered that she be compensated quickly.[38]

Perhaps the most famous oxen story of the Revolution involved a confrontation between innkeeper Pamelia Mann and Sam Houston. Mann allowed the general to impress a yoke of oxen to pull his cannon, so long as the army was headed in the same direction as she was (toward Nacogdoches). When Houston turned the army toward Harrisburg, Mann stormed after it and demanded her oxen back. Details of the confrontation vary with the witnesses, but apparently she had to resort to profanity and perhaps force to get the oxen returned. Whatever the tactics, she retrieved the oxen and continued her way eastward. Earlier Mann, who was a friend of Houston's—at least until the oxen incident—served as a courier for the government. She wrote Houston that "sum gentle men" had offered her one hundred dollars "to let them intercept them [messages] but I cannot be bought by munney." She promised to identify

---

[36] *Telegraph and Texas Register* (San Felipe), Oct. 17, 1835.

[37] Harris, "Reminiscences of Dilue Harris," *QTSHA*, IV (Jan., 1901), 157–159; Elizabeth McAnulty Owens, *The Story of Her Life* (San Antonio, 1936), 7; Mary S. Helm, *Scraps of Early Texas History, 1828–1843* (Austin, 1884), 54; *Telegraph and Texas Register* (San Felipe), Feb. 27, Mar. 5, 1836.

[38] J. W. Moody to Angelina B. Peyton, Dec. 30, 1835, John J. Jenkins (ed.), *The Papers of the Texas Revolution, 1835–1836* (10 vols.; Austin, 1974), III, 376 (quotation); David G. Burnet to J. W. Moore and DeWitt Clinton Harris, Aug. 13, 1836, ibid., VIII, 220–221; Harris to Burnet, Aug. 23, 1836, ibid., 299.

the men to Houston when she saw him. She also reported that "the inderpendance ticket went hole hog in this presenct." Other women served as couriers from time to time.[39]

Texas had its Betsy Rosses as well. Joanna Troutman of Georgia made a flag for Georgia volunteers; their commander wrote, "your flag shall yet wave over fields of victory in defiance of despotism." Moseley Baker accepted a flag made by two women of San Felipe; he pledged that it would wave triumphantly from ranks of his troops. The motto on the flag was "our country's rights or death." Sarah Dodson crafted a red, white, and blue flag for Harrisburg volunteers.[40]

As the opposing armies drew further into Texas, women, anxious for the safety of their families and themselves, evacuated eastward in the Runaway Scrape. Fear of the Mexican army, whipped up by Texan leaders in their efforts to rally men to the fight, added to the trauma of the refugees. The calls to arms raised the specter of sexual assaults and massacres. Newspapers warned, "Behold your wives and daughters, are you prepared to deliver them up to the rude embraces of a brutal soldiery [?]" "Rally . . . your homes and your firesides are assailed."[41] James Fannin wrote,

> Will the freemen of Texas calmly fold their arms, and await until the approach of their deadly enemy compels them to protect their own firesides? Can it be possible that they—that any American—can so far forget the honour of their mothers, wives, and daughters, as not to fly to their rifles and meet the Tyrant, and avenge the insults and wrongs inflicted on his own country-women on the Rio Grande? What can be expected for the *Fair Daughters* of chaste *white women,* when their own country-women are prostituted by a licensed soldiery, as an inducement to push forward into the Colonies, where they may find *fairer game?*[42]

As the danger increased, so did the virulence of the language. Moseley Baker challenged Texans: "Will anyone dare to have the effrontery to say that his interest must be alluded to, when Texas is in danger of being overrun, and the women and children in cold blood massacred. . . ." Racist pronouncements

---

[39]Andrew Forest Muir, "In Defense of Mrs. Mann," Mody C. Boatright (ed.), *Mexican Border Ballads and Other Lore* (Austin, 1946), 115–116; William Ransom Hogan, "Pamelia Mann: Texas Frontierswoman," *Southwest Review,* XX (Summer, 1935), 360–362; Pamelia Mann file, Texas Women Exhibit Archives; Pamelia Mann to Sam Houston, Feb. 3, 1836, Jenkins (ed.), *Papers,* IV, 248 (quotations); George M. Collinsworth to Margaret C. Linn, [Oct. 10, 1835], ibid., II, 84–85; *Telegraph and Texas Register* (San Felipe), Mar. 5, 1836.

[40]Hugh McLeod to Joanna Troutman, Nov. 23, 1835, Jenkins (ed.), *Papers,* II, 494 (1st quotation); Moseley Baker to Gail Borden, [Feb. 29, 1836], ibid., IV, 460 (2nd quotation); *Telegraph and Texas Register* (San Felipe), Mar. 5, 1836; Mohl, "Women of the Texas Republic and Revolution," 59–60.

[41]*Texas Republican* (Brazoria), Sept. 26, 1835 (1st quotation); *Telegraph and Texas Register* (San Felipe), Jan. 23, 1836 (2nd quotation).

[42]James Fannin to James Robinson, Feb. 7, 1836, Jenkins (ed.), *Papers,* IV, 280.

such as these undoubtedly contributed to the poisonous atmosphere after the war, which accounted for the hostility toward Hispanics.[43]

The toll of war on Texas women can be measured in deprivation, fear, insecurity, and grief. There are instances of women being harassed and threatened after their husbands had left to fight. An ugly situation in Gonzales occurred when some men, reportedly from Ayish Bayou, broke into homes, "compelled women to leave their House with their Children and seek protection from their neighbors[.]"[44]

Mexican troops took their toll as well. Women of San Antonio were in a particularly difficult position because that community was the site of two principal battles. Those women who could evacuate to the ranches along the San Antonio River did so. The Mexican commander Martín Perfecto de Cos threatened to make the citizens of Bexar sweep the public square and their women make tortillas for his men. Virtually all the residents of San Antonio were Hispanic, which put them in an anomolous position. They were in considerable danger during the battle for control of the city in December, 1835. When the Mexican army returned to Texas in early 1836, Colonel J. C. Neill reported that, as the Mexicans moved north, they placed a forced loan on all property and compelled women to grind corn and make bread. Reports circulated that influential citizens had been killed and wives and daughters prostituted.[45]

Texas families feared more than the Mexican army. The threat of Indian attack or slave uprising preoccupied some. Henry Austin wrote James Perry that Emily Perry was anxious with the enemy near, apprehensive for "a possible rising of the negroes," and worried "that the Indians may avail themselves of the opptunity *[sic]* for plunder."[46]

Traditionally women have had to stay home and wait while their kinsmen were at war. Grief was profound for those who lost loved ones. It was multiplied in Gonzales when the news arrived of the fall of the Alamo; thirty-two men from Gonzales had answered Travis's appeal for aid and lost their lives thereby.[47] One young man recalled,

> I remember most distinctively the shrieks of despair with which the soldiers' wives received the news of the death of their husbands. The piercing wails of woe that

[43]Moseley Baker to John R. Jones et al., Mar. 8, 1836, ibid., V, 23.

[44]Jno. Fisher to Austin, Nov. 3, 1835, ibid., II, 304 (quotation); L. Smither to Austin, Nov. 4, 1835 (two letters), ibid., 318, 319–320.

[45]Downs, "History of Mexicans in Texas," 234; Stiff's account of the taking of San Antonio, Jenkins (ed.), *Papers,* III, 390–391; Joseph Field, "Three Years in Texas," ibid., IX, 188–189; J. C. Neill to Provisional Government, Jan. 28, 1836, ibid., IV, 174; Robert Morris to Fannin, Feb. 6, 1836, ibid., 276.

[46]H. Austin to James Perry, Mar. 5, 1836, Jenkins (ed.), *Papers,* IV, 515 (quotations), 516.

[47]Archie P. McDonald, "Lone Star on the Rise," Donald W. Whisenhunt (ed.), *Texas: A Sesquicentennial Celebration* (Austin, 1984), 81.

> reached our camps from these bereaved women thrilled me and filled me with feelings I cannot express, nor ever forget. I now could understand that there is woe in warfare, as well as glory and labor.[48]

A grieving mother wrote her sister,

> Yes sister I must say it to you, I have lost my William. O, yes he is gone. My poor boy is gone, gone from me. The sixth of March in the morning he was slain in the Alamo, in San Antonio. Then his poor body commited to the flames. Oh, Sally, can you sympathise with and pray for me that I may have grace to help in this great time of trouble.[49]

The new widows of Gonzales joined the stream of refugees heading east in the Runaway Scrape. Some women well away from the war area remained at home; it would appear, however, that hundreds of women—free and slave—took to the roads to flee from danger.

The families in the San Patricio and Refugio areas were the first to leave their homes; as General José de Urrea advanced into Texas in February, 1836, people began the evacuation. One woman remembered, "It was a sorrowful sight to see so many women and children driven from their homes. . . ." Another referred to the evacuation as a "panic." Rebecca Westover reportedly rode a horse from her home at San Patricio to Harrisburg, accompanied by a male Mexican servant. At Harrisburg she stayed with Mrs. Jane Harris and then accompanied the Harrisses when they had to evacuate their own home.[50]

As the Mexican advance continued, General Houston ordered Colonel James Fannin to fall back to Victoria and directed him to aid the "women and children who may be desirous of leaving that place." Several families from further south had sought refuge in Victoria, but they had to leave that community when the Mexican army approached. Some went overland or by sea to New Orleans; others stayed on ranches in the area.[51]

As Santa Anna approached San Antonio, families in that town began to leave. J. M. Rodriguez, whose father was with the Texas army, recalled, "My mother undertook to act for us and decided it was best for us to go into the country to avoid being here when General Santa Ana's army should come in.

---

[48]John H. Jenkins, *Recollections of Early Texas,* ed. John H. Jenkins III (Austin, 1958), 37.

[49]Mrs. George Sutherland to sister, June 5, 1836, Jenkins (ed.), *Papers,* VII, 24.

[50]Rosalie B. Hart Priour, "The Adventures of a Family of Emmigrants [*sic*] Who Emmigrated to Texas in 1834," typescript, 42, Rosalie Bridget Hart Priour Reminiscences (BTHC); Gwen Vincent, "Runaway Scrape of the Texas Revolution: The Return and Effect on the Participants," (M.A. thesis, Hardin-Simmons University, 1976), 19–29; Mrs. T. C. Allan, "Reminiscences of Mrs. Annie Fagan Teal," *SHQ,* XXXIV (Apr., 1931), 326 (2nd quotation); Adele B. Looscan, "Sketch of the Life of Oliver Jones and of His Wife Rebecca Jones," *SHQ,* X (Oct., 1906), 177.

[51]Houston to Fannin, Mar. 11, 1836, Jenkins (ed.), *Papers,* V, 51, 52 (quotation); John J. Linn, *Reminiscences of Fifty Years in Texas* (1883; facs. reprint, Austin, 1935), 247–249; Priour, "Adventures," 45–46.

We went to the ranch of Doña Santos Ximenes. . . . We buried our money in the house, about $800.00; it took us nearly two days to get to the ranch." Later, after Fannin's defeat, they joined other San Antonio families and journeyed to East Texas, where they stayed until the war's end.[52]

As the Mexican army moved deeper into Texas more families were dislocated. Mary Rabb's experience was not atypical: "We was all drove out of ouer houses with ouer little ones to suffer with cold and hungry and little Lorenzy not three months when we started died on the road [.]" John Rabb got a furlough because Mary was sick and accompanied the family eastward. Mrs. George Sutherland, who lived west of the Colorado, retreated eastward with her family to the Colorado, then on to the Brazos, where George Sutherland "quit us and joined the army." Like the other women, she had hoped to stop at the Brazos, but when General Houston continued beyond that river, the civilians had to move as well.[53] The situation was grim for many.

> All this time you could hardly guess my feelings. My poor William gone, Sutherland in the army. Me with my three little daughters and my poor Thomas wandering about, not knowing what to do or where to go. You will guess my feelings were dreadful but even the Lord supported me and was on our side[54]

Adding to the misery of the evacuation were unusually heavy rainfall, sickness, and short supplies. At the Brazos people were "in great alarm and confusion." Crossing the river and traversing the bottoms was difficult. "It was pitiful and distressing to behold the extremity of the families, as sometimes a team would bog down, and women with their babies in their arms, surrounded by little children, had to wade almost waist deep in places." The widow Angelina Peyton recalled the scene at San Felipe: "Great commotion—destruction of property— much left on river banks—no wagons scarcely—few horses—women and children—I was the last to cross—" She gave rice and hogs to the army.[55] The "motley procession" consisted of

> all manner of vehicles, good and worn out carriages, ox and mule wagons, trucks, slides, and anything that could carry women and children. The animals were loaded with bedding and provisions, until the person guiding them was hardly perceptible. Women led donkey's packed with a few household treasures, and her more precious treasures, her children.[56]

---

[52]J. M. Rodriguez, *Memoirs of Early Texas* (San Antonio, 1913), 8–9 (quotation), 10.

[53]Rabb, *Travels,* 14 (1st quotation); Mrs. George Sutherland to sister, June 5, 1836, Jenkins (ed.), *Papers,* VII, 25 (2nd quotation).

[54]Mrs. G. Sutherland to sister, June 5, 1836, Jenkins (ed.), *Papers of the Texas Revolution,* VII, 25.

[55]Jenkins, *Recollections,* 43–44 (1st quotation); Holley, "Notes Made in Interviews," Mrs. Eberly, 21 (2nd quotation); Sinks, "Chronicles of Fayette," 53 (3rd quotation).

[56]Sinks, "Chronicles of Fayette," 53.

A report to General Houston referred to the situation at the Brazos as one of "great confusion," with the families in "deplorable condition." Some men created a "scene of drunkenness and debauchery, when ladies' proud claims to decency and respectability were insulted. . . ." The situation continued to deteriorate, although no other scenes of debauchery were noted. But as the number of persons moving eastward increased, so did the congestion along the roads and at the fords. Dilue Harris, a youngster at the time, referred to the "horrors" of the evacuation. "We left home at sunset, hauling clothes, bedding, and provisions on the sleigh with one yoke of oxen. Mother and I were walking, she with an infant in her arms. Brother drove the oxen, and my two little sisters rode in the sleigh." Her father joined them; they traveled with five other families. Her father and another man were the only white men with the group, which consisted of about fifty, about one-half slaves. At Lynch's Crossing on the San Jacinto River there were some 5,000 people and a three-day wait to cross. One observer said that the "prairie near Lynch's resembeled a camp meeting; it was covered with carts, wagons, horses, mules, tents, men, women and children, and all the baggage of a flying multitude."[57]

As the families pushed on, their hardships continued; much of the area adjacent to the Trinity River was under water. Dilue Harris remembered, "The horrors of crossing the Trinity are beyond my power to describe." Many were sick, including one of her sisters. Crossing the slough was extremely difficult, and people were in the water for several days. The situation was grim for both black and white women. Dilue's little sister died; then her family stopped for three weeks at Liberty because her mother was sick. They moved on eastward "as wretched" as could be until they got news of the Texas victory at San Jacinto.[58]

Angelina Peyton remembered "horrible confusion" at the Trinity, but "at night forgetting all—would seek out prettiest trees to camp under—visit each other—music—dancing—one marriage—" One enterprising woman wrote President Burnet asking his advice about "getting a house in your place [Harrisburg], one suitable for a Public House, if you think a living could be made at that business. . . ." Of course, by the time she wrote the letter, Harrisburg had been evacuated![59]

The government made some attempt to aid the fleeing families— though the government itself was on the run. Burnet ordered that committees should

---

[57]James Collinsworth to Houston, [Apr. 8, 1836], Jenkins (ed.), *Papers,* V, 372–373 (1st–3rd quotations); Harris, "Reminiscences of Dilue Harris," *QTSHA,* IV (Jan., 1901), 162 (4th and 5th quotations), 163; Gray, *From Virginia to Texas,* 150 (6th quotation).

[58]Harris, "Reminiscences of Dilue Harris," *QTSHA,* IV (Jan., 1901), 164, 165 (1st quotation), 166, 167 (2nd quotation), 168–169.

[59]Holley, "Notes Made in Interviews," 23 (1st and 2nd quotations); Elizabeth Beeson to Burnet, Apr. 10, 1836, Jenkins, (ed.), *Papers,* V, 416 (3rd quotation).

be organized in towns to protect women and children so the rest of the able-bodied men could fight. The government established a refugee camp on the south side of Buffalo Bayou, but this effort was insufficient to meet the needs. Burnet also ordered that food and other supplies be provided for refugees and that boats be impressed to ferry them or take them home.[60]

Not all women had to evacuate overland; some who lived close to the coast escaped by sea. Mary Wightman's family left with one cart carrying "only such things as support life" and caught a ship at Velasco. She had to nurse several sick people on board and manage meals for her party of family and servants. Unlike most, she had ample money ($2,000 sewn into her corset) to provide for their needs. They stayed in the Beaumont area until war's end. When news came of the victory at San Jacinto, "we all turned shouting Methodists." Some of the women and children evacuated by sea to New Orleans. Others sought refuge on one of several ships in Galveston Bay. Several families of Germans spent time on Galveston Island in what one woman described as "our hardest experiences." Supplies were in short measure, and many were sick.[61]

The last to be affected by the Runaway Scrape were the families of the Nacogdoches area, who were in less danger than they imagined. There were rumors of an Indian uprising and a Mexican army assault in the area. John Quitman wrote that when he arrived in Nacogdoches in mid-April not a woman or child was in town. Although he judged that there was no danger, the women and children were "in the woods on both sides of the Sabine without supplies or money. Everything was left in flight—the corn in the crib, the meat in the smokehouse, their poultry, cattle, and furniture." He found "the roads literally lined with flying families." Able-bodied men were likewise on the move.[62]

The Runaway Scrape was a traumatic experience for Texas women; however, they coped well. These women were accustomed to hardship and they attended to one another. They took care of each other's children, helped bury the dead, shared food and shelter. They comforted each other when grieved and clung to each other when frightened. In this experience the conditions of living were not so different between slave women and their mistresses. Thomas Jefferson Rusk declared grandly, "The men of Texas deserve much credit, but

[60]David G. Burnet, Proclamation, Mar. 18, 1836, Jenkins (ed.), *Papers,* V, 126–127; Burnet, Order, Mar. 25, 1836, ibid., 186–188; Burnet, Proclamation, Apr. 9, 1836, ibid., 399–400; Jesse Grimes to Burnet, Apr. 17, 1836, ibid., 497; Clarke Beach to Burnet, May 9, 1836, ibid., VI, 190.

[61]Helm, *Scraps of Early Texas History,* 11, 12 (1st quotation), 13–16, 17 (2nd quotation); "Memoirs of Mrs. Annie P. Harris," typescript, 6–7 (BTHC); James F. Perry to H. Austin, Apr. 8, 1836, Jenkins (ed.), *Papers,* V, 385–386; Burnet to James Morgan, Apr. 21, 1836, ibid., VI, 5; Burnet to Morgan, May 18, 1836, ibid., 324–325; Henson, *Anglo American Women,* 27; Rosa Kleberg, "Some of My Early Experiences in Texas," *QTSHA,* I (Apr., 1898), 302 (3rd quotation).

[62]John A. Quitman to Houston, [Apr. 15, 1836], Jenkins (ed.), *Papers,* V, 484 (quotations); John T. Mason to Edmund Gaines, Apr. 13, 1836, ibid., 459–460.

more was due the women. Armed men facing a foe could not but be brave; but the women, with their little children around them, without means of defense or power to resist, faced danger and death with unflinching courage."[63]

The return to homes and businesses ransacked and looted, sometimes destroyed, was by no means easy. Rumors of another Mexican invasion caused considerable insecurity for several months. In spite of rumors of war, however, families set about rebuilding their homes and fences, rounding up their livestock, planting crops. People returned to burned San Felipe, but not all rebuilt and stayed. Angelina Peyton found the

> place bare of every thing—ruins all my things burnt up—crockery piles of cinders—ashes and incombustibles in heaps as left by the fire. . . . [Soldiers] told me afterwards all hated to burn my tavern where they had eaten so many good meals—. . . I was lonely—nobody came—. . . wanted to build a house—call for men—troublesome—couldnt stop there—went to Columbia in self defense—

There she opened another inn.[64]

When the Rose family returned to their home at Fort Bend, they found their possessions scattered. Dilue recalled that her father immediately began to plow his corn crop, and her mother began to wash. "I was shocked, for mother had always kept the Sabbath." Before long, life for the Rose family was back to normal.[65]

The Hispanic families of San Antonio had similar experiences. When they returned to San Antonio, they found "their houses in ruins, their fields laid waste, and their cattle destroyed or dispersed." Juan Seguin found his ranch "despoiled" by Texas and Mexican troops, a scene of "ruin and misery." When Frances Sutherland returned home with her family, she found property destroyed and food in short supply. She reflected, "If we can have peace and can have preaching I wont care for the loss of what property is gone."[66]

Both peace and preaching eventually came to the Texas Republic, and women resumed their lives. The Texas Revolution had little significant long-term impact for them, except for those Hispanic women whose families left Texas permanently. Though Texas women had contributed significantly to the war effort and suffered not a little, there was no apparent change in their roles or expectations. Surely women were valued in Texas, but they were valued as

---

[63]Harris, "Reminiscences of Dilue Harris," *QTSHA*, IV (Jan., 1901), 163–168; Helm, *Scraps of Early Texas History*, 15–17; Kate Scurry Terrell, "The Runaway Scrape," Wooten (ed.), I, 670 (quotation).

[64]Holley, "Notes Made in Interviews," 24.

[65]Harris, "Reminiscences of Dilue Harris," *QTSHA*, IV (Jan., 1901), 177, 178 (quotation), 179.

[66]Juan Seguin, "Personal Memoirs," typescript, 7 (1st–3rd quotations), Juan Nepomuceno Seguin Reminiscences (BTHC); Mrs. Sutherland to sister, June 5, 1836, Jenkins (ed.), *Papers*, VII, 26 (4th quotation).

wives, mothers, helpers, supporters, and slave laborers. Within the confines of those roles Texas women created lives of integrity and service.

Women in Texas experienced pioneer life on farms and in towns in much the same way as women on other frontiers before and after. Their migrations to Texas were marked by both grief and joy, and their settlement by hardship and happiness. They coped with danger, illness, loss, isolation, and privation; yet they found strength and stamina in themselves, their families, and friends. They ministered to others, built churches and schools, ran businesses, and helped establish communities. They survived the Texas Revolution and the Runaway Scrape and helped make the Texas Republic a viable reality. Despite their "tryels and trubbles," Hispanic, black, Anglo-American, and European women were essential in creating nineteenth-century Texas.

# Human Property: The Negro Slave in Harrison County, 1850–1860

Randolph B. Campbell*

*Although slavery existed throughout the period of Spanish rule, it was not until the coming of Anglo Americans in the 1820s that the institution became a significant factor in Texas life. Even though the Mexican government discouraged slavery after independence from Spain, there were 5,000 African American slaves in the area by the time of the Texas Revolution. The numbers increased rapidly during the period of the Republic and early statehood, rising to slightly over 58,000 in 1850 and 182,000 in 1860. More than one-fourth of Texas families owned slaves by the time of the American Civil War.*

*The number of enslaved African Americans in Texas counties varied widely. The heaviest concentration was in northeast and central Texas and along the middle Texas coast. In this article Randolph Campbell of the University of North Texas, recognized as the leading authority on slavery in Texas, describes the "Peculiar Institution" in Harrison County, which had the highest number of enslaved African Americans on the eve of the Civil War. In this essay Campbell demonstrates the significance of slavery in agricultural production in Harrison County. He also points to the many complexities and contradictions in the institution of slavery.*

*For more on the subject of slavery in Texas see Campbell's book* **An Empire for Slavery: The Peculiar Institution in Texas, 1821–1865** *(Baton Rouge: Louisiana State University Press, 1989) as well as his* **A Southern Community in Crisis: Harrison County, 1850–1880** *(Austin: Texas State Historical Association, 1983).*

Harrison County provides an excellent setting for a study in microcosm of the Negro slave's role in antebellum Texas society. The federal censuses

* Randolph B. Campbell, "Human Property: The Negro Slave in Harrison County, 1850–1860," *Southwestern Historical Quarterly*, 76 (Apr., 1973), 384–396.

of 1850 and 1860 reported a larger population for this East Texas county than for any other in the state. There were 599 slaveholders in 1850 and 650 in 1860 which meant that in both census years approximately 60 percent of Harrison's white families owned at least one slave. There were 6,190 slaves reported in the first federal census of Harrison County taken in 1850. Ten years later the number stood at 8,726, an increase of 41 percent during the decade before the Civil War. Negro slaves made up 52 percent of the county's total population of 11,822 in 1850 and 58 percent of the 15,001 people living there in 1860.[1]

Thus a majority of antebellum Harrison County's free families were slaveholders and a majority of its population were black slaves. This situation was not typical of either Texas or the South in the 1850's. Only 29 percent of families in the Lone Star State and 25 percent of all southern families held slaves in 1860. In the same year, slaves composed 30 percent of Texas's population and 32 percent of the population of all fifteen slave states and the District of Columbia.[2] Harrison County's advantages for a study of slavery in microcosm do not, therefore, depend on its being "typical." Instead, the large numbers of slaveholders and slaves in a limited area and the availability of good county records provide an opportunity to combine federal census materials and local government documents in a study small enough to be exhaustive in the use of statistical information and yet large enough to test significant ideas about slavery. Quantitative information from the federal censuses establishes the broad framework of slaveholding in Harrison County and provides evidence

---

[1]Statistics on slaveholders and slaves were compiled from microfilmed manuscript returns of the Seventh Census of the United States, 1850, Schedule 1, Free Inhabitants, and Schedule 2, Slave Inhabitants; and the Eighth Census of the United States, 1860, Schedules 1 and 2. Hereinafter these manuscript returns on microfilm will be cited as Seventh Census, 1850, and Eighth Census, 1860, with appropriate schedule numbers. Total population figures are from United States Bureau of the Census, *Statistical View of the United States: A Compendium of the Seventh Census, 1850* (Washington, 1854), 314; U.S. Census Office, *Eighth Census of the United States: 1860.* Population (Washington, 1864), 485. My research relies primarily on the manuscript censuses, but in a few cases I used data from the published returns. Figures from these published returns often differ slightly from those I compiled from the manuscript censuses. For example, Bureau of the Census, *Statistical View of the United States, 1850,* p. 314, reports 6,213 slaves in Harrison County while I counted 6,190 from the manuscript returns. Minor discrepancies of this sort are to be expected when dealing with large amounts of quantitative historical data, and generally they are unimportant.

[2]There were 76,781 families and 21,878 slaveholders in Texas in 1860. U.S. Census Office, *Eighth Census of the United States: 1860. Mortality and Miscellaneous Statistics* (Washington, 1866), 348–349; ibid., *Agriculture* (Washington, 1864), 247; ibid., *Population,* 486. Some families had more than one slaveholder, but the use of these figures to determine an approximate percentage of slaveholding families should be acceptable. The idea that only 25 percent of all southern families held slaves is generally accepted. See Kenneth Stampp, *The Peculiar Institution: Slavery in the Ante-Bellum South* (New York, 1956), 30-32.

of the importance of slave labor there, while local records illustrate the social utility of the institution.[3]

Obviously slavery was a central fact in the existence of Harrison County before the Civil War. But what can be said of the slave's position and role in this society? In the first place, Negro bondsmen in Harrison County were property, chattels personal whose conduct was subject to the discipline of their owner just as their labor and services were at his disposal. Slaves were given a few civil rights by Texas law—such as the right to trial by jury when charged with a crime greater than petit larceny—but they had no religious rights, no right to lawful marriage, and virtually no property rights. State law in the 1850's declared it illegal for an owner to make a contract with a slave allowing the latter to "hire his time" by paying a set price and then be free to negotiate his own labor contract with another employer. Under no circumstances could one slave be hired to another slave or to any "free person of color." In general slaves had no legally prescribed way to earn or otherwise win their freedom.[4]

Clearly Harrison County's slaves were property, and the laws of Texas provided definitions and guarantees in this area. Nevertheless, slaves were much more than simple chattels personal; they were also human beings with human intelligence and abilities. Negro bondsmen represented a unique combination of the qualities of property and humanity, and this created a complexity in their role in slave society that must not be underestimated.

David Brion Davis's study, *The Problem of Slavery in Western Culture,* points out that the contradiction involved in holding men as things is believed to have produced tension in virtually all slave societies. Charles G. Sellers, Jr., has argued that the conflict between slave-holding in the South and the liberal and Christian ideals for humanity espoused by most free Americans constituted the "travail of slavery." Indeed a major part of the Civil War crisis was the "suggestible" psychological state produced in southerners by the tensions of holding humans as property. Their struggle was not a clear-cut contest between slaveholders and nonslaveholders or proslavery and antislavery forces, but

---

[3]Harrison County offers other advantages too. The size of slaveholdings ranged from the very small to the very large, and slaves were used in a great variety of nonagricultural as well as agricultural pursuits. See notes 13 and 16 below.

[4]This summary of the slave's legal position as property in Texas is drawn from Williamson S. Oldham and George W. White, *A Digest of the General Statute Laws of the State of Texas* (Austin, 1859). Sections pertinent to my paragraph are as follows: "Texas Constitution of 1845," p. 26; "Penal Code," 481, 521, 542–543, 559–562; "Code of Criminal Procedure," 640, 642, 670–673. Important statutes relative to slavery in Texas are found in H. P. N. Gammel (comp.), *The Laws of Texas, 1822–1891* (10 vols.; Austin, 1898), II, 345–346, 778–782, 1501–1504; III, 29, 911–912, 1502–1516; IV, 499–500, 947–949.

rather a more subtle internal conflict for those who faced the problems of conscience and belief involved in owning and controlling human beings defined as property. Ralph E. Morrow contended that much of the proslavery argument was not really aimed at its apparent targets such as the abolitionists and antislavery people. Instead it was intended to reassure those people who had no hostility to slavery and were committed to its preservation. For the South as a whole there is much evidence to support the argument that the contradictions of holding men as things resulted in internal psychological strain for many individual slaveholders.[5] Did the slave's peculiar situation as property and humanity create similar tensions for the free citizens of Harrison County?

Harrison County's slaveholders could not avoid the contradictions of their "Peculiar Institution." The slave's humanity was a fact not easily denied, and the constitution and laws of the state directed all Texans to remember it. The Constitution of 1845 called on the legislature to pass laws "which will oblige the owners of slaves to treat them with humanity." In fact, a new law was not necessary because "An Act Concerning Slavery" which had been passed in 1840 under the Republic of Texas was simply continued in effect after statehood. It outlawed unreasonable or cruel treatment and made the murder of a slave, or deliberate action causing a bondsman's death, a felony comparable to a similar act perpetrated against a white man. The Texas Supreme Court in the cases that came before it in the antebellum period, several of which began in Harrison County, was careful to read this law with emphasis on the slave as humanity rather than as property. Legislation, of course, also called for punishing the slave's criminal offenses as though committed by whites. Punishment, however, was either whipping or death, and eventually the legislature came to enact the ultimate legal recognition of the slave as humanity and property when in 1852 it passed "An Act to Indemnify the Owners for the Loss of Slaves Executed for Capital Offenses." The slave was human enough to be tried for his crimes and property enough to be paid for if destroyed.[6]

Many slaveholders in Harrison County did not need constitutional or legislative reminders that their slave property differed significantly from their other chattels personal such as cattle and horses. The county's estate and probate

---

[5]David Brion Davis, *The Problem of Slavery in Western Culture* (Ithaca, 1966), 60; Charles Grier Sellers, Jr., "The Travail of Slavery," from Sellers (ed.), *The Southerner as American* (Chapel Hill, N.C., 1960), 40–71; Ralph E. Morrow, "The Proslavery Argument Revisited," *Mississippi Valley Historical Review,* XLVIII (June, 1961), 79–94.

[6]Gammel (comp.), *Laws of Texas,* II, 345–346, 1296; III, 911–912; Oldham and White, *Digest of the Laws,* 561; A. E. Keir Nash, "The Texas Supreme Court and Trial Rights of Blacks, 1845–1860," *Journal of American History,* LVIII (December, 1971), 622–642. Important legal cases rising from Harrison County, that are discussed in this article, included *Purvis* v. *Sherrod,* 12 *Texas* 140 and *Moore* v. *Minerva,* 17 *Texas* 20. The quote from the constitution is found in Gammel (comp.), *Laws of Texas,* II, 345–346. Laws such as the "Act to Indemnify the Owners" were not unusual in the slave South.

records from the antebellum period provide evidence of this fact in the many wills which conferred special status on individual slaves or groups of bondsmen. John P. Thompson's will of August 11, 1849, for example, referred to an "old favorite Negro man . . . whom I desire to maintain on the place with his mistress and to perform easy labor, but I do not wish him to be regarded as the property of anyone." J. M. Saunders directed his wife to provide five dollars per month to a Negro man named Henry, "said Negro at no time nor under any circumstances to be subject to sale." In 1853, J. J. Webster requested "that my Negroes be so distributed as to allot the families by families in the partition [of his estate] that members of the same family may remain together."[7] When William T. Weathersby's will freeing three of his slaves was contested by would-be heirs, his brother-in-law and executor, John L. Sherrod, successfully defended Weathersby's recognition of human dignity all the way to the Texas Supreme Court in 1854.[8]

Although the cases of Thompson, Saunders, Webster, and Weathersby were probably more typical than unusual, not every slaveholder in Harrison County was concerned with the humanity of his slaves.[9] Many wills directed the division and sale of slave property without any apparent regard for the Negro family or individual. Agnes McKay, for example, directed in 1853 that her boy Andrew be reserved to serve her daughters until they were grown at which time he was to be sold and the proceeds divided among the girls. The laws protecting slaves undoubtedly were not enforced to the letter, especially since bondsmen were hardly in a position to bring charges against their masters and could not testify in criminal actions except against other slaves and free blacks.[10] Yet the fact remained—the Negro slave was a human being— and there is evidence that many slaveholders were very aware of that fact.

Did the slave's humanity, however, serve only to make him a property troublesome to the consciences of many owners, and ultimately of course, a property unacceptable in the civilized world? Perhaps slave property was valuable and socially useful in some ways precisely because it was human. This proposition may seem obvious at first glance, but it is not often considered.[11] If true, it

---

[7]Harrison County Estate Records (County Clerk's Office, Marshall), B, 266–267; E, 307–309; Harrison County Probate Minutes (ibid.), E, 353–354. Thompson's and Webster's wills are quoted from Estate Records B and E respectively. Saunders's will, made on January 2, 1861, is quoted from Probate Minutes.

[8]*Purvis* v. *Sherrod,* 12 *Texas* 140. The slaves were freed, although they could not legally remain in Texas. Weathersby's will had provided funds to settle them outside the state.

[9]My opinion that these wills were more typical than unusual is based on reading large numbers of such documents in the Harrison County courthouse.

[10]Harrison County Estate Records, E, 333–334; Oldham and White, *Digest of the Laws,* 640.

[11]The general idea is expressed in George R. Woolfolk, "Cotton Capitalism and Slave Labor in Texas," *Southwestern Social Science Quarterly,* XXXVII (June, 1956), 43–52. My research followed a number of ideas expressed in this article.

adds a dimension to the story of the Negro as a member of his society. He made the plantation system work, but he contributed much more than muscle for farm work. To provide evidence to support this idea, it is necessary to examine the variety of ways in which the slave was involved in the day to day economic affairs and social arrangements of antebellum Harrison County and the degree to which the slave's many roles depended on his humanity, and finally to consider what it meant to the master and the slave that the latter was recognized as a human in many aspects of the same institution that defined him as property.

The slave's most obvious role in the 1850's was as a supplier of labor for Harrison County's thriving agricultural economy ruled by King Cotton. It is difficult to imagine in the 1970's when there is only one gin operating in the county, but Harrison was among the major cotton producing areas in the Southwest in the years before the Civil War. According to the census of 1850, the 1849 crop of 4,560 bales was the second largest grown in any Texas county that year. Harrison's 1859 crop showed an increase of 366 percent to 21,231 bales. (Even then the county fell one spot to third in the state's cotton production.) While cotton was the main crop, it was not the sole concern of Harrison's farmers. The county's production of corn, for example, 377,902 bushels in 1849 and 647,732 bushels in 1859, ranked her first in the state in both years.[12]

Other statistics drawn from the censuses of 1850 and 1860 demonstrate how important the Negro slave was to agricultural production in Harrison County. Plantations and farms using slave workers controlled more than 90 percent of the improved acreage and represented approximately 90 percent of the cash value of the county's farms in 1850 and 1860. They produced 96 percent of the cotton in 1849 and 94 percent in 1859. The corresponding figures for corn production were 91 percent in 1849 and 88 percent in 1859. These figures are especially significant because slaveholding plantations and farms constituted only 76 percent of the county's agricultural units in 1850 and 68 percent in 1860. Non-slaveholding farmers owned a disproportionately small share of the valuable farm acreage and produced an equally small share of the important crops.[13]

---

[12]Seventh Census, 1850, Schedule 4, Agriculture; Eighth Census, 1860, Schedule 4, Agriculture. Comparisons with other counties are based on Bureau of the Census, *Statistical View of the United States, 1850*, 310–319, and Bureau of the Census, *Eighth Census: 1860. Agriculture*, 140–151. As in the case of slaves and slaveholders, my figures on agricultural production in Harrison County compiled from the manuscript census differ slightly from those in the published returns.

[13]Seventh Census, 1850, Schedules 1, 2, and 4; Eighth Census, 1860, Schedules 1, 2, and 4. Harrison County farmers, regardless of the size of their slaveholdings, did not designate themselves as "planters" in the censuses of 1850 and 1860. The great majority (79 percent in 1850 and 70 percent in 1860) held fewer than 20 slaves. However, the mean slaveholding size was relatively large—12.9 slaves in 1850 and 16.2 in 1860—and there was a high degree of concentration of slave property in the hands of big slaveholders in both years. The nine men who owned more than 50 slaves

Statistics on the value of real and personal property owned in Harrison County in 1850 and 1860 further indicate the importance of the slave to its economy. Slaveholding farmers, including those who owned farms and those who identified themselves as farmers but did not appear as landholders in the agricultural return, constituted 66 percent of the county's agricultural families in 1850. They owned 91 percent of all the real property listed as belonging to farmers. By 1860 this group had decreased to 63 percent of those who listed their occupation as farmer, but they still held 91 percent of the real property and 96 percent of the personal property claimed by the whole farming population.[14] Slaves themselves were the largest single item of personal property reported. These figures on agricultural production and property values indicate that slaveholders dominated the agricultural economy of antebellum Harrison County. The slave's productive capacity played a key part in creating this situation, although the causal connection between ownership of slaves and production is not proven here.

The Negro slave as agricultural laborer was cast primarily in the role of property. Typically his job was to work from daylight to dark at simple tasks which took advantage of his muscle power. His value generally depended on his capabilities as a field hand. A farm horse is valued on its working qualities and exploited in much the same fashion. Human qualities, however, contributed to the slave's value and potential in this role as laborer. The simplest task depended on the intelligence of the slave which permitted him to follow directions without constant supervision and guidance such as would have to be provided in working a horse. The use of one slave as a "driver" to keep the others working and enforce discipline with whippings was a common practice in Harrison County. Apparently some owners with large holdings avoided the expense of overseers by managing their own slaves with the aid of such "drivers." W. L. Sloan, according to one of his former slaves, demonstrated another more obvious way to use the slave's intelligence when he taught several bondsmen to read and write and used them to record work such as cotton picking in the field.[15]

---

in 1850 constituted only 2.3 percent of all slaveholders, and yet they held 9.7 percent of all slaves. In 1860 the 27 men who owned more than 50 slaves represented 5.7 percent of all slaveholders and owned 20.2 percent of the slaves. There was only one slaveholder, William T. Scott, who owned over 100 slaves in either census year. He held 103 in 1850 and 104 in 1860. The concentration of wealth and planter domination in Harrison County, especially as it related to agricultural production, is the subject of another study now in preparation.

[14]Seventh Census, 1850, Schedules 1 and 4; Eighth Census, 1860, Schedules 1 and 4. Agricultural families include all those who were headed by a farmer whether they owned land or not. Personal property was not reported in the census of 1850.

[15]Works Progress Administration, Federal Writers Project, *Texas Narratives,* Slave Narratives: A Folk History of Slavery in the United States from Interviews with Former Slaves, Vol. XVI in 3 parts (Washington, 1941), Part 1, pp. 191–192, 285; Part 2, pp. 195–197; Part 3, pp. 160–161.

Thus even the role of agricultural laborer depended to some extent on the slave's human qualities, and some slaveholders found methods to allow fuller exploitation of the bondsman's potential in that area.

The Negro slave's importance to the society of antebellum Harrison County did not end with his role as an agricultural laborer. Approximately 6 percent of the county's bondsmen in the 1850's apparently were not engaged in agriculture. Nonfarming slaveholders (109 in 1850 and 129 in 1860), who constituted slightly less than 20 percent of all slaveowners, held 364 bondsmen in 1850 and 584 in 1860. Living for the most part in the town of Marshall, these were generally small slaveholders (average of 3.34 slaves per owner in 1850 and 4.53 per owner in 1860) who pursued a wide variety of occupations. There were professional men including lawyers, doctors, ministers, and teachers; tradesmen such as blacksmiths, tailors, printers, and carpenters; manufacturers including ginmakers and brickmakers; public officials such as judges and county clerks; and businessmen ranging from merchants and grocers to tavern-keepers and livery-stable operators. Certainly in some cases their slaves served only as household servants or personal servants for wives and children. Perhaps in a few cases the bondsmen were hired out or else used in agricultural pursuits in a fashion that did not show up in the federal census returns. It is difficult to imagine, for example, what other use W. J. Sorrelle, a Baptist minister, could have made of the seventeen slaves he owned in 1850. Apparently many of these non-farming slaveholders employed their bondsmen in their occupations. Three examples from 1850 illustrate this possibility. G. B. Atkins, a brickmaker in Marshall, owned nine slaves, six of whom were males over eighteen years of age. J. P. Cooley, a tailor, owned one male slave over eighteen, and William P. Barrett, a grocer, held one adult male, one boy, and two girls.[16] No proof is available that these slaves and several hundred others like them assisted their owners in nonagricultural occupations, but very likely they did. Possibly some of these slaves possessed special skills. Clearly these occupations required intelligence and abilities not possessed by any other form of property.

Thus the slave provided agricultural and nonagricultural labor in antebellum Harrison County; beyond this he was thoroughly involved in the everyday social arrangements of the county's free population. The range of utility demonstrated by the slave is especially noteworthy when considering the nature of his role in society. In some cases his position was that of property pure and simple; in others, his humanity was plainly essential.

Tax records illustrate one way the slave figured heavily in his society albeit solely as a piece of property. The state of Texas and Harrison County naturally required sources of tax revenue to provide for public expenses, and slaves were

[16]Seventh Census, 1850, Schedules 1 and 2; Eighth Census, 1860, Schedules 1 and 2.

by far the largest single item on the property-tax rolls for the county in 1850 and 1860. For example, a sample of twelve of the largest slaveholders in the county in 1860 shows a total property valuation for tax purposes of $791,343 of which $557,360 or 71 percent was assessed on their slaves. Twelve small slaveholders (owning from one to nine slaves) were assessed $33,000 or 51 percent of their total property valuation of $64,359 on their slave property. State tax rates amounted to only one and one-quarter mills or .00125 cents on the dollar in 1860 so they do not seem burdensome by today's standards.[17] Nevertheless slaves were a major source of tax revenue.

Slaves were taxed as personal property; a riding horse would have been treated in precisely the same fashion. But it seems that the slave contributed to keeping tax rates low in a way possible only for a human. The Harrison County Commissioners Court Minutes for the 1850's indicate that while upkeep of the county's roads was a primary public concern, it cost local government little or nothing. The Commissioners Court simply appointed a citizen to be responsible for a particular section of road in his area and directed him to use his slaves and those of certain of his neighbors to do the work.[18] Individual responsibility and slave labor maintained most of the roads at no cost to the taxpayer. It was of course not unusual in free societies to have the citizens of an area "turn out" to maintain the roads, but the slave as human property provided a ready-made work force for the job in Harrison County.

The probate and estate records of Harrison County clearly demonstrate that the slave proved useful as a highly mobile means of conveying and distributing property in social arrangements such as marriage contracts, divorce decrees, and settlement of estates. The last will and testament of J. J. Webster, for example, probated in 1854, divided his estate into three shares of approximately $45,000 each in value for his son and the heirs of two daughters. To achieve an equitable distribution in this fashion, the son, J. B. Webster, received 29 slaves and 54 percent of the land while the two daughters' heirs received 37 and 34 slaves respectively and smaller shares of land. Stock and cash were then allocated to complete the distribution of property.[19] In this case the slave's humanity was largely unimportant, but property in slaves was almost as handily divisible as stock or cash, and it was economically more feasible to divide it rather than land into small shares.

Slave property was usually distributed in some fashion in estate settlements, but in cases where a guardian or an administrator was appointed, the

---

[17]Records of the Comptroller of Public Accounts, Ad Valorem Tax Division: County Real and Personal Property Tax Rolls, 1836–1874, Harrison County, 1850, 1860. Microfilms of these manuscript tax records may be seen in the State Finance Building, Austin.

[18]Harrison County Commissioners Court Minutes, 1850 (County Clerk's Office, Marshall), 205–207.

[19]Harrison County Estate Records, E, 307–309.

slave could be used over a period of time as an asset to the heirs. When Sheriff S. R. Perry was made administrator of the estate of S. J. Arnett in 1853, he apparently found it more profitable to hire out Arnett's slaves annually than to sell them. At the end of 1854, for example, he hired out seven slaves to the highest bidder for their services from January 2 to December 25, 1855 for a total of $431. The following year the same seven slaves hired for $549.[20] Real property could have been rented in the same fashion, but there could not have been a comparable return from any other personal property left to a typical estate in the antebellum period.

The Harrison County District Court Civil Minutes for January 17, 1851, show that when Mary Pridgen won a divorce from Wiley Pridgen the first step in their property settlement was the assignment of 29 slaves to her share. This case provides not only another example of slavery's usefulness in estate arrangements; it also suggests that the ownership of slave property could give women a degree of independence and security in Harrison County's agrarian society. The Texas Constitution of 1845 gave married females the right to hold real and personal property separate from the property of their husbands.[21] This meant that women could bring land and slaves to marriage and maintain separate ownership of them. In the event of divorce, they could take an important means of support with them from the marriage. Here the slave's human ability to work on his own was critical. The female left with hundreds of acres of land was none too secure unless adequate labor was available. When she had the land and the slaves to work it, she only needed to hire someone to direct them in producing a living.

Possession of slaves was, of course, similarly important to the security of the widowed female left with a family to support and no ability to work a farm herself. For example, John P. Thompson at his death in 1849 left his wife Elizabeth with eight children at home. He also left her a farm reported at 265 improved acres of land in the census of and a slave labor force that numbered 50 that same year. Although several of her children were grown, Elizabeth Thompson could not have produced her 1849 crops of 29 bales of cotton and 2,300 bushels of corn without slave labor. She might possibly have hired free labor, but probably the immediate expenses of operation would have been greater. Her slaves had the further advantage of being a readily negotiable, self-reproducing capital investment.[22]

[20]Harrison County Probate Minutes, D, 348–349; Estate Records, F, 444; Estate Records, H, 340.

[21]Harrison County District Court, Civil Minutes (District Clerk's Office, Marshall), 99–100, January 17, 1851; William M. McKinney, *Texas Jurisprudence* (45 vols.; San Francisco, 1929–1937), XXIII, 50.

[22]Harrison County Estate Records, B, 266–267; Seventh Census, 1850, Schedules 1, 2, and 4. The importance of the slave as liquid capital is described in Woolfolk, "Cotton Capitalism," 43–44, 51–52.

The case of Mrs. Nancy Beck provides an example of how the slave helped provide security for even a small farm operator. Isaac Beck died in 1850, leaving his wife and five children under twelve years of age with 70 acres of improved land and five young slaves. Ten years later Mrs. Beck still lived in Harrison County. From the census returns of 1860, it appears that she managed a farm of 100 improved acres worked by four slaves and produced 400 bushels of corn and five bales of cotton.[23] The slave's role in cases such as those of Elizabeth Thompson and Nancy Beck was the familiar one of agricultural worker, but no other type of property could supply intelligent labor with the same degree of utility for a female farm owner.

Women were only a small portion of Harrison County's slaveholders in 1850 and 1860. There were 48 female slaveholders in the county in 1850, and they owned 707 slaves. A decade later 52 women held 744 slaves. Females comprised a very small percentage of all slaveholders in these years, but the security provided by slave property extended to many women who did not actually hold slaves in their names.[24]

The "Peculiar Institution" proved to be so flexible and adaptable to public and private needs that the Negro slave was thoroughly worked into the economic and social arrangements of Harrison County's society in the 1850's. Evidently, no form of nonhuman property could have proved equally useful in so many ways. Even the simple role of agricultural laborer depended to some extent on the slave's humanity. And slaveholders and slaveholding society at times employed arrangements that were based especially on his human qualities.

It is impossible to determine precisely how many slaveholders were bothered by the contradiction of holding people as things or how much tension was created by the institution. In the 1850's public statements casting unfavorable light on slavery were decidedly unpopular in Harrison County. The Marshall *Texas Republican,* edited by R. W. Loughery, was quick to label anyone who favored compromising in any way on the ultrasouthern position in the 1850's as a "submissionist." Editor Loughery was angrily surprised in 1856 to find the *Harrison Flag,* an American party paper, publishing a series of articles entitled "Texas—Dark and Bright Side" which included "domestic slavery" on the dark side. This betrayed, said the *Republican,* a "very decided squinting towards abolitionism."[25] Loughery had little to fear, however. In 1860, Editor John W. Barrett of the *Flag,* although he endorsed the moderate Constitutional Union

[23]Harrison County Probate Minutes, C, 30; Seventh Census, 1850, Schedules 1, 2, and 4; Eighth Census, 1860, Schedules 1, 2, and 4.

[24]Seventh Census, 1850, Schedules 1 and 2; Eighth Census, 1860, Schedules 1 and 2. Slaveownership by females may have been underreported in the census due to combining by the enumerator of the slaves held by family members under the name of the head of the household.

[25]*Texas Republican* (Marshall), July 19, 1856.

party ticket of John Bell and Edward Everett, took great care to explain his support for the South and all southern institutions.[26]

Some slaveholders were well aware that their property was human and indicated their awareness in the special treatment of individual slaves in their wills. The County Commissioners Court demonstrated an interesting terminology in regularly referring to slaves as "hands." This may signify nothing, but it is clearly a reference to property with a word associated with humans. The constitution and laws of Texas demonstrated the free citizens' inability to think of the bondsman as property only, and the State Supreme Court regularly ruled in favor of protecting the slave from unreasonably harsh treatment in the antebellum period.[27] These recognitions of the slave's humanity, conscious or unconscious, would seem to indicate a problem of conscience for those who held men as things, but obviously the degree or effect of their sentiments cannot be positively established or measured.

The scarcity of records makes it difficult to say what recognition of the slave's humanity meant to the enslaved individual. Legally, it brought some degree of protection for his body and life although enforcement of the laws certainly was not perfect. Personally, it could mean special treatment for an old or especially favored bondsman or for a slave family. It might even mean that an owner would consider the psychological state of his workers and attempt to use good treatment as an inducement to good work. Dr. William Baldwin provided an unusual example of this approach. According to one of his former slaves, Baldwin kept a barrel of whiskey on his front porch and allowed slaves to get a drink on their way to the field. Still there was no guarantee that an individual owner would recognize his slaves' humanity. And the slave could hardly be secure in the knowledge that he was a human, let alone that he would be treated like one. Will Adams, born a slave in Harrison County in 1853, remembered years later that he had once remarked to his grandmother about how well their owners had treated them. He also remembered her answer: "Why shouldn't they—it was their money."[28]

The Negro slave was almost certainly a profit-producing part of Harrison County's antebellum society. This is not the place, however, to pursue the complicated and much-controverted question of the profitability of slavery. The matter of productivity and profitability is an important one, but it says little about the slave to differentiate him from any other piece of property. The Negro was much more than a unit of capital investment and labor supply to Harrison County in the 1850's, and, although his humanity probably created

[26] *Harrison Flag* (Marshall), August–December, 1860, passim.

[27] Harrison County Commissioners Court Minutes, 1850, pp. 205–207, and throughout the 1850's; Nash, "Texas Supreme Court and Trial Rights of Blacks," 622, 630–631, 639.

[28] *Texas Narratives,* Part 1, pp. 1–3; Part 4, pp. 89–91. The quote is from Part 1, p. 1.

tensions for many slaveholders, the Negro's utility as a slave was frequently enhanced by his qualities as a human. Slavery might have disappeared had it been unprofitable, and its destruction would have been a simpler matter had the slave been white, but the institution's social utility extended beyond profitability and racial control. The Harrison County experience suggests that possibly Sellers and Morrow underestimated the complexity of the situation. The Negro's humanity was the ultimate flaw of slavery, but, ironically, in some ways his capacities and contributions as a human only strengthened his bonds as property.

# Sarah Devereux: A Study in Southern Femininity

JOLEENE MADDOX SNIDER*

*As noted earlier, the role of women in Texas history has received more attention from historians in recent years. In this article Joleene Maddox Snider, retired history professor at Texas State University in San Marcos, describes the life and times of Sarah Ann Landrum, daughter of a Texas Revolutionary veteran, who at the age of sixteen married thirty-six-year-old Julien Sidney Devereux, a plantation owner in Rusk County, Texas. When Julien died in 1856, Sarah, only twenty-nine at the time, was left with four sons, eighty slaves, and a 10,000-acre plantation, Monte Verdi. For the next thirteen years Sarah ran the plantation, finished the uncompleted plantation mansion, raised a large cotton crop, brought up four sons, and endured the hardships of the Civil War and Reconstruction. As Snider points out, Sarah's marriage to Jim Garrison in 1869 was "a disaster and resulted in the loss of her home and property." When Sarah died at Jacksonville, Texas, in 1910 her estate was value at $600.*

*Readers interested in learning more about the Devereux plantation should see Dorman H. Winfrey,* Julien Sidney Devereux and his Monte Verdi Plantation *(Waco: Texian Press, 1962). For more on the role of Texas women see the works listed in the introduction to the article in this volume by Fane Downs, "'Tryels and Trubbles': Women in Early Nineteenth-Century Texas."*

This article will seek to illuminate more clearly the dimensions and variations of southern femininity through a biographical sketch of Sarah Devereux Garrison, an upper-class white woman from East Texas who filled all the gender roles expected of her, but also took responsibility and control for

*Joleene Maddox Snider, "Sarah Devereux: A Study in Southern Femininity," *Southwestern Historical Quarterly*, 97 (Jan., 1994), 479–508.

affairs clearly out of the theoretical domain of woman's sphere.[1] Sarah Devereux accepted the nineteenth-century cultural assumptions of southern womanhood and the "Cult of Domesticity,"[2] but the tenets of her personal philosophy had to expand in order to accommodate the changing circumstances of her life; first, to succeed as a female planter after her husband's death, then to endure the trials of the Civil War and Reconstruction, and, lastly, to cope with her disastrous second marriage. She never rebelled against society's expectations of her gender, class, and race, but she repeatedly enlarged on those expectations to meet the exigencies of her life. Ironically, even as she sought to fulfill her place as a proper southern lady of the genteel upper class, she was constantly expanding the boundaries of that place.

Sarah Ann Landrum (1827–1900) was only sixteen in 1843 when she married thirty-six-year-old Julien Sidney Devereux. When Julien died in 1856, she inherited Monte Verdi, one of the largest plantations in East Texas. Julien's death left Sarah, who was only twenty-nine at the time, with four young sons, an unfinished plantation mansion, over 10,000 acres of land, 80 slaves, 300 head of cattle and hogs, 230 head of sheep, and all the work animals, outbuildings, and equipment that a large plantation required. During the thirteen years that she ran the plantation alone, she finished the mansion, raised a profitable cotton crop most years, supervised and arranged for the upbringing and education of her sons, and endured the difficult years of the Civil War and Reconstruction. Her remarriage in 1869 was not a happy one and resulted in the loss of her home and, eventually, all her land.

In order to develop a clear and detailed portrait of Sarah Devereux, we must address the following issues and questions: how, when, and why did she begin to assume responsibility for the management of the family plantation? Was her management successful? What sort of support staff did she have? How did she exercise control and power? What impact did the Civil War have on her? Did prevailing philosophies and assumptions about women affect her self-image as a woman? What was the role of marriage and family in her life? If her

---

[1]Biography is uniquely suited to examine the role of cultural assumptions and historical events as they impact the people of a society. The southern historian Drew Gilpin Faust has often used biography as a vehicle to study social and intellectual history. She states in her book, *Southern Stories: Slaveholders in Peace and War* (Columbia: University of Missouri Press, 1992), that she has "found the point of intersection between the individual and his or her social world an extraordinarily rich—all but irresistible—locus in which to explore the opportunities and limitations that shape social action. Individual lives are the ultimate sites in which the larger forces of historical process and change operate in their fullest and . . . most intriguing and revealing complexity" (p. 2).

[2]According to Nancy F. Cott in *The Bonds of Womanhood: "Woman's Sphere" in New England, 1780–1835* (New Haven: Yale University Press, 1977), Barbara Welter first used the term "cult of true womanhood" in 1966 and Aileen S. Kraditor coined the phrase "cult of domesticity" in 1968. The nineteenth century used the terms "woman's sphere" and "woman's place" to discuss women's roles (p. 1).

management was successful, then why did she remarry in 1869? Can she be considered a feminist or protofeminist?

According to her brief, undated autobiography, written in the last few years of her life, Sarah Ann Landrum was almost three when her parents and grandparents "Emigrated to Texas during the winter of 1829 & 30" from Alabama and settled in the Austin Colony in Montgomery County.[3] Her father served in the Texas Revolution under Sam Houston's command but "was not in the Battle of Sanjacinto" because the company in which he served was "absent to remove families out of the way of the armies."[4] Nothing remains in the Devereux papers of Sarah's girlhood and early womanhood, but it is reasonable to believe that they were not atypical of a young woman of the period in southern society. For women marriages were contracted young and, in spite of the importance of marriage to the life of a young woman, often casually, but usually with a "thoughtful consideration of land and family connections."[5]

While Julien and Sarah Devereux's marriage would result in a warm, affectionate union, certainly the social position of each was important in the match. Sarah was the daughter of a Texas Revolutionary veteran and, if not a great beauty, a comely young woman of sixteen in whom Julien recognized intelligence and ability in spite of her youth. According to Sarah's autobiography, Col. Julien S. Devereux (that the exact nature of his military experience was unclear and may have been nonexistent hardly mattered; all true southern gentlemen bore titles of some variety) was already "a man of wealth and high standing" at the time of their marriage and had risen to a position as "a member of the Texas Legislature at the time of his death in 1856."[6] Julien, however, brought considerable personal baggage to the union.

Accompanied by his father, John, Julien Devereux came to Texas in 1841 from Alabama with most of the family slaves and his illegitimate young daughter, Antoinette, and left behind considerable debt, a failed marriage, and an illegitimate son, Sidney. By legal agreement Julien had separated from his first wife, Adaline Rebeccah Bradley Devereux, in 1840 but did not file a petition for divorce until February 1843. Considering the sequence of events in 1843—the divorce petition was filed in February and granted in March, and Julien

---

[3]The use of *"[sic]" to* indicate original usage or spelling has been eliminated in this manuscript except for a few critical instances. Quotations have been checked to ensure accuracy of the original. If the grammar or style appears strange to the modern reader, it is because of the erratic style and grammar of the nineteenth century.

Sarah Devereux Garrison's autobiography, undated [1898], Julien Sidney Devereux Family Papers (Eugene C. Barker Texas History Center, University of Texas, Austin).

[4]Ibid.

[5]Anne Firor Scott, *The Southern Lady: From Pedestal to Politics, 1830–1930* (Chicago: University of Chicago Press, 1970), 24.

[6]Sarah Devereux Garrison's autobiography, undated [1898], Devereux Family Papers.

married Sarah in June—it is highly likely that Julien sought the formal divorce in order to marry Sarah.

In any event, the divorce was a messy affair. John William Devereux, Julien's father, testified to Adaline's "extravagant and wasteful" behavior and her tendency to "beat and abuse the servants . . . in the most unmerciful and unwarrantable manner." Certainly the most damaging charge against Adaline was of "inconsiderate and neglectful" maternal skills. John Devereux's deposition stated that Adaline and Julien's child died of starvation because Adaline "would neither suckle the infant herself nor suffer a wet nurse to do it." Her violent outbursts of temper and later addiction "to habits of intemperance" brought on excessive uterine bleeding, which rendered her incapable of performing the "duties of a wife," and were entirely "inconsistent with the proper delicasy of a female."[7] Heirs of Adaline Bradley Devereux have challenged Julien's version of events and claimed that he deserted his wife and took the slaves contrary to their estrangement agreement.[8]

While this article tells Sarah's story and not Adaline's, the divorce is worthy of some discussion and is germane to Sarah's tale. Besides the obvious conclusion that Adaline was as shrewish as John Devereux's deposition portrayed her to be, there are other plausible explanations for her behavior. Adaline's violent outbursts and alcoholism may have been her way of reacting to Julien's financial difficulties, infidelity, and illegitimate children. Additionally, many of her problems may have had a physiological origin. The frequent hemorrhages which rendered her unfit as a wife sound more like serious gynecological problems than the result of angry fits or intemperance as her father-in-law charged. Also, it is difficult to image Adaline, Julien, or other relatives deliberately allowing an infant to succumb to starvation and not taking positive action of some sort. If Adaline had serious gynecological and obstetrical health problems, then her infant could have been afflicted in untold ways, while her ability to lactate may also have also been seriously impaired. Whether the reasons for her inappropriate behavior and physical deficiencies were related to Julien's financial problems and marital indiscretions or her health or both, her greatest failure was not fulfilling her role as a proper woman. Regardless of what beset them, women were expected to be good mothers, quietly and stoically accept whatever fate brought them, and contain and control their anger at their situation, and Adaline Devereux apparently did not do this.

---

[7]John Devereux's deposition from Divorce Petition, County of Montgomery, Republic of Texas, Feb. 10, 1843, Devereux Family Papers, as quoted in Dorman H. Winfrey, *Julien Sidney Devereux and his Monte Verdi Plantation* (Waco: Texian Press, 1962), 38 (3rd, 4th, and 6th quotations), 39 (1st, 2nd, 5th, and 7th quotations).

[8]Winfrey, *Julien Sidney Devereux,* 30.

Why was Sarah's marital relationship with Julien so different? Certainly Julien was older, presumably wiser, and more committed to his second marriage because he wanted legitimate heirs. His letters to Sarah are those of a kind, considerate, faithful husband and father to a respected and adored wife and mother of his children. If Sarah applied the management skills to her husband that she later applied so successfully to her children and plantation, then she may have simply "managed" Julien more efficiently than did Adaline. In essence, Sarah succeeded because she was a proper woman in the accepted mode: she was a good mother, she bore her disappointments and disagreements with a minimum of fuss and vocalizing, and, most importantly, she contained and submerged her anger.

Sarah apparently accepted Julien's past with graciousness and aplomb, dutifully fulfilling the role of stepmother to Antoinette and Sidney. Sidney did not come to live with Julien and Sarah for several years after their marriage, and then was often away at boarding school, but Antoinette had come to Texas with her father and would have fallen under Sarah's care immediately. While Antoinette was at boarding school in 1854, it was Sarah, the stepmother, who wrote the headstrong teenager concerning her father's disapproval of her sudden engagement. It is unclear why Julien did not write the letter himself; perhaps he thought Sarah's feminine voice would have more impact on Antoinette.

> Dear Antoinette your Papa appears to be a good deal troubled about your having made so hasty an arrangement without letting him know any thing about it before hand, and he requests me to say to you that if you set any value on his love and regard for you that you will abandon all such notions for the present, and give your entire attention to your studies and improvement of your mind, and he further says that he does not wish you to make any more apologies, explanations or any further engagements to any person at this time whatever. Dear Antoinette if you knew how much distress and anxiety you have caused to your Dear Papa by what he considers your imprudent and thoughtless engagement, you certainly would be more cautious for the future—he has no disposition to interfere with your choice or affections when you arrive at a proper age, and complete your Education, but the thoughts of your marrying at this time renders him very unhappy.[9]

Apparently the letter accomplished its goal: Antoinette did not marry for two more years. Even after Julien's death she remained close to her stepmother and half brothers, and Sarah's second husband was Antoinette's husband's brother.

Sarah's creation of a successful marriage and family with a man with a checkered background is hardly an uncommon story. In fact, it bears a striking

[9]Sarah Devereux to Antoinette Devereux, Feb. 24, 1854, Devereux Family Papers.

resemblance to the story of a more famous Texas contemporary of Sarah's, Margaret Lea Houston, Sam Houston's third wife.[10] Both women married very young to public men considerably older than themselves who were by all odds poor marital bets, yet both women managed to achieve successful marriages. In both cases their intelligence and interpersonal skills were no small part of the achievement. Both are excellent examples of women who refused to accept the culturally prescribed powerlessness of women and exercised considerable control over their lives in profound if subtle ways.

Julien and Sarah spent the early years of their marriage in Montgomery County, starting a family and farming. Sarah lost her first child at birth in January 1845 but delivered a healthy boy, named John William after his grandfather, in February 1846. The sad results of the first pregnancy caused Julien some concern and anxiety as to the outcome of the second. Julien's father was already in Rusk County setting up the new homestead when Julien wrote him of his concerns: "I hope and believe all will go well this time and the next time you hear from us the probability is that you will have a grandson (or granddaughter) entitled in all respects to our name."[11] Julien was clearly overcome with emotion when he announced the birth a few weeks later. "I have more that I wish to say and feel less qualified to express it than on any occasion I have ever written to you—on Tuesday the 24th of February about 9 Oclock at night our little boy was born. . . ."[12] Julien had more reasons than most new fathers to be emotional: he was thirty-nine, his health was already deteriorating, and his first legitimate child was a male who could inherit his holdings and carry on his name.

At the time, Sarah, Julien, John, and their entourage were in the process of moving to Rusk County in East Texas, approximately a hundred miles northeast. William Howerton, Julien's overseer, and his family made the move with the Devereuxs and Sarah's parents, the Landrums, followed within a year. The Howertons would be employees, neighbors, friends, and traveling companions for years to come. While the soil in Montgomery County was productive, the miasmic climate, unhealthy and unpleasant water supply, oppressive heat and humidity, and prevalence of yellow fever and malaria as well as other ailments all encouraged the move. Sarah had spent the summer of 1845 in Rusk County with Julien and John while they began to establish the new homestead, and she remained "very unreserved and determined in her preferences for Rusk County."[13] In spite of the fact that Sarah encouraged the move, it must have been difficult on her.

---

[10]See William Seale, *Sam Houston's Wife: A Biography of Margaret Lea Houston* (Norman: University of Oklahoma Press, 1970).

[11]Julien Devereux to John Devereux, Feb. 4, 1846, Devereux Family Papers.

[12]Julien Devereux to John Devereux, Mar. 7, 1846, ibid., as quoted in Winfrey, *Julien Sidney Devereux*, 52.

[13]Julien Devereux to John Devereux, Oct. 22, 1845, Devereux Family Papers.

Travel conditions were primitive, her baby was only two months old, food was scarce the first year, and the Rusk County farmhouse in its early stages of development could hardly have been commodious and well appointed.[14]

One of the main reasons for the move and a cause of continuing concern was Julien's health. By 1845 he was suffering from an enlarged spleen which caused him pain and general debilitation, and everyone hoped the change in climate would improve his health. His enlarged spleen could have been the result of an infectious disease such as hepatitis or tuberculosis, an autoimmune disease such as arthritis, or cancer in the form of leukemia or Hodgkin's disease. Since Julien apparently did not experience symptoms of jaundice, joint inflammation, or breathing difficulties which would have accompanied the various infectious or autoimmune disorders, however, his condition is more consistent with Hodgkin's disease or leukemia. Whatever the diagnosis, the ailment was the cause of his death in 1856.[15]

Her husband's slowly deteriorating health affected Sarah in more ways than just as a source of anxiety. In addition to her duties and responsibilities as a mother and homemaker, she took on more responsibility for the plantation than she might have assumed had Julien been healthy. Julien's illness was chronic and not the sort that confined him to bed for long periods of time, but it did cause a persistent and progressive weakness. Like other nineteenth-century patients, Julien traveled for his health while Sarah remained at home, surrounded by her growing domestic and plantation responsibilities. In addition to his illness and travels, Julien was involved in business and political affairs that took him away from home periodically. Whatever the reason for Julien's absences, they gave Sarah valuable experience in plantation affairs and may have encouraged her belief that she had earned a considerable say in where she would live.

Sometime in 1851 Julien was contemplating a move to Florida. "I am one of the few in number," he wrote a Florida real estate agent, "that are willing to admit that I have been deceived in a removal to the West."[16] By August 1852 he had apparently given up the scheme of moving, however, because he was writing to a friend on a more positive note:

> I have seen hard times in Texas, and *no mistake,* but for several years past my situation has been comfortable and I have reasons to believe that from now hence I may improve my Condition some, by prudent management, but I fear that *better times* has come to late with me, as I am getting advanced in life and my Constitution impared *[sic]* by frequent attacks of sickness.[17]

---

[14]The best source on the early years in Rusk County is John Devereux's diary for the years 1845–1847, ibid.

[15]Dr. J. P. Treadaway to author, Dec. 28, 1991, interview.

[16]Julien Devereux to unnamed real estate agent, Dec. 28, 1851, Devereux Family Papers.

[17]Julien Devereux to Gustave Cook, Aug. 20, 1852, ibid.

Clearly his health and age were factors in his decision not to move, but his wife's opinion may have been a factor as well. Sarah made it plain once again in a letter in 1855 that she "would prefer to be near" her parents, but if they chose to move it could not be helped and she had no desire to leave her home and follow them further west.[18] From the beginning and throughout the years, Sarah remained firm in her commitment to the home in Rusk County, and she was not hesitant to say so.

An unexpected secondary benefit of Julien's travels was the larger window on the world that his letters provided Sarah. In 1852 Julien went to Shreveport in March for a month for his health and to East Florida in December for the winter. In the summer of 1854, accompanied by William Howerton, he went to Kentucky with the intention of going on to New York for his health. He sent Sarah instructions about the management of the plantation and other affairs, details about his health, and his usual observations on his trip. The trip reinforced his improving opinion of Texas: "I have not seen any country that appears to be so good for farming purposes as Eastern Texas."[19] For his health he was examined by a famous Dr. Gross, diagnosed with a "neuralgia of some of the lower intestines," placed on "short allowance of coffee and tobacco," and given some prescriptions.[20] He took the waters of Grayson Springs, although they did not seem to help him.[21] He was not impressed with the rural people of Kentucky and wrote Sarah that "they must have some regulations here to keep their ugly and bad looking people out of the large cities" because most of those in the country were "swarthy, sallow, and extremely hard favored." [22] Because of the oppressive heat, his homesickness, and the lack of improvement in his health, Julien and Howerton canceled the continuation of the trip to New York and returned home after a journey of three weeks.

"The ordinary planter's wife led a very demanding life,"[23] and Sarah was no exception. By piecing together bits and scraps of information, it is possible to assemble a composite portrait of Sarah's daily existence. Altogether she had six pregnancies spaced approximately two years apart. The first child died at birth, the second in late infancy, and the last son was born in the early fall of 1855, so at almost any given time for twelve years beginning in early 1845 Sarah was pregnant or nursing a baby.

---

[18]Sarah Devereux to Julien Devereux, Dec. 6, 1855, ibid.
[19]Julien Devereux to Sarah Devereux, June 23, 1854, ibid.
[20] Ibid.
[21] Julien Devereux to Sarah Devereux, June 28, 1854, ibid.
[22]Ibid.
[23]Scott, *Southern Lady,* 28.

The family's health was a constant concern on the plantation, and the responsibility for maintaining it usually fell to the mistress of the house. Small children generally have a never-ending collection of infections and injuries, and the doctor bills indicate that Sarah's offspring were no exception. She also monitored the health of the slaves, and the doctor was frequently on the plantation for their needs as well. Sarah cared for and monitored other illnesses and injuries herself. "Mahala was very sick all the way I was afraid we would not get her home she is getting better. . . ."[24] Tabby, often referred to as Granny or Granna, was an elderly slave who often assisted Sarah with the care of the children. "[G]ranna fell down in her house and Sprained her wrist very badly so that she could not use it to sew or do any but walk about after the children it is now getting she can begin to use it some[.]"[25]

Typical of a man of his class and position, Julien was involved in many things besides his plantation business: he was a founder of the local school known as Forest Hill Academy, a director on a board to develop navigation on the Sabine River, a commissioner of a railroad company created to bring rails to Rusk County, a county commissioner in 1854, and a member of the Texas legislature in 1855–1856. Julien's involvements brought many people to Monte Verdi on business. In addition, there was the usual collection of friends and relatives, and the combination of business and social affairs kept Sarah busy as a hostess. Nor did Julien's absence diminish the flow of visitors. While he was in Austin for the legislative session, Sarah reported that "we have nearly as much company as ever scarsely a night but some person is here."[26]

Sarah was a faithful lifelong member of the Baptist church, but occasionally she attended the Methodist church. This was not unusual; Protestants in rural areas often attended whichever denomination had a service or a preacher available at a given time. Sarah's interests also included the other things expected of her gender, such as gardening and sewing. In 1851 Amanda Lawson, who was "almost entirely destitute of the useful and pretty things that grow in a yard or garden," wrote asking Sarah for whatever she could spare: "I send for a portion of your useful and ornamental Garden Herbs and Yard Shrubbery together with a few of your rose bushes."[27] Presumably Sarah complied with the request. Even if Sarah did not sew herself, she would have been responsible for overseeing the making of clothing and quilts. Surviving pieces of patterns and numerous orders for cloth, pins, thread, ribbon, lace, etc., indicate that it was a large, ongoing job.

---

[24]Sarah Devereux to Antoinette Devereux, Feb. 24, 1854, Devereux Family Papers.

[25]Sarah Devereux to Julien Devereux, Nov. 22, 1855, ibid.

[26]Sarah Devereux to Julien Devereux, Nov. 20, 1855, ibid.

[27]Amanda Lawson to Sarah Devereux, Feb. 5, 1851, ibid.

The extant correspondence between Sarah and Julien Devereux for the three months he was in Austin attending the legislative session of 1855–1856 reveals the extent of Sarah's knowledge of and involvement in the business of the plantation. Julien's absence in the late fall and winter came at a busy time. It was the end of the picking and ginning season; hog slaughtering and preservation began as soon as the weather permitted; and the fields had to be prepared for spring. Sarah passed along the instructions Julien sent home and maintained a close watch on the progress of the plantation:

> I went to the gin House and plantation on Saturday, as well as I can tell every thing is geting on very well Martin says they are trying to do their best, they finished picking the new ground Saturday and have gone this week into the Heard field. 33 bales packed. I told Ramsy what you said about ploughing etc[.] he is preparing his ploughs and grubing hoes by the time they get through the Cotton which will take about two weeks.[28]

In early December, Sarah reported that Martin was traveling to Shreveport for rope and baling to complete the ginning and baling; the output was lower than had been hoped. "I wrote to you once that Ramsy [the overseer] thought there would be 80 bales but I doubt now if it reaches 70."[29] Two days later Sarah reported that "they finished picking cotton to day and came out of the field shouting and blowing their hornes like there had been a democratic victory."[30] By late December Sarah was able to report a final total on the cotton bales. "They have packed 58 bales of cotton they say they are very heavy. July says there is six or seven more to gin yet. . . ."[31] Sarah's revised estimate of under seventy bales proved quite accurate.

Since the permanent resident population of the plantation was approximately ninety people (eighty slaves, the six Devereuxs, and the overseer and his family) and there were always visitors, the production of food was nearly as crucial as the production of cotton, and Sarah kept a running tally of the pork preservation. Martin's trip to Shreveport proved fortuitous for the upcoming hog slaughtering because the river was up with "large Boats running plenty of salt,"[32] and he returned with "four Sacks of Salt at 6.50 a Sack."[33] The hog killing commenced the week of December 8. "[T]hey have 78 killing hogs in the field Dan says he could get a hundred and forty."[34] By December 20 Sarah

[28]Sarah Devereux to Julien Devereux, Nov. 20, 1855, ibid.
[29]Sarah Devereux to Julien Devereux, Dec. 4, 1855, ibid.
[30]Sarah Devereux to Julien Devereux, Dec. 6, 1855, ibid.
[31]Sarah Devereux to Julien Devereux, Dec. 27, 1855, ibid.
[32]Sarah Devereux to Julien Devereux, Dec. 8, 1855, ibid.
[33]Sarah Devereux to Julien Devereux, Dec. 15, 1855, ibid.
[34]Sarah Devereux to Julien Devereux, Dec. 8, 1855, ibid.

Monte Verdi, Sarah and Julien Devereux's Rusk County plantation home, is a Greek Revival mansion. The earliest known photograph, from the 1920s (top), shows a full-length double gallery with Doric columns at each floor. By the time Monte Verdi was abandoned, around 1950, the second-floor gallery was gone and squared full-height columns replaced the Doric columns. In the 1961 photograph of the renovated Monte Verdi (bottom), the second-floor gallery has been restored, but with fluted full-height columns. Both of these images appear in Dorman H. Winfrey, *Julien Sidney Devereux and His Monte Verdi Plantation* (Waco: Texian Press, 1962). The author wishes to thank Binnie and David Hoffman for their analysis of these photographs. *Courtesy Texian Press, Waco.*

reported considerable progress on the meat but expressed some concern about the weather: "[T]hey have killed 7160 pounds of pork out of the woods and say they can get a good deal more yet. [W] e have not had any very cold weather but I think it is cold enough to save the meat."[35] A bitter cold snap in early January relieved her anxiety: "[I]f such weather is good for nothing else it is fine on our meat. [W]e have four large troughs full of the nicest looking meat you ever saw I dont think we will loose a bone."[36]

Sarah was also concerned that Julien's instructions for clearing and plowing in preparation for the new year were carried out. "I have reminded him [Ramsy] Several times of your ideas of early and deep ploughing which I think he will certainly pay attention too."[37] Taking the older children with her, Sarah visited the fields to check on progress. "Albert and I and Julien goes out to your little orchard field every day or two to see how they get on clearing we intend going down to the Talby field tomorrow to see how they come on ploughing."[38] The previous overseer, McKnight, had been something of a failure so Sarah watched Ramsy's performance with a bit of apprehension and offered her appraisal. "As far as I am able to judge—Ramsy seems to be geting on very well at the plantation," and in Sarah's estimation his wife, "a very clever industrious woman," was certainly an improvement over McKnight's indolent spouse.[39]

As if Sarah were not already busy enough, she and Julien were well into the building of their new plantation home when he left for Austin, and the work to complete the first floor continued under her supervision.

> Linch and Polander here yet and what they can do to stay here two days longer I can not see. I dont know what their charges will be Pass and one other Workman is geting on very well, I think, if Polander and company would ever leave, the others would get on faster as they would likely have more Workmen here. North has been down and penciled the chimneys and made a wall around the dining room fire place, and layed the Hearths, his bill comes to eighty two dollars.[40]

Some bills Sarah deferred paying until Julien's return and some she paid after consultation with her father. In anticipation of cold weather Sarah "had the large doors brought up so We can now shut up the passage, which makes it much more comfortable. . . ." She concluded that if she found "the old house geting too uncomfortable we can very easily go into that part of the new house," even though she preferred waiting until the workmen were finished.[41]

---

[35]Sarah Devereux to Julien Devereux, Dec. 20, 1855, ibid.
[36]Sarah Devereux to Julien Devereux, Jan. 4, 1856, ibid.
[37]Sarah Devereux to Julien Devereux, Dec. 4, 1855, ibid.
[38]Sarah Devereux to Julien Devereux, Jan. 4, 1856, ibid.
[39] Sarah Devereux to Julien Devereux, Dec. 15, 1855, ibid.
[40]Sarah Devereux to Julien Devereux, Nov. 22, 1855, ibid.
[41]Sarah Devereux to Julien Devereux, Dec. 4, 1855, ibid.

Although paid workmen stopped in late December because of Julien's concerns about expenditures, Sarah continued to accomplish what she could on her own initiative with the plantation's resources and labor:

> I have had one room of our old house moved up on the hill for our kitchen it is all nearly put up and Charles is laying the floors back in it again it is a better one than they could have made of new logs and much Quicker done.[42]

Apparently Sarah had decided to move into the new house before Julien's return.

Sarah also kept Julien informed on a variety of matters that concerned them both: the health of the neighborhood; land prices in the area, which would be higher, in her opinion, because of newcomers; and the price of mules.[43] She counseled him not to buy mules in Austin because she believed he "could do better at home" and had "heard of several being offered tolerable low."[44] Even politics did not escape her attention; she knew that her Democratic husband, opposed to the Know Nothing party in Texas, would be interested to learn that "Gen Houston went to Rusk during Court to make a great Know Nothing Speach. but Mr. Bowden whiped him in answer so badly that he left very early next morning."[45]

By far the largest single topic on Sarah's mind was her sons, and Julien must have relished the reports of his offsprings' activities and fretted over their occasional ill health. All the boys were growing but Charlie, the baby, was changing the most rapidly. Sarah reported he could "almost sit alone and has learned to hunt for his little feet he loves to look at them."[46] Will remained convinced Julien had gone to "de Austin to buy a pony and a little shaddle and bridle and candy" for him.[47] The older boys participated in a daily make-believe game of going to Austin to see their father with "a bundle of provisions tied up in a paper" for a camp-out with the "children and little Negroes."[48] Some of the images are so picturesque and idyllic they seem contrived:

> The boys got after Jo this evening and made him stay untill after supper to play the fiddle they are now all in the kitchen. Albert as usual looking on Julien dancing all the time as hard as he can clip and Will brought in sound asleep.[49]

---

[42]Sarah Devereux to Julien Devereux, Jan. 4, 1856, ibid.

[43]Sarah Devereux to Julien Devereux, Nov. 22, 1855, ibid.

[44]Sarah Devereux to Julien Devereux, Dec. 29 postscript to Dec. 27, 1855, ibid.

[45]Sarah Devereux to Julien Devereux, Nov. 20, 1855, ibid.

[46]Sarah Devereux to Julien Devereux, Nov. 22, 1855, ibid.

[47]Sarah Devereux to Julien Devereux, Dec. 8, 1855, ibid.

[48]Sarah Devereux to Julien Devereux, Dec. 4, 1855, ibid.

[49] Sarah Devereux to Julien Devereux, Dec. 15, 1855, ibid.

Since Julien could not be home for Christmas, Sarah provided him with a description of the boys' Christmas Eve sure to bring tears to the eyes of any absent father:

> [The boys were] enjoying themselves finely they all hung their stockings up in the chimney. . . . I had no cakes or candy so sliped a dime in each ones stocking they say the [unclear] little man put them there I told maybe he would come down the chimney. After Julien had gone to bed he raised up and looked at the fire [place] I recon he thought it was to hot he layed down and told Phebee to open the window so he come there and put something in his stocking[.][50]

The boys were not the only ones who missed their father and longed for his return. In spite of household help and the pleasure children bring, caring for four small children is difficult and tiring work. Sarah's maternal chores must have been a challenge and a drain, a condition which was exacerbated by her other responsibilities due to Julien's absence. She apologized to Julien for the disjointedness and incompleteness of her letters because "these four boys has to be attended to—and as Pa is not here, it is Ma all the time—."[51] She was subtly reminding Julien that his extended absence was a burden on her, and he was not keeping up his half of the parental bargain.

Julien's letters provided Sarah with vicarious exposure to a wider world. He wrote of Democratic and Know Nothing politics and the progress of the legislative session, provided a running account of his boarding house roommates, and, as always, reported on his health. Julien, who was homesick and eager to be on his way back to Rusk County and his family, was not tolerant of the legislature's lethargic pace. He concluded the legislature had a "considerable disposition to idle away time, thereby making this a protracted session for the sake of the per diem pay."[52] To his credit Julien recognized Sarah's managerial skills, gave her the room to exercise them, and praised her for her good work.

> I feel like that I want to write to you about things and circumstances connected with home, but I am so far off that I can not tell what is best to suggest, and as I know your prudence and good sense together with a knowledge of Papas [Sarah's father's] willingness to render any aid or assistance that you many require I therefore content myself on that score, under a belief that the general management of our affairs will be as good & in all probability better, than if I was present.[53]

His confidence in Sarah was well placed.[54]

---

[50]Sarah Devereux to Julien Devereux, Dec. 25, 1855, ibid.

[51]Sarah Devereux to Julien Devereux, Dec. 27, 1855, ibid.

[52]Julien Devereux to Sarah Devereux, Nov. 29, 1855, ibid.

[53]Julien Devereux to Sarah Devereux, Nov. 22, 1855, ibid.

[54]A much broader survey of primary source materials than this article encompasses would be in order to determine how unique Sarah Devereux's knowledge and control of plantation affairs

Whether she realized it or not, Sarah Devereux was an example of nineteenth-century womanhood as defined by the "Cult of Domesticity," which grew out of the celebration of moral virtue during the American Revolution and the Second Great Awakening, in combination with the development of the urban middle class and the market economy at the beginning of the industrial age in the Northeast. As the professional and industrial classes developed and the office and factory replaced the home as the center of production for men, women were left to oversee the domain of the home, supervise the Christian education of their children, and protect and maintain morality, virtue, and domestic felicity in the male-dominated world of monetary greed and political corruption. High standards of piousness, purity, and submissiveness were demanded of women, in addition to exemplary homemaking and parenting skills.[55]

There is no evidence that Sarah owned or had read Catherine Beecher's *A Treatise on Domestic Economy* (1841) or Lydia Maria Child's *The American Frugal Housewife* (1832), but she did have a subscription to Josepha Hale's *Godey's Magazine* (1837–1877). These three publications were the most popular homemaking manuals and dispensers of the ideology of the "Cult of Domesticity." All three placed women firmly within the confines of the domestic sphere and carried forward that philosophy through how-to manuals on homemaking combined with liberal doses of advice on such topics as how properly subordinate wives and mothers might manage recalcitrant husbands and children, together with admonitions to young girls to maintain purity; essays on unselfish, martyristic motherhood; and paeans to the glories of hearth and home.[56] To the modern, post-feminist revolution reader, the "Cult of Domesticity" may sound like a sentimental anachronism, but it has had a profound impact on women's lives and options for over a century and a half.

Julien's financial records show yearly subscriptions to *Godey's Magazine*. In 1850 he wrote to obtain some missing copies of past issues and to renew the

---

were among southern women. A quick analysis of the secondary materials indicates that hers was certainly not the normal situation. According to Catherine Clinton's *The Plantation Mistress*, the standard work on the subject, Sarah's involvement with gardening, hog preservation, sewing, medical care, and parenting was within the expected scope of a plantation mistress, but her detailed knowledge and involvement with the crops, land preparation, overseer performance, and house building were unusual. Clinton, *The Plantation Mistress: Woman's World in the Old South* (New York: Pantheon Books, 1982). Whether it was an acknowledged fact or not between Sarah and Julien Devereux, she seems to have been "in training" for her future role as a female planter, a situation probably more attributable to Julien's health than any other cause.

[55]Cott, *The Bonds of Womanhood*, and Barbara Leslie Epstein, "Domesticity and Female Subordination," chap. 3 in *The Politics of Domesticity: Women, Evangelism, and Temperance in Nineteenth-Century America* (Middletown, Conn.: Wesleyan University Press, 1981).

[56]Kathryn Kish Sklar, "The Building of a Glorious Temple, 1843," chap. 11 in *Catharine Beecher: A Study in American Domesticity* (New Haven: Yale University Press, 1973).

subscription. The renewal promotion had changed and he was informed that "the Lady's Newspaper is no longer given as a premium for the subscription. Engravings instead at no charge" were supplied.[57] Sarah remained a reader, if not a subscriber, for some years. Her scrapbooks, which contain articles clipped from *Godey's,* and her recipe book reflect the ideology of the "Cult of Domesticity."

Besides serving as a cookbook, Sarah Devereux's recipe book is a practical guide to homemaking and domestic affairs. The cookery portions contain recipes for "Pumpkin Pudding," "Ochra and Tomatos," "Egg Plant," "Savoy or Sponge Cake," and "A Rich Fruit Cake" calling for thirty eggs. The amount of work involved in "Directions for Making preserves" is enough to make a modern homemaker rush gratefully to the jam and jelly section of the local grocery store.[58]

Some of the first-aid remedies included in the recipe book inspire sympathy for a potential victim. For example: "Sweet or Olive Oil is a certain cure for the bite of a Rattle Snake. Apply it internally and externally." Victims of insect bites would have fared somewhat better: "For the sting of a wasp bee or Hornet apply cotton wet with Laudnum to the place The same for centrepeed and give spirits freely."[59] If the laudanum applied topically did not ease the pain, at least the spirits would.

Both her recipe book and scrapbooks contain other useful household hints. For instance, one could "remove bed bugs by a strong decoction of the plant called waterpepper or smart weed."[60] Additional articles gave advice on how to boil rice and wash shirts, and detailed how the French grew tomatoes.[61]

In addition to recipes, household hints, and personal clippings, the later of the two scrapbooks, compiled between 1880 and 1883, contains many articles of a more philosophical nature on marriage, parenting, and womanhood, some of which reflect the unpleasant circumstances of Sarah's second marriage. The theme of many articles she preserved is the evil of intemperance and its harmful effect on the family. "The appetite for strong drink in men has spoiled the lives of more women—ruined more hopes for them, scattered more fortunes for them, brought to them more shame, sorrow, and hardship—than any other evil that lives."[62] By the time Sarah put this clipping in her scrapbook

[57]*Godey's Magazine* to Julien Devereux, Mar. 15, 1850, Devereux Family Papers.
[58]Sarah Devereux's recipe book, ibid.
[59]Ibid.
[60]Ibid.
[61]Sarah Devereux's 1853–1881 scrapbook, ibid.
[62]Sarah Devereux's 1880–1883 scrapbook, "Women and Wine," ibid.

she was personally experiencing the misery caused by her second husband's alcoholism.

Another theme of Sarah Devereux's scrapbooks is the centrality of the mother to the happiness and success of the home. All of what makes a home happy is "not wholly, but largely in the hand of her who is the central thought and well spring of pleasure in every comfortable Christian's home—the dear, honored and graceful mother."[63] Undoubtedly, Sarah Devereux saw her purpose and place in the world as that of a wife, mother, and homemaker as prescribed by the "Cult of Domesticity." Fate, in the form of Julien's death in 1856, forced her to abandon one of those roles, but she successfully incorporated her expanded role as plantation owner and businesswoman into her personal teleology without conflicting with her values by simply expanding her homemaking role. Even though she was broadening and expanding her feminine role, she never directly challenged the patriarchal society in which she lived. She continued to ask for the counsel and support of men even though she could likely have managed without it.

Although Julien Devereux's will, written in 1852, named several trusted male friends as executors, there is no doubt that he intended Sarah, as executrix, to have control of the property and affairs and to carry forward the business of the plantation.

> It is my desire and will that my wife, Sarah Ann assisted by the counsel and advice of anyone or more of my other executors as she may choose will take upon herself the supervision of my plantation for the purposes expressed in this will. That aided by my other executors she will attend to the hiring of overseers, the sale of produce, the investing of the proceeds of the plantation. That with the aid of said executors she will plan improvements of my plantation, preserve and take care of property and above all she will attend strictly and carefully to the education of my two sons, Albert and Julien and such other children as she may have by me.[64]

In a codicil written two years later, Julien enlarged Sarah's responsibilities by making Antoinette "subject to the care and control of my beloved wife," who had the option of assuming her guardianship or entrusting Antoinette's supervision to someone else.[65] Antoinette's marriage a few weeks after her father's death relieved Sarah of the responsibility of her guardianship. While Sarah called on several executors for assistance and support, the name that most frequently appears on receipts and documents is that of her father, John

---

[63]Sarah Devereux's 1880–1883 scrapbook, "What is Home," ibid.

[64] Julien Devereux's will as quoted in Winfrey, *Julien Sidney Devereux,* 147.

[65]Ibid., 151.

Landrum. Through 1856 and 1857, the frequency of Sarah's signature increased as she took more and more active control of affairs.

Sarah was relieved of some of her parenting responsibilities when she hired Mrs. M. A. Harcourt, presumably a widow, as tutoress for the children. Julien had been favorably impressed with the woman when he briefly encountered her in the home of an acquaintance during his stay in Austin. After consulting with Sarah upon his return home, he wrote his Austin friend, Mr. Worsham, that "we are anxious to get a lady to live in our family who would be capable and willing to instruct our little boys at home," and he inquired after the availability of Mrs. Harcourt.[66] Mr. Worsham responded to Sarah after Julien's death with a recommendation of Mrs. Harcourt "as a pleasant intelligent and agreeable companion and a lady of high standing and great moral worth."[67] Mrs. Harcourt was still with the family in April 1858. While on a visit to her family, she wrote Sarah she was eager to return to the "dear Children, I do want to see them so much." The tone of her letter is warm and familiar; apparently the two women had become friends. "I have the funniest thing to tell you when I see you about Judge Ochletree, and Frank Elkens, I know you will laugh, I would write it, but I love to see your pritty white teeth, when you laugh."[68] Mrs. Harcourt encouraged Sarah to take a trip with her mother to Montgomery later that year to see old friends. Certainly the tutoress's presence at home accounted for Sarah's comfortable ease in her separation from the children: "[S]omething unusual when away from the children I did not feel uneasy about them all the time I was absent from them."[69] It is likely that Mrs. Harcourt stayed in Sarah's home until all or most of the boys were old enough to go away to school.

At the time of Julien's death only the lower floor of the Monte Verdi mansion was complete. Two months after his death, Mr. M. C. Jackson, armed with a letter of introduction from an old friend of the Devereuxs, applied to Sarah to finish the house.[70] It is unclear exactly when she hired him, but in March 1857 she paid for 326 feet of walnut plank which was likely the flooring or the walls for the second floor.[71] Two months later she paid Jackson $400 "in parte payment for work done on hur hous *[sic]*" and promised $172.75 "with intrest" by January.[72] Since there are no other receipts for construction, this may have

[66]Julien Devereux to Israel Worsham, undated [1856], Devereux Family Papers.

[67]Israel Worsham to Sarah Devereux, Aug. 26, 1856, ibid.

[68]Mrs. M. A. Harcourt to Sarah Devereux, Apr. 20, 1858, ibid.

[69]Sarah Devereux to My Dear Cousin, Oct. 11 [?], 1858, ibid.

[70]John McClarty to Sarah Devereux, July 7, 1856, ibid.

[71]Receipt, Mar. 2, 1857, Gen. Corr., ibid.

[72]Receipt from M. C. Jackson, May 9, 1857 (torn into two pieces), Gen. Corr., ibid.

completed the home, but furnishings came more slowly. As late as May 1860 Sarah ordered furniture, glass, and a rocking chair.[73]

Sarah Devereux was not a wealthy widow with nothing to do but dabble in interior decorating and oversee her children's upbringing. By necessity, she was a cotton planter, and her success in that endeavor was crucial to maintaining her home and raising her sons. In order to determine how successful or unsuccessful she was as a planter, I chose to study the year of 1858 because the records were more extensive than for other years. In that year she was also far enough past Julien's death to have become reconciled to the loss and developed her own management style, and, in regard to market conditions for cotton and other southern agricultural crops, it was a typical year on the eve of the Civil War.

As a female planter, Sarah was a minuscule part of a very elite minority within a minority. Slightly over a quarter (27.3 percent) of Texas families owned slaves in 1860 and only 3 percent owned twenty or more slaves and therefore qualified as planters. While the statistics are unavailable for Texas, the percentage of female planters must have been minute.[74] Sarah's "List of Taxable Property . . ." for 1858 shows that she had fewer slaves and land than at the time of Julien's death. Some of the slaves had been part of Antoinette's and Sidney's inheritances. Still, with 61 slaves, almost 7,000 acres of land, and a total taxable value of $57,540 she was a wealthy woman.[75] She may have undervalued her slave property for tax purposes. Her statement shows a value of $30,000 for sixty-one slaves. This is only $491.80 per slave, while the mean value per slave for the period was $765.[76] If the mean value is used to calculate the value of her slaves then their value rises to $46,665, and her total worth escalates to $74,205.

The fact that over half of Sarah Devereux's wealth and status was embodied in the human beings who formed her labor force was not atypical in the prewar south, which saw slave property as a highly valuable form of investment and a unique medium of exchange. Even on the eve of the Civil War, the south was still land-rich and labor-poor, and that situation was exacerbated in the near-frontier conditions of Texas. Coupled with the southern agriculturists' traditional skepticism of banking institutions, slave property took on even greater significance. Slaves were used as payment for debt, for collateral on loans, as investment property, as valuable inheritance in estates, and as a form of insurance

---

[73]Mercantile receipt, May 1860, Gen. Corr., ibid.

[74]Randolph Campbell, *An Empire for Slavery: The Peculiar Institution in Texas, 1821–1865* (Baton Rouge: Louisiana State University Press, 1989), 68.

[75]"List of Taxable Property Given in by Mrs. Sarah A. Devereux" [1858], Gen. Corr., Devereux Family Papers.

[76]Campbell, *An Empire for Slavery*, 73.

policy whose hired-out labor could provide for the support of widows and orphaned children.[77]

In 1858 her slaves produced 113 bales of cotton, which she sold for between ten and eleven cents per pound for a profit of $5,302.13. This was the partial crop from 1857 and 1858. Such overlapping of two years' produce was typical for any planter's sales in a calendar year. According to Randolph Campbell in *An Empire for Slavery: The Peculiar Institution in Texas, 1821–1865*, an average rate of return for a planter with fifty or more slaves in 1860 was 11.05 percent at eight cents a pound and 12.35 percent at nine cents a pound.[78] By simply extending the proportions Sarah's expected rate of return at ten and a half cents a pound would have been 14.4 percent. Although she deferred payment of some expenses until 1859, the total expenses Sarah incurred for 1858 were $3,545.65. This figure includes all personal expenses, for it is very difficult to determine which expenses were vital to plantation production and which were personal. Based on these figures her profit would have been $1,756.48, or 33 percent. Such a high profit margin is probably misleading, however. Sarah was selling part of a previous year's crop and may have incurred other expenses for which the paper work has not survived. She had an additional $1,117.08 in indebtedness for notes to be paid in later years, and $500 of Antoinette's inheritance may still have been unpaid. Theoretically, if all expenses had been paid out of the income for 1858, Sarah's profit would have still been $639.40, a rate of return of 12 percent. Therefore, her rate of return on her business as a cotton planter was within or above the expected norms, and she can be considered a successful planter.

Had the Civil War not intervened, it is conceivable that Sarah Devereux would have continued as a successful female planter. Although the plantation records in the war years are not as complete as in the prewar years, there is no doubt that the war had an enormous impact on her, as it did on all her southern sisters. Sarah's attitude toward the war was complex and possibly ambivalent.[79]

---

[77]"The Economics of Slavery in Texas," chap. 4 in ibid. Additionally, the Devereux Family Papers show that Julien and Sarah Devereux viewed their slaves as a large portion of their wealth and used them in many of the ways discussed.

[78]Campbell, *An Empire for Slavery*, 75.

[79]Two scholarly works establish the extremes of the argument over the effect the Civil War had on Southern women. Anne Firor Scott's thesis in *The Southern Lady is* that the Civil War was the catalyst that spawned a growing independence and gender consciousness on the part of southern women which encouraged growing feminism after the war. Contrarily, George C. Rable recognizes the profound impact of the Civil War on women but concludes that there was no lasting change in female awareness of societal position or status, and thus no resulting protofeminism or feminism. Rable, *Civil Wars: Women and the Crisis of Southern Nationalism* (Urbana: University of Illinois Press, 1989).

Sarah doubtless supported the Southern cause: she had early absorbed Julien's loyalty to the Southern Democratic party, and her personal wealth and position in the southern hierarchy was dependent on the continued existence of slavery. The politics of the coming crisis could hardly have escaped her attention. Most of the town of Henderson, the county seat of Rusk County only sixteen miles from her home, burned in August 1860. The fire was one of several that spring and summer which were widely believed to be the work of abolitionists. In February 1861 Rusk County voted overwhelmingly in support of secession.

Undoubtedly, the Civil War strained Sarah's finances and resources nearly to the breaking point. In 1860 she was the second-largest property holder in Rusk County with real estate valued at $70,000 and a personal estate of $66,000.[80] Prior to the war her highest tax bill had never been greater than $85. In 1861 her taxes were $147.67. In 1862 they rose to $531.71 ($304.80 in Confederate taxes and $226.91 in state and county taxes). In 1863 her state and county taxes alone were $504.73. By 1864, the year before the war's end, her combined county, state, and Confederate taxes were $935.65, an astonishing increase during the war of approximately 1,200 percent![81] If her income stayed constant or fell, merely the rise in her tax rate could have plunged Sarah Devereux from the ranks of successful cotton planters in 1858 into insolvency by the end of the war.

As a wartime planter and slaveholder, Sarah faced additional demands. The Henderson *Times* carried the following notice from County Agent W. L. McMurray on November 21, 1863:

> To the Slave-Holders of Rusk County:—
>
> The Government of the Confederate Stat[es] now requires of you one third of the ablebodied negro men between the ages of 18 and 50, to be employed immediately, and having been appointed principal agent of this County, I hope the patriotic Slaveholders will comply cheerfully and faithfully with their country's demands.
>
> The negroes will be placed in camps, near the centre of the county, until further orders from the Headquarters of this Bureau.
>
> You will be notified by the county agents or sub county agents, what time to report your negroes and obtain receipts for them.[82]

Sarah's records do not contain a receipt confirming that she delivered her slaves as required, but chances are her compliance was faithful, if not cheerful. The loss of a third of her able-bodied male slaves would have considerably affected her productive work force.

---

[80]Winfrey, *Julien Sidney Devereux*, 134.

[81]Ibid.; tax receipts, Gen. Corr., 1861-1865, Devereux Family Papers.

[82]Henderson *Times*, Nov. 21, 1863, as quoted in Winfrey, *Julien Sidney Devereux*, 132.

In 1863 the Confederacy levied a "tax in kind" of one-tenth of a landowner's produce, designed to provision the Confederate army without further cash expenditures.[83] Receipts show that over the next two years Sarah relinquished a total of 750 pounds of cotton, 3,638 pounds of bacon, 1,137 pounds plus 7½ bushels of wheat, 849 pounds of flour, 75 bushels of oats, 6,108 pounds of fodder, 1,158 bushels of corn, 685 pounds of salt pork, 5 bushels of peas, 2½ bushels of potatoes, and 3 pounds of wool.[84] Sarah's contributions in agricultural produce are indicative of the demands made on southern women during the war. With many men dead or away at the war, the Confederacy was heavily dependent on its women to produce the food and fodder which its armies required. Sarah's experience as a female planter before the war may have made her more productive than other women. While many women across the Confederacy complained about their inability to encourage or coerce their slaves to produce much of anything, Sarah's work force was clearly producing adequate crops.

Considering the demands made on Sarah Devereux's finances and work force, it is no wonder that she alluded to her problems in a letter to Caleb Garrison, Antoinette's husband, who was serving in the Confederate army near Shelbyville, Tennessee. Garrison's response proved him to be an unsympathetic audience. "You spoke of some of your home troubles but did not say any thing of their nature—what on earth can be the matter?" Garrison chastised Sarah for her complaining:

> You ought not to complain of living hard, and I am satisfied you would not if you could only see the patience and endurance of our soldiers, with the little complaining they receive the rations of bread and meat.[85]

Garrison was reminding Sarah that the male role was to persevere and fight, while women's place was to support the menfolk by sacrificing and suffering in silence, and she was not doing her part.

In spite of her difficulties, Sarah Devereux did not suffer the ravages of the Civil War that affected so many southern women. Her home was not invaded or destroyed, troops did not march across her fields, she retained an overseer through part, if not all of the war, and her slaves were far removed from the possibility of liberation or temptation by Union forces. In spite of the inflation caused by the war and the gigantic increase in her taxes, she apparently remained solvent. In March 1863 she had enough excess funds to loan a male slaveholder $775, accepting three slaves as collateral on the note.[86] She managed to keep her

---

[83]Winfrey, *Julien Sidney Devereux*, 132.

[84]Tax receipts, Gen. Corr., 1860–1865 and undated, Devereux Family Papers.

[85]Caleb Garrison to Sarah Devereux, Mar. 30, 1863, ibid.

[86]Loan agreement, Mar. 24, 1863, Gen. Corr., 1860–1865, ibid.

sons in school during at least some of the war years. In 1864 she paid a Mr. Carolan $124 for one session's tuition for all four boys.[87] The education of her sons was one of her most important responsibilities, and she likely would have found a way to pay their tuition regardless of her finances. Still, specie must have been precious to Sarah because by 1863, like many other planters, she was withholding her cotton crop from market awaiting higher prices.[88]

As the war dragged on, Sarah Devereux must have grown increasingly anxious about her two oldest sons. Albert turned sixteen in December 1864, and Julien was thirteen or fourteen by then. The conscription age had dropped only to seventeen, but that may have given Sarah scant comfort, as the Confederacy's manpower needs were so critical that boys as young as fourteen were beginning to show up in the ranks. Her wartime papers contain a receipt dated November 22, 1864, for 1,137 pounds of wheat and 849 pounds of flour signed by A. T. Rogers. Although the receipt is not on an official Confederate form, it appears to be for supplies for the Confederacy. On the bottom of the receipt Rogers added, "The boys are *all right,* don't be uneasy."[89] Of course, there is no way to know how the note relates to Sarah and her boys, but it does raise the intriguing speculation that even as Sarah Devereux was supporting the Southern cause with her taxes and produce, she was seeking reassurance about her maturing sons' safety. If this was the case, Sarah may have been among a growing number of southern women who concluded that the demands of the Confederate cause were beginning to exceed what they were willing to give.[90]

At the end of the war over half of Sarah's wealth simply evaporated with the emancipation of her slaves, and her land holdings were down to 1,300 acres by 1869.[91] The decrease in her fortune was relative, however. All slaveowners suffered the loss of their slave property and many lost land, so while Sarah appeared considerably poorer at war's end, so was everyone else in the South whose wealth was based on the ownership and labor of slaves.

By 1867 James F. Garrison's name began to appear on receipts and orders for the business. "Received of Mr. James Garrison fifty six dollars and ninety too cts for work on waggon and a lot of plows for Widow Devros farm."[92] It is

---

[87]Receipt from Carolan, 1864, Gen. Corr., ibid.

[88]Winfrey, *Julien Sidney Devereux,* 134.

[89]Receipt from A. T. Rogers, Nov. 22, 1864, Gen. Corr., 1860–1865, Devereux Family Papers.

[90]A number of recent books have centered on southern women's disenchantment and outright opposition to the Civil War. Among the most useful are Victoria E. Bynum, *Unruly Women: The Politics of Social and Sexual Control in the Old South* (Chapel Hill: University of North Carolina Press, 1992), Catherine Clinton and Nina Silber (eds.), *Divided Houses: Gender and the Civil War* (New York: Oxford University Press, 1992), and Faust, *Southern Stories: Slaveholders in Peace and War.*

[91]Sarah Devereux Garrison's autobiography, undated [1898], Devereux Family Papers.

[92]Receipt, 1867, Gen. Corr., ibid.

unclear whether Garrison was hired to help or was courting Sarah at the time. In either case, two years later, on April 1, 1869, Sarah married Garrison, an older brother to Antoinette's husband, Caleb Garrison.

At the time of the marriage Sarah was forty-three years old and her youngest child, Charlie, was nearly fourteen. According to her autobiographical sketch Sarah was still successful and solvent, albeit on a smaller scale than before the war:

> When I and J. F. Garrison were married, I owned all the property there was our home & [unclear] of 1300 of acres. He had nothing unless it was a horse. I had a home, and a good farm. (1300) thirteen hundred acres of Land. Some horses & mules cattle hoggs, and every thing belonging to a farm. And all housekeeping arrangements. I owed no debts.[93]

Why then did Sarah Devereux remarry? Obviously financial support was not a necessity, but several other possibilities are worthy of consideration.

The first and most obvious speculation is that she simply fell in love with Jim Garrison. A second and equally obvious possibility is that her sons were growing up and away from her and she did not care to grow into middle and old age alone. Another reason is more complex. If Sarah's sense of self was firmly rooted in the idea of the "Cult of Domesticity," then her proper place in the world was as a wife and mother. She was able to become a cotton planter in 1856 without any loss of self-identity by conceiving of her new role as an extension of her role as wife and mother. Julien had charged her as his dutiful and obedient wife to carry forward his business and raise and educate his children. By 1869 the children were nearly grown, the plantation business as Julien had bequeathed it to her had gone with the ravages of the Civil War, and, thus, Sarah had fulfilled Julien's charge. Maintaining her sense of self and womanhood meant renewing her role as wife.

Sarah Devereux's remarriage would have made more practical sense had it occurred during the first two or three years after Julien's death, when she was still young, in her early thirties, and wealthy. She would have been a choice mate and remarriage would have provided her assistance in raising her young sons and managing her large holdings. The fact that Sarah remarried four years after the Civil War indicates that the war and its aftermath may have had some bearing on her decision. The personal and financial tragedies of the Civil War, the difficulties of adjusting to and managing free labor after the war, and the political instability of Reconstruction broke the resolve and vanquished the hopes of many men and women, and it certainly would not be to Sarah Devereux's discredit if they affected her in the same manner.

---

[93]Sarah Devereux Garrison's autobiography, undated [1898], ibid.

Regardless of the reasons shaping her decision to remarry, Sarah Devereux's second marriage was a disaster and resulted in the loss of her home and property. According to her autobiography, Jim Garrison had a serious problem with alcohol and as a result amassed considerable debt.

> I think it was in 1873, I was induced greatly by his influence to sell my home. . . . Debts had acumulated to (2500) twenty five hundred dollars. (Our debts as he calls them. I think it was mostly Saloon debts, and to pay him out of scrapes & difficulties he would get into when he would be in his drinking carousals.) All this time the place was making tolerable good crops, corn etc. and from 15. to 30. Bales of cotton. The 2500 hundred dollars was paid out of the proceeds of my place.[94]

The financial damage Garrison inflicted so rapidly on what Sarah had worked for thirteen long and arduous years to maintain and protect was not the only source of conflict. Sarah's youngest child, Charlie, became a doctor and settled in Austin County, west of Houston, in the early 1880s. His response to Sarah's entreaties to visit her must have caused her considerable grief and pain. "Ma you must not look for me back in that country for I don't know when I will be their." Charlie admitted that "tis true that their are fond memories associated with my childhood and early youth" but "later memories" and "feelings of sadness" were so strong he could not return until he had "outgrown or forgotten to think of them."[95] Garrison, in an 1897 letter remarkable for both its candor and self-pity, listed the mistakes he had made in his marriage and shed further light on Charlie's reasons for not returning home:

> I have made Two grand mistake since we married 1st was drinking, & had it not been for that I would have not made the other, & I would have been all right, financially. & that is the matter now. . . . I do hope I will yet come out all right, while I know I have got to do it myself & all alone without any aid or comfort from my wife.
>
> 2and was Sending Charlie off to colledge. It may have been best not to have done so. & I know, it could, not have been any worse for him. not to took the profession he did. & I get nothing but consent [constant] abuse for doing it. & not Even a thank. & of I even did *[sic]*. It is a thing of the past.[96]

When Charlie died in October 1884 of internal injuries after his horse rolled over on him, he had not seen his mother in over four years.[97]

After the sale of the Monte Verdi home in 1873, Jim and Sarah Garrison lived on a nearby portion of the land still in the family called Glen Fawn, and for a time Sarah taught at the local Forest Hill Academy, which had been

---

[94] Ibid.

[95] Charles Devereux to Sarah Devereux Garrison, Jan. 1, 1882, ibid.

[96] James Garrison to Sarah Devereux Garrison, Apr. 3, 1897, ibid.

[97] Charles Devereux's obituary, Oct. 16, 1884, in Sarah Devereux's 1853–1881 scrapbook, ibid.

established by Julien in 1850.[98] By 1892 Sarah and Jim had moved to Timpson in Shelby County.[99] Her son, Julien, who suffered from tuberculosis, was employed as the county clerk in Odessa, Ector County, because he found it easier to breathe in the lower humidity of West Texas. Sarah, always the fretful, attentive mother, implored him to come to Timpson. "I think you had better pack up and come here just as soon as you can. . . . Let me hear from you right away, my dear precious child."[100] Julien died suddenly of a "severe [lung] hemorrhage at his home in Odessa" in mid-1896.[101]

In the year before Julien's death, Jim Garrison returned to the Glen Fawn farm because the "Negroes couldn't pay for it," and he and Sarah had reclaimed it.[102] The combination of Julien's death and the repossession of the farm precipitated the final separation between Sarah and Jim Garrison. The financial arrangements between Garrison and Sarah's sons are confusing, but apparently Jim Garrison owed money on notes held by her sons William and Julien:

> [W]hen I made the settlement with Jim in 1893 and gave him more than half of what he was due [unclear] that he was perfectly satisfied and he so expressed himself to me but it seems that he is still dissatisfied and dont seem to have any disposition to pay the debt. I dont know what else he wants.[103]

William was perplexed and irritated that Jim was unable "to lay up some money every year" since he had no one to support but Sarah. "I dont understand what Jim does with the cotton etc he gets from the place. You say he is not drinking and to save my life I cant understand what he does with it.'"[104] Garrison wanted Sarah to settle the notes with her portion of her son Julien's estate.[105]

A year later the situation was still unresolved and growing tenser. Jim Garrison had determined to sever his financial relationship with Sarah's sons, by court action if necessary.

> Also, I am going to wind up ever thing. That is between us & the children & see what we have got. & if nothing I will have less trouble. & know who owns farm. . . . now if the courts has got to wind it up just tell them to say so. . . .[106]

---

[98]Marcy Lowry Welch (present owner of Monte Verdi) to author, Jan. 7, 1992, interview.
[99]Sarah Devereux Garrison to Julien Devereux, July 3, 1892, Devereux Family Papers.
[100]Sarah Devereux Garrison to Julien Devereux, Feb. 1, 1895, ibid.
[101] Julien Devereux's obituary, clipping dated June 8, 1896, ibid.
[102]Sarah Devereux Garrison to Julien Devereux, Feb. 1, 1895, ibid.
[103]William Devereux to Sarah Devereux Garrison, Feb. 21, 1896, ibid.
[104]Ibid.
[105]Sarah Devereux Garrison to William Devereux, Nov. 20, 1897, ibid.
[106]Jim Garrison to Sarah Devereux Garrison, Mar. 17, 1897, ibid.

In Sarah's opinion Garrison was a litigious person who "had rather be in a law Suit than any thing in the world."[107] Since Sarah wrote her autobiography "as a memorandum" for William to "make to Judge Turner if necessary," the dispute apparently did proceed toward litigation.[108]

Jim Garrison wanted Sarah to "come to farm & stay & camp out with me. awhile," but she did not do so.[109] He missed her companionship, but he also believed he was losing his control over her:

> It seems you have no aim in future, only to Stay away. Well it's alright, when a wife can't Share the loneliness of her husband, it is getting in bad Shape & I would not be surprise any day. to find it just in the Shape it was when you went there be fore. I find I got no influence, with you. & you blame me for Everything, but that is all right too.[110]

Even from the distance of nearly a hundred years Jim Garrison's manipulative self-pity is annoying. After chastising her for not writing and reminding her of his unpleasant situation, he bitterly added, "but I guess you have other things to think about, of more importance to you."[111] In another letter, Garrison detailed for an entire page how terribly life had treated him: no work in Timpson, debts accumulating, his family's mistreatment of him, and his hardship on the farm.[112] By 1898 the separation was irreparable. After Sarah moved to Albert's home in Decatur, Texas, Garrison hired someone to run the farm and moved back to Timpson to work on the railroad. "This is my last letter to you," he wrote, "as I have wrote once a month Since you left. & no ans to any."[113]

Several weeks later Sarah wrote William requesting his assistance in retrieving her belongings from Timpson. "If you Should go or Send after my things at Timpson which I wish could be done without my going as I would rather not have to meet Jim unless I'm obliged to."[114] Sadly, there was not much left to retrieve, and Sarah poignantly requested a spoon to an existing set of silver, a few trunks, including one that had belonged to her son, Julien, and the furniture from the parlor and her bedroom to which she felt she was entitled.[115] Sarah spent the rest of her life living with her two surviving sons. When she died on April 25, 1900, at William's home in Jacksonville, Texas, her estate was valued at $600.[116]

---

[107] Sarah Devereux Garrison to William Devereux, Nov. 20, 1897, ibid.
[108] Sarah Devereux Garrison's autobiography, undated [1898], ibid.
[109] James Garrison to Sarah Devereux Garrison, Mar. 25, 1897, ibid.
[110] James Garrison to Sarah Devereux Garrison, Apr. 3, 1897, ibid.
[111] James Garrison to Sarah Devereux Garrison, Feb. 7, 1897, ibid.
[112] James Garrison to Sarah Devereux Garrison, Mar. 25, 1897, ibid.
[113] James Garrison to Sarah Devereux Garrison, Aug. 1, 1898, ibid.
[114] Sarah Devereux Garrison to William Devereux, Aug. 18, 1898, ibid.
[115] Ibid.
[116] Winfrey, *Julien Sidney Devereux,* 137.

The feud between Jim Garrison and his stepsons must have been acutely painful for Sarah because the affair directly challenged her basic assumptions about herself as a wife and mother, forcing her to choose one role over the other. Her husband's letters were clearly calculated to make Sarah feel guilty that she was neglecting her proper role as a supportive, submissive, and concerned wife. On the other hand, Sarah was dedicated to her children. "I feel more concerned on your account," she wrote William, "than anything else."[117] When she had to choose between her motherly and wifely roles, her stronger loyalty was to motherhood.

Age gave Sarah a certain philosophical distance from the situation and the courage to take control of the last few years of her life. "I have learned to be patient in all things," she wrote William.[118] To paraphrase an idea of Carolyn Heilbrun's, old age may have allowed Sarah to move beyond the acceptable categories available to women, certainly the ones Sarah conceived of as appropriate for herself, and "for the first time be woman herself."[119] There is no doubt that Sarah Devereux accepted the tenets of the "Cult of Domesticity" and her prescribed role as a wife and mother. While she was hardly a feminist or even a protofeminist, by necessity she had enlarged on her perceived role at various points in her life, and by the end of her life had liberated herself, at least in part, from some of the assumptions about her sex.

Sarah Devereux expanded her concept of the boundaries of southern femininity in response to three things: the death of her husband, the Civil War and its aftermath, and the misfortunes of her second marriage. She never stepped completely out of the bounds, but each time she pushed those perimeters a bit further. She assumed the usually male role of planter in response to Julien's death, and during the war she publicly supported the Confederate cause with her taxes and products. After her second husband proved financially irresponsible, she taught school and kept boarders to supplement their income. Finally, as an elderly woman, she left Garrison when his behavior and demands became more than she could tolerate, and actively assisted her sons in challenging him. Her final removal from her home was an act of grace and strength marked by her calmness, determination, and refusal to repent.

Perhaps this study of Sarah Devereux will add to the growing interest in women's biographies. Some historians and biographers of women have suggested that as scholars we have exhausted much of the supply and some of the purpose of biographies of uncommon, unusual women who rebelled against

---

[117]Sarah Devereux Garrison to William Devereux, May 18, 1898, Devereux Family Papers.

[118]Ibid.

[119]Carolyn G. Heilbrun, *Writing a Woman's Life* (New York: W. W. Norton and Co., 1988), 131.

society's expectations of women and dared to live their own unique lives.[120] Too often these women appear as less than women, renouncing their feminine nature, family, and children for the sake of art or profession, and emerging as women who would have made great men—if only they had been of the correct gender. If women's biographies continue to follow masculine models, then there can be no development of women's lives on feminine models. Only by broadening the study of women's lives can feminine paradigms emerge. "As long as women are isolated one from the other, not allowed to offer other women the most personal accounts of their lives, they will not be part of any narrative of their own," observes Carolyn Heilbrun.[121] In other words, if historians and biographers do not study many different women's lives, how will we ever understand how women have lived their lives in the past and develop models for future generations of women? Sarah Devereux would likely be pleased to know that the story of her life is one minuscule piece of the vibrant and ever-expanding mosaic of women's history.

---

[120]Good discussions of the problem of "exceptionalism" in women's biography and history occur in Heilbrun, *Writing a Woman's Life,* and Gerda Lerner, "Placing Women in History: Definitions and Challenges," chap. 10 in *The Majority Finds Its Past: Placing Women in History* (New York: Oxford University Press, 1979). According to Heilbrun, "exceptional women are the chief imprisoners of nonexceptional women, simultaneously proving that any woman could do it and assuring, in their uniqueness among men, that no other woman will" (p. 81).

[121]Heilbrun, *Writing a Woman's Life,* 46.

# Texas Coastal Defense, 1861–1865

Alwyn Barr*

*Fifteen years after becoming the twenty-eighth state in the Union, Texas joined ten other Southern states that withdrew from the Union and formed the Confederate States of America. In the Civil War that followed more than sixty thousand Texans took part in military campaigns, fighting in Pennsylvania, Maryland, and Virginia in the east, and in Texas and New Mexico Territory in the west.*

*As Alwyn Barr, professor of history at Texas Tech and a leading authority on Texas's role in the Civil War, points out in this article, the Union made several attempts to occupy seaports along the Texas coast. Although Union naval forces occupied Galveston briefly in autumn 1862 they were driven out on New Year's Day 1863. A major Union assault against Sabine Pass on the upper Texas coast was repulsed in September 1863, but Federal troops occupied Brownsville in the winter of that year, only to withdraw in early summer 1864 to support a major Union drive up the Red River in western Louisiana. When the war ended, Galveston was the only major seaport still in Confederate hands.*

*For more on the Civil War in Texas see Ralph A. Wooster,* **Texas and Texans in the Civil War** *(Austin: Eakin Press, 1995); B. P. Gallaway (ed.),* **Texas: The Dark Corner of the Confederacy: Contemporary Accounts of the Lone Star State in the Civil War** *(3rd ed.; Lincoln: University of Nebraska Press, 1994); and Carl Moneyhon and Bobby Roberts,* **Portraits of Conflict: A Photographic History of Texas in the Civil War** *(Fayetteville: University of Arkansas Press, 1998).*

When Abraham Lincoln established a naval blockade of the Southern coast on April 19, 1861, Texas' four hundred mile stretch of beaches and harbors rated second only to Florida in length. Although somewhat distant from the fighting fronts, it was of immediate importance to the civilian population of the state, as well as a source of military supplies for the Trans-Mississippi region of

*Alwyn Barr, "Texas Coastal Defense, 1861–1865," *Southwestern Historical Quarterly*, 65 (July, 1961), 1–31.

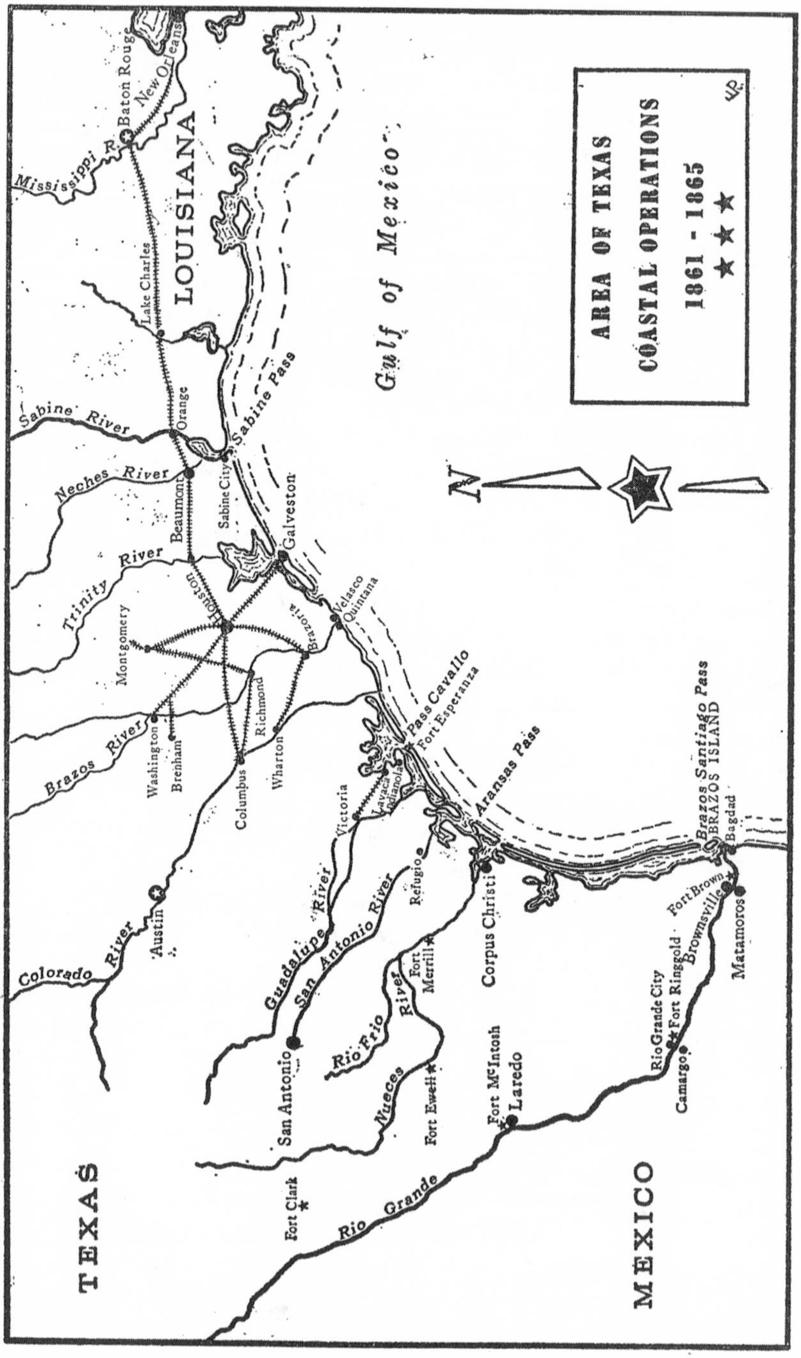
AREA OF TEXAS
COASTAL OPERATIONS
1861 - 1865
N
TEXAS
MEXICO
LOUISIANA
Gulf of Mexico
Mississippi R.
Baton Rouge
New Orleans
Lake Charles
Sabine River
Orange
Sabine Pass
Neches River
Beaumont
Sabine City
Galveston
Trinity River
Houston
Montgomery
Brazoria
Velasco
Quintana
Brazos River
Washington
Brenham
Richmond
Columbus
Wharton
Pass Cavallo
Fort Esperanza
Victoria
Lavaca
Indianola
Aransas Pass
Colorado River
Austin
Guadalupe River
San Antonio River
Refugio
Corpus Christi
Fort Merrill
Rio Frio
Nueces River
San Antonio
Fort Ewell
Fort McIntosh
Laredo
Fort Clark
Rio Grande
Rio Grande City
Fort Ringgold
Camargo
Brownsville
Fort Brown
Matamoros
Bagdad
Brazos Santiago Pass
BRAZOS ISLAND

the Confederacy. Retention of the Texas coast to keep open trade through northern Mexico also became of increasing necessity as the Federal blockade tightened on Southern ports. The need to hold open all routes for the influx of goods was compounded by Union conquest of the Mississippi River, cutting off the Trans-Mississippi area from the Southern heartland. Blockade running into Texas ports received a further stimulus from the Federal capture of most other Southern harbors as the war progressed. Thus the coast of Texas was the scene of constant activity throughout the Civil War, as its regional importance steadily increased.

Realization of the need for defense did not create the means. Texans in 1861 found themselves utterly helpless before a sea assault, and could breathe only an uneasy sigh of relief because the original Federal fleet numbered but forty-two ships for the entire Southern blockade.[1] Texas ports were guarded by no such brick fortifications as protected New Orleans, Mobile, Savannah, and Charleston. Few heavy cannon were to be found in Texas, none mounted for defense for her coastline, yet the essence of coastal attack and defense in the 1860s still lay in the artillery duel between warships and heavy artillery batteries. With batteries protected by fortifications, opposing the mobility of warships, many factors might effect the outcome. Morale and training of the men on each side, channel obstructions, the range and number of guns engaged on each side, and supporting troops in large operations all weighed to some extent in such a struggle.

During the American Civil War brick forts, such at Fort Sumter, were found to be out-of-date, and were replaced wherever possible by earthworks. Even then a Confederate engineer admitted, "No forts now built can keep out a large fleet unless the channel is obstructed."[2] For such purposes dams, sunken vessels, rocks, piles, chains, rafts, ropes, and torpedoes were employed.

Ordnance in use for warships and coastal defenses during the 1860s ranged from eighteen-pounders to twelve-inch Columbiad smoothbores, and included rifled cannon up to two-hundred-pounders. Extreme ranges for the more common pieces were:

| | | | |
|---|---|---|---|
| Eighteen-pounder | 1592 | yards at 5° | elevation |
| Twenty-four-pounder | 1834 | yards at 5° | elevation |
| Thirty-two-pounder | 1922 | yards at 5° | elevation |
| Eight-inch Columbiad | 4817 | yards at 27.30° | elevation |
| Ten-inch Columbiad | 5654 | yards at 39.15° | elevation |
| Thirty-pounder Parrott rifle | 4874 | yards at 15° | elevation |
| One-hundred-pounder Parrott rifle | 8428 | yards at 35° | elevation[3] |

[1]Charles B. Boynton, *The History of the Navy During the Rebellion* (New York, 1867), 97.

[2][Victor] Von Scheliha, *A Treatise on Coast-Defense: based on the Experience Gained by Officers of the Corps of Engineers of the Army of the Confederate States. . . .* (London, 1868), 47.

[3]U. S. War Department, *Instruction for Heavy Artillery* (New York, 1863), 236–239, 242.

In February of 1861, at the direction of the Secession Convention in Texas, Colonel John S. Ford led an expedition which captured Brazos Santiago and Fort Brown on the Rio Grande. There, from United States forces, were taken the first heavy cannon later used in defense of Texas harbors. Ford reported thirty-two guns captured, all smoothbores, including eight eight-inch howitzers, four twenty-four-pounder howitzers, twelve twenty-four-pounder siege guns, four ten-inch mortars, four twelve-pounder field guns, and 7293 rounds of ammunition. Some of the pieces, however, were without proper carriages.[4]

Twelve of the newly acquired guns were immediately forwarded to Galveston, where Sidney Sherman, a San Jacinto veteran, had been placed in charge of the city's fortification. The Secession Convention also voted during March, 1861, to entrench Sabine Pass, Matagorda Island, Aransas Pass, and Port Isabel. In April, Sherman was replaced by Captain John C. Moore, a former West Pointer and college professor from Tennessee, who later rose to brigadier general. He soon received additional cannon, taken during March at Fort Clark in West Texas. The entire confiscation of heavy ordnance there had included four twenty-four-pounders and two eight-inch howitzers.[5]

In June, 1861, Captain Walter H. Stevens, assisting in the fortification of Galveston, submitted to President Jefferson Davis the first comprehensive plan for Texas coastal defense. He suggested two twenty-four-pounders at Sabine Pass, four or five eight-inch Columbiads at Galveston, a twenty-four-pounder covering the mouth of the Brazos River, three thirty-two-pounders on Pass Cavallo, and two twenty-four-pounders at Aransas. Eight to ten companies of artillery would be normally sufficient, he felt, though reinforcements would be necessary in the event of a full scale invasion.[6]

July, 1861, brought the conflict closer to home for most Texans with the appearance of the Federal warship *South Carolina* under Commander James Alden to enforce the blockade at Galveston. Alden, an ingenious officer, armed the schooners *Dart, Shark,* and *Sam Houston* from among his first ten captures

---

[4]Ernest William Winkler (ed.), *Journal of the Secession Convention of Texas, 1861* (Austin, 1912), 352.

[5]*Ibid.*, 99, 133, 394; Francis R. Lubbock (C. W. Raines, ed.), *Six Decades In Texas, or Memoirs of Francis Richard Lubbock, Governor of Texas in War-Time, 1861–63; a Personal Experience in Business, War, and Politics* (Austin, 1900), 317; Ordnance Stores seized at U. S. A. posts in Texas, 1861 (Texas Adjutant General's Papers, Archives, Texas State Library) Fort Clark; George W. Cullum, *Biographical Register of the Officers and Graduates of the U. S. Military Academy at West Point, N. Y., . . .* (2 vols.; New York, 1868), II, 239.

[6]W. H. Stevens to Jefferson Davis, June 12, 1861, *The War of the Rebellion: A Compilation of the Official Records of the Union and Confederate Armies* (130 vols.; Washington, 1880–1901), Series I, Vol. IV, 92; cited hereafter as *Official Records.*

along the Texas coast. By their use he extended the blockade to Sabine Pass with only the original crew and guns from his single warship.[7]

With the blockade a reality enlistments in Texas coastal artillery units increased, each company being rushed to its position immediately upon mustering into the service. In Galveston the Third Battalion Texas Artillery, composed of seven companies, was organized under Major Joseph J. Cook. A graduate of the United States Naval Academy, Cook had personally raised Company A in Fayette County as the Active Company of Dixie Grays during June, 1861. When Cook was promoted to major, Captain Sidney T. Fontaine succeeded to his command.[8] Company B, raised in Galveston by Augustine S. Labuzan, came under the leadership of Captain A. R. Wier when Labuzan became major of the battalion after Cook's promotion to lieutenant colonel in December, 1861.[9] Captain E. B. H. Schneider headed Company C, while Samuel Boyer Davis, original commander of Company D, turned his battery over to Captain Charles M. Mason in late October to accept a staff appointment. Company E was raised by Captain Edward Von Harten. Captain Frederick H. Odlum commanded Company F, also known as the Davis Guards, which had been enlisted in time to accompany Ford's Rio Grande Valley expedition of February, 1861. Odlum's men were principally Irish dock workers, recruited like most of the battalion in Galveston and Houston.[10] Company G, led by Captain John H. Manly, had been a pre-war social organization known as the Houston Artillery.[11]

In September, 1861, Colonel Joseph Bates was appointed commander of the Fourth Texas Volunteer Regiment on coastal duty between San Luis Pass and Caney Creek. His unit, accepted for Confederate service as the Thirteenth Texas Infantry, actually included two artillery companies from the time of its organization. The artillery contingent was later increased to four batteries, of

[7]Commander James Alden to Lieutenant Samuel R. Knox, July 26, 1861, *Official Records of the Union and Confederate Navies in the War of Rebellion* (31 vols.; Washington, 1894–1927), Series I, Vol. XVI, 595; cited hereafter as *Official Records, Navies.*

[8]Confederate Muster Roll (73) (MS., Archives, Texas State Library); Dudley G. Wooten (ed.), *A Comprehensive History of Texas 1685–1897* (2 vols.; Dallas, 1898), II, 572; *List of Artillery Officers C. S. A.* (University of Texas Library binder's title; no title page, Marcus J. Wright lettered on spine), 134. The book is certainly the work described as U. S. War Department, Records Office, *Artillery Organization, etc. of the Confederate Army* (Washington, ?) in John Page Nicholson, *Catalogue of Library of Brevet Lieutenant-Colonel John Page Nicholson Relating to the War of the Rebellion 1861–1866* (Philadelphia, 1914), 45.

[9]*Ibid.*, 135; Confederate Muster Roll (1702) (MS., Archives, Texas State Library).

[10]*List of Artillery Officers C. S. A.*, 135; Winkler, *Journal of the Secession Convention of Texas, 1861*, p. 324; Galveston *News*, March 16, 1861; Francis Robertson Sackett, *Dick Dowling* (Houston, 1937), 16.

[11]Confederate Muster Roll (298) (MS., Archives, Texas State Library); *List of Artillery Officers C.S.A.*, 135; Houston *Tri-Weekly Telegraph*, May 6, 1859.

which Companies D and H, under Captains William G. Moseley and William E. Gibson were equipped with field guns. Companies B and F, led by Captains James S. Perry and William R. Jones, served the heavy guns at the mouth of the Brazos River near Velasco.[12]

Further south in the Matagorda Bay-Corpus Christi area three additional companies of artillery were raised for coastal service. Daniel D. Shea raised a battery known as the Van Dorn Guards, while Dr. Joseph M. Reuss recruited the Indianola Artillery Guards from Calhoun County. These units had elected officers and forwarded their rolls to the governor, even before he issued a call for three batteries to serve in their area.[13] His appeal, stemming from a requisition of three companies in August by Brigadier General Earl Van Dorn, commander of the District of Texas, was fulfilled by Captain Benjamin F. Neal's battery from the Corpus Christi area. Neal, who as a private citizen had written President Davis in April, 1861, about the need for artillery on the Texas coast, recruited his company in September and October.[14]

To complete Van Dorn's requisition of artillery, which included a request for one company at Sabine Pass, Captain J. R. Burch's Company B of Major James B. Likens' Sixth Texas Infantry Battalion was designated heavy artillery after its organization in November, 1861.[15]

While men were being recruited to serve coastal batteries a citizens' committee from Galveston left on July 25, 1861, for Richmond, armed with a requisition from General Van Dorn for heavy ordnance. Spurred on by the presence of blockaders off their city and a personal knowledge of its short ranged, inadequate batteries, William Pitt Ballinger, John S. Sydnor, and M. M. Potter arrived in Richmond on August 4.[16] On the same day Cook's men exchanged their first shots with the Federal ships, which shelled the port to test its defenses. Under a storm of protest from foreign consuls in the city Commander Alden ceased his bombardment and the blockade continued as before.[17]

In Richmond, Ballinger and his friends, unaware of events at home, were referred by the Secretary of War to Major Josiah Gorgas, Chief of the Ordnance Bureau. He offered them four ten-inch Columbiads, two eight-inch Columbiads,

---

[12]Brigadier General P. O. Hébert to Colonel J. Bates, September 26, 1861, *Official Records,* Series I, Vol. IV, 111–112; *List of Artillery Officers C.S.A.,* 48, 55, 81, 99.

[13]*Ibid.,* 52, 110, 138; Confederate Muster Roll (115) (MS., Archives, Texas State Library).

[14]Texas Adjutant General's *Report,* 1861, p. 4; B. F. Neal to Jefferson Davis, April 28, 1861, *Official Records,* Series I, Vol. I, 629–630; Confederate Muster Roll (518) (MS., Archives, Texas State Library).

[15]*List of Artillery Officers C.S.A.,* 16.

[16]William Pitt Ballinger Diary, August 4, 1861 (MS., Archives, University of Texas Library).

[17]Commander Alden to consular officers in Galveston, August 6, 1861, *Official Records, Navies,* Series I, Vol. XVI, 606–607; Oran M. Roberts, "Texas" in Vol. XI, *Confederate Military History* (Clement A. Evans, ed., 12 vols.; Atlanta, 1899), 71.

and two soon to be completed eight-inch rifled pieces, adding that carriages for the guns and some thirty-two-pounders could be had in New Orleans. The return trip, begun on August 15, proved to be a series of repeated delays, caused by railroad tie ups and the slush of fall roads in western Louisiana under incessant rains. On October 24, 1861, when Ballinger reached Galveston to assume an appointment as Receiver of Property of Alien Enemies, the cannon were still mired deep in mud east of the Sabine River. It appears probable that the guns did not reach Galveston until the early months of 1862.[18]

Despite a lack of powerful defenses as a deterrent, the Federal fleet remained relatively inactive off the Texas coast during the remainder of 1861. At Galveston a few blockade runners were taken, and on November 12 a boat attack successfully surprised and partially burned the Confederate patrol schooner *Royal Yacht*.[19]

Ashore, Commander William W. Hunter of the Confederate Navy and Brigadier General Paul O. Hébert, newly appointed Confederate commander in Texas, pushed efforts to fortify Galveston and Houston. An attempt was also made to improvise a harbor defense fleet by the purchase of river steamers and the renovation of captured government vessels.[20] Lacking heavy ordnance, however, Hébert felt that because of the

> superior naval armament of the enemy and his entire possession of the sea, it will be almost impossible to prevent a landing at some point upon this extensive and unprotected coast, I have settled upon it as a military necessity that he must be fought on shore or in the interior.[21]

After the *Royal Yacht* affair Hébert's apprehensions increased to the point of removing part of the artillery in Galveston to Virginia Point, mainland end of the island's railroad bridge. In January, 1862, however, the city's batteries were increased from eight to thirteen heavy guns, probably the pieces acquired originally by Ballinger's party in Richmond. With such an addition to the island's defenses Hébert continued to garrison both Fort Point and Pelican Spit, key positions covering the harbor mouth.[22]

At Pass Cavallo, the main entrance to Matagorda Bay, Captain Shea's battery stood guard with four twenty-four-pounders by early October. His isolated position on Matagorda Island near the lighthouse remained exposed, however,

---

[18]Ballinger Diary, August 6, 1861–October 24, 1861 (MS., Archives, University of Texas Library); Houston *Tri-Weekly Telegraph*, November 10, 1862.

[19]Galveston *Tri-Weekly Civilian*, November 9, 1861; Captain Henry Eagle to Flag Officer W. W. McKean, November 12, 1861, *Official Records, Navies*, Series I, Vol. XVI, 755–756.

[20]*Ibid.*, 835, 840–841, 844, 847–849; *Official Records*, Series I, Vol. IV, 112, 117, 122, 126–127.

[21]General Hébert to Secretary of War Judah P. Benjamin, October 24, 1861, *ibid.*, 127.

[22]*Ibid.*, 166; Ballinger Diary, November 29, 1861 (MS., Archives, University of Texas Library); Log of the *Bayou City*, *Official Records, Navies*, Series I, Vol. XVI, 869.

because of orders not to entrench until the proper point for works could be chosen by engineers.[23] Darwin M. Stapp, brigadier general of Texas militia, after inspecting Shea's position reported to General Hébert in late October that Reuss' battery, with two twelve-pounders and a six-pounder, was also present and temporary works had been thrown up to shield the guns. He also suggested the removal of both batteries to the mainland unless they were supported by other troops to protect against boat landings.[24]

Another inspection in December by Colonel Robert R. Garland found the artillery properly positioned to engage Federal warships but short of ammunition and still unsupported in an incomplete earthwork styled Fort Washington by its garrison. On December 7 and 8, during Garland's visit, Shea's men engaged a Union blockader at extreme range, firing sixteen rounds with little effect.[25]

In December, Governor Francis R. Lubbock responded to appeals from the Aransas area by requesting three or four heavy cannon from Fort Brown in Colonel Henry E. McCulloch's Western Sub-District of Texas. Such a battery, he believed, would protect intracoastal trade carried on behind the island chain with Matamoros, as well as the mail and private property in the Aransas-Corpus Christi region.[26]

Blockaders off the Texas coast in early 1862 numbered only five, thinly spread in an attempt to cover its numerous harbors while the main gulf squadron under Admiral David G. Farragut attacked New Orleans. During January the ships *Midnight, Arthur,* and *Rachel Seaman* engaged the shore batteries at Velasco and Pass Cavallo, testing their strength and range.[27] Shea, still unsupported on Matagorda Island in February, hired a patrol boat to inform him of any landing to his rear. At the same time he began earthworks to cover the land approach to his guns. Bates' defenses at Velasco were also reportedly stronger, improved by cannon originally intended for Aransas Pass.[28]

---

[23]Report of Colonel August C. Buchel, *Official Records,* Series I, Vol. IV, 116–117. Activity in the Matagorda Bay-Corpus Christi area has been well presented by Lester N. Fitzhugh, "Saluria, Fort Esperanza, and Military Operations on the Texas Coast, 1861–1864," *Southwestern Historical Quarterly,* LXI, 66–100.

[24]D. M. Stapp to General Hébert, October 17, 1861, *Official Records,* Series I, Vol. IV, 123–124.

[25]Colonel R. R. Garland to Major S. B. Davis, December 6, 14, 1861, *ibid.,* 153–154, 156–157; Captain D. D. Shea to Major S. B. Davis, December 9, 1861, *ibid.,* 155–156; Lieutenant James Trathen to Flag Officer W. W. McKean, December 18, 1861, *Official Records, Navies,* Series I, Vol. XVII, 6.

[26]Governor Francis R. Lubbock to Colonel H. E. McCulloch, December 23, 1861 (Executive Record Book 1861–1863, Archives, Texas State Library).

[27]*Official Records, Navies,* Series I, Vol. XVII, 71; Vol. XVIII, 690–691; Lieutenant James Trathen to Captain Henry Eagle, January 24, 1862, *ibid.,* Vol. XVII, 79–80.

[28]Captain D. D. Shea to Commodore W. W. Hunter, February 3, 1862, *ibid.,* 167; Major C. G. Forshey to Major S. B. Davis, February 19, 24, 1862, *Official Records,* Series I, Vol. LIII, 787–789.

Because of an almost complete lack of artillery in the Aransas vicinity, Union warships were able to shell repeatedly the off shore islands. Captain Neal, commanding the defenses there, reported his battery as equipped with two light six-pounders, and almost completely lacking in powder. Federal boat raids were also effective in destroying some property, although Shea and Neal were able to deal with most of them quickly. It was during this rather trying period that Shea received a promotion to major in command of an artillery battalion, composed of his own company under Captain John A. Vernon, and that of Captain Reuss.[29]

Activity in the Galveston area during early 1862 was limited to the burning of a beached blockade runner in San Luis Pass by a Federal boat party in April.[30] Hébert's fear of attack from the sea was heightened, however, because his district had been stripped of its supporting units to build up General Van Dorn's army in Arkansas for the Pea Ridge campaign.[31]

With the exit of most units from the Galveston garrison Lieutenant Colonel Joseph J. Cook was promoted to colonel and his battalion was increased to a full regiment, known as the First Texas Heavy Artillery. To this end Companies H, I, K, and L, under Captains Thomas J. Catching, D. M. Jackson, David G. Adams, and N. J. King, were raised and added to the command between April and June, 1862. John H. Manly, former commander of Company G, was promoted to lieutenant colonel of the new regiment, while Edward Von Harten, captain of Company E rose to the rank of major in the enlarged unit.[32]

All Hébert's nightmares seemed about to come true on May 17, 1862, when Captain Henry Eagle of the Federal frigate *Santee* demanded the surrender of Galveston. Having engaged the city's batteries two days before with the schooner *Sam Houston,* Eagle's threat of attack appeared quite real. Many guns had already been removed from the city. Those remaining on Pelican Spit were spiked by Colonel Cook, who prepared to evacuate his troops rather than fight should a landing be made. Totally without army support, Eagle ran out his bluff and the blockade again settled into normalcy.[33]

---

[29]Major D. D. Shea to Colonel R. R. Garland, February 18, 1862, *ibid.,* Series I, Vol. IX, 483–486; Captain B. F. Neal to Colonel H. E. McCulloch, February 22, 1862, *ibid.,* 562; Major W. O. Yager to Lieutenant B. E. Benton, April 25, 1862, *ibid.,* 603–604.

[30]Colonel J. Bates to Major S. B. Davis, April 6, 1862, *ibid.,* 545.

[31]Judah P. Benjamin to General Hébert, February 24, 1862, *ibid.,* 700.

[32]*List of Artillery Officers C.S.A.,* 134–136; Houston *Weekly Telegraph,* April 7, 1862.

[33]Captain H. Eagle to Admiral Farragut, June 4, 1862, *Official Records, Navies,* Series I, Vol. XVIII, 536; Ballinger Diary, May 16, 17, 1862 (MS., Archives, University of Texas Library); X. B. DeBray, *A Sketch of the History of DeBray's 26th Regiment of Texas Cavalry* (Austin, 1884), 6; Colonel J. J. Cook to General Hébert, General Hébert to Colonel J. J. Cook, May 7, 1862, *Official Records,* Series I, Vol. IX, 710–711.

Skirmishing continued along the entire coast in July with clashes at San Luis Pass, Matagorda, and Aransas Pass between small boat crews and shore patrols. Lieutenant John W. Kittredge with the bark *Arthur* was especially troublesome in the Aransas region, entering the pass to obstruct intracoastal trade and shell Neal's camp.[34] A similar bombardment was beaten off at Velasco by Bates' men with an eighteen pounder on August 11, but caused their commander to request heavier ordnance for his important post.[35]

Kittredge again captured the spotlight later in August when he took the steam gunboat *Sachem* into Corpus Christi Bay, followed by the *Bella Italia, Corypheus, Reindeer,* and *Arthur,* all sailing vessels. In the following week he captured or ran aground two Confederate patrol boats and demanded the right to inspect former government buildings in Corpus Christi. When refused by Major Alfred M. Hobby on August 14, he served forty-eight hour notice on the town.[36]

True to his word Kittredge brought his tiny fleet into the bay north of town at dawn on the 16th and opened fire with six or seven heavy guns. Protected by an old earthwork, erected by General Zachary Taylor in 1845, Hobby drove off the first attack at 9:00 A.M., and the second by 3:00 P.M. with a twelve and an eighteen-pounder. Under a rain of nearly three hundred shot and shell Hobby's men had maintained their position at a cost of one wounded.

Following a lull on Sunday the Union warships renewed their assault during the 18th. Hobby had added another cannon to his battery, and continued to hold the shore side earthworks. In a further effort to dislodge the Confederates, Kittredge sent some of his seamen ashore with a field gun. Hobby countered with a stirring southern charge, which drove the Federals back to their ships. Defeated in every effort to capture the port, Kittredge shelled the empty town, but total Southern casualties in victory were only two wounded and one killed.[37]

Once the town had been successfully defended its position was rapidly improved by subsequent events, beginning with the arrival of Captain Herman Willke's battery of two twenty-four-pounder howitzers and four twelve-pounders on August 27.[38] Hobby's local popularity increased even more when Captain

---

[34]Colonel C. Livenskiold to Brigadier General H. P. Bee, July 17, 1862, *ibid.,* 610–613; Captain B. F. Neal to Colonel C. Livenskiold, July 16, 1862, *ibid.,* 613–614.

[35]Colonel J. Bates' report, August 16, 1862, *ibid.,* 616.

[36]Captain John Harding's report, August 27, 1862, *ibid.,* 617; Captain John Sands' report, August 27, 1862, *ibid.,* 618; Lubbock, *Six Decades in Texas,* 410.

[37]Major A. M. Hobby's reports, August 16, 18, 1862, *Official Records,* Series I, Vol. IX, 621–623; *Ranchero Extra* (Corpus Christi), August 19, 1862.

[38]Brigadier General H. P. Bee's report, August 26, 1862, *Official Records,* Series I, Vol. IX, 619–621.

John Ireland's company of his battalion captured Lieutenant Kittredge, surprised while ashore south of Corpus Christi in early September.[39] To insure against heavier assaults on the community, Felix A. Blucher rebuilt the north battery, adding a bombproof, and constructed two new batteries on the south side of town. The new water battery housed two twenty-four-pounder howitzers, while a sunken position on the bluff held an eighteen-pounder.[40]

As early as July 30, 1862, Major Getulius Kellersberger reported the works at Sabine Pass to be inadequate and the battery of two thirty-two-pounders and two eighteen-pounders poorly equipped.[41] Before the engineer's suggested improvements had been made, however, three Federal vessels entered the pass and engaged the fort on September 24, 1862. Captain K. D. Keith commanding the local artillery company, a part of Ashley W. Spaight's Battalion, held the position until after dark under a continuous bombardment from beyond extreme range for his cannon. Major Josephus S. Irvine, a San Jacinto veteran commanding in Spaight's absence, ordered the pieces spiked and all stores removed from the works which were abandoned by 8:00 A.M. the next morning. Yellow fever had cut into the battalion's strength but reinforcements arrived quickly and the Union sailors limited their efforts to burning the railroad depot at Beaumont, and destroying the fort, two schooners, and later the railroad bridge over Taylor Bayou.[42]

Having struck at both ends of Texas' coastal defenses the Federal blockading fleet in early October aimed its main blow at Galveston, the commercial, military, and diplomatic center of Texas affairs. General Hébert, aware of the increased Union activity, assumed the ultimate goal to be Galveston and decided its defense was impossible. Work continued only on Fort Hébert at Virginia Point, while the heavy guns finally available in Galveston were all removed except one on Fort Point. Citizens of the island community were bitterly opposed to any retreat, accusing Hébert of greater love for his cannon than for their city.[43]

---

[39]Brigadier General H. P. Bee's report, September 24, 1862, *ibid.*, 624.

[40]Felix A. Blucher to Major E. F. Gray, October 15, 1862, *ibid.*, Series I, Vol. XV, 827–828.

[41]Major J. Kellersberg [G. Kellersberger] to Colonel X. B. DeBray, July 30, 1862, *ibid.*, Series I, Vol. IX, 729. Kellersberger, born in Switzerland in 1821, came to America in 1849, where he married and worked as an engineer in California and Mexico prior to the war.

[42]Lieutenant Colonel A. W. Spaight's reports, September 26, October 2, 1862, *ibid.*, Series I, Vol. XV, 144–145, 146–147; Acting Master Frederick Crocker to Admiral Farragut, October 24, 1862, *Official Records, Navies,* Series I, Vol. XIX, 227–229; Houston *Tri-Weekly Telegraph,* September 29, October 3, 1862.

[43]Ballinger Diary, October 4, 1862 (MS., Archives, University of Texas Library); Galveston *Weekly News,* October 15, 1862; P. W. Gray to Jefferson Davis, November 20, 1862, *Official Records,* Series I, Vol. XV, 868–869; Colonel X. B. DeBray's report, October 19, 1862, *ibid.*, 836.

Other batteries were filled with Quaker guns made of wood on October 4, 1862, when the Union gunboat *Harriet Lane* steamed into the harbor with a surrender demand for Colonel Cook. Because of a delay in replying, caused by a lack of small boats to communicate with the ship, Commander William B. Renshaw brought his remaining seven warships up the channel. The garrison of Fort Point opened on the advancing Union fleet with their ten-inch gun, only to see it dismounted by an eleven-inch shot from the gunboat *Owasco.* After fire from two twenty-four-pounders fell short, resistance ceased, for Galveston lay under the guns of Renshaw's gunboats. A four day truce was agreed to, allowing the Confederates under Colonel Cook to evacuate, since the Union fleet had no troops with which to occupy the island. Activity continued at both Virginia Point and Eagle Grove, island end of the railroad bridge, where parts of Cook's regiment improved their entrenched positions.[44]

Lavaca became the next focal point of action when Renshaw took two of his ships into Matagorda Bay later that month. On October 31 he appeared off the town, demanding its capitulation at 1:00 P.M. When refused by Major Shea, the Union commander allowed only ninety minutes for the residents to be removed, despite a yellow fever epidemic then in progress. Having thus made himself duly infamous for such harshness, Renshaw opened a close range bombardment of the town that afternoon. Shea's guns under Vernon and Reuss returned an effective crossfire on the warships, however, forcing their withdrawal beyond range of the shore batteries. Lavaca was again shelled at long range on November 1, but no further attempts to seize the town were made.[45]

Major General John Bankhead Magruder brought a fresh breath of fighting spirit to Texas in the fall of 1862, when he replaced Hébert as district commander. Magruder began immediately upon his arrival to plan an attack aimed at the recapture of Galveston, pressed onward perhaps by the hint of failures in the Seven Days' fighting near Richmond during the past summer.

For the amphibious part of his assault force "Prince John" Magruder placed two river steamers, protected by cotton bales, under Captain Leon Smith. A thirty-two-pounder rifle was placed aboard the *Bayou City* to be served by Captain A. R. Wier with volunteers from Cook's artillery. Lieutenant L. C. Harby led the men from Lieutenant Colonel William H. Griffin's Battalion who were to fire two twenty-four-pounders on the *Neptune.* Sharpshooters from the cavalry regiments of Colonels Tom Green and Arthur P. Bagby, formerly participants in

[44]Commander W. B. Renshaw to Admiral Farragut, October 8, 1862, *Official Records, Navies,* Series I, Vol. XIX, 254–260; Houston *Telegraph Supplement,* December 8, 1862; Colonel J. J. Cook's report, October 9, 1862, *Official Records,* Series I, Vol. XV, 151–153; Colonel X. B. DeBray's report, October 12, 1862, *ibid.,* 148–149.

[45]Lieutenant George E. Conklin to Major E. F. Gray, November 1, 1862, *ibid.,* 181–183; Houston *Tri-Weekly Telegraph,* November 3, 10, 1862; Lubbock, *Six Decades in Texas,* 413–414.

Brigadier General Henry Hopkins Sibley's New Mexico Expedition, also volunteered for service aboard both boats.[46]

Ashore Magruder left Lieutenant Colonel John H. Manly in charge of the Virginia Point batteries, and placed Major Edward Von Harten in command of the artillery to be moved into Galveston under cover of darkness. Fourteen field guns, including the batteries of Captains George R. Wilson and William G. Moseley, were to fan out along the city's entire waterfront prior to opening on Renshaw's fleet. An eight-inch Dahlgren gun was mounted on a railroad flat car which would be wheeled over the bridge and brought into action at short range. Captain Sidney T. Fontaine with his battery received orders to recapture Fort Point and set up three siege guns there to assist in shelling the Union warships. For support of his twenty shore pieces Magruder had an assortment of cavalry and infantry units commanded by Brigadier General William R. Scurry.[47]

The object of such a military concentration, six Federal gunboats, lay in Galveston harbor, almost completely unaware of their danger until the last minute. At anchor in the bay were the *Westfield,* flagship with six guns, another converted ferry boat, the *Clifton,* with eight heavy cannon, an altered merchant ship, *Sachem,* mounting five guns, the *Owasco,* only regular warship of the fleet, armed with four cannon, a small schooner with one gun, the *Corypheus,* and a former United States revenue cutter mounting five heavy guns, the *Harriet Lane.*[48]

Ashore on Kuhn's Wharf at the end of Eighteenth Street were 264 men and officers of the Forty-second Massachusetts Infantry, who arrived from New Orleans on December 25 as a garrison for Galveston. Because of their numerical weakness no attempt had been made to entrench the town or burn the railroad bridge connecting it with the mainland. Most of the fleet lay near the wharf, with the *Harriet Lane* in the shallow channel above it off Twenty-ninth Street.[49]

After a false start in late December, New Year's night was chosen for the surprise assault, with the hope that celebrations of the occasion would help lower

---

[46]Robert N. Franklin, *Battle of Galveston, January 1st 1863* (Galveston, 1911), 5; Major C. G. Forshey to Colonel X. B. DeBray, December 23, 1862, *Official Records,* Series I, Vol. XV, 908; General Magruder's report, February 26, 1863, *ibid.,* 211–220.

[47]*Ibid.*; Wooten, *A Comprehensive History of Texas 1685–1897,* II, 532; Houston *Tri-Weekly Telegraph,* January 19, 1863.

[48]Frank Moore, (ed.), *The Rebellion Record: A Diary of American Events* . . . (12 vols.; New York, 1862–1868), VI, 339; Franklin, *Battle of Galveston, January 1st 1863,* p. 6; Statistical Data of U. S. Ships, *Official Records, Navies,* Series II, Vol. I, 59, 67, 99, 168–169, 195, 238.

[49]Charles P. Bosson, *History of the Forty-Second Regiment Infantry, Massachusetts Volunteers 1862, 1863, 1864* (Boston, 1886), 61–77; Lieutenant Charles A. Davis' report, January 10, 1863, *Official Records,* Series I, Vol. XV, 206–207.

the efficiency of Union guards in Galveston. Artillery wheels were hard to muffle, however, and Massachusetts' pickets reported Confederate cannon in the market place by 1:00 A.M. After the moon set between 3:00 and 4:00 A.M., Southern guns opened on Federal ships from an arc of positions two and a half miles long. Colonel Cook led a pre-dawn charge through shallow water against the Union held wharf, only to be repulsed because his troops' ladders were too short.[50]

Wasting shot and shell at first, the *Sachem, Owasco,* and *Corypheus* later depressed their cannon to fire along Galveston's shadowy thoroughfares, and drove Southern gunners to cover in an unequal duel between field artillery and nine to eleven-inch naval guns. The Union flagship, *Westfield,* trying to move up channel just after midnight, went aground on Pelican Spit near the harbor's mouth. Repeated efforts by the *Clifton* were of no avail in disloding it as action began. Commander Renshaw then sent the *Clifton* to aid the other warships in silencing the Confederate guns.[51] Confederate land forces were still in action but nearing defeat at the moment when a Northern reporter penned this vivid description of the battle:

> Overhead and around night was slowly retiring before day; the dim light prevalent being rent by the frequent flashes of cannon, the soaring aloft of shell, and the omnipresent short-lived blaze of musketry, while the hellish discord beggars all description.[52]

Action was far from ending, however, for with excellent timing the *Neptune* and *Bayou City* began their rush toward the isolated *Harriet Lane* at dawn. Aided by surprise, with Federal attention centered on the shore batteries, their swift approach was hindered only by the untimely explosion of Captain Wier's heavy piece aboard the *Bayou City.* Although Wier and two of his men were killed, both river boats closed quickly to rifle range and the Texas sharpshooters swept the *Harriet Lane's* decks with fire. Attempts to ram the Union vessel failed at first and a shot from her pivot gun sank the *Neptune* in shallow water near by. Despite stiff resistance, continued heavy fire by Tom Green's sharpshooters settled the issue, forcing the Yankee seamen below decks. There they were captured when the *Bayou City* rammed and boarded her helpless adversary only moments later. Both officers of the captured vessel were found mortally wounded on her deck, their loss a key factor, no doubt, in the ship's defeat.

Fearful of injuring Federal prisoners, the *Owasco* retired after a tardy attempt to aid the *Harriet Lane.* White flags were raised by both sides and a sur-

---

[50]S. Long's report, January 10, 1863, *ibid.,* 208–210; Bosson, *History of the Forty-Second Massachusetts Infantry,* 87–95.

[51]A. J. H. Duganne, *Camps and Prisons, Twenty Months in the Department of the Gulf* (New York, 1865), 236; Major General N. P. Banks' report, January 3, 1863, *Official Records,* Series I, Vol. XV, 199–206; General Magruder's report, February 26, 1863, *ibid.,* 211–220.

[52]Moore, *The Rebellion Record,* VI, 341.

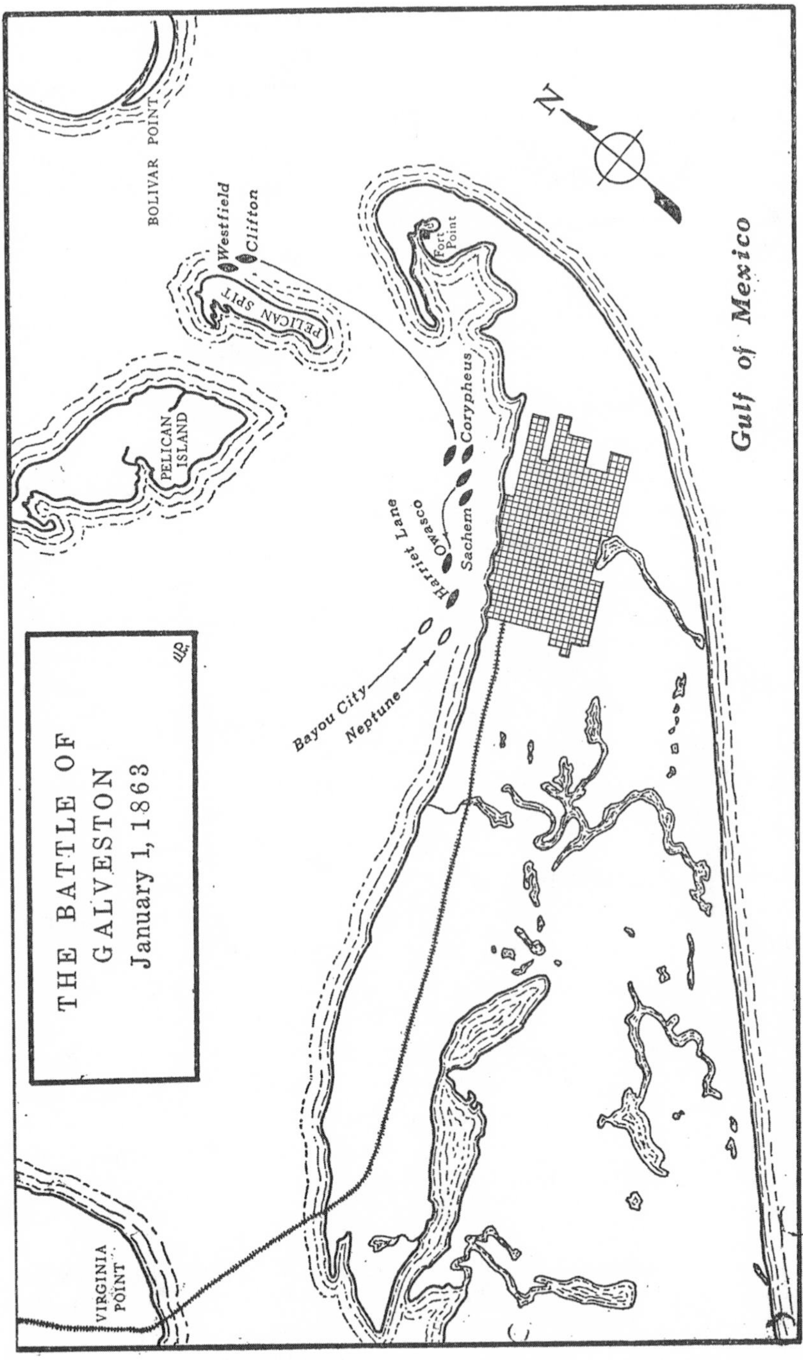
THE BATTLE OF
GALVESTON
January 1, 1863
BOLIVAR POINT
Westfield
Clifton
PELICAN SPIT
PELICAN ISLAND
Fort Point
N
Corypheus
Sachem
Owasco
Harriet Lane
Bayou City
Neptune
Gulf of Mexico
VIRGINIA POINT

render demand was presented to the nearest Union gunboat. Unable to enforce their ultimatum, the Confederates could only watch as the Federal fleet sailed out to sea. Without any central leadership each ship captain had fought his own separate fight, ending in a withdrawal by mass consent. Commander Renshaw, unable to free the *Westfield,* removed his crew and set a fuse to the ship's magazine. A premature explosion caught the commander aboard, however, killing him and his small boat crew in the concussion and wreckage. Besides the *Harriet Lane,* Magruder had captured the Massachusetts infantry who were forced to surrender when left unsupported, and inflicted over 150 casualties on the Union Navy while retaking Galveston. Even twenty-six killed, including Captain Wier and Lieutenant Sidney Sherman, Jr. of the artillery, plus 117 wounded must have seemed small price for such a success.[53]

Following up his Galveston victory, Magruder transferred Company F of Cook's regiment to Sabine Pass with an eight-inch rifled Columbiad for service on the cottonclad ram fleet there. The Davis Guards under Captain Frederick Odlum were placed aboard the *Josiah H. Bell* with their heavy piece, called "Annie" in honor of their commander's niece, the wife of Lieutenant Richard W. Dowling. Two twelve-pounders were mounted on the *Uncle Ben,* another river steamer, to be served by Captain K. D. Keith's artillerymen from Spaight's Battalion. Reinforced with riflemen of Spaight's command, the assault force moved from Beaumont down to Sabine Pass on January 20, led by Major Oscar M. Watkins. Outside the pass lay two Federal blockaders, a sloop, *Morning Light,* armed with nine heavy guns, and the schooner, *Velocity,* mounting two light howitzers. Both vessels were commanded by Captain John Dillingham.

Having removed the channel obstructions, Watkins' steamers sailed as the sun rose on January 21, 1863, heading for the blockaders. Both Union vessels ran before the attackers but were steadily overhauled on a nearly calm sea because they were strictly sailing ships. Opening at a range of over two miles, the *Bell's* gun crew exhibited uncanny accuracy in dismounting one of the *Morning Light's* cannon. Their fire was then momentarily silenced by a crudely cast shot which refused to be rammed home. Pressing on to within rifle range the *Bell's* sharpshooters cleared her opponent's decks, forcing surrender. Not to be outdone, the *Uncle Ben* brought the *Velocity* around with three solid shot and both Federal ships were towed back to Sabine Pass. Without loss Watkins had taken 109 prisoners, after inflicting thirteen casualties, while further destroying the Northern blockade of Texas' coast. After attempts to float the *Morning Light*

[53]Commander Henry Wilson to Admiral Farragut, January 8, 1863, *Official Records, Navies,* Series I, Vol. XIX, 439; General Banks' report, January 3, 1863, *Official Records,* Series I, Vol. XV, 199–206; General Magruder's report, February 26, 1863, *ibid.,* 211–220; Bosson, *History of the Forty-Second Massachusetts Infantry,* 100–115.

over the bar failed, the sloop was scuttled and burned off the pass upon the appearance of other Union warships.[54]

News of the Sabine Pass affair was an almost anticlimactic blow for Commodore Henry H. Bell, who had been sent to Galveston by Admiral Farragut to renew the blockade and if possible recapture the city. Upon his arrival on January 10, 1863, Bell bombarded the city only to be rebuked by foreign consuls, again in residence there. Entering the harbor, he found beyond his means, for Magruder had removed all channel buoys, and most of his vessels were of too deep draft to navigate the shallow bars without a pilot. Nothing was left for him, except to stand off the island watching its defenses grow, counting new guns as they were mounted.[55]

On the night of January 11, 1863, the dull boom of naval guns drifted in from the Gulf of Mexico to questioning ears ashore at Galveston. It was later found that Captain Raphael Semmes had brought the Confederate sea raider *Alabama* into the Gulf to attack the transports of a rumored invasion fleet headed for Texas. Sighting the *Alabama* off Galveston, the Federal gunboat *Hatteras* under Lieutenant Commander H. C. Blake had given chase on the eleventh, hailing after dark. Receiving the name of a British vessel in reply, Blake sent a boat party to check the stranger's papers, only to be surprised and sunk by a ripping broadside after the boat pulled away. Semmes picked up the Yankee crew and outran Bell's fleet, which arrived too late to effect the course of action.[56]

Commodore Bell would have been rudely shocked could he have seen the excellent staging which produced the vivid picture of massive defense before him at Galveston. Magruder, who believed the city untenable, nevertheless called for 2000 slaves to fortify it as part of a grand game of bluff. Works sprung up almost overnight under the skilled direction of Colonel Valery Sulakowski and Major Getulius Kellersberger.

To fill their awesome fortifications until real ordnance could arrive, the foreign born engineers improvised Quaker guns of wood, which frowned impressively on the Union blockaders. Two heavy cannon were mounted aboard railroad cars and run into the entrenchments on extended side tracks. Changing positions at night, they furthered the deception by lobbing shells at

---

[54]Duganne, *Camps and Prisons*, 243–246; Galveston *Tri-Weekly News*, February 2, 1863; Surgeon J. W. Sherfy to Secretary of Navy Gideon Welles, April 12, 1864, *Official Records, Navies*, Series I, Vol. XIX, 558–562; Major O. M. Watkins to Captain E. P. Turner, January 23, March 14, 1863, *ibid.*, 564–566, 567–570.

[55]Admiral Farragut to Commodore H. H. Bell, January 3, 1863, *ibid.*, 479; Commodore H. H. Bell to Admiral Farragut, January 24, 1863, *ibid.*, 554.

[56]Semmes to Mallory, May 12, 1863, *ibid.*, Series I, Vol. II, 683; Bell to Farragut, January 12, 1863, *ibid.*, Series I, Vol. XIX, 506.

the fleet from different batteries each day.[57] Masquerade time continued until a few days after one of the year's most intense storms, which blew over one or two of the fake cannon. Then, at a truce meeting, in a burst of gleeful satire, Federal officers informed the Confederates that "they had seen two . . . artillerymen carry a large cannon, which ordinarily weighed some 5400 pounds, into position all alone, and they did not think it adviseable to tie into such strong men as that."[58]

To improve the efficiency of defense between Matagorda Bay and Corpus Christi, Magruder combined Major Alfred M. Hobby's infantry battalion with Major Daniel D. Shea's artillery in February to form the Eighth Texas Infantry. Hobby was promoted to colonel, Shea to lieutenant colonel.[59]

May, 1863, brought a unique request to Governor Francis R. Lubbock from a citizens' committee in Houston. The group asked that Captain Henry S. Lubbock, the governor's brother, be furloughed to superintend the construction of a "Sub Marine Propeller" for attaching torpedoes to blockaders. Although no further mention was made of the project, it provided proof of Texan determination to defend their coasts, as well as ingenuity exceeded only by the partially successful use of such a vessel at Charleston in 1864.[60]

Bell's constant reports on Southern entrenching at Galveston continued into May, when he outlined the system of fortifications for his commander, Admiral Farragut. South Battery contained two rifled guns in bombproof casemates. Continuing northward along the beach were a middle battery, and the largest work of all, Fort Magruder, near the Old Hospital. Fort Point mounted eight casemate guns, while Pelican Spit held six more. Three new works covered the inner harbor and piles blocked the channel between Pelican Island and Virginia Point. He estimated that 5000 men would be necessary to conquer and garrison the island fortress.[61]

The formidable works described by Bell were inspected from within by Magruder, Governor Lubbock, and their combined staffs in June, 1863, and appeared much as Colonel Arthur Fremantle of the British Army had viewed them while passing through Texas in May. All agreed to their strength, especially since real cannon had been added. Some guns had been returned from Houston, and although the *Harriet Lane's* armament had been ordered to

---

[57]Ballinger Diary, January 5, 16, 1863 (MS., Archives, University of Texas Library); DeBray, *History of DeBray's 26th Regiment of Texas Cavalry,* 11; Getulius Kellersberger (Helen S. Sundstrom, trans.), *Memoirs of an Engineer in the Confederate Army in Texas* (Austin, 1957), 27–29.

[58]Ibid., 29.

[59]Confederate Muster Roll (95) (MS., Archives, Texas State Library).

[60]W. B. Baker and others to Governor F. R. Lubbock, May 15, 1863 (Texas State Military Board Papers, Archives, Texas State Library).

[61]Commodore H. H. Bell to Admiral Farragut, May 12, 1863, *Official Records, Navies,* Series I, Vol. XX, 183–184.

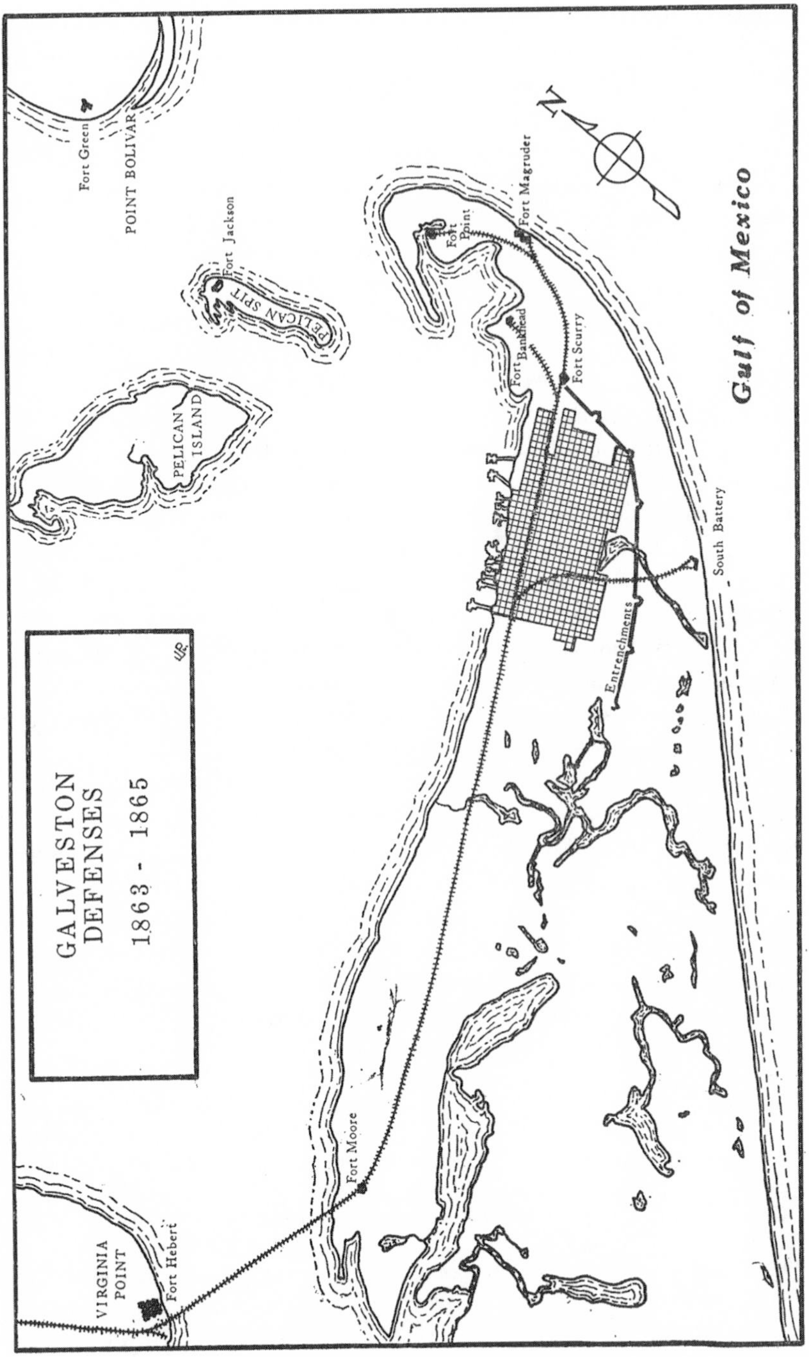

GALVESTON
DEFENSES
1863 - 1865
Gulf of Mexico
Fort Green
POINT BOLIVAR
Fort Jackson
PELICAN SPIT
PELICAN
ISLAND
Fort Point
Fort Magruder
Fort Bankhead
Fort Scurry
South Battery
Entrenchments
Fort Moore
VIRGINIA
POINT
Fort Hebert
N

Louisiana, six cannon were reclaimed from the *Westfield's* hulk.[62] By July, Commodore Bell pronounced the fortifications too strong for an assault by the normal blockading fleet without powerful army support.[63]

In August occurred a short lived mutiny by part of Galveston's garrison, surprising in view of their otherwise steady service. The refusal to drill by men of the Third Texas Infantry on August 10, 1863, followed the next day by parts of Cook's artillery, focused attention on the morale problems in coastal defense. While poor provisions and lack of pay were given as major reasons, constant exposure to disease in an unhealthy area, worry over Indian raids on their families near the frontier, and the general monotony of garrison duty with its inactivity must also be weighed in assessing the causes. The dissidents were brought quickly into line by firm yet understanding officers, well acquainted with the unmilitary quirks of volunteers.[64]

During the final four months of 1863, Confederate troops in Texas were left little time for personal problems. Once Vicksburg and Port Hudson fell, opening the Mississippi to the North, Federal efforts turned toward conquest of Texas, to forestall such a move by Maximilian's French armies in Mexico.

Sabine Pass was chosen for the first Union attack, as a weakly held point protected, supposedly, by only two thirty-two-pounders. Once in Federal hands the pass would provide access to Beaumont, a perfect base for operations in Texas because of its rail connection with Houston over flat country. To carry out his planned invasion of Texas, Major General Nathaniel P. Banks in New Orleans brought together four light draft gunboats, the *Clifton, Sachem, Arizona,* and *Granite City,* under Lieutenant Frederick Crocker. The ships were to escort and support 4000 troops of the Nineteenth Army Corps, commanded by Major General William B. Franklin. After delays caused by the imagined presence of the Confederate sea raider *Alabama* off Sabine Pass, the Federal fleet gathered late on September 7 in sight of its objective.[65]

With all hope of surprise lost it was decided to force the defenses rather than attempt a landing on the marshy coast. Crocker chose to lead the way up the Texas channel of Sabine Pass in the *Clifton,* followed by the *Granite City,*

---

[62]Lubbock, *Six Decades in Texas,* 486; Arthur James Lyon Fremantle (Walter Lord, ed.), *The Fremantle Diary* (Boston, 1954), 55–56; Houston *Tri-Weekly Telegraph,* June 4, 1863; Galveston *Tri-Weekly News,* June 10, 1863; Brigadier General W. R. Boggs to General Magruder, June 30, 1863, *Official Records,* Series I, Vol. XXVI, Part 2, 97–98.

[63]Commodore H. H. Bell to Admiral Farragut, July 3, 1863, *Official Records, Navies,* Series I, Vol. XX, 372.

[64]Lieutenant Colonel E. F. Gray's report, August 4, 1863, *Official Records,* Series I, Vol. XXVI, Part 1, 241; Colonel X. B. DeBray's reports, August 11, 12, 1863, *ibid.,* 242–245.

[65]Commodore H. H. Bell to Secretary of Navy Gideon Welles, September 4, 1863, *Official Records, Navies,* Series I, Vol. XX, 515; General N. P. Banks' report, September, 1863, *Official Records,* Series I, Vol. XXVI, Part 1, 287–292.

while the *Sachem* and *Arizona* were to pass up the Louisiana channel and take the Southern battery in reverse from Sabine Lake. Franklin agreed and ordered a transport to land troops below the works once action had begun. The infantry in turn would charge the fort when its garrison had been driven to cover by Crocker's warships.

A far different reception awaited the Union advance than was anticipated. Fort Griffin, the new Confederate battery position, lay near the head of Sabine Pass on the Texas side, above the old works abandoned in 1862. Built only that summer after word leaked out about new attempts on Texas, the fortification was a hundred yards wide and surrounded by swamps. Its armament included two thirty-two-pounders dug up and repaired under the direction of Major Kellersberger, engineer in charge of constructing the new position. To those pieces were added two twenty-four-pounders and two thirty-two-pounder howitzers, mounted only hours prior to the engagement. Captain Frederick Odlum's highly skilled Davis Guards, Company F of Cook's artillery, had been returned to the scene of their earlier success in anticipation of an invasion attempt. Daily practice on stakes driven in both channels of the pass had helped each gun crew zero in every inch of the area they would be called on to defend.[66]

Crocker opened the action on September 8, 1863, at 6:30 A.M., by lobbing twenty-six shells at the fort with a thirty-pounder Parrott rifle from a position near the Louisiana shore lighthouse. Lieutenant Richard W. Dowling, commanding in Odlum's absence, kept his men under cover, however, refusing to disclose the strength of his battery by firing on a target beyond its range. Firing ceased at 7:30 A.M., to be renewed at 11:00 A.M. when the Confederate steamer *Uncle Ben* dropped down Sabine Lake to Fort Griffin. Three shells from the *Sachem's* Parrott rifle passed over both fort and steamer, again resulting in no casualties.[67]

During the morning Colonel Leon Smith, commanding the Marine Department of Texas, had been forwarding troops from Beaumont. Hurrying to the fort that afternoon, he arrived with Captain Odlum and Captain W. Spalding Good of the ordnance department soon after all four Union gunboats got under way for their assault at 3:40 P.M. Waiting until the Federal ships were only 1200 yards away, Dick Dowling called his gunners from their bombproofs to answer the rain of shot and shell falling around them. Lieutenant Niles H. Smith, actually an

---

[66] J. Thomas Scharf, *History of the Confederate States Navy: From Its Organization to the Surrender of Its Last Vessel* (New York, 1894), 524; Moore, *The Rebellion Record*, VII, 427; Lubbock, *Six Decades in Texas*, 507; Kellersberger, *Memoirs of an Engineer in the Confederate Army in Texas*, 29–31; Sackett, *Dick Dowling*, 38–40.

[67] Lieutenant Commander W. H. Dana to Commodore H. H. Bell, September 9, 1863, *Official Records, Navies*, Series I, Vol. XX, 522; Captain F. H. Odlum's reports, September 8, 9, 1863, *Official Records*, Series I, Vol. XXVI, Part 1, 309–310.

engineer, commanded one section, Dr. George H. Bailey another, and Dowling the third. One of the howitzers ran backward off its platform on the second or third shot, cutting Confederate fire power at a crucial moment.[68]

Offsetting results came quickly, however, for Dowling's men used their practice stakes well in sighting on the *Sachem* as she steamed up the far channel. On the third or fourth round a thirty-two-pound shot found her steam drum, leaving the gunboat a helpless wreck, piled high with dead and wounded from the explosion. Having blocked the Louisiana channel to further advance, the Southern gun crews hurriedly shifted to meet the rush of Crocker's *Clifton,* rapidly approaching their works loaded with sharpshooters. When only 500 yards separated warship and battery a cannon ball carried away the gunboat's tiller rope, throwing her out of control and soon aground. From that position Crocker continued to fight until two of his three guns bearing on the Confederate works were partially disabled and the ship's boiler exploded from another direct hit. The five Southern cannon in action had fired 107 times in thirty-five minutes, or better than once every two minutes; an almost unheard of speed for heavy artillery.[69]

Rather than brave the uncanny accuracy of Dowling's gunners, the *Arizona* and *Granite City* withdrew from the pass, leaving both *Sachem* and *Clifton* in Confederate hands. Immediate results of the action were 350 prisoners and two gunboats, mounting thirteen heavy guns, all at no cost to the defenders. General Franklin saw no alternative to retreat before such a tenacious defense, and returned with his troops to New Orleans. His estimate of the fort's armament, as seven and nine inch cannon, spoke volumes for their handling which no praise could match.[70]

Reinforcements were rushed to the Beaumont area by General Magruder, who also had the fortifications strengthened and enlarged. By mid October two thirty-pounder Parrot rifles from the *Clifton* had been added to the defenses which were then quite extensive.[71] Banks, however, had given over his desire to

---

[68]Lieutenant R. W. Dowling's report, September 9, 1863, *ibid.,* 311–312; Dallas *Morning News,* April 23, 1902. Herein is an account written from articles by W. P. Doran, a reporter for the Galveston *News* and Houston *Telegraph* during the war, who talked to participants on September 9, 1863.

[69]Duganne, *Camps and Prisons,* 261–266; Henry Hall and James Hall, *Cayuga in the Field. A Record of the 75th New York Volunteers, . . .* (New York, 1873), 142–143; Lieutenant F. Crocker to Secretary of Navy Gideon Welles, April 21, 1865, *Official Records, Navies,* Series I, Vol. XX, 544–548; Lieutenant Amos Johnson to Acting Rear Admiral H. K. Thatcher, March 4, 1865, *ibid.,* 552–553; Houston *Tri-Weekly Telegraph,* October 27, 1863.

[70]Lieutenant R. W. Dowling's report, September 9, 1863, *Official Records,* Series I, Vol. XXVI, Part 1, 311–312; Major General W. B. Franklin's report, September II, 1863, *ibid.,* 294–297.

[71]Major General J. B. Magruder to Lieutenant General E. Kirby Smith, September 22, 1863, *ibid.,* Series I, Vol. XXVI, Part 2, 247–248; Assistant Inspector General Benjamin Allston to Lieutenant General E. Kirby Smith, October 14, 1863, *ibid.,* 318–321.

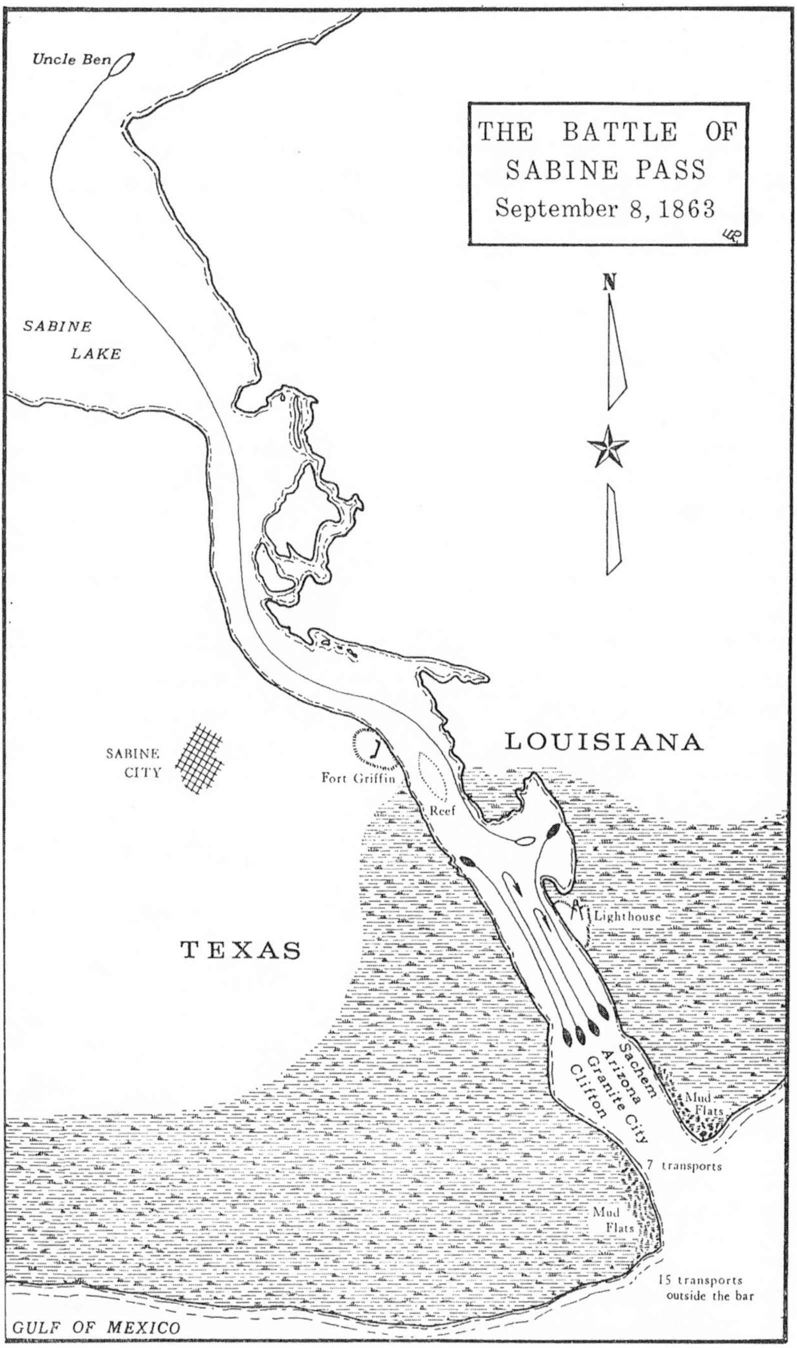
THE BATTLE OF SABINE PASS
September 8, 1863
Uncle Ben
SABINE LAKE
N
LOUISIANA
SABINE CITY
Fort Griffin
Reef
Lighthouse
TEXAS
Sachem
Arizona
Granite City
Clifton
Mud Flats
7 transports
Mud Flats
15 transports outside the bar
GULF OF MEXICO

capture Sabine Pass in favor of cutting off Confederate trade through Mexico and the Rio Grande Valley.

Landing at Brazos Santiago on November 2, 1863, Banks soon took Brownsville with a force of 7000 men. Having been reinforced by another division he sailed up the coast, intent on closing other Texas ports to blockade runners by capture and occupation. While Magruder began concentrating his forces to meet the new threat, Banks reached Mustang Island off Corpus Christi by November 17, 1863. There he landed part of his infantry which captured Captain William N. Maltby's battery of three guns after two hours of skirmishing. Maltby's cannon, twelve, eighteen, and twenty-four-pounders mounted to cover the sea approaches of Corpus Christi Bay, were engaged by the steamer *Monongahela* until their surrender.[72]

Continuing across St. Joseph Island on November 21, Major General Cadwallader C. Washburn, commanding the division ashore, crossed to Matagorda Island and moved against Fort Esperanza. The fort, an enlarged version of Shea's original works on the island's northern extremity, was garrisoned in the fall of 1863 by 500 men with eight heavy guns. Its batteries, two twelve-pounders, five twenty-four-pounders, and a ten-inch Columbiad, were mounted mainly to protect against naval attack. But with parapets ten feet high and fifteen feet thick, flanked by water on both sides, the fortification presented an awesome sight to Washburn's infantry as it loomed through the fog before them on November 27, 1863. Beset by a Texas norther, rain, sleet, and snow, the Federals dug in and brought up artillery which played on the fort during November 29. Yankee troops kept warm and amused themselves to some extent by dodging ponderous shot from the Southern batteries which bounded through their lines. Exploding Confederate magazines after midnight on November 30 gave notice of the fort's evacuation, unprepared as the garrison was for a prolonged siege. Fear of being cut off and captured, or having his position stormed by the daily increasing Union force, also affected Colonel William R. Bradfute's decision to spike his guns and retire to the mainland.[73] Casualties on both sides had been negligible.

Supported by seven warships, Washburn occupied Matagorda Peninsula and Indianola on the mainland. Probing expeditions skirmished with Magruder's forces behind the San Bernard River in December and on into the

[72]Major General N. P. Banks to Commodore H. H. Bell, November 17, 1863, *Official Records, Navies*, Series I, Vol. XX, 680–681; Houston *Tri-Weekly Telegraph*, December 15, 1863; A. T. Mahan, *The Gulf and Inland Waters* (New York, 1883), 188.

[73]Albert O. Marshall, *Army Life; From a Soldier's Journal* (Joliet, Ill., 1884), 308-337; Houston *Tri-Weekly Telegraph*, December 5, 1863; Galveston *Weekly News*, December 9, 14, 1863; Major General C. C. Washburn's reports, November 30, December 1, 6, 1863, *Official Recordes*, Series I, Vol. XXVI, Part 1, 416–421.

early spring of 1864, before being withdrawn for the Red River campaign in Louisiana. The delays involved in dislodging Texas' coastal batteries over a period of two weeks had allowed Confederate concentration of five brigades with nine field batteries in the Caney Creek area of Brazoria County, an effective deterrent to further advance.[74]

With the southern half of Texas' coast occupied by Union forces, and the majority of Confederate troops from Texas opposing Banks' Red River expedition in Louisiana as 1864 began, General Magruder found the great majority of the state's population in no real danger, and blockade running on the increase. Keeping those facts in mind, the district commander withdrew Hobby's regiment from the Matagorda Bay-Corpus Christi area as part of his decision to hold only Sabine Pass, Galveston, and Velasco at all costs. Three well fortified ports allowed some opportunity for choice by the fleet of blockade runners operating out of Havana, who had shifted their trade to Texas as other Southern harbors were closed. In May and June, 1864, most of the remaining Federal troops along the Texas coast were removed through New Orleans to support Banks' defeated army in Louisiana.[75]

Velasco's heavy batteries were estimated at six thirty-two-pounders by the blockading fleet, which showed its respect by never engaging them at close range for any period of time.[76] Galveston, where work on the fortifications never entirely ceased, contained nine companies of Cook's regiment manning thirty-one cannon. Five were mounted in South Battery, five in Fort Magruder, seven on Fort Point, five or six on Pelican Spit, and the rest scattered about in smaller works around the harbor itself. Point Bolivar and Virginia Point on the mainland were also fortified and manned by the artillery companies of Hobby's command, creating a veritable ring of fire into which an attacking fleet would have to sail. The additional problem of navigating the harbor's bars without a pilot or buoys for guidance, plus the threat of torpedoes, proved restraint enough through the final months of conflict. At the eastern terminus of Magruder's new line lay Fort Griffin at Sabine Pass, still garrisoned by the Davis Guards and supported by extensive outer works. Included among those was Fort Mannahassett, a small fortification seven miles southwest of the pass where a

---

[74]Marshall, *Army Life,* 340–361; Commander J. H. Strong to Commodore H. H. Bell, November 29, 1863, January 1, 1864, *Official Records, Navies,* Series I, Vol. XX, 702, 742–743; General Order 217, District of Texas, New Mexico, and Arizona, December 15, 1863, *Official Records,* Series I, Vol. XXVI, Part 2, 509–510.

[75]William Watson, *The Adventures of a Blockade Runner; or, Trade in Time of War* (London, 1892); Marshall, *Army Life,* 390–392; Marcus W. Price, "Ships that Tested the Blockade of the Gulf Ports, 1861–1865," *The American Neptune,* XII (1952), 154–161, 229–236.

[76]Lieutenant Commander G. H. Perkins to Captain John P. Gilles, February 16, 1864, *Official Records, Navies,* Series I, Vol. XXI, 74–75.

Federal supply ship of the same name had washed ashore and broken up in a storm.[77]

March saw another short mutiny at Galveston, in protest against parties given by ladies of the city for General Magruder and his officers, while the garrison suffered from poor food and quarters far from their homes. After the death of General Tom Green during the Red River Campaign in Louisiana that spring, the works on Bolivar Point received his name, but far more important to the troops in Galveston was the reappearance of yellow fever in September.[78]

November returns for the district showed another increase in its armament, with forty-one cannon in Galveston, nine at Sabine Pass, and eight guarding Velasco, manned by almost 1500 cannoneers. Galveston's batteries then included three ten-inch Co-lumbiads, five nine-inch Dahlgrens, three heavy rifled cannon, and eleven thirty-two-pounders, many of them unwelcome presents aboard the five Union warships taken by Texans since January, 1863.[79] Protected by such greatly strengthened batteries, blockade running into Texas grew to the extent that Gideon Welles, United States Secretary of the Navy, increased the Western Gulf Blockading Squadron off Texas' coast to twenty ships in 1865, as compared with no more than six or seven in previous years.[80] Even after such precautions only the final fall of the South ended blockade running into Texas ports. When defeat came, the surrender terms drawn up and agreed to in New Orleans, were formally signed aboard the Union gunboat *Fort Jackson* by General Edmund Kirby Smith on June 2, 1865, in Galveston harbor, the only major Southern port held by its defenders until that final hour.[81]

---

[77]H. C. Medford (Rebecca W. Smith and Marion Mullins, eds.), "The Diary of H. C. Medford, Confederate Soldier, 1864, "*Southwestern Historical Quarterly,* XXXIV, 125; *Official Records,* Series I, Vol. XXXIV, Part 2, 1010, 1044; Captain J. B. Marchand to Admiral Farragut, April 16, 1864, *Official Records, Navies,* Series I, Vol. XXI, 197.

[78]Medford, "The Diary of H. C. Medford," *Southwestern Historical Quarterly,* XXXIV, 127; Houston *Daily Telegraph,* May 29, September 19, 1864.

[79]*Official Records,* Series I, Vol. XLI, Part 4, 1066, 1117; *ibid.,* Series I, Vol. XLVIII, 1134.

[80]Secretary of Navy Gideon Welles to Acting Rear Admiral Thatcher, March 30, 1865, *Official Records, Navies,* Series I, Vol. XXII, 119; List of Vessels, January 1865 to January 1866, *ibid.,* 14–16.

[81]Report of Acting Rear Admiral Thatcher, June 8, 1865, *ibid.,* 216.

# Edmund J. Davis in the Coke-Davis Election Dispute of 1874: A Reassessment of Character

CARL H. MONEYHON*

*In spite of the success of Texans in defending the state in the Civil War as described in the previous article, Confederate forces were ultimately defeated and the Union preserved. The decade following the end of the war was a turbulent period for Texas and the nation. The end of slavery, the enfranchisement of African American males, and reconstruction of the Union brought significant changes in Texas and other southern states.*

*For the first time in Texas history a Republican, Edmund J. Davis of Corpus Christi, was elected governor. As Carl Moneyhon of the University of Arkansas at Little Rock points out in this essay, Davis was a controversial figure. Although there were some achievements in public education, road building, and frontier defense, many of Davis's policies were controversial. His determination to enforce various congressional measures of Reconstruction offended many Texans.*

*When he ran for reelection in 1873 he was defeated by Democrat Richard Coke. However, in January 1874 the state supreme court ruled the election unconstitutional because it did not strictly adhere to provisions of the state constitution. In this essay Professor Moneyhon describes controversies over the election, while at the same time reassessing Davis's character.*

*Additional information concerning the Reconstruction period in Texas may be found in Moneyhon's books* Republicanism in Reconstruction Texas *(Austin: University of Texas Press, 1980) and* Texas After the Civil War: The Struggle of Reconstruction *(College Station: Texas A&M University Press, 2004), and Barry A. Crouch, "'Unmanacling' Texas Reconstruction: A Twenty-Year Perspective,"* Southwestern Historical Quarterly, *93 (Jan., 1990), 275–302.*

---

*Carl H. Moneyhon, "Edmund J. Davis in the Coke-Davis Election Dispute of 1874: A Reassessment of Character," *Southwestern Historical Quarterly*, 100 (Oct., 1996), 131–151.

Edmund J. Davis, governor from 1869 to 1874, has long held the worst reputation of any chief executive of the state of Texas. He is a man whose character has been seen as practically irredeemable. The scholarly assessment of his administration has been the object of recent historical revision, but it is safe to say that Davis himself has continued to be perceived as dogmatic, uncompromising, and vengeful despite revisionist efforts. Charles W. Ramsdell set the interpretive tone in his 1910 study of Reconstruction in Texas, portraying Davis as "arbitrary," "self-willed," "obstinate," and "pig-headed." Although Ramsdell concluded that Davis was personally honest, he ultimately found him to be an "intense and narrow partisan," a "martinet," and that he had "no regard for the popular will, he consulted no desires but his own, and he was absolutely devoid of tact."[1]

No single event in the Davis administration appeared to provide stronger support for Ramsdell's assessment of the governor than Davis's apparent role in the Coke-Davis election dispute of 1874. The basic outline of the clash is well known. In January 1874, the state supreme court caused an electoral crisis

---

[1]Charles W. Ramsdell, *Reconstruction in Texas* (New York: Columbia University Press, 1910), 314–315, 317–318. Even though Ramsdell's interpretation remains the most commonly held view of Davis, revisionist historians of the last two decades have provided a reassessment of Reconstruction that undercuts this traditional view of the governor. The only full-scale revisionist effort at reassessing Davis is Ronald N. Gray, "Edmund J. Davis: Radical Republican and Reconstruction Governor of Texas" (Ph.D. diss., Texas Tech University, 1976), which began the process of reassessing Davis, although it does not examine the Coke-Davis conflict.

Barry A. Crouch, "'Unmanacling' Texas Reconstruction: A Twenty-Year Perspective," *Southwestern Historical Quarterly,* XCIII (Jan., 1990), 275–302 (cited hereafter as *SHQ),* provides an overview of recent revisionist studies of the Davis administration that provide a framework for a reconsideration of the governor. Among the revisionist works that deal directly with Davis and his administration and provide the framework for a reinterpretation of Davis as governor see Ann Patton Baenziger, "The Texas State Police during Reconstruction: A Reexamination," *SHQ* LXXII (Apr., 1969), 470–491; James A. Baggett, "Beginnings of Radical Rule in Texas: The Special Legislative Session of 1870," *Southwestern Journal of Social Education,* II (Spring-Summer, 1972), 28–39; James A. Baggett, "Birth of the Texas Republican Party," *SHQ* LXXVIII (July, 1974), 1–20; James A. Baggett, "Origins of Early Texas Republican Party Leadership," *Journal of Southern History,* XL (Aug., 1974), 441–454; John M. Brockman, "Railroads, Radicals, and the Militia Bill: A New Interpretation of the Quorum-Breaking Incident of 1870," *SHQ* LXXXIII (Oct., 1979), 105–122; Randolph B. Campbell, "Scalawag District Judges: The E. J. Davis Appointees, 1870–1873," *Houston Review: History and Culture of the Gulf Coast,* XIV (1992), 75–88; Randolph B. Campbell, "Carpetbagger Rule in Reconstruction Texas: An Enduring Myth," *SHQ* XCVII (Apr., 1994), 587–596; John P. Carrier, "A Political History of Texas during Reconstruction, 1865–1874" (Ph.D. diss., Vanderbilt University, 1971); William T. Field, "The Texas State Police, 1870–1873," *Texas Military History,* V (Fall, 1965), 136–141; William T. Hopper, "Governor Edmund J. Davis, Ezra Cornell, and the A&M College of Texas," *SHQ* LXXVIII (Jan., 1975), 307–312; Carl H. Moneyhon, *Republicanism in Reconstruction Texas* (Austin: University of Texas Press, 1980); Carl H. Moneyhon, "Public Education and Texas Reconstruction Politics, 1871–1874," *SHQ,* XCII (Jan., 1989), 393–416; Betty J. Sandlin, "The Texas Reconstruction Constitutional Convention of 1868–1869" (Ph.D. diss., Texas Tech University, 1970).

when it delivered the controversial *ex parte* Rodriguez decision, finding that the general election held earlier that month was unconstitutional because it did not strictly adhere to the formula provided in the constitution. The presence of a semicolon between two clauses became the key to the court's decision. A month later, Governor Davis attempted to prevent the successful candidates in that election, including new governor Richard Coke, from taking office by blocking the meeting of the Fourteenth Legislature. The Democratic victors went ahead anyway, and in January 1874 organized the legislature, inaugurated Coke as governor, and virtually threw Davis out of office.

The interpretation of the events in December and January that became the basis for later scholarly studies and ultimately the negative characterizations of Davis was developed in 1898 by Oran M. Roberts in his chapter of Dudley Wooten's *A Comprehensive History of Texas*. Roberts contended that Davis, as he had throughout Reconstruction, intended and attempted to disrupt public affairs and provoke violence that would bring about federal intervention. Only the patience and strength of the Democratic leadership, "disinterested gentlemen," according to Roberts, averted the catastrophe Davis would have brought about. Here was final proof of the illegitimacy of the Republican regime and clear evidence of the type of man that Davis was. "Perhaps the most charitable explanation of [Davis's] conduct," wrote Roberts, "is that he resorted to force blindly, under his habitual belief that it was the proper and only available mode of accomplishing any object he desired."[2] Although a participant in the events, Roberts had established himself as the state's premier historian by the time the book appeared and his interpretation was integrated into the scholarly literature.[3]

The analysis of Davis by Roberts and others is suspect, however, in part because of Roberts's political position and because even contemporary Democratic sources offer more positive assessments of Davis's character. By 1880, some six years after he left office, the Galveston *Daily News*, long a major voice of the state's Democratic Party, called Davis "a true-hearted Texan, a patriotic citizen, a liberal, progressive, and statesmanlike thinker." Upon his death in 1883, the Democratic legislature passed resolutions that recognized the Republican governor as "an honorable, honest man, a kind and obliging neighbor, and a tried and faithful friend," as well as a "fearless, earnest and honest man."[4]

---

[2]Oran M. Roberts, "Political, Legislative, and Judicial History of Texas," in Dudley G. Wooten (ed.), *A Comprehensive History of Texas, 1865–1897* (2 vols.; Dallas: William G. Scarff, 1898), II, 208.

[3]Roberts's interpretation of Reconstruction was the basic source used by Ramsdell (see his *Reconstruction in Texas*, 317), and Ramsdell's conclusions regarding Davis's character closely parallel those offered by Roberts. Ramsdell's assessment, in turn, was reflected in W. C. Nunn, *Texas Under the Carpetbaggers* (Austin: University of Texas Press, 1960), 121–132, although Nunn did not devote attention to a judgment of Davis's character.

[4]Galveston *Daily News*, Feb. 10, 1880 (1st quotation), Feb. 9, 1883 (2nd quotation).

Which characterization of Davis is correct? The answer obviously is complex, but this essay reexamines the actions of Governor Davis in the notorious Coke-Davis episode in an effort to provide at least a partial answer. Using some new sources, but primarily trying to deal with the already known sources in a more critical and analytical manner, this study traces the governor's course through the events of January 1874 to illuminate his decision-making process and to try to understand more clearly the mind and character of the enigmatic Davis.

The immediate cause of the Coke-Davis imbroglio was the state's general elections of 1873. By the time of these elections it was clear that Davis and the Republican Party's hold on the state government was over. A variety of factors had doomed the party's effort at governing the state, and both it and its leader were widely unpopular among many white Texans, at least those who voted Democratic. When the polls closed on December 2, Richard Coke had defeated Davis by an almost two-to-one margin and Democrats swept to victory in other state offices while strengthening their hold on the state legislature.[5]

In Austin, Governor Davis received reports from the polls. He expressed little surprise at the results. From the beginning, he apparently had expected no other outcome and declared his willingness to accept it. In private letters, the governor indicated that he believed that the Democrats had decisively and unquestionably won. Although aware of fraud and intimidation at some locations, he did not think that these materially changed the situation and he would do nothing to dispute the results. Even when Republicans in Houston and elsewhere challenged the election in the courts, the governor continued to hold that he had been defeated. In an interview with a reporter from the Galveston *Daily News* early in January and in correspondence with President Ulysses S. Grant, the governor maintained that he had no intention of trying to hold on to his office beyond the expiration of his term on April 28, 1874.[6]

Davis may have intended to step down at that time, but two issues ultimately complicated the peaceful transfer of power to the victorious Democrats and led to a clash between Republicans and Democrats at the state capitol. One question originated in an ambiguity in the constitution concerning terms of office that had been the object of discussion for some time and had not been resolved when the election was held. Democratic leaders contended that under the election declaration attached to the Constitution of 1869 and a clause in that constitution Davis's term expired on the second Thursday in January 1874. The constitution provided that the governor should be inaugurated on the first Thursday after the

[5]For an analysis of the election see Moneyhon, *Republicanism in Reconstruction Texas,* 183–193.

[6]E. J. Davis to W. L. Malloy, Dec. 8, 1873, Davis to Frank Green, Dec. 8, 1873, ibid.; Davis to W. P. Goff, Dec. 12, 1873, ibid.; Davis to L. J. Gallant and others, Dec. 22, 1873, Telegrams Sent, Governor's Papers: Edmund J. Davis (Archives Division, Texas State Library, Austin; cited hereafter as Governor's Papers: Davis); Davis interview, Galveston *Daily News,* Jan. 7, 9, 1874; E. J. Davis to U. S. Grant, January 6, 1874, quoted in *Daily State Journal* (Austin), Jan. 20, 1874.

organization of the legislature, or as soon thereafter as was practical. At the same time, the same section of the document provided that the governor would hold office for four years from the time of his installment, and Republicans held that meant Davis's term of office did not end until April 28, 1874.[7]

The second issue was that of the constitutionality of the election itself, a problem that grew out of a conflict between the statute that had provided for the election and the constitution. Immediately after the election, parties in Houston went to court and argued that the election law, passed by the Thirteenth Legislature and under which the general election was held, was unconstitutional. The constitution required that "all elections for State District and County officers shall be held at the county seats of the several counties, until otherwise provided by law; and the polls shall be opened for four days, from 8 o'clock, A.M. until 4 o'clock P.M. of each day." The election law provided that the election would be held only on one day. Challengers held that the semicolon separated two independent clauses, allowing the legislature to change where elections were held, but not the period of the election, while defenders, including Davis's attorney general, contended that the legislature could change both the place and extent of elections. On January 5, 1874, in the case of *ex parte* Rodriguez or what was popularly called the Semicolon Case, the state supreme court ruled the election unconstitutional.[8]

Davis's position on these issues is essential to understanding his subsequent course. The question of the timing of the transfer of the executive offices was not a new one but had actually been under discussion for some time. The fact was that the constitution provided conflicting provisions and opened up the possibility of disagreements between the parties. As early as May 1872, in an interview with John D. Elliott of the *State Gazette,* the governor stated his understanding that he held office until April 28, 1874, four years from his inaugural as civil governor. In the Democratic state convention at Corsicana in December 1873, a report argued that the term expired on December 3, 1873, four years after he was named acting governor by Gen. Joseph J. Reynolds and before the state was readmitted to the Union. In the spring of 1873, Davis and John Ireland, Democratic leader in the legislature, discussed moving the meeting of the Fourteenth Legislature to April 1874, rather than holding it in January, to bring the meeting of the legislature into line with the inauguration of the governor-elect. Their discussions, however, reached no conclusion and the disagreement was left unresolved.[9]

---

[7]San Antonio *Daily Express,* Dec. 9, 1873.

[8]Quotation from *Constitution of 1869,* in John Sayles (ed.), *The Constitutions of the State of Texas* (St. Louis: Gilbert Book Co., 1888); *Ex parte* Rodriguez, 39 *Texas Reports,* 705–776; Galveston *Daily News,* Jan. 6, 1874. For the only scholarly analysis of the court and its decision see George E. Shelley, "The Semicolon Court of Texas," *SHQ* XLVII (Apr., 1945), 449–468.

[9]San Antonio *Daily Express,* May 31, 1872; *Daily State Journal* (Austin), Sept. 19, 1872; Galveston *Daily News,* May 17, 1873.

Davis remained aware, however, that this issue needed to be resolved. In the fall of 1873 he asked Attorney General William Alexander for a ruling. Alexander issued a complex opinion on December 9. He reasoned that because the election declaration by Gen. Joseph J. Reynolds was not part of the fundamental law of the state, the term of office had to be decided exclusively on the basis of the constitution and statutes. Section 4, article 4, of the constitution set a governor's term of office for four years from the time of his installment and until his successor should be qualified. That made his term run until April 28. Alexander concluded that this interpretation of term lengths applied to other elected state and county officers as well, and that officers other than Congressmen and legislators could not take office until that date.[10] The question of the tenure of office was at this stage when the more critical question of the constitutionality of the election pushed it aside. The tenure issue re-emerged in the conflict that followed and would be critical to Davis's course of action.

On the question of the constitutionality of the election, from the first legal challenge the governor's position was that such efforts were ill-advised. There is no evidence that Davis participated in or played any role in the original court challenges to the election. In fact, one of the lawyers who took the Rodriguez case to court was Andrew J. Hamilton, who, although a prominent Austin attorney and a Republican, had been outside of the Davis faction of the party since he ran against Davis for governor in 1869. As soon as it was understood in Austin that several cases had been filed challenging the constitutionality of the election, Davis declared that he had no desire to block the results of the election and cautiously refrained from giving his opinion on the merits of the challenge as the Rodriguez case moved quickly from the lower courts to the state supreme court. In private correspondence the governor reaffirmed his public declarations.[11]

Politicians have been known to deny their participation in unpopular activities and decisions, but even Davis's enemies did not accuse him of playing a role in bringing up or trying to influence the Rodriguez case. Their major complaint, in fact, was that he had not attempted to change the mind of the court. Samuel Bell Maxey, a prominent Democrat and attorney from Paris, Bonham County, saw the whole business as an effort to subvert the will of the people by scheming politicians, but he held Davis culpable only because he had not influenced the court to come up with a different decision. The editor of the Austin *Statesman* agreed with Maxey, railing, "Who does not believe that a word from this same weak-minded, well-intentioned official, so imposed upon by stronger

[10] *Daily State Journal* (Austin), Dec. 9, 1873.

[11] E. J. Davis to Frank Green, Dec. 8, 1873, Telegrams Sent, Governor's Papers: Davis; Galveston *Daily News*, Dec. 10, 1873; see also *Daily Democratic Statesman* (Austin), Jan. 8, 1874.

natures, could have saved all this disturbance about the election and secured a very different decision from the august body of scalawags and carpetbaggers called the Supreme Court?"[12]

Once the court had ruled the election unconstitutional, however, Davis could no longer remain uninvolved. The ruling declared invalid the election of every state official, members of the Fourteenth Legislature, and county officials. In addition, it negated the ratification of two constitutional amendments that would have allowed the newly-elected governor to reorganize the state supreme court and changed the process for selecting county assessors and collectors. The governor had to take a position. He could either uphold the court, or he could ignore it and make no effort to enforce its ruling. Davis's background probably influenced the choice he would make and made his stand predictable. Forty-seven years old at the time, this native Floridian had lived in Texas since the 1850s and had been a prominent attorney and judge in South Texas prior to the Civil War. His career had been in the law and he had demonstrated a strong belief in adherence to it. He had opposed secession in 1861, at least in part because he did not believe it was a right of the state, and he had joined the Union army to sustain that belief. A man with clear ideas about the preeminence of the law, ignoring a decision of the state supreme court was unlikely.[13] Davis made an almost inevitable decision to sustain the court.

Democratic newspapers greeted his decision with condemnation and for the first time suggested that he was trying simply to hold on to office and keep the Democrats from regaining power. The Austin *Daily Statesman* saw Davis "at the bottom of all our troubles." The editor went on to conclude that he would do all that he could to keep the elected officials from taking office. "He hates the people of Texas, whom he knows he has injured and offended past all thought of pardon," the editor went on, "and he will do the worst he can—mark our words."[14]

Democratic leaders decided that they would ignore the court's ruling, seriously complicating any effort Davis might make to enforce it. Their decision to organize the government, no matter what, had been made even before the court's ruling was made. On December 23, Richard Coke requested advice from several Galveston attorneys on how to proceed if the court ruled the election unconstitutional. Coke wanted to have the legislature organize, then go

[12]S. B. Maxey to Mrs. S. B. Maxey, Jan. 6, 1874, Samuel B. Maxey Papers (Archives Division, Texas State Library; cited hereafter as Maxey Papers); *Daily Statesman* (Austin), Jan. 7, 1874 (quotation); see also Richard Coke to O. M. Roberts, Dec. 29, 1873, A. W. Terrell to Roberts, January 5, 1874, in O. M. Roberts Papers (Center for American History, University of Texas at Austin; cited hereafter as CAH).

[13]See Moneyhon, *Republicanism in Reconstruction Texas,* 129–130.

[14]*Daily Statesman,* (Austin), Jan. 8, 1874.

ahead with his inauguration. William P. Ballinger, one of the attorneys, agreed with him, but others consulted did not want to complicate the election issue with the tenure of office question and advised that the legislature organize, but that Coke wait until April 28 to be inaugurated. The question of Coke's inauguration was left unsettled, but Democratic leaders agreed to assemble the legislature in defiance of the court. The editor of the Austin *Statesman* urged the legislature to "proceed in the discharge of their duties" and "let it be seen by the people of the United States if the general government will use its bayonets to keep in subjection the peaceful State of Texas for the benefit of the Radical party."[15]

The governor was well aware of the Democratic decision, which was already announced and being discussed in party newspapers in the week prior to the court's actual ruling. To firm up his response, he met with other Republican leaders on the evening of January 5. Those attending included Secretary of State James P. Newcomb, Republican state party chairman James G. Tracy, former governor Andrew J. Hamilton (who challenged the constitutionality of the election), black legislator Ed Randall, and supreme court justices Wesley Ogden and Moses B. Walker. Newspapers reported serious disagreements among the participants on the best strategy to enforce the court's decision. Tracy urged the Thirteenth Legislature be called to order a new election. Justices Ogden and Walker urged the governor to call for federal intervention to sustain their decision and to prevent the newly elected legislature from meeting. Davis was reluctant to ask for federal troops, at least in part because he thought that it was useless and that President Grant would not intervene. Even so, Davis ultimately decided to appeal for federal support.[16]

On the evening of the January 5 meeting, probably after it had adjourned, the governor telegraphed Gen. Christopher C. Augur at San Antonio and requested him to send U.S. troops to prevent the Fourteenth Legislature from being seated.[17] Although this appeal may appear to support the traditional view of Davis's character, given the clear intention of his opponents of ignoring the Rodriguez decision and the nature of the alternatives that he possessed to

---

[15]William P. Ballinger Diary, Dec. 23, 27, 28, 29, 31, 1873, Jan. 2, 1874 (CAH); see also Richard Coke to O. M. Roberts, Dec. 29, 1873, A. W. Terrell to Roberts, Jan. 5, 1874, Roberts Papers; Galveston *Daily News,* Dec. 10, 12, 1873, Jan. 10, 1874; S. B. Maxey to Mrs. S. B. Maxey, Jan. 6, 1874, Maxey Papers; *Daily Statesman* (Austin), Jan. 6, 1874 (quotations).

[16]Galveston *Daily News,* Jan. 7, 8, 1874; *Daily Statesman* (Austin), Jan. 8, 1874. Evidence for this meeting comes only from Democratic newspapers. Even though specifics about the ideas advanced by participants vary somewhat from subsequent events, other information suggests that the meeting did take place and that the reports of its proceedings are generally accurate. The *Daily State Journal* (Austin), Jan. 8, 1874, did not admit that the meeting took place, but chided the *Daily Statesman* for being scooped by the *Daily News.*

[17]C. C. Augur to E. J. Davis, Jan. 7, 1874, Telegrams Received, Department of Texas, Record Group 393 (cited hereafter as RG 393) (National Archives; cited hereafter as NA); Galveston *Daily News,* Jan. 7, 8, 1874.

uphold it, the call for federal troops does not appear to be that of a man intent on producing a conflict or provoking a full-scale intervention by federal authorities, but the one means of avoiding such a catastrophe. Rather than a radical choice, Davis's course may be seen as a moderate one.

The position of the Democratic leaders left Governor Davis with only one choice readily at hand if he was going to uphold the court on his own. He would have to use force. Davis in fact possessed the authority to call out the state militia, a possibility overlooked in the traditional interpretation of events. It is uncertain how reliable the militia would have been in such a crisis. At least one such unit, the Travis Rifles, refused to submit to the command of the adjutant general when called out later in the imbroglio. Still, Davis was supported strongly by the state's African Americans who constituted a large part of the militia and clearly their units would have come to his support. The problem for the governor was that calling out the militia would inevitably have resulted in a large-scale conflict. Even though this action would have been the one that would have most clearly resulted in federal intervention, Davis chose not to exercise this option.

For a man who did not intend to provoke a conflict, the introduction of federal troops was the wiser course. As much as the Democrats desired to inaugurate the new government, it is very doubtful that they would have risked a confrontation with U.S. troops and gambled on a full-scale federal intervention in state affairs. In such a situation a small number of federal troops would have maintained the court decision with little risk of fighting. Unfortunately for the governor, he had no way to ensure that federal troops would be sent and, if newspaper reports are accurate, he did not believe there was much of a chance of securing them. In a sense, Davis could use the threat of federal troops only as a bluff. In effect, he gave up any hope he had of personally determining the outcome of his conflict with the legislature and left it in the hands of Washington. Federal authorities quickly made it apparent that they did not want to become involved. Even if Davis had believed Augur would send troops, that illusion was not maintained long, for the general sent word the next day, January 6, that the army could not "interfere in the *domestic troubles* of a State, without the order of the *President*."[18]

Davis's decision to pursue the less confrontational course of appealing to federal authorities to uphold the courts was apparent also in a telegram he sent to President Grant on the day after his meeting with local Republican leaders. Davis presented his view of the situation, explained the reasons for his course, and offered a solution. The reasons he advanced may have been simply his justification for a policy designed to ensure he stayed in office, but the fact that he

[18]C. C. Augur to E. J. Davis, Jan. 6, 1874, Telegrams Sent, Department of Texas, RG 393, NA.

also offered a way to have the newly elected government installed suggests that the concerns he expressed may have been the real reasons for the position that he had taken.

The central issue of the Rodriguez case for Davis, at least as he informed the president, was the question that it raised about the legitimacy of any government that took power in its wake. Every action of state and local government would be open to challenge in the courts. Potentially, he argued, the legality of every act of the Fourteenth Legislature and its successors would be tested in the courts. The state of Texas would become involved in endless litigation. Although he did not mention it in this message, subsequent letters and telegrams indicated that he believed the reorganization of the supreme court under the constitutional amendment complicated the situation even further.[19]

Davis provided the president with his assessment of the complex situation, but, suggesting that he really intended simply to avoid the complications of succession, he also outlined an answer to the problem that he found acceptable and would allow him to step down without qualms. The solution that he proposed was for the president or Congress to make a "distinct expression of opinion as to the course to be pursued." Such a sign, he believed, would, "in default of an enabling act. . . . be accepted and followed by all parties here, and prevent trouble." Such a step clearly would have secured the ends Davis asserted that he desired. It would have ensured that challenges to the legitimacy of the Democratic government would have been difficult. It would have allowed the fulfillment of the electoral majority's will. Further suggesting that the governor was seeking a moderate solution, he made no new request for troops.[20]

General Augur had replied quickly to Davis's earlier request for troops, but the White House was silent concerning the governor's request for recognition of the new legislature. Davis waited for events to move forward. The official Republican newspaper at Austin counseled calm and assured Texans that while the supreme court decision may have been "inconvenient to Austin politicians and hungry office-seekers" it would "in no wise interrupt the proper government of the State."[21] On January 7, the governor was interviewed by John D. Elliott, a personal friend even though the editor of the Democratic *State Gazette.* Davis again insisted that he had no intention of holding on to his office beyond its four-year term, but he expressed his concern that the transfer of power take place within a framework acceptable to all parties. Davis reported that he had submitted the question of the legitimacy of the government to federal authorities, apparently referring to his telegram to Grant, and stated his intention of

[19]E. J. Davis to U. S. Grant, Jan. 6, 1874, in *Daily State Journal* (Austin), Jan. 30, 1874.
[20]Ibid.
[21]Ibid., Jan. 5 (quotation), 7, 8, 1874.

abiding by whatever decision they might reach and asked the other side to do so too. The governor clearly was aware that many within the Democratic Party were pushing to go ahead and organize the legislature and inaugurate Coke, but he counseled them to wait.[22]

Democratic leaders, however, evidenced no intention of waiting for federal recognition and proceeded with their own plans. Governor-elect Coke was particularly vigorous in pushing others to organize the government. The more radical element within the Democratic Party appeared anxious for a fight. It is clear that they considered federal involvement irrelevant. In the words of the editor of the Austin *Daily Statesman,* authorities at Washington had no more interest in Texas affairs than the "man in the moon."[23]

Why they were so unwilling to accept Davis's solution to the problem is unclear, but it does not appear to have been based solely on the ambitions of some of the Democratic leadership. At least in part their attitudes probably were molded by events that had taken place elsewhere in the South. The most immediate example of federal intervention had been in Louisiana, where in 1872 an election dispute had led to the creation of two legislatures and the inauguration of two governors. That situation had not been resolved until the regular Republican government was declared legitimate by a federal district judge and the president used federal troops to support it. That many of the leaders distrusted Davis and his party and feared that if the situation continued too long without resolution some sort of mischief might be stirred up and a pretext created for intervention is also clear. From the beginning, many had seen the Rodriguez case as part of a radical conspiracy.[24]

Yet it is also apparent that the Democratic leaders already had concluded that they had little to fear from either the governor or federal authorities unless there was a major outbreak of violence. Augur's refusal to send troops was known on the streets of Austin almost as soon as the telegram arrived. As a result, there was little incentive to compromise and Democrats were willing to push Davis harder than they might have otherwise. While the Louisiana situation the year before gave cause for concern, it was also evident that the president had his fill of involvement in Southern political affairs. Assumptions that the federal government had no desire to intervene were confirmed further when President Grant, in a meeting with Democrats Dewitt C. Giddings and

---

[22]A summation of the interview presented in the *Daily Statesman* (Austin), Jan. 8, 1874.

[23]George Clark, *A Glance Backwards; or, Some Events in the Past History of My Life* (Houston: Reim & Sons Co., 1914), 78–79; *Daily Statesman* (Austin), Jan. 8, 1874 (quotation).

[24]For concerns about the situation see Coke to O. M. Roberts, Dec. 29, 1873, A. W. Terrell to O. M. Roberts, Jan. 5, 1874, in Roberts Papers; *Daily Statesman* (Austin), Jan. 7, 1874, editorial titled "The Conspiracy and the Conspirators"; San Antonio *Daily Herald,* Jan. 2, 1874, in Nunn, *Texas Under the Carpetbaggers,* 120.

John Hancock of the Texas Congressional delegation, stated that he did not believe there was any basis for using troops in Texas.[25]

Davis had his first opportunity to discuss the situation with Democratic leaders on January 10. During the weekend prior to the scheduled Tuesday assembling of the legislature, its members and Democratic Party leaders began arriving at Austin. On Saturday morning several legislators and party leaders met with Governor Davis to see if there was a way to resolve the impasse. The group included old enemies, such as former governor James W. Throckmorton, plus Senator James E. Swift, an East Texas Democrat who was a personal friend of Davis. The results were not promising. The Democrats urged the governor to recognize the legislature. Davis, however, indicated that he could not do so and urged them, in turn, not to proceed with their organization until the legal question could be resolved.[26]

The committee that met with the governor quickly relayed Davis's position to the governor-elect and other Democratic Party leaders. Throckmorton and the others met with Coke at the City Hotel from 10:00 in the morning until 1:00 that afternoon to discuss the situation. They apparently discussed some basis for compromise, but Coke was reluctant and insisted, according to George Clark, who was one of his associates, that he be inaugurated "no matter what it cost him." Subsequent events clearly showed that the rest of the Democratic leadership had not reached the same conclusion, however.[27]

With the threat of legislative organization imminent, Governor Davis telegraphed President Grant once again on the evening of January 11. He renewed his request for some sort of recognition of the election results from Washington, but this time he also requested military assistance from Grant. Davis based his request on his hopes that a "display of U.S. troops will be most likely to keep the peace till the trouble is settled."[28] The next day, while waiting for a reply from the president, the governor issued a proclamation that urged the Democratic leaders not to try to organize the legislature. Davis warned of "public injury" and "dangerous complications of public affairs" that might result from such action. The January 12 proclamation appears to have been one last effort to cause Democrats to consider waiting until the constitutional issue could be resolved.[29]

---

[25]New York *Times*, Jan. 5, 7, 11, 1874; New York *Tribune*, Jan. 13, 1874; Galveston *Daily News*, Jan. 8, 10, 1874; S. B. Maxey to Mrs. S. B. Maxey, Jan. 6, 1874, Maxey Papers.

[26]Galveston *Daily News*, Jan. 11, 1874.

[27]Clark, *A Glance Backwards*, 79 (quotation); Galveston *Daily News*, Jan. 11, 1874; Roberts, "Political, Legislative, and Judicial History of Texas," 201.

[28]E. J. Davis to U. S. Grant, Jan. 11, 1874, in *Daily State Journal* (Austin), Jan. 20, 1874 (quotation); New York *Times*, Jan. 12, 1874.

[29]Proclamation of Jan. 12, 1874, in *Daily Statesman* (Austin), Jan. 13, 1874.

Although he had called for federal support, Davis's course remained a cautious one, using the threat of federal intervention without taking steps to actually produce a confrontation. Notably, Davis still had not called out state forces to aid him. Davis himself considered his a "mild course" and later explained it as the way he believed would prevent confrontation and make it possible that "moderate counsels" among Democrats might be heard and compromises reached that would guarantee the *"de facto* legislature might universally be accepted as one of right."[30]

By the 12th, however, it is clear that Davis was convinced that "moderate counsels" would not be heard and was considering whether or not to use state troops to prevent the legislature from meeting. On the 12th the governor was joined by Maj. G. B. Russell, a member of Augur's staff who had been sent from San Antonio as a liaison to Davis, who was with Davis through most of the rest of the crisis. Russell's report to Augur on that day indicated that the governor had determined not to recognize the legislature, but he also was trying to decide how to prevent it from occupying the capitol. Force seemed to be the only means to keep that from happening, and Davis considered for the first time calling up units of the militia. Russell believed there would be trouble.[31]

On that Monday afternoon, however, Davis received a reply from Grant that denied the request for troops made the day before, again stating that the situation did not fall within constitutional guidelines for the use of federal troops. On the same day, Republican Senator James W. Flanagan informed Davis that there was no hope for federal support and advised the governor to get out of the way. The president's telegram not only offered no encouragement but still did not give a clear recognition of the legislature. Nonetheless, Grant did move in that direction and suggested that since the election law had been approved by the governor and that both parties had canvassed under it that it would be "prudent" and "right" to yield to the "will of the people." [32]

---

[30]E. J. Davis to the People of Texas, Jan. 19, 1874, in Galveston *Daily News*, Jan. 23, 1874.

[31]G. B. Russell to C. C. Augur, Jan. 12, 1874, Department of Texas, Telegrams Received, RG 393, NA. It is clear that the federal government was interested in avoiding violence, even if not in propping up the Davis government. Apparently to ensure that there was no bloodshed, General Augur sent Maj. G. B. Russell from San Antonio to Austin as an observer. Russell's presence was well known to the Democrats and added to fears they may have had of a possible military intervention. See T. B. Wheeler, "Reminiscences of Reconstruction in Texas," *Quarterly of the Texas State Historical Association,* XI (July, 1908), 57; Roberts, "Political, Legislative, and Judicial History of Texas," 206. Russell's telegrams as well as other materials related to the 1874 crisis sent from army headquarters at San Antonio were sent in code. The author would like to thank Mr. David W. Gaddy of New Carrollton, Maryland, for deciphering these telegrams.

[32]U. S. Grant to E. J. Davis, Jan. 12, 1874, *Daily State Journal* (Austin), Jan. 20, 1874 (quotation); Stephen B. Oates (ed.), *RIP Ford's Texas* (Austin: University of Texas Press, 1963), 419.

The president's telegram clearly did not satisfy Davis's need for a statement regarding the legitimacy of the government, and Davis immediately telegraphed back to the president that he did not see how he could "with propriety disregard the decision of the [state] Supreme Court." Once again, he asked that either Congress or the president himself state that they recognized the new legislature. The president's statement, supplemented by Flanagan's, was strong enough, however, that Davis decided that it was pointless to use the state forces at his disposal to keep the legislature from meeting. Major Russell noted the change in the governor's attitude and informed General Augur that the president's message had made Davis "more moderate."[33]

On the evening of the 12th, Democratic Party leaders and members of the legislature caucused in the senate chamber of the capitol, aware that Grant had refused to send troops. They made their final decision to organize the legislature. In the event that the governor tried to bar their entrance into the capitol, the leaders asked Gen. William P. Hardeman, a veteran of the Texas Revolution and a Confederate brigadier general, to seize the senate and house chambers if possible. Oran M. Roberts recalled that those who attended decided to proceed in a peaceable and prudent manner and to avoid illegal actions. On the question of inaugurating Coke, George Clark noted that some still advocated "delay and temporizing in the matter." Coke, apparently incensed at the idea, pushed the leaders to go ahead, reportedly saying "by the eternal Gods, he [Coke] intended to become Governor in obedience to the voice of the people, no matter what it cost him or the state." Other party leaders remained unconvinced of the value of this and remained uncommitted on the question.[34]

Plans to seize the legislative chambers were unnecessary, however, for Governor Davis made no effort to keep the legislature from meeting. The next morning Hardeman secured the keys to the house and senate chambers without problem. At 9 A.M. both houses of the legislature assembled at the state capitol, organized, and elected officers: John Ireland as president of the senate, and Guy M. Bryan as speaker of the house. The appearance of Republican state senators Ed Randle and Webster Flanagan convinced many that the governor was not going to use state forces against them. On the 13th the editor of the *Daily Statesman* concluded that recognition was "reasonable to suppose" although warning that anything was possible.[35]

The problem between the governor and the legislature may have ended with the occupation of the capitol, but Democratic legislative leaders soon

---

[33]E. J. Davis to U. S. Grant, Jan. 12, 1874, in *Daily State Journal* (Austin), Jan. 20, 1874 (1st quotation); G. B. Russell to C. C. Augur, Jan. 13, 1874 (2nd quotation), Department of Texas, Telegrams Received, RG 393, NA.

[34]Oates (ed.), *RIP Ford's Texas,* 418; Clark, *A Glance Backwards,* 79 (quotations); Roberts, "Political, Legislative, and Judicial History of Texas," 201.

[35]*Daily Statesman* (Austin), Jan. 13, 14, 1874; Galveston *Daily News,* Jan. 14, 1874.

made it clear that they had to have some sort of recognition from the governor.[36] Immediately after organizing, a joint committee of the senate and house was named to inform Davis that they had met and were ready to discuss the situation with him. The governor invited them to the executive offices and in the subsequent meeting committee members and Davis discussed the complexities of the case. Col. John C. Robertson stated that members of the legislature "need your recognition" in order to go to work, and David B. Culberson asked for recognition that they at least were the "de facto" legislature. In the course of the meeting John H. Reagan implied that the legislature was willing to concede the governor's view on his term of office, in return for his recognition of their organization. Davis promised a formal reply, but as he had done in his previous meeting with Democratic leaders he gave the legislative committee little hope that he would change his mind.[37]

Davis drafted his reply during the afternoon and evening of January 13 and had it delivered to the legislature the next day. The governor proved uncompromising and again declared his conviction that he did not think it advisable for the public good to disregard the supreme court decision and recognize the Fourteenth Legislature. He understood that the simplest means of resolving the difficulty would be to ignore the decision, since without the support of the executive or the legislature the court could not enforce its ruling. Davis repeated his concern, however, that this course would "leave the door open for dangerous uncertainty in the future, both in the matter of authority to enact the legislation that may be proposed by the gentlemen you represent, and the matter of Constitutional existence of the highest tribunal of our State." The governor was concerned that there might be two courts, two legislatures. Davis's solution was that the parties simply submit the issue to Congress and the executive, whose recognition would provide the necessary sanction to the government.[38]

---

[36]Why they were so insistent is unclear, but George Clark, later Richard Coke's secretary of state, contended that ensuring the legality of the amendment that reorganized the supreme court was critical. At the time the court was considering the cases of *Keuchler v. Wright* and *Bledsoe v. International Railroad,* two cases that were vital to the interests of railroad developers who considered the existing court hostile. Clark, *A Glance Backwards,* 84.

[37]The governor apparently had a stenographer present who took verbatim notes on the meeting that were then printed in the *Daily State Journal,* Jan. 20, 1874. While these contents were never published in Democratic journals, other Democratic sources suggest the substantial accuracy of the report. In a letter to Rutherford B. Hayes, Guy M. Bryan, one of the members of the committee, noted that the legislature was "perfectly willing to let him [Davis] hold over until the 28th of April next." Guy M. Bryan to Hayes, February 1, 1874, in E. W. Winkler (ed.), "The Bryan-Hayes Correspondence V," *SHQ* XXVI (Oct., 1922), 152 (quotation).

[38]Davis to B. H. Epperson et al., Jan. 13, 1874, in *Daily Statesman* (Austin), Jan. 15, 1874.

Davis's position was unacceptable to the legislative leaders. As a result, they established two joint committees to consider how to proceed. The first was to recommend a course of action and the second to seek the election returns from Secretary of State James P. Newcomb, who had earlier refused to turn them over. The first committee recommended that the legislature obtain the votes for state officials, count them, then inaugurate Coke and other officials as quickly as possible. The second committee met with the governor on January 15 and Davis agreed to turn over the votes under protest. Newcomb took the committee to his office, drafted a protest and signed it, and then gave the returns to the committee. That evening in a joint session, the legislature counted the votes, which showed Coke the victor. They then immediately inaugurated Coke as governor.[39]

Events on the 15th confronted Davis with another challenge. He had conceded to a peaceful meeting of the legislature, despite the supreme court's ruling. Now that legislature was acting to remove him from office despite the attorney general's decision regarding the tenure of office. Davis was forced once again to respond. This time he appears to have concluded that he was being dealt with in bad faith by the Democrats and was ready for a fight. During the day prior to the inauguration, Davis informed Major Russell of the Democratic leadership's intentions and his fear that they might also try to seize the executive offices by force. Davis advised Russell that he intended to resist with an armed force. Following the surrender of the ballots, the governor ordered Adj. Gen. Forbes Britton to protect the executive offices from being seized by the Coke forces, and the adjutant general moved a force of forty to fifty men, probably militia but their exact character is unknown, into the basement of the capitol. Britton also called up a local militia unit, the Travis Rifles, but these were recruited by local Coke supporters to help Governor Coke. They reported to the sergeants-at-arms of the legislature, who placed them on the second floor of the capitol to protect the legislative halls. With the injection of state militia and armed Coke supporters into the situation, for the first time a real threat of violence existed.[40]

Davis telegraphed the president again during the day, as he moved men into the capitol to defend his offices. He reported Coke's impending inauguration and informed him that he intended to use force if necessary to prevent Coke from

---

[39]*Daily State Journal* (Austin), Jan. 20, 1874; *Daily Statesman* (Austin), Jan. 16, 1874; San Antonio *Daily Express*, Jan. 17, 1874; Oates (ed.), *RIP Ford's Texas*, 420, 422; Roberts, "Political, Legislative, and Judicial History of Texas," 204, 205.

[40]G. B. Russell to C. C. Augur, Jan. 15, 1874, Department of Texas, Telegrams Received, RG 393, NA; *Daily Democratic Statesman* (Austin), Jan. 16, 17, 1874; *Daily State Journal* (Austin), Jan. 16, 17, 1874; Wheeler, "Reminiscences of Reconstruction in Texas," 56–58; V. O. Weed, "Recollections," pp. 1–2, manuscript (Travis County Rifles Collection, CAH); Roberts, "Political, Legislative, and Judicial History of Texas," 205.

entering the executive offices. Once again he asked for U.S. troops, this time to assist him in "defending the government offices and keeping the peace."[41]

There was little chance that those troops would be sent. The next day both the president and the attorney general indicated that they had received Davis's telegrams. In meetings at the White House with Democratic and Republican representatives from Texas, however, the president stated he did not believe either that Davis was in danger or that he intended to provoke a conflict. Grant surmised that the governor simply wanted to oblige the new government to dispossess him by a show of force, so that he would have the basis for a suit in the courts. Attorney General Williams indicated he did not believe that Davis had any expectation that he could hold on to his office. No communication from Austin suggests any basis for either of these conclusions, but Democratic Congressmen were convinced that Davis would "back down" at the first display of force by the new government.[42]

In Austin, the problem for the Democrats was displaying force without provoking an actual conflict that might cause the president to reconsider the use of troops. Through the night of the 15th, tension increased at the capitol and, according to some Democratic participants, their men were anxious for a fight. Several incidents nearly provoked clashes, but Democratic leaders maintained control over their men. At the same time, Davis's troops remained in their position in the executive offices in the capitol basement and did not interfere with the proceedings above, where Coke was inaugurated before the legislature.[43]

On the 16th, while the president was assuring partisans on both sides in Washington that all would be well, the threat of an armed clash actually increased. Coke, now as the "duly and constitutionally declared Governor of the State of Texas," asked that Davis turn over the executive offices. At the same time, his supporters attempted to strengthen their position. That morning the city mayor and a squad of the Travis Rifles attempted to seize state ammunition and arms in a storehouse on West Avenue for use by the Coke forces. A unit of state militia arrived and arrested Mayor Thomas B. Wheeler. Only the retreat of the Travis Rifles prevented bloodshed and Wheeler was released, but tension increased in the hours that followed and the possibility of an armed confrontation grew. If Davis wished to produce a case for federal intervention, the time had come.[44]

---

[41]E. J. Davis to U. S. Grant, Jan. 15, 1874, in *Daily State Journal* (Austin), Jan. 20, 1874.

[42]New York *Tribune,* Jan. 16, 17, 1874; New York *Times,* Jan. 16, 1874; George H. Williams to Thomas F. Purnell, Jan. 16, 1874, Justice Department, Instructions to U. S. Attorneys and Marshals, Letters Sent, RG 60 (NA).

[43]Wheeler, "Reminiscences of Reconstruction in Texas," 57–58; Oates (ed.), *RIP Ford's Texas,* 418–420.

[44]*Daily State Journal* (Austin), Jan. 17, 1874 (quotation); Oates (ed.), *RIP Ford's Texas,* 428; Wheeler, "Reminiscences of Reconstruction in Texas," 57, 59–61, 72.

Davis did not wish to produce that conflict any more than did Democratic leaders, however. At 3:30 in the afternoon the sergeants-at-arms of the legislature asked for a meeting with the governor, who received them in the executive offices. According to the *Daily State Journal* the legislative delegation agreed to disperse their men if the governor would disband the militia; they also promised that they would not use force to oust the governor. Davis reminded them that they had also promised not to inaugurate Coke. Even though he had no reason to trust them, he agreed to their terms, probably realizing that he had little other choice unless he was willing to fight them. The administration's newspaper declared that Davis intended to remain in the office, unless the president or Congress recognized the "usurpers," but the troops were sent away from the capitol.[45]

Davis's decision to disband his troops rather than to keep them in place to hold the state offices ensured that the election conflict would end peacefully. Results could easily have been otherwise, for while hundreds of Democrats hastened to the defense of Coke, hundreds of African Americans came to the capitol rallying to the support of Governor Davis. A member of the legislature informed Guy M. Bryan that the grounds in front of the capitol were "black with negroes" and that they were "swarming here from every direction to the assistance of Davis." If Davis had chosen, he could have produced at the very least a riot that may have produced military intervention.[46]

Davis chose not to use the forces at his disposal and, therefore, he, as much as the Democratic leadership, may claim some responsibility for preventing further turmoil. His political opponents declared that he feared being killed, but such an explanation is an unlikely one for the behavior of a man who had fought valiantly through the Civil War and had shown his courage repeatedly. In a letter to his private secretary the governor stated his reasons. When the U.S. government had refused to sustain him, he believed that he was left only with the alternative of "defending the constituted authorities against violence by means which I am unwilling to adopt." He had decided against the use of the state police or the militia because he believed it would "produce great public disturbance and injury to the prosperity of the state."[47]

Unwilling to precipitate an armed conflict, Davis had no means to sustain his position and no choice but to step down. After his meeting on the 16th, he determined to disband his forces and abandon all plans for the use of force in resisting what he considered Coke's usurpation. That evening the governor

---

[45]*Daily State Journal* (Austin), Jan. 17, 1874; Oates (ed.), *RIP Ford's Texas*, 428.

[46]Guy M. Bryan to RIP Ford, Mar. 2, 1891, in Oates (ed.), *RIP Ford's Texas*, 424.

[47]E. J. Davis to Jno. J. Stevens, Jan. 19, 1874, in *Weekly State Journal* (Austin), Jan. 22, 1874 (quotation). See the statement of Sheriff George B. Zimpleman in Oates (ed.), *RIP Ford's Texas*, 428, for the suggestion that Davis may have feared for his life.

left the capitol for the final time in a carriage accompanied by George B. Zimpleman, sheriff of Travis County and one of the men sent by the legislature to negotiate with him and who had promised to secure his safety. As the governor left, the militia, composed largely of African Americans, cheered their leader one last time.[48]

From the Governor's Mansion, Davis made one last effort to settle the succession question within a framework that he considered acceptable. He wrote to Coke, once again asserting his claim to hold the office until April 28. "I do not regard you as the Executive of this state or entitled to possession of the Governor's office, or any official records. I am myself governor of the State till the 28th of April next." One last time, he asked that the question be resolved by the president or Congress, who had the responsibility of sustaining state governments against domestic violence. Davis pledged himself to "abide the decision."[49]

Officials at Washington made clear their decision on the matter that evening, when Attorney General George Williams telegraphed Davis. Having already given tacit approval to the election results, Williams, responding to Davis's telegram of the 15th, now wrote that the president was "of the opinion your right to the office of governor at this time is at least so doubtful that he does not feel warranted in furnishing United States troops to aid you in holding further possession of it."[50] This telegram appears to have settled the matter. U.S. Marshal Thomas F. Purnell telegraphed Williams on January 19 that the message of the previous day had "as anticipated" secured the desired effect and the complications had been amicably settled.[51]

On Sunday morning, January 18, news quickly spread through Austin that Davis was preparing to leave the mansion and abandon the executive offices. The son of Oran M. Roberts informed his father that blacks had informed him that Davis had inquired during the morning where he could rent a house. Senator James G. Tracy, chairman of the state Republican Party, informed George Clark, Coke's secretary of state, that Davis would leave the offices the following day and that he wanted to remain in the mansion for two or three days to get his furniture out. Clark told Tracy that this was acceptable.[52] The next day the governor authorized his private secretary to turn over the executive office to the Coke forces, over his protest.[53] The Coke-Davis imbroglio had ended, except for futile efforts by Davis to be restored to his office carried out in Congress and in the courts.

---

[48]Edmund J. Davis to "The People of Texas," Jan. 19, 1874, in *Daily State-Journal* (Austin), Jan. 20, 1874; George B. Zimpleman to John S. Ford, Feb. 11, 1892, in Oates (ed.), *RIP Ford's Texas,* 428.

[49]E. J. Davis to Richard Coke, Jan. 17, 1874, Letter Press, Governor's Papers: Davis.

[50]George Williams to E. J. Davis, Jan. 17, 1874, in *Daily State Journal* (Austin), Jan. 20, 1874.

[51]Thomas E. Purnell to George H. Williams, Jan. 19, 1874, in New York *Times,* Jan. 21, 1874.

[52]Clark, *A Glance Backwards,* 82; R. P. Roberts to O. M. Roberts, Jan. 18, 1874, Roberts Papers.

[53]E. J. Davis to Jno. J. Stevens, Jan. 19, 1874, in *Weekly State Journal* (Austin), Jan. 22, 1874.

In assessing Davis's course through the crisis, there is no question that the governor attempted to block the implementation of the 1873 election results and that he tried to hold on to office. A closer look at his motives and the means that he was willing to use to sustain this position, however, suggest a much more complicated story than the traditional one. Rather than the tyrant trying to hang on to power at any cost, Davis more realistically appears to be an unwilling participant caught in the dilemma of enforcing the law he had sworn to uphold or surrendering to what he personally agreed was the will of the people. His decision was to enforce the law, while at the same time looking for an acceptable means to ensure the people of the state an uncomplicated transition of government that would exact no future cost. When it was clear that maintaining his position would undermine the goal that he sought rather than achieve it, he chose to concede rather than fight. Instead of playing the role of a partisan who hated the people of Texas, Davis backed away from partisan goals and means to protect the people of the state from further harm. His actions in this situation, in a sense, were heroic and, at least based upon his behavior in this conflict, his entire career and his reputation appear to deserve reconsideration.

# "The Lone Star State Surrenders to a Lone Woman": Frances Willard's Forgotten 1882 Texas Temperance Tour[1]

JAMES D. IVY*

*An issue in the lives of Texans and Texas politics as early as the time of the Republic, campaigns for prohibition or temperance—efforts to prohibit or limit the sale and transportation of alcoholic beverages—diminished during the Civil War and Reconstruction eras but regained momentum in the 1880s. Frances Willard, national president of the Women's Christian Temperance Union, toured Texas in the early months of 1882 and founded a number of "unions" or local organizations to support the cause. Although she spoke to large audiences and newspaper accounts of her activities were gracious and complementary, her tour was soon forgotten. Prohibition continued to be an issue until well into the twentieth century and become a legal reality in time, but Willard's efforts in Texas were rarely mentioned, even by those dedicated to the cause. The Women's Christian Temperance Union remained involved in the campaign against alcohol, but other organizations, notably the Anti-Saloon League, and other leaders dominated the activities and the news.*

*Author James Ivy's analysis of the reasons why Frances Willard's efforts in Texas were soon forgotten reveal much about attitudes and values prevalent in*

*James D. Ivy, "'The Lone Star State Surrenders to a Lone Woman'; Frances Willard's Forgotten 1882 Texas Temperance Tour," *Southwestern Historical Quarterly*, 102 (July, 1998), 415–432. An earlier version of this essay was presented at the Mid-America Conference in History at Topeka, Kan., Sept. 1996. The author is indebted to Prof. Virginia Laas of the Dept. of History at Missouri Southern College and the other panelists for their comments, and to Prof. Char Miller of Trinity University for reading two earlier drafts of this essay.

[1]Joseph E. Roy, "Miss Willard in Texas," *The Independent* (New York). Woman's Christian Temperance Union National Headquarters Historical Files (joint Ohio Historical Society-Michigan Historical Collections), Temperance and Prohibition Papers, microfilm edition, W.C.T.U. series (cited hereafter as W.C.T.U. series), reel 30, scrapbook 7; reprinted in the Union Signal (Chicago), Mar. 23, 1882.

*the late nineteenth-century South. Reluctance to support reform movements characterized the antebellum South, and remained a powerful barrier to change even as the end of the century grew near. Politics, mostly a desire to protect the Democratic Party, and resistance to any cause that might support women's equality, especially the right to vote, were more specific obstacles to leaders such as Willard. Even though she presided over an organization that included Christian in its name, certain religious leaders found her efforts, even her speaking in public, a threat and a violation of religious orthodoxy. Others merely feared her support for women's suffrage.*

*More information on the prohibition crusade can be found in James D. Ivy,* **No Saloon in the Valley: The Southern Strategy of Texas Prohibitionists in the 1880s** *(Waco: Baylor University Press, 2003) and Lewis L. Gould,* **Progressives and Prohibitionists: Texas Democrats in the Wilson Era** *(Austin: University of Texas Press, 1973).*

Texas was wet when Frances Willard left Texarkana en route to Marshall on February 3, 1882. The town of Denison recorded over three-and-a-half inches of rain the previous month. More than eight inches had fallen on Galveston. With her companion and personal secretary, Anna Gordon, Willard had been on the road for several weeks, stirring up support for the temperance cause, braving the early spring rains. Leaving Little Rock, Arkansas, they had crossed into Texas over the swollen Sabine River on a Texas and Pacific railroad bridge that would be destroyed by flood waters a week later.[2]

Willard had served as president of the Woman's Christian Temperance Union since she had defeated incumbent Annie Wittenmyer by a large majority at the 1879 convention. Even before her election propelled her into the national spotlight as the leader of the largest women's organization in America, Willard had been an important figure in reform circles. She had been president of the North Western Female College at Evanston, had won a wide reputation as a speaker and as a member of the staff of evangelist Dwight L. Moody, and had served as president of the Illinois W.C.T.U. and corresponding secretary for the national Union. Her tireless efforts and constant travel had been significant factors in a dramatic increase in the Union's membership rolls; however, the organization's strength remained in the northeastern and midwestern states.[3]

---

[2]U.S. War Dept., Signal Service, Monthly Meteorological Reports, Denison, Galveston, Jan. 1882, U.S. Dept. of Commerce, National Oceanic and Atmospheric Admin., National Environmental Satellite, Data and Information Service (National Climatic Center, Asheville, N.C.).

[3]The most recent, and the best, biography of Willard is Ruth Bordin, *Frances Willard: A Biography* (Chapel Hill: University of North Carolina Press, 1986), although Mary Earhart, *Frances Willard: From Prayers to Politics* (Chicago: University of Chicago Press, 1944) remains an important

In the principal purpose of the tour, the effort to organize local chapters of the Woman's Christian Temperance Union in the southern states, Willard had met with only modest success. For a variety of reasons, southern women had proved much more difficult to enlist in the cause. The conservatism and paternalism of southern society closely delimited the public activities of women. In the northern states evangelical churches provided many women with their first experiences in social activism, most commonly in temperance work. In contrast, southern evangelicals generally eschewed social activism and its association with antebellum abolitionism. In addition, rural isolation and the disruption of western migration made it impossible for most women to participate in the wider associations of a national reform movement. Finally, southern women were themselves suspicious of an organization based in the North, associated with female suffrage, and dedicated to the participation of women in the public sphere. Still, Willard had made significant inroads. Her excursion into Texas came toward the end of her second tour of the southern states, a tour which had attracted both record crowds and national attention. For the first time in decades, southern women were meeting and working with their counterparts in the northern states. And her reception in Texas would demonstrate that there was a significant number of reform-minded women and men who were anxious to embrace Willard and her cause.[4]

But many of the prohibitionists in Texas saw in Frances Willard more of a threat to the social and political order than a champion for the cause. Her support of female suffrage, her decidedly reformist politics, even her position as a public figure made her a problematic ally. Although her tour attracted unprecedented and wide-ranging support while she was in the state, it did not result in the galvanizing of temperance forces over the longer term. Within a few years, Texas prohibitionists, even many of those who warmly greeted her in 1882, rarely mentioned Willard. Moreover, Willard's tour has virtually disappeared from the historical record, and, where it is mentioned, the details of her visit are often recorded incorrectly. The fact is that in the years following her

---

revision of the W.C.T.U.'s more conservative orthodoxy and a significant effort to place Willard as a leader in nineteenth-century feminist circles. Willard's autobiography, *Glimpses of Fifty Years: The Autobiography of an American Woman* (Chicago: Woman's Temperance Publication Assoc., 1889), is detailed and fascinating, but suffers from being hurriedly pieced together and deals little with the southern tours. Also useful for insight into Willard's character is Carolyn De Swarte Gifford, *Writing Out My Heart: Selections from the Journal of Frances E. Willard, 1855–96* (Urbana: University of Illinois Press, 1995), although Willard was not keeping a journal at the time of her Texas visit.

[4]On the significance of Willard's southern tours see Ruth Bordin, *Woman and Temperance: The Quest for Power and Liberty, 1873–1900* (Philadelphia: Temple University Press, 1981), 76–85. On the complexities of engaging southern women in social reform the best work is still Anne Firor Scott, *The Southern Lady: From Pedestal to Politics, 1830–1930* (Chicago: University of Chicago Press, 1970).

visit to the state, Texas prohibitionists appear to have made a strategic decision to distance themselves from Frances Willard and her national organization. But historians should not overlook her tour. Frances Willard took the state by storm, the herald of a movement that would be at the center of the state's politics for the next five decades.[5]

Texas was booming when Willard arrived. The population of the state had nearly doubled between 1870 and 1880, and the growth of the towns and cities was even more dramatic. Although barely a tenth of the people of the state lived in urban areas in 1880, the rate of urban population increase for the previous decade was nearly double that in the country.[6] Most of the newcomers were from other southern states, though a significant number were from the lower Midwest. For the new and the older Texans, the years following Reconstruction were a period of disruption and change, bustle and promise. Things were not settled. The decision to build a spur line on a railway could transform the economy of an older village, or could leave it a ghost town. The Democratic Party was unsure of its grip on power, and reformers appeared to pose a real threat to the newly reconstituted Bourbons. African Americans, so recently freed from bondage and then disappointed by the failure of Reconstruction, had not yet been silenced by Jim Crow. Poor farmers had not yet slipped irredeemably into the peonage of the crop lien and shares. Roads were inadequate, governments were overwhelmed, and some people appeared to be making money by the bale. Intemperance, broadly speaking, seemed the order of the day.

If lawlessness was not pervasive it was a persistent problem in many communities, and the saloon stood as a visible sign of disruption, disorder, and vice. Willard was not the first to come to Texas to preach the temperance gospel. James Younge, lecturer and organizer for the United Friends of Temperance, had arrived over a decade before and had stayed. He organized hundreds of locals, who worked through moral suasion and occasionally the legal coercion of local option to combat drunkenness. The evangelical Protestant clergy, particularly the Methodists and the Baptists, had railed from the pulpit and in

---

[5]Willard's Texas tour merits a one-sentence mention in Alwyn Barr, *Reconstruction to Reform: Texas Politics, 1876–1906* (Austin: University of Texas Press, 1971), 86. Willard's visit is overlooked altogether in most general histories of the state; see, e.g., Rupert Richardson, Adrian Anderson, and Ernest Wallace, *Texas: The Lone Star State* (6th ed.; Englewood Cliffs, N.J.: Prentice Hall, 1993), 298; and David G. McComb, *Texas: A Modern History* (Austin: University of Texas Press, 1989), 134 (in which Carrie Nation is briefly featured). Willard's part in establishing the Texas W.C.T.U. is briefly noted in Ron Tyler, et al. (eds.), *The New Handbook of Texas* (6 vols.; Austin: Texas State Historical Association, 1996), V, 355 (the date is incorrect).

[6]196.2 percent as opposed to 89.1 percent. Char Miller and David R. Johnson, "The Rise of Urban Texas," in Char Miller and Heywood T. Sanders (eds.), *Urban Texas: Politics and Development* (College Station: Texas A&M University Press, 1990), 6.

print against the sin of drink. Greenbackers, Alliance men, and labor agitators fought the saloon. Still, Texans drank.

Willard's entrance into the state did not go unnoticed. She visited sixteen of the most populous communities in the state, and at each spoke to record crowds. The press accounts of her meetings were numerous, thorough, and with only a few exceptions flattering to the point of adulation. Her tour corresponded with, and vitalized, early efforts to impose statutory prohibition in Texas on both the local and state levels. Despite the divisive nature of the issue, she was received warmly by Texans who supported prohibition and by those who did not. When she left the state there were very few newspaper readers who were unaware of her visit and the extraordinary impression she had made.[7]

On Willard's brief foray into the state the previous year, she had met Eben L. Dohoney at Paris, Texas. Dohoney secured her a venue at Babcock's Opera House when none of the churches would condone a woman speaking from the pulpit. A former Greenbacker, a local expert on spiritualism and phrenology, and an advocate of women's rights, Dohoney was no stranger to the cause. He was responsible for the inclusion in the 1876 state constitution of a provision for local option elections. In 1884, he would run for governor of Texas on the Prohihition Party ticket and would serve with Willard on the platform committee of the national Prohibition Party. For the 1882 tour, Dohoney undertook to lay out the route of the campaign through the principal cities and towns of the state.[8]

At Marshall, the weather cleared briefly after three days of continuous rain, and despite the last-minute change in her schedule, Willard drew an audience beyond the capacity of the Cumberland Presbyterian church. Listeners crowded in, filling not only the pews but the aisles as well. Many stood in the churchyard, listening at the windows and open doors. A correspondent of a Galveston paper reported that "the lady spoke for one hour, and held the audience spellbound by her delivery." When she and Anna Gordon left Marshall for Jefferson later that evening, they left behind a newly formed local

---

[7]The Methodist paper, the *Texas Christian Advocate*, on January 28, 1882, published a detailed agenda of Willard's tour provided by the W.C.T.U. of Paris, Texas.

[8]*North Texan* (Paris), May 20, 1881, May 13, 1882, W.C.T.U. series, reel 32, scrapbook 14, pp. 140, 144; E[ben] L[afayette] Dohoney, *An average American; being a true history of leading events in the life of Lafayette, who was born in Ky.; but "went West to grow up with the country." Containing a brief outline of some of the decisive events of American history; with short sketches of representative men and women* (Paris, Tex.: E. L. Dohoney, 1907), 209–211; Seth Shepard McKay (ed.), *Debates in the Texas Constitutional Convention of* 1875 (Austin: University of Texas Press, 1930), 142–144; Ernest William Winkler (ed.), *Platforms of Political Parties in Texas*, Bulletin of the University of Texas, 1916, No. 3 (Austin: University of Texas, 1916), 244; D. Leigh Colvin, *Prohibition in the United States: A History of the Prohibition Party and of the Prohibition Movement* (New York: George H. Doran Co., 1926), 169; *Union Signal* (Chicago), Feb. 23, 1882.

W.C.T.U. with more than forty members pledged. After two appointments at Jefferson, Willard made a brief stop at Clarksville for one lecture, and then on to Paris, where she had visited the year before.[9]

It was at the invitation of the Paris union that Willard had added Texas to her itinerary, and she was embraced by the community upon her arrival. She renewed acquaintances, spoke with community leaders, visited the home of Eben Dohoney, lectured twice to a house "full and running over" despite the inclement weather, and recruited new members for the local union, already the strongest in the state. Lamar County was one of only four dry counties at the time of her visit, having enacted county-wide prohibition by popular vote under the provisions of the state constitution, and the local W.C.T.U. was credited with getting out the vote on the issue. From Paris, Willard and Gordon took the Texas and Pacific east to Sherman. The rain had not let up and rivers and streams were overflowing their banks throughout the country. Because of the danger of washout, the train was running backward to protect the engineer and fireman. Despite the hardships, Anna Gordon could report with satisfaction to Willard's mother in Evanston that they were "traveling on through the mud of this immense state planting the W.C.T.U. here and there, and having tremendous meetings all along the line."[10]

The press reports of Willard's lectures and organization activities confirm Gordon's optimism. Typical was the report of the correspondent for the *Sherman Courier-Chronicle,* who after attending Willard's lecture in that city, hailed it as "perfect, unanswerable, and cover[ing] every part of the ground. . . . Miss Willard could do no more for the temperance cause here than all the committees, papers, and temperance tracts in Christendom."[11]

Two stops were planned at Austin. As the center of the state's political attention, it was crucial to the success of her campaign that Willard be well received there. Her first meeting at the Texas capital was an affair of church and state. Joining her on the stage of Millett's Opera House that Wednesday

---

[9] *Union Signal* (Chicago), Feb. 23, 1882; *Galveston Daily News,* Feb. 7, 1882 (quotation), Feb. 5, 1887; *Texas Observer* (Dallas), undated clipping in W.C.T.U. series, reel 13, scrapbook 15, p. 13; *Daily Jimplecute* (Jefferson), Feb. 6, 1882, ibid., p. 14. The choice of the Cumberland Presbyterian church was likely a result of that denomination's greater willingness to allow for women's participation in church affairs than most southern churches. See Ben M. Barrus, Milton L. Baughn, and Thomas H. Campbell, *A People Called Cumberland Presbyterians* (Memphis, Tenn.: Frontier Press, 1972), 173–175, 279–280; and R. Douglas Brackenridge, *Voices in the Wilderness: A History of the Cumberland Presbyterian Church in Texas* (San Antonio: Trinity University Press, 1968), 130–131.

[10] *North Texan* (Paris), Feb. 4, 1882, W.C.T.U. series, reel 32, scrapbook 15, p. 14; Frances Willard, *Woman and Temperance; or, The Work and Workers of the Woman's Christian Temperance Union* (Hartford: Park Publishing Co., 1893), 574–579; Dohoney, *An Average American,* 209–211; *Texas Tribune* (Paris), Feb. 16, 1882 (1st quotation), W.C.T.U. series, reel 32, scrapbook 15, p. 14; *Denison Democrat,* Feb. 8, 1882, ibid., p. 16; Anna Gordon to Mary Hill Willard, Feb. 14, 1882 (2nd quotation), ibid., reel 12, folder 14.

[11] *Courier-Chronicle* (Sherman), Feb. 12, 1882, W.C.T.U. series, reel 32, scrapbook 15, p. 15.

evening were the ministers from three Protestant denominations and the president of the local union. Also on stage, presiding at the meeting and introducing Willard, was Capt. Thornton Hardie Bowman, who when he was not leading temperance meetings served as secretary of state in Gov. Oran Roberts's administration. In a town accustomed to political pageantry and speeches, the decidedly antiprohibitionist *Austin Statesman* reported that Willard "was listened to with the closest attention and was frequently applauded."[12]

Willard had been cautioned by her supporters in North and Central Texas to stay away from San Antonio, but she kept to the itinerary that had her in the River City between her two Austin stops. Certainly, the demographics of the city did not suggest that she would find audiences so amenable to her message as those in towns to the north and east. More than a quarter of the population of Bexar County was foreign born, and many of the natives were Tejanos and German-Texans who were unlikely to support Willard's cause. Even among the Anglo-Texans there appeared to be less support for any sort of organized reform. "Heretofore all efforts to organize a temperance society have failed on account of lack of enthusiasm on the part of the leading citizens," one editor lamented. "There are more saloons in that town than there are in Austin when the Legislature is in session."[13]

Despite the inauspicious conditions, Willard was received as enthusiastically in San Antonio as she had been elsewhere in the state. On the evening of February 23, Trinity Methodist Church was packed an hour before the lecture was scheduled to begin. Willard was joined on the platform by several ministers, newspaper editors, and prominent citizens of the city. The support of the German community was demonstrated by the address of alderman William Heofling on the deleterious effects of beer drinking, and by the music for the occasion provided by the Beethoven Glee Club. Staunchly opposed to prohibition, the principal newspapers of the city nevertheless battled to provide the most comprehensive and glowing account of the meeting.[14]

On Sunday afternoon, Willard was back in Austin, lecturing one last time at Millett's Opera House to an audience that packed the hall "from pit to dome." The meeting was called to order by the Travis County attorney, and Willard was joined on the platform by five of the city's ministers. The Musical Union of Austin provided the chorus. An invitation was proffered to the newspapers to send representatives to join Willard on stage, and a number appeared both as reporters and as participants in the proceedings. Once more Willard was able to guarantee

[12] *Austin Statesman*, Feb. 23, 1882 (quotation), ibid., p. 23; *Galveston Daily News*, Feb. 24, 1882.

[13] Tenth U.S. Census (1880), Population Statistics, Vol. 1, Table VIII; *Texas Siftings* (Austin), Mar. 4, 1882 (quotations), W.C.T.U. series, reel 32, scrapbook 15, p. 25.

[14] *Texas Siftings* (Austin), Mar. 4, 1882, W.C.T.U. series, reel 32, scrapbook 15, p. 25; *San Antonio Daily Express*, Feb. 24, 25, 1882, ibid., p. 24; *San Antonio Evening Light*, Feb. 24, 25, 1882, ibid., pp. 24, 25, 27; *Union Signal* (Chicago), Mar. 9, 1882; *Galveston Daily News*, Feb. 25, 1882.

for herself extensive and favorable press coverage, despite the skeptical attitude most of the city's editors displayed toward the cause of prohibition.[15]

From Austin the two women traveled east on the Central Texas Railway to Brenham, Houston, and Galveston. At Houston, on March 2, the forty-sixth anniversary of Texas Independence, Willard and Gordon organized one more union, then boarded a train for New Orleans. The Texas Christian Advocate bid them farewell, noting that "Miss Willard has certainly endeared herself to the people of the Lone Star State."[16]

Willard could leave the state pleased with the results of her visit. She left in her wake sixteen local unions, a state organizer, and plans for the establishment of a statewide organization. By 1885 there were sixty local unions, two "Young Ladies' Unions," and forty "Bands of Hope" in Texas. Two years later there were approximately a hundred unions. These local unions immediately began attracting attention by organizing social gatherings, reporting on their meetings and temperance work in local papers, and raising funds for reading rooms and libraries. The W.C.T.U. would be instrumental in getting out the vote for the statewide prohibition amendment in 1887, and more importantly, would have a persistent role in social reform in the decades preceding national prohibition. Many of the women recruited by Willard in her southern tours would remain active in the leadership of reform movements for years to come.[17]

Another immediate result of Willard's tour was a dramatic increase in agitation for local option. Although the state constitution of 1876 provided for local option prohibition, efforts to outlaw saloons had been sporadic and usually unsuccessful. Willard's visit galvanized the temperance forces, and elections were called all across the state in the weeks during and following her tour. In some communities her visit coincided with the campaign, and she took an active role. In other places her lectures, and the press reports of them, sparked an effort to vote out liquor. The *Texas Tribune* of Paris reported that the local

---

[15] *Austin Statesman*, Feb. 26, 1882, W.C.T.U. series, reel 32, scrapbook 15, p. 23.

[16] *Houston Daily Post*, Feb. 26, Mar. 2, 1882, ibid., pp. 26, 27; *Texas Christian Advocate*, Mar. 4, 1882 (quotation).

[17] *Union Signal* (Chicago), Apr. 13, 1882; *Galveston Daily News*, Feb. 26, 1882; *Fort Worth Daily Democrat-Advance*, Feb. 21, Mar. 3, 7, 12, 17, 1882; National W.C.T.U. minutes, 1885, W.C.T.U. series, reel 2, p. 117; May Baines, *A Story of Texas White Ribboners* (n.p., 1935), 23. On the importance of the W.C.T.U. in moving women into the ranks of social activism, see Barbara Leslie Epstein, *The Politics of Domesticity: Women, Evangelism and Temperance in Nineteenth Century America* (Middletown, Conn.: Wesleyan University Press, 1981), 115–146. For the experience of southern women in particular, see Scott, *The Southern Lady*, esp. 135–163. On the W.C.T.U.'s challenge to and accommodation with the racial order and the ideal of southern womanhood, see Glenda Elizabeth Gilmore, *Gender and Jim Crow: Women and the Politics of White Supremacy in North Carolina, 1896–1920* (Chapel Hill: University of North Carolina Press, 1996), esp. 46–56; and Anastatia Sims, *The Power of Femininity in the New South: Women's Organizations and Politics in North Carolina, 1880–1930* (Columbia: University of South Carolina Press, 1997).

option election scheduled for Marshall was "of course the result of Miss Willard's address at that place." But while Willard was able to address the issue of prohibition without generating a great deal of hostility, the local campaigns brought to the surface deep divisions regarding the issue. Accusations of fanaticism and political opportunism were made on both sides. Newspaper editors entered the fray, or else tried to remain aloof and inoffensive with studied irresolution. The *Fort Worth Daily Democrat-Advance* was a typical case. Its editors took a cautious approach to local option, suggesting that the issue be postponed until the fall elections. In the same issue the paper came out foursquare against the sale of oleomargarine, demanding that the "poisonous article" be "banished by law from the markets." The newly formed W.C.T.U. locals were active and outspoken in the campaigns, often forgetting the virtues of Willard's generous tone. When Mrs. McPherson, a reporter for the *Sherman Democrat,* opposed local option, the editor of the *Democrat-Advance* quipped that the local W.C.T.U. should "tackle" her. A Fort Worth W.C.T.U. member took the bait, replying that "the best thing to tackle any woman who advocates the whiskey traffic is a drunken husband." Agitation for the cause became so pervasive that one Fort Worth saloon keeper renamed his establishment in its honor. "While some people are worrying themselves about how to prevent men from drinking, others are inquiring where the finest wines, the purest liquors and the best cigars may be found and enjoyed," he noted. "Such men are always directed to the princely Local Option Saloon." Despite the unprecedented attention to the issue, most of the elections in the weeks immediately following Willard's visit returned large majorities for continued licensing of saloons. Willard had energized many who supported the temperance cause, and impressed a great number with her intelligence and conviction, but she had not immediately converted the state wholesale on the issue of statutory prohibition. Nevertheless, the agitation for local option continued, and within three years of her visit, scores of local option elections were held in communities throughout the state. Moreover, in 1886 the state legislature was pressured to submit a statewide prohibition amendment. The Texas W.C.T.U. played an important role in that lobbying effort, and in the unsuccessful attempt the following year to persuade voters to adopt the amendment.[18]

---

[18] *Waco Daily Examiner,* Mar. 9, 1882; *Texas Christian Advocate,* Mar. 4, 1882; *Houston Daily Post,* Feb. 19, 1882, W.C.T.U. series, reel 32, scrapbook 15, p. 26; *Texas Tribune* (Paris), undated clipping, ibid., p. 13 (1st quotation); *Fort Worth Daily Democrat-Advance,* Feb. 12, 14, 17, 24, 25 (2nd quotation), Mar. 1 (5th quotation), 3 (3rd quotation), 7 (4th quotation), 16, 23, 1882; National W.C.T.U. minutes, 1885, W.C.T.U. series, reel 2, p. 117. The success of local option prohibition was often very brief. As the state constitution allowed annual votes on the issue if citizens successfully petitioned, many counties remained dry for a year and then would vote wet in the next round of elections. Moreover, the report of twelve dry-county votes, based on W.C.T.U. records, is difficult to verify. Local governments were not required to report the results of local option elections to the state. Previous historians and partisans have reported as few as three dry counties by 1887.

The temperance movement in Texas had often skirted the blurred line between voluntarism and social control. Since the provision for local option elections in the 1876 constitution, ad hoc organizations had emerged in a number of communities to petition for local elections. There had also been more sustained efforts. The Friends of Temperance, preceding the W.C.T.U. in Texas by twelve years, was a secret fraternal society pledged to personal abstinence. The primary tool of the organization was moral suasion, but its leadership had been instrumental in an unsuccessful effort to lobby the state legislature to submit a statewide prohibition amendment to Texas voters in 1881. A second attempt to get a prohibition amendment was made after a group of Protestant ministers met at Waxahachie in December 1881, and a prohibition convention was called for April 1882. Willard's tour coincided with these efforts, and with a wave of local and statewide prohibition campaigns throughout the southern states. Willard strongly endorsed these efforts toward statutory and constitutional prohibition. There was even talk of having Willard address the increasingly politicized Farmers' Alliance on Washington's Birthday, but that plan never materialized. It was difficult for either supporters or opponents to ignore the fact that Frances Willard was conducting a political campaign.[19]

The impact on the political arena of Willard's visit brought into sharper focus issues that would be central to the prohibition campaigns in the state for decades. Despite the overwhelming success of her speaking tour, despite the visible results in local organization, prohibitionist leaders apparently decided that on balance an alliance with Frances Willard was more a liability than an asset. In the years immediately following Willard's tour, the core leadership of the prohibition movement in Texas outside the W.C.T.U. adopted a conservative strategy that excluded many potential supporters. They believed that if prohibition were to succeed it must be presented to the voters of Texas as a homegrown

---

[19] *Texas Christian Advocate*, Dec. 10, 1881, Feb. 4, 1882; *Waco Daily Examiner*, Apr. 20, 1882; *Texas Prohibitionist*, Feb. 3, 1882, W.C.T.U. series, reel 32, scrapbook 15, p. 12. On the United Friends of Temperance in Texas, see H. A. Ivy, *Rum on the Run in Texas: A Brief History of Prohibition in the Lone Star State* (Dallas: Temperance Publishing Co., 1910), 19–23. On temperance movements in other southern states, see T. J. Bailey, *Prohibition in Mississippi; or, Anti-Liquor Legislation from Territorial Days, with Its Results in the Counties* (Jackson, Miss.: Hederman Brothers, 1917); James Benson Sellers, *The Prohibition Movement in Alabama, 1702–1943* (Chapel Hill: University of North Carolina Press, 1943); Daniel Jay Whitener, *Prohibition in North Carolina, 1715–1945* (Chapel Hill: University of North Carolina Press, 1945); C. C. Pearson and J. Edwin Hendricks, *Liquor and Anti-Liquor in Virginia, 1619–1919* (Durham, N.C.: Duke University Press, 1967); and Paul E. Isaac, *Prohibition and Politics: Turbulent Decades in Tennessee, 1885–1920* (Knoxville: University of Tennessee Press, 1965). Leonard Stott Blakey, *The Sale of Liquor in the South: The History of the Development of a Normal Social Restraint in Southern Commonwealths* (New York: Columbia University, 1912) is an early overview of the region. A recent contribution is David M. Fahey, *Temperance and Racism: John Bull, Johnny Reb, and the Good Templars* (Lexington: University Press of Kentucky, 1996).

Texan (or at least southern) notion, uncorrupted by connection with northern reformers. Prohibition was pitched in such a way that it might appeal to Democrats anxious about the rise of competing political parties. A few prominent prohibitionists, such as Dohoney and James B. Cranfill, retained their loyalties to reform parties, but these were increasingly marginalized as a new generation of leaders came forward. These new men (and outside the W.C.T.U. they were inevitably men), in order to persuade local politicians and a state legislature dominated by Democrats to take up the issue, deemphasized the role played by political reformers and crusading women in stirring up support for the cause in the first place. Willard was vulnerable for two reasons. As a northerner engaging in political agitation, she posed a threat to the southern Democracy; as a woman stumping for social reform, she threatened the southern patriarchy.

In December 1881, at the beginning of her southern tour, Willard had forwarded to the *National Liberator,* a prominent reform periodical, a letter whose author she did not identify. It was a lengthy analysis of the state of reform politics in the southern states, particularly highlighting the success of William Mahone, the extraordinary leader of the Virginia Readjusters who had cooperated with that state's Republicans to turn out of office the Bourbon Democrats. This same feat could be accomplished in Texas, this anonymous writer continued, if the Greenbacker Wash Jones could be induced "to promise affiliation with the Republicans." The goal of this sort of fusion in Texas and other southern states was not to facilitate the reemergence of the Republican Party. Since the party of Lincoln had abandoned its reform roots, it would be superseded by the Prohibition Party. Willard did not explicitly endorse the arguments made in the letter, but she was impressed enough to make the document public.[20]

The printing of this letter apparently went unnoticed in the Texas press at the time. At Willard's first appearance in the state, even those few papers who regarded her critically made no mention of it. Nor was Willard implicated when, two days before her arrival in Dallas, handbills circulated in that city announcing a "grand Republican mass meeting at Fort Worth," to be addressed by, among others, Gov. John St. John of Kansas, who had pioneered the adoption of state constitutional prohibition. The *Galveston Weekly News* was one of many papers that denounced the upcoming event, warning of a "politico-theological organization [that] will join with the prohibitionists in the next State campaign, in support of a prohibition ticket." The rally never materialized. Local Republican leaders denied any knowledge of it and dismissed it as a hoax, but Democrats were put on their guard.[21]

---

[20] *National Liberator* (undated clipping), W.C.T.U. series, reel 32, scrapbook 15, pp. 43–44.

[21] *Galveston Weekly News,* Feb. 16, 1882 (quotations); *Fort Worth Daily Democrat-Advance,* Feb. 18, 1882.

Then, in mid-April, after Willard had left the state and a few days before the scheduled prohibition convention, a number of articles appeared in several Texas papers accusing Willard of complicity in plotting to destroy the Democratic Party. One account had it that Willard was the chief conspirator in a "republican religio-prohibition alliance combination [that] has been secretly organized under the patronage and fostering care of the Woman's Christian Temperance Union." Another writer reminded readers that Willard was a member of the "Northern" Methodist Church, and that her arrival preceded by only a few days the establishment of a "great morality party." The W.C.T.U., "the legitimate offspring of the prohibition failures, and the lineal descendant of Miss Willard," was little more than a front for the Republican efforts to establish libraries in Texas towns to disseminate "temperance and Republican tracts." Editors warned that "Miss Willard . . . came down South, the hireling of the Republican party, not . . . to advance religion and morality but to use her best licks in endeavoring to destroy the Democratic party."[22]

Many prohibitionist leaders rallied to Willard's defense. At the convention meeting in Waco, Eben Dohoney was the first to rise in condemnation of the newspapers. He was followed by a number of others, and a committee was formed which drafted a resolution excoriating several editors and praising Willard and her work in hagiographic terms. The Reverend John Allen was appointed to draft a rebuttal to the charges. He asserted that "Miss Willard came to Texas upon the invitation of the Christian ladies, not as the hireling of anybody." Vague about her origins, he wrote that "Miss Willard came from Mississippi to Texas . . . with [the] assurance that a courteous reception and generous hospitality would be extended to her by the people of the state." Of the Paris W.C.T.U. that sponsored the tour, he wrote that "every officer in it is a Southern lady," and that most were Southern Methodists. His reply was printed as a letter to the editor in a number of papers, but it is likely that more readers saw

[22] *State Gazette*, Apr. 18, 1882 (1st quotation), W.C.T.U. series, reel 32, scrapbook 15, p. 20; *Fort Worth Daily Democrat-Advance*, Apr. 19, 1882 (2nd quotation). Versions of the editorial also appeared in the *Dallas Times* and the *Austin Statesman*. Of course Texas Democrats were not the only southerners who recognized the threat female prohibitionists posed to the political order. Belle Kearney was an idealistic young teacher when she heard Willard speak in Jackson, Mississippi. She did not know of the W.C.T.U. until just before she attended the lecture, but was immediately drawn in and appointed state organizer within a month, becoming a successful lecturer for the cause throughout the South. She recalled: "Immediately upon entering the work of the Woman's Christian Temperance Union, I affiliated with the Prohibition party, as it was the only political body in the United States that stood for the protection of the home against the saloon. My brothers and I had stirring arguments on the subject. In their excitement they would walk rapidly up and down the long, old front gallery at the plantation home, and say, "'You are the only one of a vast relationship who has gone over to a new political faith. If you and the women associated with you, continue the agitation that has begun you will eventually break up the Democratic party.'" Belle Kearney, *A Slaveholder's Daughter* (New York: Abbey Press, 1900), 187–188.

the original accusations. Certainly Willard's critics had found a potent weapon to discredit interloping reformers. Allen's defensive regionalism only served to highlight the prohibitionists' acknowledgment of vulnerability on the point.[23]

For many of her critics, it was not only as a Yankee that Willard merited censure. As a woman, speaking from the pulpit, engaging in political discourse, working for social reform, she overstepped the bounds that circumscribed the role of women in nineteenth-century society. In the North, her caution, her moderation, and her generosity toward adversaries blunted much of the criticism. In the South, however, where gender roles were closely linked to the maintenance of the racial order, Willard's public activism posed an intolerable threat.

There were rumblings in some quarters that Willard was a suffragist, but she managed to sidestep this issue with a bit of calculated prevarication in the pages of the *Texas Christian Advocate.* More problematic was the simple fact that she was speaking publicly. From the first days of her tour of the state Willard had faced criticism for engaging in unladylike behavior. The editor of the *Denison Democrat,* while admitting that he did not attend Willard's lecture, was harsh in his denunciation. "On Saturday evening the people of Denison listened to the lecture of one of God's creatures who had stepped out of the sphere in which her Creator placed her and taken upon herself the duties belonging solely to a man," he wrote. "When Christ wanted apostles he chose men, not women; when Rome needed a general to command her armies, she sent to Cincennati [*sic*] not to his wife . . . and we do not believe that the cause of temperance, religion or education will ever be benefited by these female spouters of memorized compositions." As news of Willard's tour spread, more critics would raise questions about its propriety.[24]

---

[23] *Waco Daily Examiner,* Apr. 21, 22, 1882; *Fort Worth Daily Democrat-Advance,* Apr. 23, 1882 (quotations).

[24] *Texas Christian Advocate,* Feb. 4, 1882. Willard quoted directly from the Home Protection resolution passed by the 1881 convention (without crediting herself for its authorship or passage), and stressed that equal suffrage was only put forward as a drastic measure of last resort, when all other temperance efforts fail to produce results. "Beyond this no action was taken," she wrote, "nor has the National Women's Christian Temperance Union ever done anything whatever in the line of work for woman's ballot, either partial or complete." She also reassured readers that she "never [has] spoken, either in public or private, in favor of this branch of work for the women of the south." To the extent that this was true, it was a reflection of Willard's care to avoid jeopardizing the temperance cause by interjecting the divisive issue of suffrage at an inappropriate moment. Her letter to the *Texas Christian Advocate* was reprinted in the *Christian Advocate,* Mar. 2, 1882, W.C.T.U. series, reel 32, scrapbook 15, p. 38; *Denison Democrat,* Feb. 12, 1882 (quotations), W.C.T.U., ibid., p. 19. Willard was personally committed to the ballot for women and made every effort to gain its endorsement from the national Union. See Bordin, *Frances Willard,* 97–111. It should be noted that despite the criticism, on principle, of Willard, the *Democrat* continued to publish news of her tour and reactions from other papers, both favorable and critical.

Particularly troubling was the division that began to appear in the leadership of the Texas prohibitionists regarding Willard's role. Although most of the religious and secular newspapers sympathetic to the cause closely followed her progress in the state, there were noteworthy exceptions. In particular the *Texas Baptist*, a paper that was instrumental in organizing efforts for a statewide prohibition amendment and that reported weekly on local option elections, completely ignored Willard. Editor R. C. Buckner was not just an influential journalist. He was president of the Baptist General Association of Texas, proprietor of the Texas Baptist Publishing House, and general superintendent of the collection of funds for the Buckner Baptist Orphan's Home, the Texas Baptists' premier social welfare program that bore his name. The associate editor of the paper was Benajah Harvey Carroll, a young Waco minister who was already perceived as a rising star among Texas Baptists and who would play a leading role in the prohibition campaigns for years to come.[25]

Willard's name never appeared in print in the *Texas Baptist*, but a week after she left the state the paper published a long piece entitled "Dethroning American Queens" that offered an extensive list of charges against women speakers. "Take a woman out of her sphere and you dethrone a queen; place her before the public as a politician or an advocate from the rostrum, even of social reform or religion, and you rob her of her God-given retiring modesty and weaken her influence over man," the editorial warned. The writer then went on to present the inevitable slippery slope of women in the public sphere: preaching would lead to stump speaking which would lead to political involvement. Before long one would "hear the voices of men and maidens, of negro women and the cultivated wife and daughters of our own race, shouting . . . in our streets and at our country voting places." Only a decade before, "especially in our dear South-land, women but seldom appeared in the pulpit and on the platform; now . . . they travel the whole country over on lecturing tours, and make speeches in court-houses; and public halls." These women may be well meaning, but the inevitable result of this sort of behavior was social disorder, and the appearance of "female infidels," "female sleight-of-hand performers," "female gamblers," and "female horsejockeys."[26]

The dangers of too close an association with the likes of Willard and her organization was demonstrated to the prohibitionists when three years after her tour the citizens of McLennan County fought a bitter campaign over local option. The election was seen as a test case for the cause. The state Grand Council of the United Friends of Temperance was organized at Waco, the county seat, in 1870. Waco University would soon become the flagship institution for the

[25]On Carroll, see Alan J. Lefever, *Fighting the Good Fight: The Life and Work of Benajah Harvey Carroll* (Austin: Eakin Press, 1994).

[26]*Texas Baptist*, Mar. 9, 1882.

denomination, with the closing of Baylor College at Independence and the removal of its faculty and students to Waco. The evangelist Sam Jones had recently held a revival in Waco and his attacks on the saloons had been reported across the state. Both sides drew on the assistance of prominent political leaders to hold rallies in the contest. The antiprohibitionist forces enlisted the aid of Sen. Richard Coke. He delivered a speech at Waco, reprinted in a number of newspapers and in pamphlet form, in which he denounced interlopers from the North meddling in the affairs of Texas. Later, in an interview with a reporter for the *Waco Examiner,* he asserted that the ultimate goal of the prohibitionists was female suffrage: "Our noble women are being familiarized with the idea from the stump, the pulpit, and the lectures of strong-minded women sent to do missionary work." The Reverend Dr. B. H. Carroll expressed his frustration with the antiprohibitionist tactics, insisting that there were neither outside influences nor hidden agendas in the prohibition campaign. However, the antiprohibitionist strategy paid off when the voters of the county chose to continue licensing saloons.[27] Fearing that their opponents would again successfully use this strategy during the statewide campaign two years later in 1887, the prohibitionists scrambled to distance themselves from visiting speakers associated with the W.C.T.U. The prohibitionist *Dallas Herald* assured readers that "female speakers have not been imported from abroad by the prohibitionists." The confusion arose from the fact that "the ladies who have come to Texas from other states came under the auspices of the National Temperance Bureau of the W.C.T.U. . . . and these appointments were made before the submission of the amendment." The activities of temperance women were nothing more than an annoying coincidence. Frances Willard's central role in the early campaigns was suppressed.[28]

Historians have long been aware of the role the W.C.T.U. played in providing southern women with opportunities for involvement in public affairs that eventually led them to greater participation in all areas of reform and politics. Willard's southern tours obviously mark an important beginning in that story. But in the narrower context of Texas history, Willard's tour has faded from the record. There are some good reasons for this. Although her visit was followed by a flurry of temperance activity, there were few substantial successes. Statewide prohibition would not be accomplished in Texas until thirty-seven years after Willard left the state. When prohibition finally came, it was the Anti-Saloon League that could claim the credit. Nor in the short run did Willard's tour make it much easier for women to address the issue of prohibition publicly. Indeed, the backlash associated with the appearance of "long-haired men

[27] *Waco Daily Examiner,* Sept. 18, 1885 (quotation). B. H. Carroll, *Prohibition: Dr. B. H. Carroll's Reply to Senator Coke* (pamphlet, n.p.), (Center for American History, University of Texas at Austin; cited hereafter as CAH).

[28] *Dallas Daily Herald,* Apr. 11, 1887.

and short-haired women" on the stump for prohibition temporarily fostered a climate that made it difficult for women to play a greater role in any area of social reform. Despite the unprecedented attention and enthusiastic reception Willard received in Texas, her tour in the long run did not translate into great advances for either prohibitionists or feminists in the state.[29]

Nevertheless, there are good reasons to recover and reassess Willard's Texas tour. Excepting perhaps some denominational organizations, the W.C.T.U. provided the most acceptable and most common outlet for southern women interested in social reform in the closing decades of the nineteenth century. And within a few decades, while most of the denominational women's reform groups had been appropriated by men, the W.C.T.U. remained in the control of women. The W.C.T.U. was instrumental in lobbying for legislation regarding prison reform, the suppression of prostitution, the increase in the age of consent for females, and, close to the prohibitionist agenda, the establishment of "scientific temperance" curricula in public schools. And better than any other single event, Willard's tour of the state marks the beginning of significant public attention in Texas to the issue of prohibition, an issue that would be prominent and divisive for the next half century.[30]

---

[29]The phrase "long-haired men and short-haired women" was frequently employed by southern propagandists critical of interloping northern reformers. It had been applied to the carpetbaggers of the Reconstruction era, and seems to have served the antiprohibitionists well in their efforts to disparage imported temperance lecturers. Five years after Willard's visit, in the aftermath of the 1887 prohibition campaign, Texas W.C.T.U. president Jenny Bland Beauchamp expressed her exasperation with male prohibitionist leaders who avoided association with the more experienced female reformers rather than stand accused of consorting with "short-haired women." *Texas Baptist and Herald*, Aug. 31, 1887. In *The Southern Lady*, Anne Firor Scott wrote that "the significance of the WCTU went far beyond bringing about prohibition, though it played an important role in doing that. Like the church societies, the WCTU provided a respectable framework in which southern women could pursue their own development and social reform without drastically offending the prevailing views of the community about ladylike behavior" (p. 147). In a later work Scott asserted that "the WCTU probably contained more suffragists than did the two suffrage organizations put together." *Natural Allies: Women's Associations in American History* (Urbana: University of Illinois Press, 1991), 103. Marjorie Spruill Wheeler, *New Women of the New South: The Leaders of the Woman Suffrage Movement in the Southern States* (New York: Oxford University Press, 1993), 11. On the relationship between prohibition and women's suffrage in later years, see Lewis L. Gould, *Progressives and Prohibitionists: Texas Democrats in the Wilson Era* (Austin: University of Texas Press, 1973); and A. Elizabeth Taylor, "The Woman Suffrage Movement in Texas," *Journal of Southern History*, 17 (May, 1951), 19–215. Elizabeth Hayes Turner argues that, particularly on the urban seaboard, women's impetus for social reform did not originate in the evangelical denominations or with the temperance movement. Elizabeth Hayes Turner, "Women, Religion, and Reform in Galveston, 1880–1920," in Miller and Sanders (eds.), *Urban Texas*, 75–95.

[30] On the broad range of reforms that the W.C.T.U. undertook, see Bordin, *Woman and Temperance*, 95–139. On scientific temperance education, see Jonathan Zimmerman, "'The Queen of the Lobby': Mary Hunt, Scientific Temperance, and the Dilemma of Democratic Education in America, 1879–1906," *History of Education Quarterly*, 32 (Spring, 1992), 1–30.

Willard's decline in the story of the Texas prohibition campaigns can be attributed in part to the fact that history is written by the winners, and Willard was a loser twice over. Measured by its enforcement, by its long-term political success, or by its reputation in popular culture as a genuine reform, prohibition was an abysmal failure. Additionally, as the Anti-Saloon League could claim the credit as the eventually successful champion of the cause, its historical narrative became the definitive version. Just as Ernest Cherrington's massive work became the reference of first resort for historians of national prohibition, Texas historians in monographs and in textbooks have relied almost exclusively on the histories, tracts, and memoirs of the state Anti-Saloon League, the Texas Local Option Association, and their opponents, eclipsing the place of women in the early days of the reform. The women of the Texas W.C.T.U. did little to record their participation in the early campaigns, so that even those sources sympathetic to their efforts emerged from the later, male-dominated organizations.[31]

---

[31] As the general manager of the publishing interests of the Anti-Saloon League, Cherrington was the pen behind the movement in the later decades. Among his many works are the massive Anti-Saloon League Year Books (Westerville, Ohio: American Issue Press, [various years]), and *Evolution of Prohibition in the United States of America* (Westerville, Ohio: American Issue Press, 1920). Ivy, *Rum on the Run in Texas,* 46–52. Ivy's election returns, particularly for the 1887 statewide prohibition vote, are probably the most accurate available. Gregg Cantrell, "'Dark Tactics': Black Politics in the 1887 Texas Prohibition Campaign," *Journal of American Studies,* 25 (Apr., 1991), 85–93, n. 23. Ivy's work was a source for many of the standard texts in Texas historiography. See, e.g., Barr, *Reconstruction to Reform,* 86. The other principal sources on the Texas W.C.T.U. are a number of short sketches by Fannie Armstrong, who served as the press superintendent of the state union for nearly four decades, and Baines, *A Story of Texas White Ribboners.* Baines has Willard organize the Paris union in 1882 (instead of visit, for the second time, at their invitation) and reports that the state union was formed in 1883. A number of Armstrong's pieces are collected in the Texas Woman's Christian Temperance Union Scrapbook (CAH).

Willard's tours do not receive much attention in the various southern state histories of prohibition. In *Prohibition in Mississippi,* written by Bailey before the adoption of national prohibition, Willard is mentioned twice, once when she addressed a joint session of the state legislature during her 1882 tour. Whitener, *Prohibition in North Carolina,* does not mention Willard visiting that state until 1883, when she organized a state union. The W.C.T.U. is credited with success "through their propagandistic literature and appeals to the children," and in particular in the successful lobbying for the scientific temperance curriculum (pp. 104–107; quotation from p. 105). Sellers, *The Prohibition Movement in Alabama,* details some of the broadly ranging reform work of the W.C.T.U., but concludes that "the scattering of energy implied in this wide and varied program was undeniably a source of weakness" (p. 54). Willard is mentioned only as she opposed the use of fermented wine in churches (p. 62). Isaac, *Prohibition and Politics: Turbulent Decades in Tennessee, 1885–1920,* does not place Willard in that state until 1887. Robert Smith Bader, *Prohibition in Kansas: A History* (Lawrence: University of Kansas Press, 1986), notes Willard's visible role in the successful 1880 amendment fight in that border state, and particularly highlights the role of women generally. However, he asserts that the influence of the state W.C.T.U. has generally been overstated, and that women were most influential "as individuals and volunteers in the churches and in the sundry temperance organizations" (p. 59).

The historical record has been tainted by the false memory of these prohibitionists, but not everyone associated with those early days of the reform effort forgot Frances Willard's visit to Texas. Eben L. Dohoney, Willard's champion in Paris, Texas, outlived many of his contemporaries, and he became something of an anachronism among prohibitionists. His unorthodox religion, his support for female suffrage, and his willingness to abandon the Democratic Party left him too vulnerable for prohibitionist leaders to risk close association with him. Long before he died he was referred to in temperance histories and tracts in the past tense; he was commended primarily for his work with the 1876 Texas constitution and was designated the "Father of Texas Local Option" for his effort. But in 1903, Dohoney published a book in which he included the text of a letter that he reported receiving from Frances Willard in December 1899. Willard had been dead for nearly two years, but the communication was accomplished through the offices of a California medium. The letter praises his latest book, wishing for it "the commendation of the world," and recalls their work together in the cause of temperance. "We labored under great difficulties; it was not a bed of roses," the letter continues, "and though the numbers were few, good seed was sown." Dohoney cherished his part in that labor, but neither he nor Willard received much credit for the harvest.[32]

---

[32] Ivy, *Rum on the Run in Texas*, 24; Eben Lafayette Dohoney, *The Constitution of Man in the Physical, Psychical and Spiritual Worlds* (Denver, Colo.: Reed Publishing Co., 1903), 217–218 (quotations).

In 1914, the Texas W.C.T.U. voted Dohoney a life member, but the goodwill of the occasion was marred slightly by a dispute between Dohoney and the organization's designated historian, Fannie Armstrong, regarding the dates of Willard's visit and the establishment of the state union. A later work by the state historian of the Texas W.C.T.U. reported a third date. Dohoney had it right. E. L. Dohoney to Nannie Curtis, Texas Woman's Christian Temperance Union Scrapbook (CAH); Baines, *A Story of Texas White Ribboners*, 23.

# The Blizzard of 1886 and Its Effect on the Range Cattle Industry in the Southern Plains

DAVID L. WHEELER*

*A natural disaster such as the Galveston hurricane and flood of 1900 is a well-remembered historical experience, for the loss of human life made it a tragedy that cannot and should not be forgotten. Another natural disaster, the blizzard of 1886, is rarely remembered, for there were few human casualties, but it too affected the lives of thousands, brought bankruptcy and ruin to many, and permanently altered the practices of an entire industry.*

*In the 1880s the Great Plains, which extend from West Texas northward to Canada, were an open range where ranchers maintained huge cattle herds, a total of perhaps 2,500,000 head. A land with few natural boundaries, the only barriers dividing the plains were "drift" fences built to keep cattle from roaming too far, not to contain the animals in a particular location. There were ample signs that ranchers of the plains were producing too much beef on limited resources of a fragile land. But most cattlemen were confident and optimistic.*

*Overproduction and overgrazing would have surely challenged the optimism of the industry in time, but a natural disaster intervened and brought it to an end. For three days, January 6–9, 1886, a blizzard bearing some of the lowest temperatures ever recorded in Texas swept with high winds, snow, and ice across the center of North America. The waters of Galveston Bay froze; Austin recorded temperatures of 6.5 degrees below zero; and across the cattle country of the high plains, cattle died by the tens, probably hundreds, of thousands.*

*David L. Wheeler, "The Blizzard of 1886 and Its Effect on the Range Cattle Industry in the Southern Plains," *Southwestern Historical Quarterly*, 94 (Jan., 1991), 415–432. The research for this study was made possible by grants from Ball State University and the National Endowment for the Humanities Travel to Collections Program. The assistance of David J. Murrah, Director, Southwest Collection, who offered suggestions on the manuscript, and Mr. and Mrs. H. R. Fulton, Jr., Canyon, Texas, is gratefully acknowledged. An abbreviated account of this research was presented at the annual meeting of the Texas State Historical Association on March 4, 1989.

***Although the exact number of cattle that perished in the storm is unknown, the losses were severe enough to leave many ranchers bankrupt and to cause others who survived their losses to change their practices. Abandoning their dependence on the open range, they adopted a more conservative system of ranching, with smaller herds, fenced pastures, and improved care. Thus ended one of the more romantic episodes in the history of Texas.***

***The book gives little thought to romanticism, but E. E. Dale,* The Range Cattle Industry *(Norman: University of Oklahoma Press, 1930), remains the most useful source for information on the days of the open range.***

The seasonably mild weather on Wednesday, January 6, 1886, came as welcome relief to the young people preparing for a dance that evening at the Merchant's Hotel in Larned, Kansas. In the aftermath of the season's first storm on January 2, the weather was "settled" now, even "pleasant" with a soft, southerly breeze. If an angry cloud was seen scowling on the northern horizon no one made note of it in anticipation of the evening's revelry. The dance was in full swing when, around 9 P.M., the breeze shifted to the northwest, accelerated in velocity, and filled the air with snow. No one paid attention. By midnight, when the dance ended, snow drifts closed the streets. Swirling snow blinded the eyes and filled the lungs of those who dared to leave. The dance-goers had no alternative but to remain in the hotel for the night. Not until midday on January 7, during a respite in the storm, did anyone venture from the hotel, through enormous drifts, to the comparative safety of home.[1]

The storm stranding dancers in Larned, Kansas, began as cold, dry air settling on frozen land between the Canadian Rockies and Hudson Bay. Devoid of moisture and heavy, the air gripped the earth's surface, accumulating in a high pressure mass of "noteworthy" proportions before spilling out and flowing over the frozen ground. The overflow moved with inexorable force toward a low pressure system forming over the lower Rio Grande Valley.[2] A powerful stream of air aloft intensified the mass of high pressure and, inevitably, swept it east across the country. Fair weather preceded the rapidly moving air. A blizzard and a cold wave followed.

Before noon on January 6, it was apparent at the Signal Office in Washington City, the nation's capital, that an unprecedented cold wave was

---

[1]*Chronoscope* (Larned), Jan. 9, 1936; O. P. Beyers, "Personal Recollections of the Terrific Blizzard of 1886," in George W. Martin (ed.), *Collections: Kansas State Historical Society, 1911–1912*, XII (Topeka: State Printing Office, 1912), 110 (1st and 2nd quotations); *Irrigator* (Garden City), Jan. 16, 1886; *Chronoscope* (Larned), Jan. 9, 1936.

[2]*Monthly Weather Review* (Washington City: Signal Office, Jan., 1886), 4.

descending the Great Plains. The first of seventeen warnings and cold wave signals was dispatched to weather observers in the storm's track:

> Washington City, January 6, 1886, 4:45 P.M. To observers, Cheyenne, Wyoming; North Platte, Nebraska; Yankton, Dakota; Denver, Colorado; Dodge City, Kansas; Omaha, Nebraska; Concordia, Kansas; Leavenworth, Kansas (repeating to Wellington); Kansas City postmaster, and dispatcher Fort Scott and Gulf Railway; Lamar, Missouri:
>
> Hoist cold wave signal. Cold wave, accompanied by a "norther"; temperature will fall from 20 to 25 degrees in the next twenty-four hours at western and northern stations, and in twenty-four to thirty-six hours at southern stations.
>
> Hazen[3]

The leading edge of the cold wave was marked by a turbulent cloud accompanied by blowing sand and freezing drizzle that turned to sleet and then to driving snow. By the time the first cold wave warning reached weather observers, a blizzard extended over west Kansas and, with gale force winds, hurtled toward Indian Territory and the panhandle plains of Texas. Life and livestock throughout the plains were in grave danger from exposure to the snow and cold.[4]

With the storm's onslaught, cattle on the open range turned tail and drifted before the wind. Any obstacle in the path of drift cattle was a potential death trap. Snow-filled draws, rivers and waterholes, railroad cuts and ditches, and especially fences were instruments of destruction. Thousands of cattle were drowned, trampled, suffocated, frozen, or starved. Entire herds were lost. Cattle companies were ruined. The storm, in a single stroke, lay prostrate an industry doomed of its own excesses.

In the years following the Civil War the range cattle industry began to attract the attention of investors in the United States and Europe, especially Scotland and England. An increase in the population of the United States and a shortage of cattle created a demand for beef that could not be met by high-cost producers in the Midwest. Buyers turned attention to the Southwest where, during the war years, cattle left undisturbed on the range multiplied in considerable numbers. The range business in the Southwest required little more than a ranch, a few cowboys, and cattle. Public lands were available for grazing and, in winter, cattle required neither supplemental feed nor shelter. Production costs were low, profit margins were high. The cattle had only to be rounded up,

---

[3]Ibid., 2 (quotation), 3. Brigadier and Brevet Major General W. B. Hazen was chief signal officer of the army under whose direction the *Monthly Weather Review* was prepared.

[4]*Monthly Weather Review* (Washington City: Signal Office, Jan., 1886), 28; Ibid., 3; *Globe Live Stock Journal* (Dodge City), Jan. 12, 1886.

driven to the nearest railhead, and shipped to markets in Kansas City, St. Louis, or Chicago.[5]

By 1880 the range cattle industry entered a boom phase in its development. Improvements in refrigeration and shipping provided access to international markets and led to steadily rising prices for western beef. By 1882 prices achieved levels "rarely before reached in the history of the trade." Range cattle that sold at seven dollars a head only a few years before now brought twenty-five dollars. At the same time cattle companies were being formed at an accelerating rate and, within a few years, forty to fifty million dollars were invested in the industry. There was a widespread belief among many investors that "no other business is so safe nor so profitable as cattle-raising in the Far West."[6]

The beef bonanza resulted in "a fever of excitement" that became "almost a craze." Banks extended unlimited credit for investment in cattle. "Heavy loans" were made to investors at monthly interest rates of 1.5 or 2 percent. Large sums of money were entrusted to inexperienced or incompetent management. Herds were bought and sold on book count, a procedure in which estimates were made of the number of cattle based on an assumed rate of natural increase, calves branded, sales, and losses. This procedure expedited sales and was believed to be less stressful on cattle than an actual head count. In many instances, however, the rate of increase was overestimated and the losses were underestimated leading to "transactions . . . in which thousands of dollars changed hands over cattle herds which were purely fictitious."[7]

The boom in the cattle industry led to a rapid occupation of ranges and, by 1885, the ranges were stocked beyond their capacity to sustain the herds grazing on them. The increasingly speculative nature of the business, the desire for rapid and high returns on capital invested, led to the exploitation, indeed, to the destruction of the range and to the ruin of many investors. Even when the

---

[5]Edward Everett Dale, *The Range Cattle Industry* (Norman: University of Oklahoma Press, 1930), 94; Herbert O. Brayer, "The Influence of British Capital on the Western Range Cattle Industry," *Journal of Economic History,* IX (1949), 89; Tad Moses, "Development of the Cattle Business in Texas," *Texas Almanac and State Industrial Guide, 1949–1950* (Dallas: A. H. Belo, 1949), 258–259.

[6]Dale, *The Range Cattle Industry,* 90, 122–125; James Cox, *Historical and Biographical Record of the Cattle Industry and the Cattlemen of Texas and Adjacent Territory* (St. Louis: Woodward and Tiernan Publishing Co., 1895), 139 (1st quotation); H. R. Hilton, "Influence of Climate and Climatic Change Upon the Cattle Industry of the Plains," in *Report of the Kansas State Board of Agriculture, March 31, 1888* (Topeka: Kansas Publishing House, 1888), 144; Moses, "Development of the Cattle Business in Texas," 265; Walter Baron von Richthofen, *Cattle-Raising on the Plains of North America* (New York: D. Appleton and Co., 1885), 98 (2nd quotation).

[7]Dale, *The Range Cattle Industry,* 96 (1st and 2nd quotations), 97 (3rd quotation), 125; Richard Graham, "The Investment Boom in British-Texan Cattle Companies, 1880–1885," *Business History Review,* XXXIV (Winter, 1960), 424–425; Paul I. Wellman, *The Trampling Herd* (New York: J. B. Lippincott Co., 1939), 301 (4th quotation).

end of the boom was near, many held firm in the belief that the range cattle industry would continue to ensure the safety and the profitability of their investment. Only in retrospect did cattle interests realize they had bet their fortunes against "God Almighty and a sub-Arctic winter."[8]

The antecedents of the disaster originated in a series of events beginning in the winter of 1880–1881. It was a hard winter throughout the Great Plains, temperatures were substantially below normal and blizzards alternated with cold rains. Cattle drifted far from their home ranges with nothing to impede their progress until they reached the breaks, the rugged, broken ground along the Canadian and Red rivers in the Texas Panhandle. Thousands of cattle from Kansas, Nebraska, Colorado—even Wyoming—drifted in with each succeeding storm. Cowboys were unable to drive out the intruders. Cattle bunched up in sheltered places along the rivers nearly wiping out the winter pasture of local herds. In spring, outfits from the Beaver, Cimarron, Arkansas, and Platte river country joined the roundup on the Canadian. Panhandle cattlemen were determined that local pastures should not be imperiled again.[9]

The Panhandle Stock Raisers Association, at a meeting held in Mobeetie, Texas, resolved to string drift fences across the northern line of each member's range, or holding, to halt the encroachment of storm-driven cattle from the plains above them. Some fences were strung cooperatively by association members whose ranges were adjacent; others were strung by independent cattlemen. Fences thirty to forty miles in length were not uncommon, and a few were much longer. Each cattleman fenced where he thought best and, while the fences did not always connect, they usually overlapped to an extent that made them virtually impassable.[10]

---

[8]*The Western Range,* Doc. 199, 74th Cong., 2nd Sess., 1936 (Serial 10005), 119, 123 (quotation); Dale, *The Range Cattle Industry,* 131; Graham, "The Investment Boom in British-Texan Cattle Companies," 442.

[9]James W. Freeman, *Prose and Poetry of the Livestock Industry of the United States* (Denver and Kansas City: National Livestock Historical Association, 1904 and 1905), 703; O. H. Nelson to J. Evetts Haley, Feb. 26, 1927, interview file (Panhandle-Plains Historical Museum, Canyon, Tex.; cited hereafter as PPHM); Ray Allen Billington, *Westward Expansion: A History of the American Frontier* (New York: The MacMillan Company, 1949), 682; Arrell M. Gibson, "Ranching on the Southern Great Plains," *Journal of the West,* VI (Jan., 1967), 145–146; J. Evetts Haley, *Charles Goodnight: Cowman & Plainsman* (Norman: University of Oklahoma Press, 1949), 320–321.

[10]Nelson to Haley, Feb. 26, 1927; interview file (PPHM); Henry D. McCallum and Frances T. McCallum, *The Wire that Fenced the West* (Norman: University of Oklahoma Press, 1965), 130–131. For a general discussion of Texas drift fences see Roy D. Holt, "Barbed Wire Drift Fences," *The Cattleman,* XXI (Mar., 1935), 17–21. Charles Goodnight strung a "sixty-mile drift fence from the edge of the Plains, near the Armstrong County line, along the divide between Salt Fork and Mulberry, to Coleman and Dyer's Shoe Bar range on the east. When connected with the Shoe Bar fence, which ran east by south to near the site of Memphis, it was a hundred miles long." Haley, *Charles Goodnight: Cowman & Plainsman,* 321–322 (quotation).

Fence construction began in 1881. When completed in 1885, the fences extended from near the site of Higgins, Texas, west to the vicinity of Dalhart, and on into New Mexico, a straight-line distance of about two hundred miles. In the severe winter of 1884–1885, the drift fences saved Canadian River pastures from certain destruction. The fences were strung on the open ground above the Canadian River across the northern range lines of the Box T, Seven K, Bar C's, Turkey Track, Flying T, LX, LIT, LS, and LE. Fences were thrown across southern range lines also, to prevent local cattle from drifting beyond home ranges. The fences formed, in the words of a contemporary observer, "a clear cut line which admits of no argument. . . ."[11]

Before barbed wire, cattle drifted freely in winter storms or summer droughts. The cattle continued to drift until conditions changed or a barrier halted their progress. Cowboys followed to round up the drifting herds and drive them back to home ranges. If grass were available, cattle might even graze their way home. When barbed wire came into use, however, cattle drifting in winter storms piled up along fence lines "standing six and ten deep in rows as far as the eye can reach." The cattle could not go forward and would not turn into the storm. Huddled together cold and gaunt, and crowded by successive waves drifting in upon them, a "die-up" of catastrophic proportions was a grim possibility.[12]

The drift fences denied access to Canadian River pastures to all but local cattle. With burgeoning herds and range so scarce "a man cannot find a place to graze a goose," cattlemen in Texas and Kansas were attracted to abundant pastures in the Indian Territory. In 1883, a number of Texas cattlemen succeeded in obtaining leases on more than three million acres from Cheyenne and Arapaho Indians at $62,000 a year for ten years. This agreement enabled other cattlemen to negotiate leases opening Indian lands to large numbers of

---

[11]Thomas S. Bugbee to J. Evetts Haley, July 17 and 18, 1925, interview file (PPHM); A. L. Turner to J. Evetts Haley, July 2, 1926, interview, ibid.; Holt, "Barbed Wire Drift Fences," 18; McCallum and McCallum, *The Wire that Fenced the West,* 131; *Breeders Gazette,* Jan. 10, 1884, quoted in Ernest S. Osgood, *The Day of the Cattleman* (Chicago: University of Chicago Press, Phoenix Books, 1960), 191, 193 (quotation); Angie Debo (ed.), *The Cowman's Southwest: Reminiscences of Oliver Nelson . . .* (Glendale, Calif.: Arthur Clark Co., 1953), 230–231; Haley, *Charles Goodnight: Cowman & Plainsman,* 321; Vas Stickley to J. Evetts Haley, July 20, 1926, interview file (PPHM); J. Evetts Haley, "And Then Came Barbed Wire to Change History's Course," *The Cattleman,* XIII (Mar., 1927), 82; Clinton Leon Paine, "The History of Lipscomb County" (M.A. thesis, West Texas State Teachers College, 1941), 27–28; George Rainey, *No Man's Land: The Historic Study of a Landed Orphan* (Guthrie, Okla.: Cooperative Publishing Co., 1937), 99; M. Huffman to J. Evetts Haley, Nov. 30, 1927, interview in *The XIT Ranch: As Remembered By Its Cowboys,* III (H-M), 19 (Nita Stewart Haley Memorial Library, Midland, Tex.); Dallas *Morning News,* Nov. 29, 1885.

[12]*Daily Drovers Journal* (Chicago), Feb. 8, 1886 (quotation); Edward E. Dale, "The History of the Ranch Cattle Industry in Oklahoma," *Annual Report, American Historical Association* (Washington, D.C.: Government Printing Office, 1920), 314.

cattle. Inevitably, disputes arose over the destruction of cultivated land by wayward herds, the loss of Indian cattle, and the theft of horses. Relations between Indians and stockmen reached a low point in May 1884 when a Cheyenne was murdered in a confrontation with a Texan who was unlawfully driving horses through the territory. As a consequence, an uprising was feared. It became apparent a solution to the problem could not be obtained with cattlemen occupying land that had been reserved for the exclusive use of Indians.[13]

On July 23, 1885, Grover Cleveland issued a presidential proclamation declaring the leases invalid and ordering cattlemen to remove all stock from the Cheyenne-Arapaho reservation within forty days. The proclamation was vigorously opposed by cattlemen occupying leases in the territory. On August 4, cattlemen in the Cherokee Strip stated their opposition to the proclamation in a memorial to the president. They were opposed not so much because they were being forced to abandon their leases but because of the brief amount of time given to do so. A spokesman for the cattlemen requested the time allowed be extended to the following spring, but Cleveland was adamant. Furthermore, Gen. Philip H. Sheridan was ordered to the Indian Territory to put down any disturbance that might arise and to ensure obedience to the proclamation.[14]

There were about 210,000 cattle on the Cheyenne-Arapaho reservation when Sheridan arrived. Including cattle on other reservations in the territory, it was estimated up to four hundred thousand head had to be removed. Cattlemen did not believe it possible to remove so many cattle in so short a time but there was no alternative other than to obey the proclamation with Sheridan

---

[13]*Texas Live Stock Journal* (Ft. Worth), Sept. 30, 1882 (quotation). In 1884, the Cheyenne and Arapaho were paid $77,351.60 to lease their land, an amount equal to about two cents per acre or an average of $12.33 per capita. The total paid for leases on all Indian lands in the territory was $107,891.60. *The Range and Ranch Cattle Business of the United States,* H. Exec. Doc. 7, 48th Cong., 2nd Sess., 1885 (Serial 2295), pt. 3: 109–110; *Annual Report of the Lieutenant-General of the Army,* H. Exec. Doc. 1, 49th Cong., 1st Sess., 1885 (Serial 2369), pt. 2: 67; David J. Murrah, "C. C. Slaughter: The Cattle King of Texas" (Ph.D. diss., Texas Tech University, 1979), 147–148; Dale, "The History of the Ranch Cattle Industry in Oklahoma," 315.

[14]Prohibiting Unlawful Grazing in Indian Territory, July 23, 1885, Statutes at Large of the United States of America, from December 1885 to March 1887, and Recent Treaties, Postal Conventions, and Executive Proclamations. Proclamation No. 1, July 23, 1885, Vol. 24, 49th Cong. (Washington, D.C.: Government Printing Office, 1887), 1023; *Daily Drovers Journal* (Chicago), July 23, 1885; Cox, *Historical and Biographical Record of the Cattle Industry,* 131–133; *Daily Drovers Journal* (Chicago), July 24, 1885; Dale, "The History of the Ranch Cattle Industry in Oklahoma," 315. Sheridan confirmed the source of the difficulty was the leasing of Indian land and the presence of whites, many of whom were not authorized to be in the territory. *Annual Report of the Lieutenant-General,* H. Exec. Doc. 1, 49th Cong., 1st Sess., 1885, pt. 2: 66. Donald J. Berthrong says "200 men . . . roamed over the reservation at will. In addition, 160 cowboys employed by the cattle companies, seventy agency employees, fifty-five Ft. Reno employees, and twenty-one squawmen lived on the Indian lands." Donald J. Berthrong, "Cattlemen on the Cheyenne-Arapaho Reservation, 1883–1885," *Arizona and the West,* XIII (1971), 29.

there to enforce it. The greater problem was where to move the cattle since nearby ranges were overstocked, and in Kansas, Colorado, and New Mexico quarantines were hostile to the passage of cattle before December 1. By then the season would be too advanced to drive herds to northern ranges eight hundred to twelve hundred miles away. Consequently, most of the cattle were thrown on overstocked ranges in Texas or Kansas or sold at a loss on a market, at the time, depressed by drought in the southern plains and the Midwest. In September, fifty thousand to seventy-five thousand cattle remained on the Cheyenne-Arapaho reservation but these were removed by early November.[15]

The autumn of 1885 was unseasonably mild and, after September rain, it became increasingly dry. The weather facilitated the removal of cattle from the Indian Territory, but it increased the danger of grass fires. By November, the grass was so dry it might be ignited easily by an errant spark or a lightning strike. Precautions were taken to protect pastures by plowing fireguards parallel to fence lines. In early November the XIT assembled a crew to plow a fireguard around a pasture fence in the Texas Panhandle. One day while the crew was at work, a spark from a campfire caught the grass nearby and quickly spread beyond the cook's ability to contain it. The fire widened along a twenty-mile front creating a "vast cloud of smoke" seen by LS cowboys branding calves on Alamosa Creek. The fire is said to have burned for two days and two nights destroying an enormous amount of grass in the Panhandle and No Man's Land. Later it was believed the fire broke out in the Arkansas River country of western Kansas. Swept by sixty-mile-an-hour winds, the fire sped south, leaped the Cimarron at a narrows on the 101 range, burned No Man's Land, and entered the panhandle plains of Texas west of Buffalo Springs. The fire continued beyond the Canadian, finally burning out along the Red River.[16]

---

[15] *Annual Report of the Lieutenant-General,* H. Exec. Doc. 1, 49th Cong., 1st Sess., 1885, pt. 2: 69; Dale, "The History of the Ranch Cattle Industry in Oklahoma," 315; Debo (ed.), *The Cowman's Southwest,* 240; Cox, *Historical and Biographical Record of the Cattle Industry,* 131–133; *Daily Drovers Journal* (Chicago), July 24, 1885; *Tribune* (Greeley), July 29, 1885; Berthrong, "Cattlemen on the Cheyenne-Arapaho Reservation, 1883–1885," 30; *Tribune* (Greeley), July 29, 1885; Billington, *Westward Expansion,* 685; Murrah, "C. C. Slaughter: The Cattle King of Texas," 148–149; Lewis Nordyke, *Great Roundup: The Story of Texas and Southwestern Cowmen* (New York: William Morrow and Co., 1955), 166; *Journal* (Coffeyville), Sept. 12, 1885; Berthrong, "Cattlemen on the Cheyenne-Arapaho Reservation," 31. According to Dale, "the beginning of the decline in the prosperity of the ranch cattle industry can be quite definitely placed at the summer and autumn of 1885, though it was not until 1887 that conditions had become so bad as to show almost universal distress throughout the entire cow country." Dale, *The Range Cattle Industry,* 144–145, 146 (quotation). Dale says, also, some cattle removed from the territory eventually drifted back and it was not until 1892 that the last of them were removed. Ibid., 146.

[16] Both Dodge City, Kansas and Fort Elliott, Texas, reported temperatures 6.4°F above the mean and precipitation 50 percent to 75 percent below the mean for November. *Monthly Weather Review* (Washington City: Signal Office, Nov., 1885), 286; Dulcie Sullivan, *The LS Brand: The Story of*

Whatever its origin the fire, or fires, consumed much of the grass in the Texas Panhandle and northeastern New Mexico. It is reported that one hundred thousand head of cattle were driven away from the fire, but the XIT lost a million acres of grass including the Buffalo Springs range; the LE lost thirty miles of fence on its range along the Canadian and, in one pasture, a substantial number of cattle were believed to have perished. According to Charles Goodnight, the fire

> extended . . . a distance of 150 miles across the panhandle above and west of me. Nearly all of the country between me and New Mexico was burned. It extended southwest and west, burning to the New Mexico line and a great extent of the country on both sides of the Canadian River. The grass on one entire ranch was utterly destroyed. It came in my direction and got into my pasture [burning 200 sections].[17]

The Indian Territory was not spared the conflagration. In the middle of November, a fire burned a strip of grass forty to sixty miles wide causing damage estimated at $400, 000. The fire was reported to have originated near Wild Horse Creek and to have burned an area extending from forty miles north of Red River to twelve miles west of Red River Station. The fire destroyed "a vast amount of grass" on the Kiowa, Comanche, and Apache reservations scattering cattle and, in places, burning the range "clean as a whistle." Nearly all of the country between Fort Sill and the Wichita Agency was burned, and reports declared "not a blade of grass [was] left on the Cheyenne Reservation."[18] The range had been consumed and, in the event of a hard winter, there was not enough grass to sustain all the cattle in need of it.

---

*a Texas Panhandle Ranch* (Austin: University of Texas Press, 1968), 93 (quotation); J. Evetts Haley, *The XIT Ranch of Texas and the Early Days of the Llano Estacado* (Norman: University of Oklahoma Press, 1967), 172–173; J. Evetts Haley, "Grassfires of the Southern Plains," *West Texas Historical Association Year Book,* V (June, 1929), 30–32; M. Huffman to J. Evetts Haley, Nov. 30, 1927, interview, in *The XIT Ranch: As Remembered By Its Cowboys,* III (H-M), 28; *Daily Optic* (Las Vegas), Dec. 7, 1885. Other sources speculate the fire began on the XIT range. Howard Wright to J. Evetts Haley, Jan. 16, 1927, interview, in *Panhandle Notes,* II (L-W), 246 (Nita Stewart Haley Memorial Library, Midland, Tex.); Wellman, *The Trampling Herd,* 290–292; A. W. Thompson, "Fire, Then Snow, Wrought Destruction on the Llano Estacado," *News-Globe* (Amarillo), Aug. 14, 1938.

[17] *Journal* (Coffeyville), Nov. 7, 1885; Dallas *Morning News,* Nov. 16, 1885; *Daily Optic* (Las Vegas), Dec. 7, 1885; *Daily Drovers Journal* (Chicago), Nov. 24, 1885; Haley, *The XIT Ranch of Texas,* 80, 81, 173; M. Huffman to J. Evetts Haley, Nov. 30, 1927, interview, in *The XIT Ranch: As Remembered By Its Cowboys,* III (H-M), 29; Dallas *Morning News,* Jan. 7, 1886. About a week after this fire a pasture belonging to the Franklyn Land and Cattle Company in the Texas Panhandle was reported to have been destroyed in a fire accidentally ignited while some men were burning grass around a haystack. *Daily Drovers Journal* (Chicago), Nov. 26, 1885. In late December, according to J. Evetts Haley, another grass fire burned a hundred square miles of the south plains. Haley, *The XIT Ranch of Texas,* 87.

[18] *Free Press* (Caldwell), Nov. 21, 1885; *Daily Drovers Journal* (Chicago), Nov. 24, 1885; *Monthly Weather Review* (Washington City: Signal Office, Nov., 1885), 288; Dallas *Morning News,* Nov. 26, 1885 (1st–3rd quotations). Grass fires were a frequent occurrence with sightings reported in the vicinity of Fort Sill on November 1, 3, 4, 7, and 9–12, and near Fort Supply on November 3, 5, 10, 15, and 19. *Monthly Weather Review* (Washington City: Signal Office, Nov., 1885), 288.

In 1880 there was a perception among stockmen and others that climate in the southern plains favored unlimited expansion in the range cattle industry. While the summers might be capricious, winters were open and invigorating. Precipitation appeared to be following the march of the farmer's plow into the plains and, indeed, between 1875 and 1885 much of the plains received above average rainfall. Many interpreted this phenomenon as a change in climate ensuring abundant pastures and economic prosperity. A contemporary observer proclaimed there was "not the slightest element of uncertainty in cattle-raising" on the plains.[19]

At first the range was open and free, and often a portion was reserved for winter pasture. Cattle were driven onto winter pastures in the fall while summer grazing grounds lay at rest. As the number of cattle increased, however, the carrying capacity of the range decreased. By the summer of 1885 the range was so crowded winter pastures were in use and cattle went into the cold on ranges grazed summer and fall. Formerly cattle might have been driven to distant pastures to relieve the crowding, but now virtually all were overstocked, quarantined, or clearly delineated by fences.[20]

Many cattlemen failed to realize that their continued prosperity, their very existence, was inextricably bound to the physical environment of the plains. The pursuit of personal fortune, the ephemeral nature of land tenure on the plains, and the competition for grass led to exploitation of the range. Few appear to have questioned the assertion, "the beef business cannot be overdone" and continued to stock the range as though there was no limit to its capacity to carry the herds grazing on it. Pastures that could have sustained "a cow on every 40 acres had one on every 10 acres." Even if the winter of 1885–1886 had remained open, heavy losses from starvation and exposure were likely to have occurred. Some cattlemen would have been able to hold on, but in the weather on the plains they were dealing with an element they did not understand and could not control. Too late they learned "an overstocked range must bleed when the blizzards sit in judgement."[21]

---

[19]In the last half of the 1880s, however, precipitation was below average with the years 1885–1887 being particularly dry. Robert Claiborne, *Climate, Man and History* (New York: W. W. Norton and Co., Inc., 1970), 389. Billington, *Western Expansion,* 808; Ralph H. Brown, *Historical Geography of the United States* (New York: Harcourt, Brace, and Co., 1948), 422; von Richthofen, *Cattle-Raising on the Plains,* 59 (quotation).

[20]*Third Annual Report of the Bureau of Animal Industry, for the Year 1886,* H. Misc. Doc. 156, 49th Cong., 2nd Sess., 1887 (Serial 2493), 107; T. A. McNeal, *When Kansas Was Young* (Topeka: Capper Publications, 1934), 160.

[21]Dale, *The Range Cattle Industry,* 130–131; James S. Brisbin, *The Beef Bonanza; or How to Get Rich on the Plains . . .* (1881; reprint, Norman: University of Oklahoma Press, 1959), 49 (1st quotation); *The Western Range,* S. Doc. 199, 74th Cong., 2nd Sess., 1936, p. 123 (2nd quotation); Osgood, *The Day of the Cattleman,* 193.

December came. Weather forecasts, based on the "conjunction of planets," were reported by the Coffeyville *Journal* to be "setting up 1886 for us and predict it will be an old rip-snorter, the worst season in all respects since Washington crossed the Delaware." Yet the season continued mild. All weather stations along the middle and southern slopes of the Rocky Mountains recorded temperatures well above their monthly means. The St. Jo Weekly *Times* reported the season was

> as remarkably mild as last winter was unusually severe. A year ago the stock over the country was dying with cold, starvation, and disaster. This season the cattle and horses are generally in fine condition, and the prospects of perhaps ninety-five hundredths of them going through to spring seems a safe one.

With the promise of an open winter at hand, there did not appear to be any need for cattlemen to retain the usual complement of cowboys to tend the herds.[22]

The New Year began as the old one ended: clear, bright, and mild. It was a splendid day for a baseball game between teams from the neighboring towns of Ness City and Bazine in west Kansas. As the day progressed, however, a "peculiar yellowish-purple bordering the northern horizon" was increasingly visible to player and spectator alike. About 4 P.M., the wind shifted to the northwest bringing rain, then snow, and ending further activity out-of-doors. By 10 P.M., eight inches of snow were on the ground, and ten to twelve inches had accumulated at Spearville east of Dodge City. A "howling gale" whipped the snow, obscuring objects only a few feet away. By morning, the temperature had dropped to $-18^{\circ}$ F.[23] The force of the blizzard gradually diminished and by Tuesday, January 5, the west Kansas weather was settled once again. Wednesday was a "beautiful day," perhaps better than could have been hoped for the dance that evening at the Merchant's Hotel in Larned.

The beautiful weather was the result of a rapidly developing high pressure system. By January 6, the system had so increased in magnitude as to leave no doubt in the minds of weather observers in Washington City of the imminent approach of a cold wave. Late that afternoon the first warnings and cold wave signals were issued while even then the leading edge of the storm system knifed into Kansas.

Within hours west Kansas was in the midst of "as fine a specimen of a blizzard . . . as anyone would wish to see." Gale force winds slammed Dodge City,

---

[22]*Journal* (Coffeyville), Nov. 7, 1885; *Monthly Weather Review* (Washington City: Signal Office, Dec, 1885), 311; *Weekly Times* (Saint Jo), Jan. 3, 1886.

[23]"Blizzards," in *Clippings Book*, 2, 1935–1962 (Topeka: Kansas State Historical Society), n.p.

swirling snow reduced visibility to a "rod," and the temperature dropped rapidly, reaching $-16.2°$ F. In the aftermath of the blizzard, one observer remarked:

> If snow has a commercial value by adding fertility to the soil and hard freezing weather insures a bountiful harvest, the destiny of southwestern Kansas is fixed and her success assured beyond doubt.[24]

Heavy snows, high winds, and low temperatures descended on the southern plains. At Fort Supply, in the Indian Territory, fifty-mile-an-hour winds piled a "blinding fall of snow" into "huge" drifts; ice formed to a depth of eleven inches. Two to three feet of snow accumulated at Buffalo Springs in the Texas Panhandle blocking the road to Trinidad, New Mexico, for a month. The wind velocity at Fort Elliott in the eastern Panhandle reached fifty-eight miles an hour on January 7; the temperature huddled near $-10°$ F the day after. As the storm system swept toward the Gulf of Mexico, weather observers in Central and South Texas recorded the coldest known temperatures: $-7°$ F at Dublin, $-6.5°$ F at Sarnotz' drug store in Austin, and 0° F at Palestine.[25]

In Galveston, at 1:20 P.M. on January 7, the temperature was 65° F. Late that afternoon the wind accelerated, a strong, northerly breeze becoming a fresh gale, and the temperature plunged with "unprecedented rapidity" to 11° F. Around 9 P.M. ice began to form on Galveston Bay and within two days it was frozen to a thickness of three to four inches. The freezing cold was followed by six inches of snow. Ice three inches thick covered ponds and bayous at Indianola; not even Brownsville was spared. The *Daily Drovers Journal* reported:

> The storm which swept over Texas . . . is without parallel in the history of Texas in its extent, severity, and duration. Intelligence from the cattle regions of the state are of the gloomiest and most depressing character. The loss in cattle will be great. . . . All water pools and streams are frozen over hard, and to add to the gravity of the situation . . . Texas, from the Sabine to the Rio Grande, and from the Red River to the Gulf is covered [with] snow.[26]

Every weather station in the Rio Grande Valley and Western Gulf States recorded monthly lows on January 8 or 9, some of the lowest ever. Record-

---

[24] *Globe Live Stock Journal* (Dodge City), Jan. 12, 1886 (1st quotation); *Monthly Weather Review* (Washington City: Signal Office, Jan., 1886), 3 (2nd quotation), 20. The Dodge City *Globe*, Jan. 12, 1886, reported a temperature of -20° F during the night of January 7. Carl Coke Rister, *No Man's Land* (Norman: University of Oklahoma Press, 1948), 51 (3rd quotation).

[25] *Monthly Weather Review* (Washington City: Signal Office, Jan. 1886), 3 (1st and 2nd quotations); Abner Taylor to John V. Farwell, Jan. 30, 1886, Abner Taylor Papers (PPHM); *Monthly Weather Review* (Washington City: Signal Office, Jan., 1886), 3, 15; Austin *Daily Statesman*, Jan. 9, 1886.

[26] *Monthly Weather Review* (Washington City: Signal Office, Jan., 1886), 3 (1st quotation), 10; *Daily Drovers Journal* (Chicago), Jan. 13, 1886.

breaking temperatures occurred throughout the storm's track. Monthly low temperatures were recorded at all forty-two weather stations in the Eastern Gulf States, Florida Peninsula, South Atlantic States, Middle Atlantic States, and New England before the storm disappeared over the ocean east of Nova Scotia on January 16.[27]

The snow and cold consternated people in the south and east but nowhere, perhaps, was anyone more affected by it or less prepared for it than cattlemen on the plains of Texas and Kansas. The Dickinson County *Chronicle* reported:

> In many respects it was the worst storm ever known on the plains and it came upon the people when they were illy-prepared for it. They were deceived, too, by the child-like and bland and banana-like weather of December that was almost "as pleasant as May." The peculiarity of the recent storm was its blinding force. . . . It was a storm of sand and snow and intense cold."[28]

In the winter of 1885–1886, there were about 2,500,000 cattle on ranges in west Kansas, the Indian Territory and Neutral Strip, and the Texas Panhandle. As the storm came upon them, cattle bunched up for protection. Then, instinctively, one after another they began to drift downwind, entire herds straggling in procession behind the leaders. Cattle tumbled into snow-filled coulees, cuts, and ditches, crashed into fences, and plunged through ice. The Arkansas, Cimarron, and Canadian rivers were full of cattle who, in attempting to cross, broke through the ice and drowned or, falling, were unable to stand and were trampled or frozen. Cattle piled up along fence lines, halted in their macabre procession by frail strands of barbed wire stretching interminably across the plains.[29]

For days they stood bewildered and benumbed at a right-of-way fence along the Santa Fe tracks in west Kansas while, "passengers looked out in pity at the line of cattle 200 miles long. . . ." It was said along the Union Pacific right-of-way, "one could have walked from Ellsworth [Kansas] to Denver, a distance of more than 400 miles, on the carcasses." Workmen labored "day and night" to clear dead cattle from a cut, where they had sought protection, before trains could pass between Wright, Kansas, and Dodge City.[30]

---

[27] *Monthly Weather Review* (Washington City: Signal Office, Jan., 1886), 2, 19.

[28] Dickinson County *Chronicle,* Feb. 12, 1886.

[29] *Globe Live Stock Journal* (Dodge City), Jan. 11, 1887; Dallas *Morning News,* Nov. 29, 1885; George B. Loving to Joseph Nimmo, Jr., Jan. 20, 1885, in Joseph Nimmo, Jr., *Report in Regard to the Range and Ranch Cattle Business of the United States* (Washington, D.C.: Government Printing Office, 1885), 102; *Daily Drovers Journal* (Chicago), Feb. 8, 1886.

[30] *Times* (Leavenworth), Dec. 30, 1928 (1st quotation); Beyers, *Collections: Kansas State Historical Society, 1911–1912,* 104 (2nd quotation); *News* (Garden City), Jan. 7, 1937 (3rd quotation).

There were places where heaps of dead cattle extended back from drift fences a mile and farther. A cowboy wrote of his approach to the drift fences in the Texas Panhandle:

> I began to run into dead stock, then more and more. . . . When within a mile or two of the fence, I actually ran into piles of them. I could have walked for miles on dead animals, stepping from one to another. These were mostly natives belonging to northern ranges which had drifted across the burned prairie. As long as they could travel, cattle kept alive. Finally, the drift fence halted them. Here they stopped . . . bunched close together as for a last protection, helplessly dropped in their tracks and froze.[31]

Attempts were made to cut fences to permit cattle to continue to drift. Cowboys from a number of outfits joined to cut sixty-five miles of fence between Taylor and Mosquero, New Mexico, to let cattle through to the relative protection of breaks nearby. A similar effort in the Texas Panhandle was less successful:

> Eleven of us camped on the [drift fence] in the winter of 1885 and1886. That was the worst winter I ever saw. The boys were from different outfits: two LS men, two ZH, two OI, two OX, and others. All but the LS men were sent down by the northern outfits to look after their cattle that drifted. We didn't do much good it was so damn cold.[32]

Occasionally, however, the piles of dead cattle were stacked so high along the fences succeeding waves of drift cattle could cross to the other side on the frozen carcasses and hard-packed snow. Sometimes the weight of cattle pressing on the fences broke them, allowing the drift to continue until the cattle dropped in exhaustion or encountered another fence less yielding than the first. Weeks later, a traveler from Kansas observed:

> As I drove over the prairie from Kansas into Texas I saw thousands upon thousands of carcasses of domestic cattle which had, "drifted" before the chilling, freezing, "norther." Everyone of them had died with its tail to the blizzard, never having stopped except at its last breath, then fell dead in its tracks.[33]

The number of cattle lost in the blizzard and its aftermath may never be known with certainty; in most instances, the losses were estimated. From west Kansas came the report entire herds were destroyed while total losses varied between 20 percent and 90 percent. It was reckoned fifty thousand dead cattle

---

[31]Thompson, "Fire, Then Snow Wrought Destruction on the Llano Estacado," *News-Globe* (Amarillo), Aug. 14, 1938.

[32]J. M. Wise to L. F. Sheffy, May 11, 1935, manuscript file (PPHM); A. L. Turner to J. Evetts Haley, July 2, 1926 (quotation), interview file, ibid.

[33]O. E. Enfield to Iva Henderson, July 28, 1938, interview file (PPHM); *Daily Drovers Journal* (Chicago), Feb. 8, 1886; Dallas *Morning News*, Jan. 21, 1886; Beyers, *Collections: Kansas State Historical Society, 1911–1912*, 109 (quotation).

littered the banks of the Arkansas and the railroad tracks in the vicinity of Dodge City. Within one hundred miles of Dodge City, one hundred thousand cattle were believed frozen dead on the plains. Between Dodge City and Pueblo, Colorado, 150, 000 cattle were thought to have perished.[34]

Heavy losses were reported in the Texas Panhandle, especially along the drift fences strung between the Indian Territory and New Mexico. Ed Brainard, wagon boss and foreman of the Bar C's in Roberts and Ochiltree counties, said the loss was 150,000 while the *Daily Drovers Journal* reported two hundred thousand. These estimates did not include cattle that may have perished on ranges at some distance on either side of the fences.[35]

The blizzard was indiscriminate, sparing neither large cattle companies nor small operators. Virtually every livestock producer in southwestern Kansas was bankrupted. When the weather settled, one ranch gathered five hundred head from a herd of fifty-five hundred; another found 182 remaining in a herd of six thousand. An outfit running cattle in No Man's Land rounded up but twenty-five hundred out of a herd of twenty thousand. In the panhandle plains of Texas, a herd of XIT cattle numbering between twenty thousand and twenty-three thousand was reported to have been reduced to a "vestige," though others thought the loss did not exceed 15 percent. The Bar C's threw a herd of eleven thousand southern cattle on its range in 1885 and rounded up eight hundred the following spring. The Quarter Circle Heart, in Donley County, Texas, closed down operations after sustaining losses of about 50 percent.[36]

Losses in New Mexico were reported to have been "nominal," while in Colorado they were said to have been limited to late arriving Texas cattle, especially those on ranges along the Arkansas River. There were various reports from the Indian Territory. The Dallas Morning *News* declared, "the storm has been the most disastrous to stock growing interests ever experienced in the Indian Territory," the losses being heavy in the Cherokee nation, the Cherokee Outlet, and in the Choctaw and Chickasaw nations. The January 16 Garden

[34] *Globe* (Dodge City), Jan. 26, 1886; *Globe Live Stock Journal* (Dodge City), Jan. 19, Feb. 16, 1886.

[35] *Daily News* (Amarillo), Apr. 24, 1941; Ochiltree County Historical Survey Committee, *Wheatheart of the Plains: An Early History of Ochiltree County* (n.p.: n.p., 1969), 26; *Daily Drovers Journal* (Chicago), Feb. 8, 1886. On ranges south on Mobeetie and Fort Elliott, for example, the mortality was first reported at 90 percent but later revised to 30 percent, still a heavy loss. *Daily Drovers Journal* (Chicago), Jan. 13, 1886.

[36] *Capital* (Topeka), Jan. 19, 1940; Wellman, *The Trampling Herd,* 307–308; Rister, *No Man's Land,* 52; Dallas *Morning News,* Jan. 28 (quotation), Feb. 12, 1886; W. Maud to Abner Taylor, Apr. 1886, Abner Taylor Papers (PPHM); Haley, *The XIT Ranch of Texas,* 79, 81; E. H. Brainard to J. Evetts Haley, July 19, 1926, interview file (PPHM); E. H. Brainard to T. D. Hobart, Timothy Dwight Hobart Collection, J A Correspondence, Apr. 5, 1930 (PPHM); Haley, *Charles Goodnight: Cowman & Plainsman,* 348.

City *Irrigator* stated, "thousands" of cattle lost on the Comanche and Wichita reservations. Five days later, the San Antonio *Daily Express* reported no serious losses on the Sac and Fox Reservation. A Kansas stockman running cattle in the Indian Territory wrote his wife:

> My misfortune is that I have lost half of my cattle in the Territory which is the same as $3,500 to me which I will think I am doing well to make that amount and consequently we will not feel like giving any nice dinners or take any excursions this year.[37]

Not only did reports vary on losses for all cattle but also among cattle native to the plains, "through" cattle brought up the trail from South Texas to winter on the range, and dogies. Early reports from the Texas Panhandle indicated 25 percent of the through cattle and dogies were dead, while losses among native range cattle south of the Canadian River were 1 percent or less. The difference was said to have been the result of native cattle going into the winter in good condition while through cattle arrived on the range late in the season and in so poor condition that many perished even before the onset of inclement weather. Skeptics believed losses reported among through cattle were a "slick scheme" and the numbers "cooked" either to promote the hardiness of North Texas cattle among foreign buyers or to force down cattle prices as a means of driving speculators out of business. "It is not possible," the *Texas Livestock Journal* reported, "that on the same range and under the same conditions for the one to be wiped out and the other to lose only one percent." No, through cattle losses were deliberately overstated to cover losses accumulating among native cattle for the past two winters, at least.[38]

Ranch managers on some ranges may have taken advantage of the weather, reporting heavy losses among their herds by bringing the estimated number of cattle, or book count, into line with the actual number, or head count. The 1886 annual report of the Hansford Land and Cattle Company (Turkey Track) stated the problems involved in attempting to establish a head count:

> The conditions under which cattle ranching is carried on in Texas upon the open prairie are such as to render it all but impossible to deal with exact figures, and it is only by careful comparison of results over a series of years that a fairly trustworthy basis can be reached. The shrinkage in numbers is to be explained by a probable original shortage, and the exceptionally heavy losses of the last two winters. When the company was formed in 1882 it was the general practice that herds were taken over

---

[37]Galveston *Daily News,* Jan. 13, 1886 (1st quotation); Dallas *Morning News,* Jan. 13, 1886; *Irrigator* (Garden City), Jan. 16, 1886; *Daily Express* (San Antonio), Jan. 21, 1886; Melville C. Campbell to wife, Mar. 4, 1886 (4th quotation), Miscellaneous M. C. Campbell Collection, Manuscripts Department (Kansas State Historical Society, Topeka, Kan.).

[38]Dallas *Morning News,* Jan. 31, Feb. 4 (2nd quotation), Feb. 12, 1886; *Daily Gazette* (Ft. Worth), Jan. 28, Feb. 23, Apr. 25 (3rd quotation), 1886; Austin *Daily Statesman,* Jan. 28, 1886; Galveston *Daily News,* Jan. 28, 1886; *Texas Live Stock Journal* (Ft. Worth), Feb. 6, 1886.

on book count, after confirmation inspection and reports by a competent cattleman appointed by the purchaser. It was not until later times that head to head counts became the custom, and even now there are few examples of such counts having been fully carried out. . . .[39]

Another indication of cattle losses is provided in reports on the number of carcasses skinned and hides gathered and sold. John Hollicut, manager of the LX range in Potter and Moore counties, Texas, said cowboys lifted hides from 250 cattle to the mile for thirty miles along one section of the panhandle drift fences. Simon LeBrecht, a dealer in Medicine Lodge, Kansas, bought forty thousand hides that year. In response to an appeal from the Texas Cattle Raisers Association, stockmen delivered hides to Dodge City where an estimate could be made of the loss. By June 1, 1886, more than four hundred thousand hides were delivered and there were thought to be thousands more rotting on the plains.[40]

The blizzard and its aftermath had a devastating impact on the open range system of cattle herding in the southern plains. There is little doubt, however, the system would have collapsed from other causes. For more than a decade cattle prices had been rising in response to an insatiable demand for beef in the United States and Europe. Favorable economic conditions accelerated formation of large, highly capitalized cattle companies throughout the Great Plains. Expectations for profit on investments were high, loans were extended at lofty rates of interest, and herds were bought and sold on the basis of book count but seldom actually tallied. So feverish did expansion become that most of the range land was occupied by 1883, virtually all of it by 1885.[41]

In December 1885, there was a sudden, sharp correction in cattle prices; the blizzard and a prolonged dry spell, which spread throughout the Great Plains and into the Midwest, contributed to the ensuing collapse. With depleted pastures, dry streams, and gaunt stock, cattlemen dumped the remnants of their herds on the market, selling at any price, rather than confront the uncertainty of another winter. Cattle fetching twenty-five or thirty dollars but a few months before could not find buyers at ten dollars or less. Cattlemen not ruined by the blizzard sold out or changed operations in order to survive.[42]

---

[39]Hansford Land and Cattle Company, Ltd., 4th Annual Report (Dundee, Scotland: Hansford Land and Cattle Company, Ltd., 1887), 4.

[40]Haley, "And Then Came Barbed Wire to Change History's Course," 83; McNeal, *When Kansas Was Young,* 161; *Capital* (Topeka), Jan. 19, 1940; *Clark County Clipper* (Ashland), Nov. 12, 1942.

[41]*The Western Range,* S. Doc. 199, 74th Cong., 2nd Sess., 1936, p. 119.

[42]Frances A. Alsup, "A History of the Panhandle of Texas" (M.A. thesis, University of Southern California, 1943), 112–113; Billington, *Westward Expansion,* 685; Dale, *The Range Cattle Industry,* 121–125.

The blizzard impressed on cattlemen the open range system of herding could not endure. In a game of chance with winter storms or summer droughts, cattlemen could no longer stand pat; "the trump cards [were] in the hands of the elements." The market collapse, the weather, the advance of homesteaders into the plains forced cattlemen to change their ways or to close down operations. Circumstances cattlemen were powerless to control had turned against unrestricted herding on the open range.[43]

Laws were enacted to prohibit the running of cattle on the range, to abolish illegal fencing, and to protect the rights of homesteaders. Ranges formerly grazed by wandering herds were divided and farms established. The settlement and development of homesteads had the effect of reducing the carrying capacity of the range "out of all proportion" to the land actually occupied. Drift fences came down and farm and field fences were erected in their stead. Barbed wire was used now to contain farm animals rather than to repulse drift herds. "Now is the time," the Garden City *Irrigator* reported, to "drive 'the lonesome cow on the wild prairie' into a good barn yard, couple her with a thoroughbred bull and if you take care of her a few years, she will not only appreciate the treatment but return you a good percentage for the outlay." [44]

The blizzard persuaded even the most reluctant cattlemen that survival depended on change in the old ways of herding. Operations were reduced, herds diminished, and adequate care provided. Purebred bulls, shorthorns, herefords, and angus were introduced to improve blood lines and, eventually, to produce higher quality beef and command better prices. Cattle were placed in enclosed pastures and provided forage, shelter, and water rather than being left to rustle for themselves as best they could. Land, leased or purchased, was acquired along permanent streams where there was a dependable supply of water and where wild hay might be found. Later, with the use of windmills, land at some distance from water was brought under cultivation and corn and other feed crops grown, harvested, and stored in anticipation of the next calamity. Cattleyards, sorting pens, and loading chutes were built to facilitate stock handling; railroads alleviated the need for long drives and accelerated the transport of cattle from ranch to market. Cattle production after that terrible winter

---

[43]Granville Stuart, *Forty Years on the Frontier* . . . , ed. Paul C. Phillips (2 vols.; Cleveland: Arthur H. Clark Co., 1925), II, 227 (quotation); *Irrigator* (Garden City), June 12, 1886; *Daily Drovers Journal* (Chicago), Feb. 12, 1886.

[44]*Third Annual Report of the Bureau of Animal Industry for the Year 1886*, H. Misc. Doc. 156, 49th Cong., 2nd Sess., 1886, p. 109; Dale, *The Range Cattle Industry,* 130 (1st quotation); *Times* (Leavenworth), Dec. 30, 1928; R[oy] D. Holt, "The Saga of Barbed Wire in the Tom Green Country," *West Texas Historical Association Year Book,* IV (June, 1928), 47; *Irrigator* (Garden City), Feb. 27, 1886.

became more a business, less a gamble. The blizzard of January 1886 changed forever cattle herding on the southern plains and hastened permanent settlement. The open range would be the same no more.[45]

---

[45]*Daily Drovers Journal* (Chicago), Feb. 12, 1886; *Third Annual Report of the Bureau of Animal Industry for the Year 1886*, H. Misc. Doc. 156, 49th Cong., 2nd Sess., 1886, pp. 107, 109; *Chronoscope* (Larned), Feb. 5, 1886; *The Western Range*, S. Doc. 199, 74th Cong. 2nd Sess., 1936, p. 124; Brayer, "The Influence of British Capital on the Western Range-Cattle Industry," 97; Moses, "Development of the Cattle Business in Texas," 265. According to Dale, "The range cattle area furnished a market for a large number of well bred bulls to improve its herds and so had a great influence in promoting the breeding of fine stock in the corn belt." Dale, *The Range Cattle Industry*, 105n. In another place Dale states, "The purchase of high grade cattle in the corn belt had begun early but increased as the years went by." Ibid., 111n; Holt, "The Saga of Barbed Wire in the Tom Green Country," 47; *Times* (Leavenworth), Dec. 30, 1928; *Irrigator* (Garden City), June 12, 1886; *Capital* (Topeka), Jan. 19, 1940.

# Nineteenth-Century Farmers, Cotton, and Prosperity

Robert A. Calvert*

*The history of nineteenth-century Texas must include farmers and cotton. Cowboys and cattle kingdoms were more romantic; industrialism spoke for the future of the state. But it was cotton in the Gilded Age that brought Texans their major source of income and dominated their search for economic well-being. Prosperity never came, however. Instead, tenancy and poverty grew. Farmers tried to improve their lot through scientific agriculture, blamed their plight on others, joined third parties, and stayed with the cash crop of cotton. They had no other choice. The struggle of cotton farmers then was in large measure the story of Texas.*

*In this essay the late Robert A. Calvert, a member of the faculty of Texas A&M University for many years, views the impact of cotton culture on the family farmer as both exploitative and inevitable. He describes the monotonous labor in the fields and the hopes for a combination of high yields and high prices that might diminish their burden of debt. He also explains why farmers seldom found their hopes fulfilled but searched in vain for alternatives that might make their life in the cotton fields more rewarding.*

*Two studies, John Spratt,* The Road to Spindletop *(Dallas: Southern Methodist University Press, 1955), and Lawrence Goodwyn,* Democratic Promise: The Populist Moment *(New York: Oxford University Press, 1976), describe the plight of the nineteenth-century cotton farmer in more detail. For a look at Texas farm life in the 1920s, readers should consult Thad Sitton and Dan K. Utley,* From Can See to Can't: Texas Cotton on the Southern Prairies *(Austin: University of Texas Press, 1997).*

---

* Robert A. Calvert, "Nineteenth-Century Farmers, Cotton, and Prosperity," *Southwestern Historical Quarterly,* 73 (Apr., 1970), 509–521.

"Let us crown our snowy white monarch King again!" exulted a southern newspaper in the agricultural boom of 1867.[1] Texans endorsed this proposal heartily. After the Civil War farmers flocked to the frontier regions of the state, and by 1889 Texas led all others in the production of cotton. The monarch proved to be a fickle one, however, because prosperity for the farmer did not necessarily follow the king's growth. Indeed, from 1870 to 1930, the percentage of tenant-operated to owner-operated farms grew steadily. Tenancy cast its economic blight upon black and whites impartially. In the famous blackwaxey lands of Texas in 1929, for example, 55.7 percent of all farms were tilled by white tenants. The growth of tenancy and the poverty of the state caused agricultural experts to bemoan the southern attachment to cotton culture and to blame the king for its peasant's woes.[2]

Throughout the Gilded Age agricultural reformers offered explanations for the increasing poverty of the cotton farmer. Most saw his plight as growing from the single-crop economy that sharecropping and the crop-lien system buttressed.[3] They thought, too, that these systems began as an answer to the unwillingness of the Negro to work. One expert explained that, "It [the sharecropping system] was devised by the planters in the days when politicians and fanatics were drawing the attention of the freedmen from their work in the cotton fields, and the employers found some means necessary to make the laborers feel the effects of their own idleness."[4] Consequently the reformers began with the wrong assumption: reliance on cotton produced poverty. Actually, it was the other way around: poverty produced reliance on cotton.

The crop-lien system developed as a way to provide the sharecropper with the necessary supplies. Landlords and lienholders demanded that their debtors plant cotton, the only commercial crop to guarantee some return on their investment. One way to wed labor and the land and to produce the mythical happy yeoman, many Texans thought, would be to eliminate the no longer needed crop-lien and sharecropping systems and to destroy the single crop economy.[5]

---

[1] *Southern Argus* (Selma, Alabama), August 15, 1867.

[2] A. C. True (ed.), *The Cotton Plant: Its History, Botany, Chemistry, Culture, Enemies, and Uses* (Washington, 1896), 269; Samuel Lee Evans, "Texas Agriculture, 1880–1930" (Ph.D. dissertation, University of Texas, Austin), 319; Rupert B. Vance, *Human Factors in Cotton Culture* (Chapel Hill, N.C., 1929), 23; John S. Spratt, *The Road to Spindletop* (Dallas, 1955), 67–68.

[3] For example, see the worthy master's address in *Proceedings of the Thirteenth Annual Session of the Texas State Grange* (Dallas, 1887), Appendix, 15.

[4] M. B. Hammond, *The Cotton Industry* (New York, 1897), 225.

[5] *Proceedings of the Twelfth Annual Session of the Texas State Grange* (Austin, 1886), 42–43; *Proceedings of the Fifteenth Annual Session of the Texas State Grange* (Dallas, 1889), 6, 24; *Journal of Proceedings of the Twentieth Annual Session of the Texas State Grange* (Belton, 1894), 19–20; Spratt, *Road to Spindletop*, 4, 67–69, 162–163.

Agricultural reformers blamed other villains for the Texas farmers' plight, too. A handy one, of course, was the ubiquitous "furnishing" merchant, whose store seemed to exist at every crossroads, whose wealth seemed to be claiming all the land, and to whom most crop-liens were owed. They sympathized, too, with the farmers' charges that the merchant not only marked the price of his goods too high, but that he falsified his account books so that his debtors were cheated. Few reformers realized, as later scholars demonstrated, that the merchant lost a great deal of his profits to those who defaulted on their debts; that he paid interest in turn to wholesale houses which extended credit to his store; and that illiterate farmers who kept no books never knew how much credit they actually used.[6]

Instead reformers charged that the merchant bought cotton at the cheapest price, encouraged credit to increase profits, and used crop liens to maintain the sharecropper system and to hold the farmer in bondage. When Texas Grangers told farmers that "There are an Army of intermediate nonproducers . . . that stand between the producers and consumers that are unnecessary links in the chain of trade and should be dispensed with," they spoke of the furnishing merchant.[7]

The crop-lien and the sharecropping systems did not develop, as farmers supposed, either because of the perniciousness of merchants or the shiftlessness of the freedmen. Necessity produced them and necessity kept them alive. Texas farmers lacked capital. Consequently, by necessity, they bartered their knowledge; they promised that their farming techniques could grow a commercial crop for a profit. That commercial crop was, of course, cotton. On the basis of this promise, the storekeeper financed the farmer. The creditor demanded that the debtor plant enough cotton to retire the debt; if that debt was not retired the first year, the answer was to plant more cotton the next. It was not the system but the lack of liquid capital that doomed the cotton farmer. Texas had too few banks which could grant long-term loans. Thus the farmer paid high interest rates on short-term loans. He needed the facilities to borrow money over a long period of time, so that his debts could be retired piecemeal, while capital improvements were made on the farm.[8]

Agricultural reformers might not have agreed that Texans needed banks: they suspected banks, bankers, and credit. They suggested that farmers, instead

---

[6]Thomas D. Clark, *Pills, Petticoats and Plows: The Southern Country Store* (Norman, 1964), 258–291; C. Vann Woodward, *Origins of the New South, 1877–1913* (Baton Rouge, 1951), 184–185; Harold Woodman, *King Cotton and His Retainers* (Lexington, Ky., 1968), 270, 272–273, 275, 284, 299–300.

[7]Undated notebook, 19, Box A13/106, Archibald J. Rose Papers (Archives, University of Texas Library, Austin).

[8]William E. Laird and James R. Rinehart, "Deflation, Agriculture and Southern Development," *Agricultural History,* XLII (April, 1968), 117, 120–121.

of seeking credit, should reduce their cotton planting and diversify their farms. In urging diversification, however, farm experts probably did not mean to increase the number of commercial crops. Rather they asked that the farmer return to subsistence farming—that is, plant less cotton and produce all possible necessities on his own farm. A noted Texas economist has argued that such a proposal sailed against the tides of history. Industrialization demanded specialization; and to ask the farmer to forsake his most lucrative cash crop, cotton, was to ask him to look backward to nineteenth- and not forward to twentieth-century Texas.[9]

Economic methods alone, agricultural reformers asserted, could not end the farmers' poverty. They bewailed his poor tilling methods that ravaged the soil and limited its yield. One spokesman for the Department of Agriculture lamented that:

> Cotton is now cultivated under a very slovenly system, if it can be called a system. No manures are used, the first plowing scarcely exceeds two inches in depth, and after [later] cultivation is often delayed until the crop is materially injured by being crowded by grass.[10]

Farm organization spokesmen believed that the farmer could increase his crop yields by employing fertilizers, by studying scientific agriculture, and by learning to keep accurate account books so that he could determine the costs and profits of farm commodities.[11]

Despite admonitions of agricultural writers, farm organizations, and farm journals, Texas farmers planted more cotton each year. By 1879, some 2,176,000 acres were devoted to cotton and by the close of the century the acreage tilled by cotton farmers had increased to 6,961,000. In 1880 most of this farming was done by manual labor, with the average expense of 167 hours and 48 minutes of man-labor per acre.[12] Undoubtedly farmers continued to use methods deplored by proponents of scientific agriculture.

The rural population suspected scientific agricultural techniques. For example in 1880, many farmers would not use Paris green, a well-known insecticide designed to control the army worm that destroyed cotton, because it contained arsenic trioxide, and laborers feared that it would poison them as well as

---

[9]Spratt, *Road to Spindletop*, 61–83.

[10]U.S. Department of Agriculture, *Report of the Commissioner of Agriculture for the Year 1867* (Washington, 1867), 410.

[11]See, for example, *Proceedings of the Tenth Annual Session of the Texas State Grange* (Dallas, 1884), 18–19, 41, 43–44.

[12]Evans, "Texas Agriculture, 1880–1930," 1–2; Fred A. Shannon, *The Farmer's Last Frontier* (New York, 1945), 143.

the insects.[13] Besides it was difficult to disseminate agricultural information to illiterate farmers and for them to keep books, when they neither knew how nor understood why, was an almost impossible task. Furthermore they thought, with some justification, that fertilizers often were too expensive or did not live up to their expectations. Guanos, the generic name that farmers used for manures, frequently contained weed seeds, and many farmers believed that their use increased farm problems rather than crop yields. Commercial chemical fertilizers contained additives such as brick dust, that prompted Granges and Alliances to denounce their use and to adopt resolutions condemning them throughout the late-nineteenth century.[14] This suspicion, the fertility of the comparatively virgin soil of the state, and the farmer's illiteracy caused Texas to rank at the bottom of the list in 1880 in the amount of fertilizer used per acre of improved land.[15]

Thus the Texas cotton farmer in the Gilded Age began his cotton farming each year schooled in little but past experience. If the field previously had been cleared, he in all likelihood planted on land that had a cotton or a corn crop grown on it the last season. Crops seldom were rotated and when they were, no particular order was followed. Land was rarely "turned out" or allowed to lie fallow. Since he usually did not practice fall plowing, the farmer began each spring by removing the previous year's cotton stalks. Before the advent of mechanical stalk cutters, he knocked these down with a heavy drag, a hoe, or club, or pulled them by hand. Sometimes farmers raked the stalks into piles and burned them, even though such a practice was known to destroy humus in the soil. In the 1880's farmers began using a mechanical stalk cutter. This machine, a two-wheel device that straddled the rows, pulled sharp blades or knives that cut the stalks into bits and enabled one man to clean five to nine acres in a ten-hour day.[16]

When the stalks were removed the farmer prepared ridges in the fields—called rows or beds. To do this, he plowed out the depression between the previous year's rows with a "bull-tongue" plow. When this was completed, he replaced this implement with a turning plow, and plowed first on one side of

[13]R. H. Loughridge, "Report on the Cotton Production of the State of Texas," in U.S. Census Office, *Tenth Census of the United States: 1880. Report on Cotton Production in the United States* (Washington, 1884), 818; hereafter cited as Loughridge, "Cotton Production of Texas."

[14]True, *The Cotton Plant,* 173–175. Note too the report of a southern newspaper, Montgomery *Advertiser,* April 18, 1871, that some fertilizers contained 40 percent brick and sand.

[15]U.S. Census Office, *Tenth Census of the United States: 1880. Agriculture (Washington,* 1881), 103.

[16]Loughridge, "Cotton Production of Texas," 811–812, 813; Sam Evans, "Texas Agriculture, 1865–1880" (M.A. thesis, University of Texas, Austin, 1955), 26; Evans, "Texas Agriculture, 1880–1930," 19; True, *The Cotton Plant,* 243–244.

the furrow and then on the other until he had built a row about four feet wide and six inches high. The distances between the rows varied from three-to-four feet in the uplands areas to four-to-five feet in the bottoms where the soil was richer and the plants had a more luxuriant growth. The elevated bed permitted better drainage, allowed extra plants and weeds to be hoed out more easily, and since the bed was warmer, caused more successful germination of the seed.[17]

After the farmer prepared his ridge, he usually pulled a log across it to smooth the bed and to pulverize the soil. Then he plowed a single trench down the middle of the bed and deposited seed into it. In 1880 he probably planted the seed by hand and covered it by dragging a log afterwards. Mechanical planters, which trenched the bed, deposited the seed, and covered it in one operation, saw only limited use that year. Their employment varied from area to area. Wood County land contained too many stumps and roots for their effective use. A farmer in Nacogdoches County reported, "they have been laid aside for the next generation," but Cooke County farmers seem to have utilized them readily.[18] The types of mechanical planters employed varied from homemade ones to the manufactured keg-type machines. By 1885 the Champion and Standard machines boasted widespread popularity in the state.[19]

Farmers began planting in early March in the southern part of Texas, and most throughout the state completed the operation by mid-May. Tender cotton plants cannot survive frost, but they need to mature before the usual summer drouths. After the appearance in 1893 of the cotton-boll weevil, farmers planted as early as possible, because the infestation of the insect grew worse toward the end of the season.[20] In short, the farmer relied on experience to pick a planting date.

He planted between one-half and two bushels of seed per acre, depending once more on his location and previous experience. In 1880 most Texas farmers preferred the Schubach or storm-proof variety of seed, but farmers also expressed faith in the Dixon, Petit Gulf, Cheatham, Hurlong, Meyers, Sugarloaf, Hefley, South American, and other varieties of cotton. These seeds produced cotton with the length of the staple between ⅞ and 1 ⅛ inches. Because of public gins and cross-fertilization by insects, farmers seldom acquired superior seed, and complaints that a particular variety had "run out" were common.[21]

The new plants came up in from three to ten days. After the plants had grown for about two weeks, the grower "barred off" or plowed on either side of

---

[17]Evans, "Texas Agriculture, 1880–1930," 20–21; Loughridge, "Cotton Production of Texas," 813; Alston Hill Garside, *Cotton Goes to Market* (New York, 1935), 17.

[18]Loughridge, "Cotton Production of Texas," 813.

[19]Evans, "Texas Agriculture, 1880–1930," 35.

[20]Loughridge, "Cotton Production of Texas," 813; True, *The Cotton Plant,* 335.

[21]Loughridge, "Cotton Production of Texas," 813; True, *The Cotton Plant,* 214–215.

the row, leaving the cotton plants on a ridge about six inches in height and three inches in width. "Choppers" followed the "plowing off," and hoed out surplus plants and weeds. They left bunches of three to four plants spaced, depending upon the planter's preference and the fertility of the soil, from ten inches to four feet apart.[22] No work in the cotton field was harder. A tenant farmer, the main character in a novel by a Texas writer, explained the arduous chore:

> Through the wanning days chopping. Sending the blade slicing through the dark, hilled crumbles of earth. Killing weeds. Thinning cotton. Up, down, swing the hoe into a sort of limbo, a Nirvana, in which only a few muscles remain aware, and they not sharply. Sweat-wet clothes dragging cooly, cooly galling. And time no longer exists in minutes and hours, but in rows and acres. And even this is vague. A sea of up and down. Of bad meals. A back that aches in your sleep.[23]

After chopping, the crop was cultivated. First the planter "dirtied up" the cotton by using a turning plow to throw dirt lost in "barring off" back on the ridge around the young plants. This action gave the plants ample soil to develop strong root systems. The farmer continued cultivation of the crops, usually three plowings and two to four hoeings, until about a month or six weeks before harvest. A man could hoe from one-half to something over an acre per day. The cultivating processes kept down weeds and grass, aerated the soil, and made it more capable of absorbing moisture. Then the cotton was "laid by" or allowed to remain idle until time to pick.[24]

After 1885, the walking or riding cultivator came into use, eliminating much of that hand labor. Farmers not only welcomed its advent but advertisers promised miraculous results. One company told the farmer that:

1st. The man who buys a 'Standard' Cultivator or Planter gets the full worth of his money.
2nd. His crops are always well worked.
3rd. He takes pride in paying his debts.
4th. His daughters are comely and helpful, and his sons respected and popular.
5th. His wife always cheerful and obliging.
6th. He is accounted a man of sound judgment.
7th. About 40,000 'Standard' Cultivators have been sold in Texas.[25]

---

[22]Evans, "Texas Agriculture, 1865–1880," 31–32; Loughridge, "Cotton Production of Texas," 814.

[23]George Sessions Perry, *Hold Autumn in Your Hand* (New York, 1941), 130–131.

[24]Loughridge, "Cotton Production of Texas," 814; D. A. Tompkins, *Cotton and Cotton Oil* (2 vols.; Charlotte, N.C., 1901), I, 156; True, *The Cotton Plant,* 245.

[25]*Farm and Ranch,* VIII (October 15, 1889), 13.

In about thirty days, early May in the southern counties and late June in the northern ones, the cotton sprouted blooms. From the time of blooming until the harvesting, the cotton plant was threatened by diseases and insects. Farmers lacked the knowledge to cope with these evils. Many thought "sore shin," a fungus, was caused by either laborers carelessly nicking the stalks while hoeing or by high winds blowing the plant and breaking its bark. Another fungus, root rot, was reputed to occur because of poison soils.[26]

In addition to these and other diseases, cotton plants fell prey to such dread insects as the cotton caterpillar and, by 1895, the boll weevil. Farmers hunted desperately for cures. For the caterpillar, the scourge of the eighties, they hung lanterns or pots of molasses and vinegar in the fields to attract and kill the moths, dusted the plants with ashes, and experimented with supposedly caterpillar-resistant strains of cotton.[27]

No insect did as much damage to cotton, of course, as did the boll weevil. In 1902 it was estimated that the southern states had lost from 235,000 to 500,000 bales valued at between $8,000,000 and $25,000,000 to the weevil's depredations. In 1895 no insecticides were known to destroy the insect. It was suggested that the farmer plant early, have workers pick the affected bolls, or cultivate select plants at convenient parts in his fields, which with care would mature before the regular crop and attract the earliest beetles. These plants could then be destroyed and the damage done to the remainder lessened.[28] Given the seemingly hopelessness of the situation the farmer was more than his usual easy mark to all sorts of spurious cures or machines that promised to eradicate the insect.

At times farmers faced the insect plight with grim humor. The suggestion that the United States government might import a natural predator such as a particular species of ant from Guatemala to attack the weevil elicited an ironic anecdote from H. L. Stringfellow, a Texas horticulturist. He told readers of *Farm and Ranch* that he put a boll weevil and a native species of red ant under a glass jar and observed the following episode through a magnifying glass:

> Finally, seeing that neither showed any desire for a closer acquaintance, I moved the glass backward and forward, so as to bring them into contact repeatedly, a proreeding [*sic.* proceeding] for which the ant seemed to blame the weevil, for in a few minutes he seized his snout, close to his head, with his mandibles and a rough and tumble fight ensued for more than an hour without a single break. Over and over they turned, the ant repeatedly bringing the rear of his body in contact with the wee-

---

[26]Loughridge, "Cotton Production of Texas," 814; *Southern Cultivation,* XXXII (March, 1874), 86–87.

[27]Loughridge, "Cotton Production of Texas," 813; Evans, "Texas Agriculture, 1865–1880," 35–36.

[28]Evans, "Texas Agriculture, 1880–1930," 74; True, *The Cotton Plant,* 339–340.

vil's back in what seemed to be a vain attempt to sting him, just as a wasp would, but the magnifying glass showed no sign of a wound. In the meantime my sympathy was all with the weevil, of whom the ant had taken undue advantage by seizing him by the snout without warning . . . sometimes lifting him clear off the board and then slamming him down on his back, a position occupied by the weevil during the greatest part of the fight. Of course I thought it would soon be all over with the weevil, for his only effective weapon was in his enemy's possession and all he could do was to kick and scratch the ant's stomach, which he did vigorously from start to finish.

Finally, after about an hour, to my surprise, the ant suddenly relaxed his grip of the weevil's snout, and doubling himself up in a ball, rolled over dead.

A careful examination of the ant's body showed no wound of any kind, while the weevil also was apparently uninjured, except the loss of his left hind leg, which had been broken off close to his body in the stuggle. . . . I at once gave him a fresh cotton square and the next morning found him sitting contentedly upon it, just as if nothing had happened.

After such a contest, I could not kill him, so, after several days, holding him between finger and thumb, on my front gallery, I said to him: "Boll weevil, brave boll weevil, Fly away to Washington; And tell the entomologists, Killing ants is only fun!"[29]

Cotton had to survive inclement weather as well as insects and diseases. Too little rain, of course, produced a drouth; but too much rain or rain falling in mid-summer caused cotton to exceed the desired height of from three to four feet and "run to weed." Farmers combatted the excessive height by plowing close to the roots on either side of the plant or by pruning out the topmost branches. Rain did by far the most damage, however, after bolls had split open and exposed the lock of cotton that dried, became fluffy, and was attached only at the stem end. Then rain could cause the boll to stain the cotton, lowering its grade, or if accompanied by high winds could blow and beat the lock to earth causing a near total crop loss. For this reason Texans preferred a variety of cotton called "storm proof."[30]

The lock of cotton was the most vulnerable at the time of harvest. Consequently, at picking time, which began in July in the southern counties and early September in northern ones, all available manpower came to the fields and picked until the harvest ended. Since the bolls opened progressively, hands usually harvested the cotton two or three times per field, the picking continuing well into December and sometimes into the new year. Even then some cotton was left in the field.[31]

The necessity of quickly gathering the crop demanded that the farmer utilize all of his family and frequently hire additional labor to pick the cotton. The

---

[29]*Farm and Ranch,* XXVII (February 15, 1908), 3.

[30]Evans, "Texas Agriculture, 1865–1880," 37; Loughridge, "Cotton Production of Texas," 722–724; True, *The Cotton Plant,* 245.

[31]Loughridge, "Cotton Production of Texas," 815.

amount gathered by each worker depended on his ability. In 1895, in the prairie regions of the state, it was reported that six-year-old children had picked 100 pounds per day and that first-class pickers gathered between 500 and 600 pounds per day. The writer added that the workers took so little care that the cotton was mixed with trash and bolls.[32] A more realistic appraisal by a later student states that in Texas a good picker averaged around 250 pounds of seed cotton in a day. In 1880 it cost a farmer between fifty cents and one dollar per hundred pounds to gather cotton.[33]

The picker dragged a sack strapped to his shoulder that held a capacity of around 25 pounds of seed cotton. When the sack was filled, the cotton was weighed, deposited in a basket or wagon, and credited to the picker's account. When a farmer had enough cotton picked for a bale, he usually sent the staple to the gin. In some cases, however, cotton was stored in the fields in wagons or in cribs, giving only limited protection from the weather, until the entire crop was picked or until prices rose.[34]

The cotton was now ready for the gin and ultimately for the market. When the farmer took the seed cotton from the field to the gin, the town began to claim its share of Texas' $100,000,000 cotton crop.[35] In 1870 farmers estimated that it cost them anywhere from 3.5 cents to 10 cents per pound to produce the cotton lint, excluding the merchants' commission and the cost of transportation, storing, and insurance.[36] The average annual yield per acre of lint cotton in Texas, 1874 to 1894, was computed by the United States Department of Agriculture at 229 pounds, with the minimum average (1884) of 142 pounds and the maximum (1894) of 383 pounds.[37] In this same period the average price per pound of cotton ranged from a high of 13 cents in 1874 to a low of 4.6 cents in 1894.

Such estimates told nothing of and could not total the wear and tear of hard work on the farmer and his family. Even with the wide differences in costs and production per acre, and assuming that the farmer used all the byproducts of the cotton—such as hulls and seeds—few family farmers became prosperous. The Texas farmer realized that prosperity was not automatically rewarding his hard work. Instead his labor produced all sorts of urban enterprises that seemed to him to prosper while he grew poorer. He undoubtedly saw the phenomenal rise in this period of industries based upon cotton processing. By 1900, for example, Texas had 4,514 gins within its borders, and these gins aver-

---

[32]True, *The Cotton Plant,* 245.

[33]Evans, "Texas Agriculture, 1865–1880," 39; Loughridge, "Cotton Production of Texas," 821.

[34]True, *The Cotton Plant,* 245.

[35]Estimated value of cotton in Texas at the turn of the century, from Spratt, *Road to Spindletop,* 83.

[36]Loughridge, "Cotton Production of Texas," 821.

[37]True, *The Cotton Plant,* 269.

aged 589 bales each year, handling 34 percent of the nation's total cotton crop.[38]

Besides gins the farmer witnessed the rise of kindred business—cotton compresses and mills. A cotton compress was easily dismantled and moved. When cotton production declined in one area or increased in another, the industry followed the production, and by 1890 the shipping areas of the states were served by over 40 cotton compress companies. In addition, the same period saw an increase from 7 to 103 in the number of oil mills that pressed cotton seed. Indeed the investments in Texas in 1900 in businesses that were related to cotton processing probably ran to something around $25,000,000.[39] These enterprises were not so much to serve the farmer as they were tools of the entrepreneur.

Texas farmers resented the fact that they did not receive what they considered to be their just share of profits from the production and sale of cotton. All other industries, they pointed out, were just auxiliaries of agriculture. "The soil is the source from which we derive all that constitutes wealth," an agrarian leader told Texas farmers.[40] They particularly disliked the transportation companies and middlemen who, they believed, grew rich off of the farmers' toil. The poorer the farm population became the more agrarians attacked these "abuses." Thus, many of the same farmers who supported the 1874 statement of Grange Worthy Master William Lang that, "I am unable to discover any antagonism to railroads or to transportation companies by the Patrons of Husbandry,"[41] cheered wildly in 1888 when the Farmers Alliance demanded "that the state establish maximum freight and passenger rates on railroads."[42]

It took fifteen years of poverty to turn the conservative granger into the radical allianceman. Yet Texas farmers always denounced the city. Lang, who felt farmers and railroads could cooperate, said in 1878 that "Great cities are beginning to be plague centers of the social system. Debasing pleasures there have temples overcrowded with devotees; depravity finds cordial friendship . . . . and, as filth generates a pestilence, so this congregation of all that is offensive to virtue corrupts society."[43] He unconsciously explained the reason for rural

---

[38]U.S. Census Office, *Twelfth Census of the United States: 1900. Manufactures* (Washington, 1902), pt. 3, pp. 331–332. For the story of the rise of town gins see Raymond White, "The History of the Texas Cotton Ginning Industry, 1882–1957" (M.A. thesis, University of Texas, Austin, 1957), 46–47, 54–55. Spratt, *Road to Spindletop,* 78, places the aggregate value of these gins at $9,282,101 in 1900.

[39]Tuffly Ellis, *The Texas Cotton Compress Industry: A History* (Dallas, 1962), 31–37; U.S. Census Office, *Twelfth Census, Manufactures,* pt. 2, p. 863; Spratt, *Road to Spindletop,* 81.

[40]*Proceedings of the Twelfth Annual Session of the Texas State Grange,* 19.

[41]*Minutes of the Texas State Grange* (Waco, 1874), 7.

[42]Ernest W. Winkler, *Platforms of Political Parties in Texas* (Austin, 1916), 267.

[43]*Proceedings of the Fourth Annual Session of the Texas State Grange* (Waco, 1875), 15.

opposition to urban areas by calling on farmers to join the Patrons of Husbandry, win status, and end "the reckless yearnings of the young men of the country" for the city.[44] Farmers wondered how to keep their sons "down on the farm" long before World War I and Paris.

Thus the Texas farmer must have considered as the ultimate irony the fact that the cotton he grew not only supported subsidiary industries but was shipped to those "plague centers of the social system" and caused their growth. He saw Galveston become by the twentieth century the number one cotton port in the nation, handling at the height of the cotton season 40,000 to 50,000 bales a day.[45] He saw the city prosper while he starved. Consequently Texas farmers joined alliances and granges, experimented with economic cooperatives, and some ultimately bolted the Democratic party and formed a third political party. Yet farmers stayed with cotton: it was their only cash crop, and it could always be sold. The selling, though, seemed to bring prosperity only to others; and the hopelessness this fact engendered caused the attack of agricultural reformers upon the money crop.

Cotton continued to be the King of the state's economy, however, until events at Spindletop dethroned it. Except for a brief period before and during World War I, however, the cotton farmer never received many economic benefits from the monarch. History almost foreordained it that way. Industrialization processes exploit someone, and in the United States a large portion of that exploitation fell upon the farmer and worker. In the case of agriculture, industrialization meant the end of the family farm and of King Cotton. George Sessions Perry in 1934 had his fictional character Sam Tucker sum it up this way:

> Land just catches the culls that can't do no good in cities. Cept me. I wasn't culled here. I blong, But there's too much cotton and too much corn. We go on raisin it cause it's all we know. Ain't worth enough in money to keep us alive, but the government's a-doing for us what it done for the arrow-makers [Indians]. When their kind of work got useless an in the way. Farms ain't farms no more; not no real business. Just reservations where the government gives men money to stay there and keep off the relief. . . . An it seems strange when you know this year's cotton'll be just as good, just as white, and a better staple than it ever was; just as much work to raise. Except there ain't no use for but about half of it. Ain't nobody's fault, I guess, but ourn for raisin cotton. More of us got to crowd into factories, looks like.[46]

---

[44] *Ibid.*, 16.

[45] Galveston *Daily News*, October 12, 1913.

[46] Perry, *Hold Autumn in Your Hand*, 133.

# Curtains for Jim Crow: Law, Race, and the Texas Railroads

William S. Osborn*

*By an act of the legislature in 1891, Texas law required that railroads provide "separate coaches or compartments . . . for the accommodation of white and negro passengers," and a subsequent law of 1910 required segregation of waiting areas in the railway stations. In some parts of the state, local ordinances enforced these rules and, in some instances, preceded them. Although the state regulatory body, the Railroad Commission, at times exerted considerable pressure to ensure separation of the races, as a practical matter, enforcement of such laws customarily was the responsibility of railroads.*

*The author suggests that railroads were less than enthusiastic about segregation, primarily for economic reasons. Railroads complained that the practice required additional coaches, employees, and station facilities that were only partially utilized. Enforcement was especially difficult when the passengers involved were traveling from states where accommodations were not segregated. Moreover, public support for the measures in areas where the black population was small was limited.*

*William S. Osborn, "Curtains for Jim Crow: Law, Race, and the Texas Railroads," *Southwestern Historical Quarterly,* 105 (Jan., 2002), 393–427. The author desires to acknowledge the assistance of Connie Menninger of the Kansas History Center at Topeka, archival custodian of certain records of the Atchison, Topeka & Santa Fe Railway Company; Louis Marchiafava of the Houston Metropolitan Research Center, which holds more than four hundred boxes of files from the Santa Fe's Texas legal department dating from 1900 to 1965; the staff of the Texas State Archives; Dr. T. Lindsay Baker, who has given countless hours as a mentor and critic to the author's efforts; noted authors John Miller Morris and Carolyn Osborn; Railroad Commission Librarian Susan Rhyne; George C. Werner, who is one of the foremost experts on the history of Texas railroads; Austin attorneys Joe Osborn and Jim Cousar; former Assistant Attorney General Linward Shivers; and Santa Fe historical expert Matt Zebrowski. Law partner Philip F. Patman provided invaluable editorial comments and encouragement, and partner Ana Maria Marsland provided research assistance. Special thanks to TSHA editors Holly Zumwalt Taylor and Theresa Ann Case for their patience and careful attention to detail. Donna Osborn kindly tolerates the interruption of attention to family affairs provoked by the author's historical interests.

*Yet, upheld in* Plessy v. Ferguson, *a Louisiana case before the United States Supreme Court, railroad segregation was sometimes ignored, but rarely challenged in Texas until about the time of World War II. On the eve of the war, a Supreme Court ruling that outlawed the use of "unequal facilities" suggested that possibilities of ending segregated travel were improving. But it was World War II and the military demand of equal treatment for traveling soldiers that placed "Jim Crow" on Texas railroads in jeopardy.*

*With the return of peace, however, segregationists made clear their determination to maintain a segregated society. Local law enforcement officials in some areas and the state Railroad Commission continued efforts to enforce laws that had not changed in over fifty years. But they met increasing resistance. Opponents of the practice made considerable progress in their campaign for social justice in the 1950s, eliminating it in most respects except for certain facilities in some stations. But it was not until the early 1960s that fully integrated facilities were at last available for all.*

*For a comprehensive discussion of segregation, see the classic study, C. Vann Woodward,* The Strange Career of Jim Crow *(3rd rev. ed.; New York: Oxford University Press, 1974). The essay of F. Kenneth Jensen, "The Houston Sit-In Movement of 1960–1961," in Howard Beeth and Cary D. Wintz (eds.),* Black Dixie: Afro-Texan History and Culture in Houston *(College Station: Texas A&M University Press, 1992), describes some of the last major conflicts and the fanatical defense of the practice even in the face of obvious and certain defeat.*

On September 15, 1893, Thomas W. Cain, a black resident of Galveston, was visiting in St. Louis, Missouri. He purchased a ticket for rail travel home and paid an extra fare for a berth in a Pullman car. His trip began without incident. At Longview, Texas, this Pullman car was switched onto an International & Great Northern Railroad Company train bound for Galveston. Upon arrival at Troup, Texas, I. & G. N. trainmaster J. C. Gregory announced to Cain that his presence in the sleeping car with whites violated a new state statute. This statute, the first Texas law regarding segregation on the railways, had passed in the 1891 legislative session. It required separate coaches or compartments for white and black passengers. Trainmaster Gregory instructed Cain to move from his Pullman car to a day coach assigned to blacks only. Cain objected but to no avail. He was refunded $2, this sum being the premium fare calculated for Pullman travel on the remainder of his journey.[1]

[1] *Pullman Palace Car Co., et al. v. Cain*, 40 S.W. 220 (Tex. Civ. App., 1897).

Cain filed suit against the I. & G. N. and the Pullman companies in Galveston County District Court and a trial on the merits resulted in a verdict in his favor with an award of $100 for damages. The Pullman Company appealed but found little sympathy in the Texas Court of Civil Appeals, which sustained the award to Cain. The court held that the Pullman Company was liable for damages because it did not fulfill its contract with Cain to provide him with first-class accommodations. Chief Justice Garrett, author of the court's opinion, argued that the Pullman Company could comply with the law by furnishing separate sleeping cars for blacks and whites.[2] This would never happen. The cost of doubling the company's fleet and workforce in the South would have been prohibitive, especially given low patronage of Pullman cars by the black population, which was generally too poor to purchase first-class service. Through the end of the Jim Crow era, trains entering Texas from segregation-free states to the north and west retained integrated sleeping cars, regardless of what legislators in Austin decreed.

One surmises that the justices on the Texas Court of Civil Appeals sympathized with Cain for economic reasons. No doubt they, too, could afford the comfort of first-class accommodations. They likely viewed the railroad's decision to turn a paying customer out of his sleeping car as disconcerting, even if that customer was black. The court was less sympathetic to discrimination complaints of coach passengers, black or white. Just a year before, the same court had affirmed dismissal of a suit brought against the Galveston, Houston & San Antonio Railway Company by a black passenger who had been compelled to travel between Gonzales and Harwood in a day coach that lacked a stove, toilet facilities, and a drinking water tank.[3] Twenty years later the court also affirmed dismissal of a suit brought against the Missouri, Kansas & Texas Railway Company by white passengers forced to ride in the same car with black passengers between Austin and San Marcos when flood damage disrupted regular train service.[4]

---

[2]Ibid. The court ruled on the basis of contract law rather than civil rights law on the theory that Cain had paid for a level of service that was promised but not delivered.

[3]*Norwood v. Galveston, Houston & San Antonio Ry. Co.*, 34 S.W. 180 (Tex. Civ. App., 1896). However, see *Henderson v. Galveston, H. & S. A. Ry. Co.*, 38 S.W. 1136 (Tex. Civ. App. 1896). In this latter case, a black minister who had paid for passage from San Antonio to Hondo was compelled to ride in a coach with no toilet facilities. The court found that he was entitled to damages for his pain and humiliation. In the same year and in cases involving the same railroad, the same court ruled against one black plaintiff and for another. The only difference in those cases was in the social status of the black plaintiffs (one being a preacher).

[4]*Weller et ux. v. Missouri, K. & T. Ry. Co. et al.*, 187 S.W. 374 (Tex. Civ. App. 1916).

In both of these decisions the court's opinions stated that enforcement of the separate coach law was a matter reserved for action by the state. Only the state, it argued, could prescribe penalties against offending railway companies, and aggrieved individuals could not use such penalties as a basis for recovering damages. Yet, from the earliest years of the statute, the courts permitted recovery in damages in private suits when black passengers on Pullman cars experienced discrimination.[5] Throughout the Jim Crow era, economic status tended to trump racial status on the Texas railways. Fifty years after the *Cain* case, even the chief enforcer of Jim Crow legislation for the Railroad Commission of Texas found that he lacked the nerve to confront a prosperous black passenger traveling in a Pullman lounge car in order to require her to leave the premises.

As the Thomas Cain incident and other cases cited above suggest, several factors made interpreting and enforcing Texas segregation laws on the rails difficult. First, under certain conditions a number of whites were willing to ignore or moderate the otherwise rigid requirements of Jim Crow legislation. Second, railroad companies serving Texas and the western section of the nation from corporate centers in Chicago or San Francisco often resisted segregation laws in regard to first-class cars, as those laws required them to supply extra equipment and staff. In addition, some white Texans, particularly in the western part of the state, thought segregation of rail transportation unnecessary in their territory. Many West Texas authorities silently refused to enforce state laws designed to address circumstances in the eastern part of Texas. Indeed, the records of railroad companies, the Texas Railroad Commission, and Texas courts demonstrate that, though white Texans generally accepted segregation in principle, race relations on the rails were far more complicated and fluid than the signs marked "White" and "Colored" imply.

Segregation on the railroads, so long an institution in Texas and elsewhere in the South, came to an end in slow and halting steps during the early to mid-twentieth century. An apartheid system of transportation was always an expensive proposition for carriers, but the industry's declining fortunes during the twentieth century increasingly pushed railroad corporations to disregard Jim Crow statutes. Landmark court decisions and the need for national unity and economic efficiency during World War II led to the disintegration of Texas's enforcement of segregation on rail travel shortly after the war, a few years sooner than in the states of the Deep South. Vestigial segregation practices enforced by local police authorities remained in place, however, in many Texas railroad depots until the dawn of the Space Age, when media attention brought to bear the power of civic embarrassment on the issue. In the end, the court of public

[5]Edward L. Ayers, *The Promise of the New South: Life After Reconstruction* (New York: Oxford University Press, 1992), 141–142.

opinion proved more powerful than any court of law in closing the curtains on the Jim Crow era on the Texas railroads.

Between 1868 and 1873, when the state of Texas underwent radical Reconstruction, federal authorities generally did not tolerate segregation of the races, as the Fourteenth Amendment, adopted in 1868, provided that "no state shall make or enforce any law which shall abridge the privileges or immunities of citizens of the United States . . . nor deny to any within its jurisdiction the equal protection of the laws." But after the withdrawal of the federal occupying force, Republican control of state government ended and discriminatory practices soon resurfaced. Still, because few railroads existed in Texas during the 1870s, the issue of segregation in railcars did not much concern Texans.[6]

In 1875 Congress passed a new civil rights bill, which for the first time clearly provided that all people within the jurisdiction of the United States were entitled to full and equal enjoyment of accommodations, public transportation, theaters, and places of public amusement. The Fourteenth Amendment had not been so specific. By 1883, however, five challenges to this legislation had reached the United States Supreme Court, where they were consolidated and called "The Civil Rights Cases."[7] In these cases the Court ruled eight to one that the new civil rights law was unconstitutional. The Fourteenth Amendment, the Court held, affects only state actions, because the amendment explicitly provides: "No state shall make or enforce any law" that denies equal protection. The majority of the justices considered the federal government powerless to intrude on the regulation of social rights between private citizens; thus, they made a distinction between social and civil rights. According to this view, the owner of a hotel should be entitled to decide to whom to rent a room—the government is not entitled to say to whom a room must be rented. Such a decision was not a state action because the state did not own the hotel. The railroads of that era were, in a sense, traveling hotels operated by private companies, not by states.[8]

Justice John Marshall Harlan was a southerner, but he dissented in the Civil Rights Cases, writing that the majority was sacrificing the "substance and spirit" of the Thirteenth and Fourteenth Amendments. In his view a railroad received a state charter and therefore essentially operated as a public highway, the state even giving it the right to condemn private property to construct its route. But in 1883 he was far outnumbered. His fellow justices on the U.S. Supreme Court left to the states the power to regulate social interactions between individuals, and the southern states began in earnest to establish laws providing for what was essentially an *apartheid* social system by segregating the

---

[6]Ibid., 136; "Railroads," *The Handbook of Texas Online*, http://www.tsha.utexas.edu/handbook/online/articles/view/RR/eqr1.html [Accessed Jan. 7, 2002].

[7]*Civil Rights Cases*, 109 United States Reports 3 at 13 and 25.

[8]*Civil Rights Cases*, 109 United States Reports 3 at 24 and 25.

races in many areas of public contact.[9] Described by historian C. Vann Woodward as "the most elaborate and formal expression of sovereign white opinion upon the subject," segregation statutes in the various southern states by the end of the nineteenth century extended to schools, residential housing, restaurants, hospitals, orphanages, prisons, bus lines, railroads, funeral homes, and cemeteries.[10] Such extensive control over the geography of society was critical to whites' exercise of dominion over blacks.[11]

Black citizens who lived through this period, who were later interviewed about their experiences with segregation, frequently mentioned the particular humiliation involved in riding Jim Crow railroad cars. They easily recalled being forced to change places in railroad cars, or to leave certain cars entirely, because these incidents occurred in full public view, sometimes with vocal support for the enforcing conductor expressed by the white passengers.[12] Blacks who needed to travel in nineteenth- and twentieth-century Texas were forced to brave that humiliation in exchange for the ease and speed of movement offered by rail travel.

During the 1880s railroad construction in Texas greatly accelerated. The Texas & Pacific built west from Fort Worth and reached El Paso in 1881. A line chartered in the name of the Galveston, Harrisburg & San Antonio Railway linked El Paso with San Antonio in 1883. Three years later the Atchison, Topeka & Santa Fe built south from Oklahoma to its newly purchased subsidiary, the Gulf, Colorado & Santa Fe, which connected Galveston with points in the Midwest. Branch lines linked many of the smaller communities in East Texas. In 1880 Texas had 2, 440 miles of mainline track; more than 6,000 miles were added by 1890.[13] The impact of these connections to the outside world on the daily lives of Texans was sudden and dramatic. The new ability to move passengers and freight easily and quickly was just as significant then as the rise of electronic communication via the Internet at the end of the twentieth century. The freedom of movement brought about by the railroads was so highly valued that Congress enacted the Interstate Commerce Act in 1887 in order to prevent undue state restrictions on railroad traffic.[14]

---

[9] *Civil Rights Cases,* 109 United States Reports 3 at 26–62 (quotation on p. 26); David Delaney, *Race, Place, and the Law, 1836–1948* (Austin: University of Texas Press, 1998), 90; Ayers, *The Promise of the New South,* 136.

[10] C. Vann Woodward, *The Strange Career of Jim Crow* (1957; 3rd ed.; New York: Oxford University Press, 1974), 7.

[11] Delaney, *Race, Place, and the Law,* 1836–1948, 6.

[12] Leon F. Litwack, *Trouble in Mind: Black Southerners in the Age of Jim Crow* (New York: Alfred A. Knopf, 1998), 9–10.

[13] George C. Werner, "Railroads," in Ron Tyler, Douglas E. Barnett, Roy R. Barkley, Penelope C. Anderson, and Mark F. Odintz (eds.), *The New Handbook of Texas* (6 vols.; Austin: Texas State Historical Association, 1996), V, 412.

[14] "Interstate Commerce Act," Feb. 4, 1887, Chapter 104, 24 stat. 379.

By the 1880s a minority of black Texans could afford the luxury of first-class rail travel, which, given the slow speeds of that period, often involved overnight stays on the train. Many white Texans, influenced by Victorian ideas, worried about the sexual charge created when strangers, especially white and black strangers, were temporarily placed in intimate surroundings. At that time, interracial personal relations did not have to end in physical contact to be considered dangerously intimate and therefore damaging to a woman's reputation. Press reports demonstrate that there existed among white Texans no shortage of lurid imaginings about the consequences of racial mixing on sleeping cars.[15]

During this period many Texans were also unhappy with railroad corporations. They accused railway officials of colluding with state and federal officials, discriminating against farmers who sought to transport their agricultural commodities at a fair rate, and paying little heed to local expectations or desires for passenger train schedules or facilities.[16] The anger and bitterness of Texas voters was expressed during the 1891 legislative session, which established the Railroad Commission of Texas. Railroad companies had previously operated with little government supervision, but henceforth they were strictly regulated.[17] Following the example of other southern states, Texas legislators specifically addressed the subject of segregation on the railroads, enacting in the same year a new law that required:

> Each railway company . . . doing business in this state . . . shall provide separate coaches or compartments . . . for the accommodation of white and negro passengers, which separate coaches shall be equal in all points of comfort and convenience . . . each compartment of a railroad coach divided by good and substantial wooden partitions with a door therein shall be deemed a separate coach within the meaning of this law, and each separate coach shall bear in some conspicuous place appropriate words in plain letters indicating the race for which it is set apart.[18]

---

[15]Ayers, *The Promise of the New South*, 137–146. See also Mary Frances Berry and John W. Blassingame, *Long Memory: The Black Experience in America* (New York: Oxford University Press, 1982). Berry and Blasingame observe in Chapter Four, "Sex and Racism," that in contrast to white men, black Americans of this era were generally uninterested in pursuing intimate interracial relationships.

[16]In August 1885 the major roads organized the Texas Traffic Association to fix rates. The state attorney general filed suit alleging that collusion to set tariffs was illegal, and the Texas Supreme Court declared this activity unconstitutional in 1888. See Earle B. Young, *Tracks to the Sea: Galveston and Western Railroad Development, 1866–1900* (College Station: Texas A&M University Press, 1999), 92–94.

[17]David F. Prindle, "Railroad Commission," in Tyler, et al. (eds.) *The New Handbook of Texas*, V, 409; George C. Werner, "Railroads," in Tyler, et al. (eds.), *The New Handbook of Texas*, V, 410.

[18]"Separate Coach Law," Acts 1891, p. 44; Acts 1907, p. 58; G.L. Vol. 10, p. 46. The bill was first proposed in the 1889 session and failed to pass. Norris Wright Cuney, then chairman of the Republican Party of Texas and the state's most influential black politician, wrote a brilliantly prescient letter in opposition to the legislation to certain prominent representatives. See Maud Cuney Hare, *Norris Wright Cuney: A Tribune of the Black People* (New York: Crises, 1913; reprint, New York: Steck-Vaughn Co., 1968), 128–130.

This was the new statute the I. & G. N. invoked when it ejected Thomas Cain from his sleeping car accommodations.

Among the reasons for the passage of this and similar legislation across the South was a realization by whites that black men and women coming of age in the 1890s were the first generation to reach maturity without having experienced the social controls of slavery firsthand.[19] What the white South wanted was not so much separation as subordination. This can be clearly seen in the fact that, throughout the Jim Crow era, a black nursemaid traveling with a white invalid or a small white child was allowed to ride in the "Whites Only" railway car alongside her charge while a black man or woman traveling alone or with friends or family—in other words, independently—was not.

Railway companies operating overnight service in Texas at the time of the new legislation attempted to avoid the cost of doubling their sleeping car fleets by strictly interpreting the new statute as applicable only to coaches, not to sleeping cars. In practice, however, this policy drew fire. A February 1893 story in the *Galveston Daily News* reported a controversy over the Wagner Sleeping Car Company's policy that black porters working sleeping cars on runs between Houston and Dallas occupy upper berth number "1." One white passenger protested that "a big burly negro porter" had "crawled into the berth immediately above" his wife. The *News* reported speculation that the Texas statute could not be enforced under these circumstances.[20]

The Railroad Commission itself discussed internally whether or not the law only addressed coach travel but publicly sought more widespread observance of the state's segregation laws. One example of the commission's effort is found in a 1903 communication to the general manager of the Fort Worth & Denver City Railway Company concerning a complaint that blacks and whites were allowed to commingle in dining cars. Commission chairman, L. J. Storey, wrote of the complaint, "Technically speaking . . . the law may not include dining cars, but undoubtedly the spirit of the law . . . would seem to demand separate dining car service, as well as separate chair and sleeping car service."[21] Chairman Storey observed that, of course, nobody was compelled to use the dining car service, but passengers expected its availability and did not come prepared with a lunch basket. He mentioned wryly that, while all of the carriers had rules limiting meal service to the dining cars, "generally an extra quarter repeals the rule," meaning that offended whites might not have prepared themselves with

---

[19]Delaney, *Race, Place, and the Law,* 100; Litwack, *Trouble in Mind,* 214, 238–239.

[20]*Galveston Daily News,* Feb. 4, 1893. Husband and wife abandoned the facilities and "sat up the entire night."

[21]L. J. Storey, Chairman, Railroad Commission of Texas, to F. W. Egan, General Manager, Fort Worth & Denver City Railway Co., Aug. 21, 1903, Letterpress Book 4-2/1087, p. 244 (Archives Division, Texas State Library, Austin; hereinafter cited as TSL).

extra quarters. He concluded, "Unless the practice is discontinued the Commission will take up the question as to whether or not it has power to correct the abuse."[22]

The Fort Worth & Denver City Railway Company chose not to trifle with the Railroad Commission on this matter, as the agency's good will on rate and tariff questions was of paramount importance to it. Yet, despite railroad officials' desire to please the Railroad Commission, neither this railway company nor any other would ever provide a separate dining car for blacks due to the expense involved. Separate dining times for black and white patrons and later the use of curtains seemed to be the most expedient approach to the issue for railroad officials.

Another example of the Railroad Commission's policy of encouraging rather than requiring compliance with Jim Crow practices is seen in a 1904 letter from Commissioner Storey to the Atchison, Topeka & Santa Fe Railroad Company about a white passenger who was offended that the races were mixed at the waiting room of the company's Cleveland, Texas, depot. The commissioner declared, "[W]hile we do not claim to have the right to force you, where you have two waiting rooms, to designate one for whites and one for colored people, yet it is right that you should do so, and better for all concerned that it should be done, this I am sure you will agree with us."[23] This statement was made a few years before a new Texas statute explicitly required segregation in waiting rooms. Prior to the passage of that statute, the commission relied on the power of suggestion rather than the force of law in its dealings with railroad officials on the issue of segregation in depots.

Texas Railroad Commission records from this time period are replete with letters that freely express the venomous racial prejudices of complainants. For example, one correspondent wrote the following in August 1909 regarding the Santa Fe depot at Arcola:

> More than once I have seen this waiting room crowded with coons and if it happened to be cold or raining the white people would have to hold their noses and crowd in too. . . . When the coons occupy a place they are equal, if not better, than the white people, and their importance and impudence swells.[24]

The Railroad Commission forwarded this communication to the Santa Fe, and dryly asked its officials to "remove cause for further complaint."[25]

---

[22]Ibid.

[23]Chairman L. J. Storey to F. G. Pettibone, general manager, Feb. 23, 1904, Records of Railroad Commission of Texas, Letterpress Book 4-2/1153, p. 158 (TSL).

[24]Railroad Commission of Texas Letterbook 4-2/1149, Aug. 13, 1909, p. 327 (TSL).

[25]Railroad Commission of Texas Letterbook 4-2/1149, Aug. 13, 1909, p. 327 (TSL).

The Railroad Commission also received letters from black passengers and responded favorably to them. Writing to the Santa Fe's general manager in 1906, the agency concluded:

> We think this is a just complaint. The idea of compelling people to ride 218 miles in a car without water cooler or water closet for the benefit of passengers, who are not permitted to enter other cars, is a violation of the purpose and intent of the laws of this state, and the Commission desires to say that this must be remedied. It would not be tolerated for a moment in a car devoted to white passengers and under the laws of this state there can be no difference made as to the necessary comforts on account of race or color.[26]

The agency's position here did not contradict its commitment to segregation; it insisted only on some semblance of equality as to "the necessary comforts," not to a more general equality.

The Louisiana legislature adopted a Jim Crow railroad statute in 1890, one year before Texas did. Homer Plessy, whom the state classified as a black man because one of his great-grandparents was black, challenged the law after a deliberately provoked ejection from a "whites only" railcar. A group desiring to overturn the statute had selected Plessy as a favorable plaintiff, due to his white appearance, in a carefully planned test case. He asserted that a state law forbidding the races to mingle was by its nature a violation of the Fourteenth Amendment because it denied them the "equal protection" of the law. In 1896 the U.S. Supreme Court, with only one dissenting vote, sustained the Louisiana statute on the theory that separate accommodations must be equal. The Court reasoned, as it had in the 1883 Civil Rights Cases, that the Fourteenth Amendment was intended to enforce political equality, not social equality, as the latter could only come by voluntary consent of the individuals involved.[27] During argument of the case, the Court's attention was directed to the fact that the state of Massachusetts, the original hotbed of abolitionist sentiment, prescribed or permitted separate schools for blacks and whites, as did the District of Columbia, California, Ohio, Indiana, New York, and Kentucky. Relying on the idea that it is the natural tendency of society to segregate itself socially, the Court's majority held that a state legislature could act "with reference to the established usages, customs and traditions of the people." Justice Henry B. Brown denied that segregation "stamps the colored race with a badge of inferiority," stating: "if this be so . . . it is solely because the colored race chooses to put that construction on it."[28]

---

[26]Railroad Commission of Texas Letterbook 4-2/1071, Mar. 17, 1906, p. 245 (TSL).

[27]*Plessy v. Ferguson*, 163 U.S. 537 at 550 (1896). For background information on the *Plessy* case, see Litwack, *Trouble in Mind*, 243; Ayers, *The Promise of a New South*, 144–145; and Richard Kluger, *Simple Justice: The History of Brown v. Board of Education and Black America's Struggle for Equality* (New York: Alfred A. Knopf, 1976), 73.

[28]*Plessy v. Ferguson* (1st quotation on p. 550; 2nd quotation on p. 551).

The single dissenting justice was again John Harlan, who wrote that the decision to legitimize a "separate but equal" framework would "arouse race hate" and "perpetuate a feeling of distrust" between blacks and whites. He predicted, "The thin disguise of equal accommodations for passengers in railroad coaches will not mislead anyone."[29]

Perhaps because the quarters were less confining, segregation in Texas depots was not legally required for almost twenty years after segregation on Texas trains was decreed. At the turn of the century, only three southern states—Mississippi, Louisiana, and Arkansas—had instituted segregation in railroad stations. Within a few years, however, states throughout the Deep South and as far west as Texas and Oklahoma passed such laws. The Texas statute, enacted on May 10, 1909, provided that "[r]ailroad companies shall keep and maintain separate apartments in such depot buildings for the use of white passengers and negro passengers."[30]

For railroad companies, compliance with the new depot segregation law was expensive. The Santa Fe began a significant wave of station replacements in 1910, substituting buildings with two separate spaces for those with only a single waiting room. It was not feasible simply to add a room to an existing facility because the ticket office had to be in the middle of the two waiting rooms in order to serve each side separately. The Railroad Commission recognized the magnitude of the task and gave railway companies several years to meet the requirements of the new statute.[31] The commission also looked the other way when companies operating in West Texas chose to ignore the statute because there were few blacks in that territory.

Historians have noted with interest that no southern state ever compelled segregation in the outdoor waiting area between the depot and the train tracks it served. One scholar, Grace Elizabeth Hale, has commented that the prospect of regulating this realm of activity seemed to baffle white ingenuity.[32] The historical record is replete with photographs of integrated trackside crowds awaiting a segregated train in the shadow of a completely segregated Texas depot.

---

[29]*Plessy v. Ferguson.*

[30]Acts 1909, 2nd Civil Statutes, p. 401, recodified to *Vernon's Texas Statutes and Codes Annotated,* (Rev. Civ. St. 1911), Article 6693 and Article 6694.

[31]For examples of commission forbearance, see Letterpress Books 4-2/1174, p. 284 (Sanger, Texas depot, May 16, 1911); 4-2/1169, p. 457 (Buckholts, Texas depot, Oct. 20, 1911); and 4-2/1230, p. 117 (Wadsworth, Texas depot, Sept. 8, 1913) (TSL).

[32]Grace Elizabeth Hale, *Making Whiteness: The Culture of Segregation in the South, 1890–1940* (New York: Pantheon Press, 1998), 133–135. Hale found the Farm Security Administration photographs from the 1930s helpful in making observations about patterns of racial interaction in public places. The author has collected some 1,500 images of activity along the tracks of the Santa Fe railroad in Texas between 1890 and 1960. A study of this collection clearly supports Hale's premise that the space between the depot and the train or its tracks was never racially segregated.

Sometimes the black railway patrons in these images appear deferential to whites, but at other times they stand shoulder-to-shoulder with them. Certainly, the natural tendency of the rural South in public places was to mingle irrespective of race. The laws considered in this study would have been unnecessary if separation of the races in the South was truly natural, as alleged by Justice Brown in the *Plessy* case.

The only known case in which the Texas Railroad Commission held a hearing on a complaint about racial mixing in a Texas depot involved an area outside of the old South. Perhaps the conflict arose because of the lack of well-defined customs and patterns of racial relations in that region. The rise of cotton cultivation on the Texas High Plains and its expansion after 1920 attracted an influx of migrant black workers. In April 1923 a traveling salesman wrote the Railroad Commission a letter from the Santa Fe depot at Slaton, southeast of Lubbock, complaining that in the men's waiting room, which had a seating capacity of twenty-four, he had counted "17 Negroes, 14 white persons and 6 Mexicana [*sic*]," and a "conglomeration" in the ladies' waiting room.[33] The company answered by reporting that between May 10 and May 21, 1920, it had sold only twenty-nine tickets to blacks. Officials stated that the permanent population of the Slaton community included only about forty-three blacks out of some four thousand residents.[34]

When the railroad disputed the necessity of separate facilities, the commission held a hearing on the matter in Slaton on July 6, 1923. Commissioner Walter Splawn presided. He heard evidence that the railroad sold less than three tickets to blacks for every twenty-eight tickets sold to whites, and that most of the former group's travel was seasonal and related to the cotton harvest. Commissioner Splawn did not seem to have his heart set on enforcing segregation under these conditions. The Santa Fe's local counsel reported to its Galveston management that the commissioner "was not active or aggressive in developing the testimony."[35] Yet, the fact remained that on the day of the original complaint, blacks had outnumbered whites in the Slaton waiting room, which must have caused an unusual feeling among the whites. The commissioner asked that he be provided a transcript of the hearing within a month. By that deadline the company made a decision to construct a separate waiting room at Slaton for blacks, and it voluntarily added a waiting room for blacks to the Lubbock depot in the same year. None of the company's other Texas stations north of Lubbock

[33]J. E. Eaves of Dallas, Texas, to Railroad Commissioner of Texas, Apr. 15, 1923, RG D-4, box 41, folder 5 (Houston Metropolitan Research Center, Houston; hereinafter cited as HMRC).

[34]J. W. Terry of Terry, Cavin & Mills, Galveston, to Hon. W. A. Nabors, Commissioner, Railroad Commission of Texas, June 11, 1923, RG D-4, box 41, folder 5 (HMRC).

[35]Madden, Trulove, Ryburn & Pipkin to Terry, Cavin & Mills, July 6, 1923, RG D-4, box 41, folder 5 (HMRC).

had separate waiting rooms for black patrons, nor is there any record of a request from the commission to provide them. Amarillo is the largest community in the area, but neither the Santa Fe, the Rock Island, nor the Fort Worth & Denver City had separate waiting rooms in their depots there in the mid-1920s.[36] The station segregation law never received much consideration in the Panhandle. The state capitol in Austin was a long way away, and during this time there were not many blacks permanently residing in the Texas High Plains.

The 1920s brought a severe reduction in Texas passenger train travel as people began to purchase automobiles and as the state pumped money into road and highway construction. Intrastate passenger revenues for rail carriers fell precipitously, from $58.1 million in 1920 to $25.9 million in 1929. The onset of the Depression made an already bad situation worse, driving revenue down to a low of $6.5 million in 1933.[37] The administrative headache suffered by the Texas carriers in enforcing segregation was far outweighed by the pain of inexorably declining business, as passengers of all races deserted the rails in favor of automobiles and buses. The railway companies and the Pullman Company that served them responded by making drastic reductions in personnel. Railway labor associations used Jim Crow laws as one weapon in opposing such measures.

In 1939 the Association of Pullman Car Conductors drafted a model statute that forbade the operation of a Pullman car without a Pullman conductor. The association was fighting a financially-motivated move by the company to operate some cars under the exclusive care of Pullman porters. This was a racial as well as a labor issue, because porters were generally black, while supervising conductors were always white. The president of the Conductors Association traveled the South in 1939 pushing his bill and was successful in having it introduced in the legislatures of Arkansas, Tennessee, Florida, and Texas, among others. The Texas version almost passed as Senate Bill 395, but it died in conference committee, smothered by lobbyists for the railroads and the Pullman Company.

B. H. Vroman, assistant to the vice president of the Pullman Company, came to Austin to testify before the House Committee on Labor when it held its hearing on the conductors' bill. He said that the company had carried about 40 million sleeping car passengers in 1920, 17.7 million in 1937, and 15.5 million in 1938. He pointed out that many of the runs in question were on trains that

---

[36]F. A. Lehman, general manager, Panhandle & Santa Fe Ry. Co. to J. W. Terry, Galveston solicitor, Apr. 25, 1923, RG D-4, box 41, folder 5 (HMRC).

[37]"Petition of Common Carrier Railroads for Increase in Specified Roundtrip and Intermediate Passenger Fares," Railroad Passenger Circular No. 162, Railroad Commission of Texas, docket 3522-R, Dec. 29, 1937 (Library, Railroad Commission of Texas, Austin).

were not generating revenue adequate to pay fixed operating and personnel expenses, which he estimated to be about $9,600 per car a year. Company statistics showed that many of its cars had an average occupancy of only three or four passengers, so if the company were not permitted to enjoy economies of operating expense by leaving the car solely in charge of a porter, its only alternative would be to discontinue service entirely. Vroman provided a number of examples of runs in danger of cancellation if the bill passed. One of these was the M. K. & T. connection between Houston and Wichita Falls. This service used one Pullman car each way, which with other Pullman cars was under the supervision of a conductor between Houston and Fort Worth. But at Fort Worth, where the car split off for Wichita Falls, it was the only Pullman on a smaller train, and it was staffed by one porter. The segment from Fort Worth to Wichita Falls served an average of just four passengers per day. The same arrangement prevailed on the San Antonio, Uvalde, & Gulf connection between San Antonio and Corpus Christi and some fourteen other city pairs within Texas. Many of these represented the last link in the chain of sleeping car service to smaller communities. Most state senators and representatives came from small communities and could afford to ride in Pullman cars. The company's testimony regarding the potential for loss of service appears to have convinced the conference committee to kill the legislation.[38]

Earlier in the same legislative session House Bill 487 was introduced. It would have forbade the operation of dining cars or club cars without a white steward in charge while white passengers were served.[39] That bill, which was also a labor union move, died in committee. When the legislation was first introduced, Grady Ross, the Santa Fe's Galveston attorney, reported to his supervisors and to Fred Harvey dining company personnel, "This bill seems to carry the Jim Crow idea to the nth degree, and, of course, is quite vicious."[40]

The fight became even more vicious as it shifted from the legislature to the Railroad Commission in the summer of 1939. In August of that year, the commission on its own motion entered an order requiring white conductors on all Pullman cars. This order was stayed for a few weeks to allow a hearing on August 31, 1939. The hearing lasted two days. Although the transcript does not

---

[38]Claude Pollard, Counsel, Railway General Managers Association of Texas to Messrs. Terry, Cavin & Mills, General Attorneys, Gulf, Colorado & Santa Fe Ry. Co., June 17, 1939, RG D-4, box 188, folder 12 (HMRC). This folder contains a considerable amount of material on the controversy.

[39]Grady B. Ross of Terry, Cavin & Mills, Galveston, to W. E. Maxson et al, G. C. & S. F. Railway Co., Feb. 13, 1939, RG D-4, box 188, folder 13 (HMRC).

[40]Grady B. Ross of Terry, Cavin & Mills to W. E. Maxson et al., G. C. & S. F. Ry. Co., Feb. 13, 1939, RG D-4, box 188, folder 12 (HMRC). This folder also contains a letter, dated Feb. 25, 1939, to Mr. Ross from the Houston counsel for the Southern Pacific Lines, which commented that the proposed new law was "entirely ridiculous."

survive, it appears from the text of the resulting order that the testimony included highly charged allegations of threats to white women. The agency's directive included a finding of fact:

> [F]rom the evidence of the lady passengers who testified before this commission, the womanhood of Texas entertains a fear of serious bodily injury or personal attack from a negro man and that to subject them as passengers in Pullman cars to the service where there is only a negro porter in charge would be to such passengers . . . an undue and unjust discrimination, prejudice and abuse, . . . each berth is separated from the other berths only by these small curtains, . . . [and] on different occasions Pullman porters while on duty proceeded to drink excessively and become intoxicated.[41]

The order also contains a finding "that every Texan, both man and woman, resents any interference or instructions from a negro man or from a negro porter, and the Commission finds that a negro porter would not attempt to and could not discipline a passenger on a car, nor would he attempt to prevent any misconduct in such car." All in all, the order was a thoroughly racist diatribe that Commissioner Ernest O. Thompson, former mayor of Amarillo, refused to sign, perhaps because Amarillo did not have an entrenched history of segregation. Commissioners Lon Smith and Jerry Sadler apparently came from different traditions. They approved the order on November 4, 1939.[42] A few months later, in March 1940, Sadler entered the Democratic primary for governor to run against Thompson and others. Sadler's memoirs show that he had that move in mind for some months prior to the vote, so possibly his vote for an order of this nature, far out of line with the usual attitude of the agency, can be explained as an anticipatory appeal to the populist and racist sentiment of the Texas electorate.[43]

---

[41]Final Order, Railroad Commission of Texas, Docket 3669-R, Nov. 4, 1939 (TSL).

[42]Ibid.

[43]Jerry Sadler, *Politics, Fat-Cats & Honey-Money Boys: The Mem-wars of Jerry Sadler* (Santa Monica, Calif.: Roundtable Publishing, Inc., 1984), 190–192. Adoption of this order provoked immediate litigation by the Pullman Company, sparking a case that went all the way to the U.S. Supreme Court. Suit was filed in U.S. District Court on November 28, 1939, to enjoin enforcement of the order, and the Court entered an injunction. On direct appeal to the U.S. Supreme Court, the case was remanded to Texas state court for the purpose of determining questions of applicable state law. *Railroad Commission of Texas v. The Pullman Company*, 312 U.S. 496 (1941). The case was set for trial before the Fifty-third Judicial District in Austin but was postponed upon the commission's request. The matter drifted without resolution for almost fifteen years, while the injunction prevented the order's enforcement. On May 7, 1955, Austin counsel for the Texas Railroad Association sent a letter to the general managers and attorneys of all member lines reporting that "at long last, as an abdicating King once said," the commission had on April 11 rescinded its order that all sleeping cars be supervised by a white Pullman conductor. See Ireland Graves and Kenneth McCalla to Commissioners Thompson, William J. Murray Jr., and Olin Culberson, Apr. 5, 1955, and Kenneth McCalla to member lines, May 7, 1955, RG D-4, box 188, folder 12 (HMRC).

Segregation in rail transit went practically unchallenged from the beginning of the twentieth century to the depths of the Great Depression. Though constitutional theory held that separate facilities, if equal, were legally acceptable, in truth they were never equal at all, a reality that opened the door to the first successful challenges to segregation laws. On April 20, 1937, a black man named Arthur Mitchell left Chicago on an Illinois Central train holding a first-class ticket for Pullman car sleeping accommodations to Hot Springs, Arkansas. The next morning, just before the train's arrival in Memphis, a porter moved him to another Pullman car bound for Hot Springs. At Memphis, the car was transferred to a train operated by the Chicago, Rock Island & Pacific Railway Company. As soon as the train crossed the Mississippi River into Arkansas, a Rock Island conductor came to Mitchell and told him that Arkansas's Jim Crow laws required him to leave his Pullman car and ride the rest of the way in a Jim Crow coach. Mitchell resisted, pointing out that he had paid for a first-class ticket to Hot Springs. But the conductor was adamant. He threatened to stop the train and have Mitchell put off if he declined to move, and he made a number of rude remarks to Mitchell. Mitchell moved to a car that was dirty and smelly, had a seat above a hole in the floor that served as a toilet, and lacked access to a washbasin with running water, soap, and towels.[44]

The Rock Island had picked on the wrong man. Mitchell was a United States congressman, elected from a Chicago district in the Democratic Party's "New Deal" national landslide in 1934. President Franklin D. Roosevelt had selected him to give the opening address at the 1936 Democratic National Convention.[45] As soon as he returned home from his ill-fated trip to Hot Springs, Congressman Mitchell filed suit against the railway company in an Illinois court seeking $50,000 in damages. A few months later he also filed a complaint against the company with the Interstate Commerce Commission, asking for a cease and desist order pursuant to the Interstate Commerce Act forbidding interstate railroads from subjecting passengers "to any undue or unreasonable prejudice or discrimination whatsoever."[46]

In a split opinion issued in November 1938, the ICC narrowly sided with the railroad company, finding that the discrimination against Mitchell was "plainly not unjust or undue." There was a strongly worded dissenting opinion by the minority.[47] Mitchell appealed the decision to a Federal District Court in Chicago, which sustained the ICC. He then appealed to the U.S. Supreme

---

[44]Catherine A. Barnes, *Journey from Jim Crow: The Desegregation of Southern Transit* (New York: Columbia University Press, 1983), 1, 20.

[45]Sean Dennis Cashman, *African Americans and the Quest for Civil Rights, 1900–1990* (New York: New York University Press, 1991), 52.

[46]229 Interstate Commerce Commission Reports 703 (1938).

[47]Ibid.

Court. Then, as now, the solicitor general of the United States normally represented the ICC before the Court. But Solicitor General Francis Biddle would not swallow the ICC position and instead his office filed a brief in support of Mitchell. He authorized the ICC to file its own brief. Ten southern states banded together to file a brief as "friends of the court."[48] Only seven days after the states filed, Chief Justice Charles Evans Hughes announced the unanimous decision of the Court in Mitchell's favor. But the Court did not rule that segregation was illegal; it determined merely that the Rock Island's failure to offer exactly identical accommodation to both blacks and whites was illegal. Although the Rock Island asserted that there was too little demand for first-class space to justify a separate sleeping car for blacks, the Court was unsympathetic to this argument and held that equality of accommodations was a right of each black individual, regardless of low numbers.[49]

The black press in Texas viewed the decision as half a loaf because it covered interstate Pullman car passage only, but the half was welcomed. The *Houston Informer* gave the story a banner front-page headline, commenting, "The logical consequence will be, in a south that is already too poor to furnish two equal sets of equipment for the two races of the south, the gradual abandonment of segregation." It continued, "If there are any Americans who refuse to ride with Negroes, they should be left the burden of finding other means to gratify their luxurious taste of seclusion."[50] White southern newspaper editors noted that the Court had not overturned segregation, and for that reason they generally accepted the ruling. The Rock Island settled Congressman Mitchell's private suit by paying him $1,250.[51]

It was the railway companies that the ruling really pinched, because they, not the states, were expected to bear the expense of doubling their fleets of cars in southern service to provide separate and equal facilities. The companies rejected this path of action. Instead, they desegregated their first-class interstate service but made various efforts to maintain some degree of separation within cars. The most visible of these was the use of partitions to separate white and black passengers in dining cars.[52] Of course, for the average black traveler, who could not afford first-class travel, the Court's opinion had no impact. Coach travelers were still subjected to segregation in separate, often inferior, equipment.

---

[48]Barnes, *Journey from Jim Crow*, 27–30.

[49]*Mitchell v. U.S.*, 313 U.S. 80 (1941).

[50]"Supreme Court Outlaws Inferior R.R. Accommodations for Negroes—Negroes Entitled to Equal Facilities," *Houston Informer*, May 3, 1941, p. 1.

[51]Barnes, *Journey from Jim Crow*, 30–31.

[52]The Texas lines previously had not permitted blacks to use the dining car until all whites were finished eating. "[W]e will handle colored passengers in dining cars the same as other Texas Lines do, this is, so long as there are any white passengers in the dining car no service will be afforded colored passengers. Fred Harvey has instructed Stewards of dining cars to canvass colored passengers in

Blacks traveling through Texas in these years suffered the same humiliation experienced by Congressman Mitchell. Few had the nerve to resist. The black professional class, which might have served as a voice for change, was quite small. The 1940 U.S. census found only 2 black architects, 4 black veterinarians, 6 black engineers, 23 black lawyers, 31 black pharmacists, and 164 black doctors in all of Texas.[53]

There were a comparatively larger number of black ministers in the South and West, however, and on June 16, 1941, C. S. Stamps, a black clergyman from Kansas City, Missouri, followed Congressman Mitchell's lead. The Reverend Mr. Stamps purchased a coach ticket for travel that day from Kansas City to Houston. He rode the Santa Fe line to Dallas overnight, and the next morning at Dallas's Union Station attempted to board the Rocket for Houston. This train was a three-unit articulated streamliner that was operated north of Teague by the Rock Island and south of that point by the Burlington-Rock Island. The first unit consisted of a diesel engine, a baggage-mail compartment, and a kitchen. The second unit was a dinette and coach with six tables for four people each in the dinette, and the third unit was a parlor car with twenty-four seats. The Rocket had a scheduled running time of four hours between Dallas and Houston.

On his trip Stamps traveled with another black minister from Wichita, Kansas. When they presented their tickets, the conductor, over their protests, seated them in the baggage compartment, where there were wicker seats for four people. A black man and a black woman with a baby occupied the other two seats on this trip. There were no windows or drinking fountains; nor was there air conditioning or dining service. The seats were located directly adjacent to the diesel engine compartment, so the noise must have been considerable. Stamps endured a miserable ride to Houston and filed a complaint with the ICC asserting discriminatory treatment.[54]

The Rock Island argued to the ICC examiner that the Rocket carried only about ten black passengers per month and reported that it had subsequently

---

Jim Crow Car as to what meals they will want and has made arrangements to serve such passengers with coffee and sandwiches, also with regular table d'hôte meals, latter being served to passengers in Jim Crow Car. However, if there are any colored passengers who insist upon going to the dining car they will be accommodated after all white passengers have been served." Operating Bulletin B-1-92236, Office of Trainmaster, Southern Division, Gulf, Colorado & Santa Fe Ry. Co., Sept. 22, 1936 (copy in possession of the author). This policy dated to the turn of the century, when trains were first equipped with dining cars, reflected the will of the Railroad Commission at that time. See Commissioner L. J. Storey to F. W. Egan, general manager, Fort Worth & Denver City Railway Company, Aug. 21, 1903, Railroad Commission of Texas Letterbook 4-2/1087, p. 244 (TSL).

[53]Alwyn Barr, *Black Texas: A History of African Americans in Texas, 1528–1995* (2nd ed.; Norman: University of Oklahoma Press, 1996), 198.

[54]ICC Docket No. 28781, *C. S. Stamps v. Chicago, Rock Island and Pacific Railway Co., et al.*, decided Oct. 26, 1942.

partitioned off eight seats in each coach section and constructed toilets there for black passengers. Arrangements were made for these passengers to be served meals in their coach seats when whites occupied the diner. The agency concluded that with these changes the accommodations offered were "substantially equal" and it dismissed the complaint.[55]

The greatest cultural change affecting the administration of Jim Crow laws on the railroads came with World War II. Troop traffic dramatically increased the numbers of black passengers riding trains in Texas and throughout the South. United States War Department policy required equal treatment of black and white soldiers.[56] The Railroad Commission received a continual stream of complaints in the early war years about the increased racial mixing caused by troop movements, and its chairman responded in July 1943 by sending a circular letter addressing the situation to all of the large Texas carriers. Chairman Beauford H. Jester, later governor of Texas, acknowledged in this letter that the war effort complicated efforts to prevent the intermingling of the races in the Pullman cars and dining cars of Texas trains, and asked only that the companies "give consideration to making such plans and regulations as will sharply curtail, if not eliminate, the use of Pullman cars and dining cars by Negro passengers on trains in Texas after the war."[57] Curiously, Jester called for curtailing or completely eliminating blacks' access to first-class rail service after the war rather than for providing completely separate facilities. Few then realized that the war would permanently change key aspects of American society.

Before the end of the 1940s, the Railroad Commission's resolve to enforce the state's Jim Crow laws completely collapsed. A study of commission files for this period indicates that the collapse was driven not by black citizen complaints but by the railroads' hostility to the cost of enforcing segregation statutes. Texas was on the western edge of Jim Crow territory, and by the 1940s the western-oriented lines had adopted a form of passive resistance to the state's segregation laws as a matter of financial necessity.

The Santa Fe, the Missouri Pacific, and the M. K. & T. in particular could not justify the duplication of passenger equipment already stretched thin by wartime demands. These companies were inclined to look the other way when a black passenger sat down with whites. In November 1943 Railroad Commission Engineer C. F. Boulden wrote to F. W. Grace, general manager of the M. K. & T., stating that he had noticed mixed seating of black and white passengers on a coach on the

---

[55]Ibid.

[56]M. K. & T. Railroad Company of Texas, Circular 381, Office of Superintendent, South Texas District, Smithville, Tex., Aug. 28, 1943 (Railroad Commission of Texas, Jim Crow File, 1939–1947, copy in possession of the author).

[57]Chairman Beauford H. Jester to railway operating officials, July 26, 1943, Railroad Commission of Texas (Jim Crow File, copy in possession of the author).

southbound Texas Special, which ran from St. Louis to San Antonio. He reported, "I talked to both conductors about this and each stated that the condition of intermingling Negro and white passengers on the southbound Texas Special is customary, and each seems confused as to his authority to separate the Negroes from the whites." "As a remedy for this condition," he continued, "I suggest that, as southbound M-K-T trains approach the Texas state line near Denison, the Negro passengers thereof should, without fail, be invited to occupy the space that is regularly assigned to Negro passengers."[58]

Rather than acquiesce to Boulden's request, Grace suggested a meeting to confer about his company's views on the matter.[59] Boulden may have realized that the M. K. & T. management would not be sympathetic to the commission's concerns, for on the same day that he wrote to Grace he also informed the Oklahoma commission about his findings, stating, "[W]e earnestly solicit your cooperation in helping us to segregate the Negro and white passengers, especially on the M-K-T—Frisco trains that run through your state." He made particular reference to the Texas Special as "the train that seems to give the most trouble" and commented, "During the past year, several race riots and near race riots have been started in Texas when northern Negroes attempted to go beyond their long-established limits." His letter concluded: "I feel that proper enforcement of the separate coach law will be a big step toward keeping down racial disturbances at a time when our nation needs complete unity of its citizenship."[60] Oklahoma commission General Counsel Floyd Green replied immediately. He referred Boulden to the opinion of the U.S. Supreme Court in *E. P. McCabe, et al. v. Santa Fe*, 235 U.S. 151 (1914), which suggested that the Oklahoma Jim Crow statute could not be applied to interstate passengers.[61] Since any person crossing the Texas line from Oklahoma was an interstate passenger, the Oklahoma commission believed that it lacked the jurisdiction to sort the races as Boulden requested and declined to give any assistance.[62]

In the following year the Missouri Pacific was singled out for its resistance to the law. Joe T. Steadham, chairman of the Texas Joint Railway Labor Legislative Board, filed a formal complaint with the Railroad Commission that on Missouri Pacific Trains 207 and 208 between Texarkana and Longview the company was

---

[58]C. F. Boulden, Railroad Commission of Texas, to F. W. Grace, vice-president and general manager, Missouri-Kansas-Texas lines, Nov. 18, 1943 (Jim Crow File, copy in possession of the author).

[59]F. W. Grace to C. F. Boulden, Railroad Commission of Texas, Nov. 30, 1943 (Jim Crow File, copy in possession of the author).

[60]C. F. Boulden, Railroad Commission of Texas, to State Corporation Commission of Oklahoma, Nov. 30, 1943 (Jim Crow File, copy in possession of the author).

[61]Because of a procedural defect the court dismissed this case, but Chief Justice Hughes was openly hostile to the Oklahoma position.

[62]Floyd Green, Oklahoma Corporation Commission, to C. F. Boulden, Railroad Commission of Texas, Dec. 2, 1943 (Jim Crow File, copy in possession of the author).

"serving meals to colored passengers in the dining cars on these trains during the time white passengers are being served meals." There were no partitions in these cars to separate the races, and Steadham urged that the Texas attorney general file suit against the company for violating the Jim Crow laws.[63]

In an internal agency memorandum discussing the legal merits of the complaint, Boulden reported that the railway companies were forbidden to purchase additional equipment due to the wartime emergency needs of the defense industry and proposed that the companies instead be formally requested to use a heavy cloth curtain to separate a few tables for use by blacks, moving the curtain rod as daily needs for space fluctuated. This proposal would, in effect, have segregated interstate passengers (Texarkana being on the state line), and in his memo he acknowledged that his recommendation was illegal in view of the *Mitchell* and *Stamps* cases, both of which he cited and described. Boulden stated that he had recently seen cloth curtains used for this purpose and recommended that the idea be presented to the carriers "as a suggestion only," advising the commissioners privately that the practice could not be compelled in view of legal developments.[64] The chairman of the commission sought guidance from the governor, who responded by asking the attorney general to prepare a memorandum detailing all of the state's segregation laws.[65]

After some debate, the commission resolved to request a formal opinion of the attorney general on the question of allowing blacks and whites to eat in the same dining car. The attorney general responded with an opinion that the statute required separate dining cars, or use of the same car at different times.[66] This result was, of course, completely impractical for the railway companies. They were already operating their passenger service unprofitably in some cases, and the dining car service was particularly expensive. The cost of adding a second dining car with its own staff—just what the Brotherhood of Railroad Trainmen wanted in order to create extra jobs for its members—would be prohibitive, and

[63]Joe T. Steadham, Brotherhood of Railroad Trainmen, to Beauford H. Jester, chairman, Railroad Commission of Texas, May 18, 1944 (Jim Crow File, copy in possession of the author).

[64]C. F. Boulden, Railroad Commission of Texas, to Railroad Commissioners, May 29, 1944, memorandum (Jim Crow File, copy in possession of the author).

[65]L. H. Flewellen, assistant attorney general, to Hon. Coke R. Stevenson, governor, June 6, 1944, memorandum (Jim Crow File, copy in possession of the author).

[66]Texas Attorney General Opinion o-6424, approved Mar. 6, 1945. The attorney general cited a Pennsylvania court decision that stated, "It is not an unreasonable regulation to seat passengers so as to preserve order and decorum and to prevent contacts and collisions arising from natural or well known customary repugnances, which are likely to breed disturbances by promiscuous sitting . . . if a negro takes a seat beside a white man or his wife or daughter, the law cannot repress the anger or conquer the aversion which some will feel. However unwise it may be to indulge the feeling, human infirmity is not always proof against it. It is much wiser to avert the consequences of this repulsion of race by separation than to punish afterwards the breach of the peace it may have caused."

the commissioners knew that it was out of the question. The best choice left to the commission was a compromise that would give some effect to the spirit of the law. It was curtain time for Jim Crow, in more ways than one.

In October 1945 Boulden wrote to the management of lines entering Texas from the North:

> Because of extenuating circumstances, there has been some laxity in the enforcement of the separate coach law . . . during the recent war period. This is especially true of southbound trains entering Texas from Kansas, Oklahoma, Missouri and Arkansas. Now that the war emergency is over, we are inclined to get back to the full meaning and intent of the Texas statutes.[67]

Boulden continued by acknowledging the difficulty presented by the variable numbers of black and white passengers in coach cars and admitted, "Accordingly, it will be desirable to provide some flexibility in seating arrangements." He proposed that the new streamliner equipment under construction by many of the roads include a buffer coach with two sets of full partitions dividing the car into thirds, such sections to be assigned to either blacks or whites as needs fluctuated.[68]

Western-based companies continued to ignore the Texas agency's requests. The Burlington Rock Island's management must have been particularly chastened by the federal rulings against it in the *Mitchell* and *Stamps* cases; a Railroad Commission inspector who climbed on board the Twin Star Rocket at Houston's Union Station in January 1946 for a look at its equipment found only a "so-called partition" consisting of a panel one foot high and two seats wide on each side of the aisle. Burlington management received a letter from the Railroad Commission asking for the company's "friendly cooperation" in complying with the Texas law.[69] The company responded by installing a full partition with a door in the aisle. That train ran all the way to Minneapolis, and one wonders what the citizens of Minnesota thought about this alteration of their namesake streamliner, if they even realized the purpose of the alteration. The crew removed the "white" and "colored" signs whenever the northbound train cleared the Oklahoma line.

March 1946 found Engineer Boulden in Amarillo studying the equipment the Chicago, Rock Island & Pacific Railway Company used for its Trains 51 and 52. The Rock Island had placed curtains in its dining cars and Boulden remarked to the railroad's management, "This is acceptable practice although

[67]C. F. Boulden, Railroad Commission of Texas, to railway companies, Oct. 17, 1945 (Jim Crow File, copy in possession of the author).

[68]Ibid.

[69]C. F. Boulden, Railroad Commission of Texas, to Barwise & Wallace, general solicitor, Burlington-Rock Island Railroad Co., Jan. 31, 1946 (Jim Crow File, copy in possession of the author).

it is not in strict compliance with the statute." However, Boulden also found curtains used to separate the races in coaches and asked that they be replaced by partitions.[70] Boulden also rode the M. K. & T. between Austin and Dallas that same month, observing in a letter to its general manager that blacks and whites dined together. He requested that curtains be installed to separate the races.[71] Apparently, the Texas carriers were comparing notes with each other on this subject.

In April Boulden inspected the Missouri Pacific Train No. 2 between Austin and Hearne and reported by letter to its general manager, "Negroes and whites were seated together in the dining car with no attempt being made to segregate the two races." He asked for the placement of curtains to block off either two or four tables, and closed with a postscript noting that the statute applied to military personnel also: "A government request for a meal does not abrogate any of the Texas statutes. When in Rome, we must do as the Romans do."[72] By separate letter Boulden criticized the Missouri Pacific's coach partitions for lacking doors. When the Santa Fe ordered new Pullman cars that month for its Texas Chief service from Galveston to Chicago, it specified similar open partitions, with curtains instead of doors.[73]

In May 1946 the M. K. & T. yielded to commission pressure and ordered the installation of curtains in its dining cars, noting that in cases of resistance by black patrons, dining car stewards should "use the utmost diplomacy in endeavoring to have them sit in the seats assigned to them." These instructions, however, included a directive not to refuse service to "some officious colored person who will want to take advantage of what they consider their just rights and sit in the body of the car where white passengers are served."[74]

Boulden was heartened by the installation of curtains, but within weeks he found further fault with the line. He wrote to its general manager that on May 28, 1946, he had observed a black woman and boy riding in the lounge car of Train No. 2 between Austin and Temple. The woman was holding a ticket to

---

[70]C. F. Boulden, Railroad Commission of Texas, to F. B. Gibbs, trainmaster, C. R. I. & P. Railway Co., Mar. 22, 1946 (Jim Crow File, copy in possession of the author).

[71]C. F. Boulden, Railroad Commission of Texas, to H. M. Warden, vice president and general manager, M. K. & T. Lines, Mar. 22, 1946 (Jim Crow File, copy in possession of the author).

[72]C. F. Boulden, Railroad Commission of Texas, to A. B. Kelley, general manager, Missouri Pacific Lines, Apr. 27, 1946 (Jim Crow File, copy in possession of the author).

[73]Three coaches numbered 3187 to 3189, with fifty seats each, were delivered in August 1947. One supposes that by then the law was only observed on trains northbound out of Galveston, since Oklahoma authorities declined to order the company to "shuffle" its passengers as they headed south out of that state. For car photographs, see W. David Randall and William M. Ross, *The Official Pullman-Standard Library* (10 vols.; Godfrey, Ill.: Railway Production Classics, 1986), I, 80–84.

[74]Missouri, Kansas & Texas Railroad Company, Dining Service Department Bulletin L-20, May 3, 1946 (Jim Crow File, copy in possession of the author).

Petersburg, Virginia, and Boulden averred that she and the boy "could not have reasonably been mistaken for persons of Latin extraction." Boulden might have instructed the conductor to order the woman's removal from the lounge, but he could not seem to summon the nerve to do what he wanted company conductors to do. He stated in his complaint, "It seemed to be the proper procedure to let this Negro woman and boy continue their journey in the lounge car without calling the matter to the attention of these two individuals."[75] He then went on to ask the company for assurance that there would be no further mixing of the races in lounge cars. The company balked at this request. In his reply of June 10, 1946, General Manager H. M. Warden observed curtly that on June 3 the U.S. Supreme Court had ruled in the case of Irene Morgan against the Commonwealth of Virginia that Virginia's segregation laws could not be applied to interstate passengers.[76] Warden stated that, in the opinion of company counsel, the Texas segregation statute also was invalid against interstate passengers. He declared that the company would not enforce it any longer.[77] Word of this resistance spread to other Texas carriers and on July 11, 1946, the general superintendent of the Cotton Belt advised the Railroad Commission that it would decline to provide separate toilets for black and white passengers.[78]

In June 1947 Engineer Boulden responded to a citizen complaint about the mixing of the races on the Santa Fe's "Scout" as it crossed the Texas Panhandle. He stated:

> During the past few years, I have been interested in the enforcement of the separate coach laws in Texas, but I find that where a Negro holds an interstate ticket, the Federal laws take precedence and this Negro may sit anywhere he pleases regardless of the Texas statute to the contrary. The railroads in Texas have been reluctant to give written instructions to their employees regarding enforcement of the separate coach laws, because of the possibility of the railroad company being sued in the Federal Court for discrimination . . . . It seems we have more trouble segregating the Negroes and whites in those interstate trains that cross the corner of Texas. We do not have a great deal of difficulty with this situation "deep in the heart of Texas," because separate coaches are provided, and the Texas Negroes are accustomed to segregation.[79]

So far as can be determined, the Railroad Commission seldom enforced a proceeding against any carrier to compel compliance with Jim Crow laws, and it

---

[75]C. F. Boulden, Railroad Commission of Texas, to H. M. Warden, general manager, M. K. & T. Lines, May 29, 1946 (Jim Crow File, copy in possession of the author).

[76]*Morgan v. Virginia*, 328 U.S. 373, 90 LE 1317, 66 S. Ct. 1050 (1946).

[77]H. M. Warden, general manager, M. K. & T. Lines, to C. F. Boulden, Railroad Commission of Texas, June 20, 1946 (Jim Crow File, copy in possession of the author).

[78]K. M. Post, general superintendent, St. Louis Southwestern Railway Lines, to C. F. Boulden, Railroad Commission of Texas, July 11, 1946 (Jim Crow File, copy in possession of the author).

[79]C. F. Boulden, Railroad Commissioner of Texas, to John Bode, June 12, 1947 (Jim Crow File, copy in possession of the author).

never referred such a case to the attorney general for prosecution. It could have done so often, but after the U. S. Supreme Court's 1941 opinion in the *Mitchell* case, the commission may have feared that the outcome of such efforts would cause further judicial erosion of its railroad regulatory power, which already had been usurped by the ICC. When in June 1946 the first of the large Texas roads declined to cooperate with the commission's efforts to continue segregation, the others were greatly emboldened. Finally, the foundation for Jim Crow in Texas rail transportation began to crack severely. Within a few years the walls crumbled.

In the immediate post-war years the Santa Fe maintained segregated waiting rooms and ticket windows in its depots, but it relied mostly on local custom to enforce the separation. The company's agent at Killeen found that some black soldiers from nearby Fort Hood refused to comply with that custom and insisted on making their ticket purchases at the "White" window. They were served there.[80] The railroads' refusal to reinstate the old order of Jim Crow segregation after the conclusion of World War II reflected a growing national distaste for the kind of racial control exercised in the South, which to some seemed uncomfortably close in practice to the Nazi theories of racial supremacy that had been overcome at such great cost. Reporters began to ask "why," and the answers caused discomfort. One answer came from Albert Einstein. He told a reporter for the *Chicago Defender*, a nationally circulated black newspaper, "The Negroes were brought here by greediness. And people see in them the wrong they have done to them. There is a general trend in human nature: that people hate most those to whom they have done wrong."[81] Einstein, himself a refugee from Nazi Germany, knew the practice painfully well.

In 1950 the U.S. Supreme Court struck the next national blow to southern states' segregation of rail transportation. In May 1942 a black federal employee named Elmer Henderson was denied a seat in a Southern Railway Company diner while traveling from Washington, D.C., to Birmingham, Alabama. In the diner there were two tables behind curtains reserved for blacks. He found the curtains pulled back and the tables occupied by whites. The steward offered to bring him dinner in his Pullman car, but Henderson refused this accommodation. He filed a complaint with the ICC, which decided in his favor, but also found that the railway company had since changed its rules to temporarily reserve segregated tables for blacks at the beginning of the dinner hour. The ICC determined that the new rule met the requirement of the law. Henderson appealed, and a Federal District Court decided in his favor and sent the case

[80]I. V. Allison to William S. Osborn, Dec. 11, 1993, interview (transcript in possession of the author), 17–19.

[81]Earl Conrad, *Jim Crow America* (New York: Duell, Sloan & Pearce, 1947), 63. Conrad was New York bureau manager for the newspaper at the time that he wrote this book.

back to the ICC. On rehearing, the Southern Railway Company's witness testified that its rules had changed again. It now reserved one table for blacks throughout the entire time a dining car was open, and it planned to replace its curtains with partitions. The company said that one table was 8 percent of the table space in a diner, and black patrons ordered fewer than 5 percent of meals served. Separate but equal once again. The ICC found that this practice fulfilled the requirements of the law. Henderson went back to Federal District Court, which this time sustained the ICC ruling. Now, for the first time in the twentieth century, the stage was set for the U.S. Supreme Court to reconsider its 1896 decision in *Plessy v. Ferguson.* The Court agreed to hear Henderson's case, which was set for argument in April 1950, eight years after the dining car incident from which it began.[82]

The United States Justice Department filed a brief in support of Henderson's position, asserting that separate but equal was a "constitutional anachronism" and that the Court should overturn the 1896 decision that originally encouraged the South on its statutory course of segregation.[83] Henderson's counsel, Belford Lawson, summed up the case against segregation by curtains quite bluntly when he stated, "It was as if you were a pig or some kind of animal."[84] The Court decided for Henderson but declined to overrule *Plessy.* It found that Henderson had not been offered equal facilities and condemned the use of curtains and partitions, which it said emphasized "the artificiality of a difference in treatment which serves only to call attention" to the race of those segregated.[85] So the theory of separate but equal remained standing, but the curtains had to come down. The southern roads all desegregated their diners in response to the U.S. Supreme Court ruling. Western-oriented lines such as the Rock Island railroad, having already suffered adverse verdicts in the *Mitchell* and *Stamps* cases, reacted by completely desegregating its trains in 1951. This development was front-page news in the Texas black press.[86]

Nevertheless, most of the lines serving the South retained segregation in their coaches and southern state depots. Carl T. Rowan, a black native of

---

[82]*Henderson v. U.S.*, 339 U.S. 816 (1950); Robert G. Dixon Jr., "Civil Rights in Transportation and the ICC," *George Washington Law Review*, 31 (Oct., 1962), 208–209.

[83]Barnes, *Journey from Jim Crow*, 73.

[84]Richard Kluger, *Simple Justice* (New York: Alfred A. Knopf, 1976), 277. This is the leading work on the U.S. Supreme Court battle over school desegregation in the 1950s.

[85]*Henderson v. U.S.*, 339 U.S. 816 (1950).

[86]*Houston Informer*, Apr. 7, 1951, p. 1. The railroad company's order was quoted in full: "Supplement No. 2 to Circular 1729. Subject: Abolishing Segregation in Passenger Cars . . . In compliance with United States Supreme Court decision . . . patrons shall be accorded accommodations and services without distinction as to race or color in all passenger train cars." Like the Santa Fe, the Rock Island primarily served the western portion of the country.

Tennessee who had migrated north to take a position as a reporter with the Minneapolis *Morning Tribune*, was sent on a six thousand-mile investigative journey through the South in early 1951. Charged with reporting on the current state of race relations, he passed through every southern state except Texas. He found that if he made reference to the recent U.S. Supreme Court decision and threatened litigation against the carriers he was allowed to purchase Pullman lodging on overnight interstate trains. All of the depots he entered, however, still had segregated waiting rooms. He attempted on numerous occasions to purchase tickets at the "White" window and was usually refused service, sometimes politely and other times in an ugly fashion. For intrastate travel he was generally restricted to Jim Crow coaches, and he reported on their inferior condition.[87] Local recalcitrance of this nature, often enforced by municipal ordinance, motivated the final battles in the rail desegregation effort.

The next significant step toward Jim Crow's demise occurred on December 14, 1953, when the National Association for the Advancement of Colored People filed a complaint with the ICC against twelve railroads operating in the South, accusing them of continued segregation on their coaches and in their depots. The lines involved that operated in Texas included the St. Louis-San Francisco, the Missouri Pacific, the Kansas City Southern, the Texas & Pacific, and the state subsidiaries of the Atchison, Topeka & Santa Fe.[88] The ICC convened a hearing on the complaint against the southern railroads on July 27, 1954. Two months earlier, the U.S. Supreme Court had released its decision in *Brown v. Board of Education*, wherein it squarely repudiated the separate but equal doctrine established in 1896. Chief Justice Earl Warren spoke for the Court in *Brown*, condemning the segregation of black school children in an opinion courageous for its time. He stated, "To separate them from others of similar age and qualifications solely because of their race generates a feeling of inferiority as to their status in the community that may affect their hearts and minds in a way unlikely to ever be undone." The Court further declared that "any language in *Plessy v. Ferguson* contrary to this finding is rejected."[89]

This holding generated a great deal of national publicity, and the parties that pushed the ICC to consider the NAACP complaint cited the case often as a

---

[87]Carl T. Rowan, *South of Freedom* (New York: Alfred A. Knopf, 1952). This is a fascinating first-person account of a well-educated black man's confrontation with Jim Crow as the era drew to a close. Books such as this helped to convince southerners in some quarters that segregation had prevented regional economic advancement in the post-war era.

[88]The other named railroads were the Southern, the Louisville & Nashville, the Atlantic Coast Line, the Seaboard Air Line, the Illinois Central, and the Gulf, Mobile and Ohio. *National Association for the Advancement of Colored People et al. v. St. Louis-San Francisco Railway Company et al.*, 297 ICC 335 at 338, Nov. 7, 1955.

[89]*Brown v. Board of Education*, 347 U.S. 483 at 494–495 (1954).

significant precedent. Nine of the twelve lines present stipulated that they were still engaged in Jim Crow practices to at least some degree.[90] The Santa Fe, for instance, admitted to the ICC:

> Employees of the Santa Fe are instructed that all Negro coach passengers boarding trains in Texas and Oklahoma are to be directed to the coaches or portions of coaches provided for exclusive occupancy by Negroes. Employees of the Santa Fe are instructed that when trains enter Texas or Oklahoma and specific coaches or portions of coaches are provided on such trains for exclusive occupancy by Negro passengers, they are to advise all Negro coach passengers that such separate space is provided pursuant to the customs and laws of the state but are not to insist that they move to the coaches or portions of coaches provided for persons of their race.[91]

The NAACP offered testimony to prove the point as to the three lines that refused to make such a stipulation of fact (the Illinois Central, the Missouri Pacific, and the Seaboard Air Line). The Justice Department filed a brief in support of the NAACP position, urging the ICC "to declare unequivocally that a Negro passenger is free to travel the length and breadth of this country in the same manner as any other passenger." The ICC considered the case for more than a year and finally issued its opinion in November 1955, when it held that segregation violated the law. The agency completely rejected the separate but equal approach and ordered the railway companies to abandon all of their Jim Crow rules by January 10, 1956.[92]

The ICC decision represented one step in a larger legal, social, and political revolution transforming race relations in the United States during the 1950s and 1960s. One month after the ICC ruling, Rosa Parks refused to yield her seat to a white man on a city bus in Montgomery, Alabama. Her arrest inspired a citywide bus boycott, led by Martin Luther King Jr., that ended a year later when the U.S. Supreme Court declared Alabama's state and local laws requiring segregation on buses illegal.[93] In September 1957 President Dwight D. Eisenhower ordered the 101st Airborne Division to Little Rock, Arkansas, to protect nine black students enrolled at Central High School after Arkansas Gov. Orval Faubus vowed to prevent the school's integration by armed force.[94]

---

[90] *National Association for the Advancement of Colored People et al. v. St. Louis-San Francisco Railway Company et al.*, 297 ICC 335 at 338, Nov. 7, 1955.

[91] Ibid.

[92] Barnes, *Journey from Jim Crow*, 98 (quotation), 100. Barnes writes that the Justice Department's intervention greatly influenced the commission. The Eisenhower administration made clear its desire that Jim Crow practices cease, and the president held the power of appointing ICC commissioners. The sitting commissioners may have had some interest in job security.

[93] Cashman, *African Americans and the Quest for Civil Rights*, 126–130.

[94] Ibid., 137–139. For a thoughtful and progressive white contemporary's perspective on southern attitudes toward desegregation in the 1950s, see Robert Penn Warren, *Segregation: The Inner Conflict in the South* (New York: Random House, 1956).

Also at this time, in one of the most compelling media exposures of the era, white Texan author John Howard Griffin artificially darkened his skin and traveled across the Deep South posing as a black man. His experiences, reported in *Sepia* magazine, provided a compelling look at the continued indignities blacks were suffering behind the Jim Crow curtain. *Time* magazine and television reporter Mike Wallace both interviewed Griffin, and he was the subject of a documentary television program in France. For this effrontery Griffin was lynched in effigy on Main Street in his hometown of Mansfield, Texas. Within months, the chronicle of his 1959 journey was published in book form bearing the title *Black Like Me*, which cast a glaring light on the human face of segregation.[95]

As Griffin documented, many white southerners continued to fight the tide of change. Frustrated by the lack of progress despite favorable court opinions, black civil rights activists turned to a new tactic—the sit-in. On January 31, 1960, four black men in Greensboro, North Carolina, attempted to order coffee at a local Greyhound bus station but were refused service. The next day they asked to be served at the lunch counter of the local Woolworth store and were also rebuffed. Others joined them in the following days, and the movement soon spread across the South. A worried Woolworth management soon capitulated and integrated all of its lunch counters.[96] In December 1960 the U.S. Supreme Court ruled it unlawful for restaurants at bus stations to discriminate on the basis of race.[97] The Court's opinion, however, did not address similar practices by restaurants at train stations.

Notwithstanding the legal assault on segregation during the 1950s, segregation did not end easily on Texas railroads or in Texas culture. In 1951 no public restaurant in Alvin, located in Brazoria County, would serve black employees of the Santa Fe Railroad, even at the back door. Black railroaders' fellow white employees had to purchase hamburgers "to go" for them.[98] Marscine Simmons began work for the railroad in 1948 in Silsbee, Hardin County. When required to be out overnight on the line from there to terminals at Somerville or Longview in the 1950s, he routinely slept in the caboose since no motel would rent a room to a black person. He did not walk through the front door of a restaurant that served white people until after passage of the 1964 Civil Rights Act, but he was always allowed to walk through the front door of a grocery store to purchase food.[99] The difference was, of course, that, in a

---

[95]John Howard Griffin, *Black Like Me* (1960; 2nd ed.; Boston: Houghton Mifflin Co., 1977).

[96]Cashman, *African Americans and the Quest for Civil Rights*, 145–146.

[97]*Boynton v. Virginia*, 364 U.S. 454 (1960). See also Louis H. Pollak, "The Supreme Court and the States: Reflections on Boynton v. Virginia," *California Law Review*, 49 (Mar., 1961), 15.

[98]Harry Hughes to William S. Osborn, Jan. 13, 1995, interview (transcript in possession of the author), 19–20.

[99]Marscine Simmons to William S. Osborn, Feb. 15, 2000, interview (transcript in possession of the author), 9, 20–22.

restaurant setting, white waiters would have to be subservient to black customers—still a strongly unacceptable social construct in East Texas during the 1950s.[100] Marscine Simmons saw many customs change as he rode the Santa Fe rails over the next few years.

At the dawn of the 1960s, in Texas and throughout the South, vestigial segregation practices remained in place along the railroads, principally in their stations. One thoughtful observer described the practice in these final years as "the sad barbarism of intransigence."[101] The ensuing turn of events in Houston provides a useful lens for examining the social forces that finally ended the Jim Crow era in Texas.

Houston's Union Station had a ninety-four-seat coffee shop and restaurant that served both rail passengers and such others of the public as wandered in, so long as they were white. This restaurant was the site of the final major battleground for complete racial freedom for rail passengers in Texas. Ironically, by this time rail travel was scarcely used by either whites or blacks. First-class or standard business-class passengers traveling any distance from Houston in 1960 generally traveled by air, not train. Houston Mayor Roy Hofheinz ordered desegregation of the city's airport in 1953, and a federal court ordered desegregation of the airport restaurant in 1955, after the city received embarrassing criticism when India's ambassador to the United States was refused a meal there.[102] Foreign dignitaries of color would have had no occasion to visit the Union Station terminal restaurant in 1961, but had they done so, they would have been vehemently refused service, just as were Americans of color.[103] By this time, the Railroad Commission refused to hear complaints about such matters, having almost entirely abdicated its former rail industry oversight responsibilities to the ICC.[104]

On February 25, 1961, a group of black students from Texas Southern University and their supporters entered the Houston Union Station restaurant and seated themselves. Operator James D. Burleson refused to serve them, called the police, and filed trespass charges against the fourteen students, who were arrested. At the court hearing that evening Burleson testified: "I refuse to serve

---

[100]Hale, *Making Whiteness*, 188–189.

[101]Willie Morris, *North Towards Home* (New York: Random House, 1967), 185. Morris was editor of the *Texas Observer* during the early 1960s.

[102]Barr, *Black Texas*, 185.

[103]Public restaurants in Dallas also remained segregated in 1961. See reports of sit-in protests in Houston's *The Informer & Texas Freeman*, Jan. 14, 1961, p. 1.

[104]Former attorney general counsel Linward Shivers, who represented the agency at the time, gave this information over the telephone in response to a letter from the author, dated May 24, 2001. Before responding, Shivers first conferred with Fred Young, former general counsel of the Texas Railroad Commission, and Walter Wendlandt, former director of the agency's Transportation Division, to confirm his recollection.

Negroes because it would hurt my business. I have a separate table for them in the kitchen." As he told a reporter, "I'm running a white restaurant, not a negro restaurant." The students were released from jail later that evening after posting $10 bail each. The following evening, about seventy students from Texas Southern University quietly filed into the restaurant at about 6 P.M. and asked for service. The police were called again and at 7 P.M. they arrested forty-eight students, who sang "God Bless America . . . my segregated sweet home" and variations on other familiar themes as they were taken into custody. George Washington Jr., counsel to the students, purposefully declined to make arrangements for bail for several days, realizing that the publicity given to his clients' incarceration was favorable to the cause. Although Burleson held his ground and the city fathers refused to force the issue, the students continued to press their point, supported by the black community. Houston police were called to the station to make more arrests in July. On August 11, 1961, seven black Texas Southern students joined a mixed-race group of "Freedom Riders" in seeking service at the coffee shop. Burleson obtained eighteen arrest warrants and once again the offenders were jailed. The accused went to trial in September on a charge of unlawful assembly, and the jury found them guilty. The judge set their fines at $100 each.[105] A few months later, in April 1962, the Texas Court of Criminal Appeals reversed the trial court's decision, noting that one of those convicted had in his possession when arrested a railway ticket for travel to California and was therefore engaged in interstate commerce (the only door to the restaurant opened from the train station).[106]

Segregation of rail facilities and other public places in Houston did not end until the following year. Ultimately national media attention, and the fear of more of it, finally opened Houston's restaurant doors, including James D. Burleson's coffee shop at Union Station, to all persons. In September 1962 more than fifty thousand people gathered at the Rice University football stadium to hear President John F. Kennedy deliver a speech about the space program. Kennedy told the audience that with the decision to locate the National

---

[105]For one example of the general pattern of the black media's coverage of the arrests, see *Houston Forward Times*, July 29, 1961, p. 14. This newspaper, a voice for the Houston black community, sent a reporter and photographer to cover the protests and arrests and carried detailed stories. The coverage on this day described Burleson as "one of the biggest men in Houston. . . . Why, he's so big in his segregated cesspool of filth, that he can stroke a finger and 10 big burly cops will forget all about the murder capitol and rush to his side to arrest three little 'freedom riders' and haul them off to jail." The paper described Burleson as a slave to his prejudice and a coward who was afraid to show his face to the newspaper's photographer. In contrast, mainstream daily newspapers such as the *Houston Post* remained largely silent on the matter at the time. The *Houston Post* did carry a brief story about the controversy on September 6, 1961. It reported the prosecuting district attorney's statement: "[A] man has a right to run his own business as he sees fit." The convicting jury was all white.

[106]*Eddie Douglas Jones, et al. v. The State of Texas*, 355 S.W. 2d 727 (1962).

Aeronautics and Space Administration's manned space-flight control center in Houston, the city would become "the heart of a large scientific and engineering community" and a leader in the nation's effort to put a man on the moon by the end of the decade. He observed that Houston, which was "once the furthest outpost on the old frontier of the West will be the furthest outpost on the new frontier of science and space" and remarked "there is no strife, no prejudice, no national conflict in outer space as yet . . . its conquest deserves the best of all mankind."[107]

Houston embraced a progressive new business image as "Space City"; its professional baseball team was renamed the Astros and the team's stadium was christened the Astrodome. The NASA payroll and contracting budgets provided a welcome boost to the regional economy and local daily newspapers avidly followed the progress of the space program. On May 15, 1963, Houston's hometown astronaut, Gordon "Gordo" Cooper, blasted off on the final flight of the Mercury series and concluded with a successful splashdown. An internationally televised tickertape parade through downtown Houston was planned for May 23 to welcome him home.[108]

A group of more than one hundred Texas Southern University students prepared a special welcome for their returning fellow citizen in the form of picket signs protesting Jim Crow in Cooper's hometown. Word of the plan leaked out and Houston's civic leaders were finally galvanized into action. One of the most prominent of these, Jesse Jones, then president of the Houston Endowment, promised local black community leaders that segregation in the city's downtown restaurants and theaters would end within thirty days provided that the demonstration was canceled. The trade was made and the promise was kept—under an agreed-upon news blackout by the local media.[109] The city

[107]John F. Kennedy, "Address at Rice University on the Nation's Space Effort," Sept. 12, 1962, http://www.jfklibrary.org/j091262.htm/. Kennedy first announced the national goal of putting a man on the moon by the end of the decade in an address to a joint session of Congress on May 25, 1961.

[108]*Houston Post*, May 23, 1963, p. 1.

[109]Thomas R. Cole, *No Color is My Kind: The Life of Eldrewey Stearns and the Integration of Houston* (Austin: University of Texas Press, 1997), 64–99. See also, F. Kenneth Jensen, "The Houston Sit-In Movement of 1960–1961," in *Black Dixie: Afro-Texan History and Culture in Houston*, eds. Howard Beeth and Cary D. Wintz (College Station: Texas A&M University Press, 1992), 211–222. White Houston residents were not the only Texans who held out against integration in the early 1960s. In 1961 U.S. Attorney General Robert F. Kennedy dispatched FBI agents across the South on an undercover mission to survey for discriminatory practices in the segregation of interstate passengers at bus terminals. Their final report identified many Texas terminals that continued to maintain segregated waiting rooms, including Beaumont, Bryan, Dallas, Fort Worth, Galveston, Kerrville, Lubbock, Paris, Port Arthur, San Angelo, Tyler, and Wichita Falls. For coverage of the report, see Houston's *The Informer & Texas Freeman*, July 29, 1961, p. 1. For a summary of the outcome of the resulting ICC proceeding, see Dixon, "Civil Rights in Transportation and the ICC," 222, n. 127.

fathers would no longer allow the likes of James Burleson to "run a white restaurant." The 1964 Civil Rights Act soon prohibited similar practices by force of law in smaller Texas towns.[110]

The business necessity for Houston to present a positive media image at the dawn of the Space Age accomplished within a month's time what generations of struggle in Texas had not earlier delivered. The final blow to segregation in that community came not from any court of law but from the more powerful court of public opinion in the form of civic embarrassment. It came almost exactly one hundred years after President Abraham Lincoln issued his January 1, 1863, Emancipation Proclamation that freed all slaves in the rebelling states. Under pressure from the Kennedy administration, large cities elsewhere in the state soon abandoned segregation in public places as economic interests overcame long-established cultural patterns. It was finally curtain time for Jim Crow in Texas.

---

[110]The Dallas Union Station restaurant was integrated several months earlier in March 1963. For a comprehensive survey of segregation practices remaining in force across Texas in 1963, see "Texas is Integrating: A Special Report," *Texas Observer* (Austin), June 28, 1963, 9–14.

# "The Woman of It": Governor Miriam Ferguson's 1924 Election

SHELLEY SALLEE*

*At the time and later, many observers noted that the election of Miriam Ferguson to be the governor of Texas in 1924 was an event filled with contradictions. Ferguson was the first woman governor of Texas, the second in the nation, but she had clearly supported her husband, former governor James Ferguson, in his vigorous rejection of women in politics. The opposition of both Fergusons to the Ku Klux Klan was a matter of long standing; but in her campaign for governor, Ferguson attempted to create an image of "goodness and wholesomeness associated with traditional womanhood," an image little different from that the Klan pursued. From pulpits and political platforms, Klansmen called for restoration of the "womanly" woman and obliteration of "liberated sexuality." Meanwhile, Miriam Ferguson standing by a mule, feeding chickens, and wearing a bonnet and calico, presented the picture of a maternal woman, steadfastly resisting the temptations of an increasingly immoral society and projecting nothing but trustworthiness and virtue.*

*Leaders in the women's suffrage movement of Texas found little to their liking in the Ferguson campaign. Indeed, many considered her the "wrong" woman, a symbol of "tokenism." Recognizing the concerns of the suffragists, author Sallee concludes that the election represented an "inverse relationship between political emancipation" and the social and sexual liberation of the period. In short, political emancipation opened the way for political activity, but the possibility of political power depended on preservation of traditional values, or at least, the appearance of such. Ferguson's campaign was both shrewd and successful; it may have been more show than real. The values of "traditional womanhood" softened suspicions of dishonesty carried over from her husband's administration, diminished concerns over Prohibition, and attracted some voters who otherwise might have found the Klan an attractive alternative.*

*Shelley Sallee, "'The Woman of It': Governor Miriam Ferguson's 1924 Election," *Southwestern Historical Quarterly,* 100 (July, 1996), 1–16.

***Readers seeking more information on Miriam Ferguson and her times should consult Norman D. Brown,* Hood, Bonnet, and Little Brown Jug: Texas Politics, *1921–1928 (College Station: Texas A&M University Press, 1984).***

The story of Miriam Ferguson's election as the first woman governor of Texas in 1924 is filled with ironies. Although women's newly won voting rights made her candidacy possible, she and her husband Jim Ferguson had vigorously opposed woman suffrage. Supporters of women's enfranchisement argued that women would help purify politics; yet, as a proxy, Ferguson helped her husband, a former Texas governor whose corruption had led to impeachment, regain control of the state's highest office. Newspapers announced her election with headlines such as "First Woman Governor Created by Suffrage of People Named by Texas" and "Woman has Broken Down Another Barrier."[1] Leaders of the Texas woman suffrage movement, however, had protested Ferguson's candidacy. Some former suffragists had even vowed to vote for the Klan-backed candidate before supporting the wife of the man who had given a keynote address opposing the inclusion of a woman suffrage plank in the platform at the Democratic national convention of 1916.

While Miriam Ferguson gained support from some women leaders, others could not forget suffragists' long history of fighting Jim Ferguson. In 1918 organized women, under the leadership of Minnie Fisher Cunningham, traded Governor William P. Hobby a promise of women's votes in exchange for legislation enfranchising them for the gubernatorial primary.[2] After Jim Ferguson lost to Hobby, he blamed these women. In 1924 he must have felt sweet revenge when his wife faced Felix D. Robertson in the Democratic runoff, which essentially sealed gubernatorial victory in Texas. Robertson had the support of the Ku Klux Klan, a legitimate force in Texas politics during the early 1920s. Just two years prior to Miriam Ferguson's election her husband had lost the race for the state's U.S. Senate seat to Klan-backed Earle B. Mayfield.[3] Jim Ferguson decided "to run" his wife when the courts declared him ineligible for the ballot. As he wrote his friend, attorney John Bicket, "I am going into the woman business with

---

[1]Austin *American,* Aug. 25, 1924.

[2]Judith N. McArthur, "Motherhood and Reform in the New South: Texas Women's Political Culture in the Progressive Era" (Ph.D. diss., University of Texas at Austin, 1992), 552–555. This is the most complete account of how suffragists organized women voters against Jim Ferguson.

[3]Norman D. Brown's *Hood, Bonnet, and Little Brown Jug: Texas Politics, 1921–1928* (College Station: Texas A&M University Press, 1984) examines the history of James Ferguson's political career as well as his effort to regain control of the Texas governorship by having his wife run for the office.

renewed vigor."[4] When Jim Ferguson went into the "woman business" he exploited his wife's candidacy for all it was worth. The irony that an antisuffragist like Jim Ferguson could use women's new political potential to get his wife elected governor speaks to why contemporaries who had had high expectations for woman suffrage were already speaking of its failure in the 1920s. Examining the ironies of Miriam Ferguson's election provides insight into the larger historical debate about why women encountered such difficulty claiming significant political power after suffrage succeeded.

Whereas contemporary newspapers sought to announce with hyperbolic headlines Miriam Ferguson's role in the history of women in politics in the post-suffrage decade, historians have overlooked the contribution Ferguson's election makes to women's history and Texas history. Although a proxy for her husband, Miriam Ferguson's election as governor in the early 1920s nevertheless is exceptional. Ferguson's opponents could have made the idea of a woman governor controversial. The Fergusons instead found a strategy that kept objections to the idea of a woman governor to a minimum.[5] From the point of view of former woman suffragists she was the "wrong" woman, yet by looking at how such a woman was elected we find one reason why enfranchisement did not translate into women's political power. Ferguson's election reveals the inverse relationship between women's political emancipation and women's social and sexual liberation in the 1920s.

In her novel about Ferguson's campaign, Clare Ogden Davis, Ferguson's press secretary, explored this inverse relationship between women's new political freedom and the cultural reaction to images of women's sexual liberation. At a time when the image of young women increasingly took on a social rebelliousness, Davis saw how a female political candidate like Ferguson could find political advantage in reaffirming her own commitment to the traditions women seemed to be abdicating. Davis had worked for various Texas newspapers and in Europe before she took the position with Ferguson for the year. She had an exceptional career for a woman in her day, and the scant record she left behind suggests her commitment to woman's equality. In her 1929 novel *The Woman of It,* she used Ferguson's campaign as material for examining

[4]James Ferguson to John Bicket, Temple, June 13, 1924, James E. Ferguson Papers (Center for American History, University of Texas at Austin; cited hereafter as CAH).

[5]Judge I. W. Stephens questioned the legality of a woman gubernatorial candidate and forced Ferguson adviser Martin McNulty Crane to publish a legal argument supporting it. On the day of the runoff election attorney Charles M. Dickson attempted to block a woman from appearing on the ballot. He filed a protest with the Democratic state executive chairman against placing Miriam Ferguson or Felix Robertson's name on the official ballot for the runoff, arguing that Ferguson's sex disqualified her and Robertson's Klan connections made him ineligible. See Martin McNulty Crane to I. W. Stephens, Dallas, Aug. 7, 1924, Martin McNulty Crane Papers (CAH).

the cultural constraints that women candidates faced. The novel suggests a way to move Miriam Ferguson from the periphery of a history about her husband regaining control of the governorship to the center by focusing on the "woman of it" in this 1924 campaign.[6]

Historians have argued that a new generation of women in the 1920s turned away from politics and toward the pursuit of sexual and social freedoms.[7] This generational analysis suggests that fewer and fewer women were interested in social goals achieved through political change. Although historians continue to agree that women's political opportunities did not significantly expand in the 1920s, recent scholarship shows that rather than taking a turn away from politics women began a sustained growth of activism within voluntary organizations.[8] Women's traditional activism did not decrease, but neither did women make significant inroads into male-dominated political areas. Ferguson's campaign in 1924, and Davis's novel, suggest one reason why women's political activities continued to be confined to a traditional gender hierarchy. The Fergusons and Davis recognized that women candidates were automatically evaluated in terms of family values. In the 1920s, the family values associated with a traditional gender hierarchy appeared to be assaulted by modern images and ideas of women's sexuality. In this cultural context a woman political candidate needed a political persona that clarified where she stood on family values and gender roles.

Alienation toward women's changing social and sexual roles expressed itself politically through the popular expectation that a female political candidate's first requirement was to be "womanly." When Miriam Ferguson's name appeared on the ballot, she had no political experience beyond the insights she may have drawn as the wife of a Texas governor. She had not joined any of the state's women's clubs, and, furthermore, she had publicly supported her husband's antisuffrage position. Whereas a handful of women leaders, such as Jessie Daniel Ames, rallied for Ferguson as a way of defeating the Ku Klux Klan, those most associated with the cause of women's advancement in politics denounced her candidacy as a fraud. Former suffrage leaders like Anna J. Pennybacker made it clear that they considered Ferguson, whose most outspoken desire was to "vindicate" her family's name, the "wrong" woman. Two of the most important suffrage leaders, Minnie Fisher Cunningham and Jane McCallum, voted for the Klan candidate rather than support Ferguson.[9]

---

[6]Clare Ogden Davis, *The Woman of It* (New York: J. H. Sears and Co., 1929).

[7]See, for example, William H. Chafe, *The American Woman: Her Changing Social, Economic, and Political Roles, 1920–1970* (New York: Oxford University Press, 1972), 3–132.

[8]Nancy F. Cott, "Across the Great Divide: Women in Politics Before and After 1920," in Louise A. Tilly and Patricia Gurin (eds.), *Women, Politics, and Change* (New York: Russell Sage Foundation, 1990), 161.

[9]Patricia B. Nieuwenhuizen, "Minnie Fisher Cunningham and Jane Y. McCallum: Leaders of Texas Women for Suffrage and Beyond" (Sr. thesis, University of Texas at Austin, 1982), 97.

Miriam Ferguson and Clare Ogden Davis, ca. 1935. *Courtesy Miriam Ferguson Collection of the Bell County Museum, Belton, Texas.*

Furthermore, as the runoff election results were announced, a rumor spread that, upset with Ferguson's election, "Mrs. Percy Pennybacker of Austin might run" on an independent ticket.[10] Miriam Ferguson represented the problem of tokenism that suffrage leaders like Pennybacker found increasingly difficult to overcome. By 1929, the same year Davis published her novel, Emily Newell

[10]Austin *American*, Aug. 24, 1924.

Blair, president of the Women's National Democratic Club, observed that the fifty-fifty law that in eighteen states required a national committee woman to accompany the selection of a national committee man had fostered tokenism. Women on committees were "not improving."[11] She attributed the lack of qualified women coming to power to men's preference for "another type [that] might be easier to manage."[12] Ferguson was the epitome of what Blair meant by that other "type."

Although the differences between *The Woman of It*'s fictitious gubernatorial candidate and Ferguson are remarkable, the similarities reveal how the cultural debate about women's gender roles that took place in the 1920s impinged on women's efforts to acquire political power. Davis's ambitious fictitious candidate, Delia Lawrence, in contrast to Ferguson, represented the expectations for women in politics that turned to disappointment as the decade drew to a close. Delia served as chair of the State Federation of Women's Clubs and fought for woman suffrage. Club women drafted her to run for governor. Delia Lawrence's "ambition gleamed unashamed in her eyes, misty with sudden emotion" at the thought of being elected to the state's highest office.[13] Committed to changing the role of women in politics, Lawrence declares, "I'd give . . . five years of my life to be the first woman governor of my state."[14] "Delia was doing a wonderful thing for the women of the state," narrates Davis, "people would realize one of these days that women were . . . much more important than they had ever been given credit for being."[15] Davis created a character that represented the ambitions and hopes of those who had fought for women's enfranchisement. A model of women's political accomplishments, Davis's protagonist makes it difficult to understand Miriam Ferguson's own response on the book jacket. "We have carefully read your book *The Woman of It*" Ferguson wrote, "and both agree it is a wonderful production. . . . In your usual style the work is a real description of how things happen."[16] Although the differences between the two women make Ferguson's comment about Davis's book seem unconvincing, Ferguson may have referred to the parallels that Davis makes between her fictitious candidate's campaign image and Ferguson's campaign strategy. The Fergusons had to find a way to make a woman candidate acceptable to Jim Ferguson's constituents who had long supported his antisuffrage stance. It was reportedly a farm woman who lent Miriam Ferguson

---

[11]Emily Newell Blair, "Women in the Political Parties," *Annals of the American Academy of Political and Social Science*, CXLIII (May, 1929), 222.

[12]Ibid.

[13]Davis, *The Woman of It*, 8.

[14]Ibid., 9.

[15]Ibid., 17.

[16]Miriam Ferguson to Clare Ogden Davis, Austin, June 7, 1929. The letter is published on the back cover of the book jacket of *The Woman of It*. Copy available at CAH.

her first sunbonnet.[17] The bonnet became the icon around which the Ferguson camp constructed an elaborate political persona that turned Miriam Ferguson into "Ma" Ferguson.[18] Photos of Ferguson most often pictured her peeling peaches, feeding chickens, or standing by a mule on the family farm wearing long traditional skirts, often in calico or gingham. The photographs constructed an image for Ferguson that embodied all of the goodness and wholesomeness associated with traditional womanhood. Davis's fictitious candidate, likewise, adopts a "Ma" posture for the press. Lawrence initially tells the newspaper men that she does not plan on posing "with a baby in my arms or with pots and pans and pie crust."[19] Her political adviser, however, admonishes: "You are going to put on a gingham apron this very afternoon and let the news reel men shoot you while you peel peaches to preserve!"[20] Delia retorts, "The woman in politics has come out of the kitchen!"[21] She relents, however, when her adviser replies:

> Yeah? Maybe she has, . . . But you listen to me: politics is measured, mixed and baked for the family trade, sister. Lot of stuff's going the rounds among the antisuffragists and the Klansmen about your Paris silks and satins. Make 'em think you can bake a cake as good as your mother can.[22]

If Davis understood "the woman of it" correctly, a woman candidate, whether she had the feminist credentials of Delia Lawrence or her husband's political collateral like Miriam Ferguson, had to put on a "gingham apron," peel peaches, hold babies, and bake cakes. The need to camouflage signs of a liberated sexuality—"Paris silks and satins"—with gingham suggests that in the 1920s, especially in a state like Texas, woman's political persona was confined by concern over women abdicating traditional roles. Davis had observed in Ferguson's campaign an inverse relationship between woman's political emancipation and her social and sexual liberation. She expressed this relationship in her novel when she had Delia (a single woman who, typical of 1920s popular fiction, confronts the possibility of a love affair) hide all signs that she was a modern woman for the purposes of her campaign.[23]

---

[17]Brown, *Hood, Bonnet, and Little Brown Jug*, 227.

[18]Ferguson actually became "Ma" inadvertently when a copy editor, in an effort to shorten a headline, abbreviated Miriam Amanda Wallace Ferguson to M.A.W. This was soon shortened to "Ma" by Ferguson supporters. Frank Gibler of the Houston *Press* was the copy editor who gave Ferguson her nickname. "Behind the byline," *Austin American-Statesman*, Sept. 12, 1961, Miriam A. Ferguson Clip File (Austin History Center, Austin).

[19]Davis, *The Woman of It*, 22.

[20]Ibid., emphasis added.

[21]Ibid.

[22]Ibid.

[23]Davis defines her heroine as a modern woman not only by giving her open ambition and political credentials but also by introducing her to the thrill of sex in a heated affair that leaves her torn between remarriage and career.

Miriam Ferguson's "Ma" persona responded to the particular historical circumstances of Texas in 1924. Women won the vote in 1920 on the eve of a "revolution in morals" that, as William Leuchtenburg has observed, had the changing role of women at its center. He recognized that "sexual independence was merely the most sensational aspect of the altering status of women" that was at the root of concern over the moral order.[24] It was, nevertheless, woman's new sexuality that was the preoccupation of movies, tabloids, novelists, and the dance craze. Research indicates that the new images affected the sexual practices of the generation born after the turn of the century. Ferguson's campaign of 1924 suggests that such modern images were also influencing the political responses of the parents of a generation of sexually liberated youths. Whereas some scholars have pointed out that many of the changes in manners and morals in the 1920s had begun by the end of the nineteenth century, Leuchtenburg shows how noteworthy such changes had become by the 1920s. As the revolution in morals became more pronounced so did the reaction. The reaction to modern mores took a political form in Texas, by giving rise to the dominance of the Klan in Texas politics. The political presence of the Klan in Texas made politics "measured, mixed and baked for the family trade," as Davis put it. This political and social context set the stage for "Ma" Ferguson to be elected as the first woman governor of Texas.[25]

Charles Alexander, who has written the most comprehensive study of the Ku Klux Klan in Texas, found that the Klan perceived its mission as enforcing the moral status quo.[26] The Klan wanted women to stay home or at least remain true to the domestic ideal that had become a legacy of the nineteenth-century "cult of domesticity." As historians of nineteenth-century social life have shown, ideas of women as inherently more virtuous than men and as natural protectors of the moral welfare of the family had developed with the increasing separation between home and the work place.[27] By the 1920s the rise of cities, mass culture, and the trend toward secularization seemed to be eroding much of the middle-class cultural consensus on such domestic ideals. The Klan represented one of the most extreme reactions to the sexual mores and new gender roles

---

[24]William E. Leuchtenburg, *The Perils of Prosperity, 1914–1932* (2nd ed.; Chicago: University of Chicago Press, 1993), 169.

[25]Nellie Ross was elected governor of Wyoming the same year and took office just before Ferguson. She succeeded her deceased husband. T. A. Larson, *History of Wyoming* (Lincoln: University of Nebraska Press, 1965), 458.

[26]Charles C. Alexander, *Crusade for Conformity: The Ku Klux Klan in Texas, 1920–1930* (Houston: Texas Gulf Coast Historical Association, 1962), 7.

[27]The literature on the "cult of domesticity" and nineteenth-century domestic ideals is extensive. For an overview of how historians have dealt with these topics see Linda K. Kerber, "Separate Spheres, Female Worlds, Woman's Place: The Rhetoric of Women's History," *Journal of American History*, LXXV (June, 1988), 1.

that modern images and literature popularized. Klan ministers emphasized women remaining "womanly," such as when J. T. Renfro situated "purity," "sanctity of the American home," and the woman's place there as vital to moral order. "If the women and girls are safe," he said, "the men and boys will be safe." Look at the ruined homes, he preached, "is [there] no need of the Ku Klux Klan to check the ravage of immorality that threatens the very existence of our civilization?"[28] Clearly the Klan was willing to go to extreme lengths to punish women who seemed to be the most flagrant violators of "womanliness." After kidnapping Beulah Johnson, a young Texas woman who had allegedly participated in an extramarital affair, for instance, KKK members stripped her, chopped off her hair (in their eyes a symbol of loose sexuality), poured hot tar over her, and left her in the public square.[29] And while violent attacks on suspected wrongdoers were the most publicized, the Klan's attempts to enforce conformity ranged from assaults to acts such as stationing members near favorite parking spots so that when a car stopped a hooded Klansman could appear to urge the frightened couple to leave.[30]

The Klan became a formidable political force in Texas in part because a number of citizens were unsure of the consequences of a revolution in morals that seemed at odds with their upbringing, particularly their religious beliefs. A membership list from the Dallas Klan shows a number of professionals and businessmen from all parts of the city.[31] Martin McNulty Crane, a prominent organizer of citizens against the Klan, wrote a judge in California: "You would be surprised if I were to tell you the names of some of the people who have joined the Invisible Empire."[32] The Klan presented itself as a warrior against urban values that appeared to be encroaching on Texas cities in cultural forms such as the films *Man Handled, Marriage Cheat,* or *Unguarded Woman,* the latter the story of a "girl adrift and the man who saved her when she drifted too far."[33]

---

[28]J. T. Renfro, "The Invisible Empire: Knights of the Ku Klux Klan," a sermon given at the First Baptist Church in Sinton, Texas, June 4, 1922 (Sinton, Tex.: San Patricio Co. News Print, 1922), 50 (1st–3rd quotations), 51 (4th quotation). Copy available at CAH.

[29]Brown, *Hood, Bonnet, and Little Brown Jug,* 158. For another case of a woman being attacked by the Klan see Dallas *Morning News,* July 19, 1921. For more on hair and images of women see Valerie Steele, *Fashion and Eroticism: Ideals of Feminine Beauty, from the Victorian Age to the Jazz Age* (New York: Oxford University Press, 1985); Elizabeth Wilson, *Adorned in Dreams: Fashion and Modernity* (Berkeley: University of California Press, 1985); and Naomi Wolf, *The Beauty Myth: How Images of Beauty Are Used Against Women* (New York: William Morrow, 1991).

[30]Alexander, *Crusade for Conformity,* 17.

[31]The executive committee under the Klan's Great Titan Z. E. Marvin, for instance, included four attorneys, four businessmen, one preacher, one physician, and a commissioner of police and fire. See "Names of Members of the Ku Klux Klan" (list of members in Dallas Klan), Crane Papers.

[32]Martin McNulty Crane to Judge Bennet Hill of Los Angeles, Dallas, Apr. 2, 1922, ibid.

[33]San Antonio *Express,* Aug. 7, 1924; Houston *Post-Dispatch,* Aug 8, 16, 1924 (quotation).

The Klan represented the most extreme expression of a widely held concern over the rise of urban life. More subtle social reprimands in Texas newspapers, however, suggest that alienation from modernity was widespread.[34] Citizens who did not condone the Klan punishing a person for sexual behavior, for instance, might have approved of "editorials for women" in the Austin *American* that warned that "the kisses a girl has to give should be of as much value to us as if they were precious jewels."[35] Citizens who objected to Klansmen monitoring couples necking in parked cars likewise nodded approval to a columnist "disgusted" with "auto spooners."[36]

Ferguson's supporters tried to use her "womanly woman," "Ma" political persona to capitalize on concern that modernity undermined dearly held values. Like the Austin *American* editorial, Miriam Ferguson's matronly posture suggested that motherly advice, not the extremism of the Klan, would preserve virtue in spite of new movies, new looks, and more visible sexuality. The expectation that a woman candidate should respond to cultural debate over changing gender roles surfaced in the campaign through questions such as the one reporters asked Miriam Ferguson about girls wearing the cropped hairstyle referred to as a bob. Ferguson responded to the implicit concern over moral conduct: "I see nothing distressing in shorn locks. The important thing is what the women of Texas keep in their heads, not on them."[37] Later she added, "Girls are as good now as they were in their grandmother's day and probably a lot more interesting."[38] Miriam Ferguson sought a reassuring pose on this question of hair in the explosive cultural context that led Klansmen to actually attack the hair of women they deemed promiscuous.

The fear over what women were doing socially and sexually enhanced the political expediency of stressing a woman's commitment to traditional womanhood. The "Ma" image corresponded to widespread affirmation for women playing wholesome roles. A Houston columnist, for instance, urged women to be like Janet Brown (that is, plain Jane), whom she described as "the type . . . destined for a clean, starched gingham existence with thoughts as clean as her frocks." Janet, the columnist said, foolishly tried to impress guests by making a gourmet dinner with artichokes and caviar. She failed miserably, but found success

---

[34]A relationship between the values held by members of the mainstream white middle class and members of the Klan has been noted in recent studies such as Shawn Lay's "Imperial Outpost on the Border: El Paso's Frontier," in Shawn Lay (ed.), *The Invisible Empire in the West: Toward a New Historical Appraisal of the Ku Klux Klan of the 1920s* (Urbana: University of Illinois Press, 1992), 218.

[35]Austin *American*, Aug. 15, 1924.

[36]Ibid.

[37]Dallas *Morning News*, Aug. 1, 1924.

[38]Max Bentley, "An Interview with Governor Elect Ferguson," *Holland's Magazine*, XLIV (Jan., 1925), 5, 55 (quotation).

another evening with "steak and creamy potatoes, just a home dinner for homey people." The columnist pleaded with "other Janets to be themselves," insinuating that the world of "artichokes and caviar," like the Paris silks and satins that fictitious Delia Lawrence hid, was somehow less than wholesome and homey.[39] Ferguson's "Ma" political persona strove to fit the appeal of a "plain Jane." Just as the Houston columnist described wholesomeness in terms of a "gingham existence," one supporter "unequivocally . . . for Mrs. Ferguson" endorsed her "calico" attributes: "the fact is calico when I was a young man looked like silk to me."[40] Pictures of Ferguson swathed in the traditional domesticity represented by a gingham apron distinguished her from those cosmopolitan items like artichokes and silk, which conjured images associated with women abandoning the wholesomeness of home. "In this time of confusion," another supporter wrote, "it might not be unfortunate for us to have a *plain woman* for governor of our state for two years, during which time we might 'find ourselves' and return to the administration of government along plain and established democratic principles."[41] The supporter seemed to suggest that a "plain woman" could be trusted in a "caretaker" role until a trustworthy man could be elected to office.

Portraying trustworthiness was exactly what the Fergusons needed to do because instances of corruption peppered Jim Ferguson's political past. Martin McNulty Crane, a leader of anti-Klan forces in Dallas, decided to swallow his distaste for Jim Ferguson and help Miriam Ferguson defeat the Klan candidate. Crane recognized that Miriam Ferguson's womanhood had the potential to provide a needed edge to Jim Ferguson's political pull.[42] He understood that womanhood could be made into a political resource and perhaps even reassure friends of the university and women's suffragists that Miriam Ferguson's election would not lead to more of her husband's assaults on higher education and woman's rights. "We understand the objection to Mrs. Ferguson is that she is a woman," he wrote in his draft of an initial endorsement. Before sending a copy of his speech to the Dallas *Morning News,* however, Crane replaced the line with "Had we not better trust a woman who has no entangling alliances with law violating units . . . than to have a man whose candidacy is promoted by them only."[43] Crane shaped Ferguson's gendered political persona into a shield

---

[39]Columnist Betty [Berton?] Patterson, Houston *Post-Dispatch,* Aug. 1, 1924.

[40]Epps G. Knight to Dallas *Morning News,* Aug. 18, 1924.

[41]L. A. Carlton, "An appeal in behalf of the candidacy of Mrs. Ferguson" (pamphlet) (Texas: s.n. 1924?) (CAH), emphasis added.

[42]Crane, who supported Alfred E. Smith, Catholic governor of New York, for president that year, did not share the Fergusons' politics. He had chaired the impeachment proceedings against Jim Ferguson.

[43]Martin McNulty Crane, speech sent to the Dallas *Morning News,* n.d., [Dallas?], Crane Papers. For the published speech see "Crane Announces for Mrs. Ferguson," Dallas *Morning News,* Aug. 2, 1924.

against Jim Ferguson's corrupt past. Jim Ferguson's political record and the fact that he delivered the majority of the campaign's stump speeches made him the most likely political target for the Fergusons' opponents. Klan newspapers nonetheless indicated that their attacks may have focused on Jim Ferguson because Miriam Ferguson's image made it difficult to criticize her. Pledged to the "protection of pure womanhood," the Klan now avoided attacking a candidate who represented the virtues associated with it.[44] As *The Texas 100% American* acknowledged: "You can't touch Mrs Ferguson for that [attacking her] would be termed a mistake of the heart."[45] Instead, the paper refused to acknowledge her candidacy and demanded that Jim Ferguson "Get out of the Mother Hubbard, . . . and let us take a healthy swing at your political jaw."[46] Such attacks would have backfired if used against a woman described as having eyes "like deep sea pools of liquid color in which [is] seen buried all the sorrow, all the ecstasy and all the gentleness of life."[47] The Klan assured supporters that they were not attacking a woman candidate. In one Klan newspaper a mother tells her son, "You give me heart disease. I thought they [the Klan] were picking on a woman . . . ; that is only Mother Hubbard. Can't you see those big feet. . . of old brewery-baked Jim."[48]

The Klan also tried to undermine Jim Ferguson on his Prohibition record, only to find the shield of womanhood deflect their attacks. The Klan-backed candidate, Earle B. Mayfield, had defeated Jim Ferguson in the U.S. senatorial runoff of 1922 by winning the Prohibition vote. The money that Jim Ferguson had received from "brewers," as revealed during the impeachment proceedings, had returned to haunt him. As Robertson claimed that Jim Ferguson was "trying to inject the Klan issue to hide the interests of the old brewery gang,"[49] the Ferguson camp, in response, amplified Miriam Ferguson's Prohibition credentials with gender-based arguments. "She had such [prohibitionist] instincts implanted in her as a woman and mother," explained Crane.[50] So when Robertson dared to imply that Miriam Ferguson's record on Prohibition might not be spotless, Jim Ferguson had the clout of virtuous womanhood behind him in his reply: "He had the . . . nerve to question my wife's prohibition record. . . . You good people of Waco know better than anyone how to make the comparison between my wife and him."[51]

[44] *The Texas 100% American* (Dallas), Apr. 7, 1922, Crane Papers.

[45] *Texas 100% American* (Dallas), Aug. 15, 1924.

[46] Ibid., Sept. 8, 1924.

[47] Dallas *Morning News*, Aug. 1, 1924.

[48] *The Texas 100% American* (Dallas), Aug. 8, 1924.

[49] Waco *Times-Herald*, Aug. 17, 1924.

[50] Ibid., Sept. 3, 1924.

[51] Dallas *Morning News*, Aug. 8, 1924. Although there is not much data on how women voted

The more the Klan and Robertson tried to discredit Jim Ferguson with the Prohibition issue, the more the Ferguson camp promoted Miriam Ferguson as independent of her husband. Crane advised former Governor Ferguson to step back and leave "Mrs. Ferguson as the candidate against whom nothing on the face of the earth can be said."[52] Again and again the Ferguson camp proclaimed the choice between a *woman* who "will exact her utmost power to enforce the laws against everybody" and "a *man* [Robertson] who has shown himself to be wholly unable as Criminal District Judge of Dallas County to secure the punishment of a certain large class of law breakers."[53] To underscore the choice between an old-fashioned woman with all the virtues associated with her sex and a man with the worst traits associated with his sex, the Dallas *Morning News* subtitled an article not "Ferguson preferable" but "Woman Preferable."[54]

For a major newspaper to advocate a woman as a preferable candidate was a radical departure, but a departure that the Fergusons had made safe much the way advertisers were superficially assimilating woman's emancipation. Advertisements in the 1920s, for instance, often tried to capitalize on woman's march to freedom but were careful to keep her marching in a safe direction. One company recalled that once women won the vote, "that year we decided to let them vote on towels too."[55] Once Miriam Ferguson's unprecedented campaign received publicity, mostly from sources outside of Texas, the Fergusons also superficially assimilated it into her reassuring "Ma" appeal. Dressed in the bonnet and apron of traditional womanhood, Miriam Ferguson began speaking like a leader of women's new rights. "I never fought for women's suffrage," she admitted, "but. . . they gave us the ballot and I see no reason why we should not exercise our right."[56] Her appeal to women's new sense of citizenship escalated as her campaign drew national attention over the novelty of a woman candidate. The Fergusons republished a New York *World* article that interpreted her candidacy to mean that "the abstract equality of women and men before

---

in states where they had the vote before 1920, it was assumed that women supported Prohibition in greater numbers than men. See Cott, "Across the Great Divide," 158, 169, for evidence that four states did adopt Prohibition after women won the vote, and for information on one late-1920s women's organization that opposed Prohibition.

[52]Crane to J. E. Ferguson, Dallas, Oct. 1, 1924, Crane Papers.

[53]Dallas *Morning News*, Aug. 2, 1924.

[54]Ibid.

[55]Roland Marchand, *Advertising the American Dream: Making Way for Modernity* (Berkeley: University of California Press, 1985), 186.

[56]Bentley, "An Interview with Governor Elect Ferguson," 55 (quotation).

the law has been transformed in Texas into an actual equality before public opinion and in political custom."[57] Another optimist implored, "Think of it, a woman governor of a state . . . women can do anything nowadays."[58] Ferguson, furthermore, began courting women's votes with language such as "I appeal to my sisters to become active and urge men to go to the polls. Our sex is now on trial and we must again prove to all mankind that the handle that has rocked the cradles of men can rule the destinies of men."[59]

Ferguson, who like her husband had opposed woman suffrage, had discovered a way to present her own candidacy as a test of women's new voting rights while remaining true to her original reasons for opposing the vote. Antisuffragists like the Fergusons had lost the battle over the vote but were in the best position to win in the social and political context of the 1920s in Texas. They had opposed the vote on the grounds that women would abandon traditional roles to become more like men. By 1924, however, the revolution in morals appeared to be doing much more than woman's enfranchisement to undermine women's commitment to traditional domesticity. The Fergusons consequently stayed true to their original commitment to gender hierarchy by making a ballot for "Ma" look like a vote for traditional womanhood.

"Ma" Ferguson represented the politics of womanhood that could be most effective in a Texas gubernatorial race against a candidate heavily supported by the Klan. Ferguson defeated Robertson by 97,732 votes, with the total vote, 729,770, a record for a Texas election to that time.[60] Two days after the election the combined vote count in the sixty-two counties where returns had been finalized showed voter turnout up by 48 percent from the U.S. senatorial campaign in 1922.[61] When Jim Ferguson ran against a Klan-supported candidate for the U.S. Senate seat, only 585,000 citizens had voted, and Ferguson's loss had been attributed to losing the Prohibition vote. His wife's candidacy helped pull the Fergusons over the edge to victory by offering three political advantages. First, her "womanly woman" political persona offered the same message of commitment to the moral status quo that had helped the Klan claim political power at a time when the Klan members' reputations were increasingly tarnished by stories of their brutal excesses. The Fergusons offered "Ma" as the

[57]"Whole Country Keenly Interested in the Situation in Texas Where Woman Will be Elected Governor," *Ferguson Forum* (Temple, Tex.), July 11, 1924.

[58]"Women's Victory in Texas Battle for Governor Shows Capacity of Sex," ibid., Sept. 18, 1924.

[59]The quote ends, "who have been active in the development of our Texas citizenship and who regardless of past differences, are giving me their support in this great contest." Miriam Ferguson, "Just a Word Before We Vote," ibid., Aug. 21, 1924.

[60]Brown, *Hood, Bonnet, and Little Brown Jug*, 238.

[61]Austin *American*, Aug. 25, 1924.

more virtuous caretaker of Texans' moral health. Second, her feminized political persona offered moral credibility on the issue of Prohibition, her husband's main weak point. Finally, much like a 1920s advertisement, Miriam Ferguson's candidacy superficially assimilated women's new political rights by appealing to a sense of justice about women's right to vote while limiting what they were voting on to traditional womanhood.

By 1929, when Clare Ogden Davis published her novel, women like Davis were disappointed with the lack of progress made toward equal rights and frustrated with the barriers women encountered in efforts to claim political power. *The Woman of It* ultimately sought to change the story of Miriam Ferguson's election. Ferguson won the governorship but remained a figurehead. Davis drew from this the need for a clear distinction between manipulating popular ideas of womanhood for political advantage and making a politics based on ideas about womanhood. Although her heroine borrowed the strategy the Fergusons used to gain control of the governorship, Davis did not want Delia Lawrence to remain ineffective like Ferguson. The strategy of translating ideas about women's nature into political resources may have helped woman's suffragists win the vote, but, according to Davis, feminized politics threatened to leave women without power. In an interview about her novel she indicted the politics of womanhood. "Women consider themselves superior beings," she said, "They feel as though they have come down to the political earth to lead the multitude out of the wilderness of corruption."[62] In her analysis, "The dainty [women] are defeated by their own lady-like attitude. Shrewd men are gallant to them and soon steer them away. . . . They become mere figureheads. The strong-minded, sanitary sort begin by taking the attitude that no mere male can fool them. . . . They make enemies, and those enemies in the end prove too powerful for them."[63] In *The Woman of It*, therefore, Davis has her fictitious woman governor disregard sex in order to claim political power. "She [Lawrence] handles the cats at her headquarters like a tiger trainer in a circus," narrates Davis.[64] The lesson Davis sends is that "In politics gal, you've got to use plain language to deal with the scum of the earth." Lawrence balks, "But women . . . " only to be cut off by her friend, "Women hell! Women will have to talk to men politicians for many a year yet."[65] To "disregard sex" had become the only way women like Davis saw to avoid sex stereotyping or isolation from male-dominated centers of power. It was a position that set her apart; as the Houston *Gargoyle* reported, "the freed ladies are visibly sizzlin" over Davis's

[62]Asa Bordages, book review in *Gargoyle* (Houston), July 28, 1929. Professor Norman Brown made this review available to me from his personal file on Davis.

[63]Ibid.

[64]Davis, *The Woman of It*, 27.

[65]Ibid., 33.

interview.[66] It was, nevertheless, a position that grew out of Davis's understanding of the inverse relationship between women's political emancipation and the changing social and sexual roles of women in the 1920s. As Ferguson's campaign in the context of the Texas Klan's reaction to modernity showed her, to regard sex either invited controversy that would eliminate political possibility or forced a woman, whether an ambitious Lawrence or a proxy like Ferguson, into reducing her sex to gingham aprons and a bonnet. The lesson made it difficult for women like Davis to see clear to a feminist politics that could afford to regard sex in a way that sought to claim political power in order to improve the status of women as a group.[67]

---

[66] *Gargoyle* (Houston), July 28, 1929.

[67] Nancy F. Cott, *The Grounding of Modern Feminism* (New Haven: Yale University Press, 1987), 271–283, provides the most comprehensive analysis of why a feminist politics of sex solidarity did not become more popular in the 1920s.

# The New Deal in Dallas

ROGER BILES*

*A number of recent studies have claimed that the programs of the Democratic administration of President Franklin Roosevelt, usually known as the New Deal, failed to bring about significant reforms in matters of poverty, race, and power. Often focusing on a particular city, critics conclude that the New Deal, a collection of efforts designed to cope with the Great Depression, retained and even reenforced the inequities of the past.*

*In "The New Deal in Dallas" Professor Biles examines "hard times" conditions in the second largest Texas city of the 1930s. Dallas, he notes, fared better than many other cities in the early years of the Depression. However, by the mid-1930s rising unemployment and declining levels of construction, retail sales, bank deposits, tax collections, and wages suggested that the situation was serious and becoming critical. Responsibility for determining policy fell to the local city government, controlled throughout much of the period by a formally organized group of business interests.*

*Leaders were willing to accept federal relief funds and projects, though not to the extent of other cities. But significant change otherwise encountered determined and, in most respects, successful resistance. The New Deal in Dallas, asserts Professor Biles, brought few reforms. In support of his conclusion, he presents a carefully crafted picture of conditions in locally funded relief, organized labor, and the black community of the 1930s.*

*Biles's argument is persuasive, but should be considered with another aspect of the New Deal in mind. If voting patterns are any kind of a reliable indicator, most Dallas voters accepted, supported, and perhaps were grateful for the New Deal. In 1936, the only presidential election that can be viewed as a referendum on the New Deal, voters in Dallas County voted for Roosevelt by a margin of approximately 7 to 1. This vote was the largest percentage of support received by a Democratic presidential candidate in Dallas County in the twentieth century.*

*Roger Biles, "The New Deal in Dallas," *Southwestern Historical Quarterly*, 95 (July, 1991), 4–19.

***Typical of a number of studies presenting views similar to those of this essay is Paul K. Conkin,* The New Deal *(1967; 2nd ed.; Arlington Heights, Ill.: Harlan Davidson, 1975), but William E. Leuchtenburg,* Franklin D. Roosevelt and the New Deal, 1932–1940 *(New York: Harper and Row, 1963) presents a different perspective.***

Historians continue to analyze the New Deal and its impact on U.S. history. Did Franklin D. Roosevelt's innovative responses to hard times constitute a watershed in the nation's past? How new, in other words, was the New Deal? William E. Leuchtenburg stated the case for change, arguing in his seminal *Franklin D. Roosevelt and the New Deal:* "The New Deal, however conservative it was in some respects and however much it owed to the past, marked a radically new departure." Similarly, Carl Degler called the New Deal "a revolutionary response to a revolutionary situation." Especially since the mid-1960s, however, historians have begun to focus on the lack of reform achieved in the 1930s. New Left historians like Barton Bernstein and Paul Conkin emphasized the degree to which the New Deal overlooked the plight of the downtrodden in its desire to preserve capitalism. Although many scholars stopped short of characterizing Roosevelt's presidency as counterrevolutionary, most acknowledged the shortcomings of the New Deal in effecting meaningful economic and social reform. Clearly not a radical bent on the destruction of free enterprise capitalism, they believed, Roosevelt naturally sought limited reform within the American political consensus. The New Deal could accomplish only so much because of conservative forces in Congress and the courts. Further, James T. Patterson added, the American system of federalism bolstered the states at the expense of the national government, and the New Deal made few inroads against states' rights and strict constructionism.[1]

---

[1]William E. Leuchtenburg, *Franklin D. Roosevelt and the New Deal, 1932–1940* (New York: Harper and Row, 1963), 336 (1st quotation); Carl N. Degler, *Out of Our Past: The Forces That Shaped Modern America* (New York: Harper and Brothers, 1959), 416 (2nd quotation); James T. Patterson, *The New Deal and the States: Federalism in Transition* (Princeton: Princeton University Press, 1969), 206–207. Also see Barton J. Bernstein, "The New Deal: The Conservative Achievements of Liberal Reform" in Barton J. Bernstein (ed.), *Towards a New Past: Dissenting Essays in American History* (New York: Pantheon Books, 1968), 263–288; Paul K. Conkin, *The New Deal* (Arlington Heights, Ill.: Harlan Davidson, Inc., 1967); Barry D. Karl, *The Uneasy State: The United States from 1915 to 1945* (Chicago: University of Chicago Press, 1983); and Robert S. McElvaine, *The Great Depression: America 1929–1941* (New York: Times Books, 1984). On New Deal historiography, see Richard S. Kirkendall, "The New Deal as Watershed: The Recent Literature," *Journal of American History,* LIV (Mar., 1968), 839–852; Jerold S. Auerbach, "New Deal, Old Deal, or Raw Deal: Some Thoughts on New Left Historiography," *Journal of Southern History,* XXXV (Feb., 1969), 18–30; Alonzo L. Hamby (ed.), *The New Deal: Analysis and Interpretation* (New York: Longman, 1981); and Harvard Sitkoff (ed.), *Fifty Years Later: The New Deal Evaluated* (New York: Alfred A. Knopf, 1985).

Historians have also noted the limited impact of the New Deal in cities. In Pittsburgh, Bruce Stave concluded, the New Deal relieved unemployment and improved the housing situation somewhat, but had little effect on the more lasting problems of economic stagnation and physical decay. A number of studies suggest that, rather than undermine the strength of big city political machines, Roosevelt supported those bosses loyal to national Democratic platforms and policies. Charles H. Trout found that "during the entire New Deal policies from Washington altered Boston, but just as surely Boston modified federal programs." Or, as Zane Miller summarized: "The federal response to depression in the cities was conservative. The New Deal's urban policy neither envisaged nor produced a radical transformation of metropolitan form and structure."[2]

In recent years, however, some historians concerned with the exceptionalism of southern cities have designated the 1930s as the time when sweeping changes engendered by the New Deal began to narrow the gap between urban Dixie and northern municipalities. Although emphasizing the distinctiveness of southern cities overall, David R. Goldfield conceded that the pace of change accelerated rapidly in the twentieth century. The watershed, he contended, was the New Deal, since, "the federal government paid for the capital facilities in southern cities that northern cities had paid for themselves in earlier decades and on which they were still paying off the debt. The almost-free modernization received by southern cities would prove to be an important economic advantage in subsequent decades." In *The New Deal in the Urban South,* Douglas L. Smith looked at four southern cities—Atlanta, Birmingham, Memphis, and New Orleans—and suggested that the involvement of the federal government in local affairs during the 1930s resulted in significant changes. He concluded that public works and housing initiatives altered southern cityscapes, New Deal relief agencies paved the way for the establishment for the first time of social welfare agencies, organized labor established new footholds, and black communities mobilized to make possible significant breakthroughs in later years. Moreover, according to Smith, the New Deal helped sever the ties to the Old South and develop among southerners an urban consciousness.[3]

---

[2]Bruce M. Stave, "Pittsburgh and the New Deal," in John Braeman, Robert H. Bremner, and David Brody (eds.), *The New Deal: The State and Local Levels* (Columbus, Ohio: Ohio State University Press, 1975), 376–402; Lyle W. Dorsett, "Kansas City and the New Deal," in Braeman, Bremner, and Brody (eds.), *The New Deal,* 407–418; Roger Biles, *Big City Boss in Depression and War: Mayor Edward J. Kelly of Chicago* (DeKalb: Northern Illinois University Press, 1984); Charles Hathaway Trout, *Boston, the Great Depression, and the New Deal* (New York: Oxford University Press, 1977), 315 (1st quotation); Zane L. Miller, *The Urbanization of Modern America: A Brief History* (New York: Harcourt Brace Jovanovich, 1973), 168–169 (2nd quotation).

[3]David R. Goldfield, *Cotton Fields and Skyscrapers: Southern City and Region, 1607–1980* (Baton Rouge: Louisiana State University Press, 1982), 181–182 (quotation); Douglas L. Smith, *The New Deal in the Urban South* (Baton Rouge: Louisiana State University Press, 1988). Also see David R. Goldfield, "The Urban South: A Regional Framework," *American Historical Review,* LXXXVI (Dec., 1981), 1009–1034.

An earlier study of Memphis, Tennessee, during the 1930s saw little evidence of sweeping change or, for that matter, of substantial preparation for later departures. This study of Dallas, Texas, looking at local government, relief, labor, and race relations, similarly finds minimal impact by the New Deal. In Dallas the federal government worked through city hall but exerted no influence over who made policy there, and the rise of the Citizens' Council made the control of the city's corporate regency explicit and unmistakable. No appreciable increase in social welfare activity ensued to reflect an expanded commitment to relief. To a great extent, management successfully preserved the open shop and regional wage differentials, two ingredients local businessmen viewed as essential for industry to compete effectively with northern concerns. Black residents of Dallas survived the depression in somewhat better fashion because of federal aid, but their status remained largely unchanged. In short, New Deal largess provided welcome assistance but did not alter appreciably the traditional way of life.[4]

In Dallas the business community brought local government more firmly under its control in the 1930s. Agitation for political reform dated back to the first decade of the twentieth century with the founding of the nonpartisan Citizens Association. Interest flagged, however, and by the 1920s the association was dormant. In 1927 the Dallas *Morning News* published a series of muckraking articles exposing inefficiency in city government and proposing the city manager plan as an alternative. In 1929 over thirty men ran for mayor, nine of whom constituted one-man "parties." The eventual winner, self-styled populist J. Waddy Tate, lambasted the wealthy, removed all "keep off the grass" signs from city parks, and promised to allow "plain folks" to camp there. Largely because of Tate's eccentric behavior, Dallasites began to consider seriously the *News's* arguments for change. The remnants of the old Citizens Association formed the Citizens Charter Association (CCA) in 1930 and joined in the battle for new municipal government. Tate delayed and dissembled, but finally presented the question of charter amendments to the people in a 1930 referendum. By a two-to-one margin, the voters jettisoned the mayor-commission government for council-city manager rule. Under the new system, the nine-member council (six chosen from districts and three elected at-large) chose a mayor from its own ranks and appointed a city manager.[5]

[4]Roger Biles, *Memphis in the Great Depression* (Knoxville: University of Tennessee Press, 1986).

[5]Dallas *Morning News,* Jan. 26, 1967; Ann P. Hollingsworth, "Reform Government in Dallas, 1927–1940" (M.A. thesis, North Texas State University, 1971), 10–16; New York *Times,* Oct. 19, 1930; Roscoe C. Martin, "Dallas Makes the Manager Plan Work," *The Annals of the American Academy of Political and Social Science,* CXCIX (Sept., 1938), 64; Louis P. Head, "Dallas Joins Ranks of Manager Cities," *National Municipal Review,* XIX (Dec., 1930), 806–809; W. D. Jones, "Dallas Wins a Place in the Sun," *National Municipal Review,* XXIV (Jan., 1935), 11–14; Work Projects Administration Writers' Project, *Dallas Guide and History* (Dallas: n.p., 1940), 193–194, 202–203; New York *Times,* Apr. 12, 1931.

In 1933 the CCA's slate of candidates ran unopposed, but resistance quickly formed among the ranks of the suddenly deposed politicians. They accused the CCA of being "organized . . . financed and controlled by Wall Street trusts," and unsuccessfully sought the recall of the new council. In 1935 an opposition faction composed of seasoned pols, known as the Catfish Club, bested the CCA's candidates to gain control of the city council. A haphazardly planned counteroffensive by the CCA never got off the ground in 1937, and the brief reign of the business elite seemed finished. At that time, however, two hundred of the city's corporate presidents and chief executive officers formed the Dallas Citizens' Council to breathe new life into the dying CCA. In 1939 the candidates of the fledgling Citizens' Council parlayed rumors of graft in Mayor George Sprague's parks department into a resounding victory. The council's 1941 slate won without opposition, and its dominance of local government continued into the 1970s.[6]

The Dallas Citizens' Council sprang from the imagination of Robert Lee Thornton. A former tenant farmer who mismanaged several businesses into bankruptcy, Thornton finally struck it rich as a banker. Thornton was a maverick in the local financial community; while other banks avoided risky ventures, he had the prescience to invest in the automobile industry and gave hotel tycoon Conrad Hilton his first loan. He became one of the city's most visible and esteemed philanthropists and in later years a four-time mayor who refused to keep a desk in city hall, continuing to operate from his desk at the Mercantile Bank. By the mid-1930s he had grown tired of the ineffectiveness of local government and resolved to seize authority for the city's "natural leadership." In 1936 Thornton helped persuade the Texas Centennial Commission to hold the celebration in Dallas and then served as a member of the executive committee that planned and conducted the gala. Serving on that committee convinced him that only a small, manageable group of the city's best people could effectively make decisions about such a massive undertaking as the Texas Centennial—or for that matter, he concluded, govern the city. Therefore, Thornton set out to make the emerging Citizens' Council in the form best suited to get things done.[7]

---

[6]Dallas *Morning News,* Mar. 23, 27, 1967; "'N.M.L.' Charged With Traitorous Propaganda to Install Imperialistic Government," *National Municipal Review,* XXI (Mar., 1932), 140 (quotation); Robert B. Fairbanks, "The Good Government Machine: The Citizens Charter Association and Dallas Politics, 1930–1960," in *Essays on Sunbelt Cities and Recent Urban America,* No. 23, Walter Prescott Webb Memorial Lectures, ed. Robert B. Fairbanks and Kathleen Underwood (College Station: Texas A&M University Press, 1990), 127–132.

[7]Michael C. D. Macdonald, *America's Cities: A Report on the Myth of Urban Renaissance* (New York: Simon and Schuster, 1984), 114; Transcript of interview with R. L. Thornton, Jr., Nov. 8, 1980 (quotation), Dallas Mayors Oral History Project, Dallas Public Library; Stanley Walker, *The Dallas Story* (Dallas: Dallas Times Herald, 1956), 33–35.

Thornton wanted to call the Citizens' Council the "Yes or No Council," but others thought the title a bit unseemly and overruled him. Thornton did prevail on a number of other matters, however, including his insistence that membership be limited to chief executive officers of major corporations—no doctors, lawyers, educators, clergymen, or intellectuals who might temporize when hasty action was needed. Similarly, Thornton's no-nonsense attitude predominated with the exclusion of proxy voting. "If you don't come," the rough-hewn banker said, "you ain't there." The Citizens' Council, sometimes called "Thornton's oligarchy," centralized power in an open and complete fashion. A local newspaper observed: "In many cities, power descends from a small group of influential businessmen to the city council. What distinguishes the Dallas power group from others is that it is organized, it has a name, it is not articulately opposed and it was highly publicized." If anything, local autonomy, concentrated in the hands of a relatively few influential citizens, increased during the depression decade; the bureaucracy-laden state and federal governments held no truck with the "yes or no" men of Dallas. Other southern city halls showed equally sparse evidence of federal presence. President Roosevelt made no effort to unseat political machines in Memphis or New Orleans, and local elites continued to predominate in countless other southern communities. In Houston, for example, four-time mayor Oscar Holcombe faithfully acted upon the concerns of the business community as represented by New Dealer and financial tycoon Jesse Jones. Just as Roosevelt kept hands off the steel barons who wielded such influence in Birmingham and the commercial elite in Atlanta, he declined to support or oppose the ascendance of the Citizens' Council in Dallas.[8]

In the months following the Stock Market Crash no widespread panic ensued in Dallas. The Dallas *Morning News* dismissed the significance of the stock market collapse, noting: "Many individuals, undoubtedly have suffered a loss far heavier than they could afford. Yet economic conditions in general are sound . . . and, after the storm, the sun of prosperity will again shine on the thrift, hard work and efficient effort." Nor did city officials appreciate discouraging talk of

[8]Warren Leslie, *Dallas, Public and Private* (New York: Grossman Publishers, 1964), 64 (2nd quotation), 69, 84 (1st quotation); Lyle W. Dorsett, *Franklin D. Roosevelt and the City Bosses* (Port Washington, N.Y.: National University Publications, Kennikat Press, 1977). Dallas remains the largest city in the nation with a city-manager form of government. Stephen L. Elkin, "State and Market in City Politics: Or, the 'Real' Dallas," in Clarence N. Stone and Heywood T. Sanders (eds.), *The Politics of Urban Development* (Lawrence: University Press of Kansas, 1987), 50n; Biles, *Memphis in the Great Depression,* especially chap. 4; T. Harry Williams, *Huey Long* (New York: Alfred A. Knopf, 1969), 425–427, 675, 849–853; Betty Marie Field, "The Politics of the New Deal in Louisiana, 1933–1939" (Ph.D. diss., Tulane University, 1973), 83–85, 109–112, 286–287; Edward Shannon LaMonte, "Politics and Welfare in Birmingham, Alabama: 1900–1975" (Ph.D. diss., University of Chicago, 1976), 135–136; Douglas L. Fleming, "Atlanta, the Depression, and the New Deal" (Ph.D. diss., Emory University, 1984).

economic setbacks; when a local lawyer spoke on a radio broadcast about rising unemployment, the city commission enacted a statute requiring that any such negative remarks be submitted in advance for approval. In fact, hard times were not all that hard in Dallas for the first year of the depression. According to 1930 data the city's jobless rate stood at only 4.7 percent. The merger of North Texas Bank with Republic National Bank and Trust Company constituted the largest merger of financial institutions in the state's history. Also, thanks in large part to the booster efforts of Industrial Dallas, Incorporated, a total of 802 new businesses located in the city in 1929 and some 600 more followed suit during the first nine months of 1930.[9]

Dallas seemed to suffer less than many other cities due to the discovery of oil in East Texas at the outset of the decade. In October 1930 wildcatter Columbus M. Joiner found two hundred square miles of land floating on a veritable lake of oil about 120 miles southeast of Dallas. By 1933 over nine thousand producing oil wells operated in that field. Almost immediately Dallas profited from the newfound economic opportunity a major oil strike provided. Industrial Dallas, Incorporated, launched a promotional campaign to portray the city as headquarters of the new oil field by printing advertisements in *Oil Weekly* and *Oil and Gas Journal* and mailing over five thousand reprints to oil companies. The city quickly installed telephone and telegraph service to Tyler, Kilgore, Gladewater, Longview, and the other fledgling communities of the oil field. Several Dallas banks, most notably the First National, introduced new methods of oil financing such as production loans made against oil still in the ground. As a result of these efforts hundreds of petroleum-related businesses came to Dallas, including several oil companies that located their executive headquarters or southwest branch offices there. Several local firms, such as the Magnolia and Sun Oil Companies, and individuals, like H. L. Hunt and Clint W. Murchison, prospered from the beginning. In short order, Dallas established itself as the financial and service center for the greatest oil strike since the legendary Spindletop strike of 1901.[10]

Although the fortuitous oil discovery no doubt mitigated the economic crisis of the early depression years, Dallas did not escape hard times altogether. Unemployment became a grave problem; more than 18,500 jobless men and women applied for relief at city hall by the end of 1931. Employers discharged

---

[9]Dallas *Morning News,* Nov. 13, 1929 (quotation), June 23, 1930; Bureau of the Census, *Fifteenth Census of the United States: 1930. Unemployment* (Washington, D.C.: Government Printing Office, 1932), II, 135; Dallas *Morning News,* Oct. 13, 1929, Oct. 12, 1930.

[10]James Howard, *Big D Is For Dallas: Chapters in the Twentieth-Century History of Dallas* (Austin: University Cooperative Society, 1957), 43, 89; Dorothy De Moss, "Resourcefulness in the Financial Capital: Dallas, 1929–1933," in Robert C. Cotner et al., *Texas Cities and the Great Depression* (Austin: Texas Memorial Museum, 1973), 119–121; Dallas Chamber of Commerce, "Report of Industrial Dallas, Inc., 1928–1929–1930," Dallas Public Library (Dallas: n.p., 1931).

married female employees, and retail stores cut back to five-day work weeks. Ironically, the federal government reported in 1931 that the most serious unemployment problem in the state existed in the East Texas oil fields where an estimated ten thousand of the many thousands who arrived from around the country to get work found none. As the federal government noted, the care of these new arrivals fell on local communities, including nearby Dallas.[11]

Other economic indicators reflected the city's troubles. Dallas building permits for 1931 totaled only $7.5 million, down from $11 million the year before. By 1933 the slowdown in construction led the Dallas Carpenters' Union to offer a 50 percent reduction on all repair and remodeling work. Dallas boasted of being the merchandising capital of the South and, therefore, suffered severely when net retail sales plummeted from $189 million in 1929 to $130 million 1935. Wholesale business in 1929 totaled $729 million but only $48 million a decade later. A persistent decline in bank deposits and loans led to frequent reorganizations and mergers. In the most notable case the city's three largest banks pooled their resources to save a smaller state bank from closing. Clearly, Dallas suffered from the weight of the Great Depression.[12]

Faced with unprecedented demands on local resources, the city responded minimally. Burdened by reduced tax collections, Dallas cut expenditures—including relief—to keep from going heavily in the red. In 1931 the city stood over $32.5 million in arrears. After its initial year the newly instituted city manager government trimmed the overdraft by more than $400,000. In its second year city hall refunded the remainder of the deficit, and the budget maintained a cash surplus for the duration of the decade. By and large, this owed to the cutting of municipal workers' salaries from 5 percent to 20 percent and the release of hundreds of employees. New city manager John Edy refused to allocate funds for street paving or building a levee sewer along the Trinity River downtown—despite significant pressure from the business community. Teachers received their monthly paychecks without interruption, but the sums decreased; in the 1931–1932 school year, for example, teacher salaries averaged $ 1,669 and in the 1932–1933 year only $1,463. The Board of Education reduced the number of faculty by demanding the automatic resignation of married women employees.[13]

---

[11]Dallas *Morning News,* Dec. 11, 1931; Work Projects Administration Writers' Project, *Dallas Guide and History,* 195; J. F. Lucey to Walter S. Gifford, telegram, Oct. 27, 1931, State File: Texas, President's Organization For Unemployment Relief, Record Group 73 (National Archives).

[12]Dorothy Dell De Moss, "Dallas, Texas, During the Early Depression: The Hoover Years, 1929–1933" (M.A. thesis, University of Texas, 1966), 70–81; Dallas *Morning News,* Jan. 5, 1933; Howard, *Big D Is For Dallas,* 15–16.

[13]Roscoe C. Martin, "Dallas Makes the Manager Plan Work," *The Annals of the American Academy of Political and Social Science,* CXCIX (Sept., 1938), 65; Dallas *Morning News,* Apr. 28, 1932; Fairbanks, "The Good Government Machine," 127–128; De Moss, "Dallas, Texas, During the Early Depression," 119–122.

TABLE 1 Relief Expenditures By Government And Private Organizations, January 1 to March 31, 1931

| City | Municipal ($) | % | Private ($) | % | Total ($) |
|---|---|---|---|---|---|
| Atlanta | 20,493 | 26.7 | 56,183 | 73.2 | 76,676 |
| Birmingham | 74,544 | 50.4 | 73,326 | 49.6 | 147,870 |
| Dallas | 34,622 | 48.3 | 37,109 | 51.7 | 71,731 |
| Houston | 12,329 | 20.4 | 48,224 | 79.6 | 60,553 |
| Memphis | 11,190 | 8.8 | 115,317 | 91.2 | 126,507 |
| New Orleans | 0 | 0.0 | 27,103 | 100.0 | 27,103 |
| Total | 153,178 | 30.0 | 357,262 | 70.0 | 510,440 |

NOTE: Nationwide, local governments provided 60.4% and private sources, 39.6%.

SOURCE: U.S. Bureau of the Census, *Relief Expenditures by Government and Private Organizations, 1929 and 1931* (Washington, D.C.: Government Printing Office, 1932), 6, 32–33.

As the monthly case load of the city welfare department rose to an average of 2,800 in 1931, city officials instituted a plan whereby the unemployed labored one day per week on public works projects and were paid in groceries bought by the city wholesale. After a prolonged campaign the Laboring Men's Relief Association persuaded the welfare department to issue some cash payments in addition to food, but the city continued to focus its efforts on encouraging self-sufficiency by subsidizing the planting of four hundred acres of vegetable gardens and distributing over one thousand packages of seeds to the unemployed. The welfare department also operated a cannery so that vegetables could be preserved for winter consumption. Noting that the thirty cents an hour it currently paid day laborers "cost the city about 40 percent more than if the work were done by private contract," the municipal government cut the pay to eighteen cents an hour, to be discharged in groceries. As in other southern cities, economy continued to be the first priority.[14] (Table 1 compares Dallas, the fourth largest southern city in 1930, with the other largest cities with respect to sources of relief funding.)

With an enervated municipal government, local social welfare institutions were called on to provide relief. Their resources disappeared rapidly, however, and philanthropic activity lagged as well. An American Public Welfare Association survey concluded that "analysis of Community Chest giving in Dallas . . . indicates an unusually small proportion, both in number and amount, of gifts, by individuals as compared with business firms and corporations. . . . This is not to indicate that business firms and corporations in Dallas give too much to the

[14]De Moss, "Resourcefulness in the Financial Capital," 124, 125 (quotation), 126; Dallas *Morning News,* Apr. 12, 1932. See also American Public Welfare Association, "Dallas Welfare Survey," Southern Methodist University Library, Dallas, Texas (n.p., 1938).

Community Chest. Some should give much more." The Dallas *Morning News* editorialized: "The richest of the rich in Dallas have fallen down on the task. They have shirked in the face of the winter's desperate need."[15] With city halls closely cleaving to a policy of low taxes and limited expenditures, private giving insufficient, and state government bereft of resources, the federal government became the last resort. In the early days of the depression, the Dallas *Morning News* rejected the idea of federal relief, saying: "The *News* has steadfastly set its face against tin-cup-and-blue-goggles trips to Washington for 'relief' for Texans." But the prospect of desperately needed aid proved too attractive to spurn. The Dallas *Morning News* supported the National Recovery Administration, and the Chamber of Commerce responded so quickly and energetically that NRA chief Hugh Johnson singled out the organization for commendation. Similarly, the paper encouraged compliance with the Agricultural Adjustment Act, a reflection of the community's concern with deflated cotton prices.[16]

Of most immediate concern to Dallas, to be sure, was unemployment and the resultant relief crisis. In May 1933 Congress created the Federal Emergency Relief Administration (FERA), authorizing it to distribute $500 million for direct and work relief as well as transient care. The federal government provided funds for distribution by state and local governments, with emphasis on decentralization. In spring 1933 the state legislature created the Texas Rehabilitation and Relief Commission to distribute the largess through county agencies. From its inception in July 1933 to 1935 when the federal government turned unemployment relief over to state and local authorities, FERA general relief aided thousands of jobless in Dallas. At its peak the agency dispensed relief to 14,125 city residents monthly. Workers paved roads, dug ditches, and performed hundreds of other tasks that improved the city's appearance. And the federal government paid for over 80 percent of the relief appropriations.[17]

The Public Works Administration (PWA) opened its offices in Dallas in 1933. Unlike the other New Deal agencies concerned with unemployment, which concentrated on short-term, low-cost projects, the PWA awarded grants

---

[15]American Public Welfare Association, "Dallas Welfare Survey," 84 (1st quotation); Dallas *Morning News,* Dec. 4, 1931 (2nd quotation).

[16]Donald W. Whisenhunt, *The Depression in Texas: The Hoover Years* (New York: Garland Publishing, 1983), 9 (quotation); Dallas *Morning News,* July 23, 1933, Aug. 11, 1933; Dallas Chamber of Commerce, "Departmental Reports for 1933," *Dallas,* XII (Dec, 1933), 6.

[17]Lionel V. Patenaude, *Texans, Politics, and the New Deal* (New York: Garland Publishing, 1983), 88; United States Federal Emergency Relief Administration, *Final Statistical Report on the Federal Emergency Relief Administration,* prepared under the direction of Theodore E. Whiting, Work Projects Administration (Washington, D.C.: Government Printing Office, 1942), 177–192; Arthur E. Burns, "Federal Emergency Relief Administration," in Clarence E. Ridley and Orin F. Nolting (eds.), *The Municipal Year Book, 1937* (Chicago: The International City Managers' Association, 1937), 413–414.

to cities for large-scale efforts. (The cities had to augment these grants with sizable contributions of their own.) In PWA projects, about 70 percent of funds went for materials and the remaining 30 percent for wages. Since make work was never the primary goal, the agency directly employed relatively few men; moreover, PWA hired indiscriminately, not just from the relief rolls, so it had only an incidental impact on gross unemployment figures. In Dallas the PWA built the Museum of Natural History and added 130 beds to city-owned Parkland Hospital. In 1939 the city completed negotiations with the United States Housing Authority (negotiations originating with PWA) for its first slum clearance project, providing shelter for 626 black families.[18]

Such progams as FERA and PWA provided some succor for Dallas's destitute, but by 1935 the relief crisis remained just as critical. That year President Roosevelt created the Works Progress Administration (WPA) to employ men in greater numbers and at a wage higher than the relief rate. Recognizing that "make work" often had little intrinsic value, he nonetheless favored it to the dole. (At the same time the federal government created WPA, it turned unemployment relief back over to state and local governments.) Unlike the PWA, the WPA focused its resources on smaller scale jobs with little cost for materials so that most of the funds could be spent paying wages.[19]

By 1938 when Congress mandated draconian cuts in relief appropriations, WPA had spent thousands of dollars in Dallas, a substantial contribution but somewhat less than might have been possible. Several reasons accounted for WPA's limited success. Small payments to reliefers underscored community values. The federal government divided the nation into four regions to establish variable pay rates, and laborers in the Southwest division (which included Dallas) received the second lowest wages. Certainly relief stipends fell short of desirable levels nationwide, but workers in southern cities suffered most, receiving from 33 to 65 percent of the national average emergency standard of living expense identified by federal authorities. In 1939 in Dallas 8,939 persons received certification for relief employment, but only 4,973 actually obtained assignments. A local social worker observed that, as a result, "a large though undetermined number of individuals in varying degrees of need were thus left unprovided for by any existing agency, public or private." Without federal funds after 1935, relief virtually vanished altogether; in 1935 Dallas spent approximately $350,000 to augment federal money but in 1936 appropriated

---

[18]Otis L. Graham, Jr., and Meghan Robinson Wander (eds.), *Franklin D. Roosevelt, His Life and Times: An Encyclopedic View* (Boston: G. K. Hall, 1985), 336–337; Work Projects Administration Division of Information, "Texas," Appraisal Report File, County Reports D-E, Record Group 69 (National Archives); Work Projects Administration Writers' Project, *Dallas Guide and History*, 508.

[19]Graham and Wander (eds.), *Franklin D. Roosevelt, His Life and Times*, 461–464.

TABLE 2 Sources of Funding for Relief Programs, 1935–1936

| City and Year | | Total Spent on Relief ($) | Federal Dollars Spent on Relief ($) | Percent of Total from Federal Sources |
|---|---|---|---|---|
| Atlanta | 1935 | 5,910,810 | 5,051,153 | 86 |
| | 1936 | 0 | 0 | 0 |
| Birmingham | 1935 | 5,452,319 | 5,072,506 | 93 |
| | 1936 | 140,209 | 51,996 | 37 |
| Dallas | 1935 | 1,776,400 | 1,429,494 | 81 |
| | 1936 | 0 | 0 | 0 |
| Houston | 1935 | 2,422,159 | 1,931,037 | 80 |
| | 1936 | 0 | 0 | 0 |
| Memphis | 1935 | 2,280,031 | 2,123,861 | 93 |
| | 1936 | 0 | 0 | 0 |
| New Orleans | 1935 | 9,241,949 | 8,973,956 | 97 |
| | 1936 | 0 | 0 | 0 |

SOURCE: United States Federal Emergency Relief Administration, *Final Statistical Report of the Federal Emergency Relief Administration,* prepared under the direction of Theodore E. Whiting, Work Projects Administration (Washington, D.C.: Government Printing Office, 1942), 327, 335, 343, 374, 376, 377.

nothing. Like other southern cities Dallas increasingly relied upon external sources for care of its dependents.[20] (See tables 2 and 3.)

Indeed, substandard pay rates, paltry contributions to public relief, and the virtually total reliance on federal funds indicate a minimal commitment to social welfare by the community. The Dallas *Morning News* called WPA "evil but necessary," a succinct statement of how the agency fared in the public's esteem. The acceptance of New Deal funds provided a way to preserve traditional customs related to relief while temporarily expanding coverage to meet an emergency. Far from being infused with any new spirit of social welfare, Dallas seems not to have altered its policies on indigent care at all during the Great Depression.[21]

In Dallas resistance to labor emanated from respectable, influential businessmen's groups committed to the preservation of open shops. The Chamber of Commerce boasted that Dallas was one of the first open-shop cities in the country and advertised nationally the virtues of the city's docile labor force.

[20]Donald S. Howard, *The WPA and Federal Relief Policy* (New York: Russell Sage Foundation, 1943), 84, 95, 178; Work Projects Administration Writers' Project, *Dallas Guide and History,* 494, 495 (quotation); *Final Statistical Report of the Federal Emergency Relief Administration,* 343. The city did employ 8,000 men in construction and landscaping work on the Texas Centennial Exposition. Work Projects Administration Writers' Project, *Dallas Guide and History,* 199.

[21]Dallas *Morning News,* Mar. 30, 1935.

TABLE 3 Emergency Relief by Sources of Funds, July 1933–December 1935

| City | Total ($) | Federal Funds ($) | Total (%) | State Funds ($) | Total (%) | Local Funds ($) | Total (%) |
|---|---|---|---|---|---|---|---|
| Atlanta | 12,955,483 | 11,138,002 | 86.0 | 0 | 0.0 | 1,817,481 | 14.0 |
| Birmingham | 11,486,481 | 10,915,435 | 95.0 | 64,898 | 0.6 | 506,148 | 4.4 |
| Dallas | 4,733,623 | 3,814,125 | 80.6 | 891,230 | 18.8 | 28,268 | 0.6 |
| Houston | 5,742,238 | 4,490,605 | 78.2 | 1,241,315 | 21.6 | 10,318 | 0.2 |
| Memphis | 4,119,607 | 3,963437 | 96.2 | 0 | 0.0 | 156,170 | 3.8 |
| New Orleans | 17,422,059 | 16,990,480 | 97.5 | 0 | 0.0 | 43,579 | 2.5 |
| Total | 56,459,491 | 51,312,084 | 90.9 | 2,197,443 | 3.9 | 2,949,964 | 5.2 |

SOURCE: Arthur E. Burns, "Federal Emergency Relief Administration," in Clarence E. Ridley and Orin F. Nolting (eds.), *The Municipal Year Book, 1937* (Chicago: The International City Managers' Association, 1937), 413–414.

The chamber's Open Shop Bureau took an active role in politics, supporting candidates of antiunion persuasion. The Dallas Open Shop Association, formed in 1919 by a coterie of local businessmen, guaranteed the solvency of all its members in case of work-stopping strikes through the use of its rumored $2 million to $3 million reserve fund. Further, it subjected any member who knowingly hired union workers to, a $3,000 fine. The success of the business community in safeguarding the open shop resulted in total capitulation by the local AFL leadership, as witnessed by the Central Labor Council offering to help the Chamber of Commerce keep the CIO out of the community.[22]

The Dallas *Morning News* consistently took a hostile position toward labor unionization, opposing the National Labor Relations Act and the Fair Labor Standards Act. Moreover, it flaunted compliance of New Deal labor laws in its own business affairs, refusing to pay its employees an hourly wage with time-and-a-half for overtime. In short, the newspaper continued to treat its workers in the frankly paternalistic way it always had. It guaranteed employees a certain wage in its contracts with them and disregarded federal requirements for minimum pay levels. Nobody at the *News* ever punched a time clock, federal strictures notwithstanding. The company felt so strongly about management's right to deal freely with its own workers that it successfully withstood legal challenges by the U.S. government, first in the Fifth Circuit Court of Appeals and finally in the U.S. Supreme Court. As the most influential newspaper in Dallas, its victory lent special authority to its regular anti-labor fulminations.[23]

As in other southern cities violence against union organizers in Dallas was frequent, brutal, and shockingly open. In 1937 the United Auto Workers (UAW) initiated a campaign to organize a local Ford plant. Several union members, labor lawyers, and sympathizers suffered beatings near the automobile factory and downtown in broad daylight. Socialist Herbert Harris was knocked out, stripped, tarred and feathered, and deposited on a downtown street. A few days later several men took a UAW attorney from a downtown drugstore and beat him severely. Police did nothing. In 1939 and 1940 the UAW filed unfair labor practice charges against Ford with the National Labor Relations Board, which accused company officials in Dallas with "brutality unknown in the history of the Board." Brutal, but effective—the 1930s ended with Ford still free of UAW representation.[24]

---

[22] New York *Times,* Jan. 5, 1930; George Lambert, "Dallas Tries Terror," *The Nation,* CXLV (Oct. 9, 1937), 377. *The Craftsman,* local AFL organ, protested the Chamber of Commerce's depiction of a pliable labor force. *The Craftsman* (Dallas), Mar. 28, 1930.

[23] Stanley Walker, "The Dallas *Morning News,*" *American Mercury,* LXV (Dec, 1947), 708–711. Also see Ernest Sharpe, *G. B. Dealey of the Dallas News* (New York: Henry Holt & Co., 1955).

[24] Work Projects Administration Writers' Project, *Dallas Guide and History,* 283–284; John J. Granberry, "Civil Liberties in Texas," *Christian Century,* LIV (Oct. 27, 1937), 1326–1327; Lambert, "Dallas Tries Terror," 376–378; F. Ray Marshall, *Labor in the South* (Cambridge, Mass.: Harvard University Press, 1967), 191 (quotation).

Similar violence developed when textile unions sought to penetrate the substantial Dallas clothing industry. Hat, Cap, and Millinery Workers vice president George Baer lost sight in one eye when three men wielding blackjacks waylaid him on a busy downtown street. Baer identified his attackers, but police took no action. Sporadic violence interrupted an ILGWU strike in which hooligans stripped ten women before a crowd of hundreds in the central business district. The bitter strike dragged on for over eight months before collapsing in defeat. By 1940 several hundred garment workers belonged to two ILGWU locals, representing the signal accomplishment of labor in the city. "Nevertheless," writes labor historian George Green, "the union rated Dallas as the only Southwestern city with a considerable dress production market that was still unorganized."[25]

Both the AFL and the CIO won significant victories in the 1930s, though primarily in the smokestack cities of the Northeast and Midwest. In the tradition-laden South success came more grudgingly. Major breakthroughs, achieved earlier in other parts of the nation, were forestalled by the opposition of local authorities like Memphis's Boss Crump and organizations like the Dallas Open Shop Association. The drive to unionize the South persisted for decades; in 1946 the CIO's Operation Dixie, a comprehensive drive for closed shops from the Piedmont to Texas, commenced with great fanfare. In 1953 it ceased operation, conceding defeat. Only 14.4 percent of the region's nonagricultural workers belonged to unions as late as the mid-1960s (compared to 29.5 percent nationally). The situation in Dallas confirmed historian George Tindall's conclusion that despite nominal gains in membership and the laying of a foundation for future success, "the South remained predominantly non-union and largely antiunion."[26]

Dallas blacks suffered severely from the economy's collapse in the 1930s. Traditionally "last hired and first fired" and confined to the lowest paying jobs,

---

[25] *The Craftsman* (Dallas), Feb. 22, Mar. 8, 1935; Work Projects Administration Writers' Project, *Dallas Guide and History,* 284; John J. Granberry, "Civil Liberties in Texas," 1327; George N. Green, "The ILGWU in Texas, 1930–1970," *Journal of Mexican American History,* I (Spring, 1971), 154 (quotation). Also see George N. Green, "Discord in Dallas Auto Workers, City Fathers, and the Ford Motor Company, 1937–1941," *Labor's Heritage,* I (July, 1980), 20–33.

[26] Billy Hall Wyche, "Southern Attitudes Toward Industrial Unions, 1933–1941" (Ph.D. diss., University of Georgia, 1969), 167; George Brown Tindall, *The Emergence of the New South, 1913–1945* (Baton Route: Louisiana State University Press, 1967), 515, 522 (quotation). On unionization efforts since World War II, see Robert Emil Botsch, *We Shall Not Overcome: Populism and Southern Blue Collar Workers* (Chapel Hill: University of North Carolina Press, 1980); Marshall, *Labor in the South;* and Merl E. Reed, Leslie S. Hough, and Gary M. Fink (eds.), *Southern Workers and Their Unions, 1880–1975:* Selected Papers/The Second Labor History Conference, 1978 (Westport, Conn.: Greenwood Press, 1981). Outlining the failures of the CIO in the immediate post-World War II period is Barbara S. Griffith, *The Crisis of American Labor: Operation Dixie and the Defeat of the CIO* (Philadelphia: Temple University Press, 1988).

they constituted fully one-half of the city's unemployed by 1932. The few black-owned businesses faced extinction; no banks and one black insurance company (Excelsior Mutual) survived by 1937. Residential segregation continued to be the rule, despite court rulings outlawing discriminatory municipal ordinances. Expanding black communities in "Oak Cliff" and "Elm Thicket" were situated in the least desirable areas of the city, inching across the landscape only as bordering white residents surrendered their homes. But racial turnover occurred very slowly and construction nearly ceased in the Depression years, so inadequate housing remained a serious problem. Whites also used violence to keep blacks from occupying homes in white neighborhoods. The Dallas *Express* reported a dozen bombings during the winter of 1940–1941 and criticized Mayor Woodall Rodgers, who blamed blacks for inciting violence by not accepting residential segregation. A 1938 Dallas housing survey reported 86 percent of black homes substandard. Given the squalor in which so many blacks lived, the fact that in 1930 black mortality rates more than doubled those of whites is not surprising.[27]

The drive for equal rights and improved living conditions met formidable opposition in the courts. In Texas the white primary formed the major obstacle to black voting. In 1923 the state legislature revised the election laws to prohibit explicitly black participation in Democratic primaries. When the U.S. Supreme Court ruled the statute a violation of the Fourteenth Amendment's equal protection clause in *Nixon v. Herndon,* the state legislature rewrote the law deleting references to blacks and empowering the State Democratic Executive Committee to approve voting qualifications. In 1935 the nation's highest court approved the revision in *Grovey v. Townsend,* arrogating disfranchisement to the political party by virtue of its being a nongovernmental voluntary association.[28]

In 1936 a group of the state's most influential blacks, including Antonio Maceo Smith and Maynard H. Jackson of Dallas and Clifford Jackson and Richard Grovey of Houston, reorganized the defunct Independent Voters League as the Progressive Voters League to continue the battle against white

---

[27] Bureau of the Census, *Fifteenth Census of the United States: 1930. Unemployment* (Washington, D.C.: Government Printing Office, 1931), I, 952–953; "Minutes of the Annual Meeting, Texas Commission on Interracial Cooperation," Dec. 6, 7, 1940, Houston Metropolitan Research Center, Houston Public Library; Alwyn Barr, *Black Texans: A History of Negroes in Texas, 1528–1971* (Austin: Jenkins Publishing Co., Pemberton Press, 1973), 154–155; Work Projects Administration Writers' Project, *Dallas Guide and History,* 507, 517; Dallas *Express,* Jan. 18, Mar. 1, 1941.

[28] Robert Haynes, "Black Houstonians and the White Democratic Primary, 1920–1945," in Francisco A. Rosales and Barry J. Kaplan (eds.), *Houston: A Twentieth Century Urban Frontier* (Port Washington, N.Y.: Associated Faculty Press, 1983), 122–137; James Martin SoRelle, "The Darker Side of 'Heaven': The Black Community in Houston, Texas, 1917–1945" (Ph.D. diss., Kent State University, 1980), 172–196.

primaries. In 1938 several blacks filed a class action suit in U.S. District Court seeking an injunction against the Houston Democratic Executive Committee to prevent the exclusion of black voters in that year's primary election. The court refused to grant the injunction; the black petitioners considered an appeal but finally did nothing. Not until 1944 did the U.S. Supreme Court rule the white primary unconstitutional in the landmark *Smith v. Allright* decision. For the 1930s black efforts at contesting the Democratic party's exclusive policies fell consistently short.[29]

The inability to participate in Democratic primaries severely limited the political role played by Texas blacks in the 1930s. The Dallas Progressive Voters League remained active, registering black voters and endorsing the white candidates who seemed least objectionable. Nonetheless, few blacks voted or even paid their poll taxes—only 3,400 in Dallas and just 400 in Houston in 1935. Since neither city possessed a political machine that relied on black patronage for continued electoral success, local Democratic leaders had no reason to liberalize their voting requirements. Few blacks bothered to seek elective office. In 1935 A. S. Wells did in Dallas, in a special election to fill a vacancy in the state legislature. He placed fifth with 1,001 votes as many black registered voters stayed home, allegedly in response to the Ku Klux Klan's campaign of intimidation. In 1939 black businessman James B. Grigsby ran for election to the Houston school board but received only 689 votes. In an electorate dominated by whites, blacks' efforts consistently failed to alter election outcomes.[30]

Dallas had a black chamber of commerce, an NAACP chapter, and other voluntary associations that sought to improve conditions of their constituents. Generally, their impact was unremarkable, their achievements few. Limited local resources and the overwhelming bulwark of custom, coupled with community demoralization, meant that any attempt to improve conditions for blacks would be an uphill struggle. Most blacks had only the New Deal's relief and recovery programs to fall back on. Unfortunately, in the tradition-laden southern cities the New Deal made few inroads. Nor did southern-based federal bureaucrats launch unpopular reform campaigns. Southerners feared the New Deal's reputation as liberal on the issue of race, even though Roosevelt initiated few efforts designed specifically to aid blacks and his administration's celebrity can best be attributed to the unofficial efforts of a few activists such as Harold

---

[29]Barr, *Black Texans,* 136; SoRelle, "The Darker Side of 'Heaven,'" 203–205. Also see Darlene Clark Hine, *Black Victory: The Rise and Fall of the White Primary in Texas* (Millwood, N. Y.: KTO Press, 1979).

[30]Fairbanks, "The Good Government Machine," 130–133; Ralph J. Bunche, *The Political Status of the Negro in the Age of FDR,* ed. Dewey W. Grantham (Chicago: University of Chicago Press, 1973), 95, 466, 557; SoRelle, "The Darker Side of 'Heaven,'" 302–303.

Ickes, Aubrey Williams, and Eleanor Roosevelt. And as in politics, local administrators exercised considerable autonomy in the application of New Deal programs and policies.[31]

Segregation also proved unassailable by New Deal agencies. Many programs enforced separation, as did the WPA in its sewing rooms and the Civilian Conservation Corps in its camps. The inchoate public housing program preserved racial segregation, first under the aegis of the PWA and subsequently, the U.S. Housing Authority. Under the PWA's Harold Ickes, about half the federal housing projects in the South went to blacks, and PWA housing contracts required the hiring of black workers. Dallas began construction of public housing projects during the 1930s, designating most of them for black occupation. No question ever arose about the suitability of segregated housing units—no one, black or white, called for integrated projects—but implementation of the program aroused considerable controversy nevertheless. Construction delays developed when black projects fell too near white neighborhoods, and despite PWA and USHA housing contract stipulations that blacks be employed in construction, local authorities often failed to do so.[32]

The New Deal provided new housing, jobs, and relief for many destitute blacks in Dallas but always under the vigilant control of local authorities. Municipal officials set guidelines and implemented policies to reinforce existing racial norms—with little or no federal incursions. Even the blacks helped by New Deal programs lived in a community where segregation and second-class citizenship went largely unquestioned. In Dallas, as throughout the South, few blacks voted and none held elective office. The assault on Jim Crowism and political disfranchisement, a post-World War II movement, received little impetus from the New Deal.

The Great Depression struck hard in Dallas. Although the city fared better than some others because of the oil bonanza, problems arose to tax local resources. Businesses shut down, workers lost jobs, productivity declined, trade ebbed, and the demands for relief skyrocketed. Reduced tax collections, no heritage of social welfare, and city government's insistence upon fiscal "responsibility" combined to curtail the amount of relief offered the needy in Dallas and other southern cities. The New Deal provided some aid but, even when most generously funded, only for a fraction of the needy and at wage levels below the standards in other regions. New Deal alphabet agencies allowed

---

[31]Tempie Virginia Strange, "The Dallas Negro Chamber of Commerce: A Study of a Negro Institution" (M.A. thesis, Southern Methodist University, 1945); Barr, *Black Texans,* 147; Leedel W. Neyland, "The Negro in Louisiana Since 1900: An Economic and Social Study" (Ph.D. diss., New York University, 1958), 66.

[32]Tindall, *The Emergence of the New South, 1913–1945,* 546; Charles S. Johnson, *Patterns of Negro Segregation* (New York: Harper and Brothers, 1943), 37.

Dallas to minimize its welfare contributions, not expand them. City leadership rested more firmly than ever in the city's business elite by the end of the decade. The defenders of the status quo preserved the community's independence from union influence, at least for the immediate future.

New Deal programs never excluded blacks from benefits, and occasionally explicitly included them—on paper anyway. But the Roosevelt administration had neither the desire nor the capacity to challenge the South's rock-ribbed racial mores. The federal government's impact on Dallas in the 1930s favored continuity; resistance to change resulted from the influence of powerful elites, unvarnished fealty to long-standing values and institutions, the political powerlessness of the have-nots, and the New Deal's admittedly modest reform agenda. Comparisons with other large southern cities call into question the significance of the New Deal's impact. The forces of conservatism in Dallas and its sister cities in the South appear to have resisted—or at least slowed—the dissolution of traditional political, social, and economic customs.

# The Failed Promise of Wartime Opportunity for Mexicans in the Texas Oil Industry

EMILIO ZAMORA*

*World War II confronted the people of America with horrors of battle and sacrifices of many kinds, but it also brought opportunities, especially in matters of employment. Mexican workers hoped that wartime conditions would bring them more and better jobs, equal pay for equal work, and the end of segregation and discrimination in the workplace. Minorities employed in the oil refining industry along the Texas Gulf Coast shared these hopes. The creation of the Fair Employment Practices Committee (FEPC), a federal agency charged with the task of ending discrimination against minorities in unions, defense industries, and government employment, encouraged them.*

*When discriminatory practices continued, Mexican workers filed a number of complaints, and the FEPC conducted investigations and hearings. The management of some of the larger refineries entered into negotiations with the FEPC, and occasionally ordered a minor adjustment of a particularly egregious injustice. However, when peace returned in 1945, employment practices in the oil refineries remained essentially unchanged.*

*Author Emilio Zamora's account of the struggle reveals the difficulties involved when seeking change in a situation governed by long-standing ethnic prejudice. Ethnic issues, moreover, fueled fear based on concerns about job security and union solidarity. The result was a standoff that allowed management to do little or nothing.*

*Although there have been many fine studies in Mexican American history in recent years, writings on Mexican employment-related issues remain rare. Readers will find Robin Scott, "Wartime Labor Problems and Mexican Americans in the War," in Manuel Servin (ed.),* An Awakened Minority: The

*Emilio Zamora, "The Failed Promise of Wartime Opportunity for Mexicans in the Texas Oil Industry," *Southwestern Historical Quarterly*, 95 (Jan., 1992), 323–350.

**Mexican-Americans** ***(2nd ed.; Beverly Hills: Glencoe Press, 1974) useful; the story of the Mexican American worker over a much longer period is presented in Emilio Zamora,*** **The World of the Mexican Worker in Texas** ***(College Station: Texas A&M University Press, 1995).***

Mexicans came out of the depression facing an unprecedented opportunity to improve their traditional position as low-wage labor and to alter the generational effects of prior occupational discrimination. The wartime rhetoric of democracy, public policy measures that prohibited discrimination by defense industries, government employers and labor unions, and, above all, dramatic job growth in high-wage firms led Mexicans to believe that their time had indeed arrived. The occupational gains made during the war may have raised their hopes further. Obstacles continued, however, to deny Mexican workers equal employment opportunities. Most of them remained working for low-wage employers, and those that secured jobs in high-wage firms assumed the least-skilled and lower-paying ones.[1]

This study examines wartime discrimination as an obstacle to Mexican workers in the oil refining industry of the Texas Gulf Coast, a region bounded by Texas City, Houston, and Beaumont. Oil refineries normally denied Mexicans equal occupational, wage, and upgrading opportunities. Unionized and nonunionized Anglo workers played an important role in sustaining the resultant inequality primarily by opposing the adoption of a nondiscrimination policy in the oil industry. This opposition was cast in racial terms, though it was fun-

[1]Carlos Castañeda, "Statement on Discrimination Against Mexicans in Employment," in Alonso S. Perales, *Are We Good Neighbors* (San Antonio: Artes Graficas, 1948), 59–63; Carlos Castañeda, Testimony, U.S. Senate Subcommittee of the Committee on Education and Labor Hearings, 79th Cong., 1st Sess., Mar. 12–14, 1945 (Washington, D.C.: Government Printing Office, 1945), 131–135 (Y4.Ed8/3:Em7/3); Pauline R. Kibbe, *Latin Americans in Texas* (Albuquerque: University of New Mexico Press, 1946), 157–166. Readings on Mexicans during the war include: Mario Garcia, "Americans All: The Mexican American Generation and the Politics of Wartime Los Angeles, 1941–1945," *Social Science Quarterly,* LXV (June, 1984), 279–289; Raul Morin, *Among the Valiant; Mexican-Americans in WW II and Korea* (Los Angeles: Borden Publishing Co., 1966); Gerald Nash, "Spanish-Speaking Americans in Wartime," in Gerald D. Nash, *The American West Transformed: The Impact of the Second World War* (Bloomington: Indiana University Press, 1985), 107–127; and Robin F. Scott, "Wartime Labor Problems and Mexican-Americans in the War," in Manuel P. Servin (ed.), *An Awakened Minority; The Mexican-Americans* (Beverley Hills: Glencoe Press, 1974), 134–142. The term Mexican refers to both Mexican nationals and U.S.-born Mexicans for two reasons. Incomplete nativity and citizenship data made it impossible in most cases to make such a distinction. Also, the use of the term Mexican seems appropriate since they shared the experiences of occupational, wage, and upgrading discrimination.

damentally motivated by economic and political concerns over the issue of job control. Although more work is required before we can properly gauge the effects of persistent discrimination, this study supports the conventional yet rarely substantiated view that Mexican workers continued facing formidable barriers when they entered high-wage firms during the war.[2]

The primary focus here is the role played by the Fair Employment Practice Committee (FEPC), the agency responsible for implementing President Roosevelt's Executive Orders 8802 and 9346 prohibiting various forms of discrimination by defense industries, government employers, and labor unions.[3] The FEPC waged a 2½-year challenge against discrimination in twelve oil refineries.[4] FEPC examiners focused on group complaints submitted by Mexican workers against three of the twelve refineries (Humble, Sinclair, and Shell), a company union at Humble named the Baytown Employees' Federation and two Congress of Industrial Organizations (CIO) unions, Locals 227 and 367. FEPC officials sought favorable settlements in the three refineries as a first step in pushing for a policy of nondiscrimination in the entire regional industry. Anglo worker opposition was so strong, however, that the FEPC was unable to assure Mexicans the wartime promise of full and unobstructed job opportunities. The agency's failure to effectively combat discrimination in three major

---

[2]Publications that treat the subject of the Mexican worker and the FEPC are rare. These include the previously cited works by Garcia and Nash as well as two studies, one by a CIO organizer involved in the Oil Workers' Organizing Campaign of 1942–1943 and the other by a former head of the FEPC: Clyde Johnson, "The Battle for Baytown," June, 1984 (copy of unpublished book-length manuscript in author's possession); and Malcolm Ross, "Those Gringos," in Malcolm H. Ross, *All Manner of Men* (New York: Greenwood Press, 1948), 265–278. A study by Ray Marshall examines racial discrimination against black workers in the Texas Gulf Coast oil industry and the successful 1955 challenge against it by the government and the NAACP: "Some Factors Influencing the Upgrading of Negroes in the Southern Petroleum Refining Industry," *Social Forces,* XLII (Dec., 1963), 186–195.

[3]President Roosevelt established the FEPC on June 25, 1941, with Executive Order 8802, a measure intended to end discrimination by unions, defense industries, and government employers. On May 26, 1943, the president issued Executive Order 9346 that reorganized the agency and strengthened its effectiveness with an improved budget and regional offices in such places as Dallas and San Antonio. Book-length studies of the FEPC include: Herbert Garfinkel, *When Negroes March: The March on Washington Movement in the Organizational Policies for FEPC* (Glencoe, Ill.: The Free Press, 1959); Louis C. Kesselman, *The Social Politics of FEPC; A Study in Reform Pressure Movements* (Chapel Hill: University of North Carolina Press, 1948); and Louis Ruchames, *Race, Jobs, and Politics: The Story of FEPC* (Westport: Negro Universities Press, 1953).

[4]The twelve refineries were Sinclair (Houston), Shell (Houston), Texas Company (Houston), Texas Company (Port Neches), Pure Oil (Port Neches), Republic (Texas City) Southport (Texas City), Pan American (Texas City), Texas Company (Port Arthur), Gulf (Port Arthur), Humble (Baytown), and Magnolia (Beaumont). Fair Employment Practice Committee, *Final Report* (Washington, D.C.: U.S. Government Printing Office, 1947), 23; W. Don Ellinger, "Complete Report on Shell Situation, May 1, 1945," 1–5, Division of Field Operations, Records of the Fair Employment Practice Committee (National Archives, cited hereafter as FEPC Records).

refineries underscored its powerlessness; it also demonstrated the durable strength of a system of racial inequality.[5]

The experience of Mexican oil workers reflected a pattern of employment discrimination in other war-related industries. As the wartime expansion of the southwestern economy opened up new job opportunities, Mexicans for the first time began to obtain employment in urban-based war industries such as garment, meatpacking, construction, shipping, aircraft repair, and oil. The new-found opportunities, however, soon dried up as high-wage firms filled up their laborer positions, the jobs that were normally available for Mexicans. As a result, war industries only reached an employment level of approximately 25,000 Mexicans during the war, which represented a low utilization rate of 5 percent. The wartime gains, therefore, accompanied persistent inequality. This inconsistency was especially evident in growth industries such as oil. Employers usually assigned Mexicans unskilled jobs that paid the lowest wages and denied them the opportunity to advance into the better-paying skilled positions. They shared this condition with African American workers. Moreover, when the war ended and industrial production decreased, they were generally denied further access and displaced from the jobs they had recently acquired.[6]

The booming oil industry in the Gulf Coast offered some of the more attractive job opportunities since it claimed one of the highest wage rates for skilled and unskilled workers in the state. The sheer fact that oil refineries offered a large and growing number of jobs also attracted the attention of workers. Also, by the mid-1940s the CIO-affiliated Oil Workers' International Union (OWIU) had organized eleven of the twelve major refineries in the Gulf Coast

---

[5]The FEPC conducted preliminary investigations in the Southwest in 1942 that resulted in the discovery of widespread discrimination against Mexican workers in the oil companies of the Texas Gulf Coast. The cases against the refineries and the workers' organizations lasted until the closing of the Dallas office in 1945. Report of Clay Cochran to Dr. Castañeda, Oct. 25,1943, Administrative Division, FEPC Records; John Morton Blum, *V Was For Victory: Politics and American Culture During World War II* (New York: Harcourt Brace Jovanovich, 1976), 198; Lawrence W. Cramer to M. C. Gonzales, Nov. 26, 1941, Division of Field Operations, FEPC Records; Will Alexander to W. G. Carnahan, Dec. 26, 1941, Division of Field Operations, ibid.; Carlos Castañeda to Will Maslow, Jan. 26, 1944, Administrative Division, ibid.

[6]Castañeda, "Statement on Discrimination Against Mexicans in Employment," 59–63; Castañeda, Testimony, 1945, 131–135; Carlos Castañeda, "The Second Rate Citizen and Democracy," in Perales, *Are We Good Neighbors,* 17–20; and C. L. Golightly, "Wartime Employment of Mexican Americans, 1943," Division of Review and Analysis, FEPC Records. The Mexican population, both U.S. and Mexico-born, was at least one million, or 11.5 percent of the total population in the state. Approximately 500,000 Mexicans were gainfully employed. The 25,000 figure was calculated on the basis of a 5 percent utilization rate reported by Castañeda.

and claimed some of the most favorable contractual agreements won by labor in Texas.[7] Despite the attractiveness of oil, only between 1,041 and 1,388, or less than 5 percent of the 25,000 Mexicans in the state's war industries, were drawn into the refineries by the time of Pearl Harbor. They also represented a small portion—between 6 and 8 percent—of the industry's work force.[8]

A significant number of the Mexican oil workers may have been born in Mexico. The only known source of information on nativity characteristics, a survey conducted by the FEPC in one of the refineries in 1943, indicated that 59 percent were born in Mexico and 41 percent in the United States. According to one observer, the U.S.-born Mexicans were underrepresented because they were better informed about the discrimination that awaited them in oil and preferred to search for jobs elsewhere.[9] Mexican nationals presumably had fewer options and tended to accept the low-paying jobs. The presence of a large number of Mexican nationals explains why Anglo workers may have been especially sensitive to the possibility of a wage-cutting threat from below. It also reveals why the Mexican Consul from Houston assumed an important role in representing the Mexican complaints before the FEPC.

Mexicans rarely found employment in the pipeline and production branches of the industry. Management usually assigned them common-laborer jobs in the refineries, paid them less than Anglos that were similarly classified, and denied them opportunities to advance into better-paying skilled occupations. When Mexican and African American workers assumed skilled jobs also held by Anglos, their job classification and pay normally remained unchanged.

---

[7]For readings on the oil industry, see Carl Coke Rister, *Oil: Titan of the Southwest* (Norman: University of Oklahoma Press, 1949); Joseph A. Pratt, *The Growth of a Refining Region* (Greenwich, Conn.: JAI Press, 1980); and C. A. Warner, "Texas and the Oil Industry," *Southwestern Historical Quarterly,* L (July, 1946), 7–24. For an account by a participant in the 1941–1943 Oil Workers' Organizing Campaign, see Johnson, "The Battle for Baytown." Other studies that treat the subject of labor organizing in Texas include: Harvey O'Conner, *History of the Oil Workers' International Union* (Denver: Oil Workers' International Union, 1950); F. Ray Marshall, *Labor in the South* (Cambridge: Harvard University Press, 1967), 194–199, 230–233; Herbert Werner, "Labor Organizations in the American Petroleum Industry," in Harold F. Williamson, Ralph L. Andreano, Arnold R. Daum, and Gilbert C. Klose (eds.), *The American Petroleum Industry: The Age of Energy, 1899–1959* (Evanston: Northwestern University Press, 1963), 827–845.

[8]The figure for the Mexican work force was estimated based on a total of 17,350 workers in the twelve refineries reported by the FEPC. Kibbe suggests a lower figure of less than 3 percent. Kibbe, *Latin Americans in Texas,* 159–161.

[9]Golightly, "Wartime Employment of Mexican-Americans," 2; G. L. Farned to Lawrence Cramer, Jan. 26, 1943; pp. 4–5, Personal Collection of Clyde Johnson (Berkeley, Calif.; cited hereafter as Johnson Collection). The nativity figures suggested by the survey have to be taken with caution. They differ substantially from the overall ratio of one Mexico-born to six U.S.-born Mexicans in the state.

Rarely would management promote them to such jobs as mechanics, truck helpers, truck drivers, and bottle washers.[10]

The practice of placing minorities in the common-laborer positions and denying them upgrading opportunities created a hiring ceiling that was often maintained through contractual agreements or informal understandings with labor unions. Organized labor was thus instrumental in defining the occupational hierarchical order, a fact that became clearer when unionists openly pressured the refineries to resist FEPC directives to end discrimination. Popular anti-Mexican-immigrant feelings that resulted from fears of increased job competition had previously influenced labor's defensive posture and the industry's hiring practices regarding both Mexican nationals and U.S.-born Mexican workers. The widespread anti-Mexican agitation by Anglo workers during the tight market days of the depression, for instance, resulted in decisions by Humble, Sinclair, and Shell to temporarily halt the employment of Mexican workers. The result was a gradual depletion of their Mexican work force. More importantly, these early tensions and protests coincided with union campaigns and contractual negotiations that formally and informally defined the Mexican's bottom position in the industry.[11]

Despite the expressed displeasure of national CIO officers who publicly supported the president's executive orders, the local unions and the leadership of the OWIU rarely challenged the discriminatory practices of the companies or the racially exclusive organizing policies of company unions and AFL locals. In fact, in at least four refineries CIO locals negotiated collective bargaining agreements that established dual wage systems, segregated work areas, separate occupational categories, and upgrading procedures that effectively barred minority workers from the skilled occupations. These agreements as well as numerous informal understandings established at other refineries were negotiated with the knowledge and support of the OWIU. The OWIU and local union leaders presumably shared the sentiments of their local membership or thought that it was less than worthwhile to disturb widespread and deeply ingrained racial customs.[12]

---

[10]One important FEPC finding in the Texas Gulf Coast oil industry involved the use of a dual classification system. According to one FEPC report, all refineries in the area with the exception of the Texas Company maintained a wage differential that segregated two types of common laborers. The first group was composed of Anglos who received the higher rate of pay, which was approximately eighty-nine cents an hour. The second group was made up of Mexican and African American workers who received around seventy-nine and one-half cents an hour. Ernest G. Trimble to Francis J. Haas, July 9, 1943, Region X Files, FEPC Records.

[11]This summary of conditions has been gleaned from numerous FEPC documents cited throughout the paper.

[12]See Johnson, "The Battle for Baytown," for criticism of the union leadership. A CIO organizer assigned to the oil industry in the Gulf Coast, Mr. Johnson was especially critical of the inconsistent support that the OWIU gave the CIO-backed Oil Workers' Organizing Campaign (OWOC),

Although it may be impossible to know to what degree racial thinking motivated the union leadership, it is clear that both the unions and company representatives resisted compliance on the grounds that widespread opposition by Anglo workers threatened to disrupt production. This was a recurring claim that seriously hampered the FEPC throughout the war period. There was ample evidence and good reason to believe this claim. Some FEPC officials, however, suspected that management and union leaders were concealing their own opposition to integration and seeking to encourage dissent by stalling the compliance process. Although company representatives may have shared racial views with the Anglo work force or even entertained the idea of promoting racial thinking to ingratiate themselves with labor or to encourage divisions among the workers, their stated position was credible to an extent given the economic losses they could incur as a result of a disruption in production. The unions, on the other hand, were responding to more than just fears of possible Anglo workers' reactions. Underneath their claims of possible disruptions lay an interest in protecting the privileged position of their constituency from the FEPC threat.

Although the refineries often publicly complained of FEPC compliance pressures, they usually appeared to be projecting an image of disinterested players rather than actively provoking a reaction. Local unionist leaders, however, at times openly encouraged workers to see the intervention of the federal government as a threat to racial privilege and job control. This was evident when union leaders representing the company union at Humble and the CIO locals at Sinclair and Shell openly defied FEPC directives and defended discrimination, particularly against blacks, as the prevailing custom in the South. Among the ideas entertained by unionists and the rank and file was the notion that if concessions were made to Mexicans, blacks would follow with similar allegations, competition would intensify, and management would decrease wages and release Anglo workers.[13]

---

1941–1943, of which he was a part. Much of the conflict that occurred between the staff of the OWOC and the OWIU hinged on the general reluctance of the latter organization to support the OWOC's strong civil rights planks that called for an end to discrimination in the refineries. Clyde Johnson to E. Z., Feb. 9, 1988, interview; Clyde Johnson, "CIO Oil Workers' Organizing Campaign in Texas, 1942–1943," in Gary M. Fink and Merl E. Reed (eds.), *Essays in Southern Labor History; Selected Papers, Southern Labor History Conference, 1976* (Westport, Conn.: Greenwood Press, 1977), 173–187. See the following for copies of these contracts or references to them: Carlos Castañeda to Will Maslow, Sept. 17, 1943, Region X Files, FEPC Records; Leonard M. Brin to Will Maslow, May 24, 1944, ibid.; "Application of Seniority for Selecting Men for Jobs in New Operating Units Not Replacing Other Units," July 23, 1943, ibid.; "Mechanical Seniority," Oct. 1, 1936, ibid.; and President's Committee on Fair Employment Practice, Stipulation, In the Matter of Shell Oil Company, Incorporated, and Oil Workers' International Union, Local 367, CIO, Dec. 30, 1945, pp. 3–4, Legal Division, FEPC Records.

[13]The leadership of the OWIU freely admitted widespread discrimination by its locals in the Gulf Coast, though they claimed that it was for the most part "company inspired" and, to an extent,

Although opposition to FEPC directives significantly undermined compliance, other factors constrained the agency's work. These included the short life span of the FEPC, the lack of enforcement powers, and internal divisions that periodically surfaced on the question of whether to challenge discrimination in the entire industry or on a plant-by-plant basis. These problems, however, did not seem to seriously impair the FEPC in its work in other industries. In fact, what most often appeared to be the case is that opposition to the FEPC in oil magnified internal constraints.[14]

---

reflective of local prejudices. Oil Workers' International Union, Report of the Oil Workers' International Union Concerning Experiences in the Field of Racial and Religious Discrimination, 1944, Division of Review and Analysis, FEPC Records. There were exceptions to the general rule of discrimination by the unions. CIO Local 449 from the Southport refinery in Texas City is a case in point. When the refinery refused to end its practice of wage discrimination, the union successfully challenged the company before the War Labor Board in 1943. The WLB ordered the company to end its dual classification system and pay African American workers equal wages. Another example occurred at the Gulf refinery of Port Arthur in 1945. When 250 members of the Black CIO Union, Local 254, went on a wage strike, the president of the white CIO union announced the support of his membership. National War Labor Board, In the Matter of Southport Petroleum Company of Delaware and Oil Workers' International Union Local 449, Case No. 2898-CS-D, June 5, 1943, Johnson Collection; Castañeda to Maslow, June 16–31, 1945, Region X Files, FEPC Records.

[14]International divisions regarding the proper strategy to pursue when challenging the oil industry was an especially debilitating problem that reflected wider political concerns within the FEPC. Such differences, which contributed to important delays, usually appeared when management and union leaders proposed industry-wide hearings on the grounds that it was unfair to single out individual refineries. Differences of opinion also coincided with a related ambivalence in Washington. For instance, the FEPC entertained the idea of a general hearing that would investigate the issue of discrimination against Mexicans in the Southwest as early as 1942 but dropped its plans at the insistence of Secretary of State Sumner Welles who was concerned that revelations of discrimination against Mexicans would damage relations with Latin America. Lawrence Cramer, the executive secretary of the FEPC in 1943, on the other hand, considered a general hearing involving the oil industry but remained noncommittal because he feared that it could provoke a racial reaction much like one that occurred after the FEPC hearings in Alabama. Preparations were made once again in 1944 to hold general hearings at El Paso to investigate discrimination against Mexicans in the mining industry of Arizona, New Mexico, and West Texas. These plans were also rescinded as a result of objections raised by the State Department. Blum, *V Was For Victory,* 199; Kesselman, *The Social Politics of FEPC,* 17–18; Edwin Smith to Clyde Johnson, Nov. 6, 1942, Johnson Collection; Carlos Castañeda to Maslow, Sept. 1, 1944, Legal Division, FEPC Records.

The FEPC delayed its investigation of the oil industry on two occasions. The first delay coincided with the aborted 1943 plans for a general hearing. The second one occurred during the latter part of 1944 while Castañeda was heading an investigation of the mining industry. Although there is no evidence that these decisions against holding general hearings contributed to similar decisions in oil, the FEPC personnel in Texas, however, did express similar reservations on which strategy to pursue. Castañeda to Maslow, Jan. 26, 1944; Brin to Maslow, June 24, 1944, Division of Field Operations, FEPC Records; Stanley D. Metzger to Clarence M. Mitchell, July 11, 1944, ibid.

Mexican workers began submitting their complaints in 1941 to the Office of Production Management in San Antonio and the FEPC office in Washington, D.C. Problems associated with distance and a lack of personnel kept government officials from servicing these complaints adequately until the president's Executive Order 9346, issued on May 26, 1943, made it possible to establish the Region X office in Dallas. FEPC examiners began their oil investigations almost immediately. Although the Dallas office recorded a continuous stream of settlements in other industries throughout the state, the oil refineries, especially Humble, Sinclair, and Shell, kept it occupied until the agency ceased its operations in 1945.[15]

Dr. Carlos Castañeda, the University of Texas history professor who directed the Dallas office, was an especially important figure in FEPC work in part because of his membership in a national network of Mexican American civil rights leaders that was actively testing the sincerity of the wartime rhetoric of world democracy and pan americanism. His battles against the oil refineries, particularly the fight against Shell, thus became focal points of concern in the civil rights movement and drew attention to the importance of discrimination against Mexicans in Mexico-United States relations.[16]

Castañeda processed Mexican complaints against eight of the twelve major refineries between May 1943 and December 1944. He adopted a dual strategy

---

[15]Manuel Gonzales to Sidney Hillman, Nov. 17, 1941, Division of Field Operations, FEPC Records; Lawrence Cramer to Gonzales, Nov. 26, 1941, ibid.; W. G. Carnahan to Will W. Alexander, Dec. 1, 1941, Legal Division, FEPC Records; Carnahan to Alexander, Dec. 9, 1941, Division of Field Operations, ibid.; Gonzales to Trimble, July 29, 1942, Administrative Division, ibid. See Region X Weekly Reports, ibid., beginning in August 1943 for complaint summaries.

[16]See articles by Félix D. Almaráz, Jr., on Castañeda's highly successful career as a historian and archivist: "Carlos Eduardo Castañeda, Mexican-American Historian: The Formative Years, 1896–1927," *Pacific Historical Review,* XLII (Aug., 1973), 319–344; "The Making of a Boltonian: Carlos E. Castañeda of Texas—The Early Years," *Red River Valley Historical Review,* I (Winter, 1974), 329–350; and "Carlos E. Castañeda and *Our Catholic Heritage:* The Initial Volumes (1933–1943)," *Social Science Journal,* XIII (Apr., 1976), 27–37. A recent publication by Mario T. Garcia devotes a chapter to the life of Castañeda: *Mexican Americans: Leadership, Ideology and Identity, 1930–1960* (New Haven: Yale University Press, 1989). See the following for insightful views on Mexican civil rights and labor politics, and its international ramifications during the 1940s: Juan Gomez-Quiñones, *Chicano Politics: Reality and Promise, 1940–1990* (Albuquerque: University of New Mexico Press, 1990). Almaráz and Garcia generally ignore the work that Castañeda did with the FEPC and his active associations with other civil rights leaders of the period, preferring instead to focus on his career as a historian. This, despite the voluminous amount of information that records his civil rights work. See, for example, Carlos E. Castañeda Papers (Mexican American Archival Collection, Nettie Lee Benson Latin American Collection, University of Texas at Austin); Eleuterio Escobar Papers, ibid.; Perales, *Are We Good Neighbors;* and his various testimonies in congressional hearings, cited elsewhere in this article.

Carlos Castañeda, a University of Texas at Austin history professor and an official of the Fair Employment Practice Committee, which challenged discrimination in the oil industry, speaking at the dedication of the San Jacinto Monument, April 1939. *Courtesy Mexican American Collection, Benson Latin American Collection, University of Texas at Austin.*

that first focused on complaints against Humble, Sinclair, and Shell hoping that favorable adjustments in these refineries would compel the entire industry to enforce the president's executive orders. The second part of the strategy involved a decision to challenge the general practice of racial discrimination with complaints by Mexican workers. Since he feared stronger Anglo opposition to African American complaints, Castañeda decided first to establish the existence of racial discrimination on the basis of Mexican complaints and then direct the refineries to adopt a policy of nondiscrimination that would benefit all minority workers.[17]

W. Don Ellinger became the director of the Dallas office in December 1944, while Castañeda assumed new duties as special assistant to the FEPC director on Latin American Affairs and as director of a new regional office in San Antonio. Although Castañeda was no longer officially involved in the oil cases, he continued to advise the Dallas office. Ellinger handled the cases against the oil companies until the FEPC ceased operations in Texas during 1945.[18]

Castañeda and Ellinger normally coordinated the preparation and submission of complaints with local groups of workers, officials from the Mexican Consulate at Houston, and community leaders associated with the well-known civil rights organization, the League of United Latin American Citizens (LULAC). Preliminary fact-finding meetings also included workers and civil rights leaders from the African American community. Meetings with local minority leaders and investigations conducted immediately after the opening of the Dallas office revealed that the most blatant cases of discrimination were occurring at Humble, Sinclair, and Shell. Moreover, there were a sufficient number of Mexican workers in each plant willing to formally challenge their employers.[19] Although the FEPC handled cases against the three refineries simultaneously, Castañeda obtained the first settlement at Humble.

Humble owned four oil refineries in Texas, including the one at Baytown that became the center of early controversy for the FEPC. The Baytown plant employed approximately 3,000 workers during the war including about 75 Mexicans and 400 blacks. The complaint against Humble occurred while the CIO-led Oil Workers' Organizing Campaign (OWOC) was joining the issue of unionization with the cause of minority workers. The CIO's national leadership initially directed the OWOC and thus injected a more progressive view on minority rights than was normally the case in the area. The OWOC leadership endorsed the claim of discrimination by Mexican complainants in part because it was actively soliciting the support of minority workers for the CIO union, Local 333, in the upcoming union election. This touched off a near-violent and

---

[17]Ross, *All Manner of Men,* 273–274. Castañeda's strategy can be gleaned from his Weekly Reports on the meetings. See Castañeda's Weekly Reports, FEPC Records. The decision by Castañeda to focus on complaints by Mexican workers was based on consultations with Mexican and black complainants as well as with the Mexican Counsel and black and Mexican civil rights leaders from Houston.

[18]Fair Employment Practice Committee, *First Report* (Washington, D.C.: Government Printing Office, 1945), 107.

[19]Although Mexican workers from various refineries submitted complaints, the workers from Humble, Sinclair, and Shell registered the most and best documented ones. Also, these Mexican workers were consistent in resubmitting complaints through the Mexican Consul's office when the FEPC periodically requested additional evidence in support of the complaints.

racially inspired reaction by the company union, the Baytown Employees' Federation (BEF).[20]

In the midst of this highly controversial organizing campaign, a group of six Mexican workers charged Humble with six forms of discrimination. According to the complaint, Mexican laborers received seventy-six and one-half cents per hour for performing the same tasks as Anglo laborers who were paid eighty-nine and one-half cents an hour. While Mexican orderlies in the company hospital received a wage of $137 per month, Anglo janitors received $180 per month. Mexican and Anglo workers doing the same work in and around the acid tanks received seventy-nine and one-half cents per hour and ninety-two and one-half cents per hour, respectively. Although Mexicans cut, bent, and tied steel for seventy-six and one-half cents per hour, Anglos working for contractors on refinery property earned $1.34 for doing the same work. Mexicans were usually assigned to the labor department without opportunities for promotion, and Humble had refused to hire Mexicans since at least 1937.[21]

The company superintendent, Gordon L. Farned, responded to the complaint with a lengthy justification of Humble's record with its Mexican workers. He also broached the issue of Anglo worker opposition that was to loom over compliance negotiations in the industry. Farned cautioned the FEPC about disrupting the deep-rooted custom of discrimination against Mexicans in the state and urged a strategy of gradual change to minimize Anglo hostility.[22]

> Unless and until there is a change in public feeling and sentiment, regardless of what we as one employer may do about the matter, it is an undeniable fact that Anglo American workmen and the public generally, exclusive of the Mexicans themselves, do set themselves apart and do consider themselves to be superior mentally, physically and socially to the Mexicans . . . it probably would be to the best interests of the Mexicans to "make haste slowly"; to make social and economic gains gradually, to educate the populace at large gradually, and to promote their acceptance of the principles aimed at, rather than to take action intended to accomplish the ends you seek, which in actuality, if carried out, would most certainly start serious hostilities and lead to a harmful conflagration.[23]

---

[20]"Humble Oil and Refining Company, Baytown, Texas," typed summary of FEPC case against Humble, November 1943, Division of Review and Analysis, FEPC Records. For information on early discriminatory practices, see Henrietta M. Larson and Kenneth Wiggins Porter, *History of Humble Oil and Refining Company, A Study in Industrial Growth* (New York: Harper and Brothers, 1959), 200–201.

[21]Statement on Discrimination Against Mexican Workers at the Baytown Refinery, Humble Oil and Refining Company, Baytown, Texas, Signed by Andres Contreras, C. Beltran, J. Santana, Onofre Gonzalez, L. Herrera, and G. N. Ponce, Nov. 25, 1942, Johnson Collection.

[22]Gordon L. Farned to Cramer, Jan. 26, 1943, Johnson Collection; Johnson to Trimble, Mar. 15, 1943, ibid.

[23]Ibid. The summary of Farned's response is drawn from his letter to Cramer, Jan. 26, 1943, and from the FEPC report tided "Humble Oil and Refining Company, Baytown, Texas."

Farned added a second related reason for resisting compliance that was to plague the FEPC's work in the industry. He suggested that the FEPC seek industry-wide compliance rather than plant-by-plant settlements. Otherwise, each company that complied presumably would be made the focus of the community's wrath with the resulting disruption of production.

Subsequent investigations revealed a glaring inconsistency in the company's claims that Mexican workers were not hired or promoted because they did not meet the company's educational requirements. Company officials admitted that Anglos were frequently hired without meeting the requirements and that Mexicans were denied employment even when they met them. Moreover, the officials failed to demonstrate a lack of ability by the Mexican workers since they often performed the same tasks as Anglos. As a result of the investigation, the complaint was expanded to include charges of discriminatory skill classifications and segregated drinking and toilet facilities.[24]

While Castañeda negotiated with Humble representatives, the company union began to openly declare that Local 333 was threatening the livelihood of Anglo workers by welcoming Mexicans and blacks into the union and by supporting claims of racial discrimination in the refinery. Leaders of the BEF stepped up their race-baiting activities against both Local 333 and the FEPC during the following weeks through a widely distributed organ, *The Bulletin.*[25] The paper consistently warned that compliance would result in granting equal treatment to blacks.[26]

At one point, *The Bulletin* pointed to the association between Local 333 and the FEPC with the following observation: "A vote for the CIO is a vote for absolute equality between the white and colored races on every job in the Baytown Refinery from labor gang to Department head."[27] When the FEPC wired the BEF to cease making inflammatory statements, *The Bulletin* responded that it did not "intend to be swayed from our purpose by any telegraphed reprimands from any of the C.I.O.-owned and operated Fair Labor Practices Committees in Washington, D.C., so this is a notice to them to save stamps and telegraph costs."[28]

Despite the findings of the initial investigation, the FEPC decided to delay action on the joint complaint and an additional complaint in which Local 333 alleged discrimination in the hiring, tenure, and compensation of Mexican and

[24]Ibid.

[25]"Humble Oil and Refining Company, Baytown, Texas," 4; Victor Rothen, Memorandum for the Solicitor General, pp. 1–2, Region X Files, FEPC Records.

[26]See issues of the *CIO Campaigner,* the OWOC's organ in the Gulf Coast, for critiques of discrimination in the industry. Also, see copies of *The Bulletin* for examples of the Federation's criticisms of the union. Both are in the Johnson Collection.

[27]*The Bulletin,* May 6, 1943.

[28]*The Bulletin,* Apr. 27, 1943.

African American workers. This decision to withdraw from the conflict was made pending the outcome of the union election and FEPC deliberations in Washington regarding a proposed hearing to investigate complaints of discrimination against Mexicans in the Southwest. Also contributing to the postponement was the FEPC's indecision on whether to seek compliance on an industry or plant-by-plant basis.[29]

A renewed interest in the oil companies became evident when Castañeda obtained permission for a second investigation at Humble. By this time, the union had failed to secure certification and the FEPC had decided that the proposed hearing be confined to the mining industry in the Arizona-New Mexico-West Texas region and that action against the oil companies be pursued on an individual basis.[30] The second investigation generated complaints by three Mexican workers alleging wage discrimination. By the time Castañeda met with company officials, however, Humble had settled the complaints. A subsequent inquiry confirmed that Humble had granted the complainants a raise. The settlement, however, accompanied a decision by Humble to rid itself of its minority work force by contracting out to the Brown and Root Company all of its laboring work.[31]

One can only conjecture on the almost sudden reversal of opinion by Humble. Officials had been insistent on adhering to the local custom of denying employment opportunities to Mexican workers on the grounds that it would invite trouble. Moreover, company officials had been reluctant to fully admit the existence of discrimination or to correct past abuses supposedly because of the feared reaction by Anglo workers. Humble officials, however, may have concluded that compliance was inevitable given the FEPC's belated yet determined decision to consider one refinery at a time. The union election, on the other hand, was probably the single most important factor that opened the way for resolving the impasse.

Humble had kept the FEPC at bay while it did battle with the OWOC on its successful march through the rest of the industry. Once the union lost the election the company was free to confront the problem that it faced with the FEPC. By introducing changes in the plant that exceeded the FEPC's directives, the company rid itself of a potentially difficult conflict with the agency. Although Humble may have appeared overly compliant, it had also begun to dispose of

[29]Castañeda, Final Disposition Report, Humble, Feb. 9 and 10, 1944, Administrative Division, FEPC Records; Rothen, Memorandum for the Solicitor General, pp. 1–2; "Humble Oil and Refining Company, Baytown, Texas," 2–3.

[30]Castañeda to Maslow, Oct. 16, and Oct. 23, 1943, Region X Reports, FEPC Records.

[31]Castañeda, Final Disposition Report, Humble, Feb. 9 and 10, 1944, FEPC Records; Castañeda to Maslow, Jan. 26, 1944, p. 2, Administrative Division, ibid.

its minority work force. With this move, the company also avoided a conflict with its Anglo work force and nullified one of Local 333's most important organizational and ideological bases of operations.

Local 333 was the only union in the region known to have cooperated fully with the FEPC. This was due largely to the influence of the CIO-run OWOC, which embraced the cause of the Mexican complainants. After a successful campaign that resulted in election victories in approximately six refineries, the CIO organizers in the OWOC boldly confronted racial discrimination. Supporting the cause of the Mexican complainants, however, resulted in the OWOC's only defeat in the early 1940s. The defeat also reinforced local fears of an Anglo workers' reaction to compliance and revealed a serious division between members of the national CIO and local and state leadership around the issue of race.

The OWIU and local CIO leaders had opposed the OWOC's progressive racial policy including its endorsement of Mexican complaints during the organizing campaign at Humble. Pressure on the national CIO office eventually led to the removal of its organizers and an end to labor's expressed concern for minority workers. Prior to the election, the OWIU renegotiated its organizing agreement with the local and state CIO unionists, which resulted in the replacement of the organizers with personnel selected by the OWIU. The experience at Humble thus demonstrated that the OWIU and local leadership preferred to avoid the race issue for fear of antagonizing Anglo workers, a view that also found expression during the compliance battle at Sinclair.[32]

The Sinclair refinery located in Pasadena employed a work force of approximately 1,500 that included approximately 100 Mexicans and 250 blacks.[33] At least three joint complaints were submitted on behalf of Mexican workers. J. O. Gray, secretary-treasurer of Local 227, submitted the first complaint in April 1942 to the Office of Production Management in San Antonio. He indicated that a foreman had unfairly issued warnings to the men and that the union's Workmen's Committee had submitted a request to transfer them to another department.[34] There is no evidence that the FEPC acted on the initial complaint perhaps because around that same time a group of Mexican workers was also seeking the assistance of the FEPC with a more comprehensive complaint that charged the company as well as the union with discrimination.

---

[32]See Johnson, "The Battle for Baytown," for a description of the OWOC and the conflict with the OWIU leadership.

[33]Brin, Final Disposition Report, Sinclair, Feb. 11, 1944, FEPC Records.

[34]J. O. Gray to Carnahan, Apr. 15, 1942, Region X Files, FEPC Records; Affidavit, A. S. Sanchez, Feb. 15, 1945, ibid.

The forty Mexican complainants secured the assistance of Consul Adolfo G. Dominguez in alleging a historical pattern of discrimination by the company and Local 227.[35] One of their major allegations was that Sinclair had stopped hiring Mexicans since the early 1930s. The workers also claimed that Sinclair routinely hired blacks to replace departing Mexican workers. The complainants further charged that the company, in collaboration with union leaders, maintained a job classification system that placed Mexicans in the laboring positions at an approximate wage of seventy-eight and one-half cents. Many performed the same tasks as skilled Anglo workers though they were given job classifications as helpers at an hourly wage of ninety-eight and one-half cents. Four of them received eighty-three and one-half cents an hour. They worked as janitors along with nine African American workers, and they could only transfer to other departments if they kept their classification as common laborers. Moreover, skilled and semiskilled vacancies were never posted, and only Anglo unionists were allowed to bid for these jobs. Only one of the workers had ever been promoted; he was a naturalized citizen who worked as a foreman for a crew of black workers.

The Mexican workers also complained about the company's segregation practices. They were required to punch the time clock in a separate line shared with African American workers. Also, the company kept separate lockers and bathing facilities for minority workers. During the lunch hour, Mexican workers were given the choice of eating outdoors or joining the African American workers in a segregated section. Lastly, Mexicans and blacks were transported to work in two crowded buses while the Anglos traveled in a separate, less-crowded bus.

Once Castañeda had confirmed the allegations through on-site investigations, he submitted the joint complaint to Sinclair and Local 227. When neither responded, Castañeda visited the complainants at the Mexican Consul's office to further substantiate the charges. On the basis of this inquiry, the FEPC once again forwarded a complaint and requested a response to specific wage and upgrading allegations of discrimination against both Mexican and African American workers.[36]

The superintendent of the refinery, D. A. Young, responded with a denial of the charges. He added that despite the fact that few Mexican and African

---

[35]The discussion on the complaint is based on the following documents: Minutes of the Conference Held with Management and Labor of Sinclair Refinery, Houston, Texas, Dec. 28, 1843, pp. 2–6, Region X Files, FEPC Records; Adolfo G. Dominguez, Memorandum on Discrimination of Mexican Workers at the Refinery of the Sinclair Refining Company in Houston, Texas, June 8, 1943, Division of Review and Analysis, FEPC Records; Affidavits of J. R. Flores and Teodosio Gutierrez, Nov. 20, 1943, ibid.; and Cochran to Sinclair Refining Company, Nov. 26, 1943, ibid.

[36]Castañeda to Maslow, Dec. 25, 1943, pp. 3–4, Region X Reports, FEPC Records; Minutes of the Conference, Dec. 28, 1943.

American workers qualified for the better-paying jobs, Sinclair had upgraded three Mexican workers to semiskilled and skilled positions. Probably because he anticipated a finding in favor of the Mexican complainants, Young resorted to placing the burden of compliance on Local 227. He warned FEPC officials that the union would not "permit the commingling of the different races employed at this plant."[37] To demonstrate that this was not a ploy to evade compliance, Young furnished Cochran with correspondence in which the union expressly opposed the promotion or reclassification of Mexican workers.

During a subsequent meeting with Castañeda, Young expressed a willingness to provide upgrading opportunities to Mexican as well as African American workers if the union could be made to guarantee support for compliance. Local 227 representatives, on the other hand, admitted that the union had opposed upgrading but promised to seek the cooperation of the entire membership for a policy of nondiscrimination. Company and union representatives, however, denied that discrimination existed regarding wages, the posting of vacancy notices, and the use of transportation facilities.[38]

Two months later Castañeda was reporting that the upgrading case against Sinclair had been adjusted. The company had kept its word and the union membership had grudgingly decided not to contest what Castañeda admitted were "minor advances given Latin Americans" at Sinclair.[39] A major factor in the settlement was Castañeda's decision to settle the complaint on the basis of the admissions made by the company and union representatives. Castañeda's conciliatory approach was clearly intended to capitalize on the single admission of upgrading discrimination in order to proceed with a directive calling for the adoption of a general policy of nondiscrimination.

Although Castañeda had initially filed the case alleging discrimination against Mexicans at Sinclair, he sought a settlement that favored the entire minority work force. Consequently, when he confirmed the settlement, he made binding an agreement that benefited both Mexican and black workers. In a letter to an officer of the union, he stated:

> I am pleased to note that as the result of the meetings held your union has agreed to permit the company to abandon its discriminatory practices and to give all employees an equal opportunity for promotion in accord with their experience, ability and aptitude, regardless of race, creed, color or national origin.[40]

Although the company and the union may have been cooperative during the final settlement negotiations, they did not satisfy the concerns of the

[37]Young to Cochran, Dec. 7, 1943, pp. 1–2.

[38]Minutes of the Conference, Dec. 28, 1943, pp. 1–6.

[39]Castañeda, Final Disposition Report, Sinclair, Feb. 11, 1944, FEPC Records.

[40]Castañeda to Clyde Ingram, Mar. 1, 1944, Region X Files, FEPC Records.

Mexican workers who continued to informally complain of discrimination. One year after Castañeda had secured the settlement, the same Mexican complainants were again formally contesting Sinclair's discriminatory practices. They claimed that Sinclair was refusing to hire qualified Mexican applicants and denying them upgrading opportunities. The company had allegedly refused employment to three Mexican applicants at the same time that it had been hiring African American and Anglo workers. Moreover, Sinclair had refused to upgrade at least three Mexican workers. On the basis of this complaint, Ellinger informed Sinclair that despite the recent settlement, the FEPC had determined that discrimination against Mexicans was continuing.[41]

The company responded to the complaint by denying the charges while the union simply chose to disregard it. The FEPC, on the other hand, did not press the issue even though additional complaints continued to arrive. This was probably due to the fact that mounting political opposition to the FEPC in Washington was already signaling the end of the agency and thus discouraging forthright action. Also, the FEPC was then waging its most trying battle at Shell that may have drawn its resources and attention from the fight at Sinclair.[42]

The case against Sinclair once again demonstrated the FEPC's difficulty in securing permanent settlements. One obvious problem was the discontinuance of the agency's operations at a time when settlements were still pending. Additionally, indecision regarding the compliance strategy that the FEPC wished to pursue contributed to the initial delays.

Other more important factors included the opposition of the union and the refusal of the company to comply until it could be guaranteed that Local 227 would not strike in protest. Also, the company failed to live up to its promise to comply with the FEPC directives and continued to challenge allegations of discrimination confirmed by the FEPC. The union was generally indifferent to the second complaint, preferring instead to leave the minority workers to fend for themselves against Sinclair.

Reminiscent of the fight at Humble, the FEPC often appeared to back away as if it was facing an opponent too formidable to confront. Despite the large amount of evidence accumulated in support of the complaints, the FEPC exhibited a conciliatory attitude in the settlement process. It may have been expedient, however, for Castañeda to seek a speedy settlement in light of the trouble that the agency was having at the time with Shell. This willingness to

---

[41]Ellinger to Sinclair Refining Company, Mar. 15, 1945, Region X Files, FEPC Records; Affidavits dated February 1945 and signed by A. S. Sanchez, A. V. Salinas, Juan Robledo, S. Rodriguez, Jesse Lozano Caballero, Henry S. Mendez, and M. de la Garza, ibid.

[42]Ellinger to Sinclair Refining Company, Mar. 15, 1945; Affidavits, Feb. 1945, signed by A. S. Sanchez, A. V. Salinas, Juan Robledo, S. Rodriguez, Jesse Lozano Caballero, Henry S. Mendez, and M. de la Garza.

Oil workers at a World War II war bond rally held at Shell's Deer Park Refinery, 1943. *Courtesy Shell Deer Park Historical Society, Deer Park, Texas.*

settle allowed Castañeda to correct one case of upgrading discrimination and to justify a directive calling for the adoption of a policy of nondiscrimination. Rushing into a settlement that conceded ground on key charges, however, no doubt left the impression that the FEPC lacked the confidence and enforcement power to challenge employment discrimination, a perception that plagued the agency in its dealings with Shell.

The Shell Oil Company maintained a large refinery at Deer Park with a work force of approximately 1,200 workers that included at least one hundred Mexican and African American workers.[43] Mexican workers faced the same problems evident in the Humble and Sinclair refineries. Widespread discrimination restricted them as well as African American workers to the lowest-paying unskilled positions. Moreover, both groups of workers were limited to segregated transportation, eating, and restroom facilities. Mexican complaints against Shell resulted in one of the most bitter fights over the issue of discrimination. It involved open defiance by the union and the continuing embarrassing ineffectiveness of the FEPC.

---

[43]Summary of Shell Oil Case, May 5, 1945, p. 1, Legal Division, FEPC Records. A precise figure for the number of Mexican workers at Shell is not available.

The FEPC initiated its case against Shell in May 1943 with a complaint submitted by Consul Dominguez on behalf of thirty-four Mexican nationals who had tried unsuccessfully to settle their claims with the company during the previous two years. They had also failed to convince Local 367 to intervene on their behalf. As a result, they had quit the union and were now appealing to the Mexican Consul and local LULAC leaders as an act of last resort. The workers made the familiar charges of occupational, wage, and upgrading discrimination, a hiring ceiling, and segregated facilities.[44]

During a meeting at the Mexican Consulate that was attended by company, union, and Mexican workers' representatives, an FEPC investigator confirmed the allegations, though he was not able to settle the complaint. When Consul Dominguez asked that Mexican workers be granted a just wage and the promotional guarantees enjoyed by Anglos, management and union representatives responded that they could not give assurances because of the all too prevalent fear of antagonizing Anglo workers. They claimed that there was a widespread belief among Anglo workers that a concession to the Mexicans would encourage complaints by blacks seeking similar guarantees and that this would result in depressed wages and their eventual replacement by minority workers.[45]

The company and the union maintained that the only way to avoid a disruption was if the FEPC held an industry-wide hearing and ordered all the refineries in the area with CIO union contracts to adopt a policy of nondiscrimination. The union offered to communicate the plan to the other locals. Seeing no other option, Consul Dominguez expressed his support for the plan and recommended that the FEPC initiate such a settlement in a meeting with O. A. Knight, president of the OWIU, and D. W. Hobey, president of the Gulf Coast Refiners Association.[46]

The FEPC may have allowed Shell and the union to independently implement their proposed plan because there is no evidence that Castañeda participated in it. When months passed without any news about the implementation of the plan from Shell, the local, or the OWIU, Castañeda called on the FEPC to grant him the authority to proceed with the case. He was particularly concerned that Consul Dominguez and other Mexican leaders would become more disillusioned with the FEPC. Castañeda also expressed the view that the company and the local had called for an industry-wide hearing for the sole

[44]Dominguez, Memorandum on Racial Discrimination at the Shell Refining Co., Houston, Texas, Apr. 26, 1943, and Memorandum on Conference Held Friday, May 14, 1943, at Mexican Consulate in Houston, Texas, Relative to Discrimination of Mexican Workers at Shell Oil and Refining Company, May 15, 1943, Division of Review and Analysis, FEPC Records. The discussion that follows on the complaint is based on the Dominguez documents.

[45]Dominguez, Memorandum on Conference, May 14, 1943, pp. 1–4.

[46]Ibid.; Trimble to Haas, July 9, 1943, pp. 1–2, Region X Files, FEPC Records.

purpose of delaying the compliance process. He felt that the most reasonable and promising measure to take was individual action based on the findings of discrimination that Shell and Local 367 officers openly admitted.[47]

A worsening situation at Shell underscored the need for immediate action. On November 3, the manager suspended seven Mexican workers for insubordination. According to the workers, he had instructed them to do a temporary job for eighty-seven cents an hour in the segregated pipe-fitting department though the prevailing wage for pipefitters ranged between $.97 and $1.39 an hour. When they refused to do the work at the disputed wage, he fired them. The company subsequently advertised vacancies for these same jobs at ninety-seven cents an hour. The workers once again sought the help of Consul Dominguez. This time, however, the Mexican Consul convinced his superiors to intercede in the matter—an indication of growing concern in Mexican government circles. The Mexican ambassador to the United States, Rafael de la Colina, expressed his government's displeasure to the chairman of the FEPC by stating that continuing defiance at Shell violated the Good Neighbor Alliance and undermined the U.S. government's wartime pledge of international solidarity against racial injustice. The issue of discrimination in oil thus reached international proportions, a development that pressured the FEPC to redouble its efforts.[48]

Meanwhile, to support his contention for a hearing that would address the complaints against Shell, Castañeda called for an additional investigation, which later confirmed the prior findings. He also recommended immediate action, particularly because Shell again admitted practicing discrimination.[49] The subsequent conference that Castañeda held with Shell and Local 367 representatives in December ended on a familiar note. The manager of the refinery and the president of Local 367 admitted discrimination but insisted that they would not agree to any changes until a general hearing was held or a directive was issued by the FEPC ordering the entire industry to implement a policy of nondiscrimination.[50] When FEPC officials requested a formal statement documenting this response, the union officer answered defiantly, "The Union at this time does not propose to change without first having a hearing or order, as we consider ourselves and the company both in violation of the Executive Order."[51] The company representative added, "The position of the Management

[47]Castañeda to Maslow, Sept. 18, 1943, Region X Reports, FEPC Records.

[48]Castañeda to Maslow, Dec. 4, 1944, Region X Files, FEPC Records; Castañeda to Dominguez, Sept. 16, 1943, ibid.; Castañeda to John J. Herrera, Oct. 7, 1943, ibid.; Castañeda to Dominguez, Oct. 7, 1943, ibid.

[49]Castañeda to Maslow, Oct. 16, 23, 1943, ibid.

[50]Castañeda to O. A. Knight, Jan. 1, 1944, Region X Files, FEPC Records.

[51]Castañeda to Maslow, Dec. 31, 1943, ibid.

of the company is that the consequences of any change in this respect are so far-reaching and would have such detrimental results that we do not see any reason for change."[52]

Shell defended its bid for an industry-wide hearing and directive with the argument that a unilateral settlement would place the company in an unfair position with its competitors. With this argument, Shell placed the burden of change on the union, while the union officers openly admitted that the membership would strike if the company complied.[53] The deadlock seemed unbreakable especially since the FEPC had delayed action while its personnel debated on the proper strategy to pursue. While Castañeda insisted on an individual hearing with Shell, other officials in the Dallas office were urging an industry-wide hearing. A decision was finally reached to proceed with Castañeda's recommendation and to schedule a hearing for December 1944.[54] On the day that the public hearing was to take place, Shell officials finally conceded. They requested a private conference and promised to abide by the decision to be rendered by the Trial Examiner and a committee of four FEPC representatives that included Castañeda.[55]

In his opening statement before the committee, an FEPC official accused the company and the union of disregarding the skills and experience of Mexican workers and of restricting them to the menial jobs at wages that were lower than those paid to Anglo workers performing the same tasks. This had been accomplished through a formal contract that defined the discriminatory rates of pay, hours of work, and other terms of employment operating in the plant. Since discrimination at Shell had been directed against both Mexicans and blacks, the FEPC called for an end to all forms of discrimination.[56]

The opening statement included other observations that acknowledged the importance that the Shell case had acquired in the international arena, particularly with the major ally of the U.S. in the hemisphere, Mexico.[57] In calling for an end to racial and national origin discrimination, the FEPC described the

---

[52]Ibid.

[53]Castañeda to Maslow, Dec. 31, 1943, Jan. 1, 1944, ibid.

[54]Castañeda to Maslow, Jan. 26, 1944, Region X Files, FEPC Records; Castañeda to Brin, May 17, 1944, ibid.

[55]Opening Statement, Dec. 28, 1944, Legal Division, FEPC Records; Ellinger to Maslow, Dec. 30, 1944, Region X Reports, FEPC Records.

[56]Ibid. Also see President's Committee on Fair Employment Practice, Statement of Charges and Order for Hearing, In the Matter of Shell Oil Company, Incorporated, and Oil Workers' International Union, Local 367, CIO, Dec. 11, 1945, FEPC Records; FEPC, Statement of the Case, Jan. 27, 1945, ibid.; and FEPC, Stipulation, Dec. 30, 1945, Legal Division, ibid.

[57]Opening Statement, Dec. 28, 1944, pp. 1, 9.

denial of opportunities as a problem that undermined the war effort because it harmed relations with Latin American nations:

> The eyes of our neighbors to the south are watching with keen interest. The denial of equal opportunities for full participation in the war effort, and for advancement to workers of Latin-American extraction, negatives *[sic]* our professions of good neighborliness and reflects upon our moral leadership in the family of nations.[58]

The committee appeared to have settled the issue once and for all when it ordered the company and the union to eliminate all forms of discrimination. The company and the union agreed to expunge from the collective bargaining agreement all basis for discrimination and to stop denying Mexican and African American workers hiring and upgrading opportunities. The committee also gave specific instructions directing Shell to submit a separate wage complaint to the War Labor Board for adjustment and to upgrade two Mexican complainants to carman's helper and truck driver. The FEPC followed by rendering a decision on January 27 that directed the company and the union to comply with the president's executive order within ninety days.[59] The stage was now set to determine if compliance could proceed to its logical conclusion without setting off a reaction by Anglo workers.

The compliance process quickly became burdened with difficulties that tested the FEPC's ability to influence the ensuing course of events. When several Mexican workers, including the complainants who had been assured promotions, signed up for available jobs, a foreman and the personnel manager informed them that Shell did not intend to abide by the FEPC directive until the April 27 deadline. FEPC officials rightfully saw this as a direct challenge against the spirit, if not the letter, of the settlement. Pressure was again brought to bear on Shell.[60]

In response to the FEPC's requests for support, other government agencies reminded the company that it was obligated to honor the president's executive order or risk losing lucrative federal contracts. The FEPC had mixed results, however, in convincing labor leaders to pressure Local 367. While the national CIO office declared support for a policy of nondiscrimination, key state leaders such as O. A. Knight and Timothy Flyn, state CIO director, claimed that the parent organizations did not dictate policy to their locals. Nonetheless, pressure from government agencies finally convinced Shell to cooperate. The first upgrading occurred on March 8 when Shell appointed a Mexican worker

---

[58]Ibid.

[59]Statement of the Case, Jan. 27, 1945; Stipulation, Dec. 30, 1945.

[60]Castañeda to Maslow, Mar. 24, 1945, p. 5, Region X Reports, FEPC Records; Mitchell to Ellinger, Apr. 11, 1945, Region X Files, FEPC Records.

to a carman's helper position. A week later, a second Mexican worker was upgraded to a truck driver's job.[61]

Increased pressure by the FEPC eventually forced Shell to upgrade additional minority applicants. This, however, did not occur without Shell first announcing that the FEPC was forcing the company to integrate the work force against its will. Two vice presidents of the local added to the growing tensions by resigning from their positions as a sign of disapproval of the FEPC directives. On March 22, the company nevertheless upgraded one Mexican and seven blacks to general helpers in each of the eight separate craft departments. An incident followed that raised the developing conflict to a higher level.[62]

A company foreman who obviously sought to disassociate himself from the issue of compliance convened Anglo workers from each department and asked them to publicly state if they would work alongside the upgraded minority workers. Although some of the Anglo workers may have been inclined to accept this proposition, the fear of reprisals from coworkers was probably too great because none agreed to work with them. In opposing the upgrading decision the Anglo workers were absolving the company from any blame in the compliance conflict and accepting the major responsibility for defending the status quo. Soon after the vote, an undetermined number of Anglo workers and the two union officers that had resigned threatened to stage a strike if the minority workers were placed in their new positions. The company quickly returned the workers to their previous jobs. Emboldened by this immediate response, the protesting Anglo workers then demanded that the previously upgraded Mexican workers also be returned to their former jobs. The company again capitulated.[63]

FEPC officials called a series of conferences with company and union representatives to try to remedy the situation that had clearly gotten out of hand. The company maintained that it was forced to concede to the demands of the Anglo workers. Union representatives, on the other hand, expressed an interest in complying with the FEPC directives but requested time to convince a portion of their membership that was opposed to integration.[64] Matters deteriorated further as Shell officials continued to publicly present the company as a helpless victim and as the union membership began to more forcefully express its opposition to the issue of integration. Although the union did not guarantee

[61]Summary of Shell Oil Case, May 5, 1945, p. 1.

[62]Summary of Shell Oil Case, May 5, 1945, pp. 1–2.

[63]Ibid.; Ellinger to Ross, May 1, 1945, pp. 1–5, Region X Files, FEPC Records. The following description of events is based on information from these two reports.

[64]Also see Mitchell to Emanuel Bloch, Apr. 12, 1945, Legal Division, FEPC Records.

support for compliance, continued FEPC pressure led the company to upgrade two Mexican workers on April 27. The results were predictable.[65]

Anglo workers in the automotive department responded by walking off their jobs. Negotiations followed between the union, Shell, and a conciliator from the Department of Labor. When negotiations failed to produce any results, the FEPC brought in the assistant disputes director from the Dallas office of the War Labor Board to help resolve the issue. The result was a six-day hearing that affirmed the FEPC directive and the Smith-Connally Act, which required workers to issue a petition before waging a strike in wartime. As part of the settlement, the workers agreed to remain on the job and not insist on the removal of the upgraded Mexicans without first filing a strike petition with the NLRB. In granting the union the right to hold a vote on what was essentially a compliance matter, however, the War Labor Board undermined the FEPC directives and provided the segregationists the opportunity to legitimately defy the FEPC at a future date.[66]

The tenuous settlement involved important concessions by FEPC officials who by now seemed to be desperately seeking to regain their influence. First of all, they failed to dispute the decision by the War Labor Board that granted the union the right to challenge the compliance directive. In fact, the FEPC granted Shell and the local a thirty-day extension on the compliance order to accommodate the scheduling of the election. Moreover, a general understanding was reached whereby no more upgrading actions were to be taken until the strike ballot was cast. Although the FEPC was essentially forced to back down, the prospects of losing complete control led Ellinger to declare with a sense of relief, "we have won a tremendous victory by the skin of our teeth in the agreement of the men to work with the Latin-Americans on the job."[67]

Mexican government officials and Mexican civil rights leaders from Texas did not share Ellinger's enthusiasm. They began to more openly view the Shell case as a stark demonstration of deep-rooted racism and ineffective government intervention. Mexico's foreign minister, Ezequiel Padilla, for instance, commented while attending the first United Nations Conference at San Francisco that nothing less than the hemispheric prestige of the United States as a democratic nation was at stake. Also, Castañeda reported that Mexican leaders from throughout the state expressed "strong resentment" against Shell and felt that the FEPC was not sufficiently aggressive.[68]

---

[65]Ellinger to Ross, Re: The Attached Memorandum, May 1, 1945, pp. 1–3, Region X Files, FEPC Records; Ellinger to Ross, Re: Complete Report on Shell Situation, May 1, 1945, pp. 1–5, Division of Field Operations, ibid.

[66]Ibid.

[67]Ellinger to Ross, Re: The Attached Memorandum, May 1, 1945, p. 2, ibid.

[68]Castañeda to Maslow, May 16, 1945, p. 4, Region X Reports, FEPC Records.

Minority workers remained steadfast in support of compliance. Mexican workers called for full integration, while African American workers supported the idea of a segregated work force on a separate but equal basis. In other words, both Mexican and African American workers sought guarantees of equal access to all jobs at the same pay while the latter group did not insist on working side-by-side with Anglo workers. Minority workers also agreed that the FEPC should continue to press the company and the union with claims of discrimination by Mexican workers since they had the best chance of succeeding and setting the necessary precedent for the complete integration of the work force.[69]

Anglo workers refused to concede despite the urgings of the FEPC and the negative publicity that the case brought the oil industry and the labor movement. This became openly evident when a majority of them voted in favor of a strike on June 6, 1945. The NLRB-sanctioned election not only affirmed the segregationist posture of the union; it also demonstrated the union's newfound talent for legitimately defying the president's executive order. As a result of the election, the FEPC scuttled its compliance directive and endorsed a settlement proposed by the union. The union's plan designated a small number of skilled jobs for minority workers to be set aside in still-segregated departments. Shell representatives, on the other hand, washed their hands of the whole matter. They declared a willingness to adopt whatever plan the FEPC and the union favored.[70]

Minority workers expressed deep resentment over the strike vote and were adamant in demanding that the FEPC not relent in its dealings with the company and the union despite efforts by Anglo workers to divide them. Mexicans were told that if African American workers had not been included in the directive, Anglos would have complied. Blacks, on the other hand, were told that the Mexicans ought not be supported because they were pretentious and claimed to be better than blacks. With matters still unresolved, the FEPC first restricted and then closed its operations in Texas when Congress decided to deny the agency the needed appropriations for the postwar period. There is no record that the FEPC was able to negotiate a settlement acceptable to the minority workers. Presumably, they were left to fend for themselves against continued occupational and wage discrimination.[71]

---

[69]Ellinger to Knight, May 24, 1945, Region X Files, FEPC Records; Knight to Ellinger, June 2, 1945, ibid. See Ellinger to Ross, May 20, 1945, Legal Division, FEPC Records, for proposal by union on segregated work force.

[70]George Weaver to Ellinger, June 19, 1945, Region X Files, FEPC Records; Ellinger to Mitchell, July 14, 1945, ibid.; J. J. Hickman to Ellinger, July 24, 1945, Division of Review and Analysis, FEPC Records; Castañeda to Maslow, June 1–15, 1945, pp. 4–5, Region X Reports, ibid.

[71]Castañeda to Maslow, June 16–30, 1945, p. 4, Region X Reports, FEPC Records.

The Shell case once again demonstrated the agency's weakness. The case underwent numerous delays primarily because the company and Local 367 consistently refused to comply with the president's executive order. The Shell local acted much like the Baytown Employees' Federation and Local 227 in reinforcing racial inequality. Local 367 collaborated with management in restricting minority workers to the laboring occupations and in denying them the opportunity to advance into the higher-paying and skilled jobs in the refinery. Unlike Local 227, the Shell union was steadfast in its refusal to support compliance. This refusal, coupled with the FEPC's setbacks at Humble and Sinclair, underscored the significance of discrimination in denying Mexicans equal employment opportunities in the Texas Gulf Coast oil industry.

The problem of discrimination in the oil industry had special importance when one considers that there may never have been a better time than the period of the Second World War for Mexicans from Texas to have altered their occupational standing relative to Anglos. The wartime demand on the economy had expanded job opportunities to unprecedented levels. Increased job growth coupled with labor shortages occasioned by conscription resulted in immediate occupational gains that seemed to presage a new era of equality. Accompanying these promising developments was the rhetoric of world democracy that encouraged even higher expectations of racial justice and equality at the home front. Lastly, with the establishment of FEPC regional offices in Texas, the federal government promised Mexican workers protection against employment discrimination.

Mexican oil workers were part of the relatively small yet important wave of upwardly mobile workers making the transition from low-wage employers to high-wage and well-organized firms during the war. Their disproportionate representation in the lesser-skilled and lower-paying jobs, however, defined the limits that discrimination placed on them. The twelve oil refineries located in the Gulf Coast generally maintained low hiring quotas for Mexicans, assigned them laborer occupations, paid them a lower wage than Anglos, denied them upgrading opportunities and restricted them to segregated work, eating, and restroom areas. A key element in maintaining a racial order in the refineries were the race-conscious Anglo workers, including members of CIO-affiliated unions. Anglo workers and their representatives also assumed an important role in defending the segregated order by pressuring the companies against complying with FEPC directives. Fearing the loss of their hard-won gains during the 1930s, they claimed job prerogatives and reacted defensively toward the FEPC.

Although some improvements for minority workers resulted from the intercession of the FEPC, the agency was not able to challenge discrimination and inequality effectively at Humble, Sinclair, and Shell. Since the FEPC directed most of its attention to these three companies and other refineries do not seem to have been compelled to implement nondiscrimination policies, we can conclude that the FEPC did not make an appreciable impact in the oil industry. Its work was a positive yet minor contribution next to the demand for labor that provided Mexican workers the initial limited opportunity for employment. The FEPC's lack of enforcement powers, its short duration in Texas, internal divisions, and management's ambivalence in the face of a threatened Anglo workers' reaction no doubt contributed to the failure of governmental intervention in the oil industry. The most decisive factor in the fight over compliance, however, was the opposition of Anglo workers. The most striking result was yet another delay in the full incorporation of Mexican workers into the Texas occupational structure.

# Direct Action at the University of Texas during the Civil Rights Movement, 1960–1965

MARTIN KUHLMAN*

*Long before the turbulent Civil Rights movement of the sixties, efforts to end segregation in higher education involved the University of Texas. Under court order, the university admitted Heman Sweatt, an African American, to its law school in 1950. Black graduate students were admitted to academic programs shortly thereafter, and black undergraduates gained admission in 1956. But in most respects—housing, athletics, most extra-curricular activities, restaurants, theaters, and public facilities of all kinds—the university and the world around it remained rigidly segregated at the end of the decade.*

*Within five years, however, instances of such practices were rapidly disappearing. University officials integrated athletic programs in 1963, housing in 1964, and the elite "Forty Acre Club" admitted a black member in 1965. Meanwhile, leaders in the local business community began to end segregation in their facilities. The Civil Rights Act of 1964 was in part responsible for the progress toward racial equality, but in the opinion of author Martin Kuhlman, students of the university deserve a large measure of the credit. Members of the Students for Direct Action founded in 1960 led the way, utilizing "stand-ins," picket lines, marches, other traditional methods of direct protest, and some reliance on the courts. Students combined strategies tested elsewhere in the struggle for civil rights with some new forms of "direct action" of their own creation. Conflict and confrontation were predictable, but instances of violence were rare.*

*Although the integration struggle at the University of Texas is not as well known as some, scholars have written a number of articles, published mostly in the* **Southwestern Historical Quarterly.** *A book-length study is Almetris*

*Martin Kuhlman, "Direct Action at the University of Texas during the Civil Rights Movement, 1960–1965," *Southwestern Historical Quarterly*, 98 (Apr., 1995), 551–566.

***Marsh Duren,* Overcoming: A History of Black Integration at the University of Texas at Austin *(Austin: University of Texas Press, 1978). An interesting perspective on Chandler Davidson, one of the more important student leaders in the movement of the early 1960s, is available. His book,* Race and Class in Texas Politics *(Princeton: Princeton University Press, 1990), tells much about his views on racial injustice.***

While the war against racial segregation was waged most prominently in the Deep South, the University of Texas at Austin was also a significant site in the national struggle of African Americans for civil rights. As early as the 1940s, an NAACP chapter formed at the university—the first on a segregated campus. After a court case and years of controversy, Heman Sweatt, a graduate of all-black Wiley College in Marshall, entered the University of Texas law school in 1950, becoming the first African American to integrate a law school in a state of the former Confederacy. Students at the university had aided in the collection of funds for the *Sweatt* case.

In his article "Blacks Challenge the White University," Michael L. Gillette detailed the continuing struggle to integrate the university, during which some students and faculty members participated in rallies calling for integration. The university accepted black graduate students in 1955 and undergraduates the following year. Nevertheless, as Richard B. McCaslin has pointed out, the university's new black students had little opportunity for extracurricular activities as the vast majority of recreational events and facilities remained segregated, thus providing a target for continued direct action. Like the the better-known sit-ins in Greensboro, North Carolina, the direct action demonstrations at the University of Texas in the early 1960s did not appear spontaneously but were the outgrowth of these prior years of civil rights activism.[1]

Despite desegregation on the academic front at the University of Texas, Jim Crow continued to ride high on the campus and in Austin. Besides adhering to southern tradition, university officials also opposed desegregation activities that might upset supporters of the university. Direct action had become an important tactic in the struggle for civil rights after the Montgomery bus boycott in 1955. In 1963 the Student Interracial Committee announced that "The Negro at UT has also come to realize his responsibility for direct action in the

---

[1] Michael L. Gillette, "Blacks Challenge the White University," *Southwestern Historical Quarterly*, LXXXVI (Oct., 1982), 321–344; Richard B. McCaslin, "Steadfast in His Intent: John W. Hargis and the Integration of the University of Texas at Austin," ibid., XCV (July, 1991), 21–41; William H. Chafe, *Civilities and Civil Rights: Greensboro, North Carolina, and the Black Struggle for Freedom* (New York: Oxford University Press, 1981), 17–55.

struggle." The involvement of University of Texas students in direct action, however, occurred at least three years before this statement. Students mirrored much of the civil rights activity in the nation and even initiated some national tactics as they challenged segregation in non-academic areas on the campus and in Austin.[2] On February 1, 1960, a student-led movement of direct action challenging segregated lunch counters began in Greensboro, North Carolina. By the following month University of Texas students had adopted direct action in the struggle against segregation. A biracial group of thirty-two students, twenty-five blacks and seven whites, demonstrated outside the campus on March 11. One protester announced that they wanted to make the student body aware of segregation in university policies. The protesters passed out leaflets pointing out that only one-fifth of the university's dormitories accepted African Americans and that these segregated dormitories were substandard. The printed statement also pointed out that although the Southwest Conference had no rules against black players, the University of Texas, like other schools in the conference, did not allow African Americans to play intercollegiate sports. The university also excluded blacks from stage productions, and a protester carried a sign exclaiming, "All the World's a Stage, but Negroes Can't Participate in Drama at UT." Protest leaders urged activists to avoid "heated discussion" or actions that might be perceived as causing trouble. The picketing lasted for a few days and ended after a meeting between university officials and demonstrating students. Students labeled the meeting unsatisfactory,[3] but turned their attention to demonstrations against Austin's segregated lunch counters.

The Austin Commission on Human Relations initiated negotiations between lunch counter owners and an interracial coalition of student groups in April. When negotiations broke down, University of Texas student Lynn Goldsmith announced that unless the counters were desegregated in a week, the coalition would be forced to utilize other methods "to present the problem effectively and to find a satisfactory solution." A week later, activists from the University of Texas, St. Edwards University, Huston-Tillotson College, and the Episcopal and Presbyterian seminaries picketed Congress Avenue with signs reading "I don't want it 'to go,' I want to sit down," "Why pay for racism?" and "Sit-ins? It's up to you!" The picketing lasted for nine hours, with groups of approximately thirty students walking in one-hour shifts. Some passersby heckled the picketers while merchants made their intention to refuse service clear. One restaurant owner stated, "If I can't stop them at the door and they sit

---

[2]Release from Student Interracial Committee, Sept. 27, 1963, in Almetris Marsh Duren Papers, Center for American History, University of Texas at Austin (cited hereafter as CAH).

[3]Student flyer in ibid.; "Integration–University of Texas," scrapbook, Vertical Files: Subject, CAH.

down, I'm not going to serve them." Representatives of H. L. Green, Kress, and Woolworth announced that they would "follow community practices" in deciding whom to serve. The Austin Commission on Human Relations, however, recognized "the democratic and moral rights of Negroes to equality of service at lunch counters of stores serving the public."[4]

On April 29, seventy-five to one hundred activists launched sit-ins challenging lunch counters at seven locations on or near Congress Avenue. Before the sit-ins began, the participants received written instructions telling them to be courteous, not to laugh out loud, and not to strike back if physically attacked. Merchants responded to the sit-ins by closing counters. H. L. Green and the Continental bus station removed stools, while the Greyhound bus station directed protesters to a separate dining room for African Americans. A few black diners did eat at segregated counters as individuals or in small groups. At Woolworth the first few black students to arrive received service, but after more students appeared, the manager stated he could not "keep it [the counter] open in the face of a demonstration." Although the sit-ins did not desegregate the targeted counters, Bray and Jordan pharmacies subsequently announced their intention to serve all customers.[5]

Students also looked to national figures in their struggle for desegregation. The interracial coalition of student groups sent U.S. Sen. Lyndon Baines Johnson a letter requesting the senator to use his Austin television station, his newsletter, and his influence in the community to "bring into practice the full human rights of all the citizens of Texas." The University of Texas Young Democrats also sent a letter urging Johnson to accept his responsibility.[6]

As students continued to picket and stage sit-ins, Mayor Tom Miller and other Austin community leaders formed a biracial action group to deal with the question of desegregation of counters. Former Texas Supreme Court Associate Justice W. St. John Garwood chaired the group. During the following days individual African Americans received service at a number of lunch counters. By mid-May the situation appeared stable enough that the action group disbanded. Renfro drugstores refused to desegregate their counters, however, and faced additional demonstrations.[7] The action group had only dealt with the question

[4]Austin *American*, Mar. 12 (1st quotation), April 21, 1960 (2nd–4th quotations); Dallas *Morning News*, Apr. 28, 1960. Attempts to desegregate Austin eating places began before 1960. In 1952 Sam Gibbs, a UT graduate assemblyman, wrote fifty-three restaurants asking them to drop racial bars. Most owners refused, while others announced a willingness to do so if others desegregated first. UT Chancellor's Office Records, System-Wide, Central Administration Policy and Procedure Files, 1962–64, Desegregation, CAH.

[5]Austin *American*, Apr. 30, 1960 (quotation). Four UT students attended the National Student Conference on Sit-ins in April 1960. *Daily Texan* (Austin), Apr. 29, 1960.

[6]*Daily Texan* (Austin), Apr. 27 (quotation), 29, 1960.

[7]Austin *American*, May 2, 15, 1960.

of desegregation in lunch counters while leaving many other facilities segregated.

The University of Texas student assembly proclaimed its support for the sit-ins, as did the University Religious Council (URC), which became a prominent pro-integration group on the campus. At a meeting in the university YMCA in November 1960 members of the URC discussed passing out cards in front of segregated restaurants. URC members would ask the patrons to give the cards, which read, "I will continue to patronize this establishment if it is integrated," to cashiers. The group thus hoped to demonstrate that integration would not lead to financial losses. Resistance to the URC appeared when two university students exploded a homemade bomb outside the YMCA during a URC meeting. The Federal Bureau of Investigation joined the Austin police in investigating the explosion, and the students received sentences of thirty days in jail and $200 fines. The violence did not deter the URC, however, as the group passed out 3,800 cards in less than a month.[8]

On the first anniversary of the sit-in movement, February 1, 1961, the Student Non-Violent Coordinating Committee (SNCC) announced a "second phase" of direct action challenging segregated theaters. Civil rights supporters at the University of Texas had pioneered the new form of direct action, known as stand-ins, three months earlier. Inspired by the sit-in movement, Houston Wade suggested to fellow student and school newspaper reporter Chandler Davidson that students should utilize similar means to desegregate theaters near the campus. Together Davidson and Wade organized an active civil rights group.[9]

Students for Direct Action (SDA) formed on the campus at the end of November 1960. Davidson, the chairperson of the group, said SDA's goals included spotlighting the plight of African Americans, identifying those responsible for segregation, and taking "peaceful, lawful, but definite action to remedy the situation." Although it met under the auspices of the student government's Human Relations Committee, SDA did not want any connection with groups officially recognized by the university. SDA hoped to avoid "the formidable red tape which has hamstrung 'official' groups in the past." Davidson believed that independence from the student government would allow SDA to sidestep "the extreme conservatism" and the "jungle of bureaucratic procedures" which made direct action "virtually impossible." One of the group's first activities was to circulate a petition asking students to patronize at least one

---

[8] *Daily Texan* (Austin), May 1, 5, Dec. 20, 1960; Austin *American*, Nov. 30, 1960 (quotation); San Antonio *Register*, Dec. 9, 1960.

[9] James H. Laue, *Direct Action and Desegregation, 1960–1962: Towards a Theory of the Rationalization of Protest* (Brooklyn: Carlson Publishing, 1989), 332 (quotation); Chandler Davidson to Martin Kuhlman, Nov. 22, 1992 (interview).

integrated restaurant per week. The petition proclaimed that "Now is the time to make your voice heard in favor of civil rights."[10]

On the evening of December 2, 1960, a biracial group of two hundred University of Texas students demonstrated against the Texas Theater, which excluded African Americans. The protesting students stood in line to purchase tickets to the movie, and when they stepped up to the ticket booth asked if all Americans would be admitted. The ticket attendant refused to sell tickets to the black protesters, and although they could purchase tickets and enter the theater, white students refused "until all Americans are sold tickets." The demonstrators then returned to the back of the ticket line to begin the procedure again. Two graduate students and English instructors from the university, Claude Allen and Sandra Cason, joined the stand-ins.[11]

Reaction to the demonstrations came swiftly. The manager of the theater, Leonard Masters, told the protesters he could not sell tickets to black students because of the policy of the chain. The chain had recently reaffirmed its decision to uphold segregation. When the students continued to wait in line, the manager set up another ticket booth inside the theater and forbade the protesters to enter. Masters also threatened to call the police if demonstrations continued. The protesting students did not go into the building but remained in front of the theater urging other patrons to stay out, too. Some moviegoers continued into the theater, and a few patrons and people in passing cars jeered the protesters, but others refused to enter, and some even joined the demonstration.[12]

Stand-ins quickly spread to the Varsity, another theater near campus which excluded African Americans. As in the earlier protests, students stood in line and asked ticket sellers, "Do you still discriminate against Americans?" Picketers also appeared carrying anti-segregation signs, including one which proclaimed, "Your money spent here supports segregation." The manager of the Varsity announced over a public address system that customers should ignore the protesters and continue into the theater. Many patrons did so; a member of SDA reported that moviegoers "just look right through you. When they go into the movie, they put on their blank stare and look embarrassed." The theaters' position remained that "The company has a right to refuse service to all it chooses." The Foundation for the Advancement of Conservative Thought distributed newsletters on campus saying that businessmen should have the right to make their own decisions on whom to serve. The refusal of the theaters to negotiate

---

[10] *Texas Observer* (Austin), Dec. 9, 1960; "Integration–UT," scrapbook, CAH.

[11] Dallas *Morning News,* Dec. 3, 1960 (quotation); *Texas Observer* (Austin), Dec. 9, 1960; San Antonio *Register,* Dec. 2, 1960.

[12] *Texas Observer* (Austin), Dec. 9, 1960.

caused SDA leaders to recognize that stand-ins needed to continue at a rate of at least two to three per week in order to disrupt business enough to force the theaters to desegregate. SDA's resolve won national attention.[13]

During winter break, members of SDA spread the word about stand-ins. Sandra Cason, chairperson of the student government's Human Relations Council, met with the executive committee of the National Student Association (NSA). The committee passed a resolution commending the stand-ins and also informed NSA members of an SDA resolution calling for national demonstrations against theater chains which practiced segregation anywhere in the United States. Davidson met with many supportive college groups throughout the country. Eleanor Roosevelt sent Cason a telegram stating, "I admire so much the stand which the students at The University of Texas have taken."[14]

The demonstrations continued and gained momentum when classes convened again. *The Daily Texan*, the campus newspaper, gave favorable coverage to the stand-ins for the first few months, which aided the growth of the movement. Although the protesters remained peaceful, having been told not to retaliate against aggression, the Austin police arrested two youths for assaulting picketers. Eyewitnesses reported that the attackers had "spit on them [the protesters], pushed them, shoved them into the gutter, and threw football blocks" at them. In mid-January SDA sent material to other colleges asking for sympathy demonstrations against all segregated theater chains.[15]

SDA chose the anniversary of Abraham Lincoln's birthday for these demonstrations. The SDA executive board announced that commitments for sympathy demonstrations on February 12 had been received from campuses in San Antonio; Dallas; Houston; Shreveport; New York City; Chicago; Los Angeles; San Francisco; Ann Arbor, Michigan; Cambridge, Massachusetts; Oberlin, Ohio; and Champaign, Illinois. ABC-Paramount, the chain which owned the Varsity, experienced stand-ins on February 12 in New York City, Boston, San Francisco, and Chicago. Stand-ins also appeared in Houston, San Antonio, and Dallas. The largest stand-ins to date occurred in Austin on Lincoln's birthday. Close to 450 people participated in the demonstrations. Students from Huston-Tillotson and Concordia Lutheran colleges and St. Edwards University joined together with SDA members as protesters picketed and sought admission to the two theaters near campus. Rev. Lee Freeman of the University Baptist Church announced to his congregation that he would participate in the stand-ins. Demonstrators denounced the governors of two

---

[13]Dallas *Morning News,* Dec. 3, 1960 (2nd and 3rd quotations); *Texas Observer* (Austin), Jan. 14, 1961 (1st quotation).

[14]*Daily Texan* (Austin), Jan. 5, 1961.

[15]*Texas Observer* (Austin), Jan. 14, 1961 (quotation); *Daily Texan* (Austin), Jan. 10, 15, 1961.

University of Texas students took an active role in the movement to integrate lunch counters and other public facilities in Austin in the early 1960s. *CN 00093d. Courtesy Prints and Photographs Collection, Center for American History, University of Texas at Austin.*

southern states, Arkansas and Louisiana. They sang, "We are going to hang Orval Faubus to a sour apple tree" and "We're going to send Jimmie Davis to an integrated hell." That night, the stand-ins moved to two downtown theaters, the State and the Paramount, for the first time.[16]

A few segregationists appeared during the demonstrations carrying a sign with a quotation wrongly attributed to Abraham Lincoln's second inaugural address: "I do not believe in the social or political equality of the two races." The quote did correctly paraphrase some of Lincoln's statements in the 1850s. Charles Root, who managed the Interstate chain in Austin, which owned three theaters experiencing stand-ins, stated that the protesters should "go back to

[16]UT Chancellor's Office Records, System-Wide, Central Administration Policy and Procedure Files, 1960–1962, Desegregation, CAH (cited hereafter as UT Chancellor's Office Records, Desegregation, 1960–1962); *Daily Texan* (Austin), Feb. 13, 1961; Austin *American*, Feb. 13, 1961 (quotations); *Texas Observer* (Austin), Feb. 18, 1961; New York *Times*, Feb. 13, 1961.

Russia" if they believed the rights of minorities could ever overshadow the rights of the majority. Root said that the demonstrators had their rights but added that the theater owners also had rights. State Sen. Frank Owen of El Paso branded the demonstrations as "communist inspired" with views of overthrowing the government. Owen's statement does not appear to be completely racially motivated, as he had participated in a filibuster against newly proposed state segregation laws in 1957. The FBI office in Austin investigated Chandler Davidson for Communist ties.[17]

Opposition also came from official channels at the university. Chancellor Harry Ransom referred to picketing as "gratuitous and silly." The Board of Regents also objected to students participating in demonstrations. Speaking of SDA-led demonstrations a year later, Chairman Thornton Hardie argued that participating students should be "summarily dismissed." He believed that picketing students showed little interest in acquiring an education and did not belong in the university. Other board members stated that nothing could be done to the students since the protests took place off campus and during the students' free time. The university did investigate Claude Allen because of his pro-integration views and activities. When interviews with his students revealed that Allen did not attempt to influence their opinions, the university dropped the investigation. Allen was nonetheless shifted from working with students to a research assignment. Another volley against SDA came after the Lincoln's birthday marches when Arno Nowotny, dean of student life, proposed at a Board of Regents meeting that all organizations not officially recognized by the university be barred from the campus YMCA. The proposal appeared to be aimed specifically at the SDA, since the university had officially recognized all the other civil rights groups which met at the YMCA. Nowotny added that he had heard rumors that financial support for SDA came from northerners and outsiders, although Davidson vehemently denied the rumors. The YMCA, however, declared that it would protect "free speech and free assembly" and allow SDA to meet there. More support for SDA appeared when 227 faculty members endorsed the stand-ins while condemning "arbitrary barriers that isolate groups of individuals from each other." But not many professors actually joined the stand-ins. One professor warned his graduate students not to participate in the protests because doing so might damage their career opportunities.[18]

Stand-ins continued throughout the spring of 1961. SDA led the campaign in Austin as well as in the rest of the state. Davidson and Wade helped organize

---

[17] *Daily Texan* (Austin), Feb. 13, 1961 (1st and 3rd quotations); *Texas Observer* (Austin), Feb. 18, 1961 (2nd quotation); Davidson to Kuhlman (interview).

[18] UT Chancellor's Office Records, Desegregation, 1960–1962 (1st and 2nd quotations); *Daily Texan* (Austin), Feb. 16, 17, Mar. 17, 1961 (3rd quotation); Davidson to Kuhlman (interview).

a similar campaign in San Antonio. Civil rights activists from Southern Methodist University in Dallas, Texas Christian University in Fort Worth, Trinity and St. Mary's Universities in San Antonio, and Wiley College in Marshall met with SDA to discuss stand-in strategy. In April Davidson wrote ABC-Paramount president Leonard Goldenson and the United States State Department stating that "We seek through persuasion to improve those parts of the American system we deem defective." An open letter in *The Texas Observer* gave Goldenson's address and urged readers to write that they would patronize only integrated theater chains. The letter also solicited funds to purchase a full-page advertisement in the New York *Times* protesting ABC-Paramount's policy of segregation in southern theaters. According to the letter in *The Texas Observer, The Daily Texan* had refused to print a similar letter. SDA received more national publicity when ABC commentator Edward P. Morgan sympathetically presented the group's activities. Another sympathy demonstration appeared in New York when four members of the Young People's Socialist League acted upon the urging of SDA leaders and staged a thirty-seven-hour sit-in in Goldenson's office.[19]

University of Texas government student Booker T. Bonner played an active role in challenging theaters on an individual basis. Although a member of SDA, he often disagreed with the format of the protests, the fact that whites made most of the decisions, and the socialist bent of the organization. Bonner pondered an action which would impress upon people the seriousness of the situation. He also wanted to prove to members of the African American community that they did not need to be dependent on white leadership. He decided to hold a one-man vigil and hunger strike in hope of "bringing attention to what was happening here and to try to prevail upon a person's mind [about the unfairness of segregation]." In February Bonner sat on a stool in front of the Texas Theater forgoing food and sleep for sixty and one-half hours. During the sit-in Bonner was verbally abused and threatened by segregationists. He enacted a similar protest in June when he sat in front of the university theaters for seven days with a sign which read: "RACIAL SEGREGATION (1) A DESTROYER OF OUR GLOBAL PRESTIGE, (2) A DAMNATION IN OUR DEMOCRACY" on one side and "Racial Segregation is an imbecility, a coward's shield, and an unearned badge of superiority" on the other.[20]

---

[19] *Daily Texan* (Austin), Feb. 3, 28, Apr. 26, 1961 (quotation); *Texas Observer* (Austin), May 20, Sept. 9, 1961.

[20] *Texas Observer* (Austin), Mar. 18 (1st quotation), June 10, 1961 (2nd quotation); Booker T. Bonner to Martin Kuhlman, Nov. 11, 1992 (interview). Bonner became an important figure in direct action as he led a civil rights march in Austin in 1963, joined the struggle for a municipal city rights ordinance in Austin, and became a field representative for the Southern Christian Leadership Conference in Texas. Austin *American,* Aug. 29, 1963; Dallas *Morning News,* Apr. 17, 1964; *Texas Observer* (Austin), Aug. 6, 1965.

Direct action brought the policy of segregation in Austin theaters into the public light, but only negotiation could bring about a permanent change. Pressure applied to ABC-Paramount by members of the Austin Jewish community and the Austin Commission on Human Relations aided in bringing about negotiations. On August 4 representatives from the campus theaters; a faculty member who endorsed the stand-ins; Rabbi Charles Mintz, president of the Austin Commission on Human Relations; and Houston Wade met to discuss the situation. The Texas and Varsity theaters agreed to desegregate, but the managers reserved the right to cancel integration if it hurt business. SDA also agreed to call off all other stand-ins in the city. The State and the Paramount refused to integrate, however, until "the rest of the Austin business district is ready." University of Texas students once again demonstrated against segregation at the Paramount and State theaters beginning in March 1963.[21]

The SDA-initiated stand-in campaign seemed to be more successful than SNCC's campaign. The SDA influenced direct action in three other Texas cities and five cities across the nation. Rev. James Bevel, a civil rights activist in Nashville, reported that only in Nashville had protesters heeded SNCC's call for continuous demonstrating against segregated theaters. The amount of national recognition SDA received must have had at least some influence on SNCC's call for a "second phase."[22]

SDA became involved in other civil rights activities. In February 1961 the group joined the Young Democrats, the Student Party, and URC in soliciting money for black sharecroppers in Somerville, Tennessee, who faced economic retaliation for voting. SDA also challenged segregation on the campus. Houston Wade circulated a petition for the integration of University of Texas athletics and called for all facilities of tax-supported institutions to be opened to all students. Wade submitted the petition with six thousand signatures to the Board of Regents in September 1961. The next month an athletic integration referendum indicated that most students were satisfied with segregation.[23]

The university's dependence on state funds influenced the administration's policies concerning desegregation. The university had lost support in the state legislature because of integration during the 1950s. State Rep. Jerry Sadler of Precilla announced that he had voted against appropriations for the

---

[21] *Texas Observer* (Austin), Sept. 9, 1961 (quotation); "Blacks-Integration," scrapbook, Vertical Files: Subject, CAH. A UT student working as an usher at the Paramount quit his job during the demonstration, saying he could not work in a place opposed to his principles. *Daily Texan* (Austin), Mar. 10, 1963.

[22] Aldon D. Morris, *The Origins of the Civil Rights Movement: Black Communities Organizing for Change* (New York: The Free Press, 1984), 232.

[23] UT President's Office Records, Administrative Files, Desegregation, 1960–1966, CAH (cited hereafter as UT President's Office Records, Desegregation, 1960–1966); "Integration–UT," scrapbook, CAH; *Daily Texan* (Austin), May 8, 1957.

university "because they have Negro undergraduates." Rep. Joe Chapman of Sulphur Springs, another pro-segregation legislator, pointed out that the state legislature controlled the university through appropriations. During appropriations hearings in the late 1950s, university administrators dropped Barbara Smith, an African American, from the cast of an opera. Chapman had told UT President Logan Wilson that casting a black singer would result in bad publicity. Wilson argued that Chapman's call did not influence his decision to dismiss Smith, insisting instead that he had done so to keep the university from "becoming a battleground for extremists on both sides [of the integration question]." Board members rejected the athletic petition in the fall of 1961 because they believed they had gone further in desegregating the campus "than a majority of the citizens of Texas and of the members of the Legislature would approve" and would not be forced to desegregate by an active vocal minority of the student body.[24] The slow pace of integration, however, brought direct action onto campus.

The majority of dormitories on the University of Texas campus continued to exclude African Americans. In 1956 Tom Sealy, chairman of the Board of Regents, stated that the university would integrate for educational purposes but remain segregated for residential purposes. Black women could visit rooms in the hall, but the door had to remain closed. *De facto* segregation also banned African Americans from drinking fountains, bathrooms, and the lobby. University officials reaffirmed the policy of residential segregation in the fall of 1961. When officials announced that students violating segregation rules would be punished, fifty African Americans staged a sit-in in the lobby of Kinsolving dormitory, a white women's residence hall. Protesting students assembled in the lobby and ignored requests to leave as they sat for an hour talking, studying, or watching television. Soon after the incident, University of Texas President J. R. Smiley released a statement urging all students to keep "the real business of the University, which is the training of the intellect in a wholesome academic community," in mind. Smiley also said that the right to "The orderly expression of your thoughts and opinions" might be jeopardized by incidents such as the one at Kinsolving.[25]

Some regents planned to take steps more drastic than warning students. Chairman Hardie proclaimed:

> It is my thought that if we let these people get away without some punishment that they can understand and feel, we are inviting them to take mob action again, and they will undoubtedly do so whenever it suits them.

---

[24]Decision of Board, Fall 1961, UT President's Office Records, Desegregation, 1960–1966; "Integration–UT," scrapbook; *Daily Texan* (Austin), May 8, 1957 (1st and 2nd quotations).

[25]Almetris Marsh Duren, *Overcoming: A History of Black Integration at the University of Texas at Austin* (Austin: University of Texas Press, 1979), 6; Dallas *Morning News*, Oct. 22, 1961; Message to Student Body, Oct. 1961, UT President's Office Records, Desegregation, 1960–1966, CAH.

The dean called all black students into his office and asked if they had participated in the sit-in. Officials released students answering "no," put twenty-two students answering "yes" on disciplinary probation for the rest of the fall semester, and placed one student who refused to answer on probation until June 1. Officials charged the students with failing to comply with "properly constituted authority." The URC denounced the punishment, and student body president Maurice Olian called the actions "backward, narrow-minded, and hypocritical." Chairman Hardie demanded an apology for the statement, but Olian refused. News of the sit-in also created a stir at other colleges. President Smiley received a telegram from the student council of Brandeis University in Massachusetts protesting the disciplinary action; the council reported sending a similar telegram to U.S. Attorney General Robert Kennedy.[26] Although many university organizations denounced the probation, civil rights activists lost one ally on campus.

*The Daily Texan,* which had supported integration activities in the past, warned demonstrating students against "further agitation" that might alienate supporters. The pro-integration stand the paper had taken before the Kinsolving incident had brought the daily under the scrutiny of the Board of Regents. Hardie attacked actions of the newspaper in a letter to other board members a month before the Kinsolving sit-in. He specifically referred to editorials that criticized university officials for deciding not to integrate certain facilities. Hardie believed "that those in charge of the *Daily Texan* will, unless proper steps are taken, continuously malign and down grade The University of Texas and Board of Regents." He feared that the paper's attacks would cause the university to lose public support. Hardie suggested that students and faculty members in agreement with university policy should be encouraged to write letters and articles for the paper. In February 1962, the regents took selection of the editor away from the student body and gave a nine-member board the right to appoint the editor. The university claimed to have made the move to better journalism at the school.[27]

The faculty also voiced its opposition to university segregation policies. In May 1961 the general faculty recommended complete desegregation of the university as soon as possible. After the Kinsolving sit-in, the faculty voted 512 to 170 against dormitory segregation. Faculty opinion often conflicted with

---

[26]Thornton Hardie to Board of Regents Members, Oct. 27, 1961, UT President's Office Records, Desegregation, 1960–1966 (1st quotation); *Texas Observer* (Austin), Oct. 27, 1961. The cited number of students placed on disciplinary probation represents official university figures. The Campus Interracial Committee stated that seventy-five students received probation. Duren Papers.

[27]Dallas *Morning News,* Oct. 22, 1961 (1st quotation); Hardie to Board of Regents Members, Oct. 27, 1961, UT President's Office Records, Desegregation, 1960–1966 (2nd quotation); *Daily Texan* (Austin), July 28, 1961.

official university policy, and to some extent the university did lose public support as a result. One private citizen stopped a bequest of $10,000 to the university because of the faculty resolution opposing segregation in dormitory rest rooms. Although President Smiley received a number of letters opposing the probation given to the students involved in the Kinsolving sit-in, the majority of writers supported the action.[28]

The probation, however, did not deter civil rights activists. One hundred students singing "We Shall Not Be Moved" marched in front of Kinsolving and Whitis dormitories a few days after the sit-in and disciplinary actions. The university's Traffic and Security Division and Fire Department took pictures of the protesters for their records. Activists also utilized courts in an attempt to desegregate university dormitories. Three students, Leroy Sanders, Sherryl Griffin, and Maudie Ates, brought a lawsuit against university officials calling for the integration of dormitories. Campus groups supporting civil rights raised more than $2,500 to help finance the suit. The regents fought back by warning law professor Dr. Ernest Goldstein, who had given legal counsel to SDA, attended integration rallies, encouraged the students to file the dormitory lawsuit, and organized a petition calling for the desegregation of dormitories and dining facilities which 832 faculty members approved, not to become involved in the case or risk "disciplinary action." Although the students' lawyers argued that the federal funds borrowed for the building of Kinsolving should have precluded segregation, university officials claimed that dormitories were not part of the "educational process." Frustration over the length of the court's deliberations led to a demonstration in front of Kinsolving in January 1964. The case became moot in May 1964, when the Regents voted to end segregation in all university dormitories.[29]

Segregation hurt the university financially. In 1962 the Peace Corps canceled a $257,513 contract to train volunteers for a project in Brazil. Segregation in the Forty Acre Club, which claimed to be for "the faculty, staff, and friends of The University of Texas," first caused the Peace Corps to rethink giving the contract to the university. The university often utilized the off-campus club for meetings and official visitors. Segregation in the Forty Acre Club led to an investigation of other university practices. A Peace Corps official announced that the university's action on the dormitory integration suit represented "the catalytic agent" in the withdrawal of the contract. SDA challenged the university's association with the club. SDA cited a graduate seminar to be held in the club, the utilization of the club for official university visitors, and the club's use of university property for advertising as evidence of the association, and began to picket the club in August 1962. Four

[28]Duren Papers; UT Chancellor's Office Records, Desegregation, 1960–1962.

[29]UT President's Office Records, Desegregation, 1960–1966 (quotations); Duren Papers; "Integration–UT," scrapbook.

hundred faculty members censured the club, and some members resigned. The club accepted its first African American member in 1965.[30]

University of Texas students also demonstrated against a lounge near campus that remained segregated after passage of the federal Civil Rights Act of 1964. Roy's Lounge avoided compliance with the law by ending the service of food. Under the federal law, bars and taverns that did not serve food did not have to desegregate. Roy's remained segregated out of fear that integration would hurt business. After a nonviolent training session, the Student Interracial Committee (SIC) began protests in April 1965. Countermarchers confronted the activists, however, and strains of "Dixie" mingled with "We Shall Overcome." Opposition to desegregation came not only from blatant segregationists, such as members of the Society for the Prevention of Negroes Getting Everything (SPONGE), but also from students, such as members of Young Americans for Freedom, who opposed government telling a private business whom to serve.[31]

The university did struggle against some forms of segregation. In the fall of 1962 it canceled ice skating classes at the Austin Ice Palace because of the rink's policy of segregation. Other university policies slowly changed. Darrell Royal, the university's athletic director and head football coach, announced complete desegregation of athletics in November 1963. After the end of the dormitory case in 1964, the university adopted an official policy against discrimination in any part of the university. University students remained active in challenging segregation in Austin, subsequently supporting a city anti-bias ordinance and participating in a parade depicting the burial of Uncle Tom.[32]

University of Texas students utilized direct action to challenge segregation. Of course, only a small minority of university students participated in these demonstrations, and one student referred to them as "red pawns." But demonstrations placed the spotlight on segregated facilities in Austin and often hurt profits of businesses. Although in many cases negotiations put an end to segregation, direct action forced businessmen to negotiate. Direct action also impacted university policies. The sit-in at Kinsolving led to the lawsuit against the university. After delivering a speech at the university in 1962, Dr. Martin Luther King Jr. consulted with students about the best strategy to bring about integration.[33] University administrators, however, attempted to censor student direct action groups so as not to give the university a bad image with the majority of Texas citizens and the state legislature.

---

[30]Duren Papers; Duren, *Overcoming,* 11; *Texas Observer* (Austin), Aug. 3, Sept. 21, 1962 (2nd quotation).

[31]"Integration–UT," scrapbook.

[32]*Daily Texan* (Austin), Sept. 20, 1962; UT Chancellor's Office Records, Desegregation, 1962–1964, CAH; "Integration–UT," scrapbook.

[33]Duren, *Overcoming,* 11.

The University of Texas had made relatively large strides in integrating educational facilities in the 1950s, yet other non-academic facilities remained segregated, as the university administration attempted to slow desegregation so as not to alienate the powerful Texans who controlled the university's funding. Austin segregationists did respond with some violence and intimidation to civil rights demonstrations, but their reaction proved less violent than in the Deep South. Thus more civil rights activities could take place with less fear of retaliation. The civil rights demonstrations at the University of Texas were integrated protests, although some disagreements between participants of different races did occur.

Although the courts could order the integration of educational facilities, civil rights activists often resorted to direct action to bring about negotiations and lawsuits aimed at desegregating facilities over which the courts had less control. By the early 1960s, when the tactics of direct action spread through the south, a limited tradition of civil rights activities already existed on the University of Texas campus. The university YMCA, for example, had sponsored civil rights rallies since the 1940s.[34] This tradition and the integration struggles of the 1950s to some extent aided the introduction of direct action at the university. But University of Texas students not only applied strategies first employed elsewhere; to desegregate public facilities, they also pioneered the use of direct-action tactics which later gained national acceptance. Although not as well known as other civil rights battles, the activities on the University of Texas campus represent an important chapter in the story of the struggle for civil rights in America.

---

[34]Gillette, "Blacks Challenge the White University," 339.

# A Century and a Half of Ethnic Change in Texas, 1836–1986

Terry G. Jordan

*Historians quarrel over whether Texas is a southern or western state, or for that matter, merely unique or simply representative of frontier expansion. The question is too complex to be resolved in a short essay, but the late Terry G. Jordan, a distinguished member of the faculty of the University of Texas at Austin for many years, provides some insight. His article demonstrates that Texas was and is a very heterogeneous state that includes a wide variety of ethnic and racial groups, much more diverse than other southern states. Throughout time transoceanic and intercontinental immigrants contributed and maintained their own heritages. Texas thus has a vital, multicultural makeup that breaks down the frequently preconceived notion of a state dominated by Anglo cowboy values.*

*In the twenty years since publication of this article, the population of Texas has grown at an even more rapid pace, and the representation of non-Anglo cultures has increased to approximately 50 percent. In 2000 Hispanics accounted for almost one-third of the population; in terms of percentage of increase, Asians were growing more rapidly than other groups. Such growth patterns make Jordan's conclusion—that as a borderland or zone of contact Texans must strive to appreciate our cultural differences—particularly relevant.*

*Students who are interested in the role of cultural geography in the writing of Texas history should consult two of Jordan's books,* Texas Log Buildings: A Folk Architecture *(Austin, 1978) and* Texas Graveyards: A Cultural Legacy *(Austin, 1982), as well as the April 1986* Southwestern Historical Quarterly, *which features articles by two other well-known geographers, Robin W. Doughty and Christopher S. Davies.*

---

*Terry G. Jordan, "A Century and a Half of Ethnic Change in Texas, 1836–1986," *Southwestern Historical Quarterly,* 89 (Apr., 1986), 385–422.

In the cultural as in the environmental sense, Texas has always been a borderland or even a shatterbelt. The Amerindian regional diversity of pre-Columbian times, based partially in climatic contrasts, was obliterated, only to be replaced by an even more complex human mosaic. Those who would understand Texas, now as well as 150 years ago, must once and for all discard the myth of the typical Texan, a chauvinistic notion that, on occasion, has even penetrated the scholarly community,[1] and accept the concept of a multiethnic society. Texas is a unit only in the functional political sense; culturally it is a balkanized zone entrapped in an artificial administrative framework.[2]

Texans, in short, inhabit a border province. The state, in common with eastern Canada, Belgium, Switzerland, Alsace-Lorraine, and South Tirol, lies astride a fundamental culturo-linguistic divide between Romance and Germanic civilizations, a divide lent heightened contrast here by the addition of a large non-European, Amerindian cultural component on the Latin side.

In such situations, when an artificial political framework is imposed upon a cultural borderland, ethnic groups are created. Ethnicity implies minority status in a larger society dominated numerically, and usually socially, economically, and politically as well, by a host culture.[3] In Texas, the host/dominant group throughout the past century and a half has consisted of old-stock Anglo-Americans, here defined as whites of colonial eastern-seaboard ancestry.[4] More

---

[1]Evon Z. Vogt, "American Subcultural Continua as Exemplified by the Mormons and Texans," *American Anthropologist,* LVII (1955), 1,163–1,172; Joseph Leach, *The Typical Texan: Biography of an American Myth* (Dallas, 1952).

[2]This is the theme of Terry G. Jordan, John L. Bean, Jr., and William M. Holmes, *Texas: A Geography* (Boulder, Colo., 1984). See also Terry G. Jordan, "Population Origin Groups in Rural Texas," Map Supplement No. 13, *Annals of the Association of American Geographers,* LX (June, 1970), 404–405, plus folded map; Terry G. Jordan, "Population Origins in Texas, 1850," *Geographical Review,* LIX (Jan., 1969), 83–103; and Donald W. Meinig, *Imperial Texas: An Interpretive Essay in Cultural Geography* (Austin, 1969).

[3]Wsevolod W. Isajiw, "Definitions of Ethnicity," *Ethnicity,* I (July, 1974), 111–124; Terry G. Jordan and Lester Rowntree, "Ethnic Geography," Chapter 9 in *The Human Mosaic: A Thematic Introduction to Cultural Geography* (4th ed.; New York, 1986), 271–304.

[4]Basic sources on the southern Anglo-Americans include Terry G. Jordan, "The Texan Appalachia," *Annals of the Association of American Geographers,* LX (Sept., 1970), 409–427; Henry Stuart Foote, *Texas and the Texans; or, Advance of the Anglo-Americans to the South-West* (2 vols.; Philadelphia, 1841); Rex W. Strickland, "Anglo-American Activities in Northeastern Texas, 1803–1845" (Ph.D. diss., University of Texas, 1937); Lester G. Bugbee, "The Old Three Hundred: A List of Settlers in Austin's First Colony," *Quarterly of the Texas State Historical Association,* I (Oct., 1897), 108–117 (this journal is cited hereafter as QTSHA); Mark E. Nackman, "Anglo-American Migrants to the West: Men of Broken Fortunes? The Case of Texas, 1821–1846," *Western Historical Quarterly,* V (Oct., 1974), 441–455; Barnes F. Lathrop, *Migration into East Texas, 1835–1860* (Austin, 1949); Seymour V. Connor, *The Peters Colony of Texas* (Austin, 1959); William W. White, "Migration into West Texas, 1845–1860" (M.A. thesis, University of Texas, 1948); Homer L. Kerr, "Migration into Texas, 1865–1880" (Ph.D. diss., University of Texas, 1953); R. Marsh Smith, "Migration of Georgians to Texas, 1821–1870," *Georgia*

precisely, southern Anglos served as the host culture in Texas through most of that period. Even as early as 1830, a mere fifteen years or so after southern pioneers began settling Texas, they had acquired majority status (figure 1). The war of independence in 1836 formalized the host culture claim of southern Anglos by awarding them political, social, and economic overlordship.

Though basically British-derived, the host group was itself far from internally homogeneous. Southern Anglos numbered not just English, Scotch-Irish, and Welsh among their ancestors, but also Pennsylvania Germans, Hudson Valley Dutch, French Huguenots, Delaware Valley Finns and Swedes, and others. These diverse groups, far to the east of Texas, blended through intermarriage to form the southern Anglo population. The Texian victors of 1836 lived in Finnish log cabins, fought with German long rifles, drank Scottish whiskey, adhered to British dissenter Protestantism, and introduced the language and common law of the English. Walk among their tombstones in the graveyards of rural Texas and you will find the Scotch-Irish McLane and Ross, the Germans Snider and Buckner, the English Alsbury and Cooper, the Dutch De Witt and Kuykendall, the Welsh Williams and Jones, the Huguenots Lamar and Alley, the Swedes Swanson and Justice.

Even in colonial times, the Anglo host group had formed two distinct southern subcultures, one rooted in the coastal plain and based in the plantation system, the other resident in the mountains and practiced by slaveless yeomen. In Texas, by 1850, a Texarkana–to–San Antonio line separated the domain of the planter, or lower southerner, to the east of the line, from the western interior stronghold of the yeoman, or upper southerner (figure 2).[5] While members of these two Anglo subgroups established distinctive rural economies, spoke different dialects, and often disagreed politically, they resembled each other closely enough to function as a single host culture in Texas.

At the time of the first federal census in Texas in 1850, the southern Anglo majority was absolute, but hardly, at 53 percent of the total population, overwhelming (table 1). As the century progressed, southerners strengthened somewhat their numerical hold on Texas, though the abolition of slavery weakened their overlordship. By 1887, they constituted nearly three-fifths of the population, the highest proportional level they were ever to reach. The twentieth century witnessed a steady deterioration and eventual disappearance of the host culture majority, for as we celebrate the sesquicentennial of independence, Anglos constitute less than half of the state population.

---

*Historical Quarterly,* XX (Dec, 1936), 307–325; Ethel Zively Rather, "De Witt's Colony," QTSHA, VIII (Oct., 1904), 95–192; and Eugene C. Barker, *The Life of Stephen F. Austin, Founder of Texas, 1793–1836: A Chapter in the Westward Movement of the Anglo-American People* (Nashville, 1925).

[5]Terry G. Jordan, "The Imprint of the Upper and Lower South on Mid-Nineteenth-Century Texas," *Annals of the Association of American Geographers,* LVII (Dec, 1967), 667–690; Jordan, "Population Origins in Texas," 87–89.

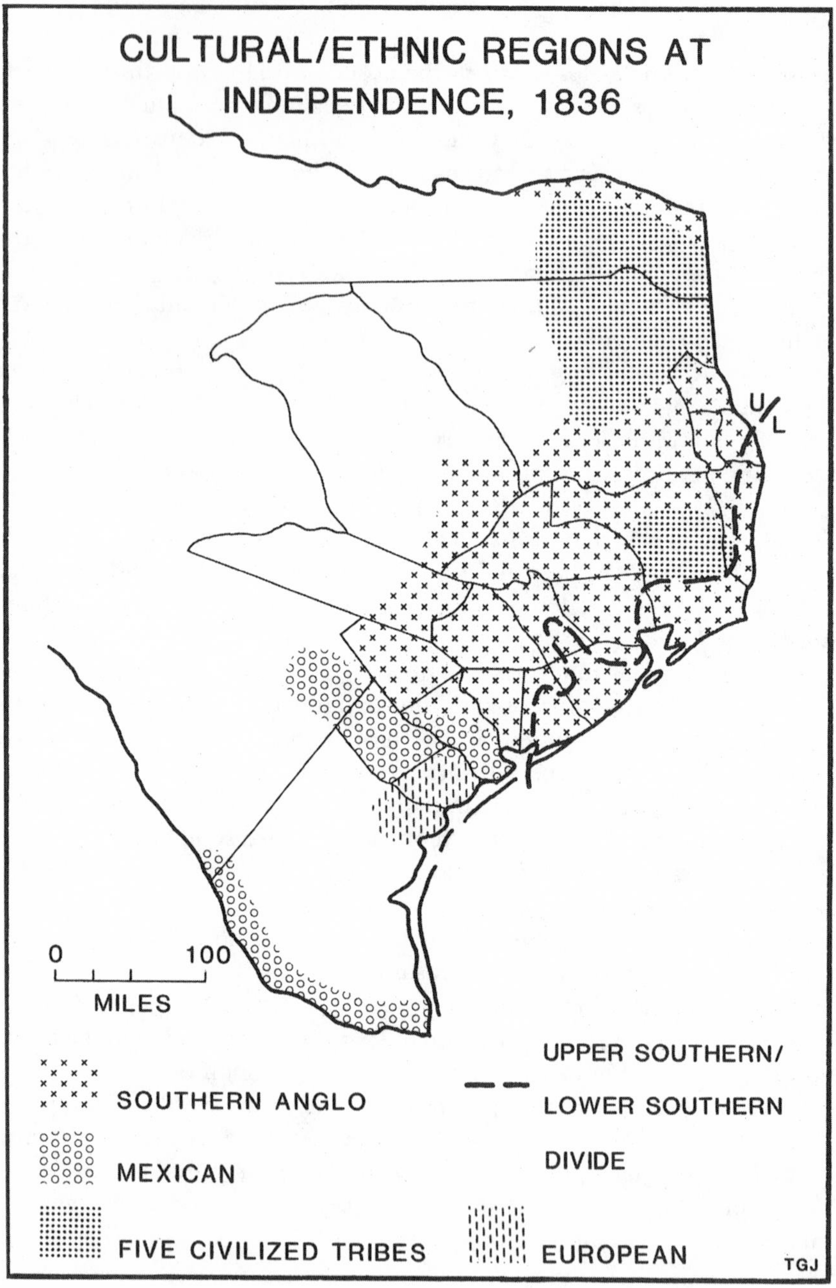


Figure 1: At the time of the Texas Revolution, Anglo settlers, mainly of upper southern origin, were concentrated in the southeastern part of Texas, while an Irish-Mexican "barrier" had been set up in their coastal path. Cherokee Indians occupied much of the northeastern Texas. (Source: Mexican censuses in the Nacogdoches Archives [Archives Division, Texas State Library, Austin] and Bexar Archives [Eugene C. Barker Texas History Center, University of Texas, Austin].)

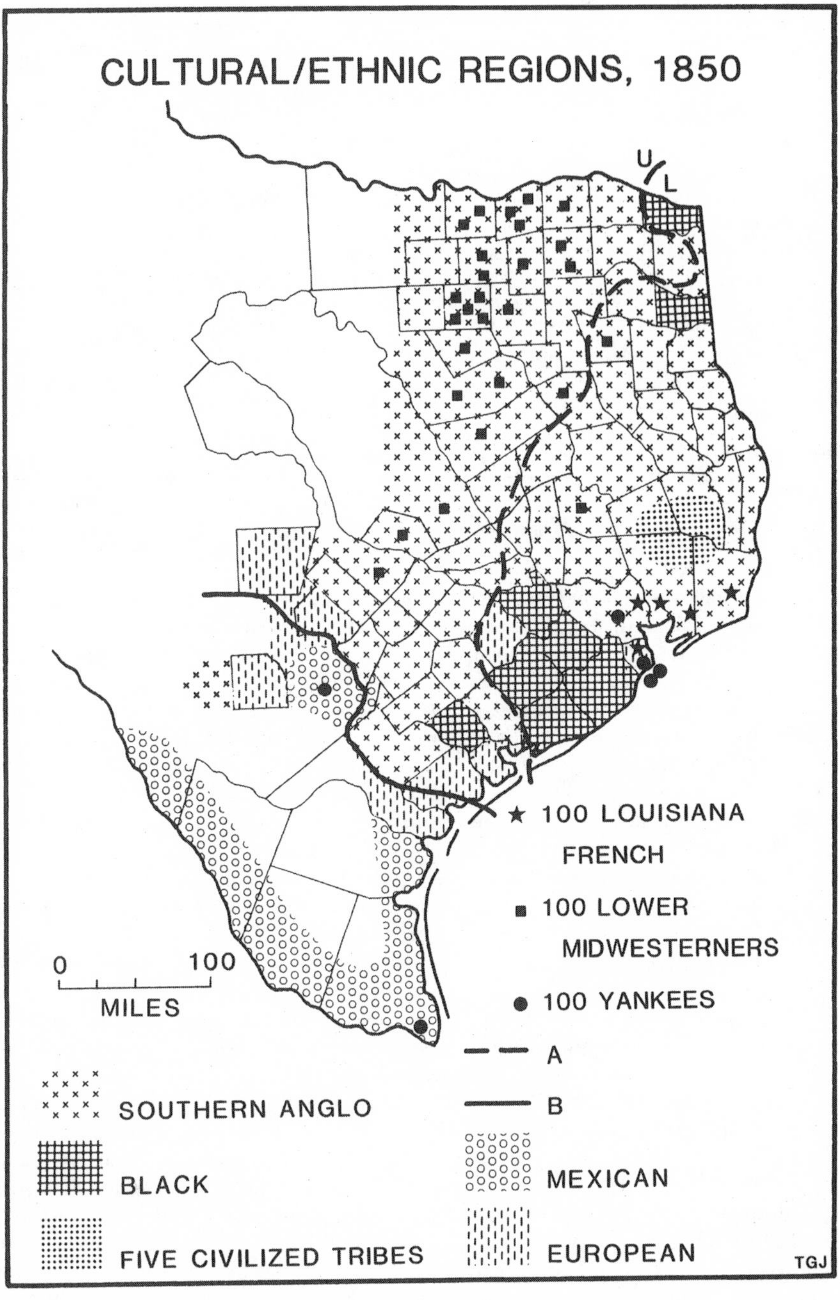


Figure 2: By mid-century, settlement had spread west to the Cross Timbers. *A* = upper southern/lower southern divide; *B* = north and east of this line, blacks outnumbered Hispanics. "Yankees" are native of New England and lower New York; "Lower Midwesterners" are natives of Ohio, Indiana, and Illinois. Military personnel at frontier posts are not included in the count. (Source: United States census of 1850, including a hand count of the manuscript population schedules.)

TABLE 1 Cultural/Ethnic/National Origin Groups in Texas, 1850–1980

| Group | 1850[a] | 1887[b] | 1980[c] |
|---|---|---|---|
| Old-Stock Southern Anglo-Americans | 114,500 (53%) | 1,156,000 (57%) | 5,100,000 (45%) (Southern and Northern combined) |
| Old-Stock Northern Anglo-Americans | 10,000 (4½%) | 148,000 (7%) | |
| Mexicans | 14,000 (6½%) | 83,000 (4%) | 2,495,000 (22%) |
| Blacks (African) | 58,600 (27%) | 396,000 (20%) | 1,368,000 (12%) |
| Louisiana French | 600 (<1%) | 2,300 (<1%) | 375,000 (3%) |
| Europeans | 16,000 (7½%) | 225,000 (11%) | 1,315,000 (12%) |
| Orientals | 0 (-) | 800 (<1%) | 120,000 (1%) |
| Amerindians | ? (-) | 800 (<1%) | 117,000 (1%) |
| Other or unknown | 2,000 (<1%) | 2,900 (<1%) | 520,000 (4%) |
| Total Population | 215,700 (100%) | 2,015,000 (100%) | 11,412,781 (100%) |

SOURCES:

[a]Hand count of the manuscript free population schedules of the 1850 United States census, including an estimate for the El Paso area, which was not enumerated. The Louisiana French total is represented by the French surnamed population of Harris, Galveston, Jefferson, and Liberty counties. The black total is from *The Seventh Census of the United States: 1850* (Washington, D.C., 1853), 504.

[b]L. L. Foster (ed.), *First Annual Report of the Agricultural Bureau of the Department of Agriculture, Insurance, Statistics, and History, 1887–88* (Austin, 1889), xlvi, 1–249. The Anglo-American population was subdivided into northern and southern groups on the basis of the United States census of 1890 (Vol. II, Pt. 1, pp. 568–571) figures for state of nativity for "native whites of native parents," with the Texas-born held neutral. For the adjustment of the Hispanic population, see Terry G. Jordan, "The 1887 Census of Texas' Hispanic Population," *Aztlan,* XII (Autumn, 1981), 274–275. The fragmentary total for American Indians was adjusted upward on the basis of the 1890 U.S. census, as was the total for Orientals, which in the state census included only Chinese (U.S. census of 1890, Vol. XI, Pt. 1, p. 609). The Louisiana French total is based on the "French" population of Galveston, Hardin, Harris, Jefferson, Liberty, and Orange counties; this total was subtracted from the European total. See Foster (ed.), *First Annual Report,* 35, 80, 95, 96, 118, 139, 173.

[c]Based upon the response to question 14 in the long form of the 1980 census: "What is this person's ancestry?" The results are available in the *1980 Census of Population and Housing,* more exactly in (1) *Ancestry of the Population by State: 1980,* Supplementary Report PC80-S1-10 (Washington, D.C., 1983), 20, 38, 44, 50, 56, 62, 68; (2) "Public-Use Microdata Samples," unpublished computer tape (Washington, D.C., 1983); and (3) "Technical Documentation," Summary Tape File 4, unpublished computer tape (Washington, D.C., 1983). Only 11,412,781 of 14,229,191 Texans gave usable responses. The "Old-Stock Anglo-American" figure is the total of persons reporting full or partial English, Irish, Welsh, or Scottish ancestry, with adjustments for internal redundancies such as "Scotch-Irish." The "Louisiana French" total is based on the "French" and "partially French" population of Chambers, Galveston, Hardin, Harris, Jefferson, Liberty, and Orange counties. The "European" total represents only those persons reporting *pure continental* European ancestry, minus the estimate for pure-blood Louisiana French and plus the total for British-born. The Amerindian total includes those persons reporting only Amerindian ancestry, and the same is true for Orientals. "Mexicans" include all persons reporting full or partial ancestral ties to Mexico and excludes all other Hispanics. The black total includes persons reporting full or partial ancestry in sub-Saharan Africa, excluding the Republic of South Africa.

In fact, one might well argue that the Anglo host culture has ceased to be "southern." A western or southwestern self-image of Anglo-Texans developed, perhaps beginning as early as postbellum times, with the result that members of the host culture began thinking of themselves in nonsouthern terms.[6] When the novelist William Humphrey left his native Clarksville, it remained a southern town, but when he returned thirty-two years later, he found that it had become western.[7] Cotton, corn, overalls, and sharecropping disappeared from East Texas; stetsons, boots, and beef cattle replaced them. The South, whose military defeat never rested gently upon the self-confident Anglo-Texans, succumbed a second time, to the West. Let the cavaliers of Virginia, accustomed to losing civil wars, keep alive the Confederate faith. Texans would turn their eyes and hearts to the setting sun.

This shift of self-image from South to West, in turn, facilitated the absorption of numerous acculturated or assimilated Europeans and northern Anglos into the host culture. Even such a redefined, enlarged group, however, cannot, on the basis of the census, claim a majority of the present population (table 2). This startling fact is revealed by the 1980 United States census, the first to include a question on remote ancestry. Even if the host culture is generously defined as those persons fully or even partially of British ancestry, the number accounts for only 45 percent of the total (table 1). This includes, for example, persons who responded that they were of English–French–German or American Indian–German–Irish ancestry, persons, in other words, who were less than half of British blood. Also included are 426,000 Texans reporting full or partial Scotch-Irish ancestry, amounting to only 4 percent of those responding. To be sure, many Anglos failed to respond to the census question, causing their numbers to be undercounted, but add the figures as you will, the total of persons claiming *any* English, Irish, Welsh, or Scotch blood falls well short of half the population.[8] Profound cultural shifts will surely accompany this loss of Anglo majority, this tipping of the ethnic balance in Texas. Increasingly, Anglo dominance retreats northward (figure 3).

As long as the Anglo host culture remained southern in character, northerners functioned much like an ethnic group in Texas. Walter Prescott Webb, recalling his youth in Stephens County, once told of a lone northern family that

---

[6] Wilbur Zelinsky, "North America's Vernacular Regions," *Annals of the Association of American Geographers*, LXX (Mar., 1980), 14.

[7]William Humphrey, *Farther Off from Heaven* (New York, 1977), 239. See also James W. Lee, "The Old South in Texas Literature," Don Graham, James W. Lee, and William T. Pilkington (eds.), *The Texas Literary Tradition: Fiction, Folklore, History* (Austin, 1983), 46, 48.

[8]United States Census of Population and Housing, 1980, Summary Tape File 4, "Technical Documentation" (Washington, D.C., 1983); and United States Census of Population, "Public-Use Microdata Samples" (Washington, D.C., 1983). Both of these sources are unpublished computer tapes.

TABLE 2 Selected Origin Groups in Texas, 1980

| Group | Number of Persons Wholly of this Origin | Number of Persons Partially of this Origin | Total | Total as a Percentage of Respondents |
|---|---|---|---|---|
| British[a] | 2,280,336 | | | |
| English | 1,639,322 | 1,444,001 | 3,083,323 | 27% |
| Irish | 572,815 | 1,847,752 | 2,420,567 | 21% |
| Scottish | 55,711 | 601,181 | 656,892 | 6% |
| German[b] | 814,152 | | | |
| Germany | 754,388 | 1,414,559 | 2,168,947 | 19% |
| Dutch | 45,838 | 251,513 | 297,351 | 2½% |
| Scandinavian[c] | 70,461 | | | |
| Swedish | 34,687 | 86,588 | 121,275 | 1% |
| Norwegian | 20,875 | 44,460 | 65,335 | < 1% |
| Slavic[d] | 191,189 | | | |
| Czech | 91,495 | 87,437 | 178,932 | 1½% |
| Polish | 70,688 | 96,777 | 167,465 | 1½% |
| Southern European[e] | 100,728 | | | |
| Italian | 78,592 | 111,207 | 189,799 | 1½% |
| Greek | 13,759 | 10,561 | 24,320 | < 1% |
| French[f] | 162,846 | | | |
| France | 152,072 | 521,605 | 673,677 | 6% |
| Europe, total[g] | 3,646,602 | | | |
| Mexican | 2,385,793 | 109,242 | 2,495,035 | 22% |
| Sub-Saharan African[h] | 1,342,915 | 24,819 | 1,367,734 | 12% |
| Asian[i] | 119,100 | 17,692 | 136,792 | 1% |
| Amerindian | 117,496 | 513,781 | 631,277 | 6% |
| Total | 7,859,393 | | | |

[a]British includes English, Irish, Scottish, Northern Irish, Welsh, and Manx.

[b]German includes also Alsatian, Austrian, Dutch, Luxembourger, 70 percent of the Swiss total, and 60 percent of the Belgian total. Many or most who responded "Dutch" are probably actually German.

[c]Scandinavian includes Danish, Norwegian, Swedish, Icelandic, and "Scandinavian."

[d]Slavic includes Belorussians, Bulgarians, Croatians, Czechs, "Eastern Europeans," Polish, Russians, Ruthenians, Serbians, "Slavic," Slovaks, Slovenes, Ukrainians, and Yugoslavians. Wends were not enumerated.

[e]Southern European includes Albanians, Basques, Cypriots, Greeks, Italians, Maltese, Portuguese, and Spaniards.

[f]French also includes French-Canadian, one-fifth of the Swiss total, and 40 percent of the Belgians.

[g]The European total also includes full-blood Estonians, Finns, Gypsies, Hungarians, Latvians, Lithuanians, Romanians, and "other Europeans."

[h]Excludes South Africa, Cape Verde Islands.

[i]Excludes Middle Easterners, includes Pakistanis.

SOURCE: 1980 Census of Population, *Ancestry of the Population by State: 1980*, Supplementary Report, PC80-S1-10 (Washington, D.C., 1983), 20, 38, 44, 50, 56, 62, 68.

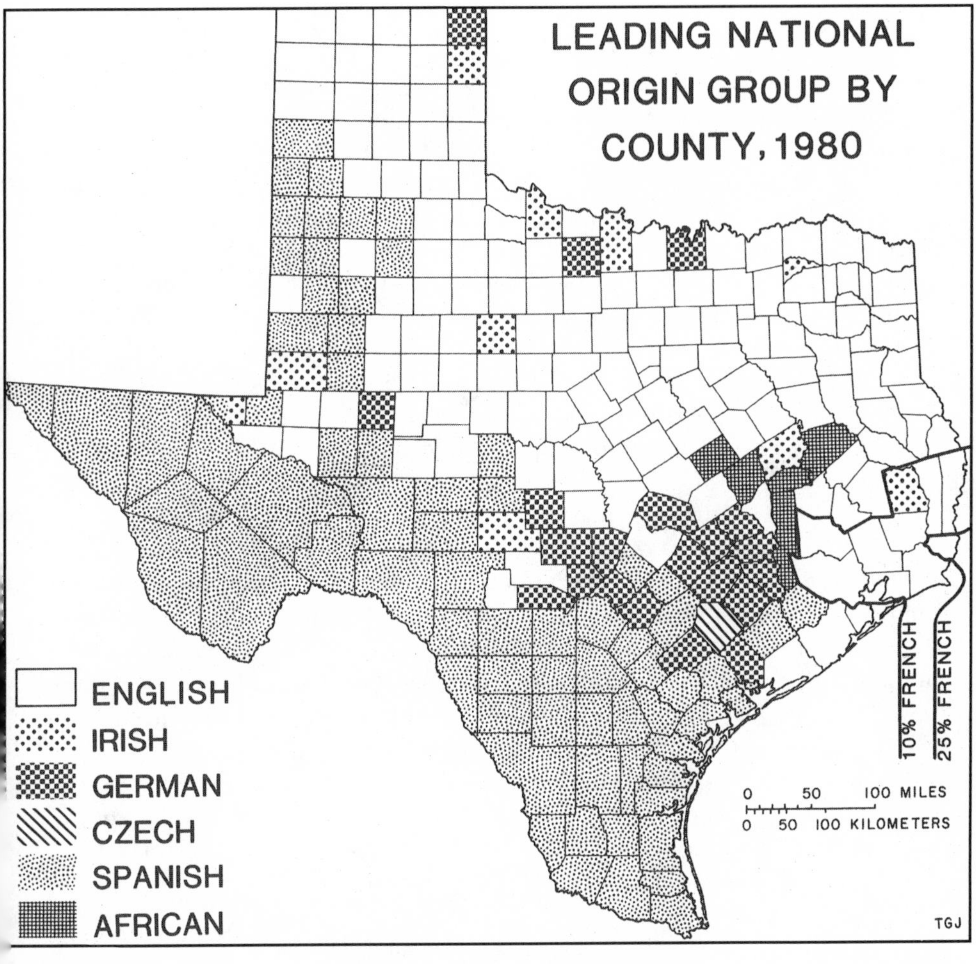


Figure 3: In each county, persons claiming full or partial ancestry from the group indicated were more numerous than any other. Had persons of English, Irish, Scottish, and Welsh ancestry been combined, the resultant "British" group would have claimed some counties shown as Spanish, German, and African. The Irish, largely Protestant or Scotch-Irish, are common wherever the English are, and the apparent islandlike character of their plurality is misleading. Loving County had precisely the same numbers of Irish and Spanish. (Source: Unites States Census of Population and Housing, 1980, Summary Tape File 4, "Technical Documentation" [Washington, D. C., 1983], unpublished computer tape.)

settled in his exclusively southern, Confederate-sympathizing neighborhood. Several quite pretty daughters graced the family, but, added Webb, "they never married, of course."[9] A segment of the northern population was Yankee—derived from New England, New York, and their daughter states of Michigan, Wisconsin, and Minnesota in the upper Midwest. Though only about 3,000 Yankees lived in Texas by 1850, they were far above average in wealth and education.[10] Typically, Yankees worked as merchants, artisans, or other professionals in the towns of antebellum Texas or as officers among soldiers on the frontier.[11] A highly distinctive group, distinguished from the bulk of southern Anglos by education, profession, place of residence, and wealth, Yankees wielded influence out of proportion to their numbers, as is suggested by the election of Connecticut native Elisha Pease as governor in 1853 and 1855.

In the period from 1865 to 1880, the Yankee states continued to provide about 2 percent of the white immigrants to Texas.[12] The leading contributing state of birth by 1890, as in 1850, was New York.[13] By the 1970s, Michigan had supplanted New York as the principal source state in an accelerating Yankee immigration. While these northerners are easily absorbed into the Anglo host culture today, their dialect remains distinctive.

Another component of the northern Anglo-American group, derived from the Ohio–to–Nebraska belt of lower midwestern states, made up 5 percent of the immigrant white population by 1850, and natives of Illinois outnumbered those from any other state in Dallas County.[14] Forty years later, Illini remained twice as numerous as natives of any other midwestern state, and the influx of lower midwesterners between 1865 and 1880 accounted for 8 percent of the whites coming to Texas in postbellum times.[15] Immigration from the Ohio–to–Nebraska belt has persisted to the present day, lending a midwestern flavor to the top two tiers of counties in the Panhandle, to the rural northern Blackland Prairie, and to parts of Dallas and Houston. Even the lower Rio Grande Valley and the Gulf Coast region display pockets of rural midwestern influence, as is suggested by

---

[9]Professor Webb told this anecdote in the classroom in the fall semester, 1960, at the University of Texas.

[10]Hand count of MSS free population schedules, United States census of 1850, including natives of New England, New York, Michigan, Wisconsin, and their Texas-born children.

[11]Arthur C. Burnett, *Yankees in the Republic of Texas: Some Notes on Their Origin and Impact* (Houston, 1952).

[12]Kerr, "Migration into Texas," 73–74.

[13]*The Seventh Census of the United States: 1850* (Washington, D.C., 1853), xxxvi–xxxvii; Eleventh Census of the United States, Vol. XI, Pt. 1, *Population of the United States, 1890* (Washington, D.C., 1894), 560–573.

[14]Hand count of MSS free population schedules, United States census of 1850; the midwestern total includes natives of Ohio, Indiana, Illinois, Iowa, Kansas, Nebraska, and their Texas-born children.

[15]Eleventh Census, Vol. XI, Pt. 1, 560–573; Kerr, "Migration into Texas," 73.

TABLE 3 The Hispanic-Black Population Shift in Texas

| Year | Number of Hispanics | Number of Blacks |
|---|---|---|
| | (% of total state population in parentheses) | |
| 1850[a] | 13,712 (6%) | 58,558 (27%) |
| 1887[b] | 83,433 (4%) | 395,576 (20%) |
| 1930[c] | 683,681 (12%) | 854,964 (15%) |
| 1940[d] | 738,440 (12%) | 924,391 (14%) |
| 1950[e] | 1,027,455 (13%) | 977,458 (13%) |
| 1960[f] | 1,417,810 (15%) | 1,187,125 (12%) |
| 1970[g] | 2,059,671 (18%) | 1,399,005 (12%) |
| 1980[h] | 2,982,583 (21%) | 1,704,741 (12%) |

NOTES AND SOURCES:

[a]Spanish-surnamed, based upon a hand count of the 1850 manuscript U.S. census schedules, with an estimate of 2,500 added for the El Paso area, which was not enumerated. *The Seventh Census of the United States: 1850* (Washington, D.C., 1853), 504.

[b]L. L. Foster (ed.), *First Annual Report of the Agricultural Bureau of the Department of Agriculture, Insurance, Statistics, and History, 1887–88* (Austin, 1889), xlvi. A refinement of the Hispanic total is based upon Terry G. Jordan, "The 1887 Census of Texas' Hispanic Population," *Aztlan,* XII (Autumn, 1981), 275.

[c]Hispanic is defined as "Mexican race." Fifteenth Census of the United States: 1930, *Population,* Vol. III, Pt. 2 (Washington, D.C., 1932), 975, 1,014.

[d]Sixteenth Census of the United States: 1940, *Population,* Vol. II, Pt. 1 (Washington, D.C., 1943), 52. Hispanics are represented by "Spanish mother tongue."

[e]United States Census of Population: 1950, Vol. II, *Characteristics of the Population,* Pt. 43, Texas (Washington, D.C., 1952), 63; and Special Report, *Persons of Spanish Surname* (Washington, D.C., 1953), p. 3C–6, which lists the Hispanic figures for 1930, 1940, and 1950.

[f]Eighteenth Census of the United States, *Census of Population: 1960,* Vol. I, Pt. 45, Texas (Washington, D.C., 1961), 64; and Subject Reports, No. PC(2)–1B, *Persons of Spanish Surname* (Washington, D.C., 1963).

[g]United States, Bureau of the Census, 1970 Census of Population, Vol. I, *Characteristics of the Population,* Pt. 45, Texas (Washington, D.C., 1973), Sec. 1, p. 103, and Sec. 2, pp. 1,269, 1,270.

[h]1980 Census of Population, Vol. I, Characteristics of the Population, Chapter C, *General Social and Economic Characteristics,* Pt. 45, Texas, Sec. 1 (Washington, D.C., 1983), 31, 59.

town names like Buckeye in Matagorda County, Bloomington in Victoria County, Iowa Colony in Brazoria County, and Ohio in Cameron County.[16]

If the enlarged old-stock Anglo host culture accounts for roughly half of the Texas population, the other half is ethnic. Between 1940 and 1950, an ethnic event of pivotal importance to the cultural future of the state occurred, entirely unnoticed at the time. Perhaps in the year 1947 or 1948, persons of Hispanic ancestry surpassed blacks in number to become the largest ethnic minority in Texas (table 3). Since that time, the Hispanic element has continued

[16]Walter Prescott Webb, H. Bailey Carroll, and Eldon Stephen Branda (eds.), *The Handbook of Texas* (3 vols.; Austin, 1952, 1976), I, 176, 237, 891, II, 303.

to grow very rapidly and may well outnumber blacks two-to-one as we observe the sesquicentennial of the war that extinguished Hispanic rule. Today perhaps one-quarter of the Texas population is Hispanic in origin, and the massive continuing immigration from Mexico has the potential further to increase the proportion in future decades.[17] Texas, in 1980, had the second largest Hispanic population among the states, ranking behind California; and the cities of San Antonio, Houston, and El Paso were among the top eight American metropolitan areas in size of Hispanic population.

Ironically, during the century-and-a-half of Spanish and Mexican colonization and rule, from 1680 to 1836, no substantial Hispanic population accumulated in Texas, while the 150 years of Anglo control produced a Spanish surnamed group of over three million. When Mexican political authority ended at San Jacinto, no more than 7,000 or 8,000 Spaniards, Christianized Indians, and mestizos resided in Texas, already for a decade a minority group in their own homeland. The 1850 census schedules suggest an Hispanic population of only about 14,000, less than 7 percent of the Texas total (tables 1, 3). Nor, in the following four decades, did the growth of the Hispanic population by natural increase and immigration keep pace with Anglos, blacks, and Europeans. In the 1850s, a mere 2.3 percent of Texas white immigrants came from Mexico, a proportion that becomes much smaller if the sizable black immigration of that decade is considered.[18] Between 1860 and

[17]Basic sources on Hispanic-Texans include Paul S. Taylor, *An American-Mexican Frontier: Nueces County, Texas* (Chapel Hill, N.C., 1934); Richard L. Nostrand, "The Hispanic-American Borderland: Delimitation of an American Culture Region," *Annals of the Association of American Geographers,* LX (Dec. 1970), 638–661; Richard L. Nostrand, "Mexican Americans circa 1850," ibid., LXV (Sept., 1975), 378–390 [a colored map serving as a companion to this article appeared in *Historical Geography Newsletter,* V (Fall, 1975), following p. 30]; Ozzie G. Simmons, "Anglo-Americans and Mexican Americans in South Texas" (Ph.D. diss., Harvard University, 1952); Pauline R. Kibbe, *Latin Americans in Texas* (Albuquerque, 1946); M. S. Handman, "The Mexican Immigrant in Texas," *Southwestern Political and Social Science Quarterly,* VII (June, 1926), 33–41; Herbert E. Bolton, *Texas in the Middle Eighteenth Century* (Berkeley, 1915); I.J. Cox, "The Early Settlers of San Fernando," *QTSHA,* V (Oct., 1901), 142–160; James A. Wilson, *Tejanos, Chicanos, and Mexicanos: A Partially Annotated, Historical Bibliography* (San Marcos, Texas, 1974); William Madsen, *The Mexican-Americans of South Texas* (2nd ed.; New York, 1973); Mary Ellen Goodman et al., *The Mexican-American Population of Houston: A Survey in the Field, 1965–1970,* Rice University Studies, LVII, No. 3 (Houston, 1971); Arnoldo De León, *The Tejano Community, 1836–1900* (Albuquerque, 1982); Arnoldo De León, *They Called Them Greasers: Anglo Attitudes toward Mexicans in Texas, 1821–1900* (Austin, 1983); Mario T. Garcia, *Desert Immigrants: The Mexicans of El Paso, 1880–1920* (New Haven, Conn., 1981); Gilberto Hinojosa, *A Borderlands Town in Transition: Laredo, 1755–1870* (College Station, Tex., 1983).

[18]White, "Migration into West Texas," 13, 20; Barnes F. Lathrop, "Migration into East Texas, 1835–1860," *Southwestern Historical Quarterly,* LII (July, 1948), 31 (the *Quarterly* is cited hereafter as *SHQ*). The total achieved by adding White's and Lathrop's samples is 7,260 immigrant families, of whom 169 were from Mexico.

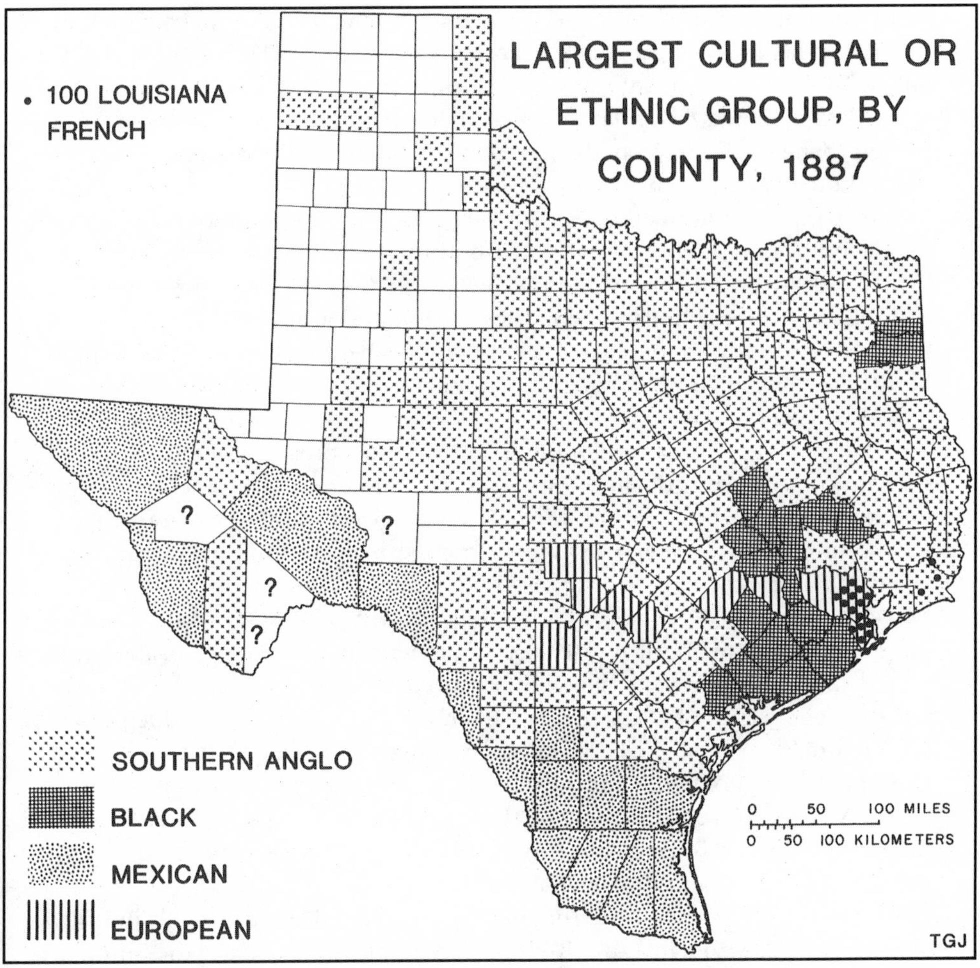


Figure 4: At the golden jubilee of Texas independence, the Anglo host culture enjoyed, proportionately and areally, its finest hour. Louisiana French were interpreted to be persons of French ancestry living in the far southeastern counties. (Source: Texas State Census of 1887, published in L. L. Foster (ed.), *First Annual Report of the Agricultural Bureau of the Department of Agriculture, Insurance, Statistics, and History, 1887–88* [Austin, 1889], 1–249. Adjustments were made for missing data for Encinal County and for flawed data for Gillespie County on the basis of manuscript population schedules of the 1880 U.S. census and the published 1890 U.S. census, *Population of the United States, 1890* [Washington, D.C., 1894].)

1880, Latin American countries, led by Mexico, accounted for 6.5 percent of the total immigration to Texas, falling from 10 percent in the 1863–1866 period to only 4.9 percent between 1875 and 1878.[19] By the time of the state census in 1887, Hispanics numbered 83,000 and formed only 4 percent of the Texas population (table 1). The Anglicization of the state seemed within reach; demographically the host culture enjoyed its finest hour.

Hispanics, outnumbered in 1887 fourteen-to-one by southern Anglos, five-to-one by blacks, almost three-to-one by Europeans, and even by Germans alone, appeared on their way to ethnic eclipse in Texas, though they continued to form majorities in thirteen counties of the border area (figures 4, 5). An observer at the beginning of the last decade of the nineteenth century could hardly have imagined what was to come.

Most observers believe the mass immigration from Mexico began about 1910, coinciding with a revolution there and the spread of railroads, which brought commercial agriculture into South Texas. In reality, however, the major influx of Mexicans began in the 1890s. The number of Mexican-born rose from 52,000 to 71,000 between 1890 and 1900; the increase in immigration alone equaled the percentage growth of the Texas population at large. By 1910, Mexican-born totaled 125,000, and an additional 108,000 native Texans reported one or both parents born in Mexico.[20] The generation 1890–1910, then, witnessed an immigration of perhaps 100,000 from Mexico, more than doubling the Hispanic population of 1887. If the old-stock Mexican group were added to the 1910 figure for first and second generation "foreign white stock," an Hispanic element of at least 300,000 would likely result. Clearly, the ethnic winds had shifted in that twenty-year span, allowing the Mexican population to grow threefold while the total number of Texas inhabitants increased by only 75 percent.

Since 1910, a tenfold growth of the Hispanic group has occurred (table 3). Key factors in the twentieth-century immigration have been the steady industrialization of Texas and an explosive birth rate in Mexico. Much of the immigration has been illegal, a situation rich in irony. In the early 1830s, harassed Mexican border troops proved incapable of halting a large-scale influx of illegal Anglo aliens ("wetnecks"?) crossing the Sabine and Red rivers; in the 1980s, the pattern is reversed. Latin American countries beyond Mexico, such as El Salvador, have begun sending substantial numbers of illegal migrants.

So lengthy and sizable an immigration is bound to be a diverse one. As a result, the Hispanic population is internally the most complex ethnic group in

---

[19]Kerr, "Migration into Texas," 74, 75, 135, 137.

[20]Eleventh Census, Vol. XI, Pt. 1, p. 606; United States, Bureau of the Census, *Abstract of the Twelfth Census of the United States, 1900* (Washington, D.C., 1904), 61; Thirteenth Census of the United States Taken in the Year 1910, Vol. III, Population, 1910 (Washington, D.C., 1913), 799.

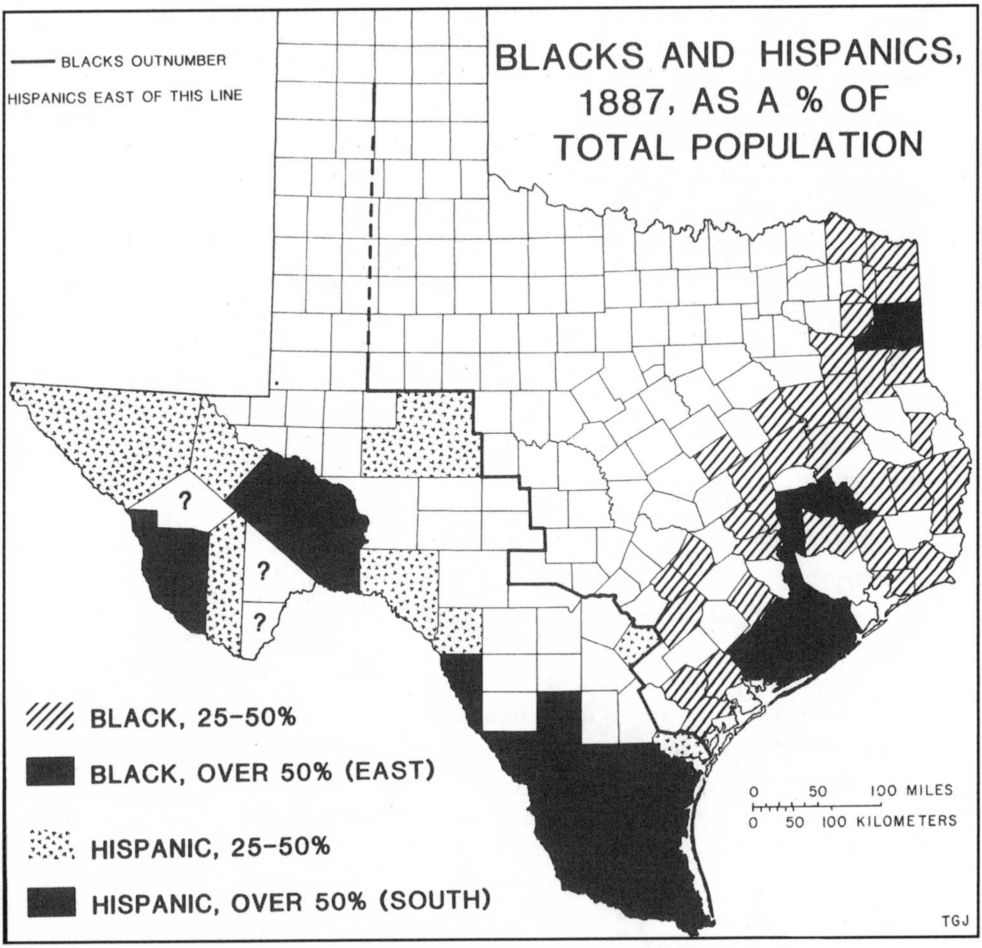


Figure 5: The spatial segregation between blacks and Hispanics is evident, and the dividing line remained much as it had been in 1850. The missing Encinal County figures were estimated, based upon a hand count of the 1880 census manuscript population schedules. (Source: Texas State Census of 1887, in Foster [ed.], *First Annual Report*, 1–249.)

Texas. It consists of many different national origin groups, though Mexicans dominate; joins Castilian Spaniard, Amerindian, and African; overlaps a complete socioeconomic range; and derives from assorted periods of migration. Not even the basic traditional defining traits—Spanish tongue and Catholic faith—suffice any longer to encompass this group. English has made inroads, as is suggested by the fact that 6 percent of the Texas Hispanic population did not list Spanish as the language of household use in 1980.[21] Protestantism, too, has spread among the Hispanics. As of 1984, various major Protestant denominations had won a total of about 140,000 Latin American converts in Texas, led by the Southern Baptists, who account for half the total.[22] By this measure, Protestantism now claims 5 percent of the Texas Hispanics. The derisive label *agringado* is applied by some of their ethnic kin to such acculturated persons.

One of the major internal divisions within the Hispanic group is based upon time of immigration. On school playgrounds, year of arrival helps determine status. Greatest prestige belongs to the Tejanos, descendants of the colonial population. In San Antonio, Canary Islander ancestry is of some social consequence, since that group constituted the first civilian settlers of Spanish Texas. Often descended from land-grant families, Tejanos tend to be wealthier than the norm, highly acculturated, and, in many cases, intermarried with Anglos. Lowest on the socio-economic scale are recently arrived laborers, many of whom live in urban slums or in rural *colonias* in the lower Rio Grande Valley.

In 1976, sixty-five *colonias* in Cameron and Hidalgo counties housed 32,000 persons, mostly agricultural laborers, 80 percent of whom had immigrated since 1960.[23] Just as there is no typical Texan, so there is no typical Hispanic-Texan.

In geographical terms, the internal Hispanic contrasts are best described by a Pecos River boundary. West of that stream, and best exemplified by the El Paso area, is found an Hispanic subculture with close links to New Mexico and Chihuahua, as is seen in such traditional architectural features as flat roofs and adobe brick. East of the Pecos, by contrast, a second Hispanic subculture prevails, exhibiting closer ties to adjacent Coahuila, Nuevo León, and Tamaulipas. Stone, caliche, and *palisadó* (picket) construction replaces adobe there, and a favored roof form features the parapet gable.

---

[21] 1980 Census of Population, Vol. I, Characteristics of the Population, Chapter C, *General Social and Economic Characteristics,* Pt. 45, Texas, Sec. 1 (Washington, D.C., 1983), 110, 141. The figures are based on the Spanish-origin population five years or more of age. Of 2,632,758 such persons, 2,484,188 reported using Spanish at home.

[22] The following 1984 figures for Hispanic members were provided by church officials: Southern Baptist Convention, 70,000; Assembly of God, 38,046; United Methodist, 16,000; Presbyterian Church, 5,300; Seventh-Day Adventist, 4,000; American Lutheran Church, 2,500; Lutheran Church–Missouri Synod, 1,947; Disciples of Christ (Christian Church), 580; Lutheran Church in America, 500. See also: Andrew J. Weigert, William V. D'Antonio, and Arthur J. Rubel, "Protestantism and Assimilation among Mexican Americans," *Journal for the Scientific Study of Religion,* X (Fall, 1971), 219–232; Martha C. M. Remy, "Protestant Churches and Mexican-Americans in South Texas" (Ph.D. diss., University of Texas, Austin, 1970); Jose Galindo-Alvirez, "Latin American Methodism in the Southwest: A History of the Rio Grande Conference" (M.A. thesis, Lamar University, 1962); and James C. Thrash, "Spanish-Speaking Presbyterians in South Texas" (M.A. thesis, Texas A&I University, 1969).

[23] *The Colonias of the Lower Rio Grande Valley of South Texas: A Policy Perspective,* Lyndon B. Johnson School of Public Affairs, Policy Research Project Report No. 18 (Austin, 1977).

These two Hispanic-Texan subcultures have been reinforced in recent years by the pattern of immigration flow from Mexico. The San Antonio district of the Immigration and Naturalization Service collected data on apprehended illegal aliens, from which it becomes clear that, as of the middle 1970s, South Texas migrants emanated mainly from an adjacent northeastern region in Mexico. Coahuila alone sent more than one-fifth of the total, and other sizable contingents arrived from Durango, Tamaulipas, San Luis Potosí, Zacatecas, and Guanajuato. Closeness to South Texas appears to be an important factor in channeling the migration. The Trans-Pecos region, by contrast, draws most heavily upon neighboring Chihuahua in the present migration, reinforcing the traditional regionalism. Surprisingly, the western Mesa Central of Mexico, centered in Jalisco and Michoacán, sends the bulk of its emigrants to California, though Texas is closer.[24]

One might expect, given the sharp rise in the Hispanic proportion of the Texas population in the last century, accompanied by the huge numerical increase, that the geographical area with a Mexican-American majority would have increased greatly. This has not been the case (figures 5, 6, 7). Indeed, the trend between 1880 and 1930 was for Mexican majorities to weaken or even be lost in South Texas. Among the river-front counties, Cameron declined from 88 percent Mexican in 1880 to 50 percent in 1930, Hidalgo from 98 to 54 percent, Zapata from 99 to 51, and Webb-Encinal from 92 to 70. Duval County, where nine of every ten persons was Mexican in 1880, was less than one-third Hispanic fifty years later.[25] Aided by a net Anglo emigration from South Texas since 1960, Mexicans have decisively reversed this trend. More notably, the past fifty years have also witnessed a significant northward movement of Hispanic people within the state, as can be seen in the significant enlargement of the area in which they form between a quarter and a half of the total population, as well as in the northward and eastward shift in the boundary of the district housing more Mexicans than blacks (figures 5, 6, 7). Four counties that had black *majorities* as recently as 1900—Brazoria, Fort Bend, Matagorda, and Wharton—housed more Hispanics than blacks by 1980.[26]

Denton County, in North Texas, provides a good example of the spread of the Mexican population into new areas. Only 14 persons of Hispanic ethnicity

---

[24]Richard C. Jones, "Undocumented Migration from Mexico: Some Geographical Questions," *Annals of the Association of American Geographers,* LXXII (Mar., 1982), 83–84.

[25]Robert C. Spillman, "A Historical Geography of Mexican American Population Patterns in the South Texas Hispanic Borderland: 1850–1970" (M.A. thesis, University of Southern Mississippi, 1977), 38, 61, based upon his hand count of the MSS population schedules of the 1880 United States census; see also Mattie L. Wooten, "Racial, National, and Nativity Trends in Texas, 1870–1930," *Southwestern Social Science Quarterly,* XIV (June, 1933), 62–69.

[26]Thirteenth Census, Vol. III, *Population,* 1910, pp. 805–851.

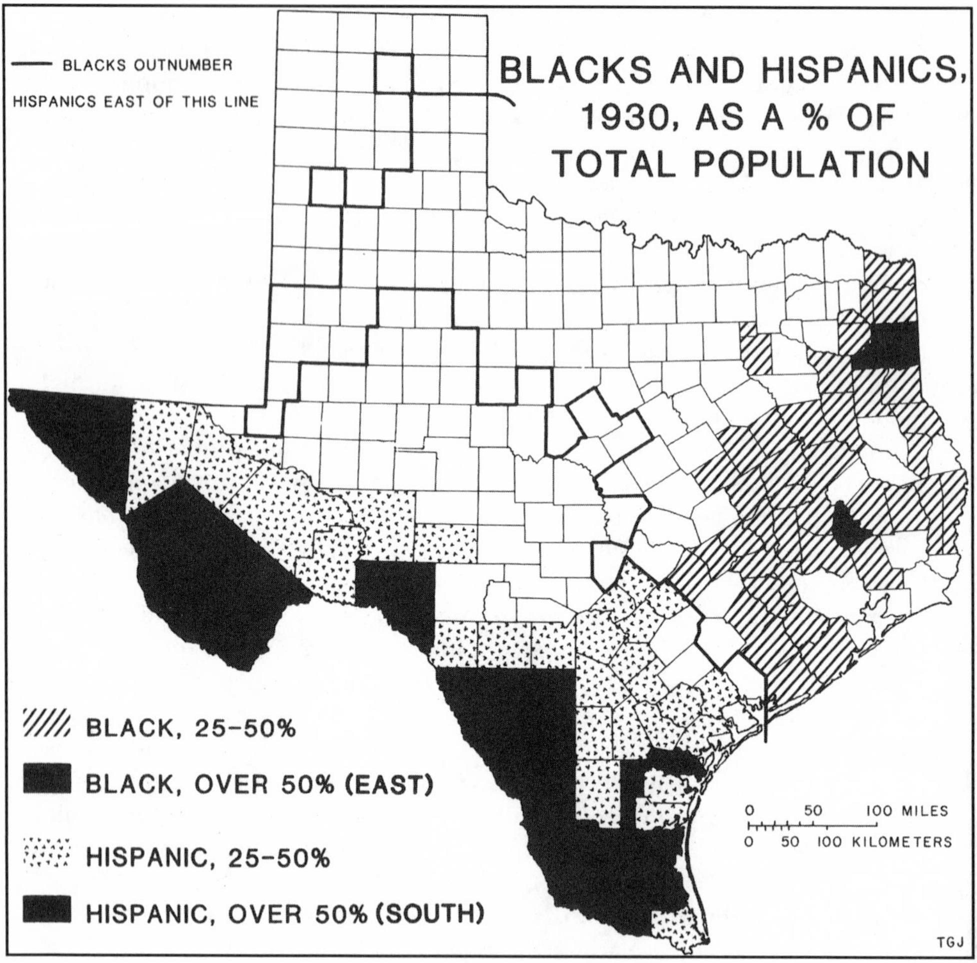


Figure 6: Note the weakening of the black areas since 1887 and the eastward shift of the Hispanic/black border. (Source: Fifteenth Census of the United States; 1930, *Population*, Vol. III, Pt. 2 [Washington. D.C., 1932], 975–990, 1,014–1,015.)

lived in Denton County in 1887, contrasted with 905 blacks; and by 1930 the Mexican total had risen to 254, still less than one-eighth the number of Afro-Americans.[27] Some had come as railroad workers, while others labored on farms and ranches in the county. Many Anglo cemeteries in rural Denton

[27]L. L. Foster (ed.), *First Annual Report of the Agricultural Bureau of the Department of Agriculture, Insurance, Statistics, and History, 1887–88* (Austin, 1889), 55; Fifteenth Census of the United States: 1930, *Population*, Vol. III, Pt. 2 (Washington, D.C., 1932), 978, 1,014.

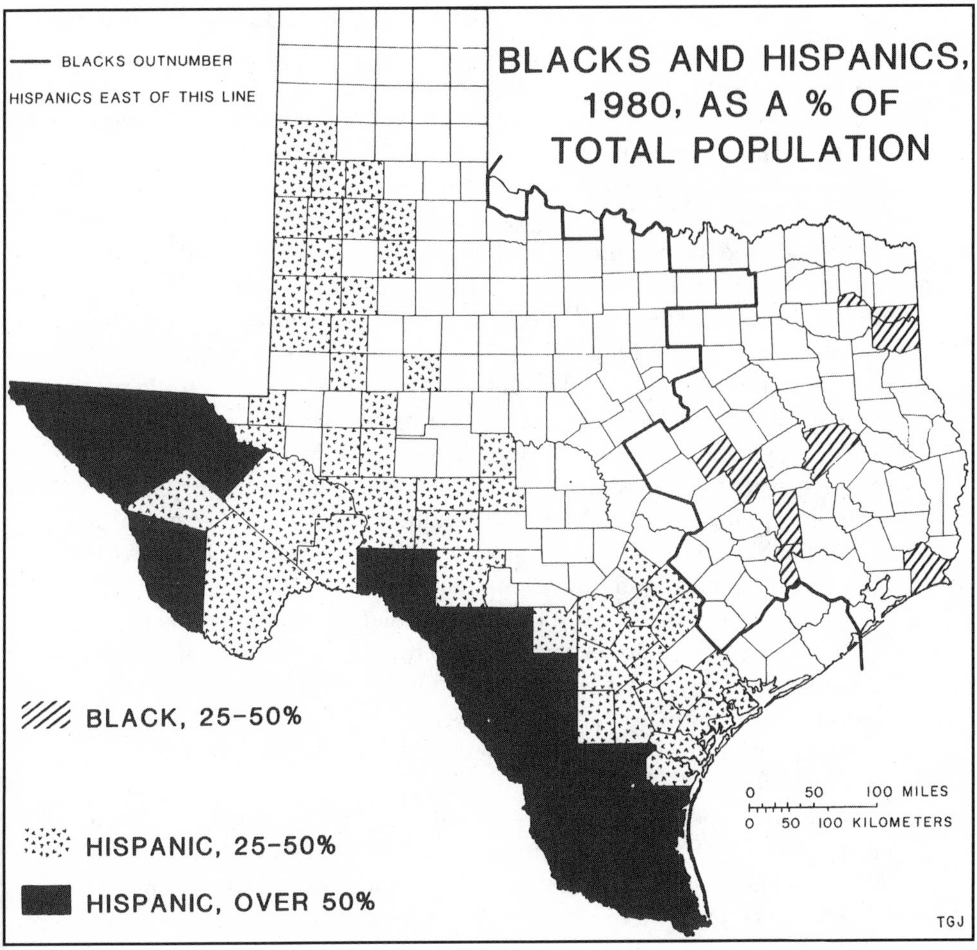


Figure 7: At the Sesquicentennial, the East Texas black stronghold has virtually vanished and the Hispanic/black border lies much farther east than in 1930. The advancing geographical Hispanicization of Texas in the last century is evident by comparing figures 5 and 7. (Source: 1980 Census of Population, Vol. I, Characteristics of the Population, Chapter C, *General Social and Economic Characteristics,* Pt. 45, Texas, Sec 1 [Washington, D.C., 1983], 49–58, 77–86.)

County contain a few, spatially segregated, Mexican graves dating from the early part of the century. The Menchaca family operated a Mexican-food cafe as early as 1916 on the east side of the Denton courthouse square. Even so, Spanish-surnamed counts revealed only 242 such persons in the county in 1950 and 885 in 1960. Beginning in the 1960s, an upswing in immigration occurred, with South Texas as the leading source, and in the following decade

Hispanics surpassed blacks to become the largest Denton County minority. The 1980 census enumerated 6,286 Hispanic persons, or 4.5 percent of the county population, surpassing the black total of 6,135.[28]

Until fairly recently, a rather orderly steplike geographical progression was evident in the northward intrastate migration of Hispanics.

The newly arrived immigrant could be expected to settle in one of the rural *colonias*, near the Rio Grande in South Texas. As acculturation progressed, the people moved farther north and up the socioeconomic ladder. In this manner, certain West Texas counties derived much or most of their Hispanic population from South Texas.[29] Today, however, sophisticated networks funnel illegal aliens far north of the border, often well beyond Texas.

The Hispanic immigration has differed from that of other ethnic minorities in some fundamental ways. Mexicans entering Texas find a familiar place. The rivers they cross, the towns and counties they settle in, even the streets they live on often bear Spanish names. Radio and television stations, newspapers, and church services employing their mother tongue await them. The century and a half of Hispanic rule is the basis of much of the sense of familiarity, providing not just toponyms and a venerable population base upon which to build, but also the unexpressed or even subconscious belief that "this land is rightfully ours." In immigration, no ocean is crossed, and the ancestral homeland remains adjacent, permitting close cultural ties. Too, the volume and duration of Mexican immigration are unrivaled by other ethnic groups and provide continual cultural reinforcement. For all these reasons, Hispanic ethnicity remains vital and acculturation is retarded.

The rapid numerical and proportional growth of the Spanish-surnamed population, coupled with the enhanced viability of Mexican ethnicity, together constitute the most significant ethnic development in Texas at the Sesquicentennial. As the Mexican element translates numbers and proportions into political power and social clout, Texas becomes increasingly Hispanicized, or better, re-Hispanicized.

Afro-Americans, forming the second largest ethnic group, have been present in Texas from Spanish times, and eighteenth-century censuses clearly acknowledge their presence, both as pure Africans and in an array of mixtures with

[28]Terry G. Jordan, "County Bicentennial Affair Rich in Spanish History," Denton *Record-Chronicle*, Feb. 11, 1976; 1980 Census of Population, Vol. I, Chapter C, Pt. 45, Texas, Sec. 1, pp. 51, 79, 101; United States Census of Population: 1950, *Persons of Spanish Surname*, Special Report (Washington, D.C., 1953), p. 3C-45; United States Census of Population: 1960, Subject Reports, PC(2)-1B, Persons of Spanish Surname (Washington, D.C., 1963).

[29]Ronald C. Sheck, "Mexican-American Migration to Selected Texas Panhandle Urban Places" (Discussion Paper No. 20, Dept. of Geography, Ohio State University, 1971).

Indians and Spaniards, in places such as San Antonio and Nacogdoches.[30] Indeed, nearly 16,000 Texas blacks claimed Hispanic ancestry in the census of 1980.[31]

Still, relatively few blacks lived in Texas prior to 1836. Anglos introduced only modest numbers of Afro-Americans prior to independence, both because the status of slaves was uncertain under Mexican law and because the large majority of early Anglo settlers came from southern mountain states, where slavery was uncommon.[32] According to the Mexican census taken in 1835, all of East Texas, which was later to become the focus of black settlement, had only 588 slaves in its population, or about 12 percent of the total. The municipality (county) of San Augustine had the highest proportion, at 23 percent, while neighboring Tenaha (present Shelby County) was lowest with only 3 percent. The largest black population at that time, numbering 243, lived in adjacent Sabine Municipality.[33] In Texas as a whole by 1836, the time of independence, no more than one-tenth of the inhabitants were black.

A dramatic increase in slave immigration occurred in the late 1830s, accompanying the first large influx of white planters from southern coastal states. The Republic legalized slavery almost at once, removing the major bar to planter immigration, and by 1840 Texans payed taxes on over twelve thousand black slaves, a total that should be adjusted upward to about 15,000 because of missing tax lists for several counties.[34] Roughly one-fifth of the total population was black in that year. The large-scale introduction of slaves accelerated still more after Texas joined the Union, and by the time of the Civil War nearly 200,000 blacks,

---

[30]See, for example, W. H. Timmons, "The Population of the El Paso Area—A Census of 1784," *New Mexico Historical Review,* LII (Oct., 1977), 314.

[31]1980 Census of Population, Vol. I, Chapter C, Pt. 45, Texas, Sec. 1, p. 59.

[32]Basic sources on Afro-Texans include Alwyn Barr, *Black Texans: A History of Negroes in Texas, 1528–1971* (Austin, 1973); Eugene C. Barker, "The Influence of Slavery in the Colonization of Texas," *SHQ,* XXVIII (July, 1924), 1–33; Lester G. Bugbee, "Slavery in Early Texas," *Political Science Quarterly,* XIII (Sept., 1898), 389–412, (Dec.), 648–668; Bruce A. Glasrud, "Black Texans, 1900–1930: A History" (Ph.D. diss., Texas Tech University, 1969); Lawrence D. Rice, "The Negro in Texas, 1874–1900" (Ph.D. diss., Texas Tech University, 1967); Neil G. Sapper, "A Survey of the History of the Black People of Texas, 1930–1954" (Ph.D. diss., Texas Tech University, 1972); Harold Schoen, "The Free Negro in the Republic of Texas," *SHQ,* XXXIX (Apr., 1936), 292–308; ibid., XL (July, 1936), 26–34, (Oct.), 85–113, (Jan., 1937), 169–199, (Apr.), 267–289; ibid., XLI (July, 1937), 83–108; Ronnie C. Tyler and Lawrence R. Murphy (eds.), *The Slave Narratives of Texas* (Austin, 1974).

[33]MSS censuses for the municipalities of Bevil, Nacogdoches, Sabine, San Augustine, and Tenaha, 1835, in the Nacogdoches Archives (Archives Division, Texas State Library, Austin), and published in Marion D. Mullins, *First Census of Texas, 1829–1836* (Washington, D.C., 1959).

[34]Gifford E. White (ed.), *The 1840 Census of the Republic of Texas* (Austin, 1966). The 1840 distribution of slaves in Texas is mapped in Stanley A. Arbingast et al., *Atlas of Texas* (5th ed.; Austin, 1976), 52 (maps compiled by Terry G. Jordan).

forming almost one-third of the total population, lived in the state.[35] Texas seemed well on its way to following the coastal southern model of black majority.

The Civil War and emancipation effectively halted the Africanization of Texas. The influx of blacks largely ended in 1865, and in the following fifteen years only 6 percent of the immigrants to the state were black, a proportion that fell even lower in later decades.[36] Indicative of the virtual cessation of black immigration is the fact that by 1880 nearly three-quarters of all Afro-Americans in the state were of Texas birth, as opposed to less than half the whites.[37] As a consequence, the proportion of blacks in the total population steadily dwindled after 1865, falling to only 12 percent at present. Actual numbers have risen modestly through natural increase, in spite of a large emigration of Texas blacks to the North and to California in the first half of the twentieth century.

The black settlement of Texas, then, occurred largely between 1836 and 1865. The major contributing states included Alabama, where nearly one-fifth of all Texas slaves were born, Virginia (13 percent), Georgia (12 percent), and Mississippi (11 percent).[38] Virginia ranked proportionately much higher as a birthplace of blacks than of Anglo-Texans, primarily because of the lively export of excess slaves from the worn-out tobacco districts of the Chesapeake Tidewater. Some Texas blacks arrived directly from Africa in an illegal trade lasting from the 1820s to the Civil War, and the census of 1880 revealed that, in number of African-born, Texas ranked highest among all the states.[39]

The region settled by blacks lay east of the Texarkana–to–San Antonio line, coinciding with the domain of the lower southern whites. Thirteen counties in that area had black majorities by 1860, led by Wharton County, where over four-fifths of the population was slave. More exactly, blacks were concentrated along the major rivers of eastern and southeastern Texas, especially the lower Brazos, Colorado, and Trinity. The Red River and some of its right-bank tributaries, most notably Cypress Bayou, also formed a major plantation district. After emancipation, black freedmen remained in these same areas, where they retained majorities in twelve counties as late as 1887.[40] Throughout the nine-

---

[35]*Population of the United States in 1860, Compiled from the Original Returns of the Eighth Census* (Washington, D.C., 1864), 479, 483, 486.

[36]Kerr, "Migration into Texas," 73–75.

[37]Tenth Census, 1880, *Statistics of the Population of the United States at the Tenth Census* (Washington, D.C., 1883), 484–492.

[38]Ninth Census, 1870, Vol. I, *The Statistics of the Population of the United States* (Washington, D.C., 1872), 328–342; *Statistics of the Population at the Tenth Census,* 488–492.

[39]*Statistics of Population at the Tenth Census,* 492. See also Eugene C. Barker, "The African Slave Trade in Texas," *QTSHA,* VI (Oct., 1902), 145–158; and Fred Robbins, "The Origin and Development of the African Slave Trade in Galveston, Texas, and Surrounding Areas from 1816 to 1836," *East Texas Historical Journal,* IX (Oct., 1971), 153–161.

[40]Foster, *First Annual Report,* 1–249.

TABLE 4 Ethnic Evolution of a Texas County, 1835–1980: Shelby County, East Texas

| Group | | 1835 | 1850 | 1887 | 1930 | 1980 |
|---|---|---|---|---|---|---|
| Old-Stock Anglos | Southern | 74% | 73% | 84% | 74% | 73% |
| | Northern | | 3% | | | |
| Afro-Americans | | 3% | 23% | 15% | 25% | 21% |
| Europeans | | 0% | 1% | < 1% | < 1% | 5% |
| Hispanics | | 0% | 0% | 0% | < 1% | < 1% |
| Amerindians | | 23% | 0% | 0% | < 1% | < 1% |

SOURCES: MSS Mexican census of the Municipality of Tenaha, 1835, in the Nacogdoches Archives (Archives Division, Texas State Library, Austin); hand count of the MSS free population schedules, United States Census of 1850; *The Seventh Census of the United States: 1850* (Washington, D.C., 1853), 504; L. L. Foster (ed.), *First Annual Report of the Agricultural Bureau of the Department of Agriculture, Insurance, Statistics, and History, 1887–88* (Austin, 1889), 202–203; Fifteenth Census of the United States: 1930, *Population,* Vol. III, Pt. 2 (Washington, D.C., 1932), 988, 1,015, 1,018, 1,022; for 1980, black, Amerindian, and Hispanic percentages are based on 1980 Census of Population, Characteristics of the Population, Chapter C, *General Social and Economic Characteristics,* Pt. 45, Texas, Sec. 1 (Washington, D.C., 1983), 57, 85; and the Old-Stock Anglo and European figures are based upon United States Census of Population and Housing, 1980, Summary Tape File 4, "Technical Documentation" (Washington, D.C., 1983), unpublished computer tape.

teenth century, there was almost no spatial overlap of blacks and Hispanics in Texas, and a clearly defined dividing line between the two groups followed the axis of the San Antonio River, coming to the Gulf along the border separating San Patricio and Refugio counties (figure 5).

The twentieth century has witnessed a severe weakening of the black rural stronghold in East Texas (table 4). Migration to Houston, Dallas, and other cities, as well as the flight to northern and western states, left only four black-majority counties by 1930 (figure 6).[41] The subsequent demise of the share-cropper system and conversion of East Texas to pasture and pine plantation undercut the remaining rural communities. At the Sesquicentennial, no Texas county has a black majority, and in only nine do Afro-Americans constitute more than one-fourth of the population (figure 7). Rural black hamlets and neighborhoods can still be found in East Texas, but they are dwindling.

Today, black population and culture are dominantly urban. Afro-Texans traded the rural river valleys for the city ghettoes. The largest concentrations are found in Houston, Dallas, and Fort Worth. Beaumont, among cities of more than 100,000 inhabitants, had the highest proportion of blacks in the total

[41]Fifteenth Census, 1930, *Population,* Vol. III, Pt. 2, pp. 975–990.

population in 1980 with 37 percent, and the other such cities in which blacks formed proportions greater than their statewide percentage were Dallas (29 percent), Houston (28), Fort Worth (23), and Waco (22).[42] In the urban setting, blacks remain highly segregated from Hispanics. Unique to the twentieth-century city, however, is the residential segregation of Anglos and blacks. Two peoples who had for several centuries shared rural and town neighborhoods as master and servant parted residential company as Texas became urbanized. While this segregation imposed many burdens and indignities upon the blacks, it permitted ethnic rejuvenation and strengthened their sense of identity. By concentrating in urban ghettoes, Texas blacks were better able to survive culturally in the century 1860 to 1960, which witnessed their fall from one-third to one-eighth of the total population.

To a great extent, the proportional decline of the Texas black population coincided with the rise of the Hispanic element (table 3). Since 1887, blacks have increased only fourfold in number while Hispanics have grown thirty-six-fold. The cultural implications of this shift are profound. Indeed, the widely held self-image of Anglo-Texans as westerners rather than southerners may be linked in part to the displacement of blacks by Mexicans as the largest ethnic minority.

Anglos, Hispanics, and blacks all represent old-stock American populations; that is, they are descended in part or whole from immigrants who entered North America in colonial times. One other major Texas ethnic group shares old-stock status—the Louisiana French (table 1).[43] Persons of French ancestry form the largest national-origin group in Louisiana and dominate a southern triangular area in that state, with apexes at the mouth of the Mississippi, Alexandria, and Lake Charles. Though this area is adjacent to Texas, notable migration across the Sabine by Louisiana French began relatively late and remained rather modest in scale.

Cajuns, or *acadiens*, who form the largest and most viable of the several Louisiana French subcultures, began entering Texas in small numbers in the 1820s, and they have from that time constituted the most sizable and important French ethnic group in the state. Most of the thousand or so ethnic French in

---

[42] 1980 Census of Population, Vol. I, Chapter C, Part 45, Texas, Sec. 1, pp. 34–49.

[43] Sources on the Louisiana French in Texas include Mary M. Withers, "The Acadians of Jefferson County, Texas," *Texas Gulf Historical and Biographical Record*, VII (Nov., 1971), 42–48; M. LeRoy Ellis, "La culture acadienne dans le sud-est du Texas," *Revue de Louisiane/Louisiana Review*, II (Summer, 1973), 99–101; Miriam Partlow, "Immigration of the Creoles," Chapter 17 in her book *Liberty, Liberty County, and the Atascosito District* (Austin, 1974); Dean R. Louder and Michael J. Leblanc, "Les Cadjins de l'Est du Texas," Dean R. Louder and Eric Waddell (eds.), *Du continent perdu à l'archipel retrouvé: le Québec et l'Amérique française*, Travaux du Département de Géographie de l'Université Laval, No. 6 (Québec, 1983), 259–271; Peveril Meigs, "An Ethno-Telephonic Survey of French Louisiana," *Annals of the Association of American Geographers*, XXXI (Dec, 1941), 243–250.

Texas by 1850 lived in the far southeastern counties and bore typically Cajun surnames, though a small contingent of Louisiana Creole French settled in the town of Liberty about that time (figure 2).[44] Most of the early Cajun settlers engaged in cattle ranching on the Coastal Prairie, and one, Taylor White (born Leblanc), owned the largest herds in that area during the 1820s and 1830s.[45] By 1887, the French element in Southeast Texas had increased very modestly to about 2,300 (table 1) (figure 4).

Following the temporal pattern of Mexican immigration, Cajuns began their major influx about the turn of the century. The trigger was the discovery of oil at Spindletop, followed by the industrialization of the Houston area and the Golden Triangle. Port Arthur bears perhaps the deepest Cajun imprint, but telephone directories for nearly every town and city from the lower Sabine westward to Houston and Galveston list numerous Cajun entries, such as Broussard, Boudreaux, Landry, Hebert, and Guedry. In 1980, about 375,000 persons claiming French ancestry lived in southeastern Texas, but nowhere do Cajuns approach majority status (table 1). Orange County is the most purely Gallic in Texas, with 26 percent of its inhabitants claiming in 1980 to be fully or partially French in origin, followed by Jefferson and Chambers counties, each at 21 percent (figure 3).

Though Texas Cajuns, in common with Mexicans, live adjacent to their ancestral homeland, unhindered even by an intervening international border, their ethnicity is at present endangered. This vulnerability stems in part from the gradual decay of the Cajun culture in Louisiana itself, where acculturation has made deep inroads, but the greater cause is likely the ease with which Cajuns can mesh into local non-French groups. Most Cajuns are white, though many have some Indian blood, and no barriers block their joining the Anglo host culture.[46] Black Cajuns, similarly, are easily absorbed into the English-speaking Afro-American population of Southeast Texas urban ghettoes. Thus, in 1970 some 91,000 Texans reported French as the mother tongue spoken during their childhood, while only 48,000 responded in 1980 that they presently use French while at home.[47] Linguistically, at least, the Louisiana French are succumbing in Southeast Texas.

---

[44]Seventh Census, 1850, MSS free population schedules, Galveston, Harris, Jefferson, and Liberty counties, Texas; Partlow, "Immigration of Creoles," 189–192.

[45]Ruth G. Francis, "The Coastal Cow Country—The Saga of James Taylor White, First," *Coastal Cattleman,* VI (Sept., 1940), 21–23; Terry G. Jordan, *Trails to Texas: Southern Roots of Western Cattle Ranching* (Lincoln, Neb., 1981), 79, 80.

[46]William F. Rushton, *The Cajuns, from Acadia to Louisiana* (New York, 1979), 5, 7, 9.

[47]United States Bureau of the Census, 1970 Census of Population, Vol. I, *Characteristics of the Population,* Pt. 45, Texas (Washington, D.C., 1973), Sec. 2, p. 1,291; 1980 Census of Population, Vol. I, Chapter C, Pt. 45, Texas, Sec. 1, p. 110.

Immigration directly from Europe played an important role in the peopling of Texas during the past century and a half. Persons involved in this migration and their Texas-born children formed about one-tenth of the state population by the turn of the century (table 5). While the 1980 census does not permit separation of old-stock persons of colonial European ancestry from those descended from the nineteenth-and twentieth-century immigration, perhaps a fair approximation can be derived by adding the total of all persons listing full-blood ancestry from non-British Europe. If enumerated in this manner, the European ethnic population of Texas in 1980 was 1,366,000, or 12 percent of those responding.[48]

The model and precedent for European immigration was established by Catholic Irish who came in the late 1820s and early 1830s, when Texas was still under Mexican rule.[49] Two Coastal Bend colonies, San Patricio and Refugio, resulted from these empresario projects, and Irish continued to dominate the counties bearing those names for at least a generation. The settlement zone, probably by design, lay between the southern Anglo and Hispanic population clusters, and the Mexican government likely sought thereby to impose a Catholic-European barrier in the path of the westward-surging Anglos. When tied to the Mexican empresario colony at Victoria and the much older mestizo-Spanish concentration in the upper San Antonio River Valley, the two Irish colonies did, indeed, by 1835 take on the appearance of links in a Celto-Romance Catholic barrier stretched thinly from Matagorda Bay to the Balcones Escarpment (figure 1).

Subsequent nineteenth-century European immigrants, though largely continental rather than British in origin, sought out the same seam between Anglo and Hispanic culture areas, causing south-central Texas to take on a balkanized ethnic character (figures 2, 4). The first groups to follow the Irish, and eventually to account for fully half the European immigration, were the Germans (table 5).[50] Forming a "German belt," ten traditionally rural counties

---

[48]1980 Census of Population, *Ancestry of the Population by State:* 1980, Supplementary Report, PC80-S1-10 (Washington, D.C., 1983), 38, 50.

[49]Sources on the Catholic Irish include William H. Oberste, *Texas Irish Empresarios and Their Colonies* (Austin, 1953); Rachel B. Hébert, *The Forgotten Colony: San Patricio de Hibernia* (Burnet, Tex., 1981); Bernadine Rice, "The Irish in Texas," *Journal of the American Irish Historical Society,* XXX (1932), 60–70.

[50]For the ethnic balkanization of Central Texas, see Jean T. Hannaford, "The Cultural Impact of European Settlement in Central Texas" (M.A. thesis, University of Texas, Austin, 1970), and Oscar Lewis, *On the Edge of the Black Waxy: A Cultural Survey of Bell County, Texas,* Washington University Studies, New Series, Social and Philosophical Sciences, No. 7 (St. Louis, 1948). Basic sources on the Germans include Terry G. Jordan, "The German Element in Texas: An Overview," *Rice University Studies,* LXIII (Summer, 1977), 1–11; Rudolph L. Biesele, *The History of the German Settlements in Texas, 1831–1861* (Austin, 1930); Terry G. Jordan, *German Seed in Texas Soil: Immigrant Farmers in Nineteenth-Century Texas* (Austin, 1966); Glen E. Lich and Dona B. Reeves (eds.), *German Culture in Texas* (Boston, 1980); Glen E. Lich, *The German Texans* (San Antonio, 1981).

in South-Central Texas—Austin, Colorado, Comal, De Witt, Fayette, Gillespie, Guadalupe, Kendall, Medina, and Washington—housed the principal Teutonic concentration. Additional strength was added by early, major urban clusters of Germans at San Antonio, Houston, and Galveston. By 1880 these cities, as well as some smaller towns, such as Victoria, were one-fifth to one-third German in population. Europeans were much more likely than southern Anglos, blacks, or Hispanics to settle in the cities and towns of nineteenth-century Texas, and one should look to the urban scene for some of the deepest continental cultural imprints. Those who would understand, for example, the evolution of San Antonio as one of the ten largest American cities must consider the fact that Germans formed one-third of its population as late as 1880. Regrettably, we lack in-depth ethnic studies of preindustrial towns and cities in Texas.[51]

Most parts of Germany, except the Catholic South, contributed significantly to the Texas migration, as did ethnic German areas in Alsace, Switzerland, and Russia. The largest groups consisted of Hessians and lower Saxons. Immigration began in the 1830s and was directed initially to lands lying between the lower Brazos and Colorado rivers, where an original colonist, a low-German Oldenburger named Friedrich Dirks (alias Ernst) had settled in 1831.[52]

German immigration followed a pattern that became typical for the European groups and depended upon a "dominant personality," a forceful, influential leader to trigger the movement. A key device often employed was the "America letter," an exaggerated, highly favorable description of the new homeland designed to encourage friends and relatives to follow.[53] Dirks's America letter, dated 1832, survives. In it, he described a land with a winterless Italian climate, abundant game and fish, immense free land grants, gold and silver to be had nearby, low taxes, and huge privately owned herds of livestock, a land where only three months' labor was necessary each year to make a living.[54]

The migration set afoot in this manner was drawn from confined districts within the mother country and can thus best be described as "cluster migration." Texas European groups, then, typically came from certain small areas and were atypical of the countries at large. Within Texas, migration was initially directed to a "mother colony." The village of Industry in Austin County, laid out on Dirks's property in the 1830s, served this function for the early German

---

[51]See, however, Ralph A. Wooster, "Foreigners in the Principal Towns of Ante-Bellum Texas," *SHQ*, LXVI (Oct., 1962), 208–220; and Fred R. von der Mehden (ed.), *The Ethnic Groups of Houston,* Rice University Studies, New Series, No. 3 (Houston, 1984).

[52]Terry G. Jordan, "The Pattern of Origins of the Adelsverein German Colonists," *Texana,* VI (Fall, 1968), 245–257; Elsie Montgomery and Austin H. Montgomery, Jr., "The Other Germans," *Texana,* IX, No. 3 (1971), 230–248.

[53]These concepts are discussed in Jordan, "German Element in Texas," 1, 3–4.

[54]The Dirks/Ernst letter appears in Detlef Dunt, *Reise nach Texas, nebst Nachrichten von diesem Lande, für Deutsche, welche nach Amerika zu gehen beabsichtigen* (Bremen, 1834), 4–16.

immigrants. Newly arrived settlers typically came to the mother colony, lived there while acquiring capital and experience, and then moved out to form daughter colonies nearby.

The Germans attracted through Dirks's influence caused Texas to become widely known in Germany. The publicity in turn helped guide an organized colonization effort led by the Adelsverein, or Society of Nobles, a group of investors drawn from the petty nobility of western Germany. This society introduced more than 7,000 Hessians and Saxons in the 1840s, mainly into the Hill Country between and including New Braunfels and Fredericksburg.[55] In a similar project, in the same decade, empresario Henri Castro brought several thousand settlers, mainly Alsatians, and founded a string of colonies in Medina County.[56]

German immigration, briefly interrupted by the Civil War, resumed at an even greater volume between 1865 and 1890, after which the Teutonic influx subsided.[57] Toward the close of the major period of immigration, in 1887, the 130,000 Germans in Texas constituted the second largest ethnic group in the state, after the blacks, and made up well over half of the European element.[58] A century later, over 750,000 Texans claimed to be wholly of German origin, a figure that perhaps accurately reflects the size of the ethnic segment of the German-descended population. An additional almost one-and-one-half million persons listed partial German ancestry, but these no doubt included many old-stock Americans descended from the colonial Pennsylvania "Dutch" and who should not be regarded as ethnics (table 2).

In the 1850s, three parallel and strikingly similar Slavic migrations to Texas began, involving Czechs, Silesian Poles, and Wends (Sorbs) (table 5). Each was prompted or led by a church figure, emanated from a confined source area, and was directed to the south-central part of Texas. Czech immigration began about 1850, spurred by the America letter of Protestant minister Ernst Bergmann (Arnost Horák); drew most heavily upon northeastern Moravia; and funneled through the mother colony of Fayetteville, near La Grange. The influx continued until 1914 and ultimately produced the largest rural Czech population of any state.[59] From a nucleus on the Fayette Prairie,

---

[55]See Hubert G. H. Wilhelm, "Organized German Settlement and Its Effects on the Frontier of South-Central Texas" (Ph.D. diss., Louisiana State University, 1968).

[56]Bobby D. Weaver, *Castro's Colony: Empresario Development in Texas, 1842–1865* (College Station, Tex., 1985).

[57]Terry G. Jordan, "The German Settlement of Texas after 1865," *SHQ*, LXXIII (Oct., 1969), 193–212.

[58]Foster (ed.), *First Annual Report*, xlvi.

[59]The only satisfactory sources on the Czechs, though largely descriptive, are Henry R. Maresh and Estelle Hudson, *Czech Pioneers of the Southwest* (Dallas, 1934); Henry R. Maresh, "The Czechs in Texas," *SHQ*, L (Oct., 1946), 236–240, plus map; Mollie E. Stasney, "The Czechs in Texas" (M.A. thesis, University of Texas, 1938); and Clinton Machann and James W. Mendl, *Krásná Amerika: A Study of the Texas Czechs, 1851–1939* (Austin, 1983).

TABLE 5 European White Stock in Texas, 1910

| Country | Persons of European Birth plus American-Born with at Least One European-Born Parent | As a Percentage of European White Stock |
|---|---|---|
| Germany[a] | 171,776 | 50% |
| Austria[b] | 53,100 | 16% |
| England | 26,260 | 8% |
| Ireland | 22,914 | 7% |
| Italy | 14,013 | 4% |
| Sweden | 11,598 | 3% |
| Russia[c] | 10,615 | 3% |
| Scotland | 6,835 | 2% |
| France[d] | 5,805 | 2% |
| Switzerland[e] | 4,616 | 1% |
| Other Europe | 13,893 | 4% |
| Total | 341,425 | 100% |
| Total Texas population | 3,896,542 | |

[a]Includes Wends, Silesian Poles, and many Jews.
[b]Mainly Czechs; includes also Galician Poles.
[c]Mainly Ashkenazic Jews.
[d]Includes many German Alsatians.
[e]Mainly ethnic Germans.
SOURCE: Thirteenth Census of the United States, 1910, Vol. III, *Population, 1910*, 799.

Czechs spread to form scores of colonies in the black-soiled grasslands of Texas, rarely venturing into adjacent, sandy-oak lands. This rich environmental base helped them become highly successful farmers. In 1980 nearly 180,000 persons claimed full or partial Czech ancestry, placing Texas second among the states (table 2).

Wendish immigration, guided by Lutheran pastor Jan Kilian, drew upon a tiny homeland in the southeastern corner of the present German Democratic Republic.[60] Serbin, or "place where the Wends live," became the mother colony in the sandy-oak forests of Lee County in the middle 1850s, and Wends later spread out to dominate the greater part of the county and to establish daughter colonies as far afield as the Corpus Christi and Vernon areas. No other Wendish settlements exist in the Americas.

[60]The best source on Wends remains George E. Engerrand, *The So-Called Wends of Germany and Their Colonies in Texas and in Australia* (Austin, 1934), but also recommended are Anne Blasig, *The Wends of Texas* (San Antonio, 1954) and Sylvia A. Grider, *The Wendish Texans* (San Antonio, 1982).

The oldest Polish colony in the United States, Panna Maria in Karnes County, was founded in 1854 by Silesians led by the Franciscan priest Leopold Moczygemba.[61] These Poles eventually founded a chain of daughter colonies along the axis of the San Antonio River, scattered among the north-bank tributaries of that stream. In postbellum times, they were joined by Galician Poles, who established colonies on old plantation lands in the Brazos and San Jacinto river valleys, most notably at Bremond. The only other rural Slavic colony was established by a small group of Lutheran Slovaks at Pakan in Wheeler County, in the Panhandle region, in 1903.[62]

Texas houses the southernmost Scandinavian rural settlements in the United States (tables 2, 5). While small in size, these colonies offer the unusual situation of Norwegians, Swedes, and Danes living in a subtropical setting. Norwegians, initially under the leadership of the liberal newspaper editor Johan Reinert Reiersen, established a mother colony, Four Mile Prairie, on the border of Kaufman and Van Zandt counties in the middle 1840s, only to see the settlement largely abandoned a decade later, when a second leader, Cleng Peerson, led the Norwegians to the hill lands of Bosque County.[63] The earliest immigrants came from hill hamlets in Aust-Agder province in southern Norway, a region bearing a startling terrain resemblance to the Bosque area. A second, and larger, contingent departed the fertile eastern shores of Lake Mjösa in Hedmark province, north of Oslo, to join the Bosque settlement.

Swedish immigration, derived very largely from the county of Jönköping in Småland province, interior southern Sweden, was drawn to Texas through the promotional and philanthropic efforts of S. M. Swenson, a native of the county who had come to Texas in the 1830s.[64] Headquartered in Austin, Swenson brought the Smålanders to that city, and many later founded farming colonies,

---

[61]The definitive work on the Silesians is T. Lindsay Baker, *The First Polish Americans: Silesian Settlements in Texas* (College Station, Tex., 1979). See also Maria Starczewska, "The Historical Geography of the Oldest Polish Settlement in the United States," *Polish Review,* XII (Spring, 1967), 11–39; and [T. Lindsay Baker], "Poles in Texas," Southwest Educational Development Laboratory, Ethnic Heritage Studies Program, Texas Heritage Unit (Poles), Resource Guide, Developmental Edition (Austin, 1975).

[62]The Pakan Slovaks remain unstudied. My remarks are based upon a visit to the settlement and informal interviews with several residents in March, 1979.

[63]On the Norwegians, see Oris E. Pierson, "Norwegian Settlements in Bosque County, Texas" (M.A. thesis, University of Texas, 1947); Axel Arneson, "Norwegian Settlements in Texas," *SHQ,* XLV (Oct., 1941), 125–135; Darwin Payne, "Early Norwegians in Northeast Texas," *SHQ,* LXV (Oct., 1961), 196–203; Peter L. Petersen, "A New Oslo on the Plains: The Anders L. Mordt Land Company and Norwegian Migration to the Texas Panhandle," *Panhandle-Plains Historical Review,* XLIX (1976), 25–54; and Odd Magnar Syversen and Derwood Johnson, *Norge i Texas* (Stange, Norway, 1982).

[64]The best study of the Swedes remains Ernest Severin, *Svenskarne i Texas i ord och bild* (2 vols.; n.p., 1919). Without acknowledging his source, Carl M. Rosenquist borrowed heavily from Severin

such as New Sweden, on the adjacent Blackland Prairie of eastern Travis and Williamson counties. The world's southernmost Danish colony was established in 1894 on the table-flat coastal prairie at Danevang, "level place where the Danes live," in Wharton County.[65] This settlement is noteworthy for the success of its farmers, based in an Old World tradition of mutual aid.

Italians, who in 1887 ranked only ninth among the European immigrant groups, rose to fifth position a generation later (table 5).[66] The bulk of the Italians came to the cities and mining towns of Texas, though agricultural colonies were established by Piemontese at Montague and by Sicilians in the Brazos Valley. Thurber, a coal-mining town in Erath County, had a notable Italian concentration. Utopian liberals from France founded La Réunion in Dallas County in the 1850s, and, though this colony soon failed, its residue of craftsmen and intellectuals perhaps played a formative role in making the infant city of Dallas something more than a typical North Texas county seat.[67] Dutch founded Nederland and several other Southeast Texas communities, while Greeks developed ethnic neighborhoods in several cities and settled as fishermen in certain port towns.[68]

Jewish migration began as a modest Sephardic influx as early as the period of Spanish and Mexican rule. They were followed, especially after 1865, by Ashkenazic Germans and still later, between 1890 and 1920, by Ashkenazic Poles and Russians. Over 2,000 Jews immigrated through the port of Galveston during the 1907–1914 period alone.[69] Today, the Jewish population is concentrated in Houston and Dallas, but synagogues in such small towns as Brenham, Corsicana, and Schulenburg serve as reminders that the Jewish presence in Texas is widespread.

---

to produce "The Swedes of Texas" (Ph.D. diss., University of Chicago, 1930). See also Mary W. Clark, *The Swenson Saga and the S M S Ranches* (Austin, 1976); and James Zambus, "Ericksdahl, a Swedish Community in Jones County, Texas," *West Texas Historical Association Year Book,* XLIX (1973), 59–68.

[65]Grace C. Grantham, "The Danes in Wharton County" (M.A. thesis, Texas A&I University, 1947); Thomas P. Christensen, "Danevang, Texas," *SHQ,* XXXII (July, 1928), 67–73.

[66]Valentine J. Belfiglio, *The Italian Experience in Texas* (Austin, 1983).

[67]William J. Hammond and Margaret F. Hammond, *La Réunion, a French Settlement in Texas* (Dallas, 1958); Ermance V. Rejebian, "La Réunion: The French Colony in Dallas County," *SHQ,* XLIII (Apr., 1940), 472–478.

[68]W. T. Block, "Tulip Transplants to East Texas: The Dutch Migration to Nederland, Port Arthur, and Winnie," *East Texas Historical Journal,* XIII (Fall, 1975), 36–50.

[69]Henry Cohen, *One Hundred Years of Jewry in Texas* (Dallas, 1936); Betty J. Maynard, *The Dallas Jewish Community Study* (Dallas, 1974); Elaine H. Maas, "The Jews of Houston: An Ethnographic Study" (Ph.D. diss., Rice University, 1973); Ronald A. Axelrod, "Rabbi Henry Cohen and the Galveston Immigration Movement, 1907–1914," *East Texas Historical Journal,* XV ([Spring], 1977), 24–37.

The Oriental element in Texas is also of long standing, though the bulk of the influx has occurred since the middle 1960s, when highly unfavorable immigration laws were modified. Chinese were the first to come, mainly as railroad workers in the 1870s, leaving as a heritage almost exclusively male groups at El Paso and in Robertson County.[70] In the latter instance, wives were found among the Brazos Valley black population, producing the fascinating, but unstudied, "black Chinese" of Calvert. The El Paso group remained bachelors and consequently died out. Harassed Chinese from Mexico accompanied General John Pershing's return from a military foray across the border in the teens. Japanese farmers from Hawaii and the West Coast founded a number of market gardening colonies in Southeast Texas, most notably at Webster and Terry.[71]

These efforts remained small and inconsequential. The total Oriental population in 1910 stood at only 943, and by 1930 had risen to but 1,576, including 703 Chinese, 519 Japanese, 288 Filipinos, 49 "Hindus," and 17 Koreans.[72] The 1980 total, by contrast, stood at about 120,000, reflecting the changed laws and the aftermath of the Korean and Vietnamese wars.[73] While many poor refugees were among these Orientals, the group as a whole is far above average in education and wealth. Included are many workers in the professions and in high-technology industries.

In the traditional view, the Amerindian population of Texas perished in epidemics and warfare or was driven across the border into Oklahoma and Mexico. All that remains, supposedly, are a few shards of tribes that immigrated from New Mexico and the southeastern states, in particular the Alabama-Coushatta of the Big Thicket; the Tigua, living in the *barrio indio* of El Paso's Ysleta community; and the Kickapoo, who seasonally come to Eagle Pass from northern Mexico.[74] Most censuses support the notion of Amerindian elimina-

[70]Nancy Farrar, *The Chinese in El Paso* (El Paso, 1972); Edward J. M. Rhoads, "The Chinese in Texas," *SHQ*, LXXXI (July, 1977), 1–36.

[71]Lillie Mae Tomlinson, "The Japanese Colony in Orange County," *University of Texas Bulletin*, No. 2746 (Dec. 1927) [The History Teachers' Bulletin, XIV (1927), 141–145]; Gwendolyn Wingate, "The Kishi Colony," in F. E. Abernethy (ed.), *The Folklore of Texan Cultures* (Austin, 1974), 327–337; Webb, Carroll, and Branda (eds.), *Handbook of Texas*, II, 875.

[72]Thirteenth Census, Vol. III, *Population*, 1910, 799; Fifteenth Census, 1930, *Population*, Vol. III, Pt. 2, p. 941.

[73]1980 Census, *Ancestry of the Population*, 44, 62.

[74]J. W. Fewkes, "The Pueblo Settlements Near El Paso," *American Anthropologist*, IV (Jan./Mar., 1902), 57–72; Alan H. Minter, "The Tigua Indians of the Pueblo de Ysleta del Sur, El Paso County, Texas," *West Texas Historical Association Year Book*, XLV (1969), 30–44; Tom Diamond, *The Tigua Indians of El Paso* (Denver, 1966); John H. Bounds, "The Alabama-Coushatta-Indians of Texas," *Journal of Geography*, LXX (Mar., 1971), 175–182; Rotha M. Berry, "The Alabama and Coushatta Indians of Texas," *Texas Geographic Magazine*, XII (Fall, 1948), 19–3; Harriet Smither, "The Alabama Indians of Texas," *SHQ*, XXXVI (Oct., 1932), 83–108; Randy E. Grothe, "The Kickapoo: Strangers in Their Own Land," Dallas *Morning News*, May 8, 1977. See also William W. Newcomb, Jr., *The Indians of Texas* (Austin, 1961).

tion from the state (table 4), for only 702 were enumerated in 1910, 1,001 in 1930, and 5,750 in 1960.[75]

Several facts combine to undermine this traditional view. First, substantial Amerindian immigration has occurred recently, drawn mainly from eastern Oklahoma and the Four Corners region of the Southwest. Navajos and Choctaws are the largest groups, and Dallas has become their principal goal. Several Amerindian ethnic neighborhoods have formed in that city, though not based upon specific tribal identity.

Second, the 1980 census delivered the startling news that 631,000 Texans claimed some measure of Amerindian ancestry (table 2). This very substantial figure did not include partially Indian persons in the Hispanic and Cajun groups, requiring the addition of perhaps another three million to the total of Texans who are partially of Amerindian ancestry. If correct, this figure suggests that one-quarter or more of the Texas white population has some measure of Indian blood. Nor does it end there. The recent upsurge in interest in Afro-American genealogy has revealed that many blacks also have Indian blood. Some such examples are well documented, including the "redbone" Ashworth family of Southeast Texas and the "Seminole Negroes" of Brackettville.[76]

Clearly, the notion of Indian elimination must be discarded, and it is time to seek the cultural imprint that so massive a genetic contribution implies. Genealogists know that a great many southern Anglo families have some Indian progenitors, and such mixing seems to have been common on the southern frontier (table 4). Could it even be that some measure of the cultural distinctiveness of the South, of Anglo-Texas, is based in partial Amerindian ancestry? A recent study of traditional funerary material culture suggests as much.[77]

Of course, the number of *ethnic* Amerindians in Texas, as defined by the Census Bureau, is much smaller, though rapidly growing. The total rose from 18,000 in 1970 to over 50,000 in 1980.[78] Curiously, more than twice that many Texans claimed pure Amerindian ancestry (table 2).

In ethnic terms, then, Texas at the Sesquicentennial remains what it has always been—a borderland, a zone of contact and friction between very different

---

[75]Thirteenth Census, Vol. III, *Population*, 1910, 799; Fifteenth Census, 1930, *Population*, Vol. III, Pt. 2, p. 1,014; Eighteenth Census of the United States, *Census of Population:* 1960, Vol. I, Characteristics of the Population, Pt. 45, Texas (Washington, D.C., 1961), 64.

[76]Kenneth Wiggins Porter, "The Seminole Negro-Indian Scouts, 1870–1881," *SHQ*, LV (Jan., 1952), 358–377; Andrew F. Muir, "The Free Negro in Jefferson and Orange Counties, Texas," *Journal of Negro History*, XXXV (Apr., 1950), 183–206; Kenneth W. Porter, "Negroes and Indians on the Texas Frontier, 1834–1874," *SHQ*, LIII (Oct., 1949), 151–163.

[77]William A. Owens, *This Stubborn Soil* (New York, 1966), 80–85; Terry G. Jordan, *Texas Graveyards: A Cultural Legacy* (Austin, 1982), 17, 34–40.

[78]1970 Census of Population, Vol. 1, Pt. 45, Sec. 2, p. 1,269; 1980 Census of Population, Vol. I, Chapter C, Pt. 45, Texas, Sec. 1, p. 31.

cultures (figure 3). The ethnic mosaic has shifted, kaleidoscope-like, during those 150 years, but the underlying diversity has proven durable. Such contact zones can be pleasant and exciting places to dwell, where multiple heritages enrich daily life. Perhaps we glimpse the future at the little Karnes County Catholic town of Cestohowa, where Poles and Mexicans now share the same parish. A glassed-in shrine in front of the church there contains, side-by-side, images of both Our Lady of Guadalupe and the Black Virgin of Czestochowa.

Borderlands can also become scenes of bigotry and conflict. Very soon, Texans of all cultural and ethnic backgrounds will have to decide whether their border province, in the coming century, will resemble troubled Belgium, where Dutch and French went separate ways, or whether it will be like Switzerland, where a long tradition of mutual respect has permitted a Teutonic majority to coexist peacefully in political union with Romance minorities.[79]

One might even wish for a hybridized culture whose practitioners value all its diverse roots, a culture produced by a lively exchange between Anglo and Latin civilizations. France, drawing from both its Germanic north and its Mediterranean south, would be a splendid model, but it required a millennium to fashion. Indeed, regardless of how Texans respond to the cultural challenge facing them, fundamental ethnic contrasts such as those in our state do not fade easily or quickly. Intra-state ethnic-based regionalism will persist for generations to come. At best, it will provide cross-cultural stimulation; at worst, it could lead to violence and even partition.

The immense popularity of the Institute of Texan Cultures museum in San Antonio and of its associated annual Texas Folklife Festival, where the state's many different ethnic minorities and the Anglo host culture are afforded due, even exaggerated and saccharine, respect, might indicate that, at the Sesquicentennial, Texans are ready to assume the needed attitude of tolerance, are ready to acknowledge their border province status. If, however, we make the wrong decisions, bleeding Ireland might even become our model. Texans should be reminded that the English, using an effective educational system, successfully destroyed the Irish Celtic language, only to find that the resultant English-speaking Irish Catholics hated them even more than before and went on to pursue political separation. Ethnicity and its baggage of prejudice often survive the demise of the associated language, and memories of ethnic oppression are well-nigh indelible.

---

[79]On the problems in Belgium, see Glen V. Stephenson, "Cultural Regionalism and the Unitary State Idea in Belgium," *Geographical Review,* LXII (Oct., 1972), 501–523.

# Index